THE COMPLETE WORKS OF
CHRISTOPHER MARLOWE

THIS volume contains the two parts of *Tamburlaine the Great*, edited by David Fuller, and *The Massacre at Paris*, edited by Edward J. Esche. It is the first time that either text has been presented in an old-spelling edition with a full critical commentary and textual annotation. The introduction to *Tamburlaine* gives a detailed account of the plays' sources, stage history, and text. The critical discussion considers the fundamental clashes which Marlowe dramatizes; the differing interpretations—often involved with opposing views of the Renaissance—to which these have given rise; and how new critical methodologies, and recent research into occult traditions in the Renaissance, might affect our reading of Marlowe. The commentary brings together the extensive modern scholarship on the plays, offers some new suggestions about their probable stage action, and cites new material from the period to contextualize Marlowe's treatment of war, medicine, religious controversy, and many other subjects. It also draws on scholarship on Elizabethan pronunciation to clarify Marlowe's poetic rhythms, and uses the revised edition of *OED* to investigate more fully than has previously been possible the originality and inventiveness of Marlowe's language.

The Massacre at Paris survives only in a severely mangled version, which bears many of the signs of a 'memorial reconstruction'; nevertheless, it provides us with the unique example of Marlowe using contemporary French history as his subject matter. The play has been edited from the copy of the Octavo once belonging to Edmund Malone, now held in the Bodleian Library. The edition also presents the single extant leaf of *Massacre* (Folger MS. J.b.8) in an authoritative form with apparatus, and argues for its legitimacy as a genuine playhouse document, although not Marlowe's autograph.

DAVID FULLER is Reader in English at the University of Durham.

EDWARD J. ESCHE is Senior Lecturer in English, Anglia Polytechnic University.

THE COMPLETE WORKS
OF
CHRISTOPHER
MARLOWE

VOLUME V

Tamburlaine the Great
Parts 1 and 2

EDITED BY
DAVID FULLER

AND

The Massacre at Paris
with the Death of the Duke of Guise

EDITED BY
EDWARD J. ESCHE

CLARENDON PRESS · OXFORD
1998

Oxford University Press, Great Clarendon Street, Oxford OX2 6DP

Oxford New York

Athens Auckland Bangkok Bogotá Buenos Aires
Calcutta Cape Town Chennai Dar es Salaam
Delhi Florence Hong Kong Istanbul Karachi
Kuala Lumpur Madrid Melbourne Mexico City
Mumbai Nairobi Paris São Paolo Singapore
Taipei Tokyo Toronto Warsaw

and associated companies in
Berlin Ibadan

Oxford is a trade mark of Oxford University Press

Published in the United States by
Oxford University Press Inc., New York

British Library Cataloguing in Publication Data

Data available

Library of Congress Cataloging in Publication Data
Marlow, Christopher, 1564–1593
[Tamburlaine the Great]
Tamburlaine the Great, parts 1 and 2 / edited by David Fuller. The
massacre of Paris : with the death of the Duke of Guise / edited by
Edward J. Esche.
— (The complete works of Christopher Marlowe ; v. 5)
Includes bibliographical references.
1. Timur, 1336–1405—Drama. 2. Saint Bartholomew's Day, Massacre
of, France, 1572—Drama. 3. Guise, Henri, duc de, 1550–1588—Drama.
4. Asia, Central—Kings and rulers—Drama. 5. Conquerors—Asia,
Central—Drama. 6. Historical drama, English. 7. Middle Ages—
Drama. I. Fuller, David, 1947– . II. Esche, Edward J., 1953–
III. Marlowe, Christopher, 1564–1593. Massacre of Paris.
IV. Title. V. Title: Massacre of Paris. VI. Series: Marlowe,
Christopher, 1564–1593. Works. 1987 ; v. 5.
PR2669.A1 1998 823'. 3—dc21 97–39062

ISBN 0-19-818320-8

1 3 5 7 9 10 8 6 4 2

Typeset by Pure Tech India Ltd, Pondicherry
Printed in Great Britain on acid-free paper by
Biddles Ltd, Guildford and King's Lynn

CONTENTS

Tamburlaine the Great

The Massacre at Paris

ACKNOWLEDGEMENTS

I AM indebted to four institutions: to the Huntington Library for the award of a Dorothy Collins Brown fellowship which allowed me to complete work on the text; to the Centre for Renaissance and Reformation Studies of Victoria University in the University of Toronto for a fellowship which allowed me to complete work on the commentary and introduction; to the British Academy, which provided a substantial part of the funding for this fellowship; and to the University of Durham, for a period of research leave in which to complete and co-ordinate the whole edition. To all of these I am very grateful for their help and support.

Various individuals gave different kinds of assistance, information and hospitality: Joseph Black, Lisa Celovsky, David Galbraith, and Brian Parker very much increased the usefulness and pleasure of my work in Toronto. Nigel Bawcutt, Edward Esche, L. C. Knights, Roger Sales, Alan Shepard, Patricia Waugh and Paul Whitfield White, at different times and in different ways, gave information, help, and Marlovian encouragement, as did Michael Schepers. Agnes Delanoy was always good-humoured about the endless production of drafts and much else. Frances Whistler and Jason Freeman, my editors at Oxford University Press, were always ideally helpful; and Christina Malkowska Zaba was a splendidly punctilious copy-editor. It is a pleasure to thank the staff of Durham University and Durham Cathedral Libraries, particularly Marilyn Hird, who assisted with technological skills, Gwynneth Thomas, whose indefatigable efforts secured a microfilm copy of Oxberry's edition of *Tamburlaine*, and Roger Norris and Wendy Stevenson, who often helped me to Ortelius.

I am especially grateful to Roma Gill, who has given constant encouragement, and from whose work on the 1993 Cambridge Marlowe conference I particularly benefited.

My greatest debt is to Professor T. W. Craik for both his friendship and his erudition. He has read and re-read these pages with an ideally careful eye for detail, and has given time and effort with the greatest generosity.

DF

ILLUSTRATIONS

In Memory of my Father
Sidney George Charles Fuller
1916–1993

REFERENCES AND ABBREVIATIONS

For *Massacre at Paris* references see p. 290 below.

Texts and Editions

Bawcutt	*The Jew of Malta*, ed. N. W. Bawcutt (Manchester, 1978).
Bevington–Rasmussen	*Doctor Faustus and Other Plays*, ed. David Bevington and Eric Rasmussen (Oxford, 1995).
Bevington–Rasmussen *Faustus*	*Doctor Faustus*, ed. David Bevington and Eric Rasmussen (Manchester, 1993).
Bowers	*The Complete Works of Christopher Marlowe*, ed. Fredson Bowers, 2 vols. (Cambridge, 1973; 2nd edn., 1981).
Brooke	*The Works of Christopher Marlowe*, ed. C. F. Tucker Brooke (Oxford, 1910).
Broughton	James Broughton's notes in his copy of Robinson, now in the British Library.
Bullen	*The Works of Christopher Marlowe*, ed. A. H. Bullen (London, 1885).
Collier	J. P. Collier's notes in his copy of Dyce[1], now in the British Library.
Craik	T. W. Craik; suggestion to editor.
F. Cunningham	*The Works of Christopher Marlowe*, ed. Francis Cunningham (London, 1870).
J. S. Cunningham	*Tamburlaine the Great*, ed. J. S. Cunningham (Manchester, 1981).
Deighton	*The Old Dramatists. Conjectural Emendations*, ed. K. Deighton (London, 1896).
Dyce[1]	*The Works of Christopher Marlowe*, ed. Alexander Dyce (London, 1850).
Dyce[2]	*The Works of Christopher Marlowe, a New Edition, Revised and Corrected*, ed. Alexander Dyce (London, 1858).

Ellis-Fermor	*Tamburlaine the Great*, ed. Una Ellis-Fermor (London, 1930; 2nd edn., revised, 1951).
Forker	*Edward II*, ed. Charles R. Forker (Manchester, 1994).
Harper	*Tamburlaine the Great*, ed. J. W. Harper (London, 1971).
Jump	*Tamburlaine the Great*, ed. John D. Jump (London, 1967).
Kirschbaum	*The Plays of Christopher Marlowe*, ed. Leo Kirschbaum (Cleveland, 1962).
MacLure	*Christopher Marlowe: The Poems*, ed. Millar MacLure (London, 1968).
Malone	MS notes by Malone in the Bodleian copy of *Q*.
O1	*Tamburlaine the Great* (London, 1590).
O2	*Tamburlaine the Great* (London, 1593).
O3	*Tamburlaine the Great* (London, 1597).
Q	*Tamburlaine the Great* (London, 1605–6: 2 vols.).
Oxberry	*Tamburlaine the Great*, ed. W. Oxberry (London, 1820).
Pendry–Maxwell	Marlowe, *Complete Plays and Poems*, ed. E. D. Pendry and J. C. Maxwell (London, 1976).
Robinson	*The Works of Christopher Marlowe*, ed. G. Robinson (London, 1826).
Wagner	*Marlowes Werke*, ed. Hermann Breymann and Albrecht Wagner (2 vols., Heilbronn, 1885–9); i, *Tamburlaine*, ed. Albrecht Wagner (1885).
Woolf	*Tamburlaine the Great*, ed. Tatiana M. Woolf (London, 1964).

Other References

Abbott	E. A. Abbott, *A Shakespearian Grammar* (Macmillan & Co., London, 1869; 2nd edn., 1870).

Ando	Sadao Ando, *A Descriptive Syntax of Christopher Marlowe's Language* (University of Tokyo Press, 1976).
Bosonnet	Felix Bosonnet, *The Function of Stage Properties in Christopher Marlowe's Plays* (Cooper Monographs on English and American Language and Literature, Franke Verlag, Bern, 1978).
Brereton	John Le Gay Brereton, 'Marlowe: Some Textual Notes', *MLR* 6 (1911), 94–6.
Cornelius	R. M. Cornelius, *Christopher Marlowe's Use of the Bible*, American University Studies, 4/23 (Peter Lang, New York, 1984).
Dent	R. W. Dent, *Proverbial Language in English Drama Exclusive of Shakespeare, 1495–1616. An Index* (University of California Press, Los Angeles, 1984).
Dobson	E. J. Dobson, *English Pronunciation, 1500–1700*, 2 vols. (Clarendon Press, Oxford, 1957; 2nd edn., 1968).
Elze	Karl Elze, *Notes on Elizabethan Dramatists with Conjectural Emendations of the Text* (Halle, 1880).
Golding	*Shakespeare's Ovid, Being Arthur Golding's Translation of the* Metamorphoses, ed. W. H. D. Rouse (Centaur Press, London, 1961).
Heninger	S. K. Heninger, Jr., *A Handbook of Renaissance Meteorology* (Duke University Press, Durham, NC, 1960).
Hoeniger	F. D. Hoeniger, *Medicine and Shakespeare in the English Renaissance* (University of Delaware Press, Newark, NJ, 1992).
Kocher	Paul H. Kocher, *Christopher Marlowe: A Study of his Thought, Learning, and Character* (University of North Carolina Press, Chapel Hill, 1946).

OED	*The Oxford English Dictionary*, 2nd edn., prepared by J. A. Simpson and E. S. C. Weiner (Clarendon Press, Oxford, 1989).
Seaton[1]	Ethel Seaton, 'Marlowe's Map', *Essays and Studies by Members of the English Association*, 10 (1924), 13–35.
Seaton[2]	Ethel Seaton, 'Fresh Sources for Marlowe', *Review of English Studies*, 5 (1929), 385–401.
Seaton[3]	Ethel Seaton, review of Una Ellis-Fermor's edition of *Tamburlaine*, *Review of English Studies*, 8 (1932), 467–72.
Seaton[4]	Ethel Seaton, 'Marlowe's Light Reading', *Elizabethan and Jacobean Studies Presented to F. P. Wilson*, ed. Herbert Davis and Helen Gardner (Clarendon Press, Oxford, 1959), 17–35.
Shakespeare	*The Complete Works: Original Spelling Edition*, ed. Stanley Wells and Gary Taylor (Clarendon Press, Oxford, 1986).
Thomas–Tydeman	Vivien Thomas and William Tydeman (eds.), *Christopher Marlowe: The Plays and their Sources* (Routledge, London, 1994).
Tilley	M. P. Tilley, *A Dictionary of the Proverbs in England in the Sixteenth and Seventeenth Centuries* (University of Michigan Press, Ann Arbor, 1950).
van Dam	B. A. P. van Dam, 'Marlowe's *Tamburlaine*', *English Studies*, 16 (1934), 1–17, 49–58.
Zucker	David Hard Zucker, *Stage and Image in the Plays of Christopher Marlowe*, Salzburg Studies in English Literature, Elizabethan Studies, 7 (Salzburg, 1972).

Periodicals

ELH	*ELH: A Journal of English Literary History*

ELR	*English Literary Renaissance*
JEGP	*Journal of English and Germanic Philology*
MLN	*Modern Language Notes*
MLQ	*Modern Language Quarterly*
MLR	*Modern Language Review*
N&Q	*Notes and Queries*
PMLA	*Publications of the Modern Language Association of America*
RES	*Review of English Studies*
RORD	*Research Opportunities in Renaissance Drama*
RQ	*Renaissance Quarterly*
SP	*Studies in Philology*
TDR	*Tulane Drama Review*
TLS	*The Times Literary Supplement*

Biblical quotations are from the 1560 Geneva Bible unless otherwise specified. Except for the B text of *Doctor Faustus* (which is not included in the edition), references to Marlowe are to *The Complete Works of Christopher Marlowe* (Clarendon Press; i. *Translations*, ed. Roma Gill, 1987; ii. *Doctor Faustus*, ed. Gill, 1990; iii. *Edward II*, ed. Richard Rowland, 1994; iv. *The Jew of Malta*, ed. Gill, 1995). References to the B text of *Doctor Faustus* are to the edition of the play (both texts) by David Bevington and Eric Rasmussen, Manchester UP, 1993. Quotations from Shakespeare are from *William Shakespeare. The Complete Works: Original Spelling Edition*, ed. Stanley Wells and Gary Taylor (Clarendon Press, Oxford, 1986). In this edition plays are numbered throughout by lines, without act and scene division. References are therefore as in *William Shakespeare. The Complete Works: Compact Edition*, ed. Stanley Wells and Gary Taylor (Clarendon Press, Oxford, 1988).

INTRODUCTION

I. Date and Authorship

THE first recorded performances of *Tamburlaine* are registered in Philip Henslowe's diary for 1594–5.[1] The first published text of the play (1590), however, refers to it as having been 'sundrie times shewed upon Stages in the Citie of London. By the right honorable the Lord Admyrall, his servantes'; and E. K. Chambers[2] suggested that we have evidence of one such showing (of Part 2), shortly before 16 November 1587. On that day Philip Gawdy reported a performance by the Lord Admiral's Men of an unspecified play, as follows:

Yow shall understande of some accydentall newes heare in this towne thoughe my self no wyttnesse thereof, yet I may be bold to veryfye it for an assured troth. My L. Admyrall his men and players having a devyse in ther playe to tye one of their fellowes to a poste and so to shoote him to deathe, having borrowed their Callyvers one of the players handes swerved his peece being charged with bullett missed the fellowe he aymed at and killed a chyld, and a woman great with chyld forthwith, and hurt an other man in the head very soore.[3]

Since no other extant play of the period offers a scene which corresponds to the stage action implied here, Chambers' suggestion that this refers to the death scene of the Governor of Babylon (*Two*, 5.1) has been generally accepted. (Though the reported tying to a post does not fit the case, given the fact of hearsay reporting some confusion of the precise circumstances is readily explicable.) If Part 2 was in performance by November 1587, and if Part 2 was actually written, as its Prologue claims, in response to the popularity of Part 1, then Part 1 must have been in performance during the summer of 1587; that is, at about the time Marlowe took his M A and left Cambridge.

[1] *Henslowe's Diary*, ed. R. A. Foakes and R. T. Rickert (Cambridge, 1961), 23–33. The diary records 22 performances between 28 Aug. 1594 and 13 Nov. 1595 (15 of Part 1, 7 of Part 2). The first performance of Part 2 took place on 19 Dec. 1594. Only once thereafter (15 Sept. 1595) does it appear that Part 1 was performed without its sequel on the following or next following day.

[2] *TLS*, 28. Aug. 1930, 684.

[3] *The Letters of Philip Gawdy*, ed. Isaac H. Jeayes (London, Roxburghe Club, 1906), 23. Quoted in E. K. Chambers, *The Elizabethan Stage* (Oxford, 1923, 4 vols), ii. 135.

Even if Philip Gawdy's letter in fact refers to the performance of some lost play, however, this would not much affect the dating of *Tamburlaine*. The first published reference to the play occurs in Robert Greene's *Perymedes the Blacksmith* of 1588,[4] in which Greene's hit at an unnamed playwright as 'daring God out of heaven with that Atheist Tamburlan'[5] clearly refers to the plays, and almost certainly to the challenge to Mahomet towards the close of Part 2 (5.1.187–202).[6] The only problem with this dating is that Paul Ive's *Practise of Fortification* of 1589 is a source for one speech of Part 2. It seems unlikely that this speech would have been added between the first performances and publication, but it does seem probable that Marlowe could have had access to Ive's treatise in manuscript.[7]

The two parts of *Tamburlaine* were therefore apparently in performance by the spring of 1588, and probably by the autumn of 1587.

There is no doubt that Marlowe wrote *Tamburlaine*, but neither is there clear external evidence that he wrote it. No author is given in any of the four early texts. The best proofs—and they have not been seriously doubted for two hundred years—are internal: in thought, feeling, and style the play is quintessentially Marlovian. Some external evidence can be adduced to support this. Robert Greene, in the preface to *Perymedes* already quoted, follows his remark on Tamburlaine with a gibe against 'scoffing poets, that have propheticall spirits as bold as *Merlins* race': the reference to Merlin here has little point unless it is a play on 'Marlin', a recorded form of Marlowe's name.[8] On this reading of the passage the play is associated with Marlowe within a year of its first performance by an authoritative source. If, as seems probable, the Dutch Church libel of 1593 (which was signed 'Tamburlaine') really is connected with

---

[4] *Perymedes* was entered in the Stationers' Register on 29 March of that year: *A Transcript of the Registers of the Company of Stationers of London; 1554–1640*, ed. Edward Arber (London, 1875–94, 5 vols.), ii. 488.

[5] *'Perymedes the Blacksmith' and 'Pandosto' by Robert Greene*, ed. Stanley Wells (New York, 1988), 3 (and see pp. xx–xxiii).

[6] Other passages which might conceivably justify such a description are also in Part 2 (particularly 2.4.102–8 and 5.3.46–53). In Part 1 the frequent references to Jove present him as Tamburlaine's mentor, never as his opponent.

[7] See Commentary, 3.2.62–82.

[8] C. F. Tucker Brooke, *The Life of Marlowe, and the Tragedy of Dido Queen of Carthage* (London, 1930) 44.

Marlowe's summons before the Privy Council in May of that year,[9] it too is contemporary evidence that he was understood to have written the play. Similarly, if Gabriel Harvey's obscure sonnet, 'Slumbring I lay in melancholy bed', does—as has been generally assumed—refer to Marlowe's death, then its allusion to 'his tamberlaine contempt' is also early evidence of the play's authorship.[10] Thomas Heywood's Cockpit prologue to *The Jew of Malta* (1633) almost certainly assumes that Marlowe wrote *Tamburlaine* (and that his audience knows this)—though, strictly, the lines say only that Edward Alleyn had a great success in the central role.[11] The play is first unequivocally assigned to Marlowe by Robert Henderson in *The Arraignment of the Whole Creature Att the Barre of Religion Reason Experience* (1632).[12] Taken together, these five pieces of evidence add up to a strong case, particularly since (though the play was one of the most commented on of its age) there is no alternative early attribution.

There are several later-seventeenth-century ascriptions to Marlowe, by Francis Kirkman (1671), Gerard Langbaine (1680), William Winstanley (1687),[13] and Anthony à Wood (1691). Wood affirms Marlowe's authorship in the process of denying Thomas Newton's, who

was author, as a certain writer saith, of two tragedies, *viz.* of the first and second parts of *Tamerline the great Scythian Emperor*, but false. For in *Tho. Newtons* time the said two parts were performed [i.e. written] by *Christop. Marlo*, sometimes a Student in *Cambridge*; afterwards, first an actor on the stage, then, (as *Shakespeare*, whose contemporary he was,) a maker of plays.[14]

In the same year the same putative authorship is denied, and the same actual authorship affirmed, in Langbaine's *An Account of the*

---

[9] Arthur Freeman, *ELR* 3 (1973), 44–52.

[10] The sonnet is printed in Tucker Brooke, *Life*, 111–12, and its veiled allusions are discussed in detail by Hale Moore, *SP* 23 (1926), 337–57. For an alternative reading see Charles Nicholl, *The Reckoning: The Murder of Christopher Marlowe* (London, 1992), 60–4.

[11] Bawcutt, *Jew*, 193.

[12] This was first pointed out by Hallett Smith in 'Tamburlaine and the Renaissance', *Elizabethan Studies... in Honour of George F. Reynolds* (Boulder, Colo., 1945), 126–31 (130–1).

[13] Kirkman, *A True, perfect, and exact Catalogue of all the Comedies, Tragedies... ever yet Printed and Published* (London, 1671), 14; Langbaine, *An Exact Catalogue of Comedies, Tragedies... Printed and Published* (Oxford, 1680), 13; Winstanley, *The Lives of the most Famous English Poets* (London, 1687), 134.

[14] *Athenae Oxonienses* (London, 1691, 2 vols.), i. 288 (a note makes clear that 'a certain writer' is Milton's nephew, Edward Phillips, in his *Theatrum Poetarum* [1675]).

English Dramatick Poets.[15] Though two other ascriptions (to Nashe and to Nicholas Breton) were later endorsed by no less an authority than the great eighteenth-century bibliophile, Edmond Malone, neither now seems at all probable, and both almost certainly depend on misreadings of the texts that gave rise to them.[16] Of Marlowe's nineteenth-century editors, only Robinson—the least competent—expresses any doubt about the play's authorship. Thereafter the relative paucity of external evidence has led no-one to doubt what the whole substance and manner of the play proclaims—that it is by Marlowe.[17]

II. Sources

The attempt systematically to trace Marlowe's sources for *Tamburlaine* began in the 1880s, with C. H. Herford and Albrecht Wagner,[1] and their work had been supplemented by Emil Koeppel,[2] Leslie Spence, and Ethel Seaton,[3] when Una Ellis-Fermor published her edition of the play in 1930. Ellis-Fermor therefore already had a considerable body of scholarship and commentary on which to draw, and her account of the main possible sources known to her is exhaustively researched and authoritative.[4] However, in her first edition Ellis-Fermor passed over one major source (George Whetstone),[5] and her account does not always distinguish between what is central and what is peripheral—

---

[15] (Oxford, 2 vols.), 344, 395.

[16] Both are discussed by Una Ellis-Fermor, 13–15.

[17] The most authoritative survey of the whole Marlowe canon, and evidence concerning attributions, is that of C. F. Tucker Brooke, *PMLA* 37 (1922), 367–417.

[1] 'The Sources of Marlowe's *Tamburlaine*', *Academy*, 24 (1883), 265–6, identifying as sources Mexía mediated through Fortescue, and Perondinus (see above).

[2] Emil Koeppel, 'Beiträge zur Geschichte des elisabethanischen Dramas', *Englische Studien*, 16 (1892), 357–74 (III: *Tamburlaine*, 362–5). To Herford and Wagner's identifications Koeppel adds Whetstone's *English Myrror*, raising precisely the problem later treated by Thomas Izard (see n. 6) that Mexía's and Marlowe's tents are in Fortescue flags. Koeppel also points out that Tamburlaine first appears in Whetstone in his *Heptameron of Civill Discourses* (1582; day 6), where he is admired for 'his vertues and invincible valure' as a modern Alexander.

[3] On Spence, see n. 6; on Seaton see Abbreviations, and *Two*, Dramatis Personae, Sigismund, *note*.

[4] *Tamburlaine the Great* (London, 1930; rev. edn., 1951), 17–52.

[5] Following Izard's essay, Ellis-Fermor added some discussion of Whetstone and one example from *The English Myrror* in her 1951 revision, but he remains peripheral to her survey.

though, as it indicates, the life of Timur had been rendered in numerous accounts which Marlowe could conceivably have read: with many possible sources we cannot tell whether or not Marlowe actually read or consulted them because their accounts share so many of the same central elements.

The repeated elements Marlowe used include Tamburlaine's low birth; his keeping the defeated Bajazeth in a cage, feeding him on scraps from his table, and using him as a mounting block; the siege ritual of white, red, and black tents; and the slaughter of a company of (women and) children sent out as ambassadors by a city which had resisted such a siege. There are also repeated elements which Marlowe excluded. Some of this is material which is simply not stageable or dramatic: the 'impregnable' castle which Tamburlaine destroys by building a taller next to it and bombarding it from above, and his adorning of Samarkand. Other exclusions suggest how pointed was Marlowe's selection and arrangement of material: Tamburlaine's lameness; the golden chains used to fetter Bajazeth; the merchant who protests against the cruelty of the slaughtered embassy of children and is furiously answered; Tamburlaine's stratagems in conquest; and the dissension between his two sons by which his empire was lost—though it may be argued that Marlowe does adumbrate the loss of empire in Part 2 in so far as the unity of his action allows.

Of those works which are sufficiently close to Marlowe for us to be certain that he read them, the two which are particularly important are those identified by the earliest commentators. Pedro Mexía's *Silva de Varia Leción* (1542; ii. 14) Marlowe probably read in both the English adaptations—Thomas Fortescue's *The Foreste or Collection of Histories* (1571; i. 15, ii. 14), and George Whetstone's *The English Myrror* (1586; i. 3, 11, and 12). Both of these were translated and adapted from a French intermediary, Claude Gruget, *Les Diverses Leçons de Pierre Messie* (1552), itself an abbreviated adaptation of Mexía. Marlowe's other main source was Petrus Perondinus (Pietro Perondino), *Magni Tamerlanis Scytharum Imperatoris Vita* (1553), which also drew in part on Mexía.

The three offer different perspectives. Fortescue introduces Tamburlaine with pious reflections: he is an agent of God's justice who, when he has completed God's work of punishing others, is himself punished as a tyrant. The biblical curse on divinely

permitted evil is invoked: 'For necessarie is it, that example of ill
happen, but woe be unto him, by whom it happeneth' (*The
Foreste*, i. 15; Matthew, 18: 7). But, though the conventional
moralizing recurs, Fortescue's actual account is full of admiration
for Tamburlaine's achievements. While his cruelty to enemies is
fully registered—particularly because, in Fortescue, Bajazeth is
allowed a degree of nobility—Fortescue also allows Tamburlaine's
courage and discipline, and (to his own people) his courtesy and
liberality. He is both 'verie cruell' and 'adorned with many rare
vertues' (ii. 14). The 'mirror' of Whetstone's title is 'a regard
Wherein al estates may behold the Conquests of Envy': envy is
the underlying subject connecting his examples. The account of
Tamburlaine indicts his cruelty, but is otherwise admiring: its
focus is the envy between his two sons by which their father's
empire was lost.[6] Perondinus is quite different: he provides a
much more full and circumstantial history, governed by no over-
riding theme or moral perspective. He gives full weight to the
violence and cruelty by which Tamburlaine gained, developed,
and maintained his power: in this Perondinus regards him as little
short of bestial, though even here there is admiration for his
courage, discipline, and general pre-eminence. However, the central and most developed episode of Perondinus' account is Tamburlaine's raising of the siege of Constantinople and the saving of
eastern Christendom from Islam. For this, and for Tamburlaine's
generosity in victory to the Palaiologos emperor, Perondinus'
admiration is enthusiastic.

Apart from Perondinus and Mexía, whether or not through
various mediations, we cannot be sure which other accounts of
Tamburlaine Marlowe consulted. Though there is nothing in them
that Marlowe could not have found in several places, in their recent
study of the sources[7] Vivien Thomas and William Tydeman select
three: Baptista Fulgosius, *De dictis factisque memorabilis collectanea*
(1509), which uses Tamburlaine to illustrate the Marlovian theme
that those born in low circumstances can nevertheless achieve great

---

[6] Leslie Spence considers the relation to Fortescue in *MP* 24 (1926–7), 181–99,
emphasizing Marlowe's transformation of his portrait of Bajazeth. J. S. Cunningham (10)
accepts Thomas Izard's view that Whetstone is Marlowe's only English conduit of Mexía,
but Izard's argument is not strong (see *One*, 4.1.49–63*n.*). Tamburlaine's various references
to 'flags', 'colours', and 'streamers' may be reminiscences of Fortescue's account of the siege
ritual.

[7] *Christopher Marlowe: The Plays and their Sources* (London, 1994).

fame; Andreas Cambinus, whose *Libro . . . della origine de Turchi et imperio delli Ottomanni* (1529) was available in English as translated by John Schute, *Two very notable Commentaries the one of the original of the Turkes by Andrewe Cambine* (1562); and the great Italian historian Paulus Jovius (Paolo Giovio, Bishop of Nocera), *Elogia virorum bellica virtute illustrium* (1551). Each of these gives a representative, brief account, such as could be duplicated from many other sources, without special bias or unusual detail.

If, as has been argued, Marlowe consulted the second edition of the Protestant martyrologist John Foxe's *Actes and Monuments* (1570),[8] he found there not only the word 'footstool' but also the perspective of militant Protestantism: Tamburlaine's treatment of Bajazeth was a just punishment for the Turkish emperor's cruelty to Christians. If, taking a recusant perspective, he consulted *Beautifull Blossomes, gathered by John Byshop from the best trees of all kyndes* (1577), he ignored one of its principal features—various tales of the origin of Tamburlaine's lameness. Thomas and Tydeman cite Bishop to suggest that his elaborate account of terrible prognostications preceding Tamburlaine's death may have influenced one detail of Marlowe's presentation.[9] Laonicus Chalcocondylas, whose history of the Turks was available to Marlowe in the Latin translation from the Greek of Conradus Clauserus (*De origine et rebus gestis Turcorum*, 1556), presents one of the few accounts in which a wife of Timur plays any significant role— though it is a role as political adviser, nothing like that of Marlowe's Zenocrate.

None of this second group of writers excerpted by Thomas and Tydeman seems more likely to have influenced Marlowe than several other possibilities discussed by Ellis-Fermor or included in her annotation, particularly Nicolas de Nicolay and Thomas Newton. Nicolay's *The Navigations, Peregrinations and Voyages made into Turkie* (1576, trans. Thomas Washington the Younger, 1585)—a work which probably provided one idea for the action of *The Jew of Malta*—seems to have contributed details to both parts of *Tamburlaine*.[10] The possible influence of Newton's translation

[8] See *One*, 4.2.1*n*.

[9] Thomas-Tydeman, 77. See Note to *Two* 5.3.67–71, which discusses the same detail traced by Seaton[2] (398–9) to André Thevet's *Cosmographie Universelle*.

[10] See notes to *One*, 1.2.88 and 3.3.46–58, and *Two*, Dramatis Personae, Calyphas and Amyras. On the *Navigations* and *The Jew of Malta* see Bawcutt, *Jew*, 6.

of Caelius Augustinus Curio's *Sarracenicae Historiae* (1567)—*A Notable History of the Saracens* (1575)—was first noted by John Payne Collier.[11] Ellis-Fermor prints the obvious Tamburlaine passage of this in her appendix of source materials, though, like Collier, she cites only one short section (1575, 129^r). The immediately following pages of the original give Callapine's name as 'Cyriscelebes', name one of his two sons as 'Orcannes', and give an account of the Battle of Varna;[12] all of which taken together suggests that Newton is a more probable source than recent studies have recognized.

For specific incidents and details of Part 2 Marlowe certainly used Antonius Bonfinius, *Rerum Ungaricarum decades quattuor cum dimidia* (1543), apparently reading in manuscript the translation of Richard Knolles (*The Generall Historie of the Turkes*, 1603) for the Orcanes/Sigismund episode; Paul Ive, *The Practise of Fortification* (1589) for one speech of technical military detail; François de Belleforest, *La cosmographie universelle de tout le monde* (1575) and Ariosto, *Orlando Furioso* (1532), both for the Olympia episode (with Belleforest perhaps supplying other details); and Philippus Lonicerus, *Chronicorum Turcicorum* (1578), his reading of which is evinced by one colourful detail of the Islamic hell. He may also have recalled George Gascoigne and Francis Kinwelmershe's *Jocasta* (1566) in relation to the king-drawn chariot.[13] Of these sources, Perondinus is given almost complete, many of the others in part, with some introductory discussion of each text and how Marlowe used it, in the study by Vivien Thomas and William Tydeman.

Apart from these sources concerned with character and incident, Marlowe also drew frequently in both Parts on the Bible, and on Virgil and Ovid (particularly on Arthur Golding's translation of the *Metamorphoses*), as well as possibly some other Roman writers, including Horace, Cicero, Lucan, and (perhaps through a Renaissance intermediary) Livy (*Two*, 4.1.93–113*n*.). His major

[11] *A Bibliographical and Critical Account of the Rarest Books in the English Language* (New York, 1866, 4 vols.), iii. 38.

[12] Newton, 129^v (cf. *Two*, 3.1.1), 130 (cf. *Two*, Dramatis Personae, Sigismund, note).

[13] On Bonfinius/Knolles see *Two*, 2.1.9*n*. and *Two*, Dramatis Personae, Sigismund, note; on Ive, *Two*, 3.2.62–82*n*.; on Belleforest and Ariosto, *Two*, 3.4.16–17 and 4.2.55–82, notes; on Lonicerus, *Two*, Dramatis Personae, Calyphas and Amyras, note, and *Two* 2.1.18 and 3.20 notes; and on Gascoigne and Kinwelmershe, *Two*, 3.5.103–7*n*.

source for the geography of the plays (particularly of Part 2) is the atlas of Abraham Ortelius.[14] He clearly draws at one point (and perhaps at others) on Spenser (see *Two*, 4.3.119–24*n*.); and may also draw on Plutarch, Machiavelli, and Holinshed.[15] The commentary gives details of all such borrowings, citing detailed discussions.[16]

It may be argued that Marlowe's handling of his sources is, in particular cases, critically indicative. But the sources in themselves give no help in resolving the central critical problem, discussed below, of the play's attitude to Tamburlaine. Unlike Marlowe, his sources are explicit in their judgements, but their range of opinion was as wide as could be, and there is no clear pattern to the different judgements: Tamburlaine was both admired and condemned, and from a variety of viewpoints. What the sources indicate morally is that Marlowe must have been aware of his subject as a ground of contest when he began to dramatize it.

Finally, in considering Marlowe's handling of his material, quite as important as what he found, selected, and arranged is that major element for which he found almost no hint in the sources: Zenocrate. Her role, with the concomitant presentation of Tamburlaine's aspirations in a wholly different and more readily sympathetic area of experience, transforms the portrait of the central character, and with it the meaning of the play as a whole.

III. The Play

Marlowe is *par excellence* a writer the interpretation of whose work is bound up with a view of his life. Most of the documents which record the known facts of that life were printed by C. F. Tucker Brooke,[1] and the facts themselves have been given many exciting

---

[14] See References and Abbreviations, Seaton[1], and the commentary, *passim*.

[15] On Marlowe and Machiavelli see *One*, 5.1.189*n*.

[16] Since *Tamburlaine* was apparently first played in the year Marlowe was awarded his MA he must have researched these sources while still at Cambridge, with access to some of the best libraries in England. We cannot, however, be sure that the library of Archbishop Parker (d. 1575), bequeathed to Corpus Christi College Cambridge, had been actually received by the college before Marlowe left in 1587. See R. I. Page, *N&Q*, n. s., 24 (1977), 510–14. (Page does not return to this subject in his recent *Matthew Parker and his Books*, Kalamazoo, Mich., 1993.)

[1] *The Life of Marlowe and The Tragedy of Dido Queen of Carthage* (London, 1930). Other documentary evidence discovered since Tucker Brooke's *Life* is given by Mark Eccles,

and tendentious interpretations.² Certain elements are clear and uncontested. Mystery—with its concomitant problems of interpretation—begins in 1587 (the year of *Tamburlaine*), probably because Marlowe had sometime earlier been recruited to Sir Francis Walsingham's network of informers and spies. Soon after his arrival in Cambridge in 1580 Marlowe had been elected to a scholarship founded by Archbishop Parker; he had taken his BA degree in 1584, and, since he continued in residence, seems then to have been intended for holy orders. But the university was apparently reluctant to award Marlowe his MA in 1587 until the Privy Council wrote instructing the authorities in interestingly obscure terms that he had been 'emploied . . . in matters touching the benefitt of his Countrie' in a way that it was apparently not prudent to specify. Thereafter Marlowe was based in London, where on several occasions he ran into trouble with the law, before he was stabbed to death at a house in Deptford on 30 May 1593.

The main interpretative issues concerning his character depend on what credence is given to various contemporary testimonies, particularly those of his fellow-dramatist (with whom he for a time shared lodgings) Thomas Kyd, and the informer Richard Baines. Both (almost certainly independently) accused Marlowe of atheism and homosexuality, and specified some of his heterodox opinions with different degrees of righteous horror and quasi-verbatim colouring. Baines' testimony, along with other documents in the case, also associates Marlowe with a supposed atheistical group centred on Raleigh—referred to by the Jesuit Robert Parsons as 'Sir Walter Rawleys school of Atheisme'—including the Wizard Earl of Northumberland and the mathematician Thomas Harriot.³ To this group Marlowe is said to have

---

Marlowe in London (Cambridge, Mass., 1934); F. S. Boas, *TLS*, 16 Sept. 1949, 608; Philip Henderson, *TLS*, 12 June 1953, 381; Arthur Freeman, *ELR* 3 (1973), 44–52; S. E. Sprott, *TLS*, 2 Aug 1974, 840; R. B. Wernham, *EHR* 91 (1976), 344–5; Willem Schrickx, *Documenta*, 1 (1983), pp. 121–31; and William Urry, *Christopher Marlowe and Canterbury* (London, 1988). The standard biography remains F. S. Boas, *Christopher Marlowe: A Biographical and Critical Study* (Oxford, 1940; rev. edn., 1964). The main evidence and the difficulties of its interpretation are summarized by John Steane in *Marlowe: A Critical Study* (Cambridge, 1964), ch. 1.

² For the most elaborate see Charles Nicholl, *The Reckoning* (London, 1992).

³ See Muriel Bradbrook, *The School of Night* (Cambridge, 1936: quotation from Parsons, 11–12). The phrase of Bradbrook's title comes from a contested reading in *Love's Labour's Lost* (4.3.253).

read an 'atheist lecture', which Paul Kocher reconstructed from the Baines note in terms of attacks on both the Old and New Testaments, and on the institution of religion *per se* as a tool of political oppression.[4] Kocher's reconstruction is professedly tentative, but its general drift (supported as it is by the corroboration of other congruent, independent testimonies) many critics have seen, and continue to see, as persuasive and important[5]—though the problem remains of what relationship one sees between the polemicist thus reconstructed and the dramatist.

The problems of interpretation of Marlowe's life have a direct bearing on opposed readings of his work generally, and *Tamburlaine* in particular. On one view Marlowe is an orthodox Elizabethan (the conception of orthodoxy may be variously defined), and his plays show the downfall of the unorthodox, their falls caused by their deviations. The fullest elaboration of this argument in relation to *Tamburlaine*, by Roy Battenhouse,[6] is simply one polemical expression of a persistent account of Marlowe's whole *œuvre*,[7] the evidence about which is: what the first audiences may be supposed to have thought as evinced by more or less

[4] *Christopher Marlowe: A Study of his Thought, Learning and Character* (Chapel Hill, 1946), 33–68.

[5] John Mebane, for example (see n. 10), specifically endorses Kocher's account of the 'atheist lecture' (234). The Kyd and Baines testimonies are examined by Jonathan Goldberg in the context of Renaissance discourses of homosexuality in David Scott Kastan and Peter Stallybrass (eds.), *Staging the Renaissance: Reinterpretations of Elizabethan and Jacobean Drama* (London, 1991), 75–82. For a recent survey of what is known about Baines, see Constance Brown Kuriyama in *'A Poet & filthy Play-maker': New Essays on Christopher Marlowe*, ed. Kenneth Friedenreich, Roma Gill, and Constance Brown Kuriyama (New York, 1988), 343–60; and Nicholl, *The Reckoning*, esp. 123–33.

[6] *Marlowe's 'Tamburlaine': A Study in Renaissance Moral Philosophy* (Nashville, 1941; 2nd edn., 1964). Battenhouse argues that *Tamburlaine* offers 'one of the most grandly moral spectacles in the whole realm of English drama' (258). Working from a fundamentally similar idea, W. Moelwyn Merchant indicts Tamburlaine for an 'impious defiance of degree and order'. That Tamburlaine defies the conservative doctrine of the homilists that all should keep to the place in the social hierarchy allotted them by birth could not be plainer. That the play treats this as corrupt is questionable. Read in this way, the play teaches us to have unaspiring minds: we should 'maintain the equipoise of the natural order': 'Marlowe the Orthodox', in Brian Morris (ed.), *Christopher Marlowe* (Mermaid Critical Commentaries, London, 1964), 177–92 (188).

[7] Broadly similar views are expressed by Molly Mahood, *Poetry and Humanism* (London, 1950), Douglas Cole, *Suffering and Evil in the Plays of Christopher Marlowe* (Princeton, 1962), and Judith Weil, *Christopher Marlowe: Merlin's Prophet* (Cambridge, 1977). Cole's account is one of the best in this kind. It is less polemical than that of Battenhouse, and so registers more of a range of effects. Cole accepts that Marlowe may give conventional forms new meanings. His observations are just, but one-sided. Dismissing all but the

official expressions of opinion; the theatrical traditions and conventions within which Marlowe worked; and a reading of the
central debated work, *Doctor Faustus*, as an Elizabethan morality
play in which there is little sympathy for the aspirations of the
scholar-magus whose damnation is just. One problem with all this
in relation to *Tamburlaine* is its claim to historicity—a claim
which, it has been argued, is implausible, given that, amongst
the considerable amount of contemporary comment on the play,
not a single voice expresses such a view.[8] The evidence of
recorded contemporary opinion suggests rather that the first audiences would have thought the Christian-moralist reading turned
the play on its head.

From the Christian-moralist perspective the alternative position—according to which Marlowe is (in various degrees)
unorthodox, subversive, and iconoclastic—is ahistorical, the con-
textually deracinated error of post-Romantic liberalism. Hazlitt set
the tone for it by finding in Marlowe, with a fine implication of
heterodoxy, 'a hunger and thirst after unrighteousness'. This has
broadly been the view of some of Marlowe's most distinguished
critics from Swinburne to Stephen Greenblatt.[9] One might argue
that, in different forms and with different emphases, this repres-
ents the consensus of two centuries—and of Marlowe's pious
contemporaries, who, far from thinking him orthodox, called

Parker-scholarship ordinand aspect of Marlowe's biography, he is unresponsive to
Marlowe's delight in the heterodox. Weil argues that Marlowe mocks his heroes with a
subtle irony of obscure allusions, and an implicit commentary of structural analogies and
spectacular devices. She admits that in *Tamburlaine* the dark allusions are peculiarly veiled
and the ironies unusually oblique (on Mahood, see n. 17.)

[8] Richard Levin, *Medieval and Renaissance Drama in England*, i. ed. J. Leeds Barroll III
(New York, 1981), 51–70. Cf. Peter Berek on imitations as a form of evidence about how the
first audiences saw the plays: '*Locrine* Revised, *Selimus*, and Early Responses to *Tamburlaine*', *Renaissance Drama*, 13 (1982), 55–82.

[9] *Renaissance Self-Fashioning: From More to Shakespeare* (Chicago, 1980). Swinburne's
comments are collected in Millar MacLure (ed.), *Christopher Marlowe: The Critical Herit-
age, 1588–1896* (London, 1979). Fundamentally similar views are expressed by Una Ellis-
Fermor, *Christopher Marlowe* (London, 1927); Paul H. Kocher (see n. 4); Harry Levin,
Christopher Marlowe: The Overreacher (London, 1952); Eugene M. Waith, *The Herculean
Hero in Marlowe, Chapman, Shakespeare and Dryden* (London, 1962); William Empson,
Faustus and the Censor, ed. John Henry Jones (Oxford, 1987); and C. L. Barber, *Creating
Elizabethan Tragedy: The Theatre of Marlowe and Kyd*, ed. Richard P. Wheeler (Chicago,
1988). (Greenblatt is broadly of this view, though with a typically Marxist turn of the screw
he sees Marlowe's rebels and sceptics as inescapably embedded in the structures of the
orthodoxies to which less determinist accounts imagine them opposed.)

him an atheist, and saw his death as God's punishment for his impiety. While the view of Marlowe as orthodox would discredit the evidence given by Kyd, Baines, and others about Marlowe's heterodox opinions, the opposite account maintains that, though this evidence may be unreliable in detail, it gives a broadly accurate indication of Marlowe's opinions, often setting these in a context of wider investigations of Elizabethan heterodox thought.[10] Invoking this tradition also recognizes that the pulpit constantly complained about the theatre, in ways which suggest that its own moral writ did not run there as the Christian-moralist reading implies—rather, that the theatre offered the possibility of experimenting in imagination with attitudes and experiences which an enforced uniformity in religion forbade in ordinary life.

The view of Marlowe as an orthodox Elizabethan in his opinions, by emphasizing elements which some versions of the earlier ('romantic') view had ignored or had passed over as artistic infelicities not in keeping with Marlowe's aims, disrupted simple identifications between Marlowe and his heroes and brought more recognition of genuine ambiguities and countercurrents in the plays. The presence of alternative ways of valuing within Marlowe's work does not, however, make them, as some critics have argued, morally neutral.[11] It is possible to sympathize with a current of feeling which acknowledges the fundamental attractiveness of the aspiring hero, while recognizing that the sceptical-

[10] How partial the invocation of Elizabethan orthodoxy is about the full intellectual context of Marlowe's work is indicated by John S. Mebane, *Renaissance Magic and the Return of the Golden Age: The Occult Tradition in Marlowe, Jonson, and Shakespeare* (Lincoln, 1989). Mebane relates to Marlowe (in particular to *Doctor Faustus*) the heterodox traditions articulated by Ficino, Pico della Mirandola, and Cornelius Agrippa. One central difference between this body of thought and the orthodox tradition's domination by original sin lies in its view of human aspiration as potentially uniting human and divine. Cf. Hilary Gatti, *The Renaissance Drama of Knowledge: Giordano Bruno in England* (London, 1989).

[11] Clifford Leech, *Christopher Marlowe: Poet for the Stage*, ed. Anne Lancashire (New York, 1986), 42–3. Cf. J. R. Mulryne and Stephen Fender, 'Marlowe and the Comic Distance', in Brian Morris (ed.), *Christopher Marlowe*, 47–64 (56). A new historicist version of a fundamentally similar view, according to which Marlowe 'frustrates discrimination', is proposed by Emily C. Bartels. Bartels develops critically the ideas of Edward Said's *Orientalism* (1978) to suggest Marlowe's subversiveness in exposing cultural stereotypes as constructs, and so persistently not demonizing as 'other' the alien (Scythian, Jew, magician, homosexual). This she relates to Stephen Greenblatt's notion of self-fashioning (see n. 9), examining how Marlowe's heroes create themselves and how others create them, and for what purposes: *Spectacles of Strangeness: Imperialism, Alienation, and Marlowe* (Philadelphia, 1993).

ironic-comic variations of tone by which the central overreachers are surrounded make Marlowe's plays morally complex, and that the aspirations they dramatize are presented as difficult and dangerous. With *Tamburlaine*, perplexity about moral attitude seems almost ostentatiously built in. The Prologue challenges ('applaud his fortunes as you please'); even Tamburlaine's enemies puzzle; and, though some are sure about his moral status, many are uncertain.[12]

There are large issues implicit in these disagreements, both about ways of reading historically and about interpretations of the Renaissance—as a period of discovery and positive new possibilities, or as a period of religious schism and breakdown in communitarian structures and social relationships. In so far as these are disagreements about contemporary values, they are likely even to involve different interpretations of the Enlightenment. It is part of *Tamburlaine*'s strength that Marlowe dramatizes so fundamental a clash, and from a perspective that imagines something of the force of opposed views. That he does so may go some way to explaining why the play is amenable to apparently opposite interpretations: on each side there is both truth and partiality. Beyond that, the presence of such distinct critical traditions—through metamorphoses of many critical methods—must indicate at least that the plays lay themselves open to substantially different readings. While it would be folly to aim for a synthesis of profoundly opposed perspectives, and while one may recognize that the partiality of some critical polemics amounts to nothing less than misreading, still, a wholly satisfying account of Marlowe must allow that the very existence of such opposed traditions of interpretation has some significance.

Crucial to an estimate of the rival views of Marlowe as they relate to *Tamburlaine* are those episodes in both parts in which the hero's cruelty is most flagrantly exhibited—his treatment of Bajazeth and the other captured Turkish kings; the killings at Damascus and Babylon; and those episodes in Part 2 which might seem in some

---

[12] See e.g. *One*, 2.7.41; *Two*, 4.1.170; *One*, 2.6.9–10. David H. Thurn attacks attempts to establish any comprehensible relation between aspiration and limitation in the play as a critical fiction of the humanist tradition. In his Lacanian account the humanist reader/ spectator, wishing to sustain an illusion of his/her own unity, cannot acknowledge that the play consistently subverts the stabilizing terms it generates: *ELR* 19 (1989), 3–21.

sense a defeat—the cowardice of Calyphas, and the deaths of Zenocrate and of Tamburlaine himself.

Understanding the emphases of Marlowe's presentation of Bajazeth requires some contextualization. The Ottoman empire had embarked on expansion into Europe during the late fourteenth century and during the fifteenth; and it did so again in the sixteenth century, defeating the Hungarians at Mohacs in 1526, and by 1529 reaching so far into Europe as briefly to besiege Vienna. When Orcanes remembers besieging that city (*Two* 1.1.) it matters less to what historical events he might refer than that, for the first audience, his taunts would suggest the contemporary Ottoman threat to Europe, most recently (and, as nobody could then know, finally) defeated at Lepanto in 1571.[13] In 1402 it had been Timur's intervention that, for the time, decisively deflected Ottoman westward expansion. That he had in effect then saved Europe from Ottoman domination was a well-informed contemporary view.[14] In the sixteenth century Europe apparently needed saving again.

For the first audience Tamburlaine therefore begins with advantages which Marlowe pointedly reinforces. He presents Bajazeth besieging the centre of eastern Christendom, boasting of his bands of forced Christian apostates, and claiming to rule Europe (*One*, 3.1.1–24), so making it, though evidently not a fact, an aim; while Tamburlaine is presented as the would-be liberator of captive Christians suffering in inhumane conditions (*One*, 3.3.46–60), and (later) the protector of a specific Christian community against Islam (*Two*, 5.1.31–3). Other aspects of Marlowe's direct presentation are in a degree even-handed: he does not use from his sources either (in Bajazeth's favour) his personal heroism at the battle of Ankara, or (on the other hand) the notion of his sufferings as retributive justice for the murder of his brother by which he came to power.[15] In terms of direct presentation

---

[13] Halil Inalcik, *The Ottoman Empire: The Classical Age, 1300–1600*, trans. Norman Itzkowitz and Colin Imber (London, 1973), Part 1 *passim*; Paul Coles, *The Ottoman Impact on Europe* (London, 1968), esp. ch. 3 *passim*, and 145–53. Cf. Samuel C. Chew, *The Crescent and the Rose: Islam and England during the Renaissance* (Oxford, 1937), which includes a brief discussion of *Tamburlaine*.

[14] Eric Voegelin, 'Machiavelli's Prince: Background and Formation', *Review of Politics*, 13 (1951), 142–68.

[15] See Thomas–Tydeman (Sources, n. 7), 86, 110, 127, 133, 135. Bajazeth's murder of his brother to obtain the throne is also reported in Whetstone, i, ch. 11, not included by Thomas and Tydeman.

Marlowe at first shows Bajazeth as good-humoured and magnanimous, though liable to flare up bombastically. With 'Turkes are ful of brags' Tamburlaine strikes out a remark in tune with this portrayal, which at times verges on comedy. Moreover, when opposed, Bajazeth becomes as violent and cruel potentially as Tamburlaine later is in fact: though its enactment depends on Tamburlaine's charismatic flamboyance, Bajazeth invents the degradation of the human chariot-horse (*One*, 3.3.77–80). The punishments which Bajazeth proposes before Ankara do not excuse Tamburlaine's brutality, but they compromise Bajazeth's grounds of protest; while his response to defeat—a loathing of Chistianity, an Islamic attitude to which Marlowe imagines brilliantly (3.3.236–40)—is calculated to alienate the sympathies of the first audience.

In Bajazeth's defeat Marlowe reverses this emphasis. In the banquet scene, where Bajazeth's sufferings serve to entertain the stage audience, for the audience in the theatre he becomes a pitiable figure. This is partly because Marlowe shifts the context: Tamburlaine is given a new tone of brutality (extended parts of the scene are, for the first time, in prose) and none of the compensatory music of sublime aspiration which earlier complicates responses to him. That compassion for Bajazeth is not an anachronistic response (one which ignores that spectacles of suffering were permitted forms of Elizabethan entertainment) is indicated by Zenocrate. She may not yet pity Bajazeth—but when she is confronted with the consequences of his suffering she regards it as a sin not to have done so (5.1.348–72); and the compassionate response she pleads for in relation to her father and her country is not validated only by the particular ties which prompt her to it. The banquet scene initiates a complication of response which is typical of Marlowe, and shows the flexibility of perspective which makes *Tamburlaine* irreducible to doctrinaire readings.

From the hateful and, at times, comic figures of Act III, and the figures of pathos in Act IV, Bajazeth and Zabina become tragic figures in Act V. The final change of tone begins with the killing of the Virgins of Damascus. Even Tamburlaine, '*verie melancholy*', shows for the first time the strain of his own cruelty. Zenocrate, whose poetry presents to the imagination sufferings the stage cannot show, offers an exemplary reaction: even beasts inured to cruelty could scarcely perform these killings. Zenocrate's lament, with its choric vision of 'the Turke and his great Emperesse' as exempla of the frailty of all earthly grandeur, draws out the response which Bajazeth's impotent curses and Zabina's madness—brilliantly contrived to exhibit an incoherence full of meaning—have already engendered. The close of Part 1 thus confirms the complication of feeling initiated by the Act IV banquet. When Tamburlaine follows up his ghoulish joke about unusually heavy rains caused by his blood-lettings with the naïveté of 'And see my Lord' as he notices the bodies of his victims, no audience that has responded adequately to the deaths and associated sufferings can accept the bodies simply as 'sights of power to grace [Tamburlaine's] victory'. The poetry, the context, and the stage picture interact to produce a complex counterpoint of tones.

The most directly similar cruelties of Part 2 evoke a comparable complexity of response. Like Bajazeth, the captured Turkish kings, had they been able, would have exercised cruelties of the kind to which they are subjected: it is they who first threaten extraordinary revenges (3.5.90). That there is, therefore, nothing to choose morally between these sufferers and their tormentor may free the audience to enjoy Tamburlaine's mental energy, which is made the more exhilarating by a degree of elegantly poised wit in the famous 'pamper'd jades' speech. But Tamburlaine's king-drawn chariot raises acutely the problem of Marlowe's manipulation of audience response through constant and subtle variation of tone, particularly in his use of comedy, the very presence as well as the character of which is often open to interpretation. Both how to judge the tone of any supposed comedy, and how to place it in relation to the other tones created and emotions stirred by the play, is one of the most difficult, contested, and crucial problems of interpretation in Marlowe's drama. Here it can be argued that Tamburlaine's ferocity towards the Turkish 'concubines' points up the tone of the 'pamper'd jades' speech by a use of immediate and subtle contrast. In Tamburlaine's dealings with the concubines, too, there is a kind of wit ('I will prefer them . . .'), but it is more crudely jeering, in line with the change of tone in the whole episode: this involves both more horrifying cruelty (the women are handed over to what is in effect group rape) and more innocent suffering. With the king-drawn chariot, Tamburlaine's jests may be uneasily echoed by laughter among the audience; with the concubines they only heighten the audience's horror.[16]

Like the cruelties to Bajazeth in Part 1 and to Orcanes and his allies in Part 2, the climactic slaughterings at Damascus and at Babylon are also in parallel. It is not only part of the drama as spectacle that, while the Virgins of Damascus are being killed (off-stage), Tamburlaine meditates on Zenocrate's beauty: this conjunction is worked into the meditation itself by Tamburlaine's contentious claim that his feelings for Zenocrate cause him more suffering than he causes others. In itself the speech is one of Marlowe's most powerful expressions of his master-theme, the aspiring mind: though its overt subject is specifically the inability of poetry wholly to capture experience, it implies an analogous feeling about experience itself, a doubt about whether a thirst for the complete can ever be entirely satisfied. The poetry is brilliantly expressive of this: the extended syntax, its skewed orderliness reinforced by irregular musical patterns, superbly enacts the striving which is Tamburlaine's subject. The insatiable nature of this struggle—the argument that a perpetual approach to plenitude can never culminate in arrival—seems to demand the paradox of a crescendo of diminishing terms for what finally escapes: 'One thought, one grace, one . . . at the least'. But 'one wonder' disturbs this pattern, and though we may supply subliminally Collier's too-sensible emendation ('at the last') to smooth out the disrupted expectation into a simple crescendo, the main sense is that a pattern of predictability cannot be applied to this struggle. Similarly it is difficult to know, even in reading, what is affirmed at the end of Tamburlaine's soliloquy, not only because the syntax is (expressively) strained, but also because the conclusion is presented as though arising logically from all that has preceded it, whereas the final assertion in fact cuts through Tamburlaine's difficulties by introducing (with all its attendant variations of meaning) the new issue, 'Vertue'. There is an underlying train

---

[16] The Turkish concubines should probably not be presented as sexually corrupt, nor even as the victims of sexual corruption, but as concubines in the sense that, on a Christian view (such as that implied by Tamburlaine's relationship with Zenocrate), Mohammedan polygamy is 'concubinage'. See *Two*, Dramatis Personae, 'concubines', *note*. On Marlowe's manipulation of tone through comedy, see Eugene M. Waith, 'Marlowe and the Jades of Asia', *Studies in English Literature*, 5 (1965), 229–45; and Mulryne and Fender (n. 11 above).

of thought: the loves of the gods show Tamburlaine—able both to appreciate beauty and control his response to it—as superior to the divine, and therefore a supreme example of 'Vertue' (*virtù*). But the different paraphrases of editors indicate that the audience is likely to grasp the final assertion unsure of the process by which it has been reached. Tamburlaine has here a puzzling eloquence on a central human subject, and Marlowe draws the audience in by this. But the dramatic context—the killing of the Virgins, and Tamburlaine's immediate plunge into his most brutal tone for the continued torturing of Bajazeth—means that the audience is simultaneously drawn in by the poetry and repelled by the action. It is a typically Marlovian effect, repeated near the close of Part 2 (4.3), with Tamburlaine's vision of himself as the earthly Jove, and (for those able to recognize the hints provided by the alexandrine and the Spenserian diction) as Prince Arthur. Even if the Spenserian echoes go unrecognized, the poetry in itself gives a genuine vision of splendour, but, as so often, poetry, stage picture (the harnessed kings), and action (the rape of the Turkish queens) are in clashing counterpoint.

The killing of the Governor of Babylon, comparable in its structural position at the climax of Part 2 to the slaughter of the Virgins of Damascus in Part 1, is also an instructive contrast. The Governor appears at first as of uncompromising courage, but, *in extremis*, this collapses into an attempt to bargain for his life with just the cowardice he condemns in others. The culpability is compound: the collapse is no momentary *volte-face*, but an escape planned while the Governor hypocritically condemned others, hoping that his profession of courage would not be tested. The Governor's hypocrisy, however, scarcely mitigates the audience's judgement of Tamburlaine. There is nothing here to redeem Tamburlaine's cruelty in the way that the struggle with contrary feelings during the murder of the Virgins of Damascus complicated the climax of Part 1. Now the absence of Zenocrate and the feelings she provoked and symbolized is crucial to Tamburlaine's plunge into new and unmitigated depths of brutality. The sack of Babylon is a scene of vileness in which Tamburlaine's unflinching cruelty to the Governor is compounded by his new violence to the captured kings. The burning of the Koran is, therefore, the climax of a movement in which Tamburlaine seems intoxicated by the desire to enact every cruelty he can conceive, as though to test whether there is any violence from which he will shrink. There proves to be none.

Throughout Part 1 Tamburlaine is continuously successful in imposing his will on circumstance. His fiat on the treatment of Bajazeth—'This is my minde, and I will have it so'—strikes a keynote. One development of Part 2 is his encounter with limitations that no human condition can dominate: the intractability of another personality, and death. The killing of Calyphas and the death of Zenocrate indicate the vulnerability—and, some would argue, finally the hopelessness—of Tamburlaine's aspirations.

Tamburlaine's behaviour to his sons is consistent with his view that honour is due not to birth but to ability. He expects his sons to inherit his character: it is only by demonstrating that inheritance in their actions that they will inherit his empire. But none of the sons are adequate to what Tamburlaine wants of them: Calyphas is only the most obviously inadequate. He has shrewd common sense, and even, in comparison with his boyish brothers, some humanity. However, as with Mycetes in his comparable indictment of Tamburlaine's warrior ethos (*One*, 2.4), the audience cannot identify with Calyphas because so much about him (his low-minded sexual jokes, his cowardice) is unsatisfactory.

We are reminded earlier of the archetypal rebellion of son against father—Jupiter against Saturn (*One*, 2.7.12): the murder of Calyphas is its horrific obverse. Tamburlaine expects the impossible: that his sons should reincarnate his unique dynamism. They do not, and Tamburlaine—having reversed one mythic pattern by being, even in age, more dynamic than his sons—reverses another and kills the son who, by his passive resistance, attempts the archetypal Oedipal task. Calyphas's cowardly evasive pacifism is the obverse not only of Tamburlaine's ethic but also of his manner. In killing him, Tamburlaine attempts to control all that can be controlled by the will. The other sons do not join Calyphas's rebellion because they are more afraid of their father than of the chances of war—wisely: death for rebellion against Tamburlaine is more certain than death in battle. But not everything can be controlled: Amyras and Celebinus may accept Tamburlaine's ethos, but he cannot impart to them his charisma. It is the impossibility of doing that—acknowledged in the case of Calyphas, but evident with his brothers—that provokes Tamburlaine to the murder: better obliterated than disgraceful. The killing presents a typical juxtaposition of brutal action with poetry of sublime aspiration. To argue that the brutal wholly undermines the sublime is to simplify the divided response Marlowe typically demands.

The extraordinary scene is symbolic in more than one way. It is an aspect of himself that Tamburlaine kills, the legacy of Zenocrate naturally symbolized in their child—an embodiment of the thoughts 'effeminate and faint', which troubled his career of violence in Part 1 (5.1.177; both words are recalled in relation to Calyphas at 4.1.164–6). It is the absence of what Tamburlaine's warrior ethic permits him to adore when exteriorized in the female, but causes him to doubt in himself and despise when exteriorized in his son, that makes the violence of the climax of Part 2 simpler than that of the close of Part 1.

Tamburlaine is twice in some sense defeated in Part 2: more important than the cowardice of Calyphas is the death of Zenocrate. Though Tamburlaine has, astonishingly, in every matter conceivably under human control made good his vaunt, 'I hold the Fates bound fast in yron chaines', the death of Zenocrate shows for the first time the limits of his power. But Tamburlaine's rage at Zenocrate's death—his refusal to accept it, even in a degree to believe it—though it has been the focus of critical remark,[17] need not be seen as the extraordinary delusion of a megalomaniac: his responses can be understood as based in ordinary experience. When Tamburlaine has Zenocrate's body wrapped in gold and her coffin kept with him, his aim is to remain in communion with what is irrevocably lost—her spiritual presence—through contact with its obvious symbol. That grief is normally moderated in more practical ways means that the audience has no power of extravagant gesture, not that it has no thrill of sympathy with one. It is the nature of heroic drama to be operatic: feelings can be exhibited unmitigated by the practical and contingent; characters need not, as Yeats put it, when deeply moved gaze into the fire. Certainly,

---

[17] See e.g. Mahood, *Poetry and Humanism*, 62. Mahood distances herself from some of Battenhouse's interpretations, but endorses his general drift. For her, 'true Humanism' (following Jacques Maritain) is a synthesis of medieval faith and Renaissance knowledge. *Tamburlaine* she fits into a pattern of development in Marlowe of enthusiasm for and disenchantment with secular humanism, which epitomizes the more general development of the next half-century. This supposed disenchantment begins to be evinced by changes in tone between Parts 1 and 2 of *Tamburlaine*.

Theridamas speaks the practical wisdom Tamburlaine has to learn: 'be patient, she is dead'. And clearly it is easy for Theridamas to do so. Similarly, the fired town is not a megalomaniac invention: this, like the king-drawn chariot, is behaviour with a recognized precedent—there Sesostris, here Alexander. The erstwhile shepherd is fashioning himself on the pattern of a semidivine hereditary ruler.

Nor is the death of Zenocrate simply a defeat: in response Tamburlaine is at his greatest. Zenocrate's dying drives him to acknowledge, in verse of a lyricism unrivalled within the play, power and beauty not involved with his own ego. His religious vocabulary—'king of kings', 'christall springs whose taste illuminates/Refined eies'—though not tied to its usual Christian frame of reference, cannot be purged of those usual connotations. The effect, however, is not blasphemous: the speech expresses awe and reverence before what is properly to be revered—his love for Zenocrate, and, through it, the intuited beauty of the divine.[18]

Some critics have seen in the presentation of Zenocrate a degree of misogyny.[19] One does not wish to dispose of interesting complications by blandly invoking a convention, but it seems clearly worked into the text that, in his treatment of Zenocrate, Tamburlaine is belying expectations (such as the Souldan's) about his Scythian barbarism by ostentatiously observing a courtly code: he will not exploit Zenocrate's position as his captive; marriage must wait until her father can give permission. Zenocrate understands this: the behaviour 'might in noble minds be counted princely'. To interpret it as frigidity,[20] or as a symbolic translation of the homosexual author's fear of women,[21] ignores the context. That Tamburlaine has problems with feelings of his own (compassion) and of Calyphas (fear), which are conventionally associated in his culture with the female, is a recognized aspect of his military

[18] The religious aspects of this scene, and of the play more generally, are well considered by John Steane, *Marlowe: A Critical Study*, 113–16.

[19] Roger Sales, *Christopher Marlowe* (New York, 1991), 81–2. Cf. Emily C. Bartels, *Spectacles of Strangeness*, 25–6. Simon Shepherd, however, argues that Marlowe explores gender difference in ways that expose contradictions and so force the audience to recognize such differences as constructs: *Marlowe and the Politics of Elizabethan Theatre* (Brighton, 1986), 178–97.

[20] Barber, *Creating Elizabethan Tragedy*, 66.

[21] Constance Brown Kuriyama, *Hammer or Anvil: Psychological Patterns in Christopher Marlowe's Plays* (New Brunswick, NJ, 1980), 29.

code. That code may not seem satisfactory to a modern ethos. Such codes have always been contentious. In any case, Tamburlaine's murder of Calyphas is not simply endorsed by the military code he invokes: this is clear both from the direct presentation and the possible Livian source. Nevertheless, it has its basis in his general scheme of values, and is consistent with the uncompromising extremism of all his actions. The first audience would not have seen Tamburlaine's feelings about Zenocrate, or his actions in relation to Calyphas, as requiring any submerged explanation.

Any estimate of Tamburlaine will be in part determined by how far his poetry gives the sense of a genuine possible grandeur and sublimity—in his vocabulary of thirsting and striving, thrusting and glutting; in his characteristic extremist formulae (more *x* than the most *x*—'lovelier than the Love of *Jove*'); in the cosmic scale implied by his comparisons with classical legend and myth— Achilles, Atlas, and, above all, Jove, as both mentor and competitor; and in his characteristic verbal music, especially the savouring by repetition of words which suggests a total (or obsessive) concentration—'Shall all we offer to *Zenocrate*, / And then my selfe to faire *Zenocrate*'; or the relished, repeated 'ride in triumph through *Persepolis*' (*One*, 2.5.50, 54).[22] Much of Marlowe's vigour as a poet lies in his verbal inventiveness—his sensitivity to a word or usage just gaining currency; the patterns of reference and imagery which are one aspect of his government of the play's tone; and, within the overall unity of the famous 'mighty line', his often expressive syntactic inflections. The early rhapsodic assertion of 'The thirst of raigne' exhibits many of Tamburlaine's (and the play's) characteristic qualities.

> The thirst of raigne and sweetnes of a crown,
> That causde the eldest sonne of heavenly *Ops*,
> To thrust his doting father from his chaire,
> And place himselfe in the Emperiall heaven,
> Moov'd me to manage armes against thy state.
> What better president than mightie *Jove*?

[22] David Daiches argues that Tamburlaine's rhetorical abilities are the index of a genuinely heroic aspiration: 'Language and Action in Marlowe's *Tamburlaine*', *More Literary Essays* (Edinburgh, 1968), 42–69. Richard A. Martin discusses how Marlowe's manipulation of tone determines the spectator's acceptance of the shocking as admirable: 'Marlowe's *Tamburlaine* and the Language of Romance', *PMLA* 93 (1978), 248–64. Daiches deals only with Part 1; Martin sees a change in Part 2, in which the imaginative freedom of romance more nearly gives way to the sense of human limitation associated with tragedy.

Nature that fram'd us of foure Elements,
Warring within our breasts for regiment,
Doth teach us all to have aspyring minds:
Our soules, whose faculties can comprehend
The wondrous Architecture of the world:
And measure every wandring plannets course:
Still climing after knowledge infinite,
And alwaies mooving as the restles Spheares,
Wils us to weare our selves and never rest,
Untill we reach the ripest fruit of all,
That perfect blisse and sole felicitie,
The sweet fruition of an earthly crowne.

(*One*, 2.7.12–29)

Part of the energy of this speech is located in its evident distortion: the myth of Saturn overthrown by Jove is applied with an inventive disregard of circumstance. Cosroe, who has thrust aside the foolish Mycetes, and who in relation to Tamburlaine has imagined himself (with evident hubris) as Jove defeating the Titans, is wrenched into a false correspondence with the supposedly 'doting' Saturn. Tamburlaine's idiosyncratic shaping of the myth implies that all authority except his own is *per se* foolish and impotent. More simply, the four elements were framed by Nature as potentially co-operative: it is Tamburlaine's indicative invention that their natural state is one of internecine struggle.[23] Likewise, though the planetary spheres may be always moving, to see this heavenly activity as 'restles' is a revelatory projection. The speech has attracted comment partly because it has an impersonal validity for the age, particularly in its stress on the new and disruptive Renaissance knowledge of the astronomer (Tycho Brahe, later Kepler and Galileo), with all the metaphysical new horizons that such observations implied. Tamburlaine becomes, for a moment, Faustus. But the characteristic emphases also make the speech perfectly in character, as, above all, does the climax. For a moralist commentator, 'the sweet fruition of an earthly crowne' is bathos which exposes the corrupt pretension of the whole. Even admirers are disappointed.[24] On another view, the evident blasphemy is

---

[23] Parallels have been sought for this idea, but not found: Kocher, 76; D. J. Palmer, 'Marlowe's Naturalism', in Brian Morris (ed.), *Christopher Marlowe*, 151–76 (163–5).

[24] Contrast Battenhouse, *Marlowe's 'Tamburlaine'*, 3, and Una Ellis-Fermor, *Christopher Marlowe*, 29 ('Marlowe . . . has broken faith with his idea').

simply the perfect fulfilment of Tamburlaine's confrontation with conventional hierarchies of value.[25] It is meant to offend pious moralist and sentimental idealist alike. Moreover, it is a climax which is soon to be acted out in gesture, as a consummation of pleasure of which Tamburlaine's poetry of aspiration has established the intensity—though one needs to remember how this pleasure is contextualized by the stage spectacle: Tamburlaine has the dying Cosroe at his feet. In a minor way, the tableau foreshadows the visionary rhapsody which is accompanied by the massacre at Damascus, or the 'sights of power to grace [his] victory'—the bleeding bodies of Bajazeth, Zabina, and Arabia—which accompany the coronation of Zenocrate.

Contemporary comments on the play suggest that such moments drew the wondering admiration of the first audiences, albeit to the scandal of contemporary moralists. Nevertheless, even some of the play's least moralistic critics feel a doubt: is not the necessary condition of Tamburlaine's dynamism perpetual dissatisfaction? C. L. Barber comments that 'there is nowhere for [Tamburlaine] to arrive'.[26] This is to distort what Tamburlaine says, and what the audience sees. The human condition is, Tamburlaine claims, to be 'aspiring...climing...alwaies mooving ...restles...Untill': we can attain points of fulfilment. Michael Goldman discusses this issue in a fine essay on what he calls 'the histrionics of ravishment'.[27] For Goldman, the Marlovian hero is a being 'ravished', with an aim which suggests the possibility of total fulfilment, an aim which can also be seen as directed obsession or infatuation; a being whose nominal objective, necessarily a thing with limits, is recognized (by the audience, and at moments by the character) as not at bottom his true provocation. In this account, Marlowe shows intense and boundless aspiration seeking an object, as well as an object with distinct bounds by which aspiration is generated. It is, therefore, part of Marlowe's conception of

[25] Cf. Harry Levin, *Christopher Marlowe*, 57. Contrast Lawrence Danson, 'Christopher Marlowe: The Questioner', *ELR* 12 (1982), 3–29 (13–15): ignoring contemporary responses to the play (see n. 8), Danson argues that mention of Jove's rebellion assumes an unstated context of Christ's obedience, by which all is then judged.

[26] *Creating Elizabethan Tragedy*, 58.

[27] 'Marlowe and the Histrionics of Ravishment', *Two Renaissance Mythmakers: Christopher Marlowe and Ben Jonson*, Selected Papers from the English Institute, 1975–76, ed. Alvin Kernan (1977), 22–40. The feelings Goldman discusses are not, he argues, confined to the central character, but are carried over into action and structure.

the ravished man that his energies should be unstable: though Tamburlaine may seem dominated by his desire for earthly crowns to which all else must give way, he also denigrates power in comparison with the love of Zenocrate, the being of his sons, the companionship of his contributory kings. Goldman accepts, however, that *Tamburlaine* is unusual in Marlowe's *œuvre* in the degree to which limitless desires—which, in other plays, turn to sources of suffering and destruction for the central figure—are here that only for others. For Tamburlaine, though there remains always a new horizon—'And shall I die, and this unconquered?'—there is also satisfaction within the aims that have been the overt focus of desire. What we see at the end of Part 1 Act 2 is (paradoxically) a transitional consummation. Tamburlaine's is not a neurotic energy: though it may not repose in any finally, it can reach points of complete satisfaction. One is reached here; another—and a greater—at the end of Part 1.

It is part of the moralist-Christian view of the play that Tamburlaine's death should be seen as punishment, that it should be accompanied by psychological suffering as a result of sin, and so give a final 'verdict' on Tamburlaine's aspirations intended from the outset. Shakespeare's Richard III would provide a near-contemporary example of such a death. The Prologue to *Tamburlaine* Part 2, however, claims that Part 1 was conceived by itself, and that Part 2 is a response to its popularity.[28] While this may be no more than the best way of presenting what Marlowe had always planned, it seems more probable that the Prologue's claim is true: Marlowe used most of the main incidents of his source material in Part 1, which he would hardly have done if he were planning a sequel. The original intention was, therefore, to end with Tamburlaine at the height of his triumphs, with none of the qualifications which can be read into Part 2—which does not mean that the two parts did not grow to form a unity, only that the first part cannot be interpreted as though always intended to lead to the second.

Even considered in itself, however, Tamburlaine's death presents interpretative difficulties: Marlowe, as usual, does not give

---

[28] The argument that the 'tragicke glasse' promised in the Prologue to Part 1 implies that Part 2 was always intended to follow is a misunderstanding. The Prologue introduces Part 1 only: 'tragic' here means serious (*OED a.* 1.a), as opposed to the drama which 'clownage keepes in pay'.

unambiguous guidance about how to view it—but it is quite different from Richard III's. Battenhouse sees Tamburlaine's challenge to Mahomet as epitomizing sacrilege, because it shows Tamburlaine's 'boastful contempt of *all* authority outside himself'.[29] But the challenge cannot properly be read in this way, because denigration of Mahomet, like the conclusion that he remains in Hell, is by Elizabethan standards orthodox. In taking the Koran as 'the Scriptures'[30] it is the moralist-Christian view that is ahistorical. Tamburlaine's challenge cannot, either, be understood as a permitted surrogate for a blasphemy which would cause objections from the censor: it is accompanied by positive theistic professions which are not merely nominal, but are consistent with attitudes Tamburlaine expresses elsewhere. Tamburlaine's 'if any God' does not imply a doubt about the existence of God: this would be at odds with what he has asserted and immediately goes on to assert. (Following 'Seeke out another Godhead to adore', it means 'if you wish to worship at all'.) If the audience connects Tamburlaine's sudden illness with the challenge to Mahomet—a possibility which Marlowe's placing of the illness permits, but by no means insists on—the effect is not to celebrate the power of a damned heathen, but, more obliquely (as Stephen Greenblatt argues), to suggest a doubt about whether the Christian heaven should be seen as the sole source of rewards and punishments.[31] Moreover, the following scenes undermine any connection that might have been made between Tamburlaine's challenge and his illness: they are a positive satire of trust in Mahomet. Certainly the challenge is related to the episode of Sigismund's oath-breaking, which is interpreted by characters in the drama as a challenge to Christ to show his power (so the non-Christian Orcanes pleads it should be; so Sigismund subsequently takes it to be). But even in that Christian context, Marlowe proposes a doubt about divine intervention: Gazellus counters Orcanes' incipient conviction with a naturalistic explanation (*Two*, 2.3.31–2).

[29] *Marlowe's 'Tamburlaine'*, 171.
[30] Ibid. 257. Similarly seeing the precise challenge as unimportant, Una Ellis-Fermor reads the episode as calling in question the validity of any religion based on the idea of a personal God who intervenes in history: *Christopher Marlowe*, 34.
[31] *Renaissance Self-Fashioning*, 202. Cf. the discussion by Ian Gaskell in the wider context of Part 2's presentation of religious issues: *English Studies in Canada*, 11 (1985), 178–92 (184–6).

However, preceding Tamburlaine's death Marlowe does generate the expectation of a profound and total reversal. Tamburlaine may have been struck down by the supernatural force which is invoked with unbounded confidence by Callapine. This possible religious sanction is explicitly combined with the natural facts of Turkish numerical superiority and universal mutability to suggest that Tamburlaine's death might be associated, at last, with military defeat. That this elaborately generated possibility is totally reversed, and Tamburlaine defeats Callapine apparently by his mere presence, transforms Tamburlaine's death, against the odds, into a final triumph of personal charisma—all the more so because he nobly accepts death as inevitable, looks forward to immortality through his sons, and, with a final lyric intensity, joys in the prospect of reunion with Zenocrate.[32] As usual, the effect is not simple: the presentation of the sons throughout Part 2, and emphatically in the final scene—in Amyras's manner of speech, and the imagery of Phaeton and Hippolytus—indicates that Tamburlaine's hopes for earthly immortality through his sons' achievements exceed all probability. Nevertheless, and despite the conclusion of the feeble Amyras, the predominant feeling of the close is not that usually thought of as tragic. The final effect is less like that of *Doctor Faustus* than of *Samson Agonistes*: Tamburlaine has quit himself like Tamburlaine; nothing is here for tears.

IV. Stage History

That *Tamburlaine* was first performed in the 1580s is clear from the printer Richard Jones's address to the readers of the 1590 octavo, as from other contemporary comments. The 1590 title page records that these performances were by 'the right honorable the Lord Admyrall, his servantes'. The first datable Elizabethan performances are those registered in the diary of Philip Henslowe in 1594–5,[1] with the great Elizabethan actor Edward Alleyn as Tamburlaine;[2] and it seems likely, from continued reference to the

---

[32] Cf. Eugene Waith, who sees the death as 'a glorification...approaching apotheosis' (*The Herculean Hero*, 85).

[1] See I. Date and Authorship, n. 1; and commentary, *One*, 4.2.1 and 4.4.1.

[2] See A. D. Wraight's copious and enthusiastic *Christopher Marlowe and Edward Alleyn* (Chichester, 1993), chs. 1 and 2.

play as still well-known in the early seventeenth century, that it continued to be performed for several years after Marlowe's death. The next recorded performances, however, are all twentieth-century. After an all-male student production of a much-truncated text of both parts edited by Edgar Montillion Woolley and Stephen Vincent Benét at Yale in 1919,[3] and an Oxford University Dramatic Society production of Part 2 only, directed by Nevill Coghill in 1933, the first professional production to give both plays in anything like a full text was that of Tyrone Guthrie, with Donald Wolfit in the title role, at the Old Vic and Stratford in 1951 (re-staged, with more elaborate sets and costumes, at Stratford, Ontario, and New York in 1956, with Anthony Quayle as Tamburlaine). The published performance text (London, 1951) shows that there were considerable cuts: whole characters of the importance of Sigismund and Olympia, as well as entire scenes, were omitted. In brief introductions Guthrie argues the play's contemporaneity following the Second World War and Wolfit the variety of its tone when prepared by actors for speaking aloud in the theatre.

A version prepared by Basil Ashmore (London, 1948), with an introduction by Eric Linklater explaining how much Ashmore improves on Marlowe, has not only cuts, but also additions and transpositions, to heighten the love interest: that Tamburlaine and Zenocrate confess their loves in a pastiche of lines from *Dido* is not so remarkable as that some of Callapine's tempting bribes to Almeda are transferred to these transformed lovers. Thus adapted the play was twice staged to honour Marlowe's quatercentenary in 1964. A production by the Glasgow Citizens' Theatre at the Edinburgh Festival in 1972 was notable mainly for having three separate actors play Tamburlaine, one in each act of the cut text: but no critic seems to have discerned an illuminating purpose in this division of labour.

The next considerable production after that of Guthrie and Wolfit—probably the most notable of modern times—was that which opened the new British National Theatre in 1976, directed by Peter Hall, with Albert Finney as Tamburlaine. The play was performed in a single evening, but with only relatively minor cuts and rearrangements. The performance was almost universally

---

[3] Published, Yale U. P., New Haven, 1919.

praised. The Woolley/Benét, Guthrie/Wolfit, and Hall/Finney productions are described in some detail (with brief reference to and documentation of other performances in the 1960s and 1970s) by George L. Gekel.[4] The Guthrie/Wolfit production is also discussed (and criticized for its excessive reliance on spectacle and its attempt at a Shakespearean style of characterization) by John Russell Brown,[5] and by Nancy T. Leslie,[6] who gives, in addition, a brief account of a London production by Robert Jones for the Marlowe quatercentenary. The Hall/Finney production has been described (with helpful detail about what actually happened on stage) by J. S. Cunningham and Roger Warren:[7] they praise its responsible and imaginative realization of the text, its extrapolations of the plays' local and larger formal symmetries, and (following Wolfit's remarks) the variousness of tone—including comedy—which, without forcing, it discovered in the lines. Most of all, their account suggests how well this production caught the flickering shiftings of sympathy and tone which contribute so much to the plays' characteristic ambiguity. The text, edited by Peter Hall and John Russell Brown, was published by Rex Collings (London, 1976). This publication, like that of the Guthrie/Wolfit productions, shows the text as prepared for rehearsals, and gives no indication of movement and stage business in the performances.

Since 1976 the most notable production has been that of Terry Hands for the Royal Shakespeare Company in 1992, with Antony Sher as a charismatic and physically exuberant Tamburlaine (climbing ropes and swinging from them, Tarzan-like), who aged wonderfully into a waddling but still powerful elder. The staging was spectacular, with African dances and chants, and violent even beyond what the text requires (a lengthy garrotting of Calyphas, the severing of one of Zabina's fingers, and—a practice reported by Perondinus which Marlowe chose to ignore—a feast of human flesh). As with Guthrie/Wolfit, the cuts were considerable: extraordinarily, given the obvious relevance in 1992 of conflict between Islamic nations and the West, these included the Sigismund/Orcanes episode.

---

[4] 'Tamburlaine' and 'Edward II': Text and Performance (Atlantic Highlands, NJ, 1988).
[5] 'Marlowe and the Actors', Tulane Drama Review, 8 (1964), 155–73.
[6] 'Tamburlaine in the Theatre: Tartar, Grand Guignol, or Janus?', Renaissance Drama, n. s., 4 (1971), 105–20.
[7] 'Tamburlaine the Great Re-Discovered', Shakespeare Survey, 31 (1978), 155–62.

V. The Text and Editorial Procedures

There are four early editions of *Tamburlaine*, published in 1590, 1593 (or 1592: the date on the unique copy's title-page is not clear), 1597—all three single-volume octavos—and 1605–6, a two-volume quarto (Part 1, 1605; Part 2, 1606). Of these, only the 1590 text has any substantive authority. Those of 1593 and 1597 derive independently from it. The text of 1605–6 derives from that of 1597.[1] The detailed evidence on which this view of the texts is based was first assembled by Albrecht Wagner (who did not, however, know of the 1597 edition, and so supposed 1605–6 dependent on 1590). The relation of 1597 to the other texts was established by Una Ellis-Fermor.[2]

One possible complication, which might attribute some substantive authority to *O2* (1593), has been suggested by Ethel Seaton, who pointed out that this edition contains six corrections accepted by all editors.[3] While each of these could be corrections guessed in the printing house, Seaton questioned whether, taken together, they were not evidence that *O2* was set up from a copy of *O1* corrected by Marlowe himself. (Since *O2* has many new errors, one would need to suppose that Marlowe did not read the proofs.) Should this be the case, several more new readings of *O2* might be considered authorial variants.[4] However, since Seaton's suggestion can be no more than a hypothesis, and in each of these latter cases the reading of *O1* is satisfactory, and since the theory does not take account of the manifest errors in *O1* not corrected in *O2*,[5] nor that *O3* (printed after Marlowe's death) actually corrects more errors

---

[1] Transcripts of the full title-pages and collations of each of the early editions are given in W. W. Greg, *A Bibliography of the Early Printed Drama to the Restoration* (4 vols., London, 1939), i. 171–4. A facsimile of *O2* (1593), edited by Roma Gill, was published by the Scolar Press (Menston, 1973).

[2] Albrecht Wagner, *Marlowes Werke. 1. 'Tamburlaine'* (Heilbronn, 1885), pp. xxii–xxxi; Ellis-Fermor, 281–2.

[3] Seaton, review of Una Ellis-Fermor's edition, *RES* 8 (1932), 467–72. The six crucial errors of *O1* properly corrected in *O2* (all in Part 1) are at: 1.1.38, 2.2.15, 2.7.50, 3.3.173, 4.2.49, 4.3.3, and 5.1.141 (see Apparatus in the present edition).

[4] Seaton points particularly to *One* 2.2.28 (*O1* are, *O2* be), 2.3.12 (*O1* some, *O2* scorne), 3.3.51 (*O1* breath and rest, *O2* rest or breath), 4.2.17 (*O1* heart, *O2* soule), and (extending the hypothesis in Part 2, in which there are no generally accepted corrections from *O2*) *Two* 4.1.79 (*O1* glories, *O2* bodies), and 5.1.209 (*O1* gaspe, *O2* gape).

[5] For example, at *One* 1.1.87, 2.1.27, 2.3.7, 2.5.32, 4.4.132, 5.1.300, or *Two* 2.4.56, and 3.2.58 (see Apparatus).

than *O2*, none of these variants has been admitted into the present text.

The text of 1590 is based on a manuscript which had probably not been used in the theatre, and which may have been written by Marlowe himself. It is unlikely that the manuscript came from a theatrical source, because the printed text lacks many indications necessary for staging, acting, and prompting. Specific features of the printed text indicating that it is based on a manuscript of non-theatrical provenance are: misnumbered scenes and omitted scene divisions; scene divisions made on inconsistent principles (there are several cases where a new scene is marked at an important entry though the stage has not been cleared); omitted entry and exit directions; omitted or inexplicit directions for necessary stage actions; the entire omission of speech prefixes; the omission from speech prefixes or stage directions of names supplied by the dialogue; and inconsistent naming in stage directions.[6] Moreover, the occasional omissions from and obscurities of the text are not ones which can be explained by the normal processes of theatrical corruption. All these features, combined with the Latin act- and scene-divisions, and punctuation which seems at times carefully

---

[6] The Apparatus gives full details of all these features. They are tabulated in J. S. Cunningham's edition (86–9), which the following observations supplement or correct. In addition to the scenes listed by Cunningham, *Two* 1.2 and 3 are incorrectly numbered 1.3 and 4, and *Two* 5.2 and 3 are incorrectly numbered 5.4 and 6. One possible explanation of some misnumbered scenes, that of omitted comedy, is suggested above; but, even if admitted, this cannot explain the unusually confused scene-numbering of Part 2, Act 3 (3.2 called 2.2; 3.3 called 3.1; 3.5.57 called 2.1). Presumably a new scene was begun in the manuscript at the present 3.5.57 to mark an important entry (as at *One*, 5.1.63 and elsewhere), though how it came to be called 2.1 (for 3.6) is inexplicable, as are the act's two other, less remarkable, misnumberings. There are unmarked exits in addition to those listed by Cunningham at the end of *One*, 3.2, 4.1 and 5.1, and *Two*, 3.3. There are further inadequate or omitted directions for necessary stage business at the ceremonial presentations to Tamburlaine in *Two*, 1.3: for the moment of death of Sigismund and the removal of his body (*Two*, 2.3.9, 41); for the kneeling and standing of various pleaders to Tamburlaine, and for Tamburlaine's stabbing of Calyphas (*Two*, 4.1.100, 106, 113); and for the burning of the Koran (*Two*, 5.1.178, 186). The changes of costume and properties to white and black are not always indicated (*One*, 4.2.1; *Two*, 5.1.62). The fates of Trebizon and Soria as implied by the dialogue are not followed through with any indication of stage action (see Apparatus, *Two*, 5.1.135). The use of the gallery is not specified where it is implied by the action at *Two*, 3.3.14; and the directions for music throughout (particularly the uses of trumpets and drums implied by the dialogue for military and ceremonial effects) are inadequate. There is one further unclear speech heading, at *One*, 5.1.193; and the names of Ceneus (at *One*, 1.1.35) and Uribassa (at *Two*, 1.1.1, 20) are given in confused forms in stage directions and a speech heading.

rhetorical, suggest a manuscript prepared in the study, possibly by Marlowe.

One problem about the text is what, if anything, can be surmised about the 'fond and frivolous Jestures' that the printer, Richard Jones, claims in his opening address to the reader to have omitted. These may have been no more than improvised actors' gags of the type reprobated by Hamlet, though that Jones should refer to them at all suggests something more elaborate. They may also have been written by Marlowe. *Doctor Faustus*, as we have it, indicates how he might have juxtaposed serious and comic material, and even as it stands, *Tamburlaine* goes a little way in this direction.[7] But it is, of course, uncertain how much of *Faustus* as we have it is of Marlowe's devising; the prologue to *Tamburlaine* Part 1 implies that there will be no 'clownage' but only 'stately' and 'tragicke' material; and both parts are, in any case, quite long. Part 1 has 2,508 lines and, Part 2 has 2,532, which already makes them Marlowe's longest plays, except for *Edward II* at 2,839 lines.[8] The length of the plays, together with the statements of the prologue, favours the view that the missing 'Jestures' were improvised in the theatre. However, Ethel Seaton again suggests a complication: that the misnumbering of scenes in *O1* may indicate that whole scenes of comedy have been cut.[9] This would indeed account for some of the misnumbering—though only some of it. If this is the case, comic scenes have been cut from before *One* 4.4 and *Two* 1.2, 4.2, 5.2, and 5.3 (the misnumbering of 5.2. as 5.4 would, on this explanation, imply two missing comic scenes). The theory in part explains a feature of the text: beyond that it is neither provable nor disprovable. Another explanation of the misnumbering of some scenes in Part 2 may be that it is a consequence of the different mode of scene division exhibited at *One* 5.1.63 and *Two* 1.1.77, 111, and 127: a new scene was

---

[7] So far, in fact, that Una Ellis-Fermor takes the text as it stands to retain disfiguring fragments of playhouse interpolations: see her notes to the opening epistle, *One*, 2.4.28–35, 3.3.215–27, 4.4.11–15, *Two* 1.3.61–3 (this edn. 2), 3.1.74–5, 3.5.100–2, and 156–7. David Bevington suggests that the comic scenes could have been the work of a collaborator, and that Marlowe might have written the prologue dismissing 'clownage' specially for Jones's publication: *From 'Mankind' to Marlowe: Growth of Structure in the Popular Drama of Tudor England* (Cambridge, Mass., 1962), 200–2.

[8] These figures are taken from David Bradley, *From Text to Performance in the Elizabethan Theatre: Preparing the Play for the Stage* (Cambridge, 1992), 231, 233.

[9] *RES* 8 (1932), 469.

marked in the manuscript at a major entry, this scene division was omitted as inconsistent by the printer, but subsequent scenes were not appropriately renumbered. Thus it may be that in the manuscript a new scene was begun with the entry of Tamburlaine after *Two* 4.1.75, and though the printer omitted the direction for this he still headed the following scene 4.3. The same explanation could apply in Act I of Part 2 (scene 1 having been divided in the manuscript at the entry of Sigismund after 1. 77), and might partially account for the misnumbering in Act V (scene 1 having been divided in the manuscript at the entry of Tamburlaine after 1. 62). This would not invalidate Seaton's suggestion about missing comic scenes: indeed, it might make it seem more probable, since one would need to suppose fewer of them.

Seaton's hypothesis implies nothing about the provenance of the manuscript from which the text was set up, since such scenes could have been written by Marlowe himself and so included in any fair copy without theatrical intervention. Bowers suggests a quite different explanation of Jones's comments: that the scenes did originate in the theatre, that Jones therefore did not have (in his non-theatrical manuscript) scenes which he knew had been successful in performance, and that he invented a high-sounding reason for not including what he could not include.[10] Since no other example is known from the period of a printer excising popular matter on artistic grounds, this explanation seems quite as probable as any other.

The play was entered in the Stationers' Register on 14 August 1590: 'Richard Jones. / Entred vnto him for his Copye / The twooe commical discourses of TOMBERLEIN the Cithian shapparde / vnder the handes of Master ABRAHAM HARTEWELL, and the wardens . . . vjd'.[11] Richard Jones is not thought to have owned a press in the years 1589–91, but the actual printer of the 1590 octavo has not been definitely identified. Robert Welsh argues plausibly, on the evidence of ornaments and initials, that the printer was probably Thomas Orwin.[12] The text collates A–K8,

[10] Bowers, I. 75.

[11] Edward Arber (ed.), *A Transcript of the Registers of the Company of Stationers of London; 1554–1640 A.D.*, 5 vols., (London, 1875–94), ii. 558.

[12] Robert Ford Welsh, *The Printing of the Early Editions of Marlowe's Plays* (University Microfilms, Ann Arbor, 1964), 12–13.

L2: both parts were probably set by the same single compositor.[13]
Part 2 is presented as a separate work: Part 1 ends, 'Finis Actus
quinti & ultimi huius primae partis'; Part 2 opens with a woodcut
(on F2^v) of a man in armour entitled 'Tamburlaine, the great',[14]
followed (on F3) by a new half-title and prologue.

Two copies of 1590 are extant, in the Bodleian and Huntington
Libraries, with a further fragment (sigs. A1–2) prefixed to the
Huntington copy of Q. The Bodleian copy is uncorrected; there
are five minor corrections in the Huntington copy.[15] The Bodleian
copy is incomplete (lacking sig. K3 and part of sig. D6), and cut
down so that line endings and final lines on some pages are
missing. Some lines, although fewer, are also missing as a result
of trimming in the Huntington copy. The copy text for this
edition is therefore the Huntington copy, supplemented as necessary by that in the Bodleian. The British Library copy of O2 and
the Huntington copies of O3 and Q have been consulted as
necessary. No copy of the edition of the play which James
Broughton said he had 'printed (but not pubd) 1818'[16] has yet
come to light. For the very rare edition of William Oxberry (1820)
I have used a copy (on microfilm) from Yale University Library.
Information on the other editions and notations consulted is given
in the References and Abbreviations.

The general editorial aim has been to show exactly what was in
the 1590 octavo, while making the text one which can be used by a
wide readership.

The apparatus performs the usual task of registering all substantive changes from O1 (including additional stage directions),
and crediting the originator or showing the text in which each was
first made. The commentary considers many emendations suggested by earlier editors which have not been incorporated into the

---

[13] Ibid. 30–1.

[14] This woodcut had been previously used in Thomas Hill, *The Contemplation of
Mankind, containing a Singuler Discourse of Phisiognomie* (1571); George Whetstone, *The
Honorable Reputation of a Souldier* (1585); and, as Bowers (I. 73) reports, Sir William
Stanley, *A Short Admonition or Warning* (1587). See Ruth Samson Luborsky and Elizabeth
Morley Ingram, *A Guide to English Illustrated Books, 1536–1603*, Medieval and Renaissance
Text Society (forthcoming).

[15] These are corrections of punctuation at *One*, 1.1.6, 10, 14, and 108, and of a mistaken
letter at 2.4.42sd.

[16] N. W. Bawcutt, 'James Broughton's Edition of Marlowe's Plays', *N&Q*, n.s., 18
(1971), 449–52.

present text. As throughout the edition, the use of i/j and u/v has been normalized silently. The names of speaking characters in stage directions, which in *O1* appear in Roman lower case, are given in capitals. The names of mute characters in stage directions remain in lower case, but, like the stage directions, are given in italic in place of *O1*'s Roman. Speech prefixes, abbreviated and with only an initial capital in *O1*, are here expanded in regularized forms, and given in capitals. (Spelling of names is not regularized in speeches or stage directions where *O1* gives a name in full, since this irregularity is a normal feature of the original and of the period.)

All other changes are registered in the collation of accidentals, as follows. Undoubted printing-house errors are emended (upnon, th'mperiall). Similarly emended is punctuation which, by Elizabethan standards, would have either been wrong, or at least highly irregular—punctuation less than a full stop at the end of a speech (as at *One*, 1.1.17); a full stop in the middle of a grammatical unit (as at *One*, 1.1.40); a comma at the end of a grammatical unit (as at *One*, 1.1.66). Question marks are added where a question is clearly asked. The occasional ampersands and contractions of names are also expanded.

The punctuation of *O1* may be at times carefully rhetorical,[17] and it has therefore been emended only modestly. However, old spelling need not imply complete retention of the original text's punctuation, since to do this would on occasion confuse the reader. With old spelling in relation to modern, there is a change of form but not of signification. (Where there are changes of signification these are, of course, noted in the commentary.) With old punctuation one may have the opposite—no change of form, but a change of signification. In keeping with the policy of the edition so far, therefore, and in keeping with the practice of other recent old-spelling editions,[18] punctuation which would actively mislead about the intended syntax has been emended. For example, at *One*, 1.1.123–34: the *O1* punctuation implies that ll.127–8 belong grammatically with the preceding lines; whereas in fact they belong with the lines which follow. To leave

[17] See Una Ellis-Fermor's edition, pp. vi–vii.
[18] See e.g. *The Shorter Poems of Edmund Spenser*, ed. William A. Oram *et al.* (Yale U. P., New Haven, 1989).

O1's punctuation would positively hinder the reader from making out the correct sense.

In *O1* metrical and non-metrical 'ed' are usually differentiated (ed/'d), except that unpronounced 'ed' may occur after a vowel (as at *One*, 1.1.14, 'denied'). In other cases where printed 'ed' should not be pronounced syllabically the spelling of *O1* is retained and a note is given in the commentary on the number of syllables to be pronounced (as at *One*, 1.1.12, 'governed', pronounced as two syllables).

Apart from the few standardized changes made throughout (i/j, u/v; speech prefixes; names in stage directions), the accidental emendations thus give full information about each non-substantive change, while a degree of modernized punctuation aims to accommodate the needs of a variety of readers.

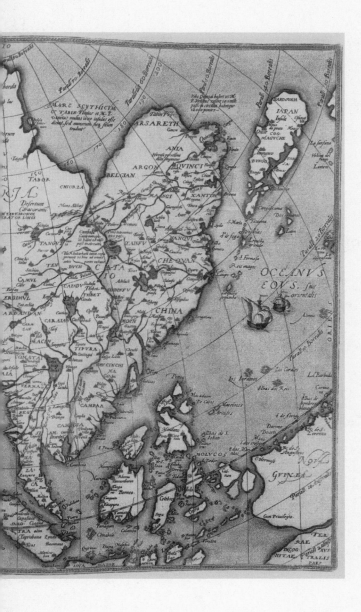

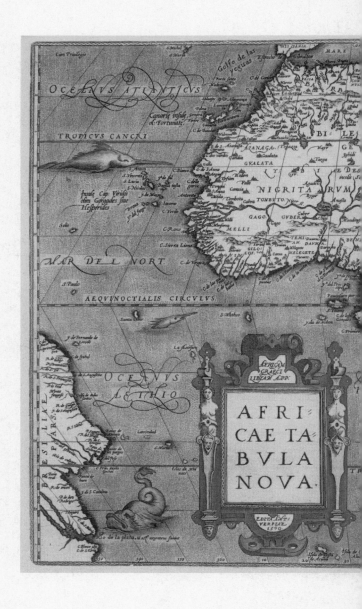

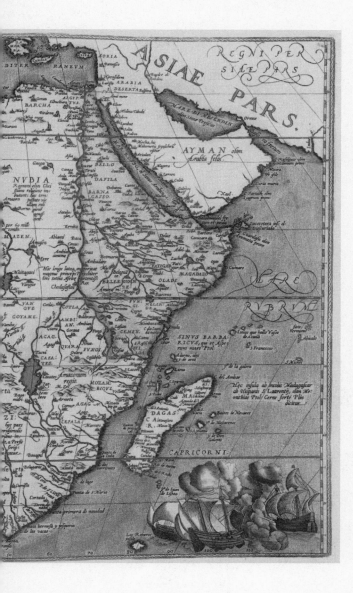

Tamburlaine

the Great.

Who, from a Scythian Shephearde,
by his rare and woonderfull Conquests,
became a most puissant and migh-
tye Monarque.

And (for his tyranny, and terrour in
Warre)was tearmed,

The Scourge of God.

Deuided into two Tragicall Dis-
courses, as they were sundrie times
shewed vpon Stages in the Citie
of London.

By the right honorable the Lord
Admyrall, his seruantes.

Now first, and newlie published.

LONDON.
Printed by Richard Ihones: at the signe
of the Rose and Crowne neere Hol-
borne Bridge. 1590.

To the Gentlemen Readers: and others that take pleasure in reading Histories.

Gentlemen, and curteous Readers whosoever: I have here published in print for your sakes, the two tragical Discourses of the Scythian Shepheard, Tamburlaine, *that became so great a Conquerour, and so mightie a Monarque: My hope is, that they wil be now no lesse acceptable unto you to read after your serious affaires and studies, then* 5
they have bene (lately) delightfull for many of you to see, when the same were shewed in London upon stages: I have (purposely) omitted and left out some fond and frivolous Jestures, digressing (and in my poore opinion) far unmeet for the matter, which I thought, might seeme more tedious unto the wise, than any way els to be regarded, though 10
(happly) they have bene of some vaine conceited fondlings greatly gaped at, what times they were shewed upon the stage in their graced deformities: nevertheles now, to be mixtured in print with such matter of worth, it wuld proove a great disgrace to so honorable and stately a historie: Great folly were it in me, to commend unto your wisedomes, 15
either the eloquence of the Authour that writ them, or the worthinesse of the matter it selfe; I therefore leave unto your learned censures, both the one and the other, and my selfe the poore printer of them unto your most curteous and favourable protection; which if you vouchsafe to accept, you shall evermore binde mee to imploy what travell and service 20
I can, to the advauncing and pleasuring of your excellent degree.

Yours, most humble at commaundement,
R. J. Printer

TAMBURLAINE
THE GREAT

Part 1

[Dramatis Personae

PROLOGUE

MYCETES, King of Persia

COSROE, his brother

MEANDER
THERIDAMAS
ORTYGIUS } Persian lords
CENEUS
MENAPHON

TAMBURLAINE, a Scythian shepherd

TECHELLES }
USUMCASANE } his followers

BAJAZETH, Emperor of the Turks

KING OF FESSE
KING OF MOROCCO } tributary kings to Bajazeth
KING OF ARGIER

ALCIDAMUS, King of Arabia

SOLDAN OF EGYPT

GOVERNOUR OF
  DAMASCUS

AGYDAS }
MAGNETES } Median lords attending Zenocrate

CAPOLIN, an Egyptian

PHILEMUS, a Messenger

SPY

Bassoes, Lords, Citizens, Moors, Soldiers, Messengers and Attendants

ZENOCRATE, daughter to the Soldan of Egypt

ANIPPE, her maid

ZABINA, wife to Bajazeth

EBEA, her maid

Virgins of Damascus]

Dramatis Personae] *Oxberry (incomplete); not in O1.*

The two tragicall Discourses of mighty Tamburlaine, the Scythian Shepheard. &c.

[Enter] The PROLOGUE.

From jygging vaines of riming mother wits,
And such conceits as clownage keepes in pay,
Weele lead you to the stately tent of War:
Where you shall heare the Scythian Tamburlaine,
Threatning the world with high astounding tearms
And scourging kingdoms with his conquering sword.
View but his picture in this tragicke glasse,
And then applaud his fortunes as you please.

OSD *Enter*] *this edn.; not in O1.*

Actus. 1. Scæna. 1.

[*Enter*] MYCETES, COSROE, MEANDER, THERIDAMAS,
ORTYGIUS, CENEUS, [MENAPHON,] *with others.*

MYCETES. Brother *Cosroe*, I find my selfe agreev'd,
  Yet insufficient to expresse the same:
  For it requires a great and thundring speech:
  Good brother tell the cause unto my Lords,
  I know you have a better wit than I.   5
COSROE. Unhappie *Persea*, that in former age
  Hast bene the seat of mightie Conquerors,
  That in their prowesse and their pollicies,
  Have triumpht over *Affrike*, and the bounds
  Of *Europe*, wher the Sun dares scarce appeare,   10
  For freezing meteors and conjealed colde:
  Now to be rulde and governed by a man,
  At whose byrth-day *Cynthia* with *Saturne* joinde,
  And *Jove*, the Sun and *Mercurie* denied
  To shed their influence in his fickle braine,   15
  Now Turkes and Tartars shake their swords at thee,
  Meaning to mangle all thy Provinces.
MYCETES. Brother, I see your meaning well enough.
  And thorough your Planets I perceive you thinke,
  I am not wise enough to be a kinge,   20
  But I refer me to my noble men,
  That knowe my wit, and can be witnesses:
  I might command you to be slaine for this,
  Meander, might I not?
MEANDER. Not for so small a fault my soveraigne Lord.   25
MYCETES. I meane it not, but yet I know I might,
  Yet live, yea, live, *Mycetes* wils it so:
  Meander, thou my faithfull Counsellor,
  Declare the cause of my conceived griefe,
  Which is (God knowes) about that *Tamburlaine*,   30

That like a Foxe in midst of harvest time,
Dooth pray upon my flockes of Passengers,
And as I heare, doth meane to pull my plumes:
Therefore tis good and meete for to be wise.

MEANDER. Oft have I heard your Majestie complain,   35
Of *Tamburlaine*, that sturdie Scythian thiefe,
That robs your merchants of *Persepolis*,
Trading by land unto the Westerne Isles,
And in your confines with his lawlesse traine,
Daily commits incivill outrages,   40
Hoping (misled by dreaming prophesies)
To raigne in *Asia*, and with barbarous Armes,
To make himselfe the Monarch of the East:
But ere he march in *Asia*, or display
His vagrant Ensigne in the Persean fields,   45
Your Grace hath taken order by *Theridimas*,
Chardg'd with a thousand horse, to apprehend
And bring him Captive to your Highnesse throne.

MYCETES. Ful true thou speakst, and like thy selfe my lord,
Whom I may tearme a *Damon* for thy love.   50
Therefore tis best, if so it lik you all,
To send my thousand horse incontinent,
To apprehend that paltrie Scythian.
How like you this, my honorable Lords?
Is it not a kingly resolution?   55

COSROE. It cannot choose, because it comes from you.

MYCETES. Then heare thy charge, valiant *Theridimas*,
The chiefest Captaine of *Mycetes* hoste,
The hope of *Persea*, and the verie legges
Whereon our state doth leane, as on a staffe,   60
That holds us up, and foiles our neighbour foes.
Thou shalt be leader of this thousand horse,
Whose foming galle with rage and high disdaine,
Have sworne the death of wicked *Tamburlaine*.
Go frowning foorth, but come thou smyling home,   65
As did Sir *Paris* with the Grecian Dame.
Returne with speed, time passeth swift away,

38 Trading] *O2*; Treading *O1*.

Our life is fraile, and we may die to day.
THERIDAMAS. Before the Moone renew her borrowed light,
Doubt not my Lord and gratious Soveraigne,   70
But *Tamburlaine*, and that Tartarian rout,
Shall either perish by our warlike hands,
Or plead for mercie at your highnesse feet.
MYCETES. Go, stout *Theridimas*, thy words are swords,
And with thy lookes thou conquerest all thy foes: 75
I long to see thee backe returne from thence,
That I may view these milk-white steeds of mine,
All loden with the heads of killed men,
And from their knees, even to their hoofes below,
Besmer'd with blood, that makes a dainty show.   80
THERIDAMAS. Then now my Lord, I humbly take my leave.

                                                    Exit.

MYCETES. *Theridamas*, farewel ten thousand times.
Ah, *Menaphon*, why staiest thou thus behind,
When other men prease forward for renowne?
Go *Menaphon*, go into *Scythia*,   85
And foot by foot follow *Theridamas*.
COSROE. Nay, pray you let him stay, a greater task
Fits *Menaphon*, than warring with a Thiefe:
Create him Prorex of *Assiria*,
That he may win the Babylonians hearts,   90
Which will revolt from Persean government,
Unlesse they have a wiser king than you.
MYCETES. Unlesse they have a wiser king than you?
These are his words, *Meander* set them downe.
COSROE. And ad this to them, that all *Asia*   95
Lament to see the follie of their King.
MYCETES. Well here I sweare by this my royal seat—
COSROE. You may doe well to kisse it then.
MYCETES. Embost with silke as best beseemes my state,
To be reveng'd for these contemptuous words.   100
O where is dutie and allegeance now?
Fled to the Caspean or the Ocean maine?
What, shall I call thee brother? No, a foe,

---

87 task] *conj. Oxberry*; feat *conj. Malone*; charge *conj. Pendry-Maxwell*; *not in O1*.
89 *Assiria*] *van Dam*; *Affrica O1*; all Africa *Oxberry*.

Monster of Nature, shame unto thy stocke,
That dar'st presume thy Soveraigne for to mocke.   105
Meander come, I am abus'd *Meander*.

                    Exit [*with* MEANDER *and others*].

        Manent COSROE *and* MENAPHON.

MENAPHON. How now my Lord, what, mated and amaz'd
    To heare the king thus threaten like himselfe?
COSROE. Ah *Menaphon*, I passe not for his threates,
    The plot is laid by Persean Noble men,   110
    And Captaines of the Medean garrisons,
    To crowne me Emperour of *Asia*.
    But this it is that doth excruciate
    The verie substance of my vexed soule:
    To see our neighbours that were woont to quake   115
    And tremble at the Persean Monarkes name,
    Now sits and laughs our regiment to scorne:
    And that which might resolve me into teares:
    Men from the farthest Equinoctiall line,
    Have swarm'd in troopes into the Easterne *Inde*:   120
    Lading their shippes with golde and pretious stones:
    And made their spoiles from all our provinces.
MENAPHON. This should intreat your highnesse to rejoice,
    Since Fortune gives you opportunity,
    To gaine the tytle of a Conquerour,   125
    By curing of this maimed Emperie.
    Affrike and *Europe* bordering on your land,
    And continent to your Dominions,
    How easely may you with a mightie hoste,
    Passe into *Græcia*, as did *Cyrus* once,   130
    And cause them to withdraw their forces home,
    Least you subdue the pride of Christendome.   [*Trumpet.*]
COSROE. But *Menaphon*, what means this trumpets sound?
MENAPHON. Behold, my Lord, *Ortigius*, and the rest,
    Bringing the Crowne to make you Emperour.   135

106 SD *with...others*] *Oxberry*; not in *O1*.   120 *Inde*] *this edn.*; *India*
O1.   132SD *Trumpet*] *this edn.*; *not in O1*.   134 Lord,] *Oxberry*; Lord *O1*.

Enter ORTIGIUS *and* CENEUS *bearing a Crowne, with others.*

ORTYGIUS. Magnificent and mightie Prince *Cosroe*,
    We in the name of other Persean states,
    And commons of this mightie Monarchie,
    Present thee with th'Emperiall Diadem.
CENEUS. The warlike Souldiers, and the Gentlemen,   140
    That heretofore have fild *Persepolis*
    With *Affrike* Captaines, taken in the field:
    Whose ransome made them martch in coates of gold,
    With costlie jewels hanging at their eares,
    And shining stones upon their loftie Crestes: 145
    Now living idle in the walled townes,
    Wanting both pay and martiall discipline,
    Begin in troopes to threaten civill warre,
    And openly exclaime against the King.
    Therefore to stay all sodaine mutinies,   150
    We will invest your Highnesse Emperour:
    Whereat the Souldiers will conceive more joy,
    Then did the Macedonians at the spoile
    Of great *Darius* and his wealthy hoast.
COSROE. Wel, since I see the state of *Persea* droope,   155
    And languish in my brothers government:
    I willingly receive th'imperiall crowne,
    And vow to weare it for my countries good:
    In spite of them shall malice my estate.
ORTYGIUS. And in assurance of desir'd successe,   160
    We here doo crowne thee Monarch of the East,
    Emperour of *Asia*, and of *Persea*,
    Great Lord of *Medea* and *Armenia*:
    Duke of *Assiria* and *Albania*,
    Mesopotamia and of *Parthia*,   165
    East *India* and the late discovered Isles,
    Chiefe Lord of all the wide vast *Euxine* sea,
    And of the ever raging Caspian Lake:
    Long live *Cosroe* mighty Emperour.
COSROE. And *Jove* may never let me longer live,   170
    Then I may seeke to gratifie your love,

135SD CENEUS] *Oxberry*; Conerus *O1*.   164 *Assiria*] *van Dam*; *Affrica O1*.

And cause the souldiers that thus honour me,
To triumph over many Provinces:
By whose desires of discipline in Armes,
I doubt not shortly but to raigne sole king,   175
And with the Armie of *Theridamas*,
Whether we presently will flie (my Lords)
To rest secure against my brothers force.

ORTYGIUS. We knew my Lord, before we brought the crowne,
Intending your investion so neere   180
The residence of your dispised brother,
The Lords would not be too exasperate,
To injure or suppresse your woorthy tytle.
Or if they would, there are in readines
Ten thousand horse to carie you from hence,   185
In spite of all suspected enemies.

COSROE. I know it wel my Lord, and thanke you all.

ORTYGIUS. Sound up the trumpets then, God save the King.

> [*Trumpets.*] *Exeunt.*

Actus. 1. Scæna. 2.

[*Enter*] TAMBURLAINE *leading* ZENOCRATE: TECHELLES,
USUMCASANE, *other Lords* [MAGNETES, AGYDAS,] *and*
Souldiers loden with treasure.

TAMBURLAINE. Come lady, let not this appal your thoughts.
The jewels and the treasure we have tane
Shall be reserv'd, and you in better state,
Than if you were arriv'd in *Siria*,
Even in the circle of your Fathers armes: 5
The mightie Souldan of *Egyptia*.

ZENOCRATE. Ah Shepheard, pity my distressed plight,
(If as thou seem'st, thou art so meane a man)
And seeke not to inrich thy followers,
By lawlesse rapine from a silly maide.   10
Who traveiling with these Medean Lords

---

182 Lords] *O3*; Lord *O1*.   188SD *Trumpets*] *this edn.; not in O1.*   OSD 1 *Enter*]
Oxberry; not in O1.   OSD 2 MAGNETES, AGYDAS] *Oxberry; not in O1.*

To *Memphis*, from my uncles country of *Medea*,
Where all my youth I have bene governed,
Have past the armie of the mightie Turke:
Bearing his privie signet and his hand: 15
To safe conduct us thorow *Affrica*.

MAGNETES. And since we have arriv'd in *Scythia*,
Besides rich presents from the puisant Cham,
We have his highnesse letters to command
Aide and assistance if we stand in need.   20

TAMBURLAINE. But now you see these letters and commandes,
Are countermanded by a greater man:
And through my provinces you must expect
Letters of conduct from my mightinesse,
If you intend to keep your treasure safe.   25
But since I love to live at liberty,
As easely may you get the Souldans crowne,
As any prizes out of my precinct.
For they are friends that help to weane my state,
Till men and kingdomes help to strengthen it: 30
And must maintaine my life exempt from servitude.
But tell me Maddam, is your grace betroth'd?

ZENOCRATE. I am (my Lord,) for so you do import.

TAMBURLAINE. I am a Lord, for so my deeds shall proove,
And yet a shepheard by my Parentage: 35
But Lady, this faire face and heavenly hew,
Must grace his bed that conquers *Asia*:
And meanes to be a terrour to the world,
Measuring the limits of his Emperie
By East and west, as *Phœbus* doth his course: 40
Lie here ye weedes that I disdaine to weare:

                    [*He takes off his shepheards cloak.*]

This compleat armor, and this curtle-axe
Are adjuncts more beseeming *Tamburlaine*.
And Maddam, whatsoever you esteeme
Of this successe, and losse unvallued,   45
Both may invest you Empresse of the East:
And these that seeme but silly country Swaines,
May have the leading of so great an host,

As with their waight shall make the mountains quake,
Even as when windy exhalations,   50
Fighting for passage, tilt within the earth.
TECHELLES. As princely Lions when they rouse themselves,
Stretching their pawes, and threatning heardes of Beastes,
So in his Armour looketh *Tamburlaine*:
Me thinks I see kings kneeling at his feet,   55
And he with frowning browes and fiery lookes,
Spurning their crownes from off their captive heads.
USUMCASANE. And making thee and me *Techelles*, kinges,
That even to death will follow *Tamburlaine*.
TAMBURLAINE. Nobly resolv'd, sweet friends and followers.   60
These Lords (perhaps) do scorne our estimates,
And thinke we prattle with distempered spirits:
But since they measure our deserts so meane,
That in conceit bear Empires on our speares,
Affecting thoughts coequall with the cloudes,   65
They shall be kept our forced followers,
Till with their eies they view us Emperours.
ZENOCRATE. The Gods, defenders of the innocent,
Will never prosper your intended driftes,
That thus oppresse poore friendles passengers.   70
Therefore at least admit us libertie,
Even as thou hop'st to be eternized,
By living *Asias* mightie Emperour.
AGYDAS. I hope our Ladies treasure and our owne,
May serve for ransome to our liberties: 75
Returne our Mules and emptie Camels backe,
That we may traveile into *Siria*,
Where her betrothed Lord *Alcidamus*,
Expects th'arrivall of her highnesse person.
MAGNETES. And wheresoever we repose our selves,   80
We will report but well of *Tamburlaine*.
TAMBURLAINE. Disdaines *Zenocrate* to live with me?
Or you my Lordes to be my followers?
Thinke you I way this treasure more than you?
Not all the Gold in *Indias* welthy armes,   85

67 they] *O2*; thee *O1*.

Shall buy the meanest souldier in my traine.
Zenocrate, lovelier than the Love of *Jove*,
Brighter than is the silver Rhodope,
Fairer than whitest snow on Scythian hils,
Thy person is more woorth to *Tamburlaine*,   90
Than the possession of the Persean Crowne,
Which gratious starres have promist at my birth.
A hundreth Tartars shall attend on thee,
Mounted on Steeds, swifter than *Pegasus*.
Thy Garments shall be made of Medean silke,   95
Enchast with precious juelles of mine owne:
More rich and valurous than *Zenocrates*.
With milke-white Hartes upon an Ivorie sled,
Thou shalt be drawen amidst the frosen Pooles,
And scale the ysie mountaines lofty tops: 100
Which with thy beautie will be soone resolv'd.
My martiall prises with five hundred men,
Wun on the fiftie headed *Vuolgas* waves,
Shall all we offer to *Zenocrate*,
And then my selfe to faire *Zenocrate*.   105

TECHELLES. What now? In love?   [*Aside.*]
TAMBURLAINE. *Techelles*, women must be flatered. [*Aside.*]
But this is she with whom I am in love.

Enter a SOULDIER.

SOULDIER. Newes, newes.
TAMBURLAINE. How now, what's the matter?   110
SOULDIER. A thousand Persean horsmen are at hand,
Sent from the King to overcome us all.
TAMBURLAINE. How now my Lords of *Egypt* and *Zenocrate*?
Now must your jewels be restor'd againe:
And I that triumpht so be overcome.   115
How say you Lordings, Is not this your hope?
AGYDAS. We hope your selfe wil willingly restore them.
TAMBURLAINE. Such hope, such fortune have the thousand
    horse.
Soft ye my Lords and sweet *Zenocrate*.

---

88 Rhodope] *Robinson*; Rhodolfe *O1*.   106SD, 107SD *Aside*] *Oxberry*; *not in O1*.

You must be forced from me ere you goe: 120
A thousand horsmen? We five hundred foote?
An ods too great, for us to stand against:
But are they rich? And is their armour good?

SOULDIER. Their plumed helmes are wrought with beaten golde.
Their swords enameld, and about their neckes   125
Hangs massie chaines of golde downe to the waste,
In every part exceeding brave and rich.

TAMBURLAINE. Then shall we fight couragiously with them.
Or looke you, I should play the Orator?

TECHELLES. No: cowards and fainthearted runawaies,   130
Looke for orations when the foe is neere.
Our swordes shall play the Orators for us.

USUMCASANE. Come let us meet them at the mountain top,
And with a sodaine and an hot alarme
Drive all their horses headlong down the hill.   135

TECHELLES. Come let us martch.

TAMBURLAINE. Stay *Techelles*, aske a parlee first.

The Souldiers enter.

Open the Males, yet guard the treasure sure,
Lay out our golden wedges to the view,
That their reflexions may amaze the Perseans.   140
And looke we friendly on them when they come:
But if they offer word or violence,
Weele fight five hundred men at armes to one,
Before we part with our possession.
And gainst the Generall we will lift our swords,   145
And either lanch his greedy thirsting throat,
Or take him prisoner, and his chaine shall serve
For Manackles, till he be ransom'd home.

TECHELLES. I heare them come, shal we encounter them?

TAMBURLAINE. Keep all your standings, and not stir a foote,   150
My selfe will bide the danger of the brunt.

Enter THERIDAMAS *with others.*

THERIDAMAS. Where is this Scythian *Tamberlaine*?

TAMBURLAINE. Whom seekst thou Persean? I am *Tamburlain*.

133 top] *Q*; foot *O1*.

THERIDAMAS. *Tamburlaine?*   [*Aside.*]
  A Scythian Shepheard, so imbellished   155
  With Natures pride, and richest furniture?
  His looks do menace heaven and dare the Gods,
  His fierie eies are fixt upon the earth,
  As if he now devis'd some Stratageme:
  Or meant to pierce *Avernus* darksome vaults,   160
  And pull the triple headed dog from hell.
TAMBURLAINE. Noble and milde this Persean seemes to be,
                            [*To* TECHELLES.]
  If outward habit judge the inward man.
TECHELLES. His deep affections make him passionate.
TAMBURLAINE. With what a majesty he rears his looks: 165
  In thee (thou valiant man of *Persea*)   [*To* THERIDAMAS.]
  I see the folly of thy Emperour:
  Art thou but Captaine of a thousand horse,
  That by Characters graven in thy browes,
  And by thy martiall face and stout aspect,
  Deserv'st to have the leading of an hoste?   170
  Forsake thy king and do but joine with me
  And we will triumph over all the world.
  I hold the Fates bound fast in yron chaines,
  And with my hand turne Fortunes wheel about,   175
  And sooner shall the Sun fall from his Spheare,
  Than *Tamburlaine* be slaine or overcome.
  Draw foorth thy sword, thou mighty man at Armes,
  Intending but to rase my charmed skin:
  And *Jove* himselfe will stretch his hand from heaven, 180
  To ward the blow, and shield me safe from harme.
  See how he raines down heaps of gold in showers,
  As if he meant to give my Souldiers pay,
  And as a sure and grounded argument,
  That I shall be the Monark of the East,   185
  He sends this Souldans daughter rich and brave,
  To be my Queen and portly Emperesse.
  If thou wilt stay with me, renowmed man,
  And lead thy thousand horse with my conduct,

154SD *Aside*] *J. S. Cunningham; not in O1.*   161 And] *catchword;* To
text.   162SD *To* TECHELLES] *J. S. Cunningham; not in O1.*   166SD *To* THER-
IDAMAS] *J. S. Cunningham; not in O1.*

Besides thy share of this Egyptian prise,   190
Those thousand horse shall sweat with martiall spoile
Of conquered kingdomes, and of Cities sackt.
Both we wil walke upon the lofty clifts,
And Christian Merchants that with Russian stems
Plow up huge furrowes in the Caspian sea,   195
Shall vaile to us, as Lords of all the Lake.
Both we will raigne as Consuls of the earth,
And mightie kings shall be our Senators.
Jove sometime masked in a Shepheards weed,
And by those steps that he hath scal'd the heavens,   200
May we become immortall like the Gods.
Joine with me now in this my meane estate,
(I cal it meane, because being yet obscure,
The Nations far remoov'd admyre me not)
And when my name and honor shall be spread,   205
As far as *Boreas* claps his brazen wings,
Or faire *Boötes* sends his cheerefull light,
Then shalt thou be Competitor with me,
And sit with *Tamburlaine* in all his majestie.
THERIDAMAS. Not *Hermes* Prolocutor to the Gods,   210
Could use perswasions more patheticall.
TAMBURLAINE. Nor are *Apollos* Oracles more true,
Then thou shalt find my vaunts substantiall.
TECHELLES. We are his friends, and if the Persean king
Should offer present Dukedomes to our state,   215
We thinke it losse to make exchange for that
We are assured of by our friends successe.
USUMCASANE. And kingdomes at the least we all expect,
Besides the honor in assured conquestes:
Where kings shall crouch unto our conquering swords,   220
And hostes of souldiers stand amaz'd at us,
When with their fearfull tongues they shall confesse
Theise are the men that all the world admires.
THERIDAMAS. What stronge enchantments tice my yeelding
     soule?
Are these resolved noble Scythians?   225
But shall I proove a Traitor to my King?
TAMBURLAINE. No, but the trustie friend of *Tamburlaine*.

THERIDAMAS. Won with thy words, and conquered with thy
　　looks,
　　I yeeld my selfe, my men and horse to thee:
　　To be partaker of thy good or ill,　　　　　　　　　230
　　As long as life maintaines *Theridamas*.
TAMBURLAINE. *Theridamas* my friend, take here my hand,
　　Which is as much as if I swore by heaven,
　　And call'd the Gods to witnesse of my vow,
　　Thus shall my heart be still combinde with thine,　　235
　　Untill our bodies turne to Elements:
　　And both our soules aspire celestiall thrones.
　　Techelles, and *Casane*, welcome him.
TECHELLES. Welcome renowmed Persean to us all.
USUMCASANE. Long may *Theridamas* remaine with us.　　240
TAMBURLAINE. These are my friends in whom I more rejoice,
　　Than dooth the King of *Persea* in his Crowne:
　　And by the love of *Pyllades* and *Orestes*,
　　Whose statutes we adore in *Scythia*,
　　Thy selfe and them shall never part from me,　　245
　　Before I crowne you kings in *Asia*.
　　Make much of them gentle *Theridamas*,
　　And they will never leave thee till the death.
THERIDAMAS. Nor thee, nor them, thrice noble *Tamburlain*,
　　Shal want my heart to be with gladnes pierc'd　　250
　　To do you honor and securitie.
TAMBURLAINE. A thousand thankes worthy *Theridamas*:
　　And now faire Madam, and my noble Lords,
　　If you will willingly remaine with me,
　　You shall have honors, as your merits be:　　255
　　Or els you shall be forc'd with slaverie.
AGYDAS. We yeeld unto thee happie *Tamburlaine*.
TAMBURLAINE. For you then Maddam, I am out of doubt.
ZENOCRATE. I must be pleasde perforce, wretched *Zenocrate*.
　　　　　　　　　　　　　　　　　　　　Exeunt.

　　　[*Finis Actus primi*.]

259 Finis…primi.] *J. S. Cunningham; not in O1*.

Actus. 2. Scæna. 1.

[*Enter*] COSROE, MENAPHON, ORTYGIUS, CENEUS, *with other Souldiers.*

COSROE. Thus farre are we towards *Theridamas*,
And valiant *Tamburlaine*, the man of fame,
The man that in the forhead of his fortune,
Beares figures of renowne and myracle:
But tell me, that hast seene him, *Menaphon*,   5
What stature wields he, and what personage?
MENAPHON. Of stature tall, and straightly fashioned,
Like his desire, lift upwards and divine,
So large of lims, his joints so strongly knit,
Such breadth of shoulders as might mainely beare   10
Olde *Atlas* burthen: twixt his manly pitch,
A pearle more worth, then all the world is plaste:
Wherein by curious soveraintie of Art,
Are fixt his piercing instruments of sight:
Whose fiery cyrcles beare encompassed   15
A heaven of heavenly bodies in their Spheares:
That guides his steps and actions to the throne,
Where honor sits invested royally:
Pale of complexion: wrought in him with passion,
Thirsting with soveraity, with love of armes: 20
His lofty browes in foldes, do figure death,
And in their smoothnesse, amitie and life:
About them hangs a knot of Amber heire,
Wrapped in curles, as fierce *Achilles* was,
On which the breath of heaven delights to play,   25
Making it daunce with wanton majestie:
His armes and fingers long and sinowy,
Betokening valour and excesse of strength:
In every part proportioned like the man,
Should make the world subdued to *Tamburlaine*.   30

---

osd 1 *Enter*] *Oxberry*; not in *O1*.   CENEUS] *Oxberry*; *Cencus O1*.   27 and
fingers...sinowy] *Dyce* 1; and...snowy *O1*; long, his fingers snowy-white *Q*; and fingers,
long, and snowy-white *Oxberry*.

COSROE. Wel hast thou pourtraid in thy tearms of life,
  The face and personage of a woondrous man:
  Nature doth strive with Fortune and his stars,
  To make him famous in accomplisht woorth:
  And well his merits show him to be made   35
  His Fortunes maister, and the king of men,
  That could perswade at such a sodaine pinch,
  With reasons of his valour and his life,
  A thousand sworne and overmatching foes:
  Then when our powers in points of swords are join'd,   40
  And closde in compasse of the killing bullet,
  Though straight the passage and the port be made,
  That leads to Pallace of my brothers life,
  Proud is his fortune if we pierce it not.
  And when the princely Persean Diadem,   45
  Shall overway his wearie witlesse head,
  And fall like mellowed fruit, with shakes of death,
  In faire *Persea* noble *Tamburlaine*
  Shall be my Regent, and remaine as King.
ORTYGIUS. In happy hower we have set the Crowne   50
  Upon your kingly head, that seeks our honor,
  In joyning with the man, ordain'd by heaven
  To further every action to the best.
CENEUS. He that with Shepheards and a litle spoile,
  Durst in disdaine of wrong and tyrannie,   55
  Defend his freedome gainst a Monarchie,
  What will he doe supported by a king,
  Leading a troope of Gentlemen and Lords,
  And stuft with treasure for his highest thoughts?
COSROE. And such shall wait on worthy *Tamburlaine*.   60
  Our army will be forty thousand strong,
  When *Tamburlain* and brave *Theridamas*
  Have met us by the river *Araris*:
  And all conjoin'd to meet the witlesse King,
  That now is marching neer to *Parthia*:   65
  And with unwilling souldiers faintly arm'd,
  To seeke revenge on me and *Tamburlaine*.
  To whom sweet *Menaphon*, direct me straight.
MENAPHON. I will my Lord.   *Exeunt.*

Actus. 2. Scæna. 2.

[*Enter*] MYCETES, MEANDER, *with other Lords and Souldiers.*

MYCETES. Come my *Meander*, let us to this geere,
    I tel you true my heart is swolne with wrath,
    On this same theevish villaine *Tamburlaine.*
    And of that false *Cosroe*, my traiterous brother.
    Would it not grieve a King to be so abusde,   5
    And have a thousand horsmen tane away?
    And which is worst to have his Diadem
    Sought for by such scalde knaves as love him not?
    I thinke it would: wel then, by heavens I sweare,
    Aurora shall not peepe out of her doores,   10
    But I will have *Cosroe* by the head,
    And kill proud *Tamburlaine* with point of sword.
    Tell you the rest (*Meander*) I have said.
MEANDER. Then having past Armenian desarts now,
    And pitcht our tents under the Georgean hilles,   15
    Whose tops are covered with Tartarian thieves,
    That lie in ambush, waiting for a pray:
    What should we doe but bid them battaile straight,
    And rid the world of those detested troopes?
    Least if we let them lynger here a while,   20
    They gather strength by power of fresh supplies.
    This countrie swarmes with vile outragious men,
    That live by rapine and by lawlesse spoile,
    Fit Souldiers for the wicked *Tamburlaine.*
    And he that could with giftes and promises   25
    Inveigle him that lead a thousand horse,
    And make him false his faith unto his King,
    Will quickly win such as are like himselfe.
    Therefore cheere up your mindes, prepare to fight.
    He that can take or slaughter *Tamburlaine*   30
    Shall rule the Province of *Albania.*
    Who brings that Traitors head *Theridamas*,
    Shal have a government in *Medea*:
    Beside the spoile of him and all his traine:

OSD *Enter*] Oxberry; *not in O1*.   15 pitcht] *O2*; pitch *O1*.

But if *Cosroe* (as our Spials say,   35
And as we know) remaines with *Tamburlaine*,
His Highnesse pleasure is that he should live,
And be reclaim'd with princely lenitie.

[*Enter a* SPY.]

A SPY. An hundred horsmen of my company
    Scowting abroad upon these champion plaines,   40
    Have view'd the army of the Scythians,
    Which make reports it far exceeds the Kings.
MEANDER. Suppose they be in number infinit,
    Yet being void of Martiall discipline,
    All running headlong after greedy spoiles: 45
    And more regarding gaine than victory:
    Like to the cruell brothers of the earth,
    Sprong of the teeth of Dragons venomous,
    Their carelesse swords shal lanch their fellowes throats
    And make us triumph in their overthrow.   50
MYCETES. Was there such brethren, sweet *Meander*, say,
    That sprong of teeth of Dragons venomous?
MEANDER. So Poets say, my Lord.
MYCETES. And tis a pretty toy to be a Poet.
    Wel, wel (*Meander*) thou art deeply read: 55
    And having thee, I have a jewell sure:
    Go on my Lord, and give your charge I say,
    Thy wit will make us Conquerors to day.
MEANDER. Then noble souldiors, to intrap these theeves,
    That live confounded in disordered troopes,   60
    If wealth or riches may prevaile with them,
    We have our Cammels laden all with gold:
    Which you that be but common souldiers,
    Shall fling in every corner of the field:
    And while the base borne Tartars take it up,   65
    You fighting more for honor than for gold,
    Shall massacre those greedy minded slaves.
    And when their scattered armie is subdu'd,
    And you march on their slaughtered carkasses,
    Share equally the gold that bought their lives,   70

38SD *Enter a* SPY] *Dyce* 1; *not in O1.*

And live like Gentlemen in *Persea*.
Strike up the Drum and martch corragiously,
Fortune her selfe dooth sit upon our Crests.

MYCETES. He tels you true, my maisters, so he does.
Drums, why sound ye not when *Meander* speaks.   [*Drums.*]
                                                    Exeunt.

Actus. 2. Scæna. 3.

[*Enter*] COSROE, TAMBURLAINE, THERIDAMAS,
TECHELLES, USUMCASANE, ORTYGIUS, *with others.*

COSROE. Now worthy *Tamburlaine*, have I reposde,
    In thy approoved Fortunes all my hope.
    What thinkst thou man, shal come of our attemptes?
    For even as from assured oracle,
    I take thy doome for satisfaction.   5
TAMBURLAINE. And so mistake you not a whit my Lord.
    For Fates and Oracles of heaven have sworne,
    To roialise the deedes of *Tamburlaine*:
    And make them blest that share in his attempts.
    And doubt you not, but if you favour me,   10
    And let my Fortunes and my valour sway,
    To some direction in your martiall deeds,
    The world will strive with hostes of men at armes,
    To swarme unto the Ensigne I support.
    The host of *Xerxes*, which by fame is said   15
    To drinke the mightie Parthian *Araris*,
    Was but a handful to that we will have.
    Our quivering Lances shaking in the aire,
    And bullets like *Joves* dreadfull Thunderbolts,
    Enrolde in flames and fiery smoldering mistes,   20
    Shall threat the Gods more than Cyclopian warres,
    And with our Sun-bright armour as we march,
    Weel chase the Stars from heaven, and dim their eies
    That stand and muse at our admyred armes.

75SD *Drums*] *Oxberry; not in O1.*   OSD *Enter*] *Oxberry; not in O1.*   7 Oracles
of heaven] *Oxberry;* Oracles, heaven *O1.*

THERIDAMAS. You see my Lord, what woorking woordes he
    hath.   25
  But when you see his actions top his speech,
  Your speech will stay, or so extol his worth,
  As I shall be commended and excusde
  For turning my poore charge to his direction.
  And these his two renowmed friends my Lord,   30
  Would make one thrust and strive to be retain'd
  In such a great degree of amitie.
TECHELLES. With dutie and with amitie we yeeld
  Our utmost service to the faire *Cosroe*.
COSROE. Which I esteeme as portion of my crown.   35
  Usumcasane and *Techelles* both,
  When she that rules in *Rhamnis* golden gates,
  And makes a passage for all prosperous Armes,
  Shall make me solely Emperour of *Asia*,
  Then shall your meeds and vallours be advaunst   40
  To roomes of honour and Nobilitie.
TAMBURLAINE. Then haste *Cosroe* to be king alone,
  That I with these my friends and all my men,
  May triumph in our long expected Fate.
  The King your Brother is now hard at hand,   45
  Meete with the foole, and rid your royall shoulders
  Of such a burthen, as outwaies the sands
  And all the craggie rockes of *Caspea*.

                [*Enter a* MESSENGER]

MESSENGER. My Lord, we have discovered the enemie
  Ready to chardge you with a mighty armie.   50
COSROE. Come *Tamburlain*, now whet thy winged sword
  And lift thy lofty arme into the cloudes,
  That it may reach the King of *Perseas* crowne,
  And set it safe on my victorious head.
TAMBURLAINE. See where it is, the keenest Cutle-axe, 55
  That ere made passage thorow Persean Armes.
  These are the wings shall make it flie as swift,

  26 top] *Dyce* 1; *conj. Oxberry*; stop *O1*.   33 and] *Q*; not *O1*.   48SD *Enter a*
MESSENGER] *Oxberry*; *not in O1*.

As dooth the lightening, or the breath of heaven,
And kill as sure as it swiftly flies.

COSROE. Thy words assure me of kind successe: 60
Go valiant Souldier, go before and charge
The fainting army of that foolish King.

TAMBURLAINE. *Usumcasane* and *Techelles* come,
We are enough to scarre the enemy,
And more than needes to make an Emperour.   65

[*Exeunt.*]

[*Actus. 2. Scæna. 4.*]

To the Battaile, and MYCETES *comes out alone with his
Crowne in his hand, offering to hide it.*

MYCETES. Accurst be he that first invented war,
They knew not, ah, they knew not, simple men,
How those were hit by pelting Cannon shot,
Stand staggering like a quivering Aspen leafe,
Fearing the force of *Boreas* boistrous blasts.   5
In what a lamentable case were I,
If Nature had not given me wisedomes lore?
For Kings are clouts that every man shoots at,
Our Crowne the pin that thousands seeke to cleave.
Therefore in pollicie I thinke it good   10
To hide it close: a goodly Stratagem,
And far from any man that is a foole.
So shall not I be knowen, or if I bee,
They cannot take away my crowne from me.
Here will I hide it in this simple hole.   15

Enter TAMBURLAIN.

TAMBURLAINE. What, fearful coward, stragling from the camp
When Kings themselves are present in the field?

MYCETES. Thou liest.

TAMBURLAINE.   Base villaine, darst thou give the lie?

MYCETES. Away, I am the King: go, touch me not.

65SD *Exeunt*] *Oxberry; not in* O1.   *Actus. 2. Scæna. 4.*] *Dyce* 1; *not in* O1.   16
What, fearful coward,] *Dyce* 1; What fearful coward O1; What fearful coward's *Oxberry.*

Thou breakst the law of Armes unlesse thou kneele,   20
And cry me mercie, noble King.
TAMBURLAINE. Are you the witty King of *Persea*?
MYCETES. I marie am I: have you any suite to me?
TAMBURLAINE. I would intreat you speak but three wise
    wordes.
MYCETES. So I can when I see my time.   25
TAMBURLAINE. Is this your Crowne?
MYCETES. I, didst thou ever see a fairer?
TAMBURLAINE. You will not sell it, wil ye?
MYCETES. Such another word, and I will have thee
    executed.   30
Come give it me.
TAMBURLAINE. No, I tooke it prisoner.
MYCETES. You lie, I gave it you.
TAMBURLAINE. Then tis mine.
MYCETES. No, I meane, I let you keep it.   35
TAMBURLAINE. Wel, I meane you shall have it againe.
Here take it for a while, I lend it thee,
Till I may see thee hem'd with armed men.
Then shalt thou see me pull it from thy head:
Thou art no match for mightie *Tamburlaine*.   [*Exit.*]
MYCETES. O Gods, is this *Tamburlaine* the thiefe,   41
I marveile much he stole it not away.

     Sound trumpets to the battell, and he runs in.

[*Actus. 2. Scæna. 5.*]

[*Enter*] COSROE, TAMBURLAINE, THERIDAMAS,
MENAPHON, MEANDER, ORTYGIUS, TECHELLES,
USUMCASANE, *with others.*

TAMBURLAINE. Holde thee *Cosroe*, weare two imperiall
    Crownes.
Thinke thee invested now as royally,

---

  24 you speak but] *F. Cunningham*; you to speak but *O1*; you but to speak *Oxberry*.
40SD *Exit*] *Oxberry*; *not in O1*.   *Actus. 2. Scæna. 5.*] *Dyce* 1; *not in O1*.   OSD 1
Enter] *Oxberry*; *not in O1*.

Even by the mighty hand of *Tamburlaine*,
As if as many kinges as could encompasse thee,
With greatest pompe had crown'd thee Emperour.   5
COSROE. So do I thrice renowmed man at armes,
And none shall keepe the crowne but *Tamburlaine*:
Thee doo I make my Regent of *Persea*,
And Generall Lieftenant of my Armies.
Meander, you that were our brothers Guide,   10
And chiefest Counsailor in all his acts,
Since he is yeelded to the stroke of War,
On your submission we with thanks excuse,
And give you equall place in our affaires.
MEANDER. Most happy Emperour in humblest tearms   15
I vow my service to your Majestie,
With utmost vertue of my faith and dutie.
COSROE. Thanks good *Meander*, then *Cosroe* raign
And governe *Persea* in her former pomp:
Now send Ambassage to thy neighbor Kings,   20
And let them know the Persean King is chang'd:
From one that knew not what a King should do,
To one that can commaund what longs thereto:
And now we will to faire *Persepolis*,
With twenty thousand expert souldiers.   25
The Lords and Captaines of my brothers campe,
With litle slaughter take *Meanders* course,
And gladly yeeld them to my gracious rule:
Ortigius and *Menaphon*, my trustie friendes,
Now will I gratify your former good,   30
And grace your calling with a greater sway.
ORTYGIUS. And as we ever aimd at your behoofe,
And sought your state all honor it deserv'd,
So will we with our powers and our lives,
Indevor to preserve and prosper it.   35
COSROE. I will not thank thee (sweet *Ortigius*):
Better replies shall proove my purposes.
And now Lord *Tamburlaine*, my brothers Campe
I leave to thee, and to *Theridamas*,
To follow me to faire *Persepolis*.   40

32 aimd] *O3*; and *O1*

Then will we march to all those Indian Mines,
My witlesse brother to the Christians lost:
And ransome them with fame and usurie.
And till thou overtake me *Tamburlaine*,
(Staying to order all the scattered troopes)   45
Farewell Lord Regent, and his happie friends:
I long to sit upon my brothers throne.
MENAPHON. Your Majestie shall shortly have your wish,
And ride in triumph through *Persepolis*.   *Exeunt.*

  Manent TAMBURLAINE, TECHELLES, THERIDAMAS,
          USUMCASANE.

TAMBURLAINE. And ride in triumph through *Persepolis*?   50
  Is it not brave to be a King, *Techelles*?
  Usumcasane and *Theridamas*,
  Is it not passing brave to be a King,
  And ride in triumph through *Persepolis*?
TECHELLES. O my Lord, tis sweet and full of pompe.   55
USUMCASANE. To be a King, is halfe to be a God.
THERIDAMAS. A God is not so glorious as a King:
  I thinke the pleasure they enjoy in heaven
  Can not compare with kingly joyes in earth:
  To weare a Crowne enchac'd with pearle and golde,   60
  Whose vertues carie with it life and death:
  To aske, and have: commaund, and be obeied.
  When looks breed love, with lookes to gaine the prize.
  Such power attractive shines in princes eies.
TAMBURLAINE. Why say *Theridamas*, wilt thou be a king?   65
THERIDAMAS. Nay, though I praise it, I can live without it.
TAMBURLAINE. What saies my other friends, wil you be kings?
TECHELLES. I, if I could with all my heart my Lord.
TAMBURLAINE. Why, that's wel said *Techelles*, so would I,
  And so would you my maisters, would you not?   70
USUMCASANE. What then my Lord?
TAMBURLAINE. Why then *Casane*, shall we wish for ought
  The world affoords in greatest noveltie,
  And rest attemplesse, faint and destitute?
  Me thinks we should not, I am strongly moov'd,   75
  That if I should desire the Persean Crowne,
  I could attaine it with a woondrous ease,

And would not all our souldiers soone consent,
If we should aime at such a dignitie?

THERIDAMAS. I know they would with our perswasions.   80

TAMBURLAINE. Why then *Theridamas*, Ile first assay,
To get the Persean Kingdome to my selfe:
Then thou for *Parthia*, they for *Scythia* and *Medea*.
And if I prosper, all shall be as sure,
As if the Turke, the Pope, *Affrike* and *Greece*,   85
Came creeping to us with their crownes apeece.

TECHELLES. Then shall we send to this triumphing King,
And bid him battell for his novell Crowne?

USUMCASANE. Nay quickly then, before his roome be hot.

TAMBURLAINE. Twil proove a pretie jest (in faith) my
friends.   90

THERIDAMAS. A jest to chardge on twenty thousand men?
I judge the purchase more important far.

TAMBURLAINE. Judge by thy selfe *Theridamas*, not me,
For presently *Techelles* here shal haste,
To bid him battaile ere he passe too farre,   95
And lose more labor than the gaine will quight.
Then shalt thou see the Scythian *Tamburlaine*,
Make but a jest to win the Persean crowne.
Techelles, take a thousand horse with thee,
And bid him turne him back to war with us,   100
That onely made him King to make us sport.
We will not steale upon him cowardly,
But give him warning and more warriours.
Haste thee *Techelles*, we will follow thee.
What saith *Theridamas*?

THERIDAMAS.   Goe on for me.   105

                                        Exeunt.

Actus. 2. Scæna. 6.

[*Enter*] COSROE, MEANDER, ORTYGIUS, MENAPHON,
with other Souldiers.

COSROE. What means this divelish shepheard to aspire

---

86 apeece] *O3*; apace *O1*.   100 turne him back] *Robinson*; turne his back *O1*.
104 Haste thee] *O2*; Haste the *O1*.   OSD1 *Enter*] *Robinson*; not in *O1*.

With such a Giantly presumption:
To cast up hils against the face of heaven:
And dare the force of angrie *Jupiter*.
But as he thrust them underneath the hils,   5
And prest out fire from their burning jawes:
So will I send this monstrous slave to hell,
Where flames shall ever feed upon his soule.
MEANDER. Some powers divine, or els infernall, mixt
   Their angry seeds at his conception: 10
   For he was never sprong of humaine race,
   Since with the spirit of his fearefull pride,
   He dares so doubtlesly resolve of rule,
   And by profession be ambitious.
ORTYGIUS. What God or Feend, or spirit of the earth,   15
   Or Monster turned to a manly shape,
   Or of what mould or mettel he be made,
   What star or state soever governe him,
   Let us put on our meet incountring mindes,
   And in detesting such a divelish Thiefe,   20
   In love of honor and defence of right,
   Be arm'd against the hate of such a foe,
   Whether from earth, or hell, or heaven he grow.
COSROE. Nobly resolv'd, my good *Ortygius*.
   And since we all have suckt one wholsome aire,   25
   And with the same proportion of Elements
   Resolve, I hope we are resembled,
   Vowing our loves to equall death and life.
   Let's cheere our souldiers to incounter him,
   That grievous image of ingratitude: 30
   That fiery thirster after Soveraigntie:
   And burne him in the fury of that flame,
   That none can quence but blood and Emperie.
   Resolve my Lords and loving souldiers now,
   To save your King and country from decay: 35
   Then strike up Drum, and all the Starres that make
   The loathsome Circle of his dated life,
   Direct my weapon to his barbarous heart,

37 his] *conj. Collier*; my *O1*.

That thus opposeth him against the Gods,
And scornes the Powers that governe *Persea*.   40
                                        [*Drums. Exeunt.*]

[*Actus. 2. Scæna. 7.*]

Enter [the armies] to the Battell, and after the battell, enter
COSROE *wounded*, THERIDAMAS, TAMBURLAINE,
TECHELLES, USUMCASANE, *with others.*

COSROE. Barbarous and bloody *Tamburlaine*,
Thus to deprive me of my crowne and life.
Treacherous and false *Theridamas*,
Even at the morning of my happy state,
Scarce being seated in my royall throne,   5
To worke my downfall and untimely end.
An uncouth paine torments my grieved soule,
And death arrests the organe of my voice,
Who entring at the breach thy sword hath made,
Sackes every vaine and artier of my heart: 10
Bloody and insatiate *Tamburlain*.
TAMBURLAINE. The thirst of raigne and sweetnes of a crown,
That causde the eldest sonne of heavenly *Ops*,
To thrust his doting father from his chaire,
And place himselfe in the Emperiall heaven,   15
Moov'd me to manage armes against thy state.
What better president than mightie *Jove*?
Nature that fram'd us of foure Elements,
Warring within our breasts for regiment,
Doth teach us all to have aspyring minds: 20
Our soules, whose faculties can comprehend
The wondrous Architecture of the world:
And measure every wandring plannets course:
Still climing after knowledge infinite,
And alwaies mooving as the restles Spheares,   25
Wils us to weare our selves and never rest,

Untill we reach the ripest fruit of all,
That perfect blisse and sole felicitie,
The sweet fruition of an earthly crowne.

THERIDAMAS. And that made me to joine with *Tamburlain*,   30
For he is grosse and like the massie earth,
That mooves not upwards, nor by princely deeds
Doth meane to soare above the highest sort.

TECHELLES. And that made us, the friends of *Tamburlaine*,
To lift our swords against the Persean King.   35

USUMCASANE. For as when *Jove* did thrust old *Saturn* down,
Neptune and *Dis* gain'd each of them a Crowne,
So do we hope to raign in *Asia*,
If *Tamburlain* be plac'd in *Persea*.

COSROE. The strangest men that ever nature made,   40
I know not how to take their tyrannies.
My bloodlesse body waxeth chill and colde,
And with my blood my life slides through my wound.
My soule begins to take her flight to hell,
And sommons all my sences to depart: 45
The heat and moisture which did feed each other,
For want of nourishment to feed them both,
Is drie and cold, and now dooth gastly death
With greedy tallents gripe my bleeding hart,
And like a Harpye tires on my life.   50
Theridamas and *Tamburlaine*, I die,
And fearefull vengeance light upon you both.   [*He dies.*]

He takes the Crowne and puts it on.

TAMBURLAINE. Not all the curses which the Furies breathe,
Shall make me leave so rich a prize as this:
Theridamas, *Techelles*, and the rest,   55
Who thinke you now is king of *Persea*?

ALL. *Tamburlaine, Tamburlaine.*

TAMBURLAINE. Though *Mars* himselfe the angrie God of
          armes,
And all the earthly Potentates conspire,
To dispossesse me of this Diadem: 60
Yet will I weare it in despight of them,

50 Harpye] *O2*; Harpyr *O1*; Harper *Q.*   52SD *He dies*] *Oxberry*; not in *O1.*

As great commander of this Easterne world,
If you but say that *Tamburlaine* shall raigne.
ALL. Long live *Tamburlaine*, and raigne in *Asia*.
TAMBURLAINE. So, now it is more surer on my head,   65
Than if the Gods had held a Parliament:
And all pronounst me king of *Persea*.

[*Exeunt.*]

Finis Actus 2.

67SD *Exeunt*] *Oxberry; not in* O1.

Actus. 3. Scæna. 1.

[*Enter*] BAJAZETH, *the kings of* FESSE, MOROCO, *and*
ARGIER, *with others* [BASSOES], *in great pompe.*

BAJAZETH. Great Kings of *Barbary*, and my portly Bassoes,
We heare, the Tartars and the Easterne theeves
Under the conduct of one *Tamburlaine*,
Presume a bickering with your Emperour:
And thinks to rouse us from our dreadful siege   5
Of the famous Grecian *Constantinople*.
You know our Armie is invincible:
As many circumcised Turkes we have,
And warlike bands of Christians renied,
As hath the Ocean or the Terrene sea   10
Small drops of water, when the Moon begins
To joine in one her semi-circled hornes:
Yet would we not be brav'd with forrain power,
Nor raise our siege before the Gretians yeeld,
Or breathles lie before the citie walles.   15
FESSE. Renowmed Emperour, and mighty Generall,
What if you sent the Bassoes of your guard,
To charge him to remaine in *Asia*.
Or els to threaten death and deadly armes,
As from the mouth of mighty *Bajazeth*.   20
BAJAZETH. Hie thee my Bassoe fast to *Persea*,
Tell him thy Lord the Turkish Emperour,
Dread Lord of *Affrike*, *Europe* and *Asia*,
Great King and conquerour of *Grecia*,
The Ocean, Terrene, and the cole-blacke sea,   25
The high and highest Monarke of the world,
Wils and commands (for say not I intreat)
Not once to set his foot in *Affrica*,
Or spread his collours here in *Grecia*,
Least he incurre the furie of my wrath.   30

Tell him, I am content to take a truce,
Because I heare he beares a valiant mind.
But if presuming on his silly power,
He be so mad to manage Armes with me,
Then stay thou with him, say I bid thee so.   35
And if before the Sun have measured heaven
With triple circuit thou regreet us not,
We meane to take his mornings next arise
For messenger, he will not be reclaim'd,
And meane to fetch thee in despight of him.   40

BASSO. Most great and puisant Monarke of the earth,
    Your Bassoe will accomplish your behest:
    And show your pleasure to the Persean,
    As fits the Legate of the stately Turk.   *Exit* BASSO.

ARGIER. They say he is the King of *Persea*.   45
    But if he dare attempt to stir your siege,
    Twere requisite he should be ten times more,
    For all flesh quakes at your magnificence.

BAJAZETH. True (*Argier*) and tremble at my lookes.

MOROCCO. The spring is hindred by your smoothering host, 50
    For neither rain can fall upon the earth,
    Nor Sun reflexe his vertuous beames thereon,
    The ground is mantled with such multitudes.

BAJAZETH. All this is true as holy *Mahomet*,
    And all the trees are blasted with our breathes.   55

FESSE. What thinks your greatnes best to be atchiev'd
    In pursuit of the Cities overthrow?

BAJAZETH. I wil the captive Pioners of *Argier*,
    Cut of the water, that by leaden pipes
    Runs to the citie from the mountain *Carnon*.   60
    Two thousand horse shall forrage up and downe,
    That no reliefe or succour come by Land.
    And all the sea my Gallies countermaund.
    Then shall our footmen lie within the trench,
    And with their Cannons mouth'd like *Orcus* gulfe   65
    Batter the walles, and we will enter in:
    And thus the Grecians shall be conquered.

                                        Exeunt.

Actus. 3. Scæna. 2.

[*Enter*] AGIDAS, ZENOCRATE, ANIPPE, *with others.*

AGYDAS. Madame *Zenocrate*, may I presume
　　To know the cause of these unquiet fits:
　　That worke such trouble to your woonted rest:
　　Tis more then pitty such a heavenly face
　　Should by hearts sorrow wax so wan and pale,   5
　　When your offensive rape by *Tamburlaine*,
　　(Which of your whole displeasures should be most)
　　Hath seem'd to be digested long agoe.
ZENOCRATE. Although it be digested long agoe,
　　As his exceding favours have deserv'd,   10
　　And might content the Queene of heaven as well
　　As it hath chang'd my first conceiv'd disdaine:
　　Yet since a farther passion feeds my thoughts,
　　With ceaselesse and disconsolate conceits,
　　Which dies my lookes so livelesse as they are.   15
　　And might, if my extreams had full events,
　　Make me the gastly counterfeit of death.
AGYDAS. Eternall heaven sooner be dissolv'd,
　　And all that pierceth *Phœbes* silver eie,
　　Before such hap fall to *Zenocrate*.   20
ZENOCRATE. Ah, life, and soule still hover in his Breast,
　　And leave my body sencelesse as the earth.
　　Or els unite you to his life and soule,
　　That I may live and die with *Tamburlaine*.

　　Enter TAMBURLAINE *with* TECHELLES *and others* [*behind*].

AGYDAS. With *Tamburlaine*? Ah faire *Zenocrate*,   25
　　Let not a man so vile and barbarous,
　　That holds you from your father in despight,
　　And keeps you from the honors of a Queene,
　　Being supposde his worthlesse Concubine,
　　Be honored with your love, but for necessity.   30
　　So now the mighty Souldan heares of you,

OSD *Enter*] Dyce *1*; *not in O1*.   1 AGYDAS] *Oxberry*; *not in O1*.   24SD *behind*]
Oxberry; *not in O1*.

Your Highnesse needs not doubt but in short time,
He will with *Tamburlaines* destruction
Redeeme you from this deadly servitude.

ZENOCRATE. *Agydas*, leave to wound me with these words,   35
And speake of *Tamburlaine* as he deserves:
The entertainment we have had of him,
Is far from villanie or servitude,
And might in noble minds be counted princely.

AGYDAS. How can you fancie one that lookes so fierce,   40
Onelie disposed to martiall Stratagems?
Who when he shall embrace you in his armes,
Will tell how many thousand men he slew.
And when you looke for amorous discourse,
Will rattle foorth his facts of war and blood: 45
Too harsh a subject for your dainty eares.

ZENOCRATE. As looks the sun through *Nilus* flowing stream,
Or when the morning holds him in her armes,
So lookes my Lordly love, faire *Tamburlaine*:
His talke much sweeter than the Muses song,   50
They sung for honor gainst *Pierides*,
Or when *Minerva* did with *Neptune* strive:
And higher would I reare my estimate,
Than *Juno*, sister to the highest God,
If I were matcht with mightie *Tamburlaine*.   55

AGYDAS. Yet be not so inconstant in your love,
But let the yong Arabian live in hope,
After your rescue to enjoy his choise.
You see though first the King of *Persea*
(Being a Shepheard) seem'd to love you much,   60
Now in his majesty he leaves those lookes,
Those words of favour, and those comfortings,
And gives no more than common courtesies.

ZENOCRATE. Thence rise the tears that so distain my cheeks,
Fearing his love through my unworthynesse.   65

TAMBURLAINE *goes to her, and takes her away lovingly by the*
hand, looking wrathfully on AGIDAS, *and sayes nothing.*

[*Exeunt. Manet* AGYDAS.]

---

35 *Agydas*,] *conj. Dyce 1; not in O1.*   65SD *Exeunt* ... AGYDAS] *Oxberry; not in O1.*

AGYDAS. Betraide by fortune and suspitious love,
    Threatned with frowning wrath and jealousie,
    Surpriz'd with feare of hideous revenge,
    I stand agast: but most astonied
    To see his choller shut in secrete thoughtes,   70
    And wrapt in silence of his angry soule.
    Upon his browes was pourtraid ugly death,
    And in his eies the furie of his hart,
    That shine as Comets, menacing revenge,
    And casts a pale complexion on his cheeks.   75
    As when the Sea-man sees the *Hyades*
    Gather an armye of Cemerian clouds,
    (*Auster* and *Aquilon* with winged Steads
    All sweating, tilt about the watery heavens,
    With shivering speares enforcing thunderclaps,   80
    And from their shieldes strike flames of lightening)
    All fearefull foldes his sailes, and sounds the maine,
    Lifting his prayers to the heavens for aid,
    Against the terrour of the winds and waves.
    So fares *Agydas* for the late felt frownes   85
    That sent a tempest to my daunted thoughtes,
    And makes my soule devine her overthrow.

           Enter TECHELLES *with a naked dagger.*

TECHELLES. See you *Agidas* how the King salutes you.
    He bids you prophesie what it imports.   *Exit.*
AGYDAS. I prophecied before and now I proove,   90
    The killing frownes of jealousie and love.
    He needed not with words confirme my feare,
    For words are vaine where working tooles present
    The naked action of my threatned end.
    It saies, *Agydas*, thou shalt surely die,   95
    And of extremities elect the least.
    More honor and lesse paine it may procure,
    To dy by this resolved hand of thine,
    Than stay the torments he and heaven have sworne.
    Then haste *Agydas*, and prevent the plagues   100
    Which thy prolonged Fates may draw on thee:
    Go wander free from feare of Tyrants rage,
    Remooved from the Torments and the hell

Wherewith he may excruciate thy soule.
And let *Agidas* by *Agidas* die,   105
And with this stab slumber eternally.   [*Stabs himselfe.*]

[*Enter* TECHELLES *and* USUMCASANE.]

TECHELLES. *Usumcasane*, see how right the man
    Hath hit the meaning of my Lord the King.
USUMCASANE. Faith, and *Techelles*, it was manly done:
    And since he was so wise and honorable,   110
    Let us affoord him now the bearing hence.
    And crave his triple worthy buriall.
TECHELLES. Agreed *Casane*, we wil honor him.
                                [*Exeunt, bearing the body.*]

Actus. 3. Scæna. 3.

[*Enter*] TAMBURLAIN, TECHELLES, USUMCASANE,
THERIDAMAS, BASSOE, ZENOCRATE, [ANIPPE,] *with
others.*

TAMBURLAINE. Bassoe, by this thy Lord and maister knowes,
    I meane to meet him in *Bithynia*:
    See how he comes? Tush. Turkes are ful of brags
    And menace more than they can wel performe:
    He meet me in the field and fetch thee hence?   5
    Alas (poore Turke) his fortune is to weake,
    T'incounter with the strength of *Tamburlaine*.
    View well my Camp, and speake indifferently,
    Doo not my captaines and my souldiers looke
    As if they meant to conquer *Affrica*?   10
BASSOE. Your men are valiant but their number few,
    And cannot terrefie his mightie hoste.
    My Lord, the great Commander of the worlde,
    Besides fifteene contributorie kings,
    Hath now in armes ten thousand Janisaries,   15

106SD *Stabs himselfe*] *Q*; *not in O1.*   Enter...USUMCASANE] *conj. Ellis-Fermor; not in
O1.*   113SD *Exeunt, bearing the body*] *Oxberry; not in O1.*   OSD1 *Enter*] *Oxberry;
not in O1.*   OSD2 ANIPPE] *Dyce 1; not in O1.*

Mounted on lusty Mauritanian Steeds,
Brought to the war by men of *Tripoly*:
Two hundred thousand footmen that have serv'd
In two set battels fought in *Grecia*:
And for the expedition of this war,   20
If he think good, can from his garrisons,
Withdraw as many more to follow him.
TECHELLES. The more he brings, the greater is the spoile,
For when they perish by our warlike hands,
We meane to seate our footmen on their Steeds,   25
And rifle all those stately Janisars.
TAMBURLAINE. But wil those Kings accompany your Lord?
BASSOE. Such as his Highnesse please, but some must stay
To rule the provinces he late subdude.
TAMBURLAINE. Then fight couragiously, their crowns are
     yours.   30
This hand shal set them on your conquering heads,
That made me Emperour of *Asia*.
USUMCASANE. Let him bring millions infinite of men,
Unpeopling Westerne *Affrica* and *Greece*:
Yet we assure us of the victorie.   35
THERIDAMAS. Even he that in a trice vanquisht two kings,
More mighty than the Turkish Emperour:
Shall rouse him out of *Europe*, and pursue
His scattered armie til they yeeld or die.
TAMBURLAINE. Wel said *Theridamas*, speake in that mood, 40
For Wil and Shall best fitteth *Tamburlain*,
Whose smiling stars gives him assured hope
Of martiall triumph, ere he meete his foes:
I that am tearm'd the Scourge and Wrath of God,
The onely feare and terrour of the world,   45
Wil first subdue the Turke, and then inlarge
Those Christian Captives, which you keep as slaves,
Burdening their bodies with your heavie chaines,
And feeding them with thin and slender fare,
That naked rowe about the Terrene sea.   50
And when they chance to breath and rest a space,
Are punisht with Bastones so grievously,
That they lie panting on the Gallies side,
And strive for life at every stroke they give.

These are the cruell pirates of *Argiere*,   55
That damned traine, the scum of *Affrica*,
Inhabited with stragling Runnagates,
That make quick havock of the Christian blood.
But as I live that towne shall curse the time
That *Tamburlaine* set foot in *Affrica*.   60

Enter BAJAZETH *with his Bassoes and contributorie Kinges*
[*of* FESSE, MOROCCO, *and* ARGIER, *and* ZABINA *and*
EBEA].

BAJAZETH. Bassoes and Janisaries of my Guard,
    Attend upon the person of your Lord,
    The greatest Potentate of *Affrica*.
TAMBURLAINE. *Techelles*, and the rest prepare your swordes:
    I meane t'incounter with that *Bajazeth*.   65
BAJAZETH. Kings of *Fesse*, *Moroccus* and *Argier*,
    He cals me *Bajazeth*, whom you call Lord.
    Note the presumption of this Scythian slave:
    I tell thee villaine, those that lead my horse
    Have to their names tytles of dignity,   70
    And dar'st thou bluntly call me *Bajazeth*?
TAMBURLAINE. And know thou Turke, that those which lead
        my horse,
    Shall lead thee Captive thorow *Affrica*.
    And dar'st thou bluntly call me *Tamburlaine*?
BAJAZETH. By *Mahomet*, my Kinsmans sepulcher,   75
    And by the holy *Alcaron* I sweare,
    He shall be made a chast and lustlesse Eunuke,
    And in my Sarell tend my Concubines:
    And all his Captaines that thus stoutly stand,
    Shall draw the chariot of my Emperesse,   80
    Whom I have brought to see their overthrow.
TAMBURLAINE. By this my sword that conquer'd *Persea*,
    Thy fall shall make me famous through the world:
    I will not tell thee how Ile handle thee,
    But every common souldier of my Camp   85
    Shall smile to see thy miserable state.

60SD2–3 *of* FESSE . . . *and* EBEA.] *Dyce 1; not in* O1.

FESSE. What meanes the mighty Turkish Emperor
   To talk with one so base as *Tamburlaine?*
MOROCCO. Ye Moores and valiant men of *Barbary*,
   How can ye suffer these indignities?   90
ARGIER. Leave words and let them feele your lances pointes,
   Which glided through the bowels of the Greekes.
BAJAZETH. Wel said my stout contributory kings,
   Your threefold armie and my hugie hoste,
   Shall swallow up these base borne Perseans.   95
TECHELLES. Puissant, renowmed and mighty *Tamburlain*,
   Why stay we thus prolonging all their lives?
THERIDAMAS. I long to see those crownes won by our swords,
   That we may raigne as kings of *Affrica*.
USUMCASANE. What Coward wold not fight for such a prize? 100
TAMBURLAINE. Fight all couragiously and be you kings.
   I speake it, and my words are oracles.
BAJAZETH. *Zabina*, mother of three braver boies
   Than *Hercules*, that in his infancie
   Did pash the jawes of Serpents venomous: 105
   Whose hands are made to gripe a warlike Lance,
   Their shoulders broad, for complet armour fit,
   Their lims more large and of a bigger size
   Than all the brats ysprong from *Typhons* loins:
   Who, when they come unto their fathers age,   110
   Will batter Turrets with their manly fists:
   Sit here upon this royal chaire of state,
   And on thy head weare my Emperiall crowne,
   Untill I bring this sturdy *Tamburlain*,
   And all his Captains bound in captive chaines.   115
ZABINA. Such good successe happen to *Bajazeth*.
TAMBURLAINE. *Zenocrate*, the loveliest Maide alive,
   Fairer than rockes of pearle and pretious stone,
   The onely Paragon of *Tamburlaine*,
   Whose eies are brighter than the Lamps of heaven,   120
   And speech more pleasant than sweet harmony:
   That with thy lookes canst cleare the darkened Sky:
   And calme the rage of thundring *Jupiter*:
   Sit downe by her: adorned with my Crowne,
   As if thou wert the Empresse of the world.   125
   Stir not *Zenocrate* untill thou see

Me martch victoriously with all my men,
Triumphing over him and these his kings,
Which I will bring as Vassals to thy feete.
Til then take thou my crowne, vaunt of my worth,   130
And manage words with her as we will armes.

ZENOCRATE. And may my Love, the king of *Persea*,
Returne with victorie, and free from wound.

BAJAZETH. Now shalt thou feel the force of Turkish arms,
Which lately made all *Europe* quake for feare: 135
I have of Turkes, Arabians, Moores and Jewes
Enough to cover all *Bythinia*.
Let thousands die, their slaughtered Carkasses
Shal serve for walles and bulwarkes to the rest:
And as the heads of *Hydra*, so my power   140
Subdued, shall stand as mighty as before:
If they should yeeld their necks unto the sword,
Thy souldiers armes could not endure to strike
So many blowes as I have heads for thee.
Thou knowest not (foolish hardy *Tamburlaine*)   145
What tis to meet me in the open field,
That leave no ground for thee to martch upon.

TAMBURLAINE. Our conquering swords shall marshal us the
        way
We use to march upon the slaughtered foe:
Trampling their bowels with our horses hooffes: 150
Brave horses, bred on the white Tartarian hils:
My Campe is like to *Julius Cæsars* Hoste,
That never fought but had the victorie:
Nor in *Pharsalia* was there such hot war,
As these my followers willingly would have: 155
Legions of Spirits fleeting in the aire,
Direct our Bullets and our weapons pointes,
And make your strokes to wound the sencelesse aire.
And when she sees our bloody Collours spread,
Then Victorie begins to take her flight,   160
Resting her selfe upon my milk-white Tent:
But come my Lords, to weapons let us fall.

---

158 your] *Dyce 1*; our *O1*.   aire] *conj. Dyce 2*; lure *O1*; lute *O2*; light *Oxberry*; wind *conj.*
F. *Cunningham*; winds *conj. Wagner*.

The field is ours, the Turk, his wife and all.

Exit, with his followers.

BAJAZETH. Come Kings and Bassoes, let us glut our swords
That thirst to drinke the feble Perseans blood.   165

Exit, with his followers.

ZABINA. Base Concubine, must thou be plac'd by me
That am the Empresse of the mighty Turke?
ZENOCRATE. Disdainful Turkesse and unreverend Bosse,
Call'st thou me Concubine that am betroath'd
Unto the great and mighty *Tamburlaine*?   170
ZABINA. To *Tamburlaine* the great Tartarian thiefe?
ZENOCRATE. Thou wilt repent these lavish words of thine,
When thy great Bassoe-maister and thy selfe,
Must plead for mercie at his kingly feet,
And sue to me to be your Advocates.   175
ZABINA. And sue to thee? I tell thee shamelesse girle,
Thou shalt be Landresse to my waiting maid.
How lik'st thou her *Ebea*, will she serve?
EBEA. Madame, she thinks perhaps she is too fine.
But I shall turne her into other weedes,   180
And make her daintie fingers fall to woorke.
ZENOCRATE. Hearst thou *Anippe*, how thy drudge doth talk,
And how my slave, her mistresse menaceth?
Both for their sausinesse shall be employed,
To dresse the common souldiers meat and drink.   185
For we will scorne they should come nere our selves.
ANIPPE. Yet somtimes let your highnesse send for them
To do the work my chamber maid disdaines.

They sound [to] the battell within, and stay.

ZENOCRATE. Ye Gods and powers that governe *Persea*,
And made my lordly Love her worthy King: 190
Now strengthen him against the Turkish *Bajazeth*,
And let his foes like flockes of fearfull Roes,
Pursude by hunters, flie his angrie lookes,

173 Bassoe-maister] *O2*; Bassoe, maister *O1*.   188SD *to*] *O3*; *not in O1*.

That I may see him issue Conquerour.

ZABINA. Now *Mahomet*, solicit God himselfe,   195
And make him raine down murthering shot from heaven
To dash the Scythians braines, and strike them dead,
That dare presume to manage armes with him,
That offered jewels to thy sacred shrine,
When first he war'd against the Christians.   200

To the battell againe.

ZENOCRATE. By this the Turks lie weltring in their blood,
And *Tamburlaine* is Lord of *Affrica*.
ZABINA. Thou art deceiv'd, I heard the Trumpets sound,
As when my Emperour overthrew the Greeks:
And led them Captive into *Affrica*.   205
Straight will I use thee as thy pride deserves:
Prepare thy selfe to live and die my slave.
ZENOCRATE. If *Mahomet* should come from heaven and sweare,
My royall Lord is slaine or conquered,
Yet should he not perswade me otherwise,   210
But that he lives and will be Conquerour.

BAJAZETH *flies* [*across the stage*], *and he* [TAMBURLAINE]
pursues him [*offstage*]. *The battell short, and they* [*re-*]*enter*
[*fighting*]. BAJAZETH *is overcome.*

TAMBURLAINE. Now king of Bassoes, who is Conqueror?
BAJAZETH. Thou, by the fortune of this damned foile.
TAMBURLAINE. Where are your stout contributorie kings?

Enter TECHELLES, THERIDAMAS, USUMCASANE.

TECHELLES. We have their crownes: their bodies strowe the
fielde.   215
TAMBURLAINE. Each man a crown? why kingly fought ifaith.
Deliver them into my treasurie.
ZENOCRATE. Now let me offer to my gracious Lord
His royall Crowne againe, so highly won.

---

198 dare presume to...him] *Craik (this edn.)*; dare to...him *O1*; dare to...*Bajazeth
Wagner.*   211SD1–2 *across the stage*...TAMBURLAINE...*offstage*...*re-*] *J. S. Cunningham*; *not in O1.*   212SD3 *fighting*] *this edn.*; *not in O1.*   213 foile] *Dyce 2*;
conj. Dyce 1; soile *O1*.

TAMBURLAINE. Nay take the Turkish Crown from her,
   Zenocrate,   220
  And crowne me Emperour of *Affrica*.
ZABINA. No *Tamburlain*, though now thou gat the best,
  Thou shalt not yet be Lord of *Affrica*.
THERIDAMAS. Give her the Crowne Turkesse you wer best.

He takes it from her, and gives it ZENOCRATE.

ZABINA. Injurious villaines, thieves, runnagates,   225
  How dare you thus abuse my Majesty?
THERIDAMAS. Here Madam, you are Empresse, she is none.
TAMBURLAINE. Not now *Theridamas*, her time is past:
  The pillers that have bolstered up those tearmes,
  Are falne in clusters at my conquering feet.   230
ZABINA. Though he be prisoner, he may be ransomed.
TAMBURLAINE. Not all the world shall ransom *Bajazeth*.
BAJAZETH. Ah faire *Zabina*, we have lost the field.
  And never had the Turkish Emperour
  So great a foile by any forraine foe.   235
  Now will the Christian miscreants be glad,
  Ringing with joy their superstitious belles:
  And making bonfires for my overthrow.
  But ere I die those foule Idolaters
  Shall make me bonfires with their filthy bones,   240
  For though the glorie of this day be lost,
  Affrik and *Greece* have garrisons enough
  To make me Soveraigne of the earth againe.
TAMBURLAINE. Those walled garrisons wil I subdue,
  And write my selfe great Lord of *Affrica*:   245
  So from the East unto the furthest West,
  Shall *Tamburlain* extend his puisant arme.
  The Gallies and those pilling Briggandines,
  That yeerely saile to the Venetian gulfe,
  And hover in the straightes for Christians wracke,   250
  Shall lie at anchor in the Isle *Asant*,
  Untill the Persean Fleete and men of war,
  Sailing along the Orientall sea,
  Have fetcht about the Indian continent:
  Even from *Persepolis* to *Mexico*,   255
  And thence unto the straightes of *Jubalter*:

Where they shall meete, and joine their force in one,
Keeping in aw the Bay of *Portingale*,
And all the Ocean by the British shore:
And by this meanes Ile win the world at last.   260

BAJAZETH. Yet set a ransome on me *Tamburlaine*.

TAMBURLAINE. What, thinkst thou *Tamburlain* esteems thy
    gold?
Ile make the kings of *India* ere I die,
Offer their mines (to sew for peace) to me,
And dig for treasure to appease my wrath: 265
Come bind them both and one lead in the Turke.
The Turkesse let my Loves maid lead away.

               They bind them.

BAJAZETH. Ah villaines, dare ye touch my sacred armes?
O *Mahomet*, Oh sleepie *Mahomet*.

ZABINA. O cursed *Mahomet* that makest us thus   270
The slaves to Scythians rude and barbarous.

TAMBURLAINE. Come bring them in, and for this happy
    conquest
Triumph, and solemnize a martiall feast.

                          Exeunt.

    Finis Actus tertii.

Actus. 4. Scæna. 1.

[*Enter*] SOULDAN *of* EGIPT *with three or four Lords,*
CAPOLIN [*and a* MESSENGER.]

SOULDAN. Awake ye men of *Memphis*, heare the clange
    Of Scythian trumpets, heare the Basiliskes,
    That roaring, shake *Damascus* turrets downe.
    The rogue of *Volga* holds *Zenocrate*,
    The Souldans daughter for his Concubine,   5
    And with a troope of theeves and vagabondes,
    Hath spread his collours to our high disgrace:
    While you faint-hearted base Egyptians,
    Lie slumbering on the flowrie bankes of *Nile*,
    As Crocodiles that unaffrighted rest,   10
    While thundring Cannons rattle on their Skins.
MESSENGER. Nay (mightie Souldan) did your greatnes see
    The frowning lookes of fiery *Tamburlaine*,
    That with his terrour and imperious eies,
    Commandes the hearts of his associates,   15
    It might amaze your royall majesty.
SOULDAN. Villain, I tell thee, were that *Tamburlaine*
    As monstrous as *Gorgon*, prince of Hell,
    The Souldane would not start a foot from him.
    But speake, what power hath he?
MESSENGER.   Mightie Lord,   20
    Three hundred thousand men in armour clad,
    Upon their pransing Steeds, disdainfully
    With wanton paces trampling on the ground.
    Five hundred thousand footmen threatning shot,
    Shaking their swords, their speares and yron bils,   25
    Environing their Standard round, that stood
    As bristle-pointed as a thorny wood.
    Their warlike Engins and munition
    Exceed the forces of their martial men.
SOULDAN. Nay could their numbers countervail the stars   30

OSD 1 *Enter*] *Oxberry; not in* O1.   OSD 2 *and a* MESSENGER] *Oxberry; not in* O1.

Or ever drisling drops of Aprill showers,
Or withered leaves that Autumne shaketh downe,
Yet would the Souldane by his conquering power
So scatter and consume them in his rage,
That not a man should live to rue their fall.   35
CAPOLIN. So might your highnesse, had you time to sort
Your fighting men, and raise your royall hoste.
But *Tamburlaine*, by expedition
Advantage takes of your unreadinesse.
SOULDAN. Let him take all th'advantages he can,   40
Were all the world conspird to fight for him,
Nay, were he Devill, as he is no man,
Yet in revenge of faire *Zenocrate*,
Whom he detayneth in despight of us,
This arme should send him downe to *Erebus*,   45
To shroud his shame in darknes of the night.
MESSENGER. Pleaseth your mightinesse to understand,
His resolution far exceedeth all:
The first day when he pitcheth downe his tentes,
White is their hew, and on his silver crest   50
A snowy Feather spangled white he beares,
To signify the mildnesse of his minde,
That satiate with spoile refuseth blood:
But when *Aurora* mounts the second time,
As red as scarlet is his furniture,   55
Then must his kindled wrath bee quencht with blood,
Not sparing any that can manage armes:
But if these threats moove not submission,
Black are his collours, blacke Pavilion,
His speare, his shield, his horse, his armour, plumes,   60
And Jetty Feathers menace death and hell,
Without respect of Sex, degree or age.
He raceth all his foes with fire and sword.
SOULDAN. Mercilesse villaine, Pesant ignorant,
Of lawfull armes, or martiall discipline: 65
Pillage and murder are his usuall trades.
The slave usurps the glorious name of war.
See, *Capolin*, the faire Arabian king,

That hath bene disapointed by this slave
Of my faire daughter, and his princely Love,   70
May have fresh warning to go war with us,
And be reveng'd for her disparagement.

                                        [*Exeunt.*]

Actus. 4. Scæna. 2.

[*Enter*] TAMBURLAIN [*all in white*], TECHELLES,
THERIDAMAS, USUMCASANE, ZENOCRATE, ANIPPE, *two*
Moores drawing BAJAZETH *in his cage, and his wife* [ZABINA]
following him.

TAMBURLAINE. Bring out my foot-stoole.

            They take him out of the cage.

BAJAZETH. Ye holy Priests of heavenly *Mahomet*,
    That sacrificing slice and cut your flesh,
    Staining his Altars with your purple blood:
    Make heaven to frowne and every fixed starre   5
    To sucke up poison from the moorish Fens,
    And poure it in this glorious Tyrants throat.
TAMBURLAINE. The chiefest God, first moover of that Spheare
    Enchac'd with thousands ever shining lamps,
    Will sooner burne the glorious frame of Heaven,   10
    Then it should so conspire my overthrow.
    But Villaine, thou that wishest this to me,
    Fall prostrate on the lowe disdainefull earth,
    And be the foot-stoole of great *Tamburlain*,
    That I may rise into my royall throne.   15
BAJAZETH. First shalt thou rip my bowels with thy sword,
    And sacrifice my heart to death and hell,
    Before I yeeld to such a slavery.
TAMBURLAINE. Base villain, vassall, slave to *Tamburlaine*:
    Unworthy to imbrace or touch the ground   20
    That beares the honor of my royall waight.
    Stoop villaine, stoope, stoope for so he bids,

72SD *Exeunt*] *Oxberry; not in O1.*   OSD 1 *Enter*] *Oxberry; not in O1.   all in white*]
J. S. Cunningham; not in O1.   OSD 3 ZABINA] *J. S. Cunningham; not in O1.*

That may command thee peecemeale to be torne,
Or scattered like the lofty Cedar trees,
Strooke with the voice of thundring *Jupiter*.   25
BAJAZETH. Then as I look downe to the damned Feends,
Feends looke on me, and thou dread God of hell,
With Eban Scepter strike this hatefull earth,
And make it swallow both of us at once.

He gets up upon him to his chaire.

TAMBURLAINE. Now cleare the triple region of the aire,   30
And let the majestie of heaven beholde
Their Scourge and Terrour treade on Emperours.
Smile Stars that raign'd at my nativity,
And dim the brightnesse of their neighbor Lamps:
Disdaine to borrow light of *Cynthia*,   35
For I the chiefest Lamp of all the earth,
First rising in the East with milde aspect,
But fixed now in the Meridian line,
Will send up fire to your turning Spheares,
And cause the Sun to borrowe light of you.   40
My sword stroke fire from his coat of steele,
Even in *Bythinia*, when I took this Turke:
As when a fiery exhalation
Wrapt in the bowels of a freezing cloude,
Fighting for passage, makes the Welkin cracke,   45
And casts a flash of lightning to the earth.
But ere I martch to wealthy *Persea*,
Or leave *Damascus* and th'Egyptian fields,
As was the fame of *Clymens* brain-sicke sonne,
That almost brent the Axeltree of heaven,   50
So shall our swords, our lances and our shot,
Fill all the aire with fiery meteors.
Then when the Sky shal waxe as red as blood,
It shall be said, I made it red my selfe,
To make me think of nought but blood and war.   55
ZABINA. Unworthy king, that by thy crueltie,
Unlawfully usurpest the Persean seat:
Dar'st thou that never saw an Emperour,

Before thou met my husband in the field,
Being thy Captive, thus abuse his state,   60
Keeping his kingly body in a Cage,
That rooffes of golde, and sun-bright Pallaces,
Should have prepar'd to entertaine his Grace?
And treading him beneath thy loathsome feet,
Whose feet the kings of *Affrica* have kist.   65

TECHELLES. You must devise some torment worsse, my Lord,
To make these captives reine their lavish tongues.

TAMBURLAINE. *Zenocrate*, looke better to your slave.

ZENOCRATE. She is my Handmaids slave, and she shal looke
That these abuses flow not from her tongue: 70
Chide her *Anippe*.

ANIPPE. Let these be warnings for you then my slave,
How you abuse the person of the king:
Or els I sweare to have you whipt stark nak'd.

BAJAZETH. Great *Tamburlaine*, great in my overthrow,   75
Ambitious pride shall make thee fall as low,
For treading on the back of *Bajazeth*,
That should be horsed on fower mightie kings.

TAMBURLAINE. Thy names and tytles, and thy dignities,
Are fled from *Bajazeth*, and remaine with me,   80
That will maintaine it against a world of Kings.
Put him in againe.

[*They put* BAJAZETH *into the cage.*]

BAJAZETH. Is this a place for mighty *Bajazeth*?
Confusion light on him that keeps thee thus.

TAMBURLAINE. There whiles he lives, shal *Bajezeth* be
    kept,   85
And where I goe be thus in triumph drawne:
And thou his wife shalt feed him with the scraps
My servitures shall bring thee from my boord.
For he that gives him other food than this:
Shall sit by him and starve to death himselfe.   90
This is my minde, and I will have it so.
Not all the Kings and Emperours of the Earth:

82SD *They...cage*] Oxberry; *not in* O1.   84 keeps] *Craik* (*this edn.*); helps
O1.   88 thee] O2; the O1.

If they would lay their crownes before my feet,
Shall ransome him, or take him from his cage.
The ages that shall talk of *Tamburlain*,   95
Even from this day to *Platoes* wondrous yeare,
Shall talke how I have handled *Bajazeth*.
These Mores that drew him from *Bythinia*,
To faire *Damascus*, where we now remaine,
Shall lead him with us wheresoere we goe.   100
Techelles, and my loving followers,
Now may we see *Damascus* lofty towers,
Like to the shadowes of *Pyramides*,
That with their beauties grac'd the Memphian fields:
The golden stature of their feathered bird   105
That spreads her wings upon the citie wals,
Shall not defend it from our battering shot.
The townes-men maske in silke and cloath of gold,
And every house is as a treasurie.
The men, the treasure, and the towne is ours.   110
THERIDAMAS. Your tentes of white now pitch'd before the
    gates
And gentle flags of amitie displaid,
I doubt not but the Governour will yeeld,
Offering *Damascus* to your Majesty.
TAMBURLAINE. So shall he have his life, and all the rest.   115
But if he stay until the bloody flag
Be once advanc'd on my vermilion Tent,
He dies, and those that kept us out so long.
And when they see me march in black aray,
With mournfull streamers hanging down their heads,   120
Were in that citie all the world contain'd,
Not one should scape: but perish by our swords.
ZENOCRATE. Yet would you have some pitie for my sake,
Because it is my countries, and my Fathers.
TAMBURLAINE. Not for the world *Zenocrate*, if I have sworn: 125
Come bring in the Turke.

                                                  Exeunt.

Actus. 4. Scæna. 3.

[*Enter*] SOULDANE, ARABIA, CAPOLINE, *with streaming collors and Souldiers.*

SOULDAN. Me thinks we martch as *Meliager* did,
 Environed with brave Argolian knightes,
 To chace the savage Calidonian Boare:
 Or *Cephalus* with lustie Thebane youths,
 Against the Woolfe that angrie *Themis* sent,   5
 To waste and spoile the sweet Aonian fieldes.
 A monster of five hundred thousand heades,
 Compact of Rapine, Pyracie, and spoile,
 The Scum of men, the hate and Scourge of God,
 Raves in *Egyptia*, and annoyeth us.   10
 My Lord it is the bloody *Tamburlaine*,
 A sturdy Felon and a base-bred Thiefe,
 By murder raised to the Persean Crowne,
 That dares controll us in our Territories.
 To tame the pride of this presumptuous Beast,   15
 Joine your Arabians with the Souldans power:
 Let us unite our royall bandes in one,
 And hasten to remoove *Damascus* siege.
 It is a blemish to the Majestie
 And high estate of mightie Emperours,   20
 That such a base usurping vagabond
 Should brave a king, or weare a princely crowne.
ARABIA. Renowmed Souldane, have ye lately heard
 The overthrow of mightie *Bajazeth*,
 About the confines of *Bythinia*?   25
 The slaverie wherewith he persecutes
 The noble Turke and his great Emperesse?
SOULDAN. I have, and sorrow for his bad successe:
 But noble Lord of great *Arabia*,
 Be so perswaded, that the Souldan is   30
 No more dismaide with tidings of his fall,
 Than in the haven when the Pilot stands
 And viewes a strangers ship rent in the winds,

0SD *Enter*] Robinson; not in *O1*.   3 Calidonian] *O2*; Caldonian *O1*.

And shivered against a craggie rocke.
Yet in compassion of his wretched state,   35
A sacred vow to heaven and him I make,
Confirming it with *Ibis* holy name,
That *Tamburlaine* shall rue the day, the hower,
Wherein he wrought such ignominious wrong,
Unto the hallowed person of a prince,   40
Or kept the faire *Zenocrate* so long,
As Concubine (I feare) to feed his lust.
ARABIA. Let griefe and furie hasten on revenge,
Let *Tamburlaine* for his offences feele
Such plagues as heaven and we can poure on him.   45
I long to breake my speare upon his crest,
And proove the waight of his victorious arme:
For Fame I feare hath bene too prodigall,
In sounding through the world his partiall praise.
SOULDAN. *Capolin*, hast thou survaid our powers?   50
CAPOLIN. Great Emperours of *Egypt* and *Arabia*,
The number of your hostes united is
A hundred and fifty thousand horse,
Two hundred thousand foot, brave men at armes,
Couragious and full of hardinesse: 55
As frolike as the hunters in the chace
Of savage beastes amid the desert woods.
ARABIA. My mind presageth fortunate successe,
And *Tamburlaine*, my spirit doth foresee
The utter ruine of thy men and thee.   60
SOULDAN. Then reare your standardes, let your sounding
     Drummes
Direct our Souldiers to *Damascus* walles.   [*Drums.*]
Now *Tamburlaine*, the mightie Souldane comes,
And leads with him the great Arabian King,
To dim thy basenesse and obscurity,   65
Famous for nothing but for theft and spoile,
To race and scatter thy inglorious crue,
Of Scythians and slavish Persians.

                                           Exeunt.

---

42 Concubine (I feare)] *Q*; Concubine, I feare *O1*.   62SD *Drums*] *this edn.; not in O1.*

Actus. 4. Scæna. 4.

The Banquet, and to it commeth TAMBURLAIN *al in scarlet,*
[ZENOCRATE,] THERIDAMAS, TECHELLES,
USUMCASANE, *the Turke* [BAJAZETH *drawn in his cage,*
ZABINA], *with others.*

TAMBURLAINE. Now hang our bloody collours by *Damascus*,
Reflexing hewes of blood upon their heads,
While they walke quivering on their citie walles,
Halfe dead for feare before they feele my wrath:
Then let us freely banquet and carouse   5
Full bowles of wine unto the God of war,
That meanes to fill your helmets full of golde:
And make *Damascus* spoiles as rich to you,
As was to *Jason Colchos* golden fleece.
And now *Bajazeth*, hast thou any stomacke?   10
BAJAZETH. I, such a stomacke (cruel *Tamburlane*) as
I could willingly feed upon thy blood-raw hart.
TAMBURLAINE. Nay, thine owne is easier to come by,
plucke out that, and twil serve thee and thy wife: Wel
Zenocrate, *Techelles*, and the rest, fall to your victuals.   15
BAJAZETH. Fall to, and never may your meat digest.
Ye Furies that can maske invisible,
Dive to the bottome of *Avernus* poole,
And in your hands bring hellish poison up,
And squease it in the cup of *Tamburlain*.   20
Or winged snakes of *Lerna* cast your stings,
And leave your venoms in this Tyrants dish.
ZABINA. And may this banquet proove as omenous,
As *Prognes* to th'adulterous Thracian King,
That fed upon the substance of his child.   25
ZENOCRATE. My Lord, how can you suffer these out-
ragious curses by these slaves of yours?
TAMBURLAINE. To let them see (divine *Zenocrate*)
I glorie in the curses of my foes,
Having the power from the Emperiall heaven,   30

Scæna. 4.] *Q*; *Scæna.5. O1*.   OSD2 ZENOCRATE] *Dyce 1*; *not in O1*.   OSD3
BAJAZETH] *Oxberry*; *not in O1*.   *drawn...cage*] *Dyce 1*; *not in O1*.   OSD4 ZABINA]
Oxberry; *not in O1*.

To turne them al upon their proper heades.

TECHELLES. I pray you give them leave Madam, this
    speech is a goodly refreshing to them.

THERIDAMAS. But if his highnesse would let them be fed,
    it would doe them more good.   35

TAMBURLAINE. Sirra, why fall you not too, are you so
    daintily brought up, you cannot eat your owne flesh?

BAJAZETH. First legions of devils shall teare thee in
    peeces.

USUMCASANE. Villain, knowest thou to whom thou   40
    speakest?

TAMBURLAINE. O let him alone: here, eat sir, take it from
    my swords point, or Ile thrust it to thy heart.

He takes it and stamps upon it.

THERIDAMAS. He stamps it under his feet my Lord.

TAMBURLAINE. Take it up Villaine, and eat it, or I   45
    will make thee slice the brawnes of thy armes into
    carbonadoes, and eat them.

USUMCASANE. Nay, twere better he kild his wife, and then
    she shall be sure not to be starv'd, and he be provided for
    a moneths victuall before hand.   50

TAMBURLAINE. Here is my dagger, dispatch her while she
    is fat, for if she live but a while longer, shee will fall into a
    consumption with freatting, and then she will not bee
    woorth the eating.

THERIDAMAS. Doost thou think that *Mahomet* wil suffer   55
    this?

TECHELLES. Tis like he wil, when he cannot let it.

TAMBURLAINE. Go to, fal to your meat: what, not a bit?
    Belike he hath not bene watered to day, give him some
    drinke.   60

They give him water to drinke, and he flings it on the ground.

Faste and welcome sir, while hunger make you eat.
How now *Zenocrate*, dooth not the Turke and his wife
make a goodly showe at a banquet?

ZENOCRATE. Yes, my Lord.

THERIDAMAS. Me thinks, tis a great deale better than a   65
    consort of musicke.

TAMBURLAINE. Yet musicke woulde doe well to cheare up
     Zenocrate: pray thee tel, why art thou so sad? If thou wilt
     have a song, the Turke shall straine his voice: but why is
     it?   70
ZENOCRATE. My lord, to see my fathers towne besieg'd,
     The countrie wasted where my selfe was borne:
     How can it but afflict my verie soule?
     If any love remaine in you my Lord,
     Or if my love unto your majesty   75
     May merit favour at your highnesse handes,
     Then raise your siege from faire *Damascus* walles,
     And with my father take a friendly truce.
TAMBURLAINE. *Zenocrate*, were *Egypt Joves* owne land,
     Yet would I with my sword make *Jove* to stoope.   80
     I will confute those blind Geographers
     That make a triple region in the world,
     Excluding Regions which I meane to trace,
     And with this pen reduce them to a Map,
     Calling the Provinces, Citties and townes   85
     After my name and thine *Zenocrate*:
     Here at *Damascus* will I make the Point
     That shall begin the Perpendicular.
     And wouldst thou have me buy thy Fathers love
     With such a losse? Tell me *Zenocrate*?   90
ZENOCRATE. Honor still waight on happy *Tamburlaine*:
     Yet give me leave to plead for him my Lord.
TAMBURLAINE. Content thy selfe, his person shall be safe,
     And all the friendes of faire *Zenocrate*,
     If with their lives they will be pleasde to yeeld,   95
     Or may be forc'd, to make me Emperour.
     For *Egypt* and *Arabia* must be mine.
[*To* BAJAZETH] Feed you slave, thou maist thinke thy selfe
     happie to be fed from my trencher.
BAJAZETH. My empty stomacke ful of idle heat,   100
     Drawes bloody humours from my feeble partes,
     Preserving life, by hasting cruell death.
     My vaines are pale, my sinowes hard and drie,
     My jointes benumb'd, unlesse I eat, I die.

98SD *To* BAJAZETH] *J. S. Cunningham; not in O1.*

ZABINA. Eat *Bajazeth*. Let us live in spite of them, looking   105
some happie power will pitie and inlarge us.

TAMBURLAINE. Here Turk, wilt thou have a cleane tren-
cher?

BAJAZETH. I Tyrant, and more meat.

TAMBURLAINE. Soft sir, you must be dieted, too much   110
eating will make you surfeit.

THERIDAMAS. So it would my lord, specially having so
smal a walke, and so litle exercise.

Enter a second course of Crownes.

TAMBURLAINE. *Theridamas*, *Techelles* and *Casane*, here
are the cates you desire to finger, are they not?   115

THERIDAMAS. I (my Lord) but none save kinges must
feede with these.

TECHELLES. Tis enough for us to see them, and for *Tamburlaine* onely to enjoy them.

TAMBURLAINE. Wel, here is now to the Souldane of   120
Egypt, the King of *Arabia*, and the Governour of *Damascus*. Now take these three crownes, and pledge me, my
contributorie Kings.
I crowne you here (*Theridamas*) King of *Argier*: *Techelles*
King of *Fesse*, and *Usumcasane* King of *Morocus*. How say   125
you to this (*Turke*)? These are not your contributorie
kings.

BAJAZETH. Nor shall they long be thine, I warrant them.

TAMBURLAINE. Kings of *Argier*, *Morocus*, and of *Fesse*,
You that have martcht with happy *Tamburlaine*,   130
As far as from the frozen plage of heaven,
Unto the watry mornings ruddy bower,
And thence by land unto the Torrid Zone,
Deserve these tytles I endow you with,
By value and by magnanimity.   135
Your byrthes shall be no blemish to your fame,
For vertue is the fount whence honor springs.
And they are worthy she investeth kings.

THERIDAMAS. And since your highnesse hath so well
vouchsaft,

131 plage] *Dyce 2*; place *O1*.   132 bower] *O3*; hower *O1*.

If we deserve them not with higher meeds   140
Then erst our states and actions have retain'd,
Take them away againe and make us slaves.
TAMBURLAINE. Wel said *Theridamas*, when holy Fates
Shall stablish me in strong *Egyptia*,
We meane to traveile to th'Antartique Pole,   145
Conquering the people underneath our feet,
And be renowm'd, as never Emperours were.
Zenocrate, I will not crowne thee yet,
Until with greater honors I be grac'd.

[Exeunt.]

Finis Actus quarti.

149SD *Exeunt*] Oxberry; *not in O1*.

Actus. 5. Scæna. 1.

[*Enter*] *The* GOVERNOUR *of* Damasco, *with three or foure*
CITIZENS, *and foure* VIRGINS, *with branches of Laurell in
their hands.*

GOVERNOUR. Stil dooth this man or rather God of war,
    Batter our walles, and beat our Turrets downe.
    And to resist with longer stubbornesse,
    Or hope of rescue from the Souldans power,
    Were but to bring our wilfull overthrow,   5
    And make us desperate of our threatned lives:
    We see his tents have now bene altered,
    With terrours to the last and cruelst hew:
    His cole-blacke collours every where advaunst,
    Threaten our citie with a generall spoile: 10
    And if we should with common rites of Armes,
    Offer our safeties to his clemencie,
    I feare the custome proper to his sword,
    Which he observes as parcell of his fame,
    Intending so to terrifie the world,   15
    By any innovation or remorse,
    Will never be dispenc'd with til our deaths.
    Therfore, for these our harmlesse virgines sakes,
    Whose honors and whose lives relie on him:
    Let us have hope that their unspotted praiers,   20
    Their blubbered cheekes and hartie humble mones,
    Will melt his furie into some remorse:
    And use us like a loving Conquerour.
1.VIRGIN. If humble suites or imprecations,
    (Uttered with teares of wretchednesse and blood,   25
    Shead from the heads and hearts of all our Sex,
    Some made your wives, and some your children)
    Might have intreated your obdurate breasts,
    To entertaine some care of our securities,
    Whiles only danger beat upon our walles,   30

These more than dangerous warrants of our death,
Had never bene erected as they bee,
Nor you depend on such weake helps as we.
GOVERNOUR. Wel, lovely Virgins, think our countries care,
Our love of honor loth to be enthral'd   35
To forraine powers, and rough imperious yokes:
Would not with too much cowardize or feare,
Before all hope of rescue were denied,
Submit your selves and us to servitude.
Therefore in that your safeties and our owne,   40
Your honors, liberties and lives were weigh'd
In equall care and ballance with our owne,
Endure as we the malice of our stars,
The wrath of *Tamburlain*, and power of warres.
Or be the means the overweighing heavens   45
Have kept to quallifie these hot extreames,
And bring us pardon in your chearfull lookes.
2. VIRGIN. Then here before the majesty of heaven,
And holy *Patrones* of *Egyptia*,
With knees and hearts submissive we intreate   50
Grace to our words and pitie to our lookes,
That this devise may proove propitious,
And through the eies and eares of *Tamburlaine*,
Convey events of mercie to his heart:
Graunt that these signes of victorie we yeeld   55
May bind the temples of his conquering head,
To hide the folded furrowes of his browes,
And shadow his displeased countenance,
With happy looks of ruthe and lenity.
Leave us my Lord, and loving countrimen,   60
What simple Virgins may perswade, we will.
GOVERNOUR. Farewell (sweet Virgins) on whose safe return
Depends our citie, libertie, and lives.

Exeunt. [Manent VIRGINS.]

63SD *Manent* VIRGINS] *Dyce 1*; *not in O1.*   63SDNo break of scene] *Dyce 1*;
Actus.5. Scæna.2. O1.

[*Enter*] TAMBURLAINE, TECHELLES, THERIDAMAS,
USUMCASANE, *with others*: TAMBURLAINE *all in blacke,
and verie melancholy*.

TAMBURLAINE. What, are the Turtles fraide out of their
    neastes?
    Alas poore fooles, must you be first shal feele   65
    The sworne destruction of *Damascus*.
    They know my custome: could they not as well
    Have sent ye out, when first my milkwhite flags
    Through which sweet mercie threw her gentle beams,
    Reflexing them on your disdainfull eies: 70
    As now when furie and incensed hate
    Flings slaughtering terrour from my coleblack tents.
    And tels for trueth, submissions comes too late.
1. VIRGIN. Most happy King and Emperour of the earth.
    Image of Honor and Nobilitie.   75
    For whome the Powers divine have made the world,
    And on whose throne the holy Graces sit.
    In whose sweete person is compriz'd the Sum
    Of natures Skill and heavenly majestie.
    Pittie our plightes, O pitie poore *Damascus*:   80
    Pitie olde age, within whose silver haires
    Honor and reverence evermore have raign'd,
    Pitie the mariage bed, where many a Lord
    In prime and glorie of his loving joy,
    Embraceth now with teares of ruth and blood,   85
    The jealous bodie of his fearfull wife,
    Whose cheekes and hearts so punisht with conceit,
    To thinke thy puisant never staied arme
    Will part their bodies, and prevent their soules
    From heavens of comfort, yet their age might beare,   90
    Now waxe all pale and withered to the death,
    As well for griefe our ruthlesse Governour
    Have thus refusde the mercie of thy hand,
    (Whose scepter Angels kisse, and Furies dread)
    As for their liberties, their loves or lives.   95
    O then for these, and such as we our selves,
    For us, for infants, and for all our bloods,

63SD2 *Enter*] *Robinson; not in O1*.

That never nourisht thought against thy rule,
Pitie, O pitie, (sacred Emperour)
The prostrate service of this wretched towne.   100
And take in signe thereof this gilded wreath,
Whereto ech man of rule hath given his hand,
And wisht as worthy subjects happy meanes,
To be investers of thy royall browes,
Even with the true Egyptian Diadem.   105
TAMBURLAINE. Virgins, in vaine ye labour to prevent
   That which mine honor sweares shal be perform'd:
   Behold my sword, what see you at the point?
VIRGINS. Nothing but feare and fatall steele my Lord.
TAMBURLAINE. Your fearfull minds are thicke and mistie
      then,   110
   For there sits Death, there sits imperious Death,
   Keeping his circuit by the slicing edge.
   But I am pleasde you shall not see him there,
   He now is seated on my horsmens speares:
   And on their points his fleshlesse bodie feedes.   115
   Techelles, straight goe charge a few of them
   To chardge these Dames, and shew my servant death:
   Sitting in scarlet on their armed speares.
OMNES. O pitie us.
TAMBURLAINE. Away with them I say and shew them death.120

                 They [TECHELLES *and others*] *take them away.*

I will not spare these proud Egyptians,
Nor change my Martiall observations,
For all the wealth of *Gehons* golden waves.
Or for the love of *Venus*, would she leave
The angrie God of Armes, and lie with me.   125
They have refusde the offer of their lives,
And know my customes are as peremptory
As wrathfull Planets, death, or destinie.

                    Enter TECHELLES.

What, have your horsmen shewen the virgins Death?
TECHELLES. They have my Lord, and on *Damascus* wals   130

           120SD TECHELLES *and others*] *Dyce 1; not in O1.*

Have hoisted up their slaughtered carcases.
TAMBURLAINE. A sight as banefull to their soules I think
As are Thessalian drugs or Mithradate.
But goe my Lords, put the rest to the sword.

Exeunt. [*Manet* TAMBURLAINE.]

Ah faire *Zenocrate*, divine *Zenocrate*,   135
Faire is too foule an Epithite for thee,
That in thy passion for thy countries love,
And feare to see thy kingly Fathers harme,
With haire discheweld wip'st thy watery cheeks:
And like to *Flora* in her mornings pride,   140
Shaking her silver tresses in the aire,
Rain'st on the earth resolved pearle in showers,
And sprinklest Saphyrs on thy shining face,
Wher Beauty, mother to the Muses sits,
And comments vollumes with her Yvory pen: 145
Taking instructions from thy flowing eies,
Eies when that *Ebena* steps to heaven,
In silence of thy solemn Evenings walk,
Making the mantle of the richest night,
The Moone, the Planets, and the Meteors light.   150
There Angels in their christal armours fight
A doubtfull battell with my tempted thoughtes,
For *Egypts* freedom and the Souldans life:
His life that so consumes *Zenocrate*,
Whose sorrowes lay more siege unto my soule,   155
Than all my Army to *Damascus* walles.
And neither *Perseas* Soveraign, nor the Turk
Troubled my sences with conceit of foile,
So much by much, as dooth *Zenocrate*.
What is beauty saith my sufferings then?   160
If all the pens that ever poets held,
Had fed the feeling of their maisters thoughts,
And every sweetnes that inspir'd their harts,
Their minds, and muses on admyred theames:
If all the heavenly Quintessence they still   165

134SD *Manet* TAMBURLAINE.] *Dyce 1*; *not in O1.*   157 *Perseas*] *Oxberry*; Perseans
O1.

From their immortall flowers of Poesy,
Wherein as in a myrrour we perceive
The highest reaches of a humaine wit:
If these had made one Poems period
And all combin'd in Beauties worthinesse,   170
Yet should ther hover in their restlesse heads,
One thought, one grace, one woonder at the least,
Which into words no vertue can digest.
But how unseemly is it for my Sex,
My discipline of armes and Chivalrie,   175
My nature and the terrour of my name,
To harbour thoughts effeminate and faint?
Save onely that in Beauties just applause,
With whose instinct the soule of man is toucht,
And every warriour that is rapt with love   180
Of fame, of valour, and of victory,
Must needs have beauty beat on his conceites,
I thus conceiving and subduing, both,
That which hath stoopt the topmost of the Gods,
Even from the fiery spangled vaile of heaven,   185
To feele the lowly warmth of shepheards flames,
And maske in cottages of strowed weeds,
Shal give the world to note, for all my byrth,
That Vertue solely is the sum of glorie,
And fashions men with true nobility.   190
Who's within there?

Enter two or three [ATTENDANTS].

Hath *Bajazeth* bene fed to day?
ATTENDANT. I, my Lord.
TAMBURLAINE. Bring him forth, and let us know if the
town be ransackt.   [*Exeunt* ATTENDANTS.]   195

Enter TECHELLES, THERIDAMAS, USUMCASANE, *and
others.*

TECHELLES. The town is ours my Lord, and fresh supply

184 stoopt] *Dyce 2*; stopped *O1*.   topmost] *Deighton*; tempest *O1*; temper *conj. Collier*;
chiefest *Dyce 2*.   186 lowly] *conj. Collier*; lovely *O1*.   187 maske] *conj.*
Broughton, Dyce 1; martch *O1*.   191SD ATTENDANTS] *Jump*; not in *O1*.   193
ATTENDANT] *Dyce 1*; An. *O1*; Anippe *Oxberry*.   195SD *Exeunt* ATTENDANTS] *Dyce*
1; not in *O1*; *Exit An. Oxberry*.

Of conquest, and of spoile is offered us.

TAMBURLAINE. Thats wel *Techelles*, what's the newes?

TECHELLES. The Souldan and the Arabian king together
March on us with such eager violence,   200
As if there were no way but one with us.

TAMBURLAINE. No more there is not I warrant thee *Techelles*.

They [ATTENDANTS] *bring in the Turke* [BAJAZETH *in his
cage, followed by* ZABINA].

THERIDAMAS. We know the victorie is ours my Lord,
But let us save the reverend Souldans life,
For faire *Zenocrate*, that so laments his state.   205

TAMBURLAINE. That will we chiefly see unto, *Theridamas*,
For sweet *Zenocrate*, whose worthinesse
Deserves a conquest over every hart:
And now my footstoole, if I loose the field,
You hope of libertie and restitution: 210
Here let him stay my maysters from the tents,
Till we have made us ready for the field.
Pray for us *Bajazeth*, we are going.

Exeunt. [*Manent* BAJAZETH *and* ZABINA.]

BAJAZETH. Go, never to returne with victorie:
Millions of men encompasse thee about,   215
And gore thy body with as many wounds.
Sharpe forked arrowes light upon thy horse:
Furies from the blacke *Cocitus* lake,
Breake up the earth, and with their firebrands,
Enforce thee run upon the banefull pikes.   220
Volleyes of shot pierce through thy charmed Skin,
And every bullet dipt in poisoned drugs,
Or roaring Cannons sever all thy joints,
Making thee mount as high as Eagles soare.

ZABINA. Let all the swords and Lances in the field,   225
Stick in his breast, as in their proper roomes.
At every pore let blood comme dropping foorth,
That lingring paines may massacre his heart.

202SD ATTENDANTS] *Dyce 1; not in* O1.   BAJAZETH...ZABINA] *Dyce 1; not in*
O1.   213SD *Manent...*ZABINA] *Dyce 1; not in* O1.

And madnesse send his damned soule to hell.

BAJAZETH. Ah faire *Zabina*, we may curse his power,   230
The heavens may frowne, the earth for anger quake,
But such a Star hath influence in his sword,
As rules the Skies, and countermands the Gods,
More than Cymerian *Stix* or Distinie:
And then shall we in this detested guyse,   235
With shame, with hungar, and with horror aie
Griping our bowels with retorqued thoughtes,
And have no hope to end our extasies.

ZABINA. Then is there left no *Mahomet*, no God,
No Feend, no Fortune, nor no hope of end   240
To our infamous monstrous slaveries?
Gape earth, and let the Feends infernall view
A hell, as hoplesse and as full of feare
As are the blasted banks of *Erebus*:
Where shaking ghosts with ever howling grones,   245
Hover about the ugly Ferriman,
To get a passage to *Elisian*.
Why should we live, O wretches, beggars, slaves,
Why live we *Bajazeth*, and build up neasts,
So high within the region of the aire,   250
By living long in this oppression,
That all the world will see and laugh to scorne,
The former triumphes of our mightines,
In this obscure infernall servitude?

BAJAZETH. O life more loathsome to my vexed thoughts,   255
Than noisome parbreak of the Stygian Snakes,
Which fils the nookes of Hell with standing aire,
Infecting all the Ghosts with curelesse griefs:
O dreary Engines of my loathed sight,
That sees my crowne, my honor and my name,   260
Thrust under yoke and thraldom of a thiefe.
Why feed ye still on daies accursed beams,
And sink not quite into my tortur'd soule.
You see my wife, my Queene and Emperesse,
Brought up and propped by the hand of fame,   265
Queen of fifteene contributory Queens,

243 A] *Oxberry*; As *O1*.

Now throwen to roomes of blacke abjection,
Smear'd with blots of basest drudgery:
And Villanesse to shame, disdaine, and misery:
Accursed *Bajazeth*, whose words of ruth,   270
That would with pity chear *Zabinas* heart,
And make our soules resolve in ceasles teares,
Sharp hunger bites upon and gripes the root
From whence the issues of my thoughts doe breake.
O poore *Zabina*, O my Queen, my Queen,   275
Fetch me some water for my burning breast,
To coole and comfort me with longer date,
That in the shortned sequel of my life,
I may poure foorth my soule into thine armes,
With words of love: whose moaning entercourse   280
Hath hetherto bin staid, with wrath and hate
Of our expreslesse band inflictions.
ZABINA. Sweet *Bajazeth*, I will prolong thy life,
As long as any blood or sparke of breath
Can quench or coole the torments of my griefe.   285

She goes out.

BAJAZETH. Now *Bajazeth*, abridge thy banefull daies,
And beat thy braines out of thy conquer'd head:
Since other meanes are all forbidden me,
That may be ministers of my decay.
O highest Lamp of everliving *Jove*,   290
Accursed day infected with my griefs,
Hide now thy stained face in endles night,
And shut the windowes of the lightsome heavens.
Let ugly darknesse with her rusty coach
Engyrt with tempests wrapt in pitchy clouds,   295
Smother the earth with never fading mistes:
And let her horses from their nostrels breathe
Rebellious winds and dreadfull thunderclaps:
That in this terrour *Tamburlaine* may live.
And my pin'd soule resolv'd in liquid ayre,   300
May styl excruciat his tormented thoughts.

300 ayre] *O3*; ay *O1*.

Then let the stony dart of sencelesse colde,
Pierce through the center of my withered heart,
And make a passage for my loathed life.

He brains himself against the cage.

Enter ZABINA.

ZABINA. What do mine eies behold, my husband dead?   305
His Skul al rivin in twain, his braines dasht out?
The braines of *Bajazeth*, my Lord and Soveraigne?
O *Bajazeth*, my husband and my Lord,
O *Bajazeth*, O Turk, O Emperor.
Give him his liquor? Not I, bring milk and fire, and my   310
blood I bring him againe, teare me in peeces, give me the
sworde with a ball of wildefire upon it. Downe with him,
downe with him. Goe to, my child, away, away, away.
Ah, save that Infant, save him, save him. I, even I, speake
to her. The Sun was downe. Streamers white, Red,   315
Blacke, here, here, here. Fling the meat in his face.
Tamburlaine, Tamburlaine. Let the souldiers be buried.
Hel, death, *Tamburlain*, Hell. Make ready my Coch, my
chaire, my jewels, I come, I come, I come.

She runs against the Cage and braines her selfe.

[*Enter*] ZENOCRATE *wyth* ANIPPE.

ZENOCRATE. Wretched *Zenocrate*, that livest to see,   320
Damascus walles di'd with Egyptian blood,
Thy Fathers subjects and thy countrimen:
Thy streetes strowed with dissevered jointes of men,
And wounded bodies gasping yet for life.
But most accurst, to see the Sun-bright troope   325
Of heavenly vyrgins and unspotted maides,
Whose lookes might make the angry God of armes,
To breake his sword, and mildly treat of love,
On horsmens Lances to be hoisted up,
And guiltlesly endure a cruell death.   330
For every fell and stout Tartarian Stead,

313 to,] *Oxberry*; to∧ *O1*.   319SD *Enter*] *Q*; *not in O1*.   320 ZENOCRATE] *Q*;
not in O1.

That stampt on others with their thundring hooves,
When al their riders chardg'd their quivering speares
Began to checke the ground, and rain themselves:
Gazing upon the beautie of their lookes: 335
Ah *Tamburlaine*, wert thou the cause of this
That tearm'st *Zenocrate* thy dearest love?
Whose lives were dearer to *Zenocrate*
Than her owne life, or ought save thine owne love.
But see another bloody spectacle.   340
Ah wretched eies, the enemies of my hart,
How are ye glutted with these grievous objects,
And tell my soule mor tales of bleeding ruth?
See, se *Anippe* if they breathe or no.

ANIPPE. No breath nor sence, nor motion in them both.   345
Ah Madam, this their slavery hath Enforc'd,
And ruthlesse cruelty of *Tamburlaine*.

ZENOCRATE. Earth cast up fountaines from thy entralles,
And wet thy cheeks for their untimely deathes:
Shake with their waight in signe of feare and griefe: 350
Blush heaven, that gave them honor at their birth,
And let them die a death so barbarous.
Those that are proud of fickle Empery,
And place their chiefest good in earthly pompe:
Behold the Turke and his great Emperesse.   355
Ah *Tamburlaine*, my love, sweet *Tamburlaine*,
That fights for Scepters and for slippery crownes,
Behold the Turk and his great Emperesse.
Thou that in conduct of thy happy stars,
Sleep'st every night with conquest on thy browes,   360
And yet wouldst shun the wavering turnes of war,
In feare and feeling of the like distresse,
Behold the Turke and his great Emperesse.
Ah myghty *Jove* and holy *Mahomet*,
Pardon my Love, oh pardon his contempt,   365
Of earthly fortune, and respect of pitie,
And let not conquest ruthlesly pursewde
Be equally against his life incenst,
In this great Turk and haplesse Emperesse.
And pardon me that was not moov'd with ruthe,   370
To see them live so long in misery:

Ah what may chance to thee *Zenocrate?*
ANIPPE. Madam content your self and be resolv'd,
   Your Love hath fortune so at his command,
   That she shall stay and turne her wheele no more,   375
   As long as life maintaines his mighty arme,
   That fights for honor to adorne your head.

       Enter [PHILEMUS,] *a Messenger.*

ZENOCRATE. What other heavie news now brings *Philemus?*
PHILEMUS. Madam, your father and th'Arabian king,
   The first affecter of your excellence,   380
   Comes now as *Turnus* gainst *Eneas* did,
   Armed with lance into the Egyptian fields,
   Ready for battaile gainst my Lord the King.
ZENOCRATE. Now shame and duty, love and feare presents
   A thousand sorrowes to my martyred soule: 385
   Whom should I wish the fatall victory,
   When my poore pleasures are devided thus,
   And rackt by dutie from my cursed heart:
   My father and my first betrothed love,
   Must fight against my life and present love: 390
   Wherin the change I use condemns my faith,
   And makes my deeds infamous through the world.
   But as the Gods to end the Troyans toile,
   Prevented *Turnus* of *Lavinia,*
   And fatally enricht *Eneas* love,   395
   So for a finall Issue to my griefes,
   To pacifie my countrie and my love,
   Must *Tamburlaine* by their resistlesse powers,
   With vertue of a gentle victorie,
   Conclude a league of honor to my hope.   400
   Then as the powers devine have preordainde,
   With happy safty of my fathers life,
   Send like defence of faire *Arabia.*

   They sound to the battaile. And TAMBURLAINE *enjoyes the*
      victory. After ARABIA *enters wounded.*

ARABIA. What cursed power guides the murthering hands,

     377SD PHILEMUS] *Oxberry; not in O1.*

Of this infamous Tyrants souldiers,   405
That no escape may save their enemies:
Nor fortune keep them selves from victory.
Lye down *Arabia*, wounded to the death,
And let *Zenocrates* faire eies beholde
That as for her thou bearst these wretched armes,   410
Even so for her thou diest in these armes:
Leaving thy blood for witnesse of thy love.

ZENOCRATE. Too deare a witnesse for such love my Lord.
Behold *Zenocrate*, the cursed object
Whose Fortunes never mastered her griefs: 415
Behold her wounded in conceit for thee,
As much as thy faire body is for me.

ARABIA. Then shal I die with full contented heart,
Having beheld devine *Zenocrate*,
Whose sight with joy would take away my life,   420
As now it bringeth sweetnesse to my wound,
If I had not bin wounded as I am.
Ah that the deadly panges I suffer now,
Would lend an howers license to my tongue:
To make discourse of some sweet accidents   425
Have chanc'd thy merits in this worthles bondage.
And that I might be privy to the state,
Of thy deserv'd contentment and thy love:
But making now a vertue of thy sight,
To drive all sorrow from my fainting soule: 430
Since Death denies me further cause of joy,
Depriv'd of care, my heart with comfort dies,
Since thy desired hand shall close mine eies.   [*He dies.*]

Enter TAMBURLAIN *leading the* SOULDANE, TECHELLES,
THERIDAMAS, USUMCASANE, *with others.*

TAMBURLAINE. Come happy Father of *Zenocrate*,
A title higher than thy Souldans name: 435
Though my right hand have thus enthralled thee,
Thy princely daughter here shall set thee free.
She that hath calmde the furie of my sword,
Which had ere this bin bathde in streames of blood,

433SD *He dies.*] Oxberry; *not in* O*1*.

As vast and deep as *Euphrates* or *Nile*. 440
ZENOCRATE. O sight thrice welcome to my joiful soule,
 To see the king my Father issue safe,
 From dangerous battel of my conquering Love.
SOULDAN. Wel met my only deare *Zenocrate*,
 Though with the losse of *Egypt* and my Crown. 445
TAMBURLAINE. Twas I my lord that gat the victory,
 And therfore grieve not at your overthrow,
 Since I shall render all into your hands,
 And ad more strength to your dominions
 Than ever yet confirm'd th'Egyptian Crown. 450
 The God of war resignes his roume to me,
 Meaning to make me Generall of the world:
 Jove viewing me in armes, lookes pale and wan,
 Fearing my power should pull him from his throne.
 Where ere I come the fatall sisters sweat, 455
 And griesly death, by running to and fro,
 To doo their ceasles homag to my sword:
 And here in *Affrick* where it seldom raines,
 Since I arriv'd with my triumphant hoste,
 Have swelling cloudes drawen from wide gasping woundes, 460
 Bene oft resolv'd in bloody purple showers,
 A meteor that might terrify the earth,
 And make it quake at every drop it drinks:
 Millions of soules sit on the bankes of *Styx*,
 Waiting the back returne of *Charons* boat, 465
 Hell and *Elisian* swarme with ghosts of men,
 That I have sent from sundry foughten fields,
 To spread my fame through hell and up to heaven:
 And see my Lord, a sight of strange import,
 Emperours and kings lie breathlesse at my feet. 470
 The Turk and his great Emperesse as it seems,
 Left to themselves while we were at the fight,
 Have desperatly dispatcht their slavish lives:
 With them *Arabia* too hath left his life,
 Al sights of power to grace my victory: 475
 And such are objects fit for *Tamburlaine*,
 Wherein as in a mirrour may be seene,
 His honor, that consists in sheading blood,
 When men presume to manage armes with him.

SOULDAN. Mighty hath God and *Mahomet* made thy hand   480
    (Renowmed *Tamburlain*) to whom all kings
    Of force must yeeld their crownes and Emperies:
    And I am pleasde with this my overthrow,
    If as beseemes a person of thy state,
    Thou hast with honor usde *Zenocrate*.   485
TAMBURLAINE. Her state and person wants no pomp you see,
    And for all blot of foule inchastity,
    I record heaven, her heavenly selfe is cleare:
    Then let me find no further time to grace
    Her princely Temples with the Persean crowne: 490
    But here these kings that on my fortunes wait,
    And have bene crown'd for prooved worthynesse,
    Even by this hand that shall establish them,
    Shal now, adjoining al their hands with mine,
    Invest her here my Queene of *Persea*.   495
    What saith the noble Souldane and *Zenocrate*?
SOULDAN. I yeeld with thanks and protestations
    Of endlesse honor to thee for her love.
TAMBURLAINE. Then doubt I not but faire *Zenocrate*
    Will soone consent to satisfy us both.   500
ZENOCRATE. Els should I much forget my self, my Lord.
THERIDAMAS. Then let us set the crowne upon her head,
    That long hath lingred for so high a seat.
TECHELLES. My hand is ready to performe the deed,
    For now her mariage time shall worke us rest.   505
USUMCASANE. And here's the crown my Lord, help set it on.
TAMBURLAINE. Then sit thou downe divine *Zenocrate*,
    And here we crowne thee Queene of *Persea*,
    And all the kingdomes and dominions
    That late the power of *Tamburlaine* subdewed: 510
    As *Juno*, when the Giants were supprest,
    That darted mountaines at her brother *Jove*:
    So lookes my Love, shadowing in her browes
    Triumphes and Trophees for my victories:
    Or as *Latonas* daughter bent to armes,   515
    Adding more courage to my conquering mind.
    To gratify thee, sweet *Zenocrate*,

517 thee,] *Dyce 2*; the‸ *O1*.

Egyptians, Moores and men of *Asia*,
From *Barbary* unto the Westerne *Inde*,
Shall pay a yearly tribute to thy Syre.   520
And from the boundes of *Affrick* to the banks
Of *Ganges*, shall his mighty arme extend.
And now my Lords and loving followers,
That purchac'd kingdomes by your martiall deeds,
Cast off your armor, put on scarlet roabes.   525
Mount up your royall places of estate,
Environed with troopes of noble men,
And there make lawes to rule your provinces:
Hang up your weapons on *Alcides* poste,
For *Tamburlaine* takes truce with al the world.   530
Thy first betrothed Love, *Arabia*,
Shall we with honor (as beseemes) entombe,
With this great Turke and his faire Emperesse:
Then after all these solemne Exequies,
We wil our rites of mariage solemnize.   535
                                       [*Exeunt.*]

Finis Actus quinti & ultimi huius primæ partis.

519 *Inde*] *Bowers*; *Indie O1*.   535 our rites] *Dyce 2*; our celebrated rites *O1*.
535SD *Exeunt*] *Dyce 2*; *not in O1*.

TAMBURLAINE
THE GREAT

Part 2

[Dramatis Personae

PROLOGUE

TAMBURLAINE,   King of Persia

CALYPHAS ⎫
AMYRAS   ⎬   his sons
CELEBINUS ⎭

THERIDAMAS,   King of Argier

TECHELLES,   King of Fez

USUMCASANE,   King of Morocco

ORCANES,   King of Natolia

URIBASSA,   a Natolian lord

KING OF TREBIZON

KING OF SORIA

KING OF JERUSALEM

KING OF AMASIA

GAZELLUS,   Viceroy of Byron

SIGISMUND,   King of Hungary

FREDERICKE,   lord of Buda

BALDWINE,   lord of Bohemia

CALLAPINE,   son to Bajazeth and prisoner of Tamburlaine

ALMEDA,   his keeper

GOVERNOUR OF
  BABYLON

CAPTAIN OF BALSERA

SON   to the Captain of Balsera

MAXIMUS,   a citizen of Babylon

PERDICAS,   companion to Calyphas

A Captain, Physicians, Lords, Citizens, Messengers, Soldiers, Pioners, Attendants and Musicians

ZENOCRATE,   wife to Tamburlaine

OLYMPIA,   wife to the Captain of Balsera

Turkish Concubines.]

Dramatis Personae] *Oxberry* (*incomplete*); *not in O1*.

The Second Part of
The bloody Conquests
of mighty Tamburlaine.

With his impassionate fury, for the death of
his Lady and love, faire Zenocrate: his fourme
of exhortation and discipline to his three
sons, and the maner of his own death.

[*Enter*] The PROLOGUE.

The generall welcomes Tamburlain *receiv'd,*
When he arrived last upon our stage,
Hath made our Poet pen his second part,
Wher death cuts off the progres of his pomp,
And murdrous Fates throwes al his triumphs down.   5
But what became of faire Zenocrate,
And with how manie cities sacrifice
He celebrated her sad funerall,
Himselfe in presence shal unfold at large.

OSD *Enter*] *this edn.; not in* O1.   8 *sad*] *Oxberry; said* O1.

Actus. *1*. Scæna. *1*.

[*Enter*] ORCANES, *king of Natolia*, GAZELLUS, *vice-roy of* BYRON, URIBASSA, *and their traine, with drums and trumpets.*

ORCANES. Egregious Viceroyes of these Eastern parts
  Plac'd by the issue of great *Bajazeth*,
  And sacred Lord, the mighty *Calapine*:
  Who lives in *Egypt*, prisoner to that slave,
  Which kept his father in an yron cage: 5
  Now have we martcht from faire *Natolia*
  Two hundred leagues, and on *Danubius* banks,
  Our warlike hoste in compleat armour rest,
  Where *Sigismond* the king of *Hungary*
  Should meet our person to conclude a truce.   10
  What? Shall we parle with the Christian?
  Or crosse the streame, and meet him in the field?
GAZELLUS. King of *Natolia*, let us treat of peace,
  We all are glutted with the Christians blood,
  And have a greater foe to fight against,   15
  Proud *Tamburlaine*, that now in *Asia*,
  Neere *Guyrons* head doth set his conquering feet,
  And means to fire *Turky* as he goes:
  Gainst him my Lord must you addresse your power.
URIBASSA. Besides, king *Sigismond* hath brought from
      Christendome,   20
  More then his Camp of stout Hungarians,
  Sclavonians, Almans, Rutters, Muffes, and Danes,
  That with the Holbard, Lance, and murthering Axe,
  Will hazard that we might with surety hold.
ORCANES. Though from the shortest Northren Paralell,   25
  Vast *Gruntland* compast with the frozen sea,
  Inhabited with tall and sturdy men,
  Gyants as big as hugie *Polypheme*,
  Millions of Souldiers cut the Artick line,

OSD1 *Enter*] Dyce *1; not in* O1.   OSD2, 20 URIBASSA] *Oxberry; Upibassa* O1.
25 ORCANES] *Oxberry; not in* O1.

Bringing the strength of *Europe* to these Armes,   30
Our Turky blades shal glide through al their throats,
And make this champion mead a bloody Fen.
Danubius stream that runs to *Trebizon*,
Shall carie wrapt within his scarlet waves,
As martiall presents to our friends at home,   35
The slaughtered bodies of these Christians.
The Terrene main wherin *Danubius* fals,
Shall by this battell be the bloody Sea.
The wandring Sailers of proud *Italy*,
Shall meet those Christians fleeting with the tyde,   40
Beating in heaps against their Argoses,
And make faire *Europe* mounted on her bull,
Trapt with the wealth and riches of the world,
Alight and weare a woful mourning weed.

GAZELLUS. Yet stout *Orcanes*, Prorex of the world,   45
Since *Tamburlaine* hath mustred all his men,
Marching from *Cairon* northward with his camp,
To *Alexandria*, and the frontier townes,
Meaning to make a conquest of our land:
Tis requisit to parle for a peace   50
With *Sigismond* the king of *Hungary*:
And save our forces for the hot assaults
Proud *Tamburlaine* intends *Natolia*.

ORCANES. Viceroy of *Byron*, wisely hast thou said:
My realme, the Center of our Empery,   55
Once lost, All *Turkie* would be overthrowne:
And for that cause the Christians shall have peace.
Slavonians, Almains, Rutters, Muffes, and Danes
Feare not *Orcanes*, but great *Tamburlaine*.
Nor he but Fortune that hath made him great.   60
We have revolted Grecians, Albanees,
Cicilians, Jewes, Arabians, Turks, and Moors,
Natolians, Sorians, blacke Egyptians,
Illirians, Thracians, and Bythinians,
Enough to swallow forcelesse *Sigismond*,   65
Yet scarse enough t'encounter *Tamburlaine*.
He brings a world of people to the field,
From *Scythia* to the Orientall Plage
Of *India*, wher raging *Lantchidol*

Beates on the regions with his boysterous blowes,   70
That never sea-man yet discovered:
All *Asia* is in Armes with *Tamburlaine.*
Even from the midst of fiery *Cancers* Tropick,
To *Amazonia* under *Capricorne,*
And thence as far as *Archipellago,*   75
All *Affrike* is in Armes with *Tamburlaine.*
Therefore Viceroies the Christians must have peace.

[*Enter*] SIGISMOND, FREDERICKE, BALDWINE, *and their*
          traine with drums and trumpets.

SIGISMOND. *Orcanes* (as our Legates promist thee)
Wee with our Peeres have crost *Danubius* stream
To treat of friendly peace or deadly war: 80
Take which thou wilt, for as the Romans usde
I here present thee with a naked sword.
Wilt thou have war, then shake this blade at me:
If peace, restore it to my hands againe,
And I wil sheath it to confirme the same.   85
ORCANES. Stay *Sigismond,* forgetst thou I am he
That with the Cannon shooke *Vienna* walles,
And made it dance upon the Continent:
As when the massy substance of the earth,
Quiver about the Axeltree of heaven.   90
Forgetst thou that I sent a shower of dartes
Mingled with powdered shot and fethered steele
So thick upon the blink-ei'd Burghers heads,
That thou thy self, then County-Pallatine,
The king of *Boheme,* and the *Austrich* Duke,   95
Sent Herralds out, which basely on their knees
In all your names desirde a truce of me?
Forgetst thou, that to have me raise my siege,
Wagons of gold were set before my tent:
Stampt with the princely Foule that in her wings   100
Caries the fearfull thunderbolts of *Jove.*
How canst thou think of this and offer war?
SIGISMOND. *Vienna* was besieg'd, and I was there,

77SD No break of scene] *Oxberry; Act.1. Scæna.2, O1.   Enter*] *Oxberry; not in O1.*

Then County-Pallatine, but now a king:
And what we did, was in extremity: 105
But now *Orcanes*, view my royall hoste,
That hides these plaines, and seems as vast and wide,
As dooth the Desart of *Arabia*
To those that stand on *Badgeths* lofty Tower,
Or as the Ocean to the Traveiler   110
That restes upon the snowy Appenines:
And tell me whether I should stoope so low,
Or treat of peace with the Natolian king?
GAZELLUS. Kings of *Natolia* and of *Hungarie*,
We came from *Turky* to confirme a league,   115
And not to dare ech other to the field:
A friendly parle might become ye both.
FREDERICKE. And we from *Europe* to the same intent,
Which if your General refuse or scorne,
Our Tents are pitcht, our men stand in array,   120
Ready to charge you ere you stir your feet.
ORCANES. So prest are we, but yet if *Sigismond*
Speake as a friend, and stand not upon tearmes,
Here is his sword, let peace be ratified
On these conditions specified before,   125
Drawen with advise of our Ambassadors.
SIGISMOND. Then here I sheath it, and give thee my hand,
Never to draw it out, or manage armes
Against thy selfe or thy confederates:
But whilst I live will be at truce with thee.   130
ORCANES. But (*Sigismond*) confirme it with an oath,
And sweare in sight of heaven and by thy Christ.
SIGISMOND. By him that made the world and sav'd my soule,
The sonne of God and issue of a Mayd,
Sweet Jesus Christ, I sollemnly protest,   135
And vow to keepe this peace inviolable.
ORCANES. By sacred *Mahomet*, the friend of God,
Whose holy Alcaron remaines with us,
Whose glorious body when he left the world,
Closde in a coffyn mounted up the aire,   140
And hung on stately *Mecas* Temple roofe,
I sweare to keepe this truce inviolable:
Of whose conditions, and our solemne othes

Sign'd with our handes, each shal retaine a scrowle
As memorable witnesse of our league.   145
Now *Sigismond*, if any Christian King
Encroche upon the confines of thy realme,
Send woord, *Orcanes* of *Natolia*
Confirm'd this league beyond *Danubius* streame,
And they will (trembling) sound a quicke retreat,   150
So am I fear'd among all Nations.

SIGISMOND. If any heathen potentate or king
Invade *Natolia*, *Sigismond* will send
A hundred thousand horse train'd to the war,
And backt by stout Lanceres of *Germany*,   155
The strength and sinewes of the imperiall seat.

ORCANES. I thank thee *Sigismond*, but when I war
All *Asia Minor*, *Affrica*, and *Greece*
Follow my Standard and my thundring Drums:
Come let us goe and banquet in our tents: 160
I will dispatch chiefe of my army hence
To faire *Natolia*, and to *Trebizon*,
To stay my comming gainst proud *Tamburlaine*.
Freend *Sigismond*, and peeres of *Hungary*,
Come banquet and carouse with us a while,   165
And then depart we to our territories.

                                        Exeunt.

Actus. *1*. Scæna. *2*.

[*Enter*] CALLAPINE *with* ALMEDA, *his keeper.*

CALLAPINE. Sweet *Almeda*, pity the ruthfull plight
Of *Callapine*, the sonne of *Bajazeth*,
Born to be Monarch of the Western world:
Yet here detain'd by cruell *Tamburlaine*.

ALMEDA. My Lord I pitie it, and with my heart   5
Wish your release, but he whose wrath is death,
My soveraigne Lord, renowmed *Tamburlain*,
Forbids you further liberty than this.

Scæna.2.] Oxberry; Scæna.3. O1.   OSD Enter] Dyce 1; not in O1; ... keeper, discovered Oxberry.

CALLAPINE. Ah were I now but halfe so eloquent
  To paint in woords, what Ile perfourme in deeds,   10
  I know thou wouldst depart from hence with me.
ALMEDA. Not for all *Affrike*, therefore moove me not.
CALLAPINE. Yet heare me speake my gentle *Almeda*.
ALMEDA. No speach to that end, by your favour sir.
CALLAPINE. By *Cairo* runs—   15
ALMEDA. No talke of running, I tell you sir.
CALLAPINE. A litle further, gentle *Almeda*.
ALMEDA. Wel sir, what of this?
CALLAPINE. By *Cairo* runs to *Alexandria* Bay,
  Darotes streames, wherin at anchor lies   20
  A Turkish Gally of my royall fleet,
  Waiting my comming to the river side,
  Hoping by some means I shall be releast,
  Which when I come aboord will hoist up saile,
  And soon put foorth into the Terrene sea: 25
  Where twixt the Isles of *Cyprus* and of *Creete*,
  We quickly may in Turkish seas arrive.
  Then shalt thou see a hundred kings and more
  Upon their knees, all bid me welcome home.
  Amongst so many crownes of burnisht gold,   30
  Choose which thou wilt, all are at thy command.
  A thousand Gallies mann'd with Christian slaves
  I freely give thee, which shall cut the straights,
  And bring Armados from the coasts of *Spaine*,
  Fraughted with golde of rich *America*:   35
  The Grecian virgins shall attend on thee,
  Skilful in musicke and in amorous laies:
  As faire as was *Pigmalions* Ivory gyrle,
  Or lovely *Io* metamorphosed.
  With naked Negros shall thy coach be drawen,   40
  And as thou rid'st in triumph through the streets,
  The pavement underneath thy chariot wheels
  With Turky Carpets shall be covered:
  And cloath of Arras hung about the walles,
  Fit objects for thy princely eie to pierce.   45
  A hundred Bassoes cloath'd in crimson silk

Shall ride before thee on Barbarian Steeds:
And when thou goest, a golden Canapie
Enchac'd with pretious stones, which shine as bright
As that faire vail that covers all the world: 50
When *Phœbus* leaping from his Hemi-Spheare,
Discendeth downward to th'Antipodes.
And more than this, for all I cannot tell.

ALMEDA. How far hence lies the Galley, say you?

CALLAPINE. Sweet *Almeda*, scarse halfe a league from hence. 55

ALMEDA. But need we not be spied going aboord?

CALLAPINE. Betwixt the hollow hanging of a hill
And crooked bending of a craggy rock,
The sailes wrapt up, the mast and tacklings downe,
She lies so close that none can find her out.   60

ALMEDA. I like that well: but tel me my Lord, if I should
let you goe, would you bee as good as your word? Shall I
be made a king for my labour?

CALLAPINE. As I am *Callapine* the Emperour,
And by the hand of *Mahomet* I sweare,   65
Thou shalt be crown'd a king and be my mate.

ALMEDA. Then here I sweare, as I am *Almeda*,
Your Keeper under *Tamburlaine* the great,
(For that's the style and tytle I have yet)
Although he sent a thousand armed men   70
To intercept this haughty enterprize,
Yet would I venture to conduct your Grace,
And die before I brought you backe again.

CALLAPINE. Thanks gentle *Almeda*, then let us haste,
Least time be past, and lingring let us both.   75

ALMEDA. When you will my Lord, I am ready.

CALLAPINE. Even straight: and farewell cursed *Tamburlaine*.
Now goe I to revenge my fathers death.

                                                    Exeunt.

Actus. 1. Scæna. 3.

[*Enter*] TAMBURLAINE *with* ZENOCRATE, *and his three*
sonnes, CALYPHAS, AMYRAS, *and* CELEBINUS, *with*
drummes and trumpets.

TAMBURLAINE. Now bright *Zenocrate,* the worlds faire eie,
   Whose beames illuminate the lamps of heaven,
   Whose chearful looks do cleare the clowdy aire
   And cloath it in a christall liverie,
   Now rest thee here on faire *Larissa* Plaines,   5
   Where *Egypt* and the Turkish Empire parts,
   Betweene thy sons that shall be Emperours,
   And every one Commander of a world.
ZENOCRATE. Sweet *Tamburlain,* when wilt thou leave these
      armes
   And save thy sacred person free from scathe: 10
   And dangerous chances of the wrathfull war?
TAMBURLAINE. When heaven shal cease to moove on both the
      poles,
   And when the ground wheron my souldiers march
   Shal rise aloft and touch the horned Moon,
   And not before, my sweet *Zenocrate*:   15
   Sit up and rest thee like a lovely Queene.
   So, now she sits in pompe and majestie:
   When these my sonnes, more precious in mine eies
   Than all the wealthy kingdomes I subdewed,
   Plac'd by her side, looke on their mothers face.   20
   But yet me thinks their looks are amorous,
   Not martiall as the sons of *Tamburlaine.*
   Water and ayre being simbolisde in one,
   Argue their want of courage and of wit.
   Their haire as white as milke and soft as Downe,   25
   Which should be like the quilles of Porcupines,
   As blacke as Jeat, and hard as Iron or steel,
   Bewraies they are too dainty for the wars.
   Their fingers made to quaver on a Lute,
   Their armes to hang about a Ladies necke: 30

Scæna.3.] Oxberry; *Scæna.4.* O1.   OSD I *Enter*] Oxberry; not in O1.

Their legs to dance and caper in the aire:
Would make me thinke them Bastards, not my sons,
But that I know they issued from thy wombe,
That never look'd on man but *Tamburlaine*.

ZENOCRATE. My gratious Lord, they have their mothers
    looks,   35
But when they list, their conquering fathers hart:
This lovely boy the yongest of the three,
Not long agoe bestrid a Scythian Steed:
Trotting the ring, and tilting at a glove:
Which when he tainted with his slender rod,   40
He raign'd him straight and made him so curvet,
As I cried out for feare he should have falne.

TAMBURLAINE. Wel done my boy, thou shalt have shield and
    lance,
Armour of proofe, horse, helme, and Curtle-axe,
And I will teach thee how to charge thy foe,   45
And harmelesse run among the deadly pikes.
If thou wilt love the warres and follow me,
Thou shalt be made a King and raigne with me,
Keeping in yron cages Emperours.
If thou exceed thy elder Brothers worth,   50
And shine in compleat vertue more than they,
Thou shalt be king before them, and thy seed
Shall issue crowned from their mothers wombe.

CELEBINUS. Yes father, you shal see me if I live,
Have under me as many kings as you,   55
And martch with such a multitude of men,
As all the world shall tremble at their view.

TAMBURLAINE. These words assure me boy, thou art my sonne.
When I am old and cannot mannage armes,
Be thou the scourge and terrour of the world.   60

AMYRAS. Why may not I my Lord, as wel as he,
Be tearm'd the scourge and terrour of the world?

TAMBURLAINE. Be al a scourge and terror to the world,
Or els you are not sons of *Tamburlaine*.

CALYPHAS. But while my brothers follow armes my lord   65
Let me accompany my gratious mother.
They are enough to conquer all the world
And you have won enough for me to keep.

TAMBURLAINE. Bastardly boy, sprong from some cowards loins,
　　And not the issue of great *Tamburlaine*,　　　　　　70
　　Of all the provinces I have subdued
　　Thou shalt not have a foot, unlesse thou beare
　　A mind corragious and invincible:
　　For he shall weare the crowne of *Persea*
　　Whose head hath deepest scarres, whose breast most
　　　　woundes,　　　　　　75
　　Which being wroth, sends lightning from his eies,
　　And in the furrowes of his frowning browes,
　　Harbors revenge, war, death and cruelty:
　　For in a field whose superficies
　　Is covered with a liquid purple veile,　　　　　　80
　　And sprinkled with the braines of slaughtered men,
　　My royal chaire of state shall be advanc'd:
　　And he that meanes to place himselfe therein
　　Must armed wade up to the chin in blood.
ZENOCRATE. My Lord, such speeches to our princely
　　　　sonnes,　　　　　　85
　　Dismaies their mindes before they come to proove
　　The wounding troubles angry war affoords.
CELEBINUS. No Madam, these are speeches fit for us,
　　For if his chaire were in a sea of blood,
　　I would prepare a ship and saile to it,　　　　　　90
　　Ere I would loose the tytle of a king.
AMYRAS. And I would strive to swim through pooles of blood,
　　Or make a bridge of murthered Carcases,
　　Whose arches should be fram'd with bones of Turks,
　　Ere I would loose the tytle of a king.　　　　　　95
TAMBURLAINE. Wel lovely boies, you shal be Emperours both,
　　Stretching your conquering armes from east to west:
　　And sirha, if you meane to weare a crowne,
　　When we shall meet the Turkish Deputie
　　And all his Viceroies, snatch it from his head,　　　　　　100
　　And cleave his Pericranion with thy sword.
CALYPHAS. If any man will hold him, I will strike,
　　And cleave him to the channell with my sword.

---

79 superficies] *Oxberry*; superfluities *O1*.　　　101 Pericranion] *Dyce 1*; Pecicranion *O1*;
pericranium *Oxberry*.

TAMBURLAINE. Hold him, and cleave him too, or Ile cleave thee,
For we will martch against them presently.   105
Theridamas, Techelles, and *Casane*
Promist to meet me on *Larissa* plaines
With hostes apeece against this Turkish crue,
For I have sworne by sacred *Mahomet,*
To make it parcel of my Empery.   110
The trumpets sound, *Zenocrate,* they come.

Enter THERIDAMAS, *and his traine with Drums and Trumpets.*

TAMBURLAINE. Welcome *Theridamas,* king of *Argier.*
THERIDAMAS. My Lord the great and mighty *Tamburlain,*
Arch-Monarke of the world, I offer here,
My crowne, my selfe, and all the power I have,   115
In all affection at thy kingly feet.

[*He presents his crown to* TAMBURLAINE.]

TAMBURLAINE. Thanks good *Theridamas.*
THERIDAMAS. Under my collors march ten thousand Greeks,
And of *Argier* and *Affriks* frontier townes
Twise twenty thousand valiant men at armes,   120
All which have sworne to sacke *Natolia:*
Five hundred Briggandines are under saile,
Meet for your service on the sea, my Lord,
That lanching from *Argier* to *Tripoly,*
Will quickly ride before *Natolia:*   125
And batter downe the castles on the shore.
TAMBURLAINE. Wel said *Argier,* receive thy crowne againe.

[*He returns* THERIDAMAS *crown.*]

Enter TECHELLES *and* USUMCASANE *together.*

TAMBURLAINE. Kings of *Morocus* and of *Fesse,* welcome.
USUMCASANE. [*Presenting his crown to* TAMBURLAINE]
Magnificent and peerlesse *Tamburlaine,*

111SD No break of scene] *Oxberry; Actus:1. Scæna.5. O1.*   116SD *He...* TAM-
BURLAINE] *Bevington–Rasmussen* ('He lays his crown at Tamburlaine's feet'); *not in O1.*
127SD *He...crown.*] *Bevington–Rasmussen; not in O1.*   No break of scene] *Oxberry;
Actus.1. Scæna.6. O1.*   129SD *Presenting...* TAMBURLAINE] *Bevington–Rasmussen*
('laying his crown before...'); *not in O1.*

I and my neighbor King of *Fesse* have brought   130
To aide thee in this Turkish expedition,
A hundred thousand expert souldiers:
From *Azamor* to *Tunys* neare the sea,
Is *Barbary* unpeopled for thy sake,
And all the men in armour under me,   135
Which with my crowne I gladly offer thee.

TAMBURLAINE. [*Returning* USUMCASANES *crown*] Thanks king
 of *Morocus*, take your crown again.

TECHELLES. [*Presenting his crown to* TAMBURLAINE] And
 mighty *Tamburlaine*, our earthly God,
Whose lookes make this inferiour world to quake,
I here present thee with the crowne of *Fesse*,   140
And with an hoste of Moores trainde to the war,
Whose coleblacke faces make their foes retire,
And quake for feare, as if infernall *Jove*,
Meaning to aid thee in these Turkish armes,
Should pierce the blacke circumference of hell,   145
With ugly Furies bearing fiery flags,
And millions of his strong tormenting spirits:
From strong *Tesella* unto *Biledull*,
All *Barbary* is unpeopled for thy sake.

TAMBURLAINE. [*Returning* TECHELLES *crown*] Thanks king of
 Fesse, take here thy crowne again.   150
Your presence (loving friends and fellow kings)
Makes me to surfet in conceiving joy.
If all the christall gates of *Joves* high court
Were opened wide, and I might enter in
To see the state and majesty of heaven,   155
It could not more delight me than your sight.
Now will we banquet on these plaines a while,
And after martch to *Turky* with our Campe,
In number more than are the drops that fall
When *Boreas* rents a thousand swelling cloudes,   160
And proud *Orcanes* of *Natolia*,
With all his viceroies shall be so affraide,

137SD *Returning...crown*] Bevington–Rasmussen; not in *O1*.   138SD *Presenting...*
TAMBURLAINE] Bevington–Rasmussen ('*laying his crown before...*'); not in *O1*.   144
thee] Oxberry; them *O1*.   these] *O3*; this *O1*.   150SD *Returning...crown*] Bevington–Rasmussen; not in *O1*.

That though the stones, as at *Deucalions* flood,
Were turnde to men, he should be overcome:
Such lavish will I make of Turkish blood,   165
That *Jove* shall send his winged Messenger
To bid me sheath my sword, and leave the field:
The Sun unable to sustaine the sight,
Shall hide his head in *Thetis* watery lap,
And leave his steeds to faire *Boetes* charge: 170
For halfe the world shall perish in this fight:
But now my friends, let me examine ye,
How have ye spent your absent time from me?
USUMCASANE. My Lord our men of *Barbary* have martcht
    Foure hundred miles with armour on their backes,   175
And laine in leagre fifteene moneths and more,
For since we left you at the Souldans court,
We have subdude the Southerne *Guallatia*,
And all the land unto the coast of *Spaine*.
We kept the narrow straight of *Gibralter*,   180
And made *Canarea* cal us kings and Lords,
Yet never did they recreate themselves,
Or cease one day from war and hot alarms,
And therefore let them rest a while my Lord.
TAMBURLAINE. They shal *Casane*, and tis time yfaith.   185
TECHELLES. And I have martch'd along the river *Nile*,
To *Machda*, where the mighty Christian Priest
Cal'd *John* the great, sits in a milk-white robe,
Whose triple Myter I did take by force,
And made him sweare obedience to my crowne.   190
From thence unto *Cazates* did I martch,
Wher Amazonians met me in the field:
With whom (being women) I vouchsaft a league,
And with my power did march to *Zansibar*,
The Westerne part of *Affrike*, where I view'd   195
The Ethiopian sea, rivers and lakes:
But neither man nor child in al the land:
Therfore I tooke my course to *Manico*,
Where unresisted I remoov'd my campe:
And by the coast of *Byather* at last,   200
I came to *Cubar*, where the Negros dwell,
And conquering that, made haste to *Nubia*:

There having sackt *Borno*, the Kingly seat,
I took the king, and lead him bound in chaines
Unto *Damasco*, where I staid before.   205
TAMBURLAINE. Well done *Techelles*: what saith *Theridamas?*
THERIDAMAS. I left the confines and the bounds of *Affrike*
And made a voyage into *Europe*,
Where by the river *Tyros* I subdew'd
Stoka, *Padalia*, and *Codemia*.   210
Then crost the sea and came to *Oblia*,
And *Nigra Silva*, where the Devils dance,
Which in despight of them I set on fire:
From thence I crost the Gulfe, call'd by the name
Mare magiore, of th'inhabitantes: 215
Yet shall my souldiers make no period
Untill *Natolia* kneele before your feet.
TAMBURLAINE. Then wil we triumph, banquet and carouse,
Cookes shall have pensions to provide us cates,
And glut us with the dainties of the world,   220
Lachrima Christi and Calabrian wines
Shall common Souldiers drink in quaffing boules,
I, liquid golde when we have conquer'd him,
Mingled with corrall and with orient pearle:
Come let us banquet and carrouse the whiles.   225
                                        Exeunt.

        Finis Actus primi.

        224 orient] *Oxberry*; orientall *O1*.

Actus. 2. Scæna. 1.

[*Enter*] SIGISMOND, FREDERICKE, BALDWINE, *with their traine.*

SIGISMOND. Now say my Lords of *Buda* and *Bohemia*,
What motion is it that inflames your thoughts,
And stirs your valures to such soddaine armes?
FREDERICKE. Your Majesty remembers I am sure
What cruell slaughter of our Christian bloods,   5
These heathnish Turks and Pagans lately made,
Betwixt the citie *Zula* and *Danubius*,
How through the midst of *Verna* and *Bulgaria*
And almost to the very walles of *Rome*,
They have not long since massacred our Camp.   10
It resteth now then that your Majesty
Take all advantages of time and power,
And worke revenge upon these Infidels:
Your Highnesse knowes for *Tamburlaines* repaire,
That strikes a terrour to all Turkish hearts,   15
Natolia hath dismist the greatest part
Of all his armie, pitcht against our power
Betwixt *Cutheia* and *Orminius* mount:
And sent them marching up to *Belgasar*,
Acantha, *Antioch*, and *Cæsaria*,   20
To aid the kings of *Soria* and *Jerusalem*.
Now then my Lord, advantage take hereof,
And issue sodainly upon the rest:
That in the fortune of their overthrow,
We may discourage all the pagan troope,   25
That dare attempt to war with Christians.
SIGISMOND. But cals not then your Grace to memorie
The league we lately made with king *Orcanes*,
Confirm'd by oth and Articles of peace,
And calling Christ for record of our truethes?   30
This should be treacherie and violence,
Against the grace of our profession.

OSD *Enter*] Oxberry; not in O1.

BALDWINE. No whit my Lord: for with such Infidels,
    In whom no faith nor true religion rests,
    We are not bound to those accomplishments,   35
    The holy lawes of Christendome injoine:
    But as the faith which they prophanely plight
    Is not by necessary pollycy,
    To be esteem'd assurance for our selves,
    So what we vow to them should not infringe   40
    Our liberty of armes and victory.
SIGISMOND. Though I confesse the othes they undertake,
    Breed litle strength to our securitie,
    Yet those infirmities that thus defame
    Their faiths, their honors, their religion,   45
    Should not give us presumption to the like.
    Our faiths are sound, and must be consumate,
    Religious, righteous, and inviolate.
FREDERICKE. Assure your Grace tis superstition
    To stand so strictly on dispensive faith: 50
    And should we lose the opportunity
    That God hath given to venge our Christians death
    And scourge their foule blasphemous Paganisme,
    As fell to *Saule*, to *Balaam* and the rest,
    That would not kill and curse at Gods command,   55
    So surely will the vengeance of the highest
    And jealous anger of his fearefull arme
    Be pour'd with rigour on our sinfull heads,
    If we neglect this offered victory.
SIGISMOND. Then arme my Lords, and issue sodainly,   60
    Giving commandement to our generall hoste,
    With expedition to assaile the Pagan,
    And take the victorie our God hath given.

                                                          Exeunt.

---

45 honors, their] *this edn.*; honors, and their *O1*; honors, and *Oxberry*.   47 con-
sumate] *conj. Dyce 1, Dyce 2*; consinuate *O1*; continuate *Oxberry*.

Actus. 2. Scæna. 2.

[*Enter*] ORCANES, GAZELLUS, URIBASSA *with their traine.*

ORCANES. *Gazellus, Uribassa,* and the rest,
    Now will we march from proud *Orminius* mount
    To faire *Natolia,* where our neighbour kings
    Expect our power and our royall presence,
    T'incounter with the cruell *Tamburlain,*   5
    That nigh *Larissa* swaies a mighty hoste,
    And with the thunder of his martial tooles
    Makes Earthquakes in the hearts of men and heaven.
GAZELLUS. And now come we to make his sinowes shake,
    With greater power than erst his pride hath felt: 10
    An hundred kings by scores wil bid him armes,
    And hundred thousands subjects to each score:
    Which if a shower of wounding thunderbolts
    Should breake out off the bowels of the clowdes
    And fall as thick as haile upon our heads,   15
    In partiall aid of that proud Scythian,
    Yet should our courages and steeled crestes,
    And numbers more than infinit of men,
    Be able to withstand and conquer him.
URIBASSA. Me thinks I see how glad the christian King   20
    Is made, for joy of your admitted truce:
    That could not but before be terrified
    With unacquainted power of our hoste.

Enter a MESSENGER.

MESSENGER. Arme, arme dread Soveraign and my noble Lords.
    The treacherous army of the Christians,   25
    Taking advantage of your slender power,
    Comes marching on us, and determines straight,
    To bid us battaile for our dearest lives.
ORCANES. Traitors, villaines, damned Christians.
    Have I not here the articles of peace,   30
    And solemne covenants we have both confirm'd,
    He by his Christ, and I by *Mahomet?*

OSD *Enter*] *Oxberry; not in O1.*   24 Arme, arme] *Craik (this edn.);* Arme *O1.*

GAZELLUS. Hel and confusion light upon their heads,
    That with such treason seek our overthrow,
    And cares so litle for their prophet Christ.   35
ORCANES. Can there be such deceit in Christians,
    Or treason in the fleshly heart of man,
    Whose shape is figure of the highest God?
    Then if there be a Christ, as Christians say,
    But in their deeds deny him for their Christ: 40
    If he be son to everliving *Jove*,
    And hath the power of his outstretched arme,
    If he be jealous of his name and honor,
    As is our holy prophet *Mahomet*,
    Take here these papers as our sacrifice   45
    And witnesse of thy servants perjury.
                       [*He tears to pieces the articles of peace.*]
    Open thou shining vaile of *Cynthia*
    And make a passage from the imperiall heaven
    That he that sits on high and never sleeps,
    Nor in one place is circumscriptible,   50
    But every where fils every Continent,
    With strange infusion of his sacred vigor,
    May in his endlesse power and puritie
    Behold and venge this Traitors perjury.
    Thou Christ that art esteem'd omnipotent,   55
    If thou wilt proove thy selfe a perfect God,
    Worthy the worship of all faithfull hearts,
    Be now reveng'd upon this Traitors soule,
    And make the power I have left behind
    (Too litle to defend our guiltlesse lives)   60
    Sufficient to discomfort and confound
    The trustlesse force of those false Christians.
    To armes my Lords, on Christ still let us crie,
    If there be Christ, we shall have victorie.
                             [*Exeunt.*]

46SD *He . . . peace*] Robinson; *not in O1.*   64SD *Exeunt*] Oxberry; *not in O1.*

[*Actus. 2. Scæna. 3.*]

Sound to the battell, and SIGISMOND *comes out wounded.*

SIGISMOND. Discomfited is all the Christian hoste,
  And God hath thundered vengeance from on high,
  For my accurst and hatefull perjurie.
  O just and dreadfull punisher of sinne,
  Let the dishonor of the paines I feele,   5
  In this my mortall well deserved wound,
  End all my penance in my sodaine death,
  And let this death wherein to sinne I die,
  Conceive a second life in endlesse mercie.   [*He dies.*]

Enter ORCANES, GAZELLUS, URIBASSA, *with others.*

ORCANES. Now lie the Christians bathing in their bloods,   10
  And Christ or *Mahomet* hath bene my friend.
GAZELLUS. See here the perjur'd traitor *Hungary*,
  Bloody and breathlesse for his villany.
ORCANES. Now shall his barbarous body be a pray
  To beasts and foules, and al the winds shall breath   15
  Through shady leaves of every sencelesse tree,
  Murmures and hisses for his hainous sin.
  Now scaldes his soule in the Tartarian streames,
  And feeds upon the banefull tree of hell,
  That *Zoacum*, that fruit of bytternesse,   20
  That in the midst of fire is ingraft,
  Yet flourisheth as *Flora* in her pride,
  With apples like the heads of damned Feends.
  The Dyvils there in chaines of quencelesse flame,
  Shall lead his soule through *Orcus* burning gulfe,   25
  From paine to paine, whose change shal never end:
  What saiest thou yet *Gazellus* to his foile:
  Which we referd to justice of his Christ,
  And to his power, which here appeares as full
  As raies of *Cynthia* to the clearest sight?   30
GAZELLUS. Tis but the fortune of the wars my Lord,
  Whose power is often proov'd a myracle.

Actus.2. Scæna.3.] *Dyce 1; not in O1.*   9SD *He dies*] *Oxberry; not in O1.*

ORCANES. Yet in my thoughts shall Christ be honoured,
    Not dooing *Mahomet* an injurie,
    Whose power had share in this our victory: 35
    And since this miscreant hath disgrac'd his faith,
    And died a traitor both to heaven and earth,
    We wil both watch and ward shall keepe his trunke
    Amidst these plaines, for Foules to pray upon.
    Go *Uribassa*, give it straight in charge.   40
URIBASSA. I will my Lord.
              Exit URIBASSA [*and souldiers with the body*].
ORCANES. And now *Gazellus*, let us haste and meete
    Our Army and our brothers of *Jerusalem*,
    Of *Soria*, *Trebizon* and *Amasia*,
    And happily with full Natolian bowles   45
    Of Greekish wine now let us celebrate
    Our happy conquest, and his angry fate.
                                   Exeunt.

Actus. 2. Scæna ultima. [4]

The Arras is drawen and ZENOCRATE *lies in her bed of state,*
TAMBURLAINE *sitting by her: three* PHISITIANS *about her*
bed, tempering potions. THERIDAMAS, TECHELLES,
USUMCASANE, *and the three sonnes* [CALYPHAS, AMYRAS,
CELEBINUS].

TAMBURLAINE. Blacke is the beauty of the brightest day,
    The golden balle of heavens eternal fire,
    That danc'd with glorie on the silver waves,
    Now wants the fewell that enflamde his beames:
    And all with faintnesse and for foule disgrace,   5
    He bindes his temples with a frowning cloude,
    Ready to darken earth with endlesse night:
    Zenocrate that gave him light and life,
    Whose eies shot fire from their Ivory bowers,
    And tempered every soule with lively heat,   10

41SD *and...body*] *Bowers; not in O1.*   43 brothers] *Oxberry;* brother *O1.*
OSD4–5 CALYPHAS...CELEBINUS] *Dyce 1; not in O1.*

Now by the malice of the angry Skies,
Whose jealousie admits no second Mate,
Drawes in the comfort of her latest breath
All dasled with the hellish mists of death.
Now walk the angels on the walles of heaven,   15
As Centinels to warne th'immortall soules,
To entertaine devine *Zenocrate*.
Apollo, *Cynthia*, and the ceaslesse lamps
That gently look'd upon this loathsome earth,
Shine downwards now no more, but deck the heavens   20
To entertaine divine *Zenocrate*.
The christall springs whose taste illuminates
Refined eies with an eternall sight,
Like tried silver runs through Paradice
To entertaine divine *Zenocrate*.   25
The Cherubins and holy Seraphins
That sing and play before the king of kings,
Use all their voices and their instruments
To entertaine divine *Zenocrate*.
And in this sweet and currious harmony,   30
The God that tunes this musicke to our soules
Holds out his hand in highest majesty
To entertaine divine *Zenocrate*.
Then let some holy trance convay my thoughts,
Up to the pallace of th'imperiall heaven: 35
That this my life may be as short to me
As are the daies of sweet *Zenocrate*:
Phisitions, wil no phisicke do her good?
1. PHYSICIAN. My Lord, your Majesty shall soone perceive:
And if she passe this fit, the worst is past.   40
TAMBURLAINE. Tell me, how fares my faire *Zenocrate*?
ZENOCRATE. I fare my Lord, as other Emperesses,
That when this fraile and transitory flesh
Hath suckt the measure of that vitall aire
That feeds the body with his dated health,   45
Wanes with enforst and necessary change.
TAMBURLAINE. May never such a change transfourme my love
In whose sweet being I repose my life,
Whose heavenly presence beautified with health,
Gives light to *Phœbus* and the fixed stars,   50

Whose absence makes the sun and Moone as darke
As when, opposde in one Diamiter,
Their Spheares are mounted on the serpents head,
Or els discended to his winding traine:
Live still my Love and so conserve my life,   55
Or dieng, be the author of my death.
ZENOCRATE. Live still my Lord, O let my soveraigne live,
And sooner let the fiery Element
Dissolve, and make your kingdome in the Sky,
Than this base earth should shroud your majesty: 60
For should I but suspect your death by mine,
The comfort of my future happinesse
And hope to meet your highnesse in the heavens,
Turn'd to dispaire, would break my wretched breast,
And furie would confound my present rest.   65
But let me die my Love, yet let me die,
With love and patience let your true love die:
Your griefe and furie hurtes my second life.
Yet let me kisse my Lord before I die,
And let me die with kissing of my Lord.   70

                                        [*He kisses her.*]

But since my life is lengthened yet a while,
Let me take leave of these my loving sonnes,
And of my Lords whose true nobilitie
Have merited my latest memorie:
Sweet sons farewell, in death resemble me,   75
And in your lives your fathers excellency.
Some musicke, and my fit wil cease my Lord.

                    They call musicke.

TAMBURLAINE. Proud furie and intollorable fit,
That dares torment the body of my Love,
And scourge the Scourge of the immortall God: 80
Now are those Spheares where *Cupid* usde to sit,
Wounding the world with woonder and with love,
Sadly supplied with pale and ghastly death,
Whose darts do pierce the Center of my soule:

---

51 makes] *O3*; make *O1*.   56 author] *Q*; anchor *O1*.   70SD *He...her.*]
Bowers; *not in O1*.

Her sacred beauty hath enchaunted heaven,   85
And had she liv'd before the siege of *Troy*,
Hellen, whose beauty sommond *Greece* to armes,
And drew a thousand ships to *Tenedos*,
Had not bene nam'd in *Homers* Iliads:
Her name had bene in every line he wrote: 90
Or had those wanton Poets, for whose byrth
Olde *Rome* was proud, but gasde a while on her,
Nor *Lesbia*, nor *Corinna* had bene nam'd,
Zenocrate had bene the argument
Of every Epigram or Eligie.   95

       The musicke sounds, and she dies.

What, is she dead? *Techelles*, draw thy sword,
And wound the earth, that it may cleave in twaine,
And we discend into th'infernall vaults,
To haile the fatall Sisters by the haire,
And throw them in the triple mote of Hell,   100
For taking hence my faire *Zenocrate*.
Casane and *Theridamas* to armes:
Raise Cavalieros higher than the cloudes,
And with the cannon breake the frame of heaven,
Batter the shining pallace of the Sun,   105
And shiver all the starry firmament:
For amorous *Jove* hath snatcht my love from hence,
Meaning to make her stately Queene of heaven.
What God so ever holds thee in his armes,
Giving thee Nectar and Ambrosia,   110
Behold me here divine *Zenocrate*,
Raving, impatient, desperate and mad,
Breaking my steeled lance, with which I burst
The rusty beames of *Janus* Temple doores,
Letting out death and tyrannising war,   115
To martch with me under this bloody flag:
And if thou pitiest *Tamburlain* the great,
Come downe from heaven and live with me againe.
THERIDAMAS.   Ah good my Lord be patient, she is dead,
And all this raging cannot make her live.   120
If woords might serve, our voice hath rent the aire,
If teares, our eies have watered all the earth:

If griefe, our murthered harts have straind forth blood.
Nothing prevailes, for she is dead my Lord.   124
TAMBURLAINE. For she is dead? thy words doo pierce my soule.
Ah sweet *Theridamas*, say so no more:
Though she be dead, yet let me think she lives,
And feed my mind that dies for want of her:
Where ere her soule be, thou shalt stay with me
Embalm'd with Cassia, Amber Greece and Myrre,   130
Not lapt in lead but in a sheet of gold,
And till I die thou shalt not be interr'd.
Then in as rich a tombe as *Mausolus*,
We both will rest and have one Epitaph
Writ in as many severall languages,   135
As I have conquered kingdomes with my sword.
This cursed towne will I consume with fire,
Because this place bereft me of my Love:
The houses burnt, wil looke as if they mourn'd,
And here will I set up her statua,   140
And martch about it with my mourning campe,
Drooping and pining for *Zenocrate*.

The Arras is drawen.

[*Finis Actus secundi.*]

140 statua] *Broughton, conj. Dyce 1*; stature *O1*; Statue *O3*.   142SD2; *Finis…se-
cundi.*] *J. S. Cunningham*; not in *O1*.

Actus. 3. Scæna. 1.

Enter the kings of TREBISOND *and* SORIA, *one bringing a
sword, and another a scepter: Next* NATOLIA *and*
JERUSALEM *with the Emperiall crowne: After* CALAPINE,
and after him other Lordes [*and* ALMEDA]: ORCANES *and*
JERUSALEM *crowne him, and the other give him the scepter*
[*and the sword*].

ORCANES. *Calepinus Cyricelibes*, otherwise *Cybelius*, son
and successive heire to the late mighty Emperour *Baja-*
zeth, by the aid of God and his friend *Mahomet*, Emperour of *Natolia*, *Jerusalem*, *Trebizon*, *Soria*, *Amasia*,
Thracia, *Illyria*, *Carmonia* and al the hundred and thirty   5
Kingdomes late contributory to his mighty father. Long
live *Callepinus*, Emperour of *Turky*.

CALLAPINE.   Thrice worthy kings, *Natolia*, and the rest,
I will requite your royall gratitudes
With all the benefits my Empire yeelds: 10
And were the sinowes of th'imperiall seat
So knit and strengthned, as when *Bajazeth*
My royall Lord and father fild the throne,
Whose cursed fate hath so dismembred it,
Then should you see this Thiefe of *Scythia*,   15
This proud usurping king of *Persea*,
Do us such honor and supremacie,
Bearing the vengeance of our fathers wrongs,
As all the world should blot our dignities
Out of the booke of base borne infamies.   20
And now I doubt not but your royall cares
Hath so provided for this cursed foe,
That since the heire of mighty *Bajazeth*
(An Emperour so honoured for his vertues)
Revives the spirits of true Turkish heartes,   25
In grievous memorie of his fathers shame,
We shall not need to nourish any doubt,

OSD4 *and* ALMEDA] *Dyce 1; not in* O1.   OSD6 *and...sword*] *this edn.; not in*
O1.   8 kings, *Natolia*] *this edn.; kings of* Natolia O1.

But that proud Fortune, who hath followed long
The martiall sword of mighty *Tamburlaine*,
Will now retaine her olde inconstancie,   30
And raise our honors to as high a pitch
In this our strong and fortunate encounter.
For so hath heaven provided my escape,
From al the crueltie my soule sustaind,
By this my friendly keepers happy meanes,   35
That *Jove* surchardg'd with pity of our wrongs,
Will poure it downe in showers on our heads:
Scourging the pride of cursed *Tamburlain*.

ORCANES. I have a hundred thousand men in armes,
Some, that in conquest of the perjur'd Christian,   40
Being a handfull to a mighty hoste,
Thinke them in number yet sufficient,
To drinke the river *Nile* or *Euphrates*,
And for their power, ynow to win the world.

JERUSALEM. And I as many from *Jerusalem*,   45
Judæa, *Gaza*, and *Scalonias* bounds,
That on mount *Sinay* with their ensignes spread,
Looke like the parti-coloured cloudes of heaven,
That shew faire weather to the neighbor morne.

TREBIZON. And I as many bring from *Trebizon*,   50
Chio, *Famastro*, and *Amasia*,
All bordring on the *Mare-major* sea:
Riso, *Sancina*, and the bordering townes,
That touch the end of famous *Euphrates*.
Whose courages are kindled with the flames,   55
The cursed Scythian sets on all their townes,
And vow to burne the villaines cruell heart.

SORIA. From *Soria* with seventy thousand strong,
Tane from *Aleppo*, *Soldino*, *Tripoly*,
And so unto my citie of *Damasco*,   60
I march to meet and aide my neigbor kings,
All which will joine against this *Tamburlain*,
And bring him captive to your highnesse feet.

ORCANES. Our battaile then in martiall maner pitcht,

---

46 *Scalonias*] *J. S. Cunningham*; *Scalonians O1*; *Sclavonians Q*; Sclavonian *Oxberry*; Sclavonia's *Robinson*.

According to our ancient use, shall beare   65
The figure of the semi-circled Moone:
Whose hornes shall sprinkle through the tainted aire,
The poisoned braines of this proud Scythian.

CALLAPINE. Wel then my noble Lords, for this my friend,
That freed me from the bondage of my foe: 70
I thinke it requisite and honorable,
To keep my promise, and to make him king,
That is a Gentleman (I know) at least.

ALMEDA. That's no matter sir, for being a king, for *Tam-*
burlain came up of nothing.   75

JERUSALEM. Your Majesty may choose some pointed time,
Perfourming all your promise to the full:
Tis nought for your majesty to give a kingdome.

CALLAPINE. Then wil I shortly keep my promise *Almeda.*

ALMEDA. Why, I thank your Majesty.   80

Exeunt.

Actus. 3. Scæna. 2.

[*Enter*] TAMBURLAINE *with* USUMCASANE, *and his three*
sons, [CALYPHAS, AMYRAS, *and* CELEBINUS,] *foure*
[*souldiers*] *bearing the hearse of* ZENOCRATE, *and the drums*
sounding a dolefull martch, the Towne burning.

TAMBURLAINE. So, burne the turrets of this cursed towne,
Flame to the highest region of the aire:
And kindle heaps of exhalations,
That being fiery meteors, may presage,
Death and destruction to th'inhabitants.   5
Over my Zenith hang a blazing star,
That may endure till heaven be dissolv'd,
Fed with the fresh supply of earthly dregs,
Threatning a dearth and famine to this land,
Flieng Dragons, lightning, fearfull thunderclaps,   10

74 king, for] *Ellis-Fermor*; king,/For *O1*.   *Actus.3.*] *Robinson*; *Actus.2. O1*.
OSD1 *Enter*] *Robinson*; *not in O1*.   OSD2 CALYPHAS...CELEBINUS] *Dyce 1*; *not in*
O1.   OSD3 *souldiers*] *J. S. Cunningham*; *not in O1*.   9 dearth] *Dyce 1*; death *O1*.

Sindge these fair plaines, and make them seeme as black
As is the Island where the Furies maske,
Compast with *Lethe*, *Styx*, and *Phlegeton*,
Because my deare *Zenocrate* is dead.

CALYPHAS. This Piller plac'd in memorie of her,   15
Where in Arabian, Hebrew, Greek, is writ
This towne being burnt by Tamburlaine *the great*,
Forbids the world to build it up againe.

AMYRAS. And here this mournful streamer shal be plac'd,
Wrought with the Persean and Egyptian armes,   20
To signifie she was a princesse borne,
And wife unto the Monarke of the East.

CELEBINUS. And here this table as a Register
Of all her vertues and perfections.

TAMBURLAINE. And here the picture of *Zenocrate*,   25
To shew her beautie, which the world admyr'd.
Sweet picture of divine *Zenocrate*,
That hanging here, wil draw the Gods from heaven:
And cause the stars fixt in the Southern arke,
Whose lovely faces never any viewed,   30
That have not past the Centers latitude,
As Pilgrimes traveile to our Hemi-spheare,
Onely to gaze upon *Zenocrate*:
Thou shalt not beautifie *Larissa* plaines,
But keep within the circle of mine armes.   35
At every towne and castle I besiege,
Thou shalt be set upon my royall tent,
And when I meet an armie in the field:
Whose looks will shed such influence in my campe,
As if *Bellona*, Goddesse of the war,   40
Threw naked swords and sulphur bals of fire,
Upon the heads of all our enemies.
And now my Lords, advance your speares againe,
Sorrow no more my sweet *Casane* now:
Boyes, leave to mourne, this towne shall ever mourne,   45
Being burnt to cynders for your mothers death.

CALYPHAS. If I had wept a sea of teares for her,
It would not ease the sorrow I sustaine.

AMYRAS. As is that towne, so is my heart consum'd,
With griefe and sorrow for my mothers death.   50

CELEBINUS. My mothers death hath mortified my mind,
　And sorrow stops the passage of my speech.
TAMBURLAINE. But now my boies, leave off, and list to me,
　That meane to teach you rudiments of war:
　Ile have you learne to sleepe upon the ground,　　　　55
　March in your armour thorow watery Fens,
　Sustaine the scortching heat and freezing cold,
　Hunger and thirst, right adjuncts of the war.
　And after this, to scale a castle wal,
　Besiege a fort, to undermine a towne,　　　　　　　　60
　And make whole cyties caper in the aire.
　Then next, the way to fortifie your men,
　In champion grounds, what figure serves you best,
　For which the quinque-angle fourme is meet,
　Because the corners there may fall more flat　　　　　65
　Whereas the Fort may fittest be assailde,
　And sharpest where th'assault is desperate.
　The ditches must be deepe, the Counterscarps
　Narrow and steepe, the wals made high and broad,
　The Bulwarks and the rampiers large and strong,　　　70
　With Cavalieros and thicke counterforts,
　And roome within to lodge sixe thousand men.
　It must have privy ditches, countermines,
　And secret issuings to defend the ditch.
　It must have high Argins and covered waies　　　　　75
　To keep the bulwark fronts from battery,
　And Parapets to hide the Muscatters:
　Casemates to place the great Artillery,
　And store of ordinance that from every flanke
　May scoure the outward curtaines of the Fort,　　　　80
　Dismount the Cannon of the adverse part,
　Murther the Foe and save the walles from breach.
　When this is learn'd for service on the land,
　By plaine and easie demonstration,
　Ile teach you how to make the water mount,　　　　　85
　That you may dryfoot martch through lakes and pooles,
　Deep rivers, havens, creekes, and litle seas,

---

58 thirst,] _Q_; cold_∧_ _O1_.　　64 which] _Robinson_; with _O1_.　　82 the walles]
Oxberry; their walles _O1_.

And make a Fortresse in the raging waves,
Fenc'd with the concave of a monstrous rocke,
Invincible by nature of the place.   90
When this is done, then are ye souldiers,
And worthy sonnes of *Tamburlain* the great.
CALYPHAS. My Lord, but this is dangerous to be done,
We may be slaine or wounded ere we learne.
TAMBURLAINE. Villain, art thou the sonne of *Tamburlaine*,   95
And fear'st to die, or with a Curtle-axe
To hew thy flesh and make a gaping wound?
Hast thou beheld a peale of ordinance strike
A ring of pikes, mingled with shot and horse,
Whose shattered lims, being tost as high as heaven,   100
Hang in the aire as thicke as sunny motes,
And canst thou Coward stand in feare of death?
Hast thou not seene my horsemen charge the foe,
Shot through the armes, cut overthwart the hands,
Dieng their lances with their streaming blood,   105
And yet at night carrouse within my tent,
Filling their empty vaines with aiery wine,
That being concocted, turnes to crimson blood,
And wilt thou shun the field for feare of woundes?
View me thy father that hath conquered kings,   110
And with his hoste marcht round about the earth,
Quite voide of skars, and cleare from any wound,
That by the warres lost not a dram of blood,
And see him lance his flesh to teach you all   *He cuts his arme.*
A wound is nothing be it nere so deepe: 115
Blood is the God of Wars rich livery.
Now look I like a souldier, and this wound
As great a grace and majesty to me,
As if a chaire of gold enameled,
Enchac'd with Diamondes, Saphyres, Rubies   120
And fairest pearle of welthie *India*
Were mounted here under a Canapie:
And I sat downe, cloth'd with the massie robe,
That late adorn'd the Affrike Potentate,

111 marcht] *O3*; martch *O1*.   114–15 all/A wound … deepe:] *this edn.*; all./A
wound … deepe, *O1*.

Whom I brought bound unto *Damascus* walles.   125
Come boyes and with your fingers search my wound,
And in my blood wash all your hands at once,
While I sit smiling to behold the sight.
Now my boyes, what think you of a wound?

CALYPHAS. I know not what I should think of it. Me thinks   130
tis a pitifull sight.

CELEBINUS. Tis nothing: give me a wound father.

AMYRAS. And me another my Lord.

TAMBURLAINE. Come sirra, give me your arme.

CELEBINUS. Here father, cut it bravely as you did your own.   135

TAMBURLAINE. It shall suffice thou darst abide a wound.
My boy, thou shalt not loose a drop of blood,
Before we meet the armie of the Turke.
But then run desperate through the thickest throngs,
Dreadlesse of blowes, of bloody wounds and death: 140
And let the burning of *Larissa* wals,
My speech of war, and this my wound you see,
Teach you my boyes to beare couragious minds,
Fit for the followers of great *Tamburlaine*.
Usumcasane now come let us martch   145
Towards *Techelles* and *Theridamas*,
That we have sent before to fire the townes,
The towers and cities of these hatefull Turks,
And hunt that Coward, faintheart runaway,
With that accursed traitor *Almeda*,   150
Til fire and sword have found them at a bay.

USUMCASANE. I long to pierce his bowels with my sword,
That hath betraied my gracious Soveraigne,
That curst and damned Traitor *Almeda*.

TAMBURLAINE. Then let us see if coward *Calapine*   155
Dare levie armes against our puissance,
That we may tread upon his captive necke,
And treble all his fathers slaveries.

                                              Exeunt.

Actus. 3. Scæna. 3.

[*Enter*] TECHELLES, THERIDAMAS *and their traine* [*souldiers and pioners*].

THERIDAMAS. Thus have wee martcht Northwarde from *Tam-burlaine*,
 Unto the frontier point of *Soria*:
 And this is *Balsera* their chiefest hold,
 Wherein is all the treasure of the land.
TECHELLES. Then let us bring our light Artilery,   5
 Minions, Fauknets, and Sakars to the trench,
 Filling the ditches with the walles wide breach,
 And enter in, to seaze upon the gold:
 How say ye Souldiers, shal we not?
SOLDIERS. Yes, my Lord, yes, come lets about it.   10
THERIDAMAS. But stay a while, summon a parle, Drum,
 It may be they will yeeld it quietly,
 Knowing two kings, the friendes to *Tamburlain*,
 Stand at the walles, with such a mighty power.

Summon the battell.

[*Enter above*] CAPTAINE *with his wife* [OLYMPIA] *and*
SONNE.

CAPTAIN. What requier you my maisters?   15
THERIDAMAS. Captaine, that thou yeeld up thy hold to us.
CAPTAIN. To you? Why, do you thinke me weary of it?
TECHELLES. Nay Captain, thou art weary of thy life,
 If thou withstand the friends of *Tamburlain*.
THERIDAMAS. These Pioners of *Argier* in *Affrica*,   20
 Even in the cannons face shall raise a hill
 Of earth and fagots higher than thy Fort,
 And over thy Argins and covered waies
 Shal play upon the bulwarks of thy hold
 Volleies of ordinance til the breach be made,   25
 That with his ruine fils up all the trench.

Scæna.3.] *Robinson; Scæna.1, O1.*   OSD1 *Enter*] *Oxberry; not in O1.*   OSD1–2
souldiers and pioners] *Jump; not in O1.*   13 *friendes*] *O3; friend O1.*   14SD2 *Enter
above*] *Oxberry; not in O1.*   OLYMPIA] *Dyce 1; not in O1.*

And when we enter in, not heaven it selfe
Shall ransome thee, thy wife and family.
TECHELLES. Captaine, these Moores shall cut the leaden
    pipes,
    That bring fresh water to thy men and thee: 30
    And lie in trench before thy castle walles,
    That no supply of victuall shall come in,
    Nor any issue foorth, but they shall die:
    And therefore Captaine, yeeld it quietly.
CAPTAIN. Were you that are the friends of *Tamburlain*   35
    Brothers to holy *Mahomet* himselfe,
    I would not yeeld it: therefore doo your worst.
    Raise mounts, batter, intrench, and undermine,
    Cut off the water, all convoies, that you can,
    Yet I am resolute, and so farewell.   40

               [Exeunt above.]

THERIDAMAS. Pioners away, and where I stuck the stake,
    Intrench with those dimensions I prescribed:
    Cast up the earth towards the castle wall,
    Which til it may defend you, labour low:
    And few or none shall perish by their shot.   45
PIONERS. We will my Lord.   *Exeunt [pioners].*
TECHELLES. A hundred horse shall scout about the plaines
    To spie what force comes to relieve the holde.
    Both we (*Theridamas*) wil intrench our men,
    And with the Jacobs staffe measure the height   50
    And distance of the castle from the trench,
    That we may know if our artillery
    Will carie full point blancke unto their wals.
THERIDAMAS. Then see the bringing of our ordinance
    Along the trench into the battery,   55
    Where we will have Gabions of sixe foot broad,
    To save our Cannoniers from musket shot,
    Betwixt which, shall our ordinance thunder foorth,
    And with the breaches fall, smoake, fire, and dust,

33 any] *Oxberry*; *not in O1*.   39 convoies, that you can] *Craik* (*this edn.*); convoies
that can *O1*; convoys that come *Oxberry*; convoys you can *F. Cunningham*.   40SD
Exeunt above] *Oxberry*; *not in O1*.   46SD *pioners*] *Oxberry*; *not in O1*.   56
Gabions] *conj. Broughton, conj. Collier, F. Cunningham*; Galions *O1*.

The cracke, the Ecchoe and the souldiers crie   60
Make deafe the aire, and dim the Christall Sky.
TECHELLES. Trumpets and drums, alarum presently,
And souldiers play the men, the hold is yours.

[*Exeunt.*]

[*Actus. 3. Scæna. 4.*]

Enter [below] the CAPTAINE [*wounded*] *with his wife*
[OLYMPIA] *and* SONNE.

OLYMPIA. Come good my Lord, and let us haste from hence
Along the cave that leads beyond the foe.
No hope is left to save this conquered hold.
CAPTAIN. A deadly bullet gliding through my side,
Lies heavy on my heart, I cannot live.   5
I feele my liver pierc'd and all my vaines,
That there begin and nourish every part,
Mangled and torne, and all my entrals bath'd
In blood that straineth from their orifex.
Farewell sweet wife, sweet son farewell, I die.   10
[*He dies.*]

OLYMPIA. Death, whether art thou gone that both we live?
Come back again (sweet death) and strike us both:
One minute end our daies, one sepulcher
Containe our bodies: death, why comm'st thou not?
Wel, this must be the messenger for thee.   15
[*She draws a dagger.*]

Now ugly death stretch out thy Sable wings,
And carie both our soules, where his remaines.
Tell me sweet boie, art thou content to die?
These barbarous Scythians full of cruelty,
And Moores, in whom was never pitie found,   20
Will hew us peecemeale, put us to the wheele,

63 hold] *O3*; holds *O1*.   SD *Exeunt*] Oxberry; not in *O1*.   Actus.3.Scæna.4.]
Dyce 1; not in *O1*.   OSD1 below] Bowers; not in *O1*.   wounded] Craik (this edn.);
not in *O1*.   1SD2 OLYMPIA] Dyce 1; not in *O1*.   10SD He dies] Oxberry; not in
O1.   13 daies, one] Craik (this edn); daies, and one *O1*.   15SD She...dagger]
Dyce 1; not in *O1*.

Or els invent some torture worse than that.
Therefore die by thy loving mothers hand,
Who gently now wil lance thy Ivory throat,
And quickly rid thee both of paine and life.   25
SON. Mother dispatch me, or Ile kil my selfe,
For think ye I can live, and see him dead?
Give me your knife (good mother) or strike home:
The Scythians shall not tyrannise on me.
Sweet mother strike, that I may meet my father.   30

She stabs him.

OLYMPIA. Ah sacred *Mahomet*, if this be sin,
Intreat a pardon of the God of heaven,
And purge my soule before it come to thee.

[*She burns the bodies.*]

Enter THERIDAMAS, TECHELLES *and all their traine.*

THERIDAMAS. How now Madam, what are you doing?
OLYMPIA. Killing my selfe, as I have done my sonne,   35
Whose body with his fathers I have burnt,
Least cruell Scythians should dismember him.
TECHELLES. Twas bravely done, and like a souldiers wife.
Thou shalt with us to *Tamburlaine* the great,
Who when he heares how resolute thou wert,   40
Wil match thee with a viceroy or a king.
OLYMPIA. My Lord deceast, was dearer unto me,
Than any Viceroy, King or Emperour.
And for his sake here will I end my daies.
THERIDAMAS. But Lady goe with us to *Tamburlaine*,   45
And see a man greater than *Mahomet*,
In whose high lookes is much more majesty
Than from the Concave superficies,
Of *Joves* vast pallace the imperiall Orbe,
Unto the shining bower where *Cynthia* sits,   50
Like lovely *Thetis* in a Christall robe:

33SD *She . . . bodies*] Dyce *1; not in* O1.   46 And see a man greater] *this edn.*; And
thou shalt see a man greater O1; thou shalt see a greater *conj. Brooke.*

That treadeth Fortune underneath his feete,
And makes the mighty God of armes his slave:
On whom death and the fatall sisters waite,
With naked swords and scarlet liveries: 55
Before whom (mounted on a Lions backe)
Rhamnusia beares a helmet ful of blood,
And strowes the way with braines of slaughtered men:
By whose proud side the ugly furies run,
Harkening when he shall bid them plague the world: 60
Over whose Zenith cloth'd in windy aire,
And Eagles wings join'd to her feathered breast,
Fame hovereth, sounding of her golden Trumpe:
That to the adverse poles of that straight line,
Which measureth the glorious frame of heaven,   65
The name of mightie *Tamburlain* is spread:
And him faire Lady shall thy eies behold.
Come.

OLYMPIA. Take pitie of a Ladies ruthfull teares,
That humbly craves upon her knees to stay,   70
And cast her bodie in the burning flame,
That feeds upon her sonnes and husbands flesh.

TECHELLES. Madam, sooner shall fire consume us both,
Then scortch a face so beautiful as this,
In frame of which, Nature hath shewed more skill,   75
Than when she gave eternall *Chaos* forme,
Drawing from it the shining Lamps of heaven.

THERIDAMAS. Madam, I am so far in love with you,
That you must goe with us, no remedy.

OLYMPIA. Then carie me I care not where you will,   80
And let the end of this my fatall journey,
Be likewise end to my accursed life.

TECHELLES. No Madam, but beginning of your joy,
Come willinglie, therfore.

THERIDAMAS. Souldiers now let us meet the Generall,   85
Who by this time is at *Natolia*,
Ready to charge the army of the Turke.
The gold, the silver, and the pearle ye got,
Rifling this Fort, devide in equall shares:

83 but beginning] *conj. Dyce 1*, *F. Cunningham*; but the beginning *O1*.

This Lady shall have twice so much againe,　　　90
Out of the coffers of our treasurie.

Exeunt.

Actus. 3. Scæna. 5.

[*Enter*] CALLEPINE, ORCANES, JERUSALEM, TREBIZON,
SORIA, ALMEDA, *with their traine.* [*Enter to them a*
MESSENGER.]

MESSENGER. Renowmed Emperour, mighty *Callepine*,
Gods great lieftenant over all the world:
Here at *Alepo* with an hoste of men
Lies *Tamburlaine*, this king of *Persea*:
In number more than are the quyvering leaves　　　5
Of *Idas* forrest, where your highnesse hounds,
With open crie pursues the wounded Stag:
Who meanes to gyrt *Natolias* walles with siege,
Fire the towne and overrun the land.
CALLAPINE. My royal army is as great as his,　　　10
That from the bounds of *Phrigia* to the sea
Which washeth *Cyprus* with his brinish waves,
Covers the hils, the valleies and the plaines.
Viceroies and Peeres of *Turky* play the men,
Whet all your swords to mangle *Tamburlain*,　　　15
His sonnes, his Captaines and his followers:
By *Mahomet* not one of them shal live.
The field wherin this battaile shall be fought,
For ever terme, the Perseans sepulchre,
In memorie of this our victory.　　　20
ORCANES. Now, he that cals himself the scourge of *Jove*,
The Emperour of the world, and earthly God,
Shal end the warlike progresse he intends,
And traveile hedlong to the lake of hell:
Where legions of devils (knowing he must die　　　25
Here in *Natolia*, by your highnesse hands)
All brandishing their brands of quenchlesse fire,

OSD1 *Enter*] *Oxberry; not in O1.*　　　OSD2–3 *Enter*...MESSENGER] *Oxberry; not in O1.*

Streching their monstrous pawes, grin with their teeth,
And guard the gates to entertaine his soule.

CALLAPINE. Tel me Viceroies the number of your men,   30
And what our Army royall is esteem'd.

JERUSALEM. From *Palestina* and *Jerusalem*,
Of Hebrewes, three score thousand fighting men
Are come since last we shewed your majesty.

ORCANES. So from *Arabia* desart, and the bounds   35
Of that sweet land, whose brave Metropolis
Reedified the faire *Semyramis*,
Came forty thousand warlike foot and horse,
Since last we numbred to your Majesty.

TREBIZON. From *Trebizon* in *Asia* the lesse,   40
Naturalized Turks and stout Bythinians
Came to my bands full fifty thousand more,
That fighting, knowes not what retreat doth meane,
Nor ere returne but with the victory,
Since last we numbred to your majesty.   45

SORIA. Of Sorians from *Halla* is repair'd
And neighbor cities of your highnesse land,
Ten thousand horse, and thirty thousand foot,
Since last we numbred to your majestie:
So that the Army royall is esteem'd   50
Six hundred thousand valiant fighting men.

CALLAPINE. Then welcome *Tamburlaine* unto thy death.
Come puissant Viceroies, let us to the field,
(The Perseans Sepulchre) and sacrifice
Mountaines of breathlesse men to *Mahomet*,   55
Who now with *Jove* opens the firmament,
To see the slaughter of our enemies.

[*Enter*] TAMBURLAINE *with his three sonnes* [CALYPHAS,
AMYRAS, CELEBINUS], USUMCASANE *with other*
[*souldiers*].

TAMBURLAINE. How now *Casane*? See, a knot of kings,
Sitting as if they were a telling ridles.

57SD no break of scene] *Oxberry*; *Actus.2.Scæna.1. in O1*.   57SD1 *Enter*] *Oxberry*;
not in O1.   SD1–2 CALYPHAS...CELEBINUS] *Dyce 1; not in O1*.   SD3 *souldiers*] *J. S. Cunningham; not in O1*.

USUMCASANE. My Lord, your presence makes them pale and
    wan.   60
    Poore soules they looke as if their deaths were neere.

TAMBURLAINE. Why, so he is *Casane*, I am here,
    But yet Ile save their lives and make them slaves.
    Ye petty kings of *Turkye* I am come,
    As *Hector* did into the Grecian campe,   65
    To overdare the pride of *Græcia*,
    And set his warlike person to the view
    Of fierce *Achilles*, rivall of his fame.
    I doe you honor in the simile,
    For if I should as *Hector* did *Achilles*,   70
    (The worthiest knight that ever brandisht sword)
    Challenge in combat any of you all,
    I see how fearfully ye would refuse,
    And fly my glove as from a Scorpion.

ORCANES. Now thou art fearfull of thy armies strength,   75
    Thou wouldst with overmatch of person fight,
    But Shepheards issue, base borne *Tamburlaine*,
    Thinke of thy end, this sword shall lance thy throat.

TAMBURLAINE. Villain, the shepheards issue, at whose byrth
    Heaven did affoord a gratious aspect,   80
    And join'd those stars that shall be opposite,
    Even till the dissolution of the world,
    And never meant to make a Conquerour,
    So famous as is mighty *Tamburlain*:
    Shall so torment thee and that *Callapine*,   85
    That like a roguish runnaway, suborn'd
    That villaine there, that slave, that Turkish dog,
    To false his service to his Soveraigne,
    As ye shal curse the byrth of *Tamburlaine*.

CALLAPINE. Raile not proud Scythian, I shall now revenge   90
    My fathers vile abuses and mine owne.

JERUSALEM. By *Mahomet* he shal be tied in chaines,
    Rowing with Christians in a Brigandine,
    About the Grecian Isles to rob and spoile:
    And turne him to his ancient trade againe.   95
    Me thinks the slave should make a lusty theefe.

CALLAPINE. Nay, when the battaile ends, al we wil meet,
    And sit in councell to invent some paine,

That most may vex his body and his soule.

TAMBURLAINE. Sirha, *Callapine*, Ile hang a clogge about   100
    your necke for running away againe, you shall not trouble
    me thus to come and fetch you.
    But as for you (Viceroys) you shal have bits,
    And harnest like my horses, draw my coch,
    And when ye stay, be lasht with whips of wier: 105
    Ile have you learne to feed on provander,
    And in a stable lie upon the planks.

ORCANES. But *Tamburlaine*, first thou shalt kneele to us
    And humbly crave a pardon for thy life.

TREBIZON. The common souldiers of our mighty hoste   110
    Shal bring thee bound unto the Generals tent.

SORIA. And all have jointly sworne thy cruell death,
    Or bind thee in eternall torments wrath.

TAMBURLAINE. Wel sirs, diet your selves, you knowe I
    shall have occasion shortly to journey you.   115

CELEBINUS. See father, how *Almeda* the Jaylor lookes
    upon us.

TAMBURLAINE. Villaine, traitor, damned fugitive,
    Ile make thee wish the earth had swallowed thee:
    Seest thou not death within my wrathfull looks?   120
    Goe villaine, cast thee headlong from a rock,
    Or rip thy bowels, and rend out thy heart,
    T'appease my wrath, or els Ile torture thee,
    Searing thy hatefull flesh with burning yrons,
    And drops of scalding lead, while all thy joints   125
    Be rackt and beat asunder with the wheele,
    For if thou livest, not any Element
    Shal shrowde thee from the wrath of *Tamburlaine*.

CALLAPINE. Wel, in despight of thee he shall be king:
    Come *Almeda*, receive this crowne of me,   130
    I here invest thee king of *Ariadan*,
    Bordering on *Mare Roso* neere to *Meca*.

ORCANES. What, take it man.

ALMEDA. Good my Lord, let me take it.

CALLAPINE. Doost thou aske him leave? Here, take it.   135

---

103 Viceroys] *Oxberry*; Viceroy *O1*.

TAMBURLAINE. Go too sirha, take your crown, and make
up the halfe dozen.
So sirha, now you are a king you must give armes.

ORCANES. So he shal, and weare thy head in his Scutchion.

TAMBURLAINE. No, let him hang a bunch of keies on his   140
standerd, to put him in remembrance he was a Jailor, that
when I take him, I may knocke out his braines with them,
and lock you in the stable, when you shall come sweating
from my chariot.

TREBIZON. Away, let us to the field, that the villaine may   145
be slaine.

TAMBURLAINE. Sirha [*to a souldier*], prepare whips, and
bring my chariot to my Tent: For as soone as the battaile
is done, Ile ride in triumph through the Camp.

    Enter THERIDAMAS, TECHELLES, *and their traine.*

How now ye pety kings, loe, here are Bugges   150
Wil make the haire stand upright on your heads,
And cast your crownes in slavery at their feet.
Welcome *Theridamas* and *Techelles* both,
See ye this rout, and know ye this same king?

THERIDAMAS. I, my lord, he was *Calapines* keeper.   155

TAMBURLAINE. Wel, now you see hee is a king, looke to
him *Theridamas*, when we are fighting, least hee hide his
crowne as the foolish king of *Persea* did.

SORIA. No *Tamburlaine*, hee shall not be put to that exi-
gent, I warrant thee.   160

TAMBURLAINE. You knowe not sir:
But now my followers and my loving friends,
Fight as you ever did, like Conquerours:
The glorie of this happy day is yours:
My sterne aspect shall make faire Victory,   165
Hovering betwixt our armies, light on me,
Loden with Lawrell wreathes to crowne us all.

TECHELLES. I smile to think, how when this field is fought,

147SD *to a souldier] this edn.; not in O1.*

And rich *Natolia* ours, our men shall sweat
With carrieng pearle and treasure on their backes.   170
TAMBURLAINE. You shall be princes all immediatly:
  Come fight ye Turks, or yeeld us victory.
ORCANES. No, we wil meet thee slavish *Tamburlain.*

Exeunt [*severally*].

[*Finis Actus tertii.*]

173SD *severally*] Dyce *1*; *not in* O*1*.   Finis Actus tertii.] *J. S. Cunningham*; *not in* O*1*.

Actus. 4. Scæna. 1.

Alarme: AMYRAS *and* CELEBINUS, *issues from the tent where*
CALIPHAS *sits a sleepe.*

AMYRAS. Now in their glories shine the golden crownes
    Of these proud Turks, much like so many suns
    That halfe dismay the majesty of heaven:
    Now brother, follow we our fathers sword,
    That flies with fury swifter than our thoughts,   5
    And cuts down armies with his conquering wings.

CELEBINUS. Call foorth our laisie brother from the tent,
    For if my father misse him in the field,
    Wrath kindled in the furnace of his breast,
    Wil send a deadly lightening to his heart.   10

AMYRAS. Brother, ho, what, given so much to sleep
    You cannot leave it, when our enemies drums
    And ratling cannons thunder in our eares
    Our proper ruine, and our fathers soile?

CALYPHAS. Away ye fools, my father needs not me,   15
    Nor you in faith, but that you wil be thought
    More childish valourous than manly wise:
    If halfe our campe should sit and sleepe with me,
    My father were enough to scar the foe:
    You doo dishonor to his majesty,   20
    To think our helps will doe him any good.

AMYRAS. What, dar'st thou then be absent from the fight,
    Knowing my father hates thy cowardise,
    And oft hath warn'd thee to be stil in field,
    When he himselfe amidst the thickest troopes   25
    Beats downe our foes to flesh our taintlesse swords?

CALYPHAS. I know sir, what it is to kil a man,
    It works remorse of conscience in me,
    I take no pleasure to be murtherous,
    Nor care for blood when wine wil quench my thirst.   30

---

1 AMYRAS] *Oxberry*; *not in O1*.   6 conquering] *O2*; conquerings *O1*; conquering's
Brereton.

CELEBINUS. O cowardly boy, fie for shame, come foorth.
   Thou doost dishonor manhood, and thy house.
CALYPHAS. Goe, goe tall stripling, fight you for us both,
   And take my other toward brother here,
   For person like to proove a second *Mars*.   35
   Twill please my mind as wel to heare both you
   Have won a heape of honor in the field,
   And left your slender carkasses behind,
   As if I lay with you for company.
AMYRAS. You wil not goe then?   40
CALYPHAS. You say true.
AMYRAS. Were all the lofty mounts of *Zona mundi*,
   That fill the midst of farthest *Tartary*,
   Turn'd into pearle and proffered for my stay,
   I would not bide the furie of my father,   45
   When, made a victor in these hautie arms,
   He comes and findes his sonnes have had no shares
   In all the honors he proposde for us.
CALYPHAS. Take you the honor, I will take my ease,
   My wisedome shall excuse my cowardise: 50
   I goe into the field before I need?

    Alarme, and AMYRAS *and* CELEBINUS *run in.*

The bullets fly at random where they list.
And should I goe and kill a thousand men,
I were as soone rewarded with a shot,
And sooner far than he that never fights.   55
And should I goe and do nor harme nor good,
I might have harme, which all the good I have
Join'd with my fathers crowne would never cure.
Ile to cardes: *Perdicas*.

     [*Enter* PERDICAS]

PERDICAS. Here my Lord.   60
CALYPHAS. Come, thou and I wil goe to cardes to drive
   away the time.
PERDICAS. Content my Lord, but what shal we play for?

CALYPHAS. Who shal kisse the fairest of the Turkes
    Concubines first, when my father hath conquered them.   65
PERDICAS. Agreed yfaith.

They play [*in the open tent*].

CALYPHAS. They say I am a coward, (*Perdicas*) and I feare
    as litle their *tara*, *tantaras*, their swordes or their cannons,
    as I doe a naked Lady in a net of golde, and for feare I
    should be affraid, would put it off and come to bed with   70
    me.
PERDICAS. Such a feare (my Lord) would never make yee
    retire.
CALYPHAS. I would my father would let me be put in the
    front of such a battaile once, to trie my valour.   75

Alarme.

What a coyle they keepe, I beleeve there will be some hurt
done anon amongst them.

Enter TAMBURLAIN, THERIDAMAS, TECHELLES,
USUMCASANE, [*and souldiers:*] AMYRAS, [*and*] CELEBINUS
leading the Turkish kings [ORCANES *of* NATOLIA,
JERUSALEM, TREBIZON *and* SORIA].

TAMBURLAINE. See now ye slaves, my children stoops your
    pride
    And leads your glories sheep-like to the sword.
    Bring them my boyes, and tel me if the warres   80
    Be not a life that may illustrate Gods,
    And tickle not your Spirits with desire
    Stil to be train'd in armes and chivalry?
AMYRAS. Shal we let goe these kings again my Lord
    To gather greater numbers gainst our power,   85
    That they may say, it is not chance doth this,
    But matchlesse strength and magnanimity?
TAMBURLAINE. No, no *Amyras*, tempt not Fortune so,
    Cherish thy valour stil with fresh supplies:
    And glut it not with stale and daunted foes.   90

66SD *in the open tent*] *J. S. Cunningham; not in* O*1*.   77SD2 *and souldiers*] *Dyce 1; not*
in O*1*.   SD3–4 ORCANES ... SORIA] *Dyce 1; not in* O*1*.

But wher's this coward, villaine, not my sonne,
But traitor to my name and majesty.

He goes in and brings him out.

Image of sloth, and picture of a slave,
The obloquie and skorne of my renowne,
How may my hart, thus fired with mine eies,   95
Wounded with shame, and kill'd with discontent,
Shrowd any thought may holde my striving hands
From martiall justice on thy wretched soule?

THERIDAMAS. Yet pardon him I pray your Majesty.

TECHELLES AND USUMCASANE. Let al of us intreat your
   highnesse pardon.   [*They kneel.*]

TAMBURLAINE. Stand up, ye base unworthy souldiers,   101
   Know ye not yet the argument of Armes?

[AMYRAS *and* CELEBINUS *kneel.*]

AMYRAS. Good my Lord, let him be forgiven for once,
   And we wil force him to the field hereafter.   104

TAMBURLAINE. Stand up my boyes, and I wil teach ye arms,
   And what the jealousie of warres must doe.   [*All stand.*]
O *Samarcanda*, where I breathed first,
And joy'd the fire of this martiall flesh,
Blush, blush faire citie, at thine honors foile,
And shame of nature which Jaertis streame,   110
Embracing thee with deepest of his love,
Can never wash from thy distained browes.
Here *Jove*, receive his fainting soule againe,
                            [*He stabs* CALYPHAS.]
A Forme not meet to give that subject essence,
Whose matter is the flesh of *Tamburlain*,   115
Wherein an incorporeall spirit mooves,
Made of the mould whereof thy selfe consists,
Which makes me valiant, proud, ambitious,
Ready to levie power against thy throne,

That I might moove the turning Spheares of heaven,   120
For earth and al this aery region
Cannot containe the state of *Tamburlaine*.
By *Mahomet*, thy mighty friend I sweare,
In sending to my issue such a soule,
Created of the massy dregges of earth,   125
The scum and tartar of the Elements,
Wherein was neither corrage, strength or wit,
But follie, sloth, and damned idlenesse:
Thou hast procur'd a greater enemie,
Than he that darted mountaines at thy head,   130
Shaking the burthen mighty *Atlas* beares:
Whereat thou trembling hid'st thee in the aire,
Cloth'd with a pitchy cloud for being seene.
And now ye cankred curres of *Asia*,
That will not see the strength of *Tamburlaine*,   135
Although it shine as brightly as the Sun:
Now you shal feele the strength of *Tamburlain*,
And by the state of his supremacie,
Approove the difference twixt himself and you.
ORCANES. Thou shewest the difference twixt our selves
    and thee   140
  In this thy barbarous damned tyranny.
JERUSALEM. Thy victories are growne so violent,
  That shortly heaven, fild with the meteors
  Of blood and fire thy tyrannies have made,
  Will poure down blood and fire on thy head: 145
  Whose scalding drops wil pierce thy seething braines,
  And with our bloods, revenge our bloods on thee.
TAMBURLAINE. Villaines, these terrours and these tyrannies
  (If tyrannies wars justice ye repute)
  I execute, enjoin'd me from above,   150
  To scourge the pride of such as heaven abhors:
  Nor am I made Arch-monark of the world,
  Crown'd and invested by the hand of *Jove*,
  For deeds of bounty or nobility:
  But since I exercise a greater name,   155
  The Scourge of God and terrour of the world,
  I must apply my selfe to fit those tearmes,
  In war, in blood, in death, in crueltie,

And plague such Pesants as resist in me
The power of heavens eternall majesty.   160
Theridamas, *Techelles*, and *Casane*,
Ransacke the tents and the pavilions
Of these proud Turks, and take their Concubines,
Making them burie this effeminate brat,
For not a common Souldier shall defile   165
His manly fingers with so faint a boy.
Then bring those Turkish harlots to my tent,
And Ile dispose them as it likes me best,
Meane while take him in.
SOLDIERS.   We will my Lord.

[*Exeunt souldiers with the body of* CALYPHAS.]

JERUSALEM. O damned monster, nay a Feend of Hell,   170
Whose cruelties are not so harsh as thine,
Nor yet imposd, with such a bitter hate.
ORCANES. Revenge it *Radamanth* and *Eacus*,
And let your hates extended in his paines,
Excell the hate wherewith he paines our soules.   175
TREBIZON. May never day give vertue to his eies,
Whose sight composde of furie and of fire
Doth send such sterne affections to his heart.
SORIA. May never spirit, vaine or Artier feed
The cursed substance of that cruel heart,   180
But (wanting moisture and remorsefull blood)
Drie up with anger, and consume with heat.
TAMBURLAINE. Wel, bark ye dogs. Ile bridle al your tongues
And bind them close with bits of burnisht steele,
Downe to the channels of your hatefull throats,   185
And with the paines my rigour shall inflict,
Ile make ye roare, that earth may eccho foorth
The far resounding torments ye sustaine,
As when an heard of lusty Cymbrian Buls,
Run mourning round about the Femals misse,   190
And stung with furie of their following,

159 resist in me] *conj. Broughton, Dyce* 1; resisting me *O1*; resisting me / [Resist]
Oxberry.   169SD *Exeunt* ... CALYPHAS] *Dyce 1*; *not in O1.*   175 Excell] *Dyce*
1; Expell *O1*.

Fill all the aire with troublous bellowing:
I will with Engines, never exercisde,
Conquer, sacke, and utterly consume
Your cities and your golden pallaces,   195
And with the flames that beat against the clowdes
Incense the heavens, and make the starres to melt,
As if they were the teares of *Mahomet*
For hot consumption of his countries pride:
And til by vision, or by speach I heare   200
Immortall *Jove* say, Cease my *Tamburlaine*,
I will persist a terrour to the world,
Making the Meteors, that like armed men
Are seene to march upon the towers of heaven,
Run tilting round about the firmament,   205
And breake their burning Lances in the aire,
For honor of my woondrous victories.
Come bring them in to our Pavilion.

                                             Exeunt.

Actus. 4. Scæna. 2.

[*Enter*] OLYMPIA *alone.*

OLYMPIA. Distrest *Olympia*, whose weeping eies
Since thy arrivall here beheld no Sun,
But closde within the compasse of a tent,
Hath stain'd thy cheekes, and made thee look like death,
Devise some meanes to rid thee of thy life,   5
Rather than yeeld to his detested suit,
Whose drift is onely to dishonor thee.
And since this earth, dew'd with thy brinish teares,
Affoords no hearbs, whose taste may poison thee,
Nor yet this aier, beat often with thy sighes,   10
Contagious smels, and vapors to infect thee,
Nor thy close Cave a sword to murther thee,
Let this invention be the instrument.

Scæna.2.] *Dyce 1*; *Scæna.3, O1.*   OSD *Enter*] *Dyce 1*; *not in O1*; OLYMPIA *discovered
alone Oxberry.*

Enter THERIDAMAS.

THERIDAMAS. Wel met *Olympia*, I sought thee in my tent,
    But when I saw the place obscure and darke,   15
    Which with thy beauty thou wast woont to light,
    Enrag'd, I ran about the fields for thee,
    Supposing amorous *Jove* had sent his sonne,
    The winged *Hermes*, to convay thee hence:
    But now I finde thee, and that feare is past.   20
    Tell me *Olympia*, wilt thou graunt my suit?

OLYMPIA. My Lord and husbandes death, with my sweete sons,
    With whom I buried al affections,
    Save griefe and sorrow which torment my heart,
    Forbids my mind to entertaine a thought   25
    That tends to love, but meditate on death,
    A fitter subject for a pensive soule.

THERIDAMAS. *Olympia*, pitie him, in whom thy looks
    Have greater operation and more force
    Than *Cynthias* in the watery wildernes,   30
    For with thy view my joyes are at the full,
    And eb againe, as thou departst from me.

OLYMPIA. Ah, pity me my Lord, and draw your sword,
    Making a passage for my troubled soule,
    Which beates against this prison to get out,   35
    And meet my husband and my loving sonne.

THERIDAMAS. Nothing, but stil thy husband and thy sonne?
    Leave this my Love, and listen more to me.
    Thou shalt be stately Queene of faire *Argier*,
    And cloth'd in costly cloath of massy gold,   40
    Upon the marble turrets of my Court
    Sit like to *Venus* in her chaire of state,
    Commanding all thy princely eie desires,
    And I will cast off armes and sit with thee,
    Spending my life in sweet discourse of love.   45

OLYMPIA. No such discourse is pleasant in mine eares,
    But that where every period ends with death,
    And every line begins with death againe:
    I cannot love, to be an Emperesse.

49 love, to] *Oxberry*; love to *O1*.

THERIDAMAS. Nay Lady, then if nothing wil prevaile,   50
     Ile use some other means to make you yeeld,
     Such is the sodaine fury of my love,
     I must and wil be pleasde, and you shall yeeld:
     Come to the tent againe.
OLYMPIA. Stay good my Lord, and wil you save my honor,   55
     Ile give your Grace a present of such price,
     As all the world cannot affoord the like.
THERIDAMAS. What is it?
OLYMPIA. An ointment which a cunning Alcumist
     Distilled from the purest Balsamum,   60
     And simplest extracts of all Minerals,
     In which the essentiall fourme of Marble stone,
     Tempered by science metaphisicall,
     And Spels of magicke from the mouthes of spirits,
     With which if you but noint your tender Skin,   65
     Nor Pistol, Sword, nor Lance can pierce your flesh.
THERIDAMAS. Why Madam, thinke ye to mocke me thus
     palpably?
OLYMPIA. To proove it, I wil noint my naked throat,
     Which when you stab, looke on your weapons point,   70
     And you shall se't rebated with the blow.
THERIDAMAS. Why gave you not your husband some of it,
     If you loved him, and it so precious?
OLYMPIA. My purpose was (my Lord) to spend it so,
     But was prevented by his sodaine end.   75
     And for a present easie proofe hereof,
     That I dissemble not, trie it on me.
THERIDAMAS. I wil *Olympia*, and will keep it for
     The richest present of this Easterne world.

            She noints her throat.

OLYMPIA. Now stab my Lord, and mark your weapons point
     That wil be blunted if the blow be great.   81
THERIDAMAS. Here then *Olympia*.   [*He stabs her.*]
     What, have I slaine her? Villaine, stab thy selfe:
     Cut off this arme that murthered my Love:

72–3 it, / If] *Oxberry*; it, if *O1*.   82SD *He stabs her*] *Oxberry*; *not in O1*.

In whom the learned Rabies of this age,   85
Might find as many woondrous myracles,
As in the Theoria of the world.
Now Hell is fairer than *Elisian*.
A greater Lamp than that bright eie of heaven,
From whence the starres doo borrow all their light,   90
Wanders about the black circumference,
And now the damned soules are free from paine,
For every Fury gazeth on her lookes:
Infernall *Dis* is courting of my Love,
Inventing maskes and stately showes for her,   95
Opening the doores of his rich treasurie,
To entertaine this Queene of chastitie,
Whose body shall be tomb'd with all the pompe
The treasure of my kingdome may affoord.

> *Exit, taking her away.*

Actus. 4. Scæna. 3.

[*Enter*] TAMBURLAINE *drawen in his chariot by* TREBIZON
and SORIA *with bittes in their mouthes, reines in his left hand, in
his right hand a whip, with which he scourgeth them,*
TECHELLES, THERIDAMAS, USUMCASANE, AMYRAS,
CELEBINUS: [ORCANES *king of*] NATOLIA, *and*
JERUSALEM *led by with five or six common souldiers.*

TAMBURLAINE. Holla, ye pampered Jades of *Asia*:
What, can ye draw but twenty miles a day,
And have so proud a chariot at your heeles,
And such a Coachman as great *Tamburlaine*?
But from *Asphaltis*, where I conquer'd you,   5
To *Byron* here where thus I honor you?
The horse that guide the golden eie of heaven,
And blow the morning from their nosterils,
Making their fiery gate above the cloudes,
Are not so honoured in their Governour,   10

Scæna.3.] *Dyce* 1; Scæna.4. O1.   OSD1 *Enter*] *Robinson; not in* O1.   OSD5
ORCANES...*of*] *Dyce* 1; *not in* O1.

As you (ye slaves) in mighty *Tamburlain*.
The headstrong Jades of *Thrace*, *Alcides* tam'd,
That King *Egeus* fed with humaine flesh,
And made so wanton that they knew their strengths,
Were not subdew'd with valour more divine,   15
Than you by this unconquered arme of mine.
To make you fierce, and fit my appetite,
You shal be fed with flesh as raw as blood,
And drinke in pailes the strongest Muscadell:
If you can live with it, then live, and draw   20
My chariot swifter than the racking cloudes:
If not, then dy like beasts, and fit for nought
But perches for the black and fatall Ravens.
Thus am I right the Scourge of highest *Jove*,
And see the figure of my dignitie, [*He raises his whip.*]   25
By which I hold my name and majesty.

AMYRAS. Let me have coach my Lord, that I may ride,
And thus be drawen with these two idle kings.

TAMBURLAINE. Thy youth forbids such ease my kingly boy,
They shall to morrow draw my chariot,   30
While these their fellow kings may be refresht.

ORCANES. O thou that swaiest the region under earth,
And art a king as absolute as *Jove*,
Come as thou didst in fruitfull *Scicilie*,
Survaieng all the glories of the land: 35
And as thou took'st the faire *Proserpina*,
Joying the fruit of *Ceres* garden plot,
For love, for honor, and to make her Queene,
So for just hate, for shame, and to subdew
This proud contemner of thy dreadfull power,   40
Come once in furie and survay his pride,
Haling him headlong to the lowest hell.

THERIDAMAS. Your Majesty must get some byts for these,
To bridle their contemptuous cursing tongues,
That like unruly never broken Jades,   45
Breake through the hedges of their hateful mouthes,
And passe their fixed boundes exceedingly.

TECHELLES. Nay, we wil break the hedges of their mouths

25SD *He . . . whip*] *this edn.; not in* O1.

And pul their kicking colts out of their pastures.

USUMCASANE. Your Majesty already hath devisde   50
A meane, as fit as may be to restraine
These coltish coach-horse tongues from blasphemy.

CELEBINUS. [*To* TREBIZON] How like you that sir king?
why speak you not?

JERUSALEM. Ah cruel Brat, sprung from a tyrants loines,
How like his cursed father he begins   55
To practize tauntes and bitter tyrannies.

TAMBURLAINE. I Turke, I tel thee, this same Boy is he,
That must (advaunst in higher pompe than this)
Rifle the kingdomes I shall leave unsackt,
If *Jove* esteeming me too good for earth,   60
Raise me to match the faire *Aldeboran*,
Above the threefold Astracisme of heaven,
Before I conquere all the triple world.
Now fetch me out the Turkish Concubines,
I will prefer them for the funerall   65
They have bestowed on my abortive sonne.

The Concubines are brought in.

Where are my common souldiers now that fought
So Lion-like upon *Asphaltis* plaines?

SOLDIERS. Here my Lord.

TAMBURLAINE. Hold ye tal souldiers, take ye Queens apeece 70
(I meane such Queens as were kings Concubines)
Take them, devide them and their jewels too,
And let them equally serve all your turnes.

SOLDIERS. We thank your majesty.

TAMBURLAINE. Brawle not (I warne you) for your lechery,   75
For every man that so offends shall die.

ORCANES. Injurious tyrant, wilt thou so defame
The hatefull fortunes of thy victory,
To exercise upon such guiltlesse Dames,
The violence of thy common Souldiours lust?   80

TAMBURLAINE. Live continent then (ye slaves) and meet not me
With troopes of harlots at your sloothful heeles.

53SD *To* TREBIZON] *this edn.; not in O1;* CELEBINUS *bridles* ORCANES *J. S. Cunning-*
ham.   81 continent] *Oxberry;* content *O1.*

LADIES. O pity us my Lord, and save our honours.
TAMBURLAINE. Are ye not gone ye villaines with your
    spoiles?

They run away with the Ladies.

JERUSALEM. O mercilesse infernall cruelty.   85
TAMBURLAINE. Save your honours? twere but time indeed,
    Lost long before you knew what honour meant.
THERIDAMAS. It seemes they meant to conquer us my Lord,
    And make us jeasting Pageants for their Trulles.
TAMBURLAINE. And now themselves shal make our Pageant,   90
    And common souldiers jest with all their Truls.
    Let them take pleasure soundly in their spoiles,
    Till we prepare our martch to *Babylon*,
    Whether we next make expedition.
TECHELLES. Let us not be idle then my Lord,   95
    But presently be prest to conquer it.
TAMBURLAINE. We wil *Techelles*, forward then ye Jades:
    Now crowch ye kings of greatest *Asia*,
    And tremble when ye heare this Scourge wil come,
    That whips downe cities, and controwleth crownes,   100
    Adding their wealth and treasure to my store.
    The Euxine sea North to *Natolia*,
    The Terrene west, the Caspian north north-east,
    And on the south *Senus Arabicus*,
    Shal al be loden with the martiall spoiles   105
    We will convay with us to *Persea*.
    Then shal my native city *Samarcanda*
    And christall waves of fresh *Jaertis* streame,
    The pride and beautie of her princely seat,
    Be famous through the furthest continents,   110
    For there my Pallace royal shal be plac'd:
    Whose shyning Turrets shal dismay the heavens,
    And cast the fame of *Ilions* Tower to hell.
    Thorow the streets with troops of conquered kings,
    Ile ride in golden armour like the Sun,   115
    And in my helme a triple plume shal spring,
    Spangled with Diamonds dancing in the aire,
    To note me Emperour of the three fold world:
    Like to an almond tree ymounted high,

Upon the lofty and celestiall mount,   120
Of ever greene *Selinus* queintly dect
With bloomes more white than *Hericinas* browes,
Whose tender blossoms tremble every one,
At every litle breath that thorow heaven is blowen:
Then in my coach like *Saturnes* royal son,   125
Mounted his shining chariot, gilt with fire,
And drawen with princely Eagles through the path,
Pav'd with bright Christall, and enchac'd with starres,
When all the Gods stand gazing at his pomp:
So will I ride through *Samarcanda* streets,   130
Until my soule dissevered from this flesh,
Shall mount the milk-white way and meet him there.
To *Babylon* my Lords, to *Babylon*.

                                        Exeunt.

            Finis Actus quarti.

121 ever greene] *Robinson*; every greene *O1*.   126 chariot] *Dyce 1*; chariots *O1*.

Actus. 5. Scæna. 1.

Enter the GOVERNOUR *of* BABYLON *upon the walles with*
[MAXIMUS *and*] *others.*

GOVERNOUR. What saith *Maximus?*
MAXIMUS. My Lord, the breach the enimie hath made
  Gives such assurance of our overthrow,
  That litle hope is left to save our lives,
  Or hold our citie from the Conquerours hands.   5
  Then hang out flagges (my Lord) of humble truce,
  And satisfie the peoples generall praiers,
  That *Tamburlains* intollorable wrath
  May be supprest by our submission.
GOVERNOUR. Villaine, respects thou more thy slavish life,   10
  Than honor of thy countrie or thy name?
  Is not my life and state as deere to me,
  The citie and my native countries weale,
  As any thing of price with thy conceit?
  Have we not hope, for all our battered walles,   15
  To live secure, and keep his forces out,
  When this our famous lake of *Limnasphaltis*
  Makes walles a fresh with every thing that falles
  Into the liquid substance of his streame,
  More strong than are the gates of death or hel?   20
  What faintnesse should dismay our courages,
  When we are thus defenc'd against our Foe,
  And have no terrour but his threatning lookes?

Enter another [I. CITIZEN, *above*], *kneeling to the*
GOVERNOUR.

I. CITIZEN. My Lord, if ever you did deed of ruth,
  And now will work a refuge to our lives,   25
  Offer submission, hang up flags of truce,
  That *Tamburlaine* may pitie our distresse,
  And use us like a loving Conquerour.

OSD2 MAXIMUS *and*] *Oxberry; not in* O1.   23SD I. CITIZEN] *Oxberry; not in*
O1.   *above*] *Dyce* 1; *not in* O1.   24 I. CITIZEN] *Oxberry; not in* O1.

Though this be held his last daies dreadfull siege,
Wherein he spareth neither man nor child,   30
Yet are there Christians of *Georgia* here,
Whose state he ever pitied and reliev'd,
Wil get his pardon if your grace would send.
GOVERNOUR. How is my soule environed with cares,
And this eternisde citie *Babylon*,   35
Fill'd with a packe of faintheart Fugitives,
That thus intreat their shame and servitude?

[Enter 2. CITIZEN, *above.]*

2. CITIZEN. My Lord, if ever you wil win our hearts,
Yeeld up the towne, and save our wives and children:
For I wil cast my selfe from off these walles,
Or die some death of quickest violence,   40
Before I bide the wrath of *Tamburlaine*.
GOVERNOUR. Villaines, cowards, Traitors to our state,
Fall to the earth, and pierce the pit of Hel,
That legions of tormenting spirits may vex   45
Your slavish bosomes with continuall paines,
I care not, nor the towne will never yeeld
As long as any life is in my breast.

Enter THERIDAMAS *and* TECHELLES, *with other souldiers.*

THERIDAMAS. Thou desperate Governour of *Babylon*,
To save thy life, and us a litle labour,   50
Yeeld speedily the citie to our hands,
Or els be sure thou shalt be forc'd with paines,
More exquisite than ever Traitor felt.
GOVERNOUR. Tyrant, I turne the traitor in thy throat,
And wil defend it in despight of thee.   55
Call up the souldiers to defend these wals.
TECHELLES. Yeeld foolish Governour, we offer more
Than ever yet we did to such proud slaves,
As durst resist us till our third daies siege:
Thou seest us prest to give the last assault,   60

34 with cares] *conj. Broughton, Bullen*; environed ∧ *O1*; with grief *conj. Dyce 1*; with fears *conj. Craik (this edn.)*.   37SD *Enter...above] Dyce 1*; *not in O1*.   39 towne, and save] *Q*; towne, save *O1*.   49 THERIDAMAS] *Oxberry*; *not in O1*.

And that shal bide no more regard of parlie.
GOVERNOUR. Assault and spare not, we wil never yeeld.

Alarme, and they scale the walles. [Exeunt above.]

Enter TAMBURLAIN, [*all in black, drawn in his chariot by the
kings of* TREBIZON *and* SORIA,] *with* USUMCASANE,
AMYRAS, *and* CELEBINUS, *with others, the two spare kings*
[ORCANES *of* NATOLIA, *and* JERUSALEM, *led by souldiers*].

TAMBURLAINE. The stately buildings of faire *Babylon*,
Whose lofty Pillers, higher than the cloudes,
Were woont to guide the seaman in the deepe,   65
Being caried thither by the cannons force,
Now fil the mouth of *Limnasphaltes* lake,
And make a bridge unto the battered walles.
Where *Belus*, *Ninus* and great *Alexander*
Have rode in triumph, triumphs *Tamburlaine*,   70
Whose chariot wheeles have burst th'Assirians bones,
Drawen with these kings on heaps of carkasses.
Now in the place where faire *Semiramis*,
Courted by kings and peeres of *Asia*,
Hath trode the Meisures, do my souldiers martch,   75
And in the streets, where brave Assirian Dames
Have rid in pompe like rich *Saturnia*,
With furious words and frowning visages,
My horsmen brandish their unruly blades.

Enter [below] THERIDAMAS *and* TECHELLES *bringing the*
GOVERNOR *of* BABYLON.

Who have ye there my Lordes?   80
THERIDAMAS. The sturdy Governour of *Babylon*,
That made us all the labour for the towne,
And usde such slender reckning of your majesty.
TAMBURLAINE. Go bind the villaine, he shall hang in chaines,
Upon the ruines of this conquered towne.   85
Sirha, the view of our vermillion tents,
Which threatned more than if the region

62SD1 *Exeunt above*] *Jump*; *not in* O1.   2 *all...black*] *J. S. Cunningham*; *not. in*
O1.   2–3 *drawn...*SORIA,] *Dyce 1*; *not in* O1.   5 ORCANES...*souldiers*] *Dyce 1*;
not in O1.   79SD *below*] *Bowers*; *not in* O1.   83 *your*] O2; *you* O1.

Next underneath the Element of fire,
Were full of Commets and of blazing stars,
Whose flaming traines should reach down to the earth 90
Could not affright you, no, nor I my selfe,
The wrathfull messenger of mighty *Jove*,
That with his sword hath quail'd all earthly kings,
Could not perswade you to submission,
But stil the ports were shut: villaine I say, 95
Should I but touch the rusty gates of hell,
The triple headed *Cerberus* would howle,
And wake blacke *Jove* to crouch and kneele to me,
But I have sent volleies of shot to you,
Yet could not enter till the breach was made. 100

GOVERNOUR. Nor if my body could have stopt the breach,
Shouldst thou have entred, cruel *Tamburlaine*:
Tis not thy bloody tents can make me yeeld,
Nor yet thy selfe, the anger of the highest,
For though thy cannon shooke the citie walles, 105
My heart did never quake, or corrage faint.

TAMBURLAINE. Wel, now Ile make it quake, go draw him up,
Hang him in chaines upon the citie walles,
And let my souldiers shoot the slave to death.

GOVERNOUR. Vile monster, borne of some infernal hag, 110
And sent from hell to tyrannise on earth,
Do all thy wurst, nor death, nor *Tamburlaine*,
Torture or paine can daunt my dreadlesse minde.

TAMBURLAINE. Up with him then, his body shal be scard.

GOVERNOUR. But *Tamburlain*, in *Lymnasphaltis* lake, 115
There lies more gold than *Babylon* is worth,
Which when the citie was besieg'd I hid:
Save but my life and I wil give it thee.

TAMBURLAINE. Then for all your valour, you would save your
life?
Where about lies it? 120

GOVERNOUR. Under a hollow bank, right opposite
Against the Westerne gate of *Babylon*.

TAMBURLAINE. Go thither some of you and take his gold.

108 him in] *Oxberry*; him up in *O1*.

[*Exeunt souldiers.*]

The rest forward with execution,
Away with him hence, let him speake no more:
I think I make your courage something quaile.   125

[*Exeunt souldiers with the* GOVERNOUR.]

When this is done, we'll martch from *Babylon*,
And make our greatest haste to *Persea*:
These Jades are broken winded, and halfe tyr'd,
Unharnesse them, and let me have fresh horse.   130

[*Souldiers unharness* TREBIZON *and* SORIA.]

So, now their best is done to honour me,
Take them, and hang them both up presently.
TREBIZON. Vild Tyrant, barbarous bloody *Tamburlain*.
TAMBURLAINE. Take them away *Theridamas*, see them
   dispatcht.
THERIDAMAS. I will my Lord.   135

[*Exit* THERIDAMAS *and souldiers, with the Kings of*
      TREBIZON *and* SORIA.]

TAMBURLAINE. Come Asian Viceroies, to your taskes a while
   And take such fortune as your fellowes felt.
ORCANES. First let thy Scythyan horse teare both our limmes
   Rather then we should draw thy chariot,
   And like base slaves abject our princely mindes   140
   To vile and ignominious servitude.
JERUSALEM. Rather lend me thy weapon *Tamburlain*,
   That I may sheath it in this breast of mine,
   A thousand deathes could not torment our hearts
   More than the thought of this dooth vexe our soules.   145
AMYRAS. They will talk still my Lord, if you doe not
   bridle them.
TAMBURLAINE. Bridle them, and let me to my coach.

123SD *Exeunt souldiers*] *Dyce 1; not in* O1.   126SD *Exeunt...* GOVERNOUR] *Dyce 1;*
not in O1.   130SD *Souldiers...* SORIA] *Dyce 1; not in* O1.   135SD *Exit...*
SORIA] *Robinson; not in* O1.

They bridle them.

[*Souldiers hang the* GOVERNOUR *of* BABYLON *in chaines on
the walles. Enter* THERIDAMAS *below.*]

AMYRAS. See now my Lord how brave the Captaine hangs.
TAMBURLAINE. Tis brave indeed my boy, wel done,   150
Shoot first my Lord, and then the rest shall follow.
THERIDAMAS. Then have at him to begin withall.

THERIDAMAS *shootes.*

GOVERNOUR. Yet save my life, and let this wound appease
The mortall furie of great *Tamburlain.*
TAMBURLAINE. No, though *Asphaltis* lake were liquid gold, 155
And offer'd me as ransome for thy life,
Yet shouldst thou die: shoot at him all at once.

They shoote.

So now he hangs like *Bagdets* Governour,
Having as many bullets in his flesh,
As there be breaches in her battered wall.   160
Goe now and bind the Burghers hand and foot,
And cast them headlong in the cities lake:
Tartars and Perseans shall inhabit there,
And to command the citie, I will build
A Cytadell, that all *Assiria*   165
Which hath bene subject to the Persean king,
Shall pay me tribute for, in *Babylon.*
TECHELLES. What shal be done with their wives and chil-
dren my Lord?
TAMBURLAINE. *Techelles,* drowne them all, man, woman,
and child,   170
Leave not a Babylonian in the towne.
TECHELLES. I will about it straight, come Souldiers.
                    Exit [TECHELLES *with souldiers*].
TAMBURLAINE. Now *Casane,* wher's the Turkish *Alcaron,*
And all the heapes of supersticious bookes,
Found in the Temples of that *Mahomet,*   175

148SD *Souldiers...below*] *Dyce 1; not in O1.*   165 *Assiria*] *van Dam;* Affrica *O1;*
Arabia *conj. Broughton.*   172SD TECHELLES ...*souldiers*] *Oxberry; not in O1.*

Whom I have thought a God? they shal be burnt.
USUMCASANE. Here they are my Lord.
TAMBURLAINE. Wel said, let there be a fire presently.

[They light a fire.]

In vaine I see men worship *Mahomet*.
My sword hath sent millions of Turks to hell,   180
Slew all his Priests, his kinsmen, and his friends,
And yet I live untoucht by *Mahomet*:
There is a God full of revenging wrath,
From whom the thunder and the lightning breaks,
Whose Scourge I am, and him will I obey.   185
So *Casane*, fling them in the fire.

[They burn the books.]

Now *Mahomet*, if thou have any power,
Come downe thy selfe and worke a myracle,
Thou art not woorthy to be worshipped,
That suffers flames of fire to burne the writ   190
Wherein the sum of thy religion rests.
Why send'st thou not a furious whyrlwind downe,
To blow thy *Alcaron* up to thy throne,
Where men report, thou sitt'st by God himselfe,
Or vengeance on the head of *Tamburlain*,   195
That shakes his sword against thy majesty,
And spurns the Abstracts of thy foolish lawes.
Wel souldiers, *Mahomet* remaines in hell,
He cannot heare the voice of *Tamburlain*:
Seeke out another Godhead to adore,   200
The God that sits in heaven, if any God,
For he is God alone, and none but he.

[Enter TECHELLES.]

TECHELLES. I have fulfil'd your highnes wil, my Lord,
Thousands of men drown'd in *Asphaltis* Lake,
Have made the water swell above the bankes,   205
And fishes fed by humaine carkasses,

178SD *They...fire*] Dyce *1; not in* O1.   186SD *They...books*] Dyce *1; not in*
O1.   202SD *Enter* TECHELLES] Oxberry; *not in* O1.   206 fed] Oxberry; feed O1.

Amasde, swim up and downe upon the waves,
As when they swallow *Assafitida*,
Which makes them fleet aloft and gaspe for aire.

TAMBURLAINE. Wel then my friendly Lordes, what now
   remaines   210
But that we leave sufficient garrison
And presently depart to *Persea*,
To triumph after all our victories.

THERIDAMAS. I, good my Lord, let us in hast to *Persea*,
And let this Captaine be remoov'd the walles,   215
To some high hill about the citie here.

TAMBURLAINE. Let it be so, about it souldiers:
But stay, I feele my selfe distempered sudainly.

TECHELLES. What is it dares distemper *Tamburlain*?

TAMBURLAINE. Something *Techelles*, but I know not what.   220
But foorth ye vassals, what so ere it be:
Sicknes or death can never conquer me.

                                      Exeunt.

Actus. 5. Scæna. 2.

Enter CALLAPINE, AMASIA, [*a* CAPTAIN, *Souldiers,*] *with
drums and trumpets.*

CALLAPINE. King of *Amasia*, now our mighty hoste,
Marcheth in *Asia major* where the streames
Of *Euphrates* and *Tigris* swiftly runs,
And here may we behold great *Babylon*,
Circled about with *Limnasphaltis* Lake,   5
Where *Tamburlaine* with all his armie lies,
Which being faint and weary with the siege,
Wee may lie ready to encounter him,
Before his hoste be full from *Babylon*,
And so revenge our latest grievous losse,   10
If God or *Mahomet* send any aide.

AMASIA. Doubt not my lord, but we shal conquer him.

   Scæna.2.] *Robinson; Scæna.4. O1.*   OSD1 *a* CAPTAIN] *Dyce 2; not in O1.*
Souldiers] *Oxberry; not in O1.*

The Monster that hath drunke a sea of blood,
And yet gapes stil for more to quench his thirst,
Our Turkish swords shal headlong send to hell,   15
And that vile Carkasse drawne by warlike kings,
The Foules shall eate, for never sepulchre
Shall grace that base-borne Tyrant *Tamburlaine.*

CALLAPINE. When I record my Parents slavish life,
Their cruel death, mine owne captivity,   20
My Viceroies bondage under *Tamburlaine,*
Me thinks I could sustaine a thousand deaths,
To be reveng'd of all his Villanie.
Ah sacred *Mahomet,* thou that hast seene
Millions of Turkes perish by *Tamburlaine,*   25
Kingdomes made waste, brave cities sackt and burnt,
And but one hoste is left to honor thee:
Aid thy obedient servant *Callapine,*
And make him after all these overthrowes,
To triumph over cursed *Tamburlaine.*   30

AMASIA. Feare not my Lord, I see great *Mahomet*
Clothed in purple clowdes, and on his head
A Chaplet brighter than *Apollos* crowne,
Marching about the ayer with armed men,
To joine with you against this *Tamburlaine.*   35

CAPTAIN. Renowmed Generall mighty *Callapine,*
Though God himselfe and holy *Mahomet,*
Should come in person to resist your power,
Yet might your mighty hoste incounter all,
And pull proud *Tamburlaine* upon his knees,   40
To sue for mercie at your highnesse feete.

CALLAPINE. Captaine the force of *Tamburlaine* is great,
His fortune greater, and the victories
Wherewith he hath so sore dismaide the world,
Are greatest to discourage all our drifts,   45
Yet when the pride of *Cynthia* is at full,
She waines againe, and so shall his I hope,
For we have here the chiefe selected men
Of twenty severall kingdomes at the least:
Nor plowman, Priest, nor Merchant staies at home: 50

36 CAPTAIN] *Dyce 2; not in O1.*

All *Turkie* is in armes with *Callapine*.
And never wil we sunder camps and armes,
Before himselfe or his be conquered.
This is the time that must eternize me,
For conquering the Tyrant of the world.   55
Come Souldiers, let us lie in wait for him
And if we find him absent from his campe,
Or that it be rejoin'd again at full,
Assaile it and be sure of victorie.

Exeunt.

Actus. 5. Scæna. 3.

[*Enter*] THERIDAMAS, TECHELLES, USUMCASANE.

THERIDAMAS. Weepe heavens, and vanish into liquid teares,
    Fal starres that governe his nativity,
    And sommon al the shining lamps of heaven
    To cast their bootlesse fires to the earth,
    And shed their feble influence in the aire.   5
    Muffle your beauties with eternall clowdes,
    For hell and darknesse pitch their pitchy tentes,
    And Death with armies of Cymerian spirits
    Gives battile gainst the heart of *Tamburlaine*.
    Now in defiance of that woonted love,   10
    Your sacred vertues pour'd upon his throne,
    And made his state an honor to the heavens,
    These cowards invisiblie assaile hys soule,
    And threaten conquest on our Soveraigne:
    But if he die, your glories are disgrac'd,   15
    Earth droopes and saies, that hell in heaven is plac'd.
TECHELLES. O then ye Powers that sway eternal seates,
    And guide this massy substance of the earthe,
    If you retaine desert of holinesse,
    As your supreame estates instruct our thoughts,   20
    Be not inconstant, carelesse of your fame,

    *Scæna.*3.] *Robinson; Scæna.*6. *O1.*   OSD *Enter*] *Oxberry; not in O1.*   1 THER-
IDAMAS] *Oxberry; not in O1.*

Beare not the burthen of your enemies joyes,
Triumphing in his fall whom you advaunst,
But as his birth, life, health and majesty
Were strangely blest and governed by heaven,   25
So honour heaven til heaven dissolved be,
His byrth, his life, his health and majesty.

USUMCASANE. Blush heaven to loose the honor of thy name,
To see thy foot-stoole set upon thy head,
And let no basenesse in thy haughty breast,   30
Sustaine a shame of such inexcellence:
To see the devils mount in Angels throanes,
And Angels dive into the pooles of hell.
And though they think their painfull date is out,
And that their power is puissant as *Joves*,   35
Which makes them manage armes against thy state,
Yet make them feele the strength of *Tamburlain*,
Thy instrument and note of Majesty,
Is greater far, than they can thus subdue.
For if he die, thy glorie is disgrac'd,   40
Earth droopes and saies that hel in heaven is plac'd.

[*Enter* TAMBURLAINE, *drawn by the captive kings*, ORCANES
of NATOLIA, *and* JERUSALEM; AMYRAS, CELEBINUS, *and*
PHYSITIANS.]

TAMBURLAINE. What daring God torments my body thus,
And seeks to conquer mighty *Tamburlaine*?
Shall sicknesse proove me now to be a man,
That have bene tearm'd the terrour of the world?   45
Techelles and the rest, come take your swords,
And threaten him whose hand afflicts my soul.
Come let us march against the powers of heaven,
And set blacke streamers in the firmament,
To signifie the slaughter of the Gods.   50
Ah friends, what shal I doe, I cannot stand,
Come carie me to war against the Gods,
That thus invie the health of *Tamburlaine*.

THERIDAMAS. Ah good my Lord, leave these impatient words,

41SD *Enter*...PHYSITIANS] *Dyce 1; not in O1;* TAMBURLAINE, AMYRAS *and* PHYSI-
CIAN *Oxberry.*

Which ad much danger to your malladie.   55
TAMBURLAINE. Why, shal I sit and languish in this paine?
  No, strike the drums, and in revenge of this,
  Come let us chardge our speares and pierce his breast,
  Whose shoulders beare the Axis of the world,
  That if I perish, heaven and earth may fade.   60
  Theridamas, haste to the court of *Jove*,
  Will him to send *Apollo* hether straight,
  To cure me, or Ile fetch him downe my selfe.
TECHELLES. Sit stil my gratious Lord, this griefe wil cease,
  And cannot last, it is so violent.   65
TAMBURLAINE. Not last *Techelles*, no, for I shall die.
  See where my slave, the uglie monster death
  Shaking and quivering, pale and wan for feare,
  Stands aiming at me with his murthering dart,
  Who flies away at every glance I give,   70
  And when I look away, comes stealing on:
  Villaine away, and hie thee to the field,
  I and myne armie come to lode thy barke
  With soules of thousand mangled carkasses.
  Looke where he goes, but see, he comes againe   75
  Because I stay: *Techelles* let us march,
  And weary Death with bearing soules to hell.
PHYSICIAN. Pleaseth your Majesty to drink this potion,
  Which wil abate the furie of your fit,
  And cause some milder spirits governe you.   80
TAMBURLAINE. Tel me, what think you of my sicknes
      now?
PHYSICIAN. I view'd your urine, and the Hipostasis
  Thick and obscure doth make your danger great,
  Your vaines are full of accidentall heat,
  Whereby the moisture of your blood is dried,   85
  The *Humidum* and *Calor*, which some holde
  Is not a parcell of the Elements,
  But of a substance more divine and pure,
  Is almost cleane extinguished and spent,
  Which being the cause of life, imports your death.   90
  Besides my Lord, this day is Criticall,

---

82 Hipostasis] *Robinson*; Hipostates *O1*.

Dangerous to those, whose Chrisis is as yours:
Your Artiers which alongst the vaines convey
The lively spirits which the heart ingenders
Are partcht and void of spirit, that the soule   95
Wanting those Organnons by which it mooves,
Can not indure by argument of art.
Yet if your majesty may escape this day,
No doubt, but you shal soone recover all.
TAMBURLAINE. Then will I comfort all my vital parts,   100
And live in spight of death above a day.

Alarme within.

[*Enter a* MESSENGER.]

MESSENGER. My Lord, yong *Callapine* that lately fled
from your majesty, hath nowe gathered a fresh Armie,
and hearing your absence in the field, offers to set upon
us presently.   105
TAMBURLAINE. See my Phisitions now, how *Jove* hath
sent
A present medicine to recure my paine:
My looks shall make them flie, and might I follow,
There should not one of all the villaines power
Live to give offer of another fight.   110
USUMCASANE. I joy my Lord, your highnesse is so strong,
That can endure so well your royall presence,
Which onely will dismay the enemy.
TAMBURLAINE. I know it wil *Casane*: draw you slaves,
In spight of death I will goe show my face.   115

Alarme, TAMBURLAINE *goes in, and comes out againe with al
the rest.*

Thus are the villaines, cowards fled for feare,
Like Summers vapours, vanish by the Sun.
And could I but a while pursue the field,
That *Callapine* should be my slave againe.
But I perceive my martial strength is spent,   120
In vaine I strive and raile against those powers,

101SD2 *Enter* ... MESSENGER] *Oxberry; not in* O1.

That meane t'invest me in a higher throane,
As much too high for this disdainfull earth.
Give me a Map, then let me see how much
Is left for me to conquer all the world,   125
That these my boies may finish all my wantes.

One brings a Map.

Here I began to martch towards *Persea*,
Along *Armenia* and the Caspian sea,
And thence unto *Bythinia*, where I tooke
The Turke and his great Empresse prisoners,   130
Then martcht I into *Egypt* and *Arabia*,
And here not far from *Alexandria*,
Whereas the Terren and the red sea meet,
Being distant lesse than ful a hundred leagues,
I meant to cut a channell to them both,   135
That men might quickly saile to *India*.
From thence to *Nubia* neere *Borno* Lake,
And so along the Ethiopian sea,
Cutting the Tropicke line of *Capricorne*,
I conquered all as far as *Zansibar*.   140
Then by the Northerne part of *Affrica*,
I came at last to *Græcia*, and from thence
To *Asia*, where I stay against my will,
Which is from *Scythia*, where I first began,
Backeward and forwards nere five thousand leagues.   145
Looke here my boies, see what a world of ground,
Lies westward from the midst of *Cancers* line,
Unto the rising of this earthly globe,
Whereas the Sun declining from our sight,
Begins the day with our Antypodes: 150
And shall I die, and this unconquered?
Loe here my sonnes, are all the golden Mines,
Inestimable drugs and precious stones,
More worth than *Asia*, and the world beside,
And from th'Antartique Pole, Eastward behold   155
As much more land, which never was descried,
Wherein are rockes of Pearle, that shine as bright
As all the Lamps that beautifie the Sky:
And shal I die, and this unconquered?

Here lovely boies [*giving them the map*], what death forbids
   my life,   160
That let your lives commaund in spight of death.

AMYRAS. Alas my Lord, how should our bleeding harts
  Wounded and broken with your Highnesse griefe,
  Retaine a thought of joy, or sparke of life?
  Your soul gives essence to our wretched subjects,   165
  Whose matter is incorporat in your flesh.

CELEBINUS. Your paines do pierce our soules, no hope survives,
  For by your life we entertaine our lives.

TAMBURLAINE. But sons, this subject not of force enough,
  To hold the fiery spirit it containes,   170
  Must part, imparting his impressions,
  By equall portions into both your breasts:
  My flesh devided in your precious shapes,
  Shal still retaine my spirit, though I die,
  And live in all your seedes immortally: 175
  Then now remoove me, that I may resigne
  My place and proper tytle to my sonne:
  First take my Scourge and my imperiall Crowne,   [*To* AMYRAS.]
  And mount my royall chariot of estate,
  That I may see thee crown'd before I die.   180
  Help me (my Lords) to make my last remoove.

THERIDAMAS. A woful change my Lord, that daunts our
   thoughts,
  More than the ruine of our proper soules.

TAMBURLAINE. Sit up my sonne, and let me see how well
  Thou wilt become thy fathers majestie.   185

They crowne him.

AMYRAS. With what a flinty bosome should I joy
  The breath of life, and burthen of my soule,
  If not resolv'd into resolved paines,
  My bodies mortified lineaments
  Should exercise the motions of my heart,   190
  Pierc'd with the joy of any dignity?
  O father, if the unrelenting eares

160SD *giving . . . map*] Craik (this edn.); *not in O1*   178SD *To* AMYRAS] Bowers; *not*
in O1.   184 and] Oxberry; *not in O1.*

Of death and hell be shut against my praiers,
And that the spightfull influence of heaven,
Denie my soule fruition of her joy,   195
How should I step or stir my hatefull feete,
Against the inward powers of my heart,
Leading a life that onely strives to die,
And plead in vaine, unpleasing soveraimy.

TAMBURLAINE. Let not thy love exceed thyne honor sonne, 200
Nor bar thy mind that magnanimitie,
That nobly must admit necessity:
Sit up my boy, and with those silken raines,
Bridle the steeled stomackes of those Jades.

THERIDAMAS. My Lord, you must obey his majesty,   205
Since Fate commands, and proud necessity.

AMYRAS. Heavens witnes me, with what a broken hart
And damned spirit I ascend this seat,
And send my soule before my father die,
His anguish and his burning agony.   210

TAMBURLAINE. Now fetch the hearse of faire *Zenocrate*,
Let it be plac'd by this my fatall chaire,
And serve as parcell of my funerall.

USUMCASANE. Then feeles your majesty no soveraigne ease,
Nor may our hearts all drown'd in teares of blood,   215
Joy any hope of your recovery?

TAMBURLAINE. *Casane* no, the Monarke of the earth,
And eielesse Monster that torments my soule,
Cannot behold the teares ye shed for me,
And therefore stil augments his cruelty.   220

TECHELLES. Then let some God oppose his holy power,
Against the wrath and tyranny of death,
That his teare-thyrsty and unquenched hate,
May be upon himselfe reverberate.

They bring in the hearse.

TAMBURLAINE. Now eies, injoy your latest benefite,   225
And when my soule hath vertue of your sight,
Pierce through the coffin and the sheet of gold,
And glut your longings with a heaven of joy.
So, raigne my sonne, scourge and controlle those slaves,
Guiding thy chariot with thy Fathers hand.   230

As precious is the charge thou undertak'st
As that which *Clymens* brainsicke sonne did guide,
When wandring *Phœbes* Ivory cheeks were scortcht
And all the earth like *Ætna* breathing fire:
Be warn'd by him, then learne with awfull eie   235
To sway a throane as dangerous as his:
For if thy body thrive not full of thoughtes
As pure and fiery as *Phyteus* beames,
The nature of these proud rebelling Jades
Wil take occasion by the slenderest haire,   240
And draw thee peecemeale like *Hyppolitus*,
Through rocks more steepe and sharp than Caspian cliftes.
The nature of thy chariot wil not beare
A guide of baser temper than my selfe,
More then heavens coach, the pride of *Phaeton*.   245
Farewel my boies, my dearest friends, farewel,
My body feeles, my soule dooth weepe to see
Your sweet desires depriv'd my company,
For *Tamburlaine*, the Scourge of God must die.   [*He dies.*]
AMYRAS. Meet heaven and earth, and here let al things end, 250
For earth hath spent the pride of all her fruit,
And heaven consum'd his choisest living fire.
Let earth and heaven his timelesse death deplore,
For both their woorths wil equall him no more.

                        [*Exeunt.*]

FINIS.

232 *Clymens*] O2 (*Clymenes*); *Clymeus* O1.   249SD *He dies*] Oxberry; *not in*
O1.   254SD *Exeunt*] Dyce 2; *not in* O1.

ACCIDENTAL EMENDATIONS

PART 1

To the Gentlemen Readers
14 and] &

Prologue
3 *War:*] ~.   4 Tamburlaine,] ~:   6 *sword.*] ~ₐ

1.1.

16 thee] thₐ   17 Provinces.] ~,   25 Lord.] ~ₐ   30 *Tamburlaine,*]
~.   32 upon] upnon   Passengers,] ~.   33 plumes:] ~,   40 outrages,]
~.   48 throne.] ~,   49, 140, 187 and] &   49 lord,] ~ₐ   54
Lords?] ~¿   55 resolution?] ~¿   58 *Theridimas,*] ~ₐ   66 Dame.]
~,   74 swords,] ~ₐ   77 mine,] ~.   78 men,] ~.   82 *Theridamas,*]
Therid. times.] ~,   84 renowne?] ~:   86 *Theridamas.*] ~:   97 seat—]
~.   99 state,] ~.   106SD, 135SD *and*] &   108 threaten] thraten
112 *Asia.*] ~,   117 scorne:] ~,   126 Emperie.] ~,   128 Dominions,] ~:
130 once,] ~.   132 Christendome.] ~.?   133 *Menaphon,*] *Menaph.* sound?] ~ₐ
135 *Crowne,*] ~ₐ   145 Crestes:] ~,   147 discipline,] ~.   148 warre,] ~.
157 th'imperiall] th'mperiall   173 Provinces:] ~.   180 neereₐ] ~,   188 then,
God] then,/God

1.2.

Scæna.2.] *Scæna.2:*   OSD I USUMCASANE] *Vsumeasane (so spelt throughout)*
1 thoughts.] ~ₐ   4 *Siria,*] ~.   16 *Affrica.*] ~:   18 Cham] *Cham*
21, 113, 228, 229 and] &   40 *Phœbus*] *Phœbus*   41 weare:] ~,
49 quake,] ~.   53 Beastes,] ~.   60 followers.] ~,   61 estimates,]
~:   62 spirits:] ~,   91 Crowne,] ~.   92 birth.] ~,   103 waves,] ~.
137 first.] ~,   145 swords,] ~.   154–5 *Tamburlaine?*/A Scythian] *Tamburlaine?* A Scythian   156 furniture?] ~,   158 earth,] ~.   160 *Avernus*] *Avernas* vaults,] ~.   162 Persean] Perseau   163 man.] ~,   166,
242 *Persea*] Persea   180 heaven,] ~.   181 harme.] ~,   182 showers,]
~.   185 East,] ~.   187 Emperesse.] ~,   192 sackt.] ~,   195 sea,]
~.   198 Senators.] ~,   207 *Boötes*] *Botëes* light,] ~.   216 thatₐ] ~,
218 expect,] ~.   223 admires.] ~,   224 soule?] ~ₐ   232 hand,] ~.
240, 252 *Theridamas*] *theridamas*   244 *Scythia*] Scythia   249 *Tamburlain,*]
~ₐ   256 with] wtth   258 doubt.] ~ₐ

2.1.

Scæna] *Scæna*   11 burthen:] ~,   20 Thirsting] Thrirsting   soverainty,]
~ₐ   armes:] ~,   23 heire,] ~.   35 madeₐ] ~:   36 men,] ~.
40 join'd,] ~ₐ   48 *Tamburlaine*] *tamburlaine*   49 King.] ~:   56 Monarchie,] ~ₐ   57 king,] ~?   59 treasure] trasure   thoughts?] ~,   64 King,]
~.   65 *Parthia:*] Parthia.

2.2.

Actus] *Act* 2.]~,   3, 30, 36 *Tamburlaine*] *tamburlaine*   4 brother.]
~ₐ   5 abusde,] ~.   8 not?] ~¿   15 hilles,] ~.   25 promisesₐ] ~.

29 fight.] ~,   32 *Theridamas*] *theridamas*   51 say,] ~∧   52 venomous?] ~.
68 subdu'd,] ~:   70 equally] equallly   71 *Persea.*] ~,   75 when]
whe   *Meander*] *Meand.*   75SD *Exeunt.*] ~∧

2.3.

   OSD2 ORTYGIUS,] ~.   2 hope.] ~,   3 attemptes?] ~.   8 *Tamburlaine*]
tamburlaine   13 armes,]   ~.   14 support.] ~,   36,   63 *Techelles*]
techelles   38 Armes,] ~:   42 alone,] ~.   44 Fate.] ~,   48 *Caspea*]
Caspea   51 *Tamburlain*] *tamburlain*   53 *Perseas*] Perseas   55 Cutle-
axe,] ~.   56 Armes.] ~,   58 lightening,] ~:

2.4.

2 not, simple]~∧ ~   17 field?] ~.   18 liest. Base] liest./Base
20 kneele,] ~.   27 didst] Didst   41 *Tamburlaine*] *tamburlaine*   42SD *and*]
aud

2.5.

   OSD2 ORTYGIUS, TECHELLES,] ~. ~.   3, 7, 38, 44, 97 *Tamburlaine*] *tambur-*
laine   8 *Persea*] Persea   16 Majestie,] ~.   19 *Persea*] Persea   23 com-
maund] commauud   29 *Menaphon*] *menaphon*   33 state∧] ~,   36 *Orti-*
gius):] ~∧   39, 52, 65, 81, 93, 105 *Theridamas*] *theridamas*   46 friends:] ~,
47 throne.] ~,   48 wish,] ~.   49SD TAMBURLAINE…USUMCASANE]
Tamb. Tech. Ther. Vsum.   51, 69, 94, 99, 104 *Techelles*] *techelles*   59 earth:] ~,
61 death:] ~,   67 What] what   72 Casane,] Casanes∧   74 attemplesse,] ~∧

2.6.

2 presumption:] ~.   13 rule,] ~.   21 and] &   26 Elements∧] ~,
28 life.] ~,   30 ingratitude] ingratude   31 Soveraigntie] Soveraingtie

2.7.

   OSD1 *and*] &   OSD2 THERIDAMAS] T*heridamas*   TAMBURLAINE]
tamburlaine   3 *Theridamas*] *theridamas*   8 voice,] ~.   10 heart:] ~,
23 course:] ~.   25 Spheares,] ~.   26 rest,] ~.   27 all,] ~.   28 felicitie,] ~.   30 *Tamburlain,*] *tamburlain*∧   34 us,] ~∧   *Tamburlaine,*] ~.
37 Crowne,] ~.   39, 57, 63, 64 *Tamburlain*] *tamburlain*   39 *Persea*]
Persea   44 hell,] ~.   47 both,] ~.   49 hart,] ~.   53 Furies]
furies   55 *Techelles*] *techelles*   67 *Persea*] Persea

3.1.

   OSD1 FESSE] *Fess.*   ARGIER,] ~.   2 and] &   14 yeeld,] ~.   16 Generall,] ~∧   17 guard,] ~.   23 *Asia,*] ~.   24 *Grecia*] Grecia   26 high-
est] higest   world,] ~.   29 *Grecia,*] Grecia.   38 arise∧] ~.   43 Persean,]
~.   44SD BASSO] *Bass.*   52 thereon,] ~.   60 *Carnon.*] ~,   67SD
Exeunt.] ~∧

3.2.

5 pale,] ~.   6, 24, 25, 36, 49, 55 *Tamburlaine*] *tamburlaine*   9 agoe,]
(turned comma)   11 well∧] ~:   12 disdaine:] ~.   14 conceits,] ~.
15 are,]~.   18 dissolv'd,] ~.   20 *Zenocrate*] *zenocrate*   21 Breast,]
~.   25 *Zenocrate,*] *zenocrate.*   28 Queene,] ~.   29 Concubine,] ~.
35 words,] ~.   38 servitude,] ~.   45 blood:] ~.   48 armes,] ~.
51 Pierides,] ~.   52 strive:] ~,   54 *Juno,*] ~∧   God,] ~.   58 en-

joy] ejoy   65SD1 TAMBURLAINE] *Tamburlaine   and*] *&*   66 love,] ~.
67 jealousie,] ~.   68 revenge,] ~.   73 hart,] ~.   74 revenge,] ~.
80 thunderclaps,] ~.   87SD TECHELLES] *Techelles*   95 die,] ~.   96 least.]
~,   100 plagues∧ ~:   102 rage,] ~.   103 hell∧ ~:   105 die,] ~.
109 *Techelles*] *techelles*

3.3.
      3.]~,   0SD2 ZENOCRATE] *Zenocrate*   1 Bassoe] *Bassoe*   3 See] see
10 *Affrica?*] ~.   12 hoste.] ~,   16 Steeds,] ~.   17 *Tripoly:*] ~.   19 *Grecia*]
Grecia   25 Steeds,] ~.   30 yours.] ~∧   31 heads,] ~:   38 *Europe*]
Europe   40, 228 *Theridamas*] *theridamas*   48 chaines,] ~.   53 side,]
~.   54 give.] ~,   55 *Argiere*] *Argeire*   56 *Affrica,*] ~.   60 *Affrica.*]
Affrica   64 swordes:] ~∧   73, 99, 205, 221, 223 *Affrica*] Affrica   74,
119, 170, 171, 202, 261 *Tamburlaine*] *tamburlaine*   75 sepulcher,] ~.   80 Emperesse,] ~.   88 *Tamburlaine?*] *tamburlaine.*   89 *Barbary,*] ~.   90 indignities?]
~.   91 pointes,] ~.   95 Perseans.] ~,   96, 114, 222, 247, 262 *Tamburlain*]
tamburlain   98 swordes,] ~∧   103 boies∧ ~,   106 Lance,] ~.   111
fists:] ~.   117, 126 *Zenocrate*] *zenocrate*   120 heaven,] ~.   128
kings,] ~.   132 *Persea,*] ~∧   135 *Europe*] Europe   137 *Bythinia.*] ~,   139 Shal] *text*; Shall (*catchword*)   157 pointes,] ~∧   158 aire.]
~,   159 spread,] ~.   166 Bassoes,] ~∧   169 Call'st] *text*; Cal'st
(*catchword*)   173 selfe,] ~.   180 weedes,] ~.   182 Hearst] hearst
183 menaceth?] ~.   188SD stay.]~∧   189 *Persea,*] Persea.   199 shrine,]
~.   201 blood,] ~∧   202 *Affrica.*] ~:   209 conquered,] ~.
210 otherwise,] ~.   211SD2 enter.] ~,   213 foile.] ~,   215 crownes:]
~∧   216 ifaith.] ~∧   218 Lord∧] ~.   219 won.] ~:   220 *Zenocrate,*] zen.   222 best,] ~∧   224SD her,] ~.   ZENOCRATE.] ~,   231 ransomed.] ~:   233 Zabina] zabina   241 lost,] ~.   248 Gallies] Galles
251 *Asant,*] ~.   257 one,] ~.   258 *Portingale,*] ~.   262 gold?] ~,
268 armes?] ~.   272 and] &

4.1.
      4 *Zenocrate*] *zenocrate*   6 vagabondes,] ~.   17 Villain,] ~.   *Tamburlaine∧*]
tamburlaine.   32 Autumne] *O3*; Autume *O1*.   downe,] ~.   33 power∧] ~:
35 fall.] ~,   38 *Tamburlaine*] *tamburlaine*   44 detayneth] *O2*; detameth *O1*.
45 *Erebus,*] ~.   52 minde,] ~.   56 blood,] ~.   58 submission,] ~.
68 *Capolin,*] ~∧   69 slave,] ~:   70 Love,] ~:   72 disparagement] *O3*;
dispardgement *O1*.

4.2.
      0SD2 ZENOCRATE] *Zenocrate*   8 God,] ~∧   Spheare∧] ~.   10 Heaven,]
~.   13 earth,] ~.   20 ground∧] ~.   26 Feends,] ~.   27 hell,]
~.   32 Emperours.] ~,   33 nativity,] ~:   34 Lamps:] ~,   50 heaven,] ~.   51 shot,] ~.   66 Lord,] ~∧   68 *Zenocrate*] *zenocrate*   slave.]
~:   75 *Tamburlaine*] *tamburlaine*   76 low,] ~.   79 dignities,] ~∧
104 Memphian] Memphion   108 gold,] ~.   112 displaid,] ~.
121 contain'd,] ~.

4.3.
      Actus] Act   3.] ~,   1SD1 SOULDANE,] ~.   streaming] *O3*; steaming *O1*
2 knightes,] ~:   3 Boare:] ~,   4 youths,] ~.   5 sent,] ~.   8 spoile,]
~.   11 *Tamburlaine,*] ~.   12 Thiefe,] ~.   13 Crowne,] ~.
15 presumptuous] *O2*; presumotuous *O1*   27 Emperesse?] ~.

34 rock.] ~,   39 wrong,] ~.   41 Zenocrate] zenocrate   long,] ~.   47 And]
text; An (catchword)   48 prodigall,] ~:   49 praise.] ~:   50 powers?]
~.   51 Arabia,] ~.   52 is,] is,   56 chace∧] ~:   59 Tamburlaine]
tamburlaine   64 Arabian King,] Arabian King.   65 obscurity,] ~.

4.4.
   Actus.] ~:   osd1 The] The   tamburlaine] Tamburlaine   osd2
theridamas,]   ~.   techelles] Techelles   Turke] Turke   1 Damascus,]
Damascns.   2 heads,] ~.   11 Tamburlane] tamburlane   12 could willingly]
could/Willingly   14 that, and] that,/And   14 Zenocrate, Techelles] zenocrate,/
techelles   18 Avernus] Avernas   19 up,] ~.   20 Tamburlain] tamburlain   24 King,] ~.   27 curses by] curses/By   28, 68, 86, 90, 148 Zeno-
crate] zenocrate   29 foes,] ~.   41 speakest?] ~∧   45 Villaine,] ~∧
48, 49 and] &   56 this?] ~∧   58 what,] ~∧   59 Belike] belike
72 borne:] ~,   78 friendly] frindly   79 Egypt] Egypt   80 stoope.]
~,   84 Map,] ~.   91, 118–19 Tamburlaine] tamburlaine   93 safe,] ~.
96 forc'd,] ~∧   97 Egypt and Arabia] Egypt and Arabia   mine] (turned m)
98 Feed] text; Feede (catchword)   105 Bajazeth.] ~,   them, looking] them,/
Looking   114, 124 Theridamas] Theridamas   114 Techelles] techelles
120 here] Here   121 Egypt,] ~∧   Governour] Governout   124 Techelles]
Techelles   126 (Turke)?] ~∧   These] these   128 them.] ~,   129 Fesse,]
~.   131 heaven,] ~.   132 bower,] ~.   134 with,] ~.   136 fame,]
~.   144 Egyptia,] ~.   145 Antartique] O2; Antatique O1.   146 feet,] ~.

5.1.
   Actus.] ~:   2 downe.] (inverted full stop)   14 fame,] ~:   17 deaths.]
~,   20 praiers,] ~∧   21 mones,] ~∧   25 Uttered] uttered   26 Sex,]
~.   28 breasts,] ~.   29 securities,] ~.   31 death,] ~.   33 we.]
~∧   34 care,] ~∧   40 owne,] ~∧   43 stars,] ~.   46 extreames,] ~.
50 intreate∧] ~,   51 lookes,] ~∧   53, 299, 356 (twice) Tamburlaine] tamburlaine
59 lenity.] ~,   63sd1 TAMBURLAINE, TECHELLES,] ~. ~∧ USUMCAS-
ANE] Vsumeasan   63sd3 verie] veri   69 beams,] ~∧   84 joy,] ~.
95 lives.] ~,   110 then] ~∧   111 imperious Death,] ~.   121 Egyptians,] ~.   123 Gehons] Gehons   141 tresses] O2; treshes O1.   aire,] ~.
147 heaven,] ~.   148 walk,] ~.   149 night,] ~.   150 light.] ~,
153 Egypts] Egypts   159, 207, 372, 517 Zenocrate] zenocrate   168 wit:] ~.
173 digest.] ~:   174 Sex,] ~∧   176 name,] ~.   179 toucht,] ~.
180 love∧] ~,   181 victory,] ~∧   183 subduing, both,] subduing both:
186 flames,] ~.   188 note,] ~∧   194 and] &   195sd, 433sd1 TECHEL-
LES] Techelles   195sd, 433sd2 THERIDAMAS] Theridamas   195sd USUMCAS-
ANE, and] Vsumeasan∧ &   198 Techelles] techelles   202 Techelles.] techelles∧
202sd1 Turke] Turke   206 Theridamas,] theridamas.   215 about,] ~.
216 wounds.] ~,   221 Skin,] ~.   223 joints,] ~.   226 roomes.] ~,
227 foorth,] ~.   230, 275 Zabina] zabina   233 Gods,] ~.   240 end∧]
~?   241 slaveries?] ~:   242 view∧] ~,   246–7 Ferriman,/To] Ferriman,
to   247 Elisian.] ~∧   248 Why] why   beggars, slaves,] beggars∧ slaves∧
253 scorne,] ~.   271 Zabinas heart,] zabinas heart: 273 root∧] ~:
274 breake.] ~,   282 inflictions.] inflictious: 285sd out.] ~:   293 heavens.] ~,   304sd2 Enter] text; Zab (catchword)   309 Bajazeth] Baiazet
309–10 Emperor./Give] Emperor, give   310 liquor?] ~∧   314 I, speake]
I∧ speake   315 her. The] her, the   white,] ~.   317 Tamburlaine, Tamburlaine.] Tamburlaine, tamburlaine,   318 Tamburlain, Hell. Make] tamburlain, Hell, make

319SD1 selfe.] ~∧   SD2 ZENOCRATE] Zenocrate   ANIPPE.] ~,   320, 337,
338, 434, 444, 485, 496 Zenocrate] Zenocrate   321 blood,] ~.   332 hooves,]
~∧   345 both.] ~∧   350 and] &   358 Emperesse.] ~,   361 war,] ~.
379 Arabian] Arabian   381 did,] ~.   394 Lavinia,] ~.   395 love,] ~.
400 hope.] ~,   403SD2 victory. After] victory, after   405 souldiers,]
~.   410 armes,] ~.   413 Lord.] ~,   431 joy,] ~.   432 dies,]
~.   436 thee,] ~∧   438 sword,] ~.   441 soule,] ~.   445 Egypt]
Egypt   447 overthrow,] ~.   448 hands,] ~.   452 world:] ~,
456 death,] ~∧   457 ceasles] ceaslles   458 Affrick] Affrick   459 trium-
phant] triumphat   460 woundes,] ~.   467 fields,] ~.   470 feet.] ~,
472 fight,] ~.   476 Tamburlaine,] ~.   480 and] &   481 Tambur-
lain] tamburlain   482 Emperies:] ~,   483 overthrow,] ~:   491 wait,]
~:   495 Persea.] ~,   501 Lord.] ~,   505 rest.] ~:   506 here's]
her's   on.] ~∧   516 mind.] ~,   518 Asia] Asia   524 martiall] O2; matiall
O1.   531 betrothed Love,] betrothed, Love

PART 2

Title

The... of] capitals in O1.

Prologue

1 Tamburlain] Tamburlain (rom.)   4 pomp,] ~.   5 down.] ~,   6 Zeno-
crate] Zenocrate (rom.)

I.I.

2 Bajazeth,] ~:   3 Lord,] ~∧   12 field?] ~.   13, 45, 114 GAZEL-
LUS] Byr.   18, 115 Turky] Turky   28 Polypheme,] ~:   30 Armes,] ~.
32 Fen.] ~,   35 home,] ~.   41 Argoses,] ~.   55 Empery,] ~∧
56 Turkie] Turkie   64 Illirians] O3; Illicians O1.   65 Sigismond,] ~∧
72 Tamburlaine.] tamburlaine,   74 Capricorne,] ~.   75 Archipellago,] ~.
76 Tamburlaine] tamburlaine   80 To] to   82 sword.] ~,   83 me:] ~,
84 againe,] ~:   87 walles,] ~.   101 Jove.] ~,   108 Arabia∧] ~.
120 array,] ~.   122, 131, 137, 157 ORCANES] Nat.   133 soule,] ~∧
144 scrowle∧] ~:   155 Germany,] ~.

I.2.

7 Tamburlain,] tamburlain.   15 runs—] ~.   16 running] rnnning
30 many] mady   31 command.] ~,   34 Spaine] Spaine   47 thee] O2;
the∧ O1   60 out.] ~.   66 mate.] ~,   76 ready.] ~,   78SD Exeunt.]
~∧

I.3.

0SD1 ZENOCRATE] Zenocrate   0SD2 CELEBINUS,] ~.   1, 15 Zenocrate]
zenocrate   6 Egypt] Egypt   9 Tamburlain] tamburlain   11 war?] ~.
12poles,] ~∧   13 And] &   15 before,] ~∧   18 precious] procions
19 subdewed,] ~:   20 face.] ~,   22 Tamburlaine.] ~∧   23 one,] ~:
24 wit.] ~,   25 Downe,] ~.   26 Porcupines,] ~.   35 looks,] ~∧
42 falne.] ~,   43 lance,] ~∧   44, 129 and] &   44 -axe,] ~∧
48 me,] ~.   53 wombe.] ~,   58 sonne.] ~,   60 world.] ~,   66 mother.] ~,   69 loins,] ~:   74 Persea∧] ~,   76 eies,] ~.   90 it,] ~.
91 king.] ~,   96 both,] ~∧   103 sword.] ~,   104 thee,] ~∧

110 Empery.] ~,   111 sound,] ~∧   112 *Argier.*] ~,   117 *Theridamas*] *ther-idamas*   118   Greeks,]   ~∧   119   townes∧]   ~,   121   sworne] sworue   124   *Tripoly*]   *Tripoly*   127SD   TECHELLES]   *Techelles*   133 *Tunys*]   *Tunys*   143   *Jove,*] ~∧   148   *Tesella*]   *Tesella*   150   again.] ~∧ 152 joy.] ~,   158   *Turky*]   Turky   169   *Thetis*]   *thetis*   179   *Spaine*]   Spaine 186 Nile,] *punctuation uncertain*   194   *Zansibar,*]   *zansibar*∧   195   view'd∧] ~. 198 *Manico,*] ~.   202   *Nubia:*] ~,   203   *Borno,*] ~∧   211   *Oblia,*] ~. 223 him,] ~.

2.1.

   10 Camp.] ~,   53 Paganisme,] ~?

2.2.

   2 *Orminius*] *O2*; *Orminus O1.*   5   *Tamburlain*]   *tamburlain*   8   heaven.] ~,   10 felt:] ~,   22 terrified∧] ~:   24 Lords.] ~∧

2.3.

   OSD *to*] *ro*   20   *Zoacum*]   *zoacum*   23   Feends.] ~,   25   gulfe,] ~: 41SD URIBASSA] *Vrib.*

2.4.

   3 waves,] ~:   4 beames:] ~∧   25, 94, 101, 111, 142 *Zenocrate*] *zeno-crate*   31 soules∧] ~:   39 1. PHYSICIAN] *Phis.*   52 when,] ~∧   Dia-miter,] ~:   64 breast,] ~.   68 life.] ~,   77SD *They*] *They*   83 death,] ~:   84 soule:] ~,   86 *Troy*] Troy   87 *Greece*] Greece   88 *Tenedos*] *Tenedos*   93 *Corinna*] *Corrinna*   95SD *The*] The   96 ∧What] *tam.* What   *Techelles*] *Techelles*   102, 126 *Theridamas*] *theridamas*   102 armes:] ~, 103 cloudes,] ~:   108 heaven.] ~,   115 war,] ~:   116 flag:] ~, 120 live.] ~,   123 blood.] ~∧   125 soule.] ~∧   126 more:] ~, 136 sword.] ~,   139 mourn'd,] ~∧

3.1.

   Scæna.1.] ~,   OSD2 *sword, and*] *sword, &*   2 mighty] mtghty   4 *Trebi-zon*] *Trebizon*   5 *Thracia*] *Thracia*   and] And   7 *Turky*] Turky 32 encounter.] ~,   38 *Tamburlain*] *tamburlain*   39 thousand] thousad 40 Christian,] ~.   51 *Chio*∧] ~,   58 strong,] ~.

3.2.

   5 inhabitants.] ~∧   11 Sindge] sindge   12 maske,] ~∧   17 Tam-burlaine] *Tamburlaine* (*rom.*)   19 mournful] mourful   plac'd,] ~∧   25 *Zeno-crate*] *zenocrate*   26 admyr'd.] ~,   31 latitude,] ~.   32 Hemi-spheare,] ~. 33 *Zenocrate:*] ~.   34 plaines,] ~.   37 tent,] ~.   38 field:] ~, 40 war,] ~∧   45 Boyes,] ~∧   53 list] ∧ist   56 thorow] *O2*; throwe *O1*   64 quinque-] *quinque-*   65 flat∧] ~:   86 and] &   92 great.] ~, 124 Potentate,] ~.   130 it. Me] it,/Me *O1.*   135 own.] *punctuation uncertain*   136 wound.] ~∧   137 thou] Thou   141 wals,] ~∧   142 see,] ~∧   144 *Tamburlaine*] *tamburlaine*   149 faintheart∧] ~,

3.3.

   9 shal] Shal   10 it.]~,   13 *Tamburlain*] *tamburlain*   17 you?] ~∧ 20 *Affrica*] Affrica   30 thee:] ~,   31 walles,] ~:   49 *Theridamas*] *ther-idamas*

3.4.

1, 12 and] &   2 foe.] ~,   15 thee.] ~,   22 that.] ~,   28 knife
(good] knife, good   33SD2 *Enter*] *Entert*   THERIDAMAS] *Theridamas*   TECHEL-
LES] *Techelles*   38 wife.] ~,   46 *Mahomet*,] ~.   48 superficies,]
~.   50 shining] *shinining*   51 *Thetis*] *thetis*   robe:] ~,   57 *Rhamnusia*]
O2; *Rhammusia O1*   59 run,] ~.   60 world:] ~.   67–8 behold./Come]
behold. Come   74 this,] ~.

3.5.

Actus.] ~:   OSD1 CALLEPINE] (*first e inverted*)   14 *Turky*] Turky
15 *Tamburlain,*] ~∧   16 followers:] ~,   19 ever∧] ~,   28 teeth,] ~.
40 *Trebizon*] trebizon   the] *the*   52, 158 *Tamburlaine*] Tamburlaine   55 *Mahomet,*] *punctuation uncertain*   57SD1 TAMBURLAINE] *Tamburlaine*   58 See,] ~∧
64 *Turkye*] Turkye   65 campe,] ~.   66 *Grœcia*,] Grœcia.   68 fame.] ~,
69 simile,] *simile.*   77, 128 *Tamburlaine*] tamburlaine   104 coch,] ~:
105 wier:] ~,   107 planks.] ~:   120 looks?] ~.   153, 157 *Theridamas*] *theridamas*   153 *Techelles*] techelles   159–60 that exigent] that/Exigent   163 Conquerours:] ~,   170 backes.] ~,   173 *Tamburlain*] tamburlain   SD *Exeunt.*]
~∧

4.1.

6 wings.] ~,   19 were] ware   26 swords?] ~.   35 *Mars.*] ~,   45
father,] ~:   46 When,] ~∧   arms,] ~.   51SD AMYRAS] *Amy.*   CELEBI-
NUS] *Celeb.*   77SD TAMBURLAINE] *Tamburlaine*   THERIDAMAS] *Theridamas*   TECHELLES] *Techelles*   Turkish] *Turkish*   87 magnanimity?] ~.   90
foes.] ~,   93 and] and and   98 soule?] ~.   100 pardon.] ~∧   117
consists,] ~.   130 head,] ~.   132 aire,] ~.   136 Sun:] ~.   140 thee∧]
~.   150 above,] ~:   151 abhors:] ~,   159 me∧] ~,   161 *Theridamas*]
Theridamas Techelles] techelles   163 Concubines,] ~.   178 heart.]
~,   183 dogs.] ~,   190 about∧] ~,   197 heavens,] ~.

4.2.

4 and] &   death,] ~∧   5 life,] ~.   14 tent,] ~∧   18 Supposing∧] ~,
38 me.] ~,   58 it?] ~.   68 wil] mil   88 *Elisian.*] ~,

4.3.

OSD3 scourgeth] scourgerh   12 *Thrace*] Thrace   31 refresht.] ~,   49 pastures.] ~,   55 begins∧] ~,   56 tyrannies.] ~?   59 unsackt,] ~.   76
die.] ~,   80 lust?] ~.   82 heeles.] ~∧   91 Truls.] ~,   97 *Techelles*]
techelles   101 store.] ~,   118 world:] ~.   129 pomp:] ~.

5.1.

6 Lord)] ~∧   20 hel?] ~.   28 Conquerour.] ~,   32 reliev'd,] ~:
38 2. CITIZEN] *Another*   62SD3 USUMCASANE,] *Vsumeasane.*   65 deepe,] ~.
68 walles.] ~,   72 carkasses.] ~,   79SD1, 152SD THERIDAMAS] *Theridamas*
79SD1 TECHELLES] *Techelles*   85 towne.] ~,   100 made.] ~,   102 *Tamburlaine*] tamburlaine   114 shal be] shalbe   117 hid:] ~,   119 life?] ~,
123 gold.] ~,   126 quaile.] ~,   130 horse.] ~:   133 *Tamburlain.*] ~∧
139 chariot,] ~.   157 die:] ~,   157SD *They*] They   169 Lord?] ~.
170 *Techelles*] Techelles   drowne] Drowne   175 *Mahomet*,] ~?   176 God?] ~,
178 presently.] ~,   179 *Mahomet.*] ~,   180 hell,] ~.   193 *Alcaron*] Alcaron   196 majesty,] ~.   199 *Tamburlain:*] ~,   209 aire.] ~,
220 *Techelles*] techelles   what.] ~,   221 be:] ~,   221SD *Exeunt.*] ~∧

5.2.

2 streames∧] ~,   4 *Babylon*] Babylon   6, 18, 21 *Tamburlaine*]
tamburlaine   8 him,] ~.   12 him.] ~∧   22 sustaine] sustaiue   24
seene∧] ~,   26 and] &   27 thee:] ~.   28 *Callapine*,] ~.   41 feete.]
~,   50 home:] *punctuation uncertain*   51 *Turkie*] Turkie

5.3.

OSD THERIDAMAS] T*heridamas*   1 THERIDAMAS] *not in O1.*   teares,] ~∧
4 earth,] ~.   38 Majesty,] Maisty.   41 plac'd.] ~∧   43 *Tamburlaine?*] ~,
47 soul.] ~,   50 Gods.] ~,   51 doe,] ~∧   53 *Tamburlaine.*] ~,
56 Why,] ~∧   paine?] ~,   60 fade.] ~,   61 *Theridamas*] *theridamas*
64 cease,] ~.   66, 76 *Techelles*] *techelles*   66 die.] ~,   74 carkasses.] ~,
76 stay:] ~,   78 potion,] ~.   89 spent,] ~.   95 spirit,] ~∧   107 med-
icine] medicince   115SD TAMBURLAINE] *Tamb.*   126 wantes.] ~,
140 *Zansibar.*] ~,   141 *Affrica*,] ~.   145 leagues.] ~,   157 bright]
kright   158 Sky:] ~,   160 life,] ~.   165 subjects,] ~.   166 incor-
porat] incorporoat   168 lives.] ~,   171 Must] must   180 die.] ~,
186 joy∧] ~,   190 Should] should   194 heaven,] ~.   229 slaves,] ~∧
234 *Ætna*] AEtna   250 and earth, and] & earth, &   end,] ~∧

COMMENTARY

In keeping with the practice established by Roma Gill in earlier volumes of the edition, annotation is predominantly factual rather than interpretative.

All verbal definitions are from *OED*. Where *OED* gives only a single definition no reference is specified. Where *OED* gives more than a single definition the number and, where necessary, letter of that used is given, thus: *OED* 1.a (first definition, first subsection). Where *OED* gives more than a single entry the reference also designates the part of speech and, where there is more than a single entry for the same part of speech, the superscript number, thus: *OED sb.*¹ 1.a (substantive, first entry, first definition, first subsection). Within the commentary on Part 1 references specify the Part only when Part 2 is intended; within the commentary on Part 2 references specify the Part only when Part 1 is intended. Thus in the commentary on Part 1, 5.1.20 means *One*, 5.1.20, and would be given in the latter form in the commentary on Part 2.

PART 1

Dramatis Personae

COSROE] The name can be pronounced with two syllables (1.1.1) or with three (1.1.169), as required by the metre.

CENEUS] Conj. Oxberry; the character appears in 1.1. and 2.1 only, and the stage directions and speech headings for this small role are inconsistent (see Apparatus, 1.1.135SD, 2.1.1SD1).

TAMBURLAINE] The historical Mongol Khan, Timur (1336–1405)—known, as the result of an injured right leg, arm, and hand, as Timur-i-Lenk ('the lame')—created an empire which stretched from modern Russia to India, from Persia to Afghanistan. He was a Moslem, famous as a conqueror, known for cruelty (the piles of severed heads with which he surrounded captured towns), and for magnificence, especially in the adornment and cultivation of his capital, Samarkand. He was particularly famous in sixteenth-century Europe for having raised the siege of Constantinople by the Ottoman Turkish ruler, Bayezid I, in 1402, since, by this, Eastern Christendom was saved for half a century. (The lameness which Marlowe ignored is mentioned by his sources, some of which connect it with Tamburlaine's name: see, for example, Thomas–Tydeman, 118, 124, 132). For modern accounts of Timur see Hilda Hookham,

Tamburlaine the Conqueror (London, 1962), and Dennis Wapman, *Tamerlane* (New York, 1987).

USUMCASANE] Usancasan is a later Persian king mentioned by Mexía (Thomas–Tydeman, 89).

BAJAZETH] Bayezid I, defeated by Timur-i-Lenk at Angora (Ankara) in 1402. He died (perhaps by suicide) in captivity in 1403.

FESSE] Marlowe used the maps of Abraham Ortelius (1527–98), whose *Theatrum orbis terrarum* was first published in 1570. Ortelius shows 'Fessa' as on the north coast of Africa, just east of the Straits of Gibraltar, in the region he calls 'Barbaria' (Barbary: cf. 3.1.1*n*.).

MOROCCO] Shown by Ortelius as to the south-west of 'Fessa', on the Atlantic coast of North Africa.

ARGIER] Ortelius shows 'Alger' as in North Africa to the east of 'Fessa', directly south of the border between Spain and France.

ALCIDAMUS] Accented on the second syllable (as at 1.2.78).

SOLDAN] Sultan.

AGYDAS] Accented on the second syllable (as at 3.2.85).

MAGNETES] Conj. Oxberry, by analogy with Mycetes; the speech headings (1.2.17 and 80) read only *Mag*.

Bassoes] Bashaws, pashas.

ZENOCRATE] Marlowe's sources make no mention of a special wife of the polygamous Timur. Like the character, the name was invented by Marlowe. J. S. Cunningham points out that its Greek elements (*zeno-kratos*) mean 'the power of Zeus'. *OED* registers 'zenocratically' as a nonce word, 1588 ('with the power or authority of Zeus').

ZABINA] Seaton[2] (p. 393) suggests that this may be Marlowe's attempt to give a Turkish inflection to the Greek form of the name or title of Bajazeth's wife, 'Despina'.

David Bevington shows how, by having some actors take two or three roles, the speaking parts could be performed by eleven men and four boys (*From 'Mankind' to Marlowe: Growth of Structure in the Popular Drama of Tudor England*, Cambridge, Mass., 1962, 205).

To the Gentlemen Readers

2 *Discourses*] written treatments of a subject in which it is handled at length (*OED sb.* 5). When entered in the Stationers' Register the plays were described as '*The twooe commicall discourses of TOMBERLEIN the Cithian shepparde*' (Edward Arber (ed.), *A Transcript of the Registers of the Company of Stationers of London* (London, 5 vols., 1875–94), ii. 558.

7–15 *omitted... historie*] See Introduction, v. (pp. xlix–l)

8 *fond*] foolish, silly (*OED a.* 2).

Jestures] *OED* records this only as an obsolete spelling of 'gestures', though Jones perhaps intended some variant of 'jests' (possibly with the suggestion that these involved low-comedy actions).

11 *happly*] perhaps, maybe.

vaine] foolish, thoughtless (*OED* 3).

conceited] having an intelligence, wit (of such a kind) (*OED ppl. a.* 1).

fondlings] foolish persons (*OED* 1).

12 *graced*] Either, endowed with grace, embellished (by the actors) (*OED ppl. a.*); or, shown favour (by the audience), applauded (*OED v.* 2).

17 *censures*] judgements, opinions (*OED sb.* 3).

19 *which*] '*them*' (l. 19), that is (ultimately), '*the two tragical Discourses*' (l. 2).

20 *travell*] travail; bodily or mental labour (*OED sb.*¹ 1).

21 *advauncing*] promotion, advancement (*OED vbl. sb.*).

pleasuring] pleasing, delectation (*OED* 1).

degree] position (in a scale of rank), station (*OED sb.* 4.a).

24 *R. J.*] Richard Jones; see Introduction, v. (p. l).

(Heading) *Discourses*] Cf. 'To the Gentlemen Readers', l. 2*n*.

Prologue

1 *jygging*] The context suggests a figurative meaning about verse— with a flat, over-emphatic, simple metre; also with reference to the comic entertainments given at the end, or during the intervals, of plays (*OED*, jig, *sb.*¹ 4).

vaines] styles of language (*OED*, 'vein', *sb.* 12).

riming] using rhyme to set off lame matter or metre (*OED*, first cited use).

mother wits] those who possess natural wit, that is (ironic) *only* natural wit—the uneducated.

2 *conceits*] mental capacities (*OED sb.* 2.b).

clownage] *OED*, earliest cited use.

5 *astounding*] shocking with surprise or wonder (*OED ppl. a.*, earliest cited use).

7 *tragicke*] Part 1 is not 'tragic' in any usual sense: Marlowe stresses the play's serious character, antithetical to the comedy dismissed in ll. 1–2.

1.1

2 insufficient] of inadequate ability, incompetent (*OED a.* 1).

7 mightie Conquerors] Cyrus the Great (reigned *c.*558–29 BC) founded the Persian empire and conquered Media, Lydia, and Babylonia. Cambyses (529–22 BC) conquered Egypt ('*Affrike*'). Darius I (522–486 BC) extended the empire into Scythia (modern south-eastern Russia).

11 freezing meteors] sleet, snow, hail (Heninger, 3–4); meteor (*OED* 1), any atmospheric phenomenon.

12 governed] Pronounced as two syllables (as though spelled 'govern'd').

13–14 *Cynthia ... Mercurie*] Cynthia (the moon) signifies vacillation, Saturn dullness and the feebleness of age. Jove and the sun signify kingliness, Mercury eloquence. All are cited on the common Elizabethan supposition that the position of the planets at a person's birth influenced his personality and fate. Johnstone Parr shows that the conjunction of Saturn and the moon was held to endow a person with weak mental faculties: *PQ* 25 (1946), 371–7.

15 influence] the supposed flowing or streaming from the stars or heavens of an ethereal fluid acting upon the character and destiny of men, and affecting sublunary things generally (*OED sb.* 2.a).

19 thorough] 'through' (*O3, Q*) is perhaps more likely, since there seems no reason for the metrical irregularity of *O1–2*.

Planets] astrological citations.

29 my ... grief] the grief which my mind entertains; conceive (*OED v.* 6), to take into the mind, to become affected or possessed with.

32 Passengers] travellers, wayfarers (*OED* 1.b); birds of passage (*OED* 5.a).

33 pull ... plumes] that is, rob me, dethrone me; proverbial (Dent, P441.1); *OED*, pull, *v.* 1, pluck (citing this example). After 'Foxe' the metaphor suggests that Mycetes is a goose, since geese were fattened on grain that lay in fields after reaping ('in ... harvest time').

36 Scythian] Ortelius (see Dramatis Personae, Fesse, *n.*) shows Scythia as on the northern shore of the Black Sea. The Scythians were at this time a branch of the Tartar race (Ellis-Fermor). Cf. l. 71*n.*

37 *Persepolis*] Ancient capital of Persia, modern Takht-e Jamshid, situated on the river Kor north-east of Shiraz.

38 Westerne Isles] 'possibly Britain, or the West Indies' (J. S. Cunningham). But the islands of the Aegean and North Mediterranean

('western', from the viewpoint of the Persian empire) accord better with any probable geography, as well as approach 'by land'.

39 confines] territories (*OED sb.*² 2); accented on the first syllable.

40 incivill] uncivil, barbarous (*OED* 3, citing this example only); Abbott (402) gives examples of in- for modern un- (incharitable, infortunate).

45 vagrant] not fixed or stationary, moving hither and thither (*OED* 5, earliest cited use).

49 like . . . selfe] to do (etc.) like oneself was proverbial (Dent, O64.01); cf. l. 107 and *Dido*, 2.1.100.

50 *Damon*] The beloved friend of Pythias (Cicero, *De officiis*, III, x. 45). The pair were the classical examplars of friendship for the Elizabethans (see e.g. *The Faerie Queene*, IV.x.27). If, like most Renaissance writers (even those widely read in classical literature, such as Jonson and Milton), Marlowe used mythological dictionaries, he would be most likely to have used Thomas Cooper's *Thesaurus Linguae Romanae et Britannicae* (1565, with four reprintings to 1587), one section of which was a 'Dictionarium historicum & poeticum propria locorum & personarum vocabula breviter complectens'. Cooper's *Thesaurus* was the most widely recognized authority on its subject in late-sixteenth-century England: see DeWitt T. Starnes and Ernest W. Gilbert, *Classical Myth and Legend in Renaissance Dictionaries* (Chapel Hill, 1955), who note that Cooper was particularly recommended by Archbishop Parker, the patron of Marlowe's Cambridge scholarship (15–16). Cooper's entry on Damon and Pythias illustrates the *Thesaurus*'s scope and method.

Two philosophers of Pythagoras his secte, in the league of frendshyppe beyng eche to other moste faythfull. For when Dionyse the tyranne of Syracuse, had condemned the one of them to death, and he had required certayne dayes respite to goe home and dispose such thynges as he had: the other became suertie for him on this condition, that if his frinde retourned not, he would be content to suffer death for him. But when he at the daye appointed according to his promyse did retourne: the tyranne wondryng at their faythfulnesse, pardoned the offender, and requested that he might be received as thirde into their knotte and league of amitie.

Other dictionaries which Marlowe would know from Cambridge, for example that of Robert Stephanus (1531), cited (as Cooper did not) principal classical sources for their accounts.

52 incontinent] immediately (*OED adv.*).

54 like] *OED v.*¹ 6.f, earliest cited use 1596.

61 foiles] overthrows, defeats (*OED v.*¹ 4); with a play (suggested by 'legges' and the opposition to 'holds . . . up') on the sense to tread underfoot, trample down (*OED v.*¹ 1).

66 Sir] title applied retrospectively to noble persons of ancient history, typically in medieval romance (*OED sb.* 2). Cf. *Faustus*, A-text, 12.13, 'when sir *Paris* crost the seas with her' (Helen).

the Grecian Dame] Helen, whose abduction by the Trojan prince, Paris, from her Greek husband, Menelaus, was the cause of the Trojan war.

67–8 time . . . fraile] Proverbial sentiments to which there are analogues, though nothing precisely similar, in Tilley (T323/327, F363 ('Flesh is frail').

69 borrowed light] reflected light (*OED*, borrow, *v.*¹ 2.a; example from 1834). That the moon reflected light from the sun was known in antiquity (see Plutarch, *De facie in orbe lunae*, 16).

71 Tartarian] of or pertaining to Tartary and its people (*OED adj.* B), with a play on sense *a.*² (= Tartarean *a.*¹), pertaining to Tartarus, infernal (first cited use, 1623).

74 thy . . . swords] Cf. Tilley W839, 'Words hurt (cut) more than swords'.

89 Prorex] deputy king, viceroy (*OED*, earliest cited use).

Assiria] The metrical irregularity of *O1–3* ('*Affrica*') is corrected by Q ('all *Affrica*'), but the emendation '*Assiria*' (van Dam) both corrects the metre and helps the sense: creating Menaphon viceroy of Africa can do nothing to win hearts in Babylon. Cf. l. 164 and *Two*, 5.1.165*n*.

90–1 Persean government] Cyrus the Great captured Babylon in 539 BC.

95 *Asia*] Pronounced as three syllables (as also at l. 112 and elsewhere).

97 my . . . seat] his throne. In Cosroe's retort (alluding to kissing any sacred object by which one swears) there is a play on 'seat', the sitting part of the body, the posteriors (*OED sb.* 9.a), though *OED* gives 1607 as the first cited use of this sense, and 1701 for the contemptuous expression which a punning sense presupposes (*OED*, 'kiss', *v.* 6.l).

99 state] rank, status (*OED sb.* 15.a).

104 Monster] a misshapen birth, an abortion (*OED A.sb.* 2).

107 mated] confounded, amazed (*OED ppl. a.*¹).

109 passe] care for, regard (*OED v.* 23.d).

111 Medean] See ll. 162–5*n*.

113 excruciate] torture mentally, inflict extreme mental anguish upon (*OED v.* 2, earliest cited use).

114 substance] vital part (*OED* 12).

117 sits . . . laughs] The third person singular form of the verb with a plural subject was not uncommon in Elizabethan English. See Abbott (333).

regiment] government, authority (*OED sb.* 1).

118 resolve] melt, dissolve (*OED v.* 1).

119 Equinoctiall line] terrestrial equator (*OED* B. *sb.* 2), the farthest point on which, relevant to an invasion of eastern India, would be Ortelius's 'Malaca' (Malaya) and the East Indian islands Java, Borneo, and Sumatra.

120 *Inde*] a form Marlowe uses elsewhere (for example *Ed. II*, 4.50), and which is more regular metrically than *o1*'s '*India*'. cf. 5.1.518.

121 Lading] loading (*OED* 1).

123 intreat] persuade by pleading (*OED*, entreat, *v.* 10).

126 Emperie] territory ruled by an emperor, or by any absolute or powerful ruler (*OED sb.* 2)—Marlowe's preferred form of 'empire' (as in *Jew*, Prol., 19).

128 continent to] connected with (*OED a.* 6.b); see *Doctor Faustus* (A text), 3. 108—the earliest instance cited in *OED*.

130 *Cyrus*] Cyrus the Great conquered the Greek cities of Asia Minor, but the Persians actually attempted to conquer Greece itself under Darius I (defeated at Marathon, 490 BC) and Xerxes I (defeated at Salamis, 480 BC).

134 my Lord,] See Apparatus: a form of address to Cosroe, not a title of Ortygius.

135SD *Crowne*] Not Mycetes' crown, which he retains (2.4). Cosroe's triumph is symbolized by his uniting that (at 2.5.1) with the usurped crown he now accepts.

137 states] persons of high rank, princes (*OED sb.* 24).

145 Crestes] crest (*OED sb.*¹ 4), the apex or 'cone' of a helmet.

150 stay] stop (*OED v.*¹ 20.a).

151 invest . . . Emperour] 'invest' with a noun as indirect object is a construction not recorded by *OED* (Ando, 75).

153–4 Macedonians . . . *Darius*] Alexander the Great defeated Darius III at Issus (333 BC). Plutarch mentions the richness of the spoils in his *Life of Alexander*.

155 state] the condition of the country with regard to its welfare and polity (*OED sb.* 27).

159 malice] seek or desire to injure (*OED v.* 1).

162–5 *Asia . . . Parthia*] Ancient Media lay west, Albania south-west, and Parthia south-east of the Caspian Sea, and Armenia lay adjacent to the Black Sea. Assyria and Mesopotamia lay between the rivers Tigris and Euphrates. In the maps of Ortelius the Persian Empire extends into modern Afghanistan and Pakistan. Cosroe becomes monarch of an area extending from the Black Sea to India. On '*Assiria*', see l. 89*n.* above.

162 *Persea*] Pronounced as three syllables.

166 the . . . Isles] F. D. Hoeniger (in J. S. Cunningham) suggests islands in the region of Indonesia discovered by Drake during his circumnavigation. (Jump's suggestion of the West Indies fits neither the logic of Ortygius' geography nor any plausible extent of the Persian empire.)

167 *Euxine*] Roman 'Pontus Euxinus', the Black Sea.

168 ever . . . Lake] The Caspian Sea's storms were notorious: see e.g. Horace, *Odes*, 2.ix.1–3 (the comparison is between unmitigated fixity and the temporary flux found in even the most apparently permanent conditions): 'Non semper . . . mare Caspium / vexant inaequales procellae' ('Not always . . . do rough tempests violently toss the Caspian Sea').

169 Long . . . Emperour] That *O3* (and *Q*) assigns this line to '*All*' may reflect an early (and effective) stage practice of repeating Ortygius' acclamation.

170 *Jove* may] may Jove (see *OED*, may, *v.*^{1} B. 8.b, citing this as the first example).

171 gratifie] requite (*OED v.* 1).

180 investion] the action of investing (*OED*, earliest cited use); pronounced as four syllables. Dobson (276) shows that one- and two-syllable pronunciations of the suffixes -ion / -ian were possible in the period. Marlowe accommodates pronunciation to the demands of the metre. Variations from modern norms are noted throughout.

182–3 too exasperate / To] so exasperated as to; too, (as an intensive) extremely, exceedingly (*OED adv.* 3); exasperate, enraged, incensed (*OED* A. *pa.pple.*, in sense of *v.* 6).

186 In spite of] in defiance of, notwithstanding (*OED*, spite, *sb.* 5.a).

I.2

3 reserv'd] kept in store (*OED v.*^{1} 9.a); cf. *Doctor Faustus* (B text), III.ii.47.

better state] a more prosperous condition (*OED*, state, *sb.* 6.a).

10 rapine] plunder, pillage.

silly] helpless, defenceless (*OED* A.a. 1.a).

11 Medean] Accented on the second syllable (but '*Medea*', l.12, is accented on the first).

12 of *Medea*] *Medea*: accented on the first syllable. The metre of the line is irregular. C. Brennan, *Beiblatt zur Anglia*, 16 (1905), 207–9 (208) suggests that 'of Medea' be dropped, and (citing *2HVI*, 1.1.206) that 'country' be pronounced as trisyllabic—but *OED*'s spellings offer no support for this. It is possible to elide 'of', though such a harsh elision would be unusual in Marlowe; 'my uncles country, *Medea*' would retain the sense and restore the metre.

13 governed] looked after (*OED v.* 6).

15 hand] signature (*OED sb.* 17).

16 *Affrica*] '?i.e. (full extent of) Turkish empire' (Pendry–Maxwell). Cf. 3.3.202, 221, and *Two*, 3.2.124*n*.

18 Cham] ruler of Tartary (an obsolete form of Khan).

24 conduct] (permission) granted to ensure safe passage (*OED sb.*[1] 2).

28 precinct] province over which a person has jurisdiction (*OED sb.* 3); accented on the second syllable.

29 they] i.e. the 'prizes'; not 'they that help . . . are friends': wealth is prelusive to the human assistance it attracts.

weane] 'assist the growth of' (J. S. Cunningham). Noting that *OED* does not record this sense of 'wean', Cunningham compares the senses of 'wean to' recorded in *OED* 5.

state] greatness, power (*OED sb.* 16.b).

33 import] imply, indicate (*OED v.* 5.a) (yourself to be).

35 shepheard . . . Parentage] The historical Timur claimed descent from Genghis Khan, but Marlowe's sources present him as of obscure parentage (see Mexía, Whetstone, and Perondinus in Thomas–Tydeman, 83, 93, 97). Cf. *Doctor Faustus* [A-text], Prologue, 11.

37 *Asia*] Cf. 1.1.95*n*.

39 Emperie] Cf. 1.1.126*n*.

40 *Phoebus*] Apollo, the sun; Tamburlaine plans to rule the whole world.

41 Lie . . . weare] The line is given to Juniper (a cobbler) in Jonson's *The Case is Altered* (1597; 1.1.23). Critics disagree on the stage business here, some supposing that Tamburlaine should take off his shepherd's outer garments to reveal the armour he is already wearing (see e.g.

Clifford Leech, *Christopher Marlowe: Poet for the Stage*, New York, 1986, 51), others that he should, after taking off his shepherd's clothes, cere- monially don armour just captured from Zenocrate's company (see e.g. Roger Sales, *Christopher Marlowe*, New York, 1991, 55). The imitation in Jonson indicates that the line became well-known, and this may favour the supposition that it was marked by the more elaborate stage business of divesting and re-costuming. On this view, the audience first sees Tamburlaine actually occupying the low social position from which he begins his career (as advertised by the title page of *O1*: 'Who, from a Scythian Shephearde...'), and then watches his first quasi-actorly piece of self-fashioning (by dressing the part, beginning to become the lord his deeds will prove him to be).

weedes] garments (*OED sb.*^{2} 1).

42 compleat] Accented on the first syllable.

curtle-axe] broad cutting sword (a variant of 'cutlass').

45 successe] upshot, result (*OED* 1.a).

unvallued] extremely great (*OED* 1, first cited use).

47 silly] of humble rank or state, lowly (*OED* A.*a*. 3.b).

49 their waight... quake] Seaton[4] (21–2) suggests romance analogies for this hyperbole.

50–51 windy... tilt] Heninger (128) quotes Arthur Golding, *A Discourse upon the Earthquake* (London, 1580): 'Earthquakes are sayde to be gendred by winds goten into the bowels of the earth... where by their stryving and struggling of themselves to get oute... they shake the earth for want of sufficient vent to issue out at'.

50 exhalations] Pronounced as five syllables.

51 tilt] thrust with violence (*OED v.*^{1} 6.c).

62 distempered] mentally disordered, insane (*OED ppl. a.*^{1} 3.b, first cited use 1594).

64 conceit] conception, thought (*OED sb.* 1).

65 Affecting] aiming at, aspiring to (*OED*, affect, *v.*^{1} 1).

69 driftes] schemes, plots (*OED sb.* 5).

70 passengers] cf. 1.1.32*n*. (first meaning only).

71 admit] grant (*OED v.* 2.a).

72 eternized] made perpetually famous (*OED*, eternize, 3; first cited use 1610).

75 to... liberties] for our liberties; see Abbott (186).

87 the Love of *Jove*] Juno.

88 Rhodope] A mountain range in Thrace. Ellis-Fermor cites Nicolas de Nicolay, *The Navigations, Peregrinations and Voyages, made into Turkie* (1576, trans. T. Washington the Younger, London, 1585), Book I, ch. i (sig. A1^r): 'the height and sharpnesse of the mount Rhodope vulgarly called the mountes of silver, because of the silver mynes that there are found'. The uncorrected error of the early texts suggests that this vulgar appellation may have been obscure.

92 at my birth] Perondinus assumes that Tamburlaine was born under an auspicious conjunction of stars (Thomas–Tydeman, 118); Marlowe frequently reverts to the theme.

94 *Pegasus*] Winged horse of Greek and Roman mythology.

96 Enchast] embroidered with gems (*OED v.*^{2} 2—though *OED* refers only to setting precious metals with gems, as, elsewhere, does Marlowe: e.g. 2.5.60; *Two*, 1.2.49).

97 valurous] valuable (*OED* cites only this instance). Ellis-Fermor compares 'valourous' in the sense 'worthy'. Cf. 4.4.126*n*.

98 sled] sledge or sleigh (*OED sb.*^{1} 2.a; first cited use of this sense).

101 resolv'd] melted, dissolved (*OED ppl.a.* 5); cf. 1.1.118*n*.

103 fiftie... *Vuolgas*] The numerous tributaries of the Volga are clearly shown in Ortelius.

104 all we] all of us; cf. John 1: 16 (Geneva and Bishops' Bible), 'of his fulnesse have all we received'; and *Hamlet*, 2.2.150–1, 'Into the madnes wherein now he raues, / And all we waile for'. (That *O2* has 'Shall we', and *Q* 'We all shall', suggests that the usage was unusual.) Comparing 'Both we' at 1.2.196, J. S. Cunningham glosses 'all of these we shall'; but 'Both we' (meaning 'Both of us') supports the sense 'all of us', and his gloss assumes a usage without parallel.

119 Soft] an exclamation with imperative force, used to enjoin silence or deprecate haste (*OED, adv.* 8.a).

127 exceeding] exceedingly (*OED ppl. a.* B).

brave] splendid, grand (*OED A.a.* 2).

129 play the Orator] A set phrase (Dent, O74.1).

133 top] This emendation in *Q* has been widely adopted. Bowers retains *O1–3* 'foot' without comment. Ellis-Fermor retains it on the grounds that 'a mountain top was no place to meet an opposing army' and 'most mountains have foothills'—which explains why the emendation is necessary. *OED* gives no support for taking 'foot' to mean 'foothill' ('foot' is therefore inconsistent with l. 135), and offering to dare the course most militarily difficult is exactly Usumcasane's proposition.

138 Males] bags (*OED*, mail, *sb.*^{3} 1).

139 wedges] ingots (*OED sb.* 3).

144 possession] Pronounced as four syllables.

146 lanch] cut, slit (*OED*, launch, *v.* 1).

150 all] all of you.

standings] stations (*OED vbl.sb.* 4, citing this example).

151 brunt] assault, charge (*OED sb.*[1] 2).

156 furniture] equipment of body and mind (*OED* 2.a).

158–9 His . . . Stratageme] Citing *Iliad*, III. 216 (Odysseus), and *Metamorphoses*, XIII. 2–4 and 124–6 (Ajax and Ulysses), J. S. Cunningham reports J. C. Maxwell's suggestion that merged here with an Herculean image of heroic anger are classical instances of a conventional brooding posture prior to a rhetorical outburst.

160 *Avernus*] lake in southern Italy near the cave of the Cumaean Sybil through which Aeneas entered the Underworld (Virgil, *Aeneid*, VI); hence a name for Hades itself.

161 And] Bowers was the first to prefer this catchword reading (the last word of sig. A8[v]) to the text's 'To', on the grounds that when the compositor began setting B1 he would read over some preceding text, and it is easier to explain 'To pull' as by contamination with 'to pierce' (l. 160) than to explain a catchword error. Craik (this edn.) suggests the possibility of a missing line ('vaults / And . . . / To pull'), pointing to the analogy with *Two*, 2.4.98–100.

triple . . . dog] Cerberus, guardian of the entrance to the Underworld. It was one of the labours of Hercules to fetch Cerberus from Hades. There are numerous references to the story in writers Marlowe knew, e.g. Ovid, *Metamorphoses*, VII. 409 ff.

163 habit] appearance (*OED sb.* 1.e).

judge] is a test or criterion of (*OED v.* 9.b, citing this example only).

164 affections] emotions (*OED a.* 2.a).

passionate] Perhaps inclined to pity, compassionate (*OED a.* 5.b): Techelles agrees with Tamburlaine's estimate ('mild'), and suggests an explanation. But, comparing *Ed.II*, 17.55 (also a comment on an aside), Craik (this edn.) suggests that 'make him passionate' means 'cause him to show deep feeling' (*OED*, passionate, *a.* 2). On either reading the line is a comment on Theridamas' silence during which (as his preceding speech indicates) he is struggling to come to terms with surprise.

166 *Persea*] Cf. 1.1.162*n*.

169 Characters] figurative use of the literal sense, 'distinctive marks' (*OED sb.* 1.b, earliest cited use); accented on the second syllable. Cf. 2.1.3*n.*

170 stout] resolute, defiant (*OED a.* 4.c).

aspect] expression of face (*OED sb.* 10, earliest cited use); accented on the second syllable.

174 the Fates] The Greek Moirai, Roman Parcae: three sisters (Clotho, Lachesis, and Atropos) who govern the courses of destiny. On some views even the gods are subject to their decrees.

175 Fortunes wheel] Cf. 5.1.374–5 and *Two*, 3.4.52. Fortune's wheel was a conventional Elizabethan emblem of her mutability. Various of Marlowe's sources stress that Tamburlaine was never deserted by Fortune (see e.g. Thomas–Tydeman, 106, 128).

176 Spheare] one of the concentric hollow globes of pre-Copernican astronomy supposed to be revolving round the earth, each carrying one of the planets (*OED* 2.a).

179 rase] scratch, cut (*OED v.*^{1} 1).

184 grounded] strongly founded, firmly established (*OED ppl. a.*^{1} 1.a).

187 portly] dignified, majestic (*OED*, citing this example).

Emperesse] Pronounced as three syllables.

188 renowmed] A form which reflects the derivation, ultimately from L. (*re-*, again, *nomen*, a name); so spelt throughout.

189 conduct] guidance, leading (*OED sb.*^{1} 1); here accented on the second syllable.

194 Merchants] trading vessels (*OED A.sb.* 4, citing this example).

stems] stem, the curved upright bow of a ship (*OED sb.*^{2} 2, citing this example), used metonymically for the whole ship. But Craik (this edn.), taking 'merchant' in its usual sense, suggests that the line means 'Christian merchants sailing in Russian ships'.

196 vaile] lower the sail [as an act of homage] (*OED v.*^{2} 9).

199 masked] disguised himself (*OED v.*^{4} 1.b, earliest example 1847, though the earliest citation for 'mask' as a substantive meaning 'disguise' is 1577 (*sb.*^{3} 2.a). Jove appeared as a shepherd to Mnemosyne (*Metamorphoses*, VI. 114).

weed] clothing (*OED, sb.*^{2} 2).

200 that] by means of which. Prepositions are not uncommonly omitted in Elizabethan English (Abbott, 200), and the omission here avoids repetition of 'by'; 'that' for 'which' is common.

204 admyre] wonder, marvel at (*OED v.* 2).

206 *Boreas*] The north wind.

brazen] as strong as brass (*OED a.* 1.b).

207 *Boötes*] a northern constellation, the Wagoner; also called Arcturus, the Bear (*OED*'s first citation is 1656).

208 Competitor] associate, partner (*OED* 2).

209 And ... majestie] An alexandrine: on Marlowe's occasional use of these (and other aspects of his versification and style) see C. F. Tucker Brooke, *SP* 19 (1922), 186–205.

210 *Hermes*] Messenger of the gods, and god of eloquence.

Prolocutor] spokesman (often with a specialized legal sense of 'advocate').

211 patheticall] moving, affecting (*OED*, = pathetic, *a.* 1).

212 *Apollos* Oracles] As god of the sun, and so identified with light penetrating darkness, Apollo was god of many oracles, of which that at Delphi was the most famous.

213 vaunts] boasts, brags (*OED sb.*[1] 3).

substantiall] of solid worth (*OED a.* 10); pronounced as four syllables.

215 present] immediately available (*OED a.* 5.a).

to our state] in addition to our present rank (*OED*, to, A.*prep.* 15; state, *sb.* 15.a).

217 assured] pronounced as two syllables (as though spelled 'assur'd'). Similarly at l. 219, where 'conquestes' is accented on the second syllable.

222 fearfull] frightened (*OED* 3, citing this example).

confesse] acknowledge, concede (*OED* 2).

224–5 What ... Scythians?] Various emendations have been proposed in these two lines, the smallest of which is that adopted here. There is no punctuation at the end of l. 224 in *O1*, but 'soule' had to be squeezed in on the line above, and there is little room for punctuation—circumstances in which omission is not unusual. Oxberry emended 'Are' to 'To'. Brooke (following the conjecture of J. Le Gay Brereton, *Beiblatt zur Anglia*, 16 (1905), 203–7) emended 'Are' to 'Ah'. Both emendations give good sense, but 'Are' is (as Seaton[3] pointed out, p. 469) corroborated by the catchword. Bullen proposes a transposition: 'These are resolved'. Albert S. Cook, *MLN* 21 (1906), 112–13 conjectures 'to' for 'tice' (entice)—but, though this also gives a good sense, a common word is unlikely to have been mistaken for an unusual one. Bowers retains *O1* (punctuating as here), taking the sense to be 'are these not mere shepherds, as I had believed, but instead noble and resolved Scythian warriors whom I should join?' J. S. Cunningham retains *O1*, italicizing '*Scythians*', to express 'astonishment that, of all people, *Scythians* should prove dignified and resolute'. No emendation, and no construction of the text as it stands here, is entirely satisfactory. Bowers proposes the best solution.

225 resolved] resolute (*OED ppl. a.* 4, earliest cited use).

236 Elements] the constituents of all material bodies in ancient and medieval philosophy: earth, water, air, and fire (*OED sb.* 1.a).

237 aspire] either seek to attain (*OED* 3); or mount up to, reach (*OED* 8). Ellis-Fermor notes the reminiscence of Ecclesiastes 12: 7.

243 *Pyllades ... Orestes*] Pylades was the companion of Orestes who assisted him in the killing of his mother, Clytemnestra (in revenge for the murder of his father, Agamemnon), and who accompanied him through the expiatory sufferings which followed. These included an expedition to Tauris in Scythia where, when captured, they offered to die on each other's behalf. Their friendship was proverbial (as in Marlowe's translation, *All Ovids Elegies*, II.6.15–16). L. J. Mills traces a likely source for the idea that they were worshipped in Scythia to a standard text of the Elizabethan grammar schools, Erasmus' translation of Lucian's dialogue *Toxaris*, *MLN* 52 (1937), 101–3. B. P. Fisher elaborates the point, *N&Q*, n.s., 34 (1987), 190–1.

244 statutes] statues (*OED sb.* 7).

245 them] J. S. Cunningham compares *King John*, 4.2.50–1, 'Your safety: for the which, my selfe and them / Bend their best studies'; the usage is apparently unusual—this is the only example in Abbott (214)— though it occurs again at l. 249 ('thee' for 'thou', 'them' for 'they').

246 *Asia*] Cf. 1.1.95*n.*

249–50 Nor ... pierc'd] 'neither to you nor to them ... shall my heart be found lacking' (Jump) (see *OED*, want, *v.* 1.a).

254–6 me / ... be / ... slaverie] A triple rhyme.

255 honors] Ellis-Fermor's recording of this word in (the Huntington copy of) *O1* as 'herors' is incorrect: the word is poorly printed, but does read 'honors'.

257 happie] fortunate (*OED a.* 3). J. S. Cunningham points out that the word is applied to Tamburlaine repeatedly.

2.1

1 Thus farre] Already aware of the defection of Theridamas (ll. 35–9), Cosroe is on his way from Persepolis (see 1.1.37*n.*) to join with Ther-

idamas and Tamburlaine, now his allies (see 1.1.176–7), at the River Araris (see l. 63*n*.) to the west of the Black Sea.

3 forhead] Cf. Tamburlaine's comment on Theridamas, 1.2.169. Ellis-Fermor refers this to the Islamic 'belief in the secret signs of destiny which Allah writes upon every man's forehead'.

5 that] thou that: Abbott (399).

6 wields] owns, possesses (*OED v.* 2, citing this example).

7–30] Ellis-Fermor points out that this description, the emblematic quality of which is pointed up by Cosroe's response, draws little from the sources: except in details of a not very specific kind it is Marlowe's invention.

8 lift] lifted (an obsolete form of the past participle).

10 mainely] mightily, vigorously (*OED*, citing this example).

11 *Atlas*] One of the Titans who, for having made war on Zeus, was condemned to carry the heavens.

pitch] shoulders (*OED sb.*² 16, first cited use).

12 pearle] i.e. his head. Cornelius (p. 146) remarks the reminiscence of Matt. 13: 46.

15–17 Whose . . . throne] Tamburlaine's glowing eyes seem to contain a tutelary arrangement of planets and stars propitious to his gaining power.

21 in foldes] furrowed.

figure] image, symbolize (*OED v.* 6).

23–24 Amber . . . curles] Homer gives Achilles a colour of hair which Chapman renders as both yellow and golden (*Iliad*, 1. 197, XXIII. 141). Achilles has curls in Chapman (1. 200).

26 wanton] unrestrained (*OED a.* 3.c).

27 sinowy] Dyce's emendation 'sinowy' (sinewy) is clearly correct. Sinews is spelt 'sinowes' elsewhere in *O1* (*One*, 4.4.103, *Two*, 2.2.9 and 3.1.11), and Marlowe uses 'sinewy' in *Hero* 371 (*O1* 'sinowie') and *All Ovids Elegies*, 1.1.27.

31 pourtraid] vividly described (*OED v.* 4, citing this example).

tearms of life] lively manner of expression (*OED*, life, *sb.* 4.a). Pendry–Maxwell suggest 'lifelike terms', Bevington–Rasmussen 'lifelike description': these suit the context, but there is no warrant for them in *OED*.

34 accomplisht] fulfilled, perfected (*OED ppl. a.* 1).

37 pinch] critical juncture (*OED sb.* 4.a).

38 With ... life] Offering (implicitly) as reasons his own boldness and general conduct (*OED*, life, III). J. S. Cunningham suggests, for 'life', 'under threat of sudden death'; but this is grammatically strained (the first 'his' must refer to Tamburlaine, the second to Theridamas), not consistent with what Cosroe is admiring (Tamburlaine's persuasive powers), and not what the audience saw.

41 compasse] range (*OED sb.*¹ 9.a).

42 straight] strait, narrow.

port] gateway (*OED sb.*³ 1.a). Cosroe conceives of his brother's body as a walled town under siege, in which the heart (of central importance to the whole) is a palace. Ellis-Fermor points out the closeness of the phraseology to Matt. 7: 14.

48 *Persea*] Cf. 1.1.162*n*. The metre here and elsewhere suggests that the word should be pronounced with three syllables, here (unusually) with the stress on the second.

59 stuft] well provided (*OED ppl. a.* 1.a).

for] with the purpose of gratifying (*OED* 16.a).

60 such] i.e. both followers and rewards.

63 *Araris*] Marlowe also mentions a River Araris in *Lucans First Booke* (ll. 434–5) where 'swift *Rhodanus* / Drives *Araris* to sea', that is, the Rhone is a tributary, and so, of possible rivers, the lines must refer to the Saône. In *Tamburlaine* Marlowe must intend a river in the Caspian Sea area, either the Ararus in Scythia, listed in several Renaissance diction-aries (Don Cameron Allen, *TLS*, 24.9.1931), or the Araxes (modern Araks) in Armenia. This ancient river is not shown on Ortelius's maps of the contemporary world, but it is listed in his 'Nomenclator Ptole-maicus' as one of the two rivers of Armenia Major (1584 edn., sig. e4ʳ). Marlowe could have known the name from this or from many classical sources, but that the river is also mentioned by Perondinus (Thomas–Tydeman, 99) makes it altogether the more probable. J. Oliver Thom-son, *MLR* 48 (1953), 323–4, explains Marlowe's transformation of the name as resulting from a probable misunderstanding of Virgil (*Eclogues*, I. 61–2). Cf. 2.3.15–16*n*. (That Herodotus, invoked there, mentions the Araxes, offers no help, since he confuses under that name different rivers.)

65 *Parthia*] South-east of the Caspian Sea.

2.2

Location: the remainder of Act II takes place 'neer to *Parthia*' (2.1.65 and *n*.). Marlowe is vague about the geography, perhaps because his material is not historical. Both armies have apparently marched east through Armenia and Media and are now in the foothills of Georgia (l. 15), that is, at the eastern tip of the Caspian Sea.

1 geere] matter, business (*OED* 11.c, where the examples indicate that the tone is colloquial).

3–4 On . . . of] Both can be used interchangeably to mean 'about', 'concerning' (Abbott, 174, 181).

5 abusde] wronged or deceived (*OED*, *ppl. a.* 2 or 3).

8 scalde] scurvy, contemptible (*OED a.*[1] 2.a).

10 *Aurora*] Goddess of the dawn.

13 have said] have finished speaking (*OED*, say, *v.*[1] 3.e); a set phrase (Dent, S118.1).

18 straight] immediately, without delay (*OED* C.*adv.* 2.a).

22 outragious] violent (*OED* 2); excessive in cruelty (*OED* 3).

27 false] break, violate (*OED v.* 4.a).

31, 33 *Albania . . . Medea*] Cf. 1.1.162–5*n*.

34 Beside] in addition to, as well as (*OED* B.*prep.* 2).

spoile] spoliation (*OED sb.* 2.a).

35 Spials] spies, scouts (*OED* 2).

40 champion] level and open (*OED*, champian, B.*a.* 1).

42 Which] Who (Abbott, 265), i.e. the horsemen.

45 greedy] greedily pursued (*OED* 5, citing this example).

47–8 Like . . . venomous] Having slain the dragon which guarded the well of Ares, Cadmus, on the advice of Athena, sowed its teeth in the earth. Armed men grew from them and attacked each other. All but five were killed. The story is told in Ovid, *Metamorphoses*, III. 1–130. (On the not uncommon noun–adjective transposition, 'Dragons venomous', see Abbott, 419.)

49 carelesse] wielded negligently or wildly (*OED* 4.a).

lanch] Cf. 1.2.146*n*.

54 toy] a thing of little or no value, a trifle (*OED sb.* 5) (here, unusually, commendatory).

56 jewell] Often applied figuratively to a person or thing of great worth (*OED sb.* 3).

58 wit] intellectual ability, cleverness (*OED sb.* 5.a).

59–67 to intrap . . . slaves] Kocher (247–8) quotes a sixteenth-century translation of the *Stratagems* of Frontinus which recommends this device, and cites its repetition in three other works, the last being Barnabe Rich's *A Path-Way to Military Practice* (1587).

60 confounded] confused (*OED ppl. a.* 1).

63 souldiers] Pronounced as three syllables; see Dobson (276).

69 slaughtered] Pronounced as two syllables (as though spelt 'slaughter'd').

71 *Persea*] Cf. 1.1.162*n*.

2.3

2 approoved] proved or established by experience (*OED ppl. a.* 1.a).

5 doome] judgement, especially one formally pronounced (*OED sb.* 2).

for satisfaction] as carrying complete conviction (*OED* 6.a, earliest cited use); satisfaction pronounced with five syllables.

8 roialise] render famous, celebrate (*OED v.* 1.b, earliest cited use).

11–12 sway ... direction] sway, have a preponderating influence (*OED v.* 11); to, with a view to (Abbott, 186); direction, guidance, instruction (*OED* 1.c; cf. l. 29): hence 'take some degree of overall command'.

15–17 The host ... handful] Cf. on Xerxes 1.1.130*n.*, and on the Araris 2.1.63*n.* For the legend that Xerxes led against Greece an army so vast that it drank rivers dry Ellis-Fermor refers to Herodotus, VII. 21. (Herodotus mentions the Araris, but not in this connection.) Marlowe is more likely to have known this fantasy from a joke about Greek lying in Juvenal (*Satires*, X. 177–8). In Marlowe's sources Tamburlaine's army is often compared for size to that of Xerxes; see Thomas–Tydeman (86, 94, 105).

21 Cyclopian warres] Perhaps following Hesiod (*Theogony*, 139–44), Marlowe identifies the Cyclopes (in Homer a race of one-eyed giants) with the Titans, sons of Uranus who made war unsuccessfully against Zeus. (*OED*'s first cited use of 'Cyclopian' is 1641).

25 woorking] effective (*OED ppl. a.* 1.b, earliest cited use).

26 top] surpass, outdo (*OED v.*[1] 12.b, earliest cited use). Oxberry's conjecture has been accepted by almost all editors.

27 stay] cease (from a specified activity) (*OED v.*[1] 2); that is, you will not be able to find words adequate to express his worth.

29 turning ... direction] putting my thousand horsemen under his command.

31 thrust] make one's way against obstacles (*OED v.* 3.a). This, the reading of *O1–3*, is evidently correct. Dyce's emendation of *Q*'s 'thrist' to

'thirst' gives a Marlovian sense, but is based on a simple compositor's error.

33 and] Brereton (94) defends *O1* (see Apparatus): 'Techelles politely disclaims any intention of presuming to claim terms of friendship; he and his companions are bound in duty to pay their utmost service to Cosroe'. This is indeed a way of making sense of *O1*'s reading, but the more obvious possible construction—that Techelles offers his service only grudgingly—makes it improbable.

37 she . . . gates] Nemesis, goddess of destiny, called '*Rhamnusia*' (as at *Two* 3.4.57) after her sanctuary at Rhamnus in Attica (described by Pausanias, *Attica*, XXXIII). Ellis-Fermor cites references to Rhamnusia in Ovid, *Tristia*, V. viii. 9, and *Metamorphoses*, III. 406 (also XIV. 694). The spelling '*Rhamnis*' is without parallel, and may be a compositorial error.

40 meeds] merits (*OED sb.* 3).

41 roomes] offices, situations (*OED sb.*[1] 12.a); since Cosroe is promising offices of rule it may also be relevant that the word could mean 'dominions, territories' (*OED sb.*[1] 7.a, *obs.*, last cited use 1570).

48 *Caspea*] The Caspian Sea.

49 discovered the enemie] discovered, descried, espied (*OED v.* 8.c). Marlowe may have intended a double elision, 'discover'd th'enemie', without which the metre is defective; 'descried' (conj. Craik, this edn.) would be metrically smoother.

55 Cutle-axe] an uncommon variant form of 'curtal-axe'; cf. 1.2.42n. Perhaps, as Bowers suggests, simply an error for 'curtle-axe' (the form elsewhere in the play).

57 These . . . wings] It is natural to stress 'These', implying some extension of Cosroe's 'winged' (l. 51). Craik (this edn.) suggests that Tamburlaine gesticulates with his fingers 'long and sinewy'. (J. S. Cunningham glosses, 'literally, the cross-piece to his cutlass'; but it would be untypical for Tamburlaine to refer his strength to his weapon rather than himself.)

57–8 as swift . . . heaven] The speed of lightning and of winds was proverbial (Tilley, L279, W411).

59–60 sure . . . assure] Ellis-Fermor supposes that Marlowe scanned these words here as having respectively two and three syllables. This was a possibility in the period (Dobson, II. 218), but Marlowe scans the words in this way nowhere else. 'Sure' is a not unusual form of the adverb (*OED* B. 2, citing this example), but on metrical grounds the lines should perhaps read 'surely' and (as Bevington–Rasmussen propose) 'assure me of a kind successe' (or perhaps more idiomatically 'thy kind successe').

kind successe] good issue (*OED*, success, *sb.* 1.a).

64 scarre] frighten away, drive off (*OED v.* 1.c).

2.4

Scaena.4] Though *O1* does not begin a new scene at this point, since the stage is cleared it is appropriate to mark one in the text. Similarly with scene 5 (see Apparatus). Since scene 6 is correctly numbered in *O1* it is probable that scenes 4 and 5 were headed separately in the manuscript from which *O1* was set up.

osd *offering*] attempting (*OED v.* 5.b).

1 Accurst] J. C. Maxwell (in J. S. Cunningham) points to analogous ideas in the elegies of Tibullus (1. 3 and 10), and in the *Ajax* of Sophocles (ll. 1192 ff.). Lamentation about the invention of war is a standard element of classical accounts of the fall from the Golden Age (see e.g. Ovid, *Metamorphoses*, 1. 89 ff.; Virgil, *Georgics*, II. 539–40).

3 were] i.e. who have been; on the omitted relative, see Abbott (244).

4–5 Stand . . . blasts] Mary Matheson Wills, *PMLA* 52 (1937), 902–5 (903), compares lines from Golding's Ovid (*Metamorphoses*, 1. 66, 73, and 3. 46), but the resemblences are not remarkable, and the trembling of the aspen leaf was proverbial (Tilley, L140). On *Boreas* see 1.2.206*n*.

8 clouts] in archery, the marks shot at (*OED sb.*[1] 6, citing this example).

9 pin] a peg, nail, or stud fixed in the centre of a target (*OED sb.*[1] 1.c); 'to cleave the pin' was the regular term for hitting the target in the very centre of the white of the butts (*OED*, cleave, *v.*[1] 1.e, first cited use).

10 pollicie] political sagacity, but also political cunning (*OED sb.*[1] 3); the associations are Machiavellian.

11 close] secretly (*OED adv.* 2).

16 fearful] timorous (*OED* 3).

18 give the lie] accuse me to my face of lying (*OED*, lie, *sb.*[1] 2.a).

22 witty] (ironic) intelligent, clever (*OED* 2.a).

23 I] Ay (similarly l. 28).

marie] certainly (*OED int.* a).

24 I . . . wordes] Francis Cunningham's emendation (see Apparatus) corrects the metre; for the omission of 'to' see Abbott (349).

26–34] On the grounds that Mycetes here 'degenerates . . . into a conventional imbecile', Ellis-Fermor supposes that this part of the scene may be a residue of the '*fond and frivolous Jestures*' rejected by Richard Jones ('To the Gentlemen Readers'). However, throughout her edition Ellis-Fermor takes prose as a sign of textual corruption, though often it may also be seen as a deliberate change of medium for expressive purposes.

42SD *Sound . . . to*] give a signal to resume (*OED v.*[1] 9.a).

2.5

1 Holde thee] Here! take it! (imperative used in offering or presenting, *OED*, hold, *v.* 15.b).

7 keepe] defend, protect (*OED v.* 14). 'Conceivably, Cosroe returns Mycetes's crown to Tamburlaine as his regent in Persia, but more probably Tamburlaine has no crown of his own until he takes Cosroe's at 2.7.52SD' (Bevington–Rasmussen).

8 my] The line is metrically awkward: 'my' may have entered by anticipation from l. 9. On the syllabic value and possible stressing of '*Persea*', cf. 2.1.48n.

12 is yeelded . . . War] i.e. has been killed.

13 excuse] excuse you (your former opposition).

17 vertue] vigour (*OED sb.* 9.e).

20 Ambassage] either ambassadorial message (*OED* 2), or an ambassador and his retinue (*OED*, embassage, 4, earliest cited use 1621); accented on the second syllable.

23 longs] is appropriate to, pertains to (*OED v.*[2] 1).

25 expert] tried, proved by experience (*OED a.*[1] 3).

souldiers] Cf. 2.2.63n.

26 campe] army (*OED sb.*[1] 2.a); similarly at l. 38.

29 *Ortigius . . . friendes*] Probably Marlowe intended here that (exceptionally) '*Ortigius*' be pronounced as having three syllables, and that 'and' be elided to give an irregular pentameter; but the line may be scanned (as Ellis-Fermor proposes) as an alexandrine.

30 gratify] Cf. 1.1.171n.

good] good services (*OED* C. II).

31 calling] position, station in life (*OED vbl. sb.* 10).

32 behoofe] benefit, advantage (*OED* 1).

33 sought . . . state] On the common omission of the preposition (for) see Abbott (200); on 'state', cf. 1.2.29n.

34 powers] either personal abilities (*OED sb.*^{1} 1.a); or (possibly) armies (*OED sb.*^{1} 9).

35 Indevor] the normal modern use, of which *OED*'s earliest example is 1594 (*v.* 3.a).

37 Better replies] i.e. the response of actions.

41 Indian Mines] Particularly famed for their wealth; cf. *Jew*, I.i.19.

43 with . . . usurie] 'to our renown and profit' (Jump); *OED*, usury, 4. *transf.*, advantage.

51 brave] Cf. 1.2.127*n.*

53 passing] surpassingly, in the highest degree (*OED* B.*adv.* a).

59 in] on (Abbott, 160).

60 enchac'd] Cf. 1.2.96*n.*

61 vertues] powers (*OED sb.* 11).

62 aske, and have] Tilley, A343.

67 saies] For the plural subject with singular verb cf. 1.1.117*n.*

68 I] Ay.

73 in . . . noveltie] of the newest or most unusual character (*OED*, novelty, 2.a).

74 rest] remain (*OED v.*^{2} 2.a).

attemplesse] without attempting (*OED*, attemptless, citing only this example. The spelling, not retained in *O2*, may be a compositorial error.)

faint] cowardly (*OED a.* 3).

75 strongly moov'd] very much inclined to think (*OED*, move, *v.* II.a, citing this example).

80 perswasions] Pronounced as four syllables.

82 to] for (*OED* 30, citing this example).

83 they] i.e. Techelles (to Scythia) and Usumcasane (to Media).

85 the Turke] The Turkish Emperor, i.e. Bajazeth.

Affrike] The Sultan of Egypt.

Greece] Cf. 3.1.6; the ruler of the Byzantine Empire, eastern Christendom (and so complementary to the Pope, as is '*Affrike*' to 'The Turke'). As Ellis-Fermor remarks, the submission of these four rulers would virtually make Tamburlaine ruler of the world (cf. 1.2.40*n.*).

86 apeece] individually; *O3*'s emendation is supported by the similar use at *Two*, 4.3.70, and restores the rhyme with which Tamburlaine resoundingly concludes his resolution.

87 triumphing] Accented on the second syllable.

88 novell] newly acquired (*OED a.* 1.c, citing this example only).

89 before . . . hot] 'before he has had time to warm his throne by sitting in it' (Bevington–Rasmussen) (*OED*, room, *sb.* II.a); cf. 2.7.5. J. S. Cunningham suggests 'before he has established his authority by wielding it eagerly', citing *OED*, hot, *a.* 6 and 7; but, though 'room' in the sense 'authority' is possible (*OED sb.*¹ 12.b), these definitions of 'hot' will hardly bear this sense, and the whole paraphrase misses the confidently dismissive tone of Usumcasane's remark.

92 purchase] attempt, endeavour (*OED sb.* 2.a).

94 presently] immediately (*OED adv.* 3).

96 lose . . . quight] waste more effort (getting to Persepolis) than the gain (of riding in triumph there) will repay (*OED*, lose, *v.* 9.a, cause the loss of; quit, *v.* 10, requite); 'to lose one's labour' is a set phrase (Tilley, L9).

103 give . . . warriours] either, with typical bravado, give Cosroe some of our own (ex-Persian) troops; or, on the assumption that Cosroe's army is bigger than Tamburlaine's, allow him the advantage of numbers.

105 for me] as far as I am concerned (*OED*, for, 26.a).

2.6

2 Giantly] giantlike (*OED* A).

3–6 To cast . . . jawes] The giants (sons of Uranus and Gea) attacked heaven, but were repelled by Jupiter who crushed them with Mount Pelion (*Metamorphoses*, I. 151–62). Line 6 with its apparent reference to volcanoes suggests that, like some classical writers, Marlowe confounds the giants with the Titans (whom Jupiter overthrew and buried beneath Tartarus), or with some other gigantic figures of classical myth such as Typhoeus or Enceladus, both buried by Jupiter under Mount Aetna. The story of Typhoeus is told in *Metamorphoses*, V. 315 ff.

10 conception] Pronounced as four syllables.

12 fearefull] to be feared (*OED* 1.a).

13 doubtlesly] certainly: the only meaning given by *OED*, but the word could perhaps also mean 'fearlessly' (cf. *OED*, doubtless, *adj.* A).

resolve of rule] determine to achieve power (*OED*, resolve, *v.* 23.c, first cited use).

14 by profession] professedly, avowedly (*OED* 4.a).

ambitious] Pronouced as four syllables.

17 mettel] temperament (*OED*, mettle, 1); but ll. 15–16 also suggest *OED*, metal (of which 'mettel' is a possible sixteenth-century spelling), 8, substance. 'Metal' could also carry a figurative meaning (*OED* 1.f), the 'stuff' of which a man is made.

19 meet...mindes] 'a proper frame of mind for facing the challenge' (Jump); meet, suitable (for the purpose expressed) (*OED a.* 3); incountring, that encounters (*OED ppl. a.*, first cited use).

25 suckt] drawn into the mouth, breathed (*OED v.* 6).

26–7 with...Resolve] 'are to decompose at death into the same proportions of earth, water, air, and fire' (Jump); on 'resolve' cf. 1.1.118*n.*, and on the elements 1.2.236 (a line also concerned with dissolution at death) and *n.*

27 resembled] made like (one another) (*OED*, resemble, *v.*¹ 4, citing this example); pronounced as four syllables ('re-sem-ble-ed').

28 Vowing...life] pledging to be true to each other whether we live or die.

29 incounter] confront in battle (*OED v.* 1).

33 quence] obsolete form of 'quench' (cf. *Two*, 2.3.24).

Emperie] absolute power (*OED sb.* 1.b): only violence and power can slake Tamburlaine's aspirations ('that flame'). Denied these satisfactions, they will recoil destructively on themselves.

35 decay] destruction, ruin (*OED sb.* 1.b).

37 Circle...life] the completed course of time in which he is destined to live (*OED*, circle, *sb.* 17.a; dated, *ppl.a.* 2, citing this as the earliest use).

his] All editors retain *O1*'s 'my', explaining it variously: 'Cosroe... has reason to feel weary of his life' (Ellis-Fermor—though she admits 'the sentiment is a little unexpected'); 'Cosroe's defeatism... reflects his conviction that Tamburlaine is invincible' (J. S. Cunningham). But Cosroe has, up to this point, expressed no such feeling and no such conviction, and no audience could understand so complete and sudden a change of psychological direction from just one word the supposed sense of which is immediately contradicted by the resolution of the following lines. Collier's conjectural 'his' is consistent with everything else Cosroe says, and the compositorial mistake it assumes is one easy to make, with both 'my' and 'his' in the following line.

40 *Persea*] Cf. 1.1.162*n.*

2.7

OSD1 *the armies*] Following Oxberry Bowers here emends '*Enter*' to '*Exeunt*'. The Bevington–Rasmussen solution is preferable, both as a lesser emendation of *O1* and because some on-stage action is to be preferred to an empty stage. There should be, as Bevington–Rasmussen comment, a 'to-and-fro action of alarums and excursions', after which the wounded Cosroe enters.

7 uncouth] both unfamiliar, previously unfelt, and unpleasant (*OED*, 2 and 4).

10 artier] artery, supposed at this date, before Harvey's discovery of the circulation of the blood, to contain an ethereal fluid distinct from that in the veins, the 'spiritual blood' or 'vital spirits' (*OED sb.* 2.a).

13–14 the eldest . . . father] Jupiter (Jove), son of Saturn and Ops, who deposed his father as ruler of the gods. Ops was the goddess of earthly fertility, associated particularly with agriculture, and so to refer to her as 'heavenly' can be regarded (as by Pendry–Maxwell) as ironical or inept. A. B. Taylor traces in this speech the first of a series of references in the scene to Ovid's account of Creation (*Metamorphoses*, I. 5–451), specifically in Arthur Golding's translation, *N&Q*, n.s., 34 (1987), 192–3. He elsewhere argues that the speech also contains verbal echoes of a passage from *The Mirror for Magistrates*, *N&Q*, n.s., 33 (1986), 336–7.

15 Emperiall] Pertaining to the highest heaven (*OED*, empyreal, 1). In traditional Renaissance cosmology the empyrean was the last of the concentric spheres surrounding the earth. The only sphere which was stationary, it was the abode of God and the angels. Tamburlaine invokes it three more times—*One*, 4.4.30, *Two*, 2.4.35 and (most notably) *Two*, 2.2.47–54; Mephistopheles discusses it with Faustus (A-text, 5.242). 'Empyreal' is distinct from 'imperial', pertaining to an empire, though the two words shared common forms (see e.g. 1.1.139). See Francis R. Johnson, *ELH* 12 (1945), 35–44.

16 manage armes] fight (a set phrase; see *OED*, manage, *v.* 2.a, which cites 3.1.34).

18 foure Elements] Cf. 1.2.236*n*. The Aristotelian physiology of these lines was conventional for the late sixteenth century. Cf. ll. 46–8*n*.

19 regiment] Cf. 1.1.117*n*.

21–9 Our soules . . . crowne] A. B. Taylor, *ELN* 27 (1989), 30–31, argues for a specific debt here to Calvin's *Institutes*; more simply, Kocher (76) sees an account within the Christian tradition until the sudden blasphemy of 'earthly' at the close.

22 Architecture] structure (*OED sb.* 5, first cited use).

25 the . . . Spheares] All the heavenly spheres except the empyrean (cf. note to l. 15) were in perpetual motion: Tamburlaine claims that earth ('Nature') and the heavens provide models for his ethos.

26 Wils] Cf. 1.1.117*n*., and ll. 46–8 below (the obverse, plural subject with singular verb).

weare . . . selves] expend our energies (*OED*, wear, *v.*¹ 10.a).

31 he] With forward reference: he who moves not upwards is gross.

36–7 when . . . Crowne] Cf. ll. 13–14*n*. When Jupiter deposed Saturn his brothers Neptune and Dis became (respectively) rulers of the sea and of the underworld.

38–9 *Asia . . . Persea*] a rhyme (on the pronunciation of '*Persea*' see 1.1.162*n*.; '*Asia*' is here also trisyllabic).

41 take] either suffer (*OED v.* 34.b); or understand (*OED v.* 46).

46–8 The heat . . . cold] In mediaeval physiology heat, moisture, dryness, and cold are fundamental qualities of humours, elements (on which see l. 18*n*. above), and bodies in general; see *OED*, cold, *a.* 6; dry, *a.* 1.b; heat, *sb.* 5; hot, *a.* 4; moisture, *sb.* 2.c. On the importance of heat, and the relation of the four elements, see Hoeniger (99–107). Cf. *Two*, 5.3.84–5. On 'Is' see l. 26*n*. above.

49 tallents] talons (*OED*'s first cited figurative use of this sense, 2.d). Mary Matheson Wills (see 2.4.4–5*n*.) compares Golding's Ovid, VI. 673, 'The greedie Hauke that did hir late with griping talants teare'.

51 Harpye] Rapacious winged monsters with female faces. The classic account is Virgil's (*Aeneid*, III. 209 ff.). Bowers retains *O1*'s 'Harpyr', but this may be no more than a foul-case error for 'Harpye'. If correct it is a unique form, though *Macbeth*, 4.1.3 ('Harpier cries', usually taken as the name of a familiar), may be seen as giving it some support. *Q*'s 'Harper' may be a spelling of 'harpier', and so also provide some support—though it may be no more than a guessing correction of *O3* (on which *Q* is based), identical here with *O1*.

tires] preys, or feeds greedily upon (an image from hawking), *OED v.*² b (earliest cited use, 1598) and c; pronounced as two syllables. Cf. *Dido*, 5.1.317.

53 the Furies] The avenging goddesses of classical mythology.

65 more surer] The doubled comparative adjective for greater emphasis was not uncommon in Elizabethan English. See Abbott, 11.

67 *Persea*] Cf. 1.1.162*n*.

3.1

Location: the siege of Constantinople.

1 *Barbary*] In the maps of Ortelius 'Barbaria' covers the whole north and north-east African coast west of Egypt, and includes the kingdoms of Morocco, Fesse, and Argier.

portly] Cf. 1.2.187*n*.

3 conduct] Cf. 1.2.189*n*. (here accented on the first syllable).

4 bickering] skirmishing (*OED vbl. sb.*[1]).

5 thinks] Cf. 1.1.117*n*., though the singular form is perhaps influenced by a transition to Tamburlaine as the real focus of Bajazeth's thought: cf. the obverse (plural form for the expected singular) at l. 49 below.

dreadful] inspiring fear (*OED a.* 2.a).

6 *Constantinople*] See Dramatis Personae, Tamburlaine, *n*. Lifting the siege of Constantinople by Bayezid I in 1402 was, as Marlowe's sources make clear, among the last acts of the historical Timur's reign. That Marlowe gives it a quite different place in Tamburlaine's career constitutes a major change to his sources.

9 renied] apostate (*OED*, renayed, *ppl. a.*).

10–12 As... hornes] That is, at the full moon, when the tides are highest. Kocher (228–9) traces the idea that there is actually more water in the sea at high tide to Galen, and cites a near-contemporary source in William Cunningham's *The Cosmographical Glasse* (1559). 'As many as drops in the sea' is a standard comparison (Dent, D615.11); cf. *Dido*, 4.4.63.

10 the Terrene sea] The eastern Mediterranean (as in Ortelius).

12 semi-circled] *OED*, first cited use.

13 brav'd] threatened (*OED v.* 2).

power] army (*OED sb.*[1] 9).

18 *Asia*] Cf. 1.1.95*n*.

21 *Persea*] That is, to Tamburlaine, now King of Persia.

23–4 Dread... *Grecia*] Transparently Bajazeth is not yet 'conquerour of *Grecia*', and never has been 'Lord of... *Europe*'; lordship of Asia is also claimed by Cosroe (1.1.112). 'Monarke of the world' (l. 26) makes clear how inflated Bajazeth's claims are (cf. 3.3.243, 'Soveraigne of the earth').

23 *Asia*] Cf. 1.1.95*n*.

25 the cole-blacke sea] The Black Sea.

29 here . . . *Grecia*] In *O1* the metre is defective. Craik's conjecture, 'here', reads more naturally than the alternatives (see Apparatus), and helps emphasise the scene's location. J. S. Cunningham's suggestion that '*Grecia*' be pronounced with four syllables ignores *O1*'s spelling and the syllabic value of the word everywhere else in the play.

31 take] make (*OED*, truce, *sb.* 1.a).

33 silly] weak, feeble (*OED* A.*a.* 2).

34 mad to] mad as to (Abbott, 281).

manage Armes] Cf. 2.7.16*n*.

37 regreet us] greet us anew (*OED v.* 1, first cited use).

38–9 We . . . reclaim'd] We shall interpret the next morning's sunrise as a token that Tamburlaine will not acknowledge the duty he owes.

38 his] the sun's.

arise] rising (*OED*, first cited use, 1590).

39 For messenger] as being a token (Abbott, 148).

he] Tamburlaine.

reclaim'd] brought back to the right way (*OED v.* 2.b).

43 pleasure] will (*OED sb.* 2).

Persean] Pronounced as three syllables.

45 *Persea*] Cf. 1.1.162*n*.

46 stir] shift, displace (*OED v.* 1.f).

47 more] i.e. more powerful than he is.

49 tremble] A rare third person plural of the verb with a grammatically singular subject (emended by Oxberry and others to 'trembles'; but perhaps influenced by the fact that 'all flesh' is collective). For the common obverse (plural subject, singular verb) cf. 1.1.117*n*.

50–4 The spring . . . multitudes] S. Artemel sees in these lines an allusion to the proverb 'Where the Turk's horse once treads the grass never grows' (Tilley, T610; Tilley's earliest reference is 1639, but Artemel cites one in an Italian work of 1595 translated into English in 1601), and relates the proverb, and the image of the Turk it summons up, to biblical warnings and prophetic utterances about agents of divine punishment: *N&Q*, n.s., 18 (1971), 216–23.

52 reflexe] cast (*OED v.* 2.b, first cited use).

vertuous] powerful (*OED* 5.a).

53 mantled] covered (*OED v.* 2).

54 *Mahomet*] Accented on the first syllable (and so throughout).

56 your greatnes] Used as a title (*OED* 4.c; cf. 'your highness').

57 pursuit] Accented on the first syllable.

58 wil] decree, give order (that) (*OED v.* 3).

Pioners] pioneers, members of an army engaged in trench-digging or similar work (*OED sb.* 1).

59 of] off.

60 *Carnon*] 'A mountain range in Servia, near Belgrade, south of the Danube, near the ancient city of Carnuntum. The underground reservoirs of Constantinople...were supplied with water from these hills.' E. H. Sugden, *A Topographical Dictionary of Shakespeare and his Fellow Dramatists* (London, 1925), 102.

63 countermaund] control, keep under command (*OED v.* 8, first cited use).

65 *Orcus* gulfe] The entrance to Hell (*Orcus*: the Roman name for Hades, the Underworld).

3.2

6 rape] abduction (*OED sb.*² 2).

7 displeasures] griefs, sorrows (*OED sb.* 2).

should] presumably is, ought according to expectation to be (*OED*, shall, *v.* 18.b; earliest cited use 1605).

8 digested] got over (*OED v.* 6.b).

11 Queene of heaven] Juno.

12 it] Anomalous: not Zenocrate's abduction ('it' in l. 9), but Tamburlaine's 'exceding favours'.

13 since] since then.

14 conceits] Cf. 1.2.64*n.*

15 dies] changes the colours of (making paler); *OED* (*v.* 1.a) offers one comparable example from Milton: 'Death...di'd her Cheeks with pale' (*Paradise Lost*, X. 1009–10).

16 if...events] 'if my violent feelings were to produce their full consequences' (Jump); 'if my fears of catastrophe were to be fulfilled' (Bevington–Rasmussen; cf. l. 65). Zenocrate's 'extreams' combines both meanings.

17 counterfeit] image, likeness (*OED* C.*sb.* 3).

19 all...eie] 'all that the moon beholds' (Jump).

Phœbes] Diana's, the moon's.

20 hap] chance (*OED sb.*[1] 1).

23 you] Her own 'life, and soule' (l. 21).

27 despight] disregard of opposition, defiance (*OED sb.* 2.b).

30 but for necessity] except in so far as circumstances make a profession of love unavoidable.

31 So now] provided that (*OED* 30).

33 destruction] Pronounced as four syllables.

37 entertainment] treatment (*OED* 5).

38 villanie] action characteristic of one base-born or low-minded (*OED sb.* 1; and 'villain', *sb.* 1); hence 'boorishness' (Jump).

40 fancie] fall in love with (*OED v.* 8).

45 facts] noble or brave deeds, exploits (*OED sb.* 1.b, citing this example).

47 *Nilus*] The River Nile's.

48 him] The sun (conceived as the god, Apollo, held in the arms of Aurora, goddess of dawn).

50–1 the Muses... *Pierides*] Challenged by the daughters of Pierus, the nine Muses (goddesses of various arts and sciences) competed with and defeated them in a song contest (Ovid, *Metamorphoses*, V. 302 ff, where only one Muse, Calliope, sings).

52 *Minerva*... strive] Minerva (Athena) contended with Neptune (Poseidon) over the possession of Athens. The gods resolved to award the city to whichever produced the gift most useful to mortals. Poseidon created the horse; Athena won by planting the olive. Despite the implication of Marlowe's reference, and though, as goddess of Wisdom and creator of the court of the Areopagus, Athena/Minerva is naturally associated with eloquence, Athena's contest with Poseidon had nothing to do with expressive power.

53 estimate] i.e. of my own worth.

57 yong Arabian] Alcidamus, King of Arabia, to whom Zenocrate was betrothed (1.2.32–3).

59 *Persea*] Cf. 1.1.162*n*.

61 in his majesty] being a king (as opposed to 'Being a Shepheard').

64 distain] stain (*OED v.* 1, citing this example).

65 Fearing] doubting (*OED vbl. sb.* b).

67 jealousie] anger (*OED* 1); similarly at l. 91.

69 astonied] bewildered, dismayed (*OED* 3).

72 pourtraid] represented (*OED*, portray, *v.* 3); accented on the first syllable.

74 Comets...revenge] Comets were widely regarded as omens of disaster; cf. *Two*, 5.1.87–90*n.*, and Heninger (26–8, 89–91). The line is in effect parenthetical (describing 'eies'), and the syntax of the whole unit free: 'the fury he feels, which is expressed in his eyes, casts...'.

76 *Hyades*] 'The Rainers', a group of seven stars in the head of Taurus, which, when they rose simultaneously with the sun, prognosticated rain. Marlowe might know of them, for example, from Horace (*Odes*, I. iii. 14).

77 Cemerian] proverbially used as a qualification of intense darkness (*OED* B.*a.* b, earliest cited use 1598; Dent, C389.1); from the Cimmerii, a legendary people mentioned by Homer (*Odyssey*, XI. 14), who lived enveloped in perpetual mists and darkness.

78–81 *Auster*...lightening] The parentheses are from *O1*, but the lines may be best understood as still governed by 'sees' (l. 76).

78 *Auster*] The south (or south-west) wind, bringer of fogs and rain, on the character of which Heninger (123) quotes Golding's Ovid (*Metamorphoses*, I. 315–18).

Aquilon] The north (or north-east) wind (and so opposite to Auster).

79–81 tilt...lightening] On 'tilt' cf. 1.2.51*n.* One ancient and Renaissance explanation of thunder and lightning was that they were caused by the collision of winds and clouds: see Heninger (74); Lucretius, *De rerum natura* (VI. 96 ff.); and *Lucans First Booke* (l. 152).

80 enforcing] producing by force (*OED v.* 11, first cited use).

82 sounds...maine] measures the depth of the sea (*OED*, sound, $v.^2$ 4.a).

83 prayers] Pronounced as two syllables.

87 devine] have a presentiment of (*OED v.* 3).

90 proove] know by experience (*OED v.* 3).

91 jealousie] either anger (*OED* 1); or (possibly) suspicion, mistrust (*OED* 5).

93 working] Cf. 2.3.25*n.*

96 of extremities...least] Proverbial: see Tilley, E207.

99 stay] wait for (*OED $v.^1$* 19).

102 Go...rage] Ellis-Fermor compares Seneca, *De beneficiis* (I. xi. 2); but there is no close verbal similarity, and Seneca is discussing escaping tyranny to live, not by dying.

104 excruciate] torture (*OED v.* 1.a); cf. 1.1.113*n.*

106SD *Enter...*USUMCASANE] *O1* marks the exit of Techelles at l. 89, but marks no re-entry for Techelles or Usumcasane. *O3* and *Q* omit the l. 89 exit: Techelles remains on stage throughout. Usumcasane must enter at some point. Oxberry and others bring him in with Techelles after l. 87, and keep both on stage throughout. But this may distract from Agydas' soliloquy and death, and Techelles' address to Usumcasane at ll. 107–8 reads more naturally if they discover Agydas' body and do not witness his suicide.

113 Agreed] As Ando points out (168), this antedates by some way the first citation of this sense in *OED* (as a rejoinder: granted, accepted; *ppl. a.* 6, 1794).

3.3

1 by this] by this time.

2 *Bithynia*] An area of north-west Asia Minor, bordering on the Black Sea and the Sea of Marmara in the region of Constantinople. This battle, which Marlowe presents as if it took place during the 1360s, was actually fought at Angora (Ankara) in 1402.

3 See how he comes] ironic; i.e., not at all.

8 Camp] Cf. 2.5.26*n.* (similarly at l. 152).

indifferently] impartially (*OED* 2).

11 their...few] Not only, as Ellis-Fermor remarks, 'a deliberate departure from the records', but also a short-term one contradicted by ll. 143–4.

14 contributorie] tributary (*OED* A.*a.* 1.b, citing this example).

15 Janisaries] properly Turkish foot-soldiers; but, by extension, any Turkish soldier (*OED* 2).

16 Mauritanian] Mauritania, in north-west Africa, was famous for its horses.

17 *Tripoly*] On the north-east coast of Africa, part of 'Barbary' (3.1.1*n.*).

20 expedition] expediting, prompt execution (*OED* 1).

26 rifle] plunder (*OED v.*[1] 1.b).

29 late] recently (*OED adv.* 4.a).

32 *Asia*] Cf. 1.1.95*n.*

33 millions infinite] On the noun–adjective transposition, cf. 2.2.47–8*n.*

34 Unpeopling] emptying of people (*OED v.* 1.a).

38 rouse] cause (game) to issue from cover (*OED v.*[1] 2); J. S. Cunningham points out that *OED*'s first figurative citation is from 1589.

42 gives] Cf. 1.1.117*n*.

44 Scourge . . . God] Similar descriptions of Tamburlaine are found in Marlowe's sources, including Mexía, Fortescue, and Perondinus (Thomas–Tydeman, 82, 91, and 117). The Old Testament enemies of Israel are also often depicted in comparable terms, as instruments (usually unknowing) of God's corrective wrath; see, for example, Isaiah 10: 5–16 on Assyria as 'the rod of [the Lord's] anger'. Cornelius traces and discusses numerous other biblical references (65–6, 151–3). Roy W. Battenhouse illustrates, in relation to *Tamburlaine*, how this view was developed by Calvin and others to explain why, in a world ruled by God's providence, tyrants flourish: they are the instruments by which God punishes sin: *PMLA*, 56 (1941), 337–48. William J. Brown argues that Marlowe's association of this idea with retribution against Bajazeth for his persecution of Christians indicates Marlowe's dependence on John Foxe: *RQ* 24 (1971), 38–48. The phrase 'Scourge . . . of God' is highlighted by its appearance on the title-page of *O1*, where the context ('for his tyranny, and terrour in / Warre') suggests rather the sense intended by the Souldan at 4.3.9 (see *n*.).

45 feare] object of fear (*OED sb.*[1] 4.d).

terrour . . . world] The phrase is specifically used of Tamburlaine by Foxe (Thomas–Tydeman, 137).

46 inlarge] set free (*OED* 6.a).

47–58 Christian . . . blood] Marlowe keeps Tamburlaine's religious position uncertain (see especially *Two*, 5.1.173–202), but in presenting him here as a pro-Christian opponent of Islam Marlowe changes at least some of his sources (for example, Chalcocondylas) in which Tamburlaine and Bajazeth are presented as fellow Muslims (Thomas–Tydeman, 143). On the treatment of Christian captives in Argier, Ellis-Fermor cites Nicolas de Nicolay (see 1.2.88*n*.):

The most part of the Turkes of Alger, whether they be of the kings houshold or the Gallies, are Christians reneid, or Mahumatised, of al Nations, but most of them, Spaniards, Italians, and of Provence, of the Ilands and Coastes of the Sea Mediterane, given all to whoredome, sodometrie, theft, and all other most detestable vices, lyving onely of rovings, spoyles, & pilling at the Seas, and the Ilands, being about them: and with their practick art bryng dayly to Alger a number of pore Christians, which they sell unto the Moores, and other merchaunts of Barbarie for slaves, doo imploy and constraine them too worke in the fields, and in all other vile and abject occupations and servitude almost intollerable. (Book I, ch. 8; sig. B4^r)

A number of details suggest that Marlowe may have read Nicolay (cf. l. 75 below *n*.; and *Two*, Dramatis Personae, Amyras, *n*.).

50 Terrene] Cf. 3.1.10*n*.

52 Bastones] cudgels (*OED* 1).

54 they] either the slaves (the stroke is that of the oar); or their captors (the stroke is that of the 'bastone').

55 These] i.e. those who keep the galley-slaves just described.

56 traine] troop (*OED sb.*^{1} 9.a).

scum] *OED sb.* 3. *transf.*, first cited use of this sense.

57 Inhabited] i.e. Argier (l. 55), 'that towne' of l. 59.

Runnagates] vagabonds (*OED* 3).

59 as I live] Cf. Tilley, L374.

70 to] in addition to (Abbott, 186).

75 *Mahomet*...Kinsmans] Nicolay (cf. 1.2.88*n*.), iii. ch. 20, concerns an Islamic sect, 'Of those which do cal themselves kinsemen to Mahomet'.

76 *Alcaron*] Koran.

78 Sarell] seraglio, harem (*OED*, serail, 1, citing this example).

79 stoutly] arrogantly (*OED* 2).

80 Emperesse] Cf. 1.2.187*n*.

82 *Persea*] Cf. 1.1.162*n*.

90 suffer] put up with, tolerate (*OED* 12).

92 glided through] pierced: used in poetry of a weapon, perhaps with a notion of unresisted movement (*OED v.* 4.b; latest cited use, apart from Dryden's Chaucer, 1513).

93 stout] valiant, brave (*OED a.* 3.a).

94 hugie] huge.

95 Perseans] Cf. 3.1.43*n*.

102 my...oracles] Cf. Tilley, O74, To speak like an oracle, i.e. with certain truthfulness.

104–5 *Hercules*...venomous] Hercules was the son of Zeus by the mortal, Alcmene; Hera (the wife of Zeus) sent two serpents to destroy the child in his cradle, but he strangled them.

105 pash] dash in pieces, crush (*OED v.* 2).

Serpents venomous] On this noun–adjective transposition, cf. 2.2.47–8*n*.

107 complet] embracing all the requisite items (*OED a.* 1.a, citing this example); cf. 1.2.42*n*.

109 all . . . loins] According to Hesiod (*Theogony*, 306–24) the offspring of Typhon (by Echidna) were Orthus, the many-headed dog of the three-headed giant, Geryon; Cerberus, the three-headed dog which guarded the entrance to Hades; the nine-headed Lernean Hydra; and the Chimaera, a fire-breathing creature with the body of a lion (forepart), a goat (middle), and a dragon (hindquarters). In some accounts Typhon also fathered other monsters, including the Theban Sphinx (part-human, part-lion), who devoured those who could not solve her riddle. Typhon was himself of monstrous size, but none of his bizarre offspring were notable for largeness of limb.

ysprong] obsolete p. ppl. of 'spring', *v.*¹ (a rare form in Marlowe; *OED* cites this example).

116 successe] Cf. 1.2.45*n*.

119 Paragon] consort (in marriage) (*OED sb.* 2); the more general sense, 'a person supreme in merit or excellence', is also relevant (*OED sb.* 1.a).

128 Triumphing] Cf. 2.5.87*n*.

130 vaunt of] boast about (*OED v.* 1.b).

131 manage words] Cf. 3.1.34*n*.

132 *Persea*] Cf. 1.1.162*n*.

137 *Bythinia*] Cf. l. 2*n*.

140 heads of *Hydra*] Cf. l. 109*n*.; a standard comparison (Tilley, H278). When one of the Lernean Hydra's heads was cut off two grew in its place.

power] Cf. 3.1.13*n*.

142 they] i.e. my soldiers.

148 marshal] guide (*OED v.* 6, earliest cited use).

152–4 My . . . war] Marlowe translated the first book of Lucan's *Pharsalia*, on the Roman Civil Wars, probably while still at Cambridge.

154 *Pharsalia*] The plain near the town of Pharsalus where Julius Caesar defeated Pompey the Great in 48 BC.

156 fleeting] floating (*OED*, fleet, *v.*¹ 3).

158 your . . . aire] See Apparatus. *O1*'s 'lure' has found defenders. It is retained by Ellis-Fermor on the grounds that the passage is hopelessly

corrupt, but she offers no possible sense, pointing only to what Dyce admits, that the repetition produced by his emendation (ll. 156, 158) is feeble. J. G. Flynn (*TLS*, 18.7.1935, 464) suggests the imitation bird used in training hawks (*OED sb.*² 1) as a metaphor 'referring to the enemy... enticing Tamburlaine to his capture'. Harper accepts 'lure' in the same sense, but explains, 'Tamburlaine regards his adversaries as imitation men, just as the lure is the imitation of a bird.' Either explanation would strain comprehension in the theatre. Bowers defends *O1*'s 'our' on the grounds that the speech is addressed as much to Tamburlaine's followers as to Bajazeth, and that 'to wound the air is not necessarily futile... but instead to make one's strokes more fearsome'. But 'these my followers' indicates that by l. 155 (probably from l. 153) Tamburlaine is addressing Bajazeth, and Bowers' interpretation would be strained even without 'sencelesse' (reinforcing the redundancy already evident in the idea of wounding the air), the finely antithetical double action of the spirits produced by the emendation 'your' (they help Tamburlaine, they injure Bajazeth), and the obvious source of the probable error ('our' twice in the previous line). J. S. Cunningham remarks the parallels in Peele's 'makes their weapons wound the senceless winds' (*David and Bethsabe*, *c*.1594, sig. B3ᵛ, possibly modelled on Marlowe's line), and Hamlet's 'hit the woundlesse ayre' (*Q2*, 4.1.44). In both cases it is clear that the action described is useless.

159 bloody Collours] Cf. 4.1.49–63*n*.

160 take... flight] i.e. spread her wings (not 'flee').

168 Turkesse] a nonce-word, invented by Marlowe (*OED* gives this example only), perhaps by analogy with 'the Turk' (i.e. the Sultan of Turkey) to mean (as a title) the Wife of the Sultan; see ll. 266–7, 'the Turk. / The Turkess'.

unreverend] irreverent (*OED a.* 1; common *c*.1580–1660).

Bosse] fat woman (*OED sb.*¹ 1.e).

172 lavish] unrestrained (*OED a.* 1.a).

173 Bassoe-maister] *O2*'s emendation gives a contemptuous nonce-word not recorded by *OED*; cf. l. 212, 'king of Bassoes'.

175 your Advocates] advocates for you both. The supposition that this may be a feminine form ('advocatess'; Wagner, followed by Ellis-Fermor) ignores the rhythm of the line, and has no support from *OED*, which gives only one doubtful instance of this form, from 1647.

180 weedes] Cf. 1.2.42*n*.

185 To dresse... drink] dresse, prepare (*OED v.* 13.a); Ellis-Fermor points out that this was the fate of Bayezid's wife, according to Perondinus and other writers.

188SD *sound ... stay*] Cf. 2.4.42SD*n*.; stay, desist (*OED v.*[1] 2).

198 presume] Cf. 5.1.479. Most editors ignore the metrically imperfect line. Wagner's emendation (see apparatus) makes the unlikely assumption that the *O1* compositor substituted a pronoun for a proper noun.

201 By this] Cf. l. 1*n*.

202 *Affrica*] Cf. 1.2.16*n*.

211SD BAJAZETH ... *overcome*] J. S. Cunningham's additional stage directions are extrapolations implied by the directions of *O1*: '*enter*' must mean '*re-enter*', which implies previous exits for both men. Cunningham (87) supposes that Bajazeth is overcome off-stage, but the stage directions he actually gives rightly dictate another action. The protagonists '[*re*]-*enter*' before 'BAJAZETH *is overcome*': it is the off-stage battle which is '*short*'. This is the only time Tamburlaine fights on stage (see 2.7.0SD and *n*.), and the climactic combat should be an extended one.

213 foile] defeat (*OED sb.*[2] 2); cf. l. 235 (which helps confirm Dyce's emendation).

216 kingly] as an adverb, *OED*'s first cited use.

222 gat the best] got the mastery (*OED*, best, 9.a; earliest cited use 1593; cf. *OED*, better, II. 8).

225 runnagates] Cf. l. 57*n*.

227 Here Madam] Giving Zenocrate the crown (l. 224SD).

229 tearmes] statues or busts terminating below in a pillar (*OED sb.* 15; earliest cited use 1604); with a play on the sense 'expressions' (such as 'empress').

235 foile] Cf. l. 213*n*.

236 miscreants] misbelievers, heretics (*OED* B. *sb.* 1); Bajazeth speaks as a Moslem to whom all Christians are infidels, and perhaps 'Idolaters' (l. 239) in the specific sense that images, permitted in Christian worship, are forbidden in Islam.

238 bonfires] specifically, fires of bones (cf. l. 240) (*OED sb.* 1, citing this example).

248 pilling] plundering, thieving (*OED ppl.a.*, first cited use).

Briggandines] small vessels, often used for plundering and piracy (*OED*, brigantine).

250 the straightes] '? i.e. of Otranto' (Pendry–Maxwell), off the southeast tip of Italy (at the opposite end of the Adriatic Sea from the Gulf of Venice).

wracke] destruction (*OED sb.*¹ 2).

251 the Isle *Asant*] Zante in Ortelius (the usual Elizabethan form); modern Zakinthos, in the Ionian Sea, off the west coast of Greece.

253 the Orientall sea] Bevington–Rasmussen plausibly suppose that this includes the Indian Ocean, though in Ortelius the Pacific specifically is called 'Oceanus Orientalis'.

254 fetcht about] taken a course around (*OED v.* 10.e, first cited use).

255 from . . . to *Mexico*] i.e. across the Pacific.

256 unto . . . *Jubalter*] to Gibraltar (*Jubalter* accented on the first and last syllables), i.e. across the Atlantic. Tamburlaine's fleet circumnavigates the globe, sailing east. If the fleet travels straight from Mexico to Gibraltar Tamburlaine apparently implies (as Ellis-Fermor notes) that he will build something like the Panama Canal, as was proposed in the mid-sixteenth century by the Portuguese navigator, Antonio Galvao, in 1550, and by the Spanish historiographer, Francisco Lopez de Gomara in 1551. Cf. *Two*, 5.3.135 (and *note*), where Tamburlaine explicitly proposes to build the Suez Canal.

258 Bay of *Portingale*] Bay of Biscay (*Portingale* is Portugal).

259 Ocean . . . shore] The English Channel.

273 Triumph] Accented on the second syllable.

4.1

Location: near Damascus (see l. 1*n.*).

1 men . . . *Memphis*] Perhaps (by synecdoche) Egyptians (the accompanying '*three or four Lords*'). However, 4.2.48, 102–4, and 124, and 4.4.71–80 suggest that Marlowe was confused about the geography and supposed Damascus (in Syria) to be near Memphis (in lower Egypt). Alternatively 'the Sultan may also speak hyperbolically, asking his hearers to imagine Tamburlaine, at the siege of Damascus, as an imminent threat to Egypt' (Bevington–Rasmussen).

2 Basiliskes] large cannons, generally made of brass, and throwing a shot of about 100 kilos (*OED* 3).

4 rogue . . . *Volga*] Marlowe is later explicit in making Tamburlaine a native of Samarkand (*Two*, 4.1.107 and 3.107); but, as Ellis-Fermor notes, he also at times associates him with the district north and west of the Caspian Sea (cf. e.g. 1.2.103).

8 Egyptians] Pronounced as four syllables.

10 unaffrighted] *OED*, first cited use.

18 monstrous] deviating congenitally from the normal type, malformed (*OED* 2.b, citing this example); pronounced as three syllables (probably mon-ster-ous, a possible sixteenth-century spelling).

Gorgon] Demogorgon, one of the powers of hell invoked by Faustus (A text, 3.18).

20 power] Pronounced as two syllables.

23 wanton] frisky (*OED a.* 3.b).

25 bils] halberds; also weapons with a long wooden handle, a concave axe with a spike at the back, and a shaft terminating in a spear head (cf. l. 27) (*OED sb.*[1] 2.a).

26–7 stood ... wood] A rare mid-scene couplet.

28 Engins] large assault weapons (*OED sb.* 5).

munition] military equipment (*OED sb.* 2.a); pronounced as four syllables.

30 countervail] equal, match (*OED v.* 2).

30–2 stars ... leaves] Stars and leaves are proverbial examples of numberlessness: Dent, S825.1, L141.12.

38 expedition] speed (*OED* 5); pronounced as five syllables.

45 *Erebus*] The dark region under the earth through which the souls of the dead pass to Hades (cf. 5.1.242–6).

47 your mightinesse] Used as a title (cf. 3.1.56*n.*).

49–63 The first ... sword] This siege ritual, with its symbolically coloured tents and their significance, is derived directly from Marlowe's sources: see, for example, Thomas–Tydeman, 95 (Whetstone) and 115 (Perondinus). The extension of this symbolism to matching costumes and 'furniture' is Marlowe's. That in Fortescue's translation of Mexía the symbolic colours are paraded in the form of an 'ensign' Thomas Izard deploys as part of an argument that Marlowe did not use Fortescue, *MLN* 58 (1943), 411–17; but if Marlowe had to choose between different ways of presenting this symbolism, clearly more effective in the theatre is the spectacular total change of costumes, properties and sets implied by the text here and the opening stage direction of 4.4 (and cf. 4.2.0SD). J. P. Cutts suggests an analogy between the symbolic colours and the white, red, and black horses which herald Death in Revelation 6: 2–8: *N&Q*, n.s., 5 (1958), 146–7. Cf. Cornelius, 65 and 155. Seaton[4] (19–20) suggests a parallel in the three days' tournament of chivalric romance, in which a knight's allegience was often indicated by a single matching colour of armour and accoutrements. It would not be lost on Marlowe that the practices condemned by the Sultan as barbaric closely resemble the tripartite scheme of mercy for some cities, partial and total destruction for others, enjoined on Moses by Jehovah in accomplishing the conquest of Canaan (Deuteronomy 20: 10–17). Marlowe may also, as Roger Sales suggests (*Christopher Marlowe*, New York, 1991, 57–9), have known of the policy adopted in Ireland by Raleigh's half-brother, Humphrey Gilbert, described in Thomas Churchyard's *A General Rehearsall of Warres* (1579; sig. Qi–iv). Gilbert's policy with any fortification he wished to subdue was to offer mercy once, but if this was refused 'he caused every creature of them, of all sortes and ages, to passe by the sworde without remission'. Gilbert also had his tent surrounded by the decapitated heads of those killed, which 'did...bryng great terrour to the people, when thei sawe the heddes of their dedde fathers, brothers, children, kinsfolke, and freendes, lye on the grounde before their faces'. Churchyard defends the policy.

51 spangled] speckled (*OED ppl. a.* 2; earliest cited use).

54 *Aurora*] Cf. 2.2.10*n*.

55 furniture] armour, accoutrements (*OED* 4.b).

57 manage] Cf. 2.7.16*n*.

58 submission] Pronounced as four syllables.

59 Pavilion] Pronounced as four syllables.

61 Jetty] jet-black (*OED a.*[1], first cited use).

62 degree] Cf. 'To the Gentlemen Readers', 23*n*.

63 raceth] completely destroys (*OED*, raze, *v.* 5.a).

68 See] See to it that (*OED v.* 8.a).

71 warning] notification (*OED vbl. sb.*[1] 8.a).

with] i.e. in alliance with.

72 disparagement] dishonouring, disgrace (*OED* 2).

4.2

osd 1 *all...white*] See 4.1.49–63 and *note*, and 4.4.osd 1, and ll. 111–22 below.

osd 2–3 BAJAZETH...*cage*] The diary of the actor-manager, Philip Henslowe, by whose company, the Admiral's Men, *Tamburlaine* was performed in the 1590s, contains in its inventory of 1598 a note of 'j cage'—presumably Bajazeth's (*Henslowe's Diary*, ed. R. A. Foakes and R. T. Rickert, Cambridge U. P., Cambridge, 1961, 319).

1 foot-stoole] This treatment of Bajazeth is reported in many of Marlowe's sources; see, for example, Thomas–Tydeman 109, 127. In

some sources it is justified, as it is not by Marlowe, as recompense for Bajazid's seizure of the throne by murdering his elder brother (Thomas-Tydeman, 133). The analogy with Valerian as the prisoner of Saporis (reported by Ellis-Fermor from Raleigh's *History*) is also drawn in Marlowe's sources (Thomas-Tydeman, 136). Seaton[4] (33–4) points to a parallel in historical legend (in William of Tyre's *Godffrey of Boloyne*); John J. O'Connor to a parallel in the romance *The History of Gerileon of England* (1578), *N&Q*, n.s., 2 (1955), 332. The specific term 'foot-stoole' is part of William J. Brown's argument for Marlowe's dependence on John Foxe (see 3.3.44*n*.).

3 sacrificing... flesh] Seaton[2] (396–7) cites a possible source for this allusion to Islamic sacrifical ritual in Belleforest, *Cosmographie Universelle*. Cornelius (156) notes the similarity to the frenzies of the priests of Baal (1 Kings 18: 28).

5–6 every... Fens] Heninger refers these lines to 'the fundamental principle that the Sun and stars exhale evaporations from the earth' (173). Kocher (237–8) quotes Abraham Fleming, *A Treatise of Blazing Starres* (1618), on such exhalations as poisonous. Cf. *Doctor Faustus*, A text, 13.85–8.

7 glorious] boastful, proud, vainglorious (*OED* a. 1).

8 chiefest... moover] The conception of God as the *primus motor* (the 'first unmoved mover', cf. *Jew*, 1.2.164) of the outermost heavenly sphere of the fixed stars (and of that sphere, the *primum mobile*, as governing the motion of the others) is Aristotelian (Aristotle, *Metaphysics*, XII. vi ff.; Kocher, 217–18).

that Spheare] Cf. 2.7.15*n*. and 25*n*.

9 Enchac'd] Cf. 1.2.96*n*.

thousands] thousands of.

13 disdainefull] hateful (*OED* 3, citing this example).

22 stoope for] The line lacks a syllable, but the conjecture of an extra (fourth) 'stoope' (Dyce[1]) smooths out a metrical irregularity which is expressively appropriate.

27 God of hell] Pluto.

28 Eban] black, dark (*OED*, ebon, B.*a*. 2; first cited example 1592).

30 triple region] The orthodox threefold division of the atmosphere between the earth and the stratum of fire encircled by the sphere of the moon (Kocher, 231); cf. *OED*, region, 4.a, one of the successive portions into which the air is theoretically divided according to height (the quotation from 1704 distinguishes three). Heninger (40) offers a sixteenth-century diagram.

31 majestie of heaven] i.e. the gods.

34 their] The reading of all the early texts. Nevertheless, Dyce''s conjecture, 'your', has some probability: it is more harmonious with the following 'your'/'you' (ll. 39–40), and follows more naturally from the imperative 'Smile'. The error could be explained by contamination with 'Their' in l. 32.

35 borrow light] Cf. 1.1.69n. (similarly at l. 40).

Cynthia] the moon.

37 aspect] Cf. 1.2.170n.; also relevant is *OED sb.* 4, the relative positions of the heavenly bodies as they appear to an observer on the earth's surface at a given time.

38 Meridian line] the great circle (of the celestial sphere) which passes through the celestial poles and the zenith of any place on the earth's surface (*OED sb.* 4.a). To be 'fixed' at such a point is to have attained an immutable preeminence. That 'the sun at its highest declines' is proverbial (Dent, S980.11).

39 Spheares] Cf. 2.7.25n.

40 the... you] An inversion of one standard supposition of the period (illustrated by Kocher, 224), that the stars took their light from the sun.

43–6 As when... earth] Cf. 3.2.79–81n.

43 exhalation] enkindled vapour, meteor (*OED* 3); pronounced as five syllables.

44 freezing] *OED*'s first cited example of the *ppl.a.* is 1611.

45 Welkin] heaven (*OED* 2.c).

47 *Persea*] Cf. 1.1.162n.

49 fame] report (*OED sb.*[1] 1.a).

Clymens... sonne] Phaëton, son of Clymene and Helios (Apollo, the Sun), given charge of the chariot of the sun, drove it so near the earth that Zeus was forced to kill him. Tamburlaine implies both comparison and contrast between himself and his examplar: Phaëton is legendary (Tamburlaine is real) and presumes beyond his abilities (Tamburlaine will perform his boast). The story is in Ovid, *Metamorphoses*, I. 750 ff. and II. 1–366. J. S. Cunningham points out that some verbal similarities suggest Marlowe may have remembered Golding's translation. (Marlowe repeats these epithets for Phaëton at *Two*, 5.3.233.)

50 brent] burned.

Axeltree] the pole of heaven (which forms the axis of its revolutions) (*OED* 4.b).

51–2 our lances...fiery meteors] Referring to Aristotle, *On the Heavens* (II. vii.), Kocher (234) suggests a reference to 'the belief held in antiquity that missiles flying through the air caught fire'. The belief is echoed in various Roman writers including Ovid (*Metamorphoses*, II. 727, XIV. 825). On meteors, cf. 1.1.11*n*.

53 Sky...blood] Discussing the influence of what they call the 'prophetic dooms' here and elsewhere in *Tamburlaine*, L. and E. Feasey note that blood in the heavens is one of the signs of the apocalypse in Joel (2: 30–31) and Revelation (6: 12), *N&Q* 195 (1950), 356–9, 404–7, 419–21.

60 state] greatness, high rank (*OED sb.* 16.b).

63 entertaine] receive (as a guest), show hospitality to (*OED* 13).

67 lavish] unrestrained (*OED a.* 1.a).

69 she...looke] Anippe shall make sure that (*OED*, look, *v.* 3.b).

76 Ambitious...low] Varied from the proverb, 'pride goes before a fall' (Tilley, P581).

84 keeps] The reading of *O1* (see apparatus) makes grammatical sense ('thee' refers to Tamburlaine, 'him' to the supernatural power that Bajazeth implies must assist such otherwise unnatural success)—though it would be unusual to imprecate confusion on a god (or devil). But Craik's emendation means that Tamburlaine's retort (by repeating what Bajazeth has actually said) follows with a more natural emphasis; 'him' now refers to Tamburlaine, 'thee' to Bajazeth (who is still referring to himself, as in the previous line, not in the first person). The emendation is reinforced by the repetition of 'thus' (ll. 84, 86).

86 thus...triumph] that is, in his cage as an exhibited captive in Tamburlaine's triumphal procession.

88 servitures] obsolete form of servitor.

96 *Platoes*...yeare] In the *Timaeus* (39D) Plato postulates a time (the so-called Great Year) when all the planets will return to the positions relative to each other from which they began; hence, at some very far distant time.

103 shadowes] delusive semblances (*OED sb.* 6.a).

Pyramides] any structure of pyramidal form, as a spire, pinnacle, obelisk (*OED sb.* 3); pronounced as four syllables.

105 stature] effigy, statue (*OED* 3). (Possibly Marlowe wrote, as at 1.2.244, 'statute'.)

105–6 their...wals] The ibis (see 4.3.37); not, as Seaton[4] suggests, (18) the eagle.

108 maske] masquerade, dress richly as though for a masque (*OED v.*[4] 4.a; though neither example of the figurative use precisely parallels this).

115 all...rest] all the rest will have theirs.

116 stay] delay (*OED v.*[1] 7.a).

120 streamers] pennons (*OED sb.* 1).

124 my countries ... Fathers] that is, Damascus is their city; cf. 4.1.1*n*.

4.3

1 *Meliager*] Meleager, King of Calydon, with a company of Greek heroes, killed the monstrous wild boar sent by Artemis when the inhabitants of Calydon neglected her worship. The boar (Tamburlaine, in the Souldan's analogy) is thus the instrument of a divinity in a sense which the Souldan does not intend (l. 9); and Meleager is a dubious type of the successful leader, since his killing of the boar led directly to his own death. The full story is in Ovid, *Metamorphoses*, VIII. 270 ff.

2 Argolian] From Argolis (strictly a district of the Peloponnesus), that is, Greek.

4 *Cephalus*] Using the hound and javelin given him by his wife Procris (who had them from Artemis), Cephalus put an end to the ravages of the wild beast sent by the goddess Themis (l. 5) to lay waste Thebes in Aonia in revenge for Oedipus's destruction of the Sphinx. Again, the story is one in which success is followed at once by disaster: Cephalus accidentally kills Procris with the javelin she gave him (Ovid, *Metamorphoses*, VII. 762 ff.). Marlowe's 'Woolfe' is in Ovid *fera*—(Golding translates 'cruell beast', VII. 991)—and in the brief account in Pausanias (IX. 19. 1) is a fox.

lustie] strong, vigorous (*OED* 5.a).

7–8 monster ... spoile] *OED* cites these lines under 'monster' *sb.* 3.a, an imaginary animal, partly brute and partly human, or compounded from elements of two or more animal forms; but the Souldan's image has a literal and entirely human sense: Tamburlaine has an army of 500,000 men.

9 Scourge of God] Cf. 3.3.44 and *n.* The Souldan intends a sense opposite to that in which Tamburlaine rejoices: in this view, Tamburlaine is not God's agent, but his enemy.

10 Raves] either rages (*OED v.*[1], but when this refers not to madness but to violent action, sense 2, it is used only of natural forces, so here would be unusually metaphorical); or roves (*OED v.*[2], but this is a rare northern dialectal form).

annoyeth] injures, harms (*OED v.* 4.a).

14 controll us] restrain our free actions, command (*OED v.* 4); perhaps with the sense 'challenge' also present (3.b).

18 remoove] raise (*OED v.* 3.c, citing this example).

20 estate] rank (*OED sb.* 3.a).

25 confines] borders (*OED sb.*² 1.a).

27 Emperesse] Cf. 1.2.187*n*.

28, 58 successe] Cf. 1.2.45*n*.

32–3 in... winds] Ellis-Fermor remarks that Lucretius, *De rerum natura*, II, begins with just this image of security contrasted with distress.

37 *Ibis*] A sacred bird of the Egyptians; cf. 4.2.105–6.

46 crest] helmet (*OED sb.*¹ 4).

47 proove] Cf. 3.2.90*n*.

49 his... praise] praise biased in his favour (*OED*, partial, *a.* 1.b).

53 hundred] Pronounced as three syllables (hundered, a possible sixteenth-century spelling). Though no text by Marlowe has the trisyllabic spelling, the metre suggests Marlowe also expected the trisyllabic pronounciation at *Jew*, 1.2.184.

55 Couragious] Pronounced as four syllables.

56 frolike] joyous, mirthful (*OED a.* 1.a).

61 sounding] resonant, reverberant (*OED ppl. a.*¹ 1.a).

65 basenesse... obscurity] On Tamburlaine's low birth, cf. 1.2.35*n*.

67 race] Cf. 4.1.63*n*.

4.4

0SD 1 *al in scarlet*] Cf. 4.2.0SD 1*n*. Henslowe's diary (cf. 4.2.0SD 2–3*n*.; inventory for 13 March 1598) lists amongst the properties of the Admiral's Men 'Tamberlanes breches of crymson vellvet' (*Diary*, 322). Also listed is another indicatively splendid costume, 'Tamberlyne's cotte, with coper lace' (ornamental braid trimmings, presumably meant to imitate gold lace).

2 Reflexing] Cf. 3.1.52*n*.; *OED*'s first cited use of the *ppl. a.* is 1606.

9 *Jason*... fleece] The Greek hero, Jason, won the golden fleece of King Aeëtes of Colchis as part of the process by which he recovered the kingdom of Iolcos, which had formerly belonged to his father. The story is told at length in Ovid, *Metamorphoses*, VII. 1 ff.

10, 11 stomacke] appetite, relish for food (*OED sb.* 5.a); courage (*OED sb.* 8.a). Tamburlaine intends primarily the first meaning; with grim wit Bajazeth plays on both.

11 I] Ay. In this scene, as elsewhere, Ellis-Fermor argues that prose is evidence that the lines are not by Marlowe; but the change of register can also be seen as expressing the brutality of Tamburlaine's treatment of Bajazeth.

16 digest] undergo digestion (*OED v.* 4.d).

17 Furies] Cf. 2.7.53n.

maske] go in disguise, hide your real form or character under an outward show (*OED v.*⁴ 5.a). However, Craik (this edn.), commenting that the Furies have no need to disguise themselves in their natural habitat (and comparing *OED*'s citation from Spenser, *v.*⁴ 4.a), suggests an idiosyncratic use meaning 'go', 'parade'. Cf. *Two*, 3.2.12 (where the word is also used of the Furies).

18 *Avernus*] Cf. 1.2.160n.

21 snakes . . . *Lerna*] The Lernean Hydra was a many-headed serpent killed by Hercules (cf. 3.3.140n.), who then poisoned his arrows with its bile, thereby inflicting incurable wounds. (The Hydra was a single creature and had no wings, so that, while Marlowe's plural may be justified by the multiplicity of the Hydra's heads, it may also be that he here confuses the creature with other serpents of classical myth.)

23–5 banquet . . . child] Tereus, King of Thrace, raped Philomela, the sister of his wife, Procne. In revenge, with the assistance of Philomela Procne murdered her own son by Tereus, Itys, cooked his flesh, and served it up to his father. The story is told in Ovid, *Metamorphoses*, VI. 424 ff.

26–7 My Lord . . . yours] Some editors print these lines as verse, dividing 'these / Outragious' (and see Accidental Emendations); and some attempt to supply the two missing syllables in the first of the blank verse lines so created (Dyce, 'tamely suffer'; Wagner, 'My gracious lord'; Bullen, 'My lord, my lord').

27 outragious] violent, excessively bold; grossly offensive (*OED* 2 and 3).

30 Emperiall heaven] Cf. 2.7.15n.

31 proper] own (*OED a.* 1).

36 fall . . . too] begin eating (*OED v.* 67.e).

37 daintily] delicately, in an over-refined way (*OED* 3).

46 slice] That *O3* reads 'flice' and *Q* 'fleece' is one of a small number of *Q* conjectural emendations which show that *Q* was set up from *O3* without reference to *O1* or *O2*.

brawnes] fleshy part, muscle (*OED sb.* 1.a).

47 carbonadoes] a piece of flesh scored across and grilled on the coals (*OED sb.*[1], first cited use).

55 suffer] allow (*OED* 13.a).

57 let] hinder, prevent (*OED v.*[2] 1.a).

58 Go to] come on (*OED*, go, *v.* 93.a).

59 Belike] probably, possibly (*OED* A. *adv.*).

watered] given water (used of animals only) (*OED v.* 1.a).

61 while] until (*OED adv.* 3.a, citing this example).

66 consort] harmonious combination of voices or instruments (*OED sb.*[2] 3.b, first cited use).

82 triple region] that is, Asia, Europe and Africa; supposedly speaking in the early fifteenth century, and addressing an audience of the late sixteenth century, Tamburlaine is in effect proposing to discover America: J. C. Maxwell, *N&Q* 197 (1952), 444.

83 trace] travel; also, chart (*OED v.*[1] 1 and 10); *OED* registers no use of the sense 'discover' before 1642 (*v.*[1] 8.a).

84 pen] that is, his sword.

reduce...to] draw (specifically on a map) (*OED v.* 12.b); with a suggestion (following 'this pen' (= sword)) of make subject (*OED v.* 19.b).

87–8 Point . . . Perpendicular] Either Tamburlaine is thinking in terms of the so-called T-in-O map, with Damascus replacing the conventional Jerusalem as centre of the world (Donald K. Anderson, Jr., *N&Q*, n.s., 21 (1974), 284–6); or the perpendicular is the initial longitudinal meridian, variable in Renaissance maps (Seaton[1] 14). Whichever kind of map is envisaged, the point of Tamburlaine's comments remains the centrality of Damascus.

91 still] invariably, always (*OED adv.* 3.a).

94 friendes] kinsmen, near relations (*OED sb.* 3).

99 trencher] plate (*OED sb.*[1] 3).

100–2 stomacke . . . death] Hunger saps Bajazeth's strength, and the body's attempt to deal with this is further deleterious. Idle, serving no useful purpose (*OED* 3.a); on humours, see 2.7.46–8*n*. And cf. *Two*, 5.2.84–5 and *n*.: there the heat of fever saps the blood which is essential to health.

105 looking] expecting, awaiting the time when (*OED*, look, *v.* 3.c).

106 happie] Cf. 1.2.257*n*.

inlarge] Cf. 3.3.46*n*.

109, 116 I] Ay.

110 Soft] Cf. 1.2.119*n*.

113SD *second... Crownes*] The first course of the banquet was set at the opening of the scene. It is usually supposed, as e.g. (with an admitted uncertainty) by Eugene M. Waith, *Ideas of Greatness: Heroic Drama in England* (1971), 54, that a second banquet, of 'cates' in the form of crowns, is brought in and offered to Theridamas, Techelles, and Usumcasane, while the actual crowns of the kings of Argier, Fesse, and Morocco are taken to Tamburlaine. On this view the ensuing dialogue then plays on the contrast between the mock crowns, which Tamburlaine's followers may legitimately finger, and the genuine crowns, to bestow which is an index of Tamburlaine's power. Craik (this edn.) suggests that the real crowns are brought to the table as if for a banquet. Tamburlaine jestingly calls them 'cates' (cf. 'pen' for sword, l. 84), and this jest is then taken up by Theridamas and Techelles. The stage action thus has the single focus of Tamburlaine's gift of the crowns.

115 cates] delicacies (*OED sb.*[1] 2).

122–7 Now... kings] Ellis-Fermor prints these lines as somewhat free blank verse.

131 plage] region, zone (*OED sb.*[1] 1, citing this example); Dyce's emendation (see apparatus) is supported by *Two*, 1.1.68; and cf. Seaton[2], 397.

131–3 As far... Zone] From the cold far north, to the east (where the sun rises), to the region between the tropics, *OED*, torrid, 1.b; citing this example; 'torrid zone' (*zona torrida*) suggests that in l. 122 Marlowe had in mind the usual antithesis, *zona frigida*, the Arctic (see *OED*, zone, *sb.* 1).

135 value] worth in terms of personal qualities; manliness, valour (*OED sb.* 5.a and b).

magnanimity] A central virtue of both Aristotelian and mediaeval ethics, with associations of fortitude and nobility of feeling (*OED* meanings 1 to 4 are all relevant).

136 byrthes] lineage, position inherited from parents (*OED sb.*[1] 5.a)— in this case, a lowly one.

137 vertue] unusual ability; courage, valour (*OED* 5.a and 7); here an inherent quality as opposed to any estimation based on inherited position. Cf. 5.1.189 and 189–90 and *notes*.

138 they] those who.

139 vouchsaft] graciously bestowed (these titles) (*OED v.* 2).

140 meeds] Cf. 2.3.40*n*.

141 erst] formerly (*OED* 4).

states] Cf. 1.2.29*n* and 215*n*.

143 holy Fates] Ellis-Fermor remarks the blend of Christian and pagan.

144 stablish me] make me secure (*OED v.* 7, citing this example).

146 underneath ... feet] 'in the southern hemisphere' (Jump), but with a suggestion also of 'trampled by us' (Bevington–Rasmussen); cf. *Two*, 3.4.52.

5.1

OSD2 *Laurell*] As emblem of Tamburlaine's victory (see ll. 55 and 101–4). This is Marlowe's change to his sources, in which branches of olive are carried, symbolizing peace (Thomas–Tydeman, 88, 95, 116).

6 desperate] despairing, hopeless (*OED a.* 1).

8 terrours] actions causing terror (*OED sb.* 2.a).

10 spoile] spoliation (*OED sb.* 2.a).

13 proper ... sword] peculiar to his mode of warfare (*OED*, proper, *a.* 2.a; sword, *sb.* 3).

14 parcell of] an essential constituent of (*OED sb.* 1.a).

16–17 By ... with] by no alteration of his established practice or feeling of pity will ever be done away with (*OED*, innovation, 1.a; remorse, *sb.* 3.a).

18 harmlesse] innocent (*OED a.* 3).

21 blubbered] flooded with tears (*OED ppl.a.* 1).

hartie] heartfelt (*OED a.* 4.a).

22 remorse] Cf. ll. 16–17*n*.

23 use] perhaps elliptical: cause him to use. Craik (this edn.) suggests a line may be missing after l. 22.

24 imprecations] prayers, entreaties (*OED sb.* 2); pronounced as five syllables.

27 made] being (J. S. Cunningham); but perhaps with a more emphatic transitive sense, 'some of whom you have married, some of whom you have fathered'.

children] Pronounced as three syllables (childeren, a possible sixteenth-century spelling; and see Dobson, sect. 328, *n.* 3). Though no text by Marlowe has the trisyllabic spelling, the metre suggests that he also expected the trisyllabic pronunciation at *Jew*, 1.1.133.

28 obdurate] hardened against pity (*OED a.* 1.b, first cited use); accented on the second syllable.

29 securities] safeties (*OED sb.* 1.a).

30 only danger] nothing worse than danger (not the present threat of extermination).

31 warrants] tokens (*OED sb.* 7.b) (Tamburlaine's black tents).

34 think . . . care] 'consider that concern for our country' (Bevington–Rasmussen).

35 enthral'd] enslaved (*OED* 1; first citation of the literal sense, 1600).

43–4 stars . . . warres] An unusual mid-speech couplet.

45 overweighing] overruling (Ellis-Fermor); *OED* offers no precisely similar use, and this is its first cited example of the *ppl. a.*

46 quallifie] moderate, mitigate (*OED v.* 8.a).

48 majesty . . . heaven] Cf. 4.2.31*n*.

49 *Egyptia*] Pronounced as four syllables.

52 propitious] Pronounced as four syllables.

54 Convey . . . mercie] 'prompt thoughts of a merciful resolution' (Bevington–Rasmussen); *OED*, event, *sb.* 3.a; cf. 3.2.16 and *n*.

55 Graunt] Addressed to the gods (ll. 48–9).

signes . . . victorie] Cf. OSD 2*n*.

58 shadow] screen, conceal (a sense parallel to 'hide' in l. 57 is required; *OED v.* 6.a offers the nearest).

59 happy] Cf. 1.2.257*n*. The Virgins use the word insistently: cf. ll. 74 and 103.

63SD *Manent* VIRGINS] O1 begins a new scene at this point, but since the stage is not cleared ('Leave us', l. 60), and the action is continuous, there is in effect no break of scene.

64 Turtles] turtle-doves (*OED sb.*[1] 1.a).

fraide] frightened (*OED*, fray, *v.*[1] 2, citing this example).

65 poore fooles] 'a form of address expressing pity' (Jump).

first] the first who; Abbott, 244.

66 The . . . *Damascus*] The metre is defective, but Bullen's emendation, 'Damascus walls', is misleading in suggesting less than complete annihilation.

68 flags] Cf. 4.1.49–63*n* (and 4.2.112 and 116).

70 Reflexing] Cf. 4.4.2*n*. The incomplete syntax may be regarded as expressive of Tamburlaine's disturbed state (*'verie melancholy'*), though some editors follow Oxberry in emending to 'Reflexed'.

your] The abrupt shift from 'they' to 'your' within the same syntactic unit may similarly be regarded as expressive, though some editors see further evidence of corruption and follow Dyce in emending 'your' to 'their'. (J. S. Cunningham supposes that 'your' refers specifically to the Virgins, but Tamburlaine means 'you of Damascus' generally; it is not the Virgins who have shown disdain.)

73 submissions] acts of submitting to a conquering power (*OED* 3.a; the plural is usual for sense 2.b, demonstrations of submissiveness, first cited use 1617).

comes] Cf. 1.1.117*n*.

77 the... Graces] Euphrosyne, Aglaia, and Thalia, daughters of Zeus, the personification of grace and beauty.

86 jealous] apprehensive, fearful (*OED* 5).

87 conceit] the conception described in the following lines (see *OED*, conceit, I).

88 staied] halted (*OED* $v.^1$ 1).

89–90 prevent... From] deprive of (*OED v.* 6).

94 Furies] Cf. 2.7.53*n*.

97 bloods] lives (*OED sb.* 4.a).

100 service] profession of allegiance (*OED sb.*^{1} 8).

102 of rule] 'in a position of authority' (Bevington–Rasmussen).

103 meanes] opportunity (*OED sb.*^{2} 11).

104 investers] those who clothe or invest (*OED* 1.a, earliest cited use).

109 fatall] deadly, death-dealing (*OED* 6).

111 imperious] Both dictatorial and overmastering (*OED* 3 and 4).

112 circuit] the appointed area of a judge (*OED sb.* 4.a), reinforced by 'Sitting in scarlet', in a judge's robes (*OED*, scarlet, *sb.* 3)—and in blood; the sweep of a sword (reinforced by 'slicing edge').

slicing] cutting cleanly (*OED ppl. a.*, citing this example).

115 fleshlesse] *OED*, first cited use in this sense; Death, the judge, is also a skeleton.

116–17 charge... chardge] command... attack (*OED v.* 14.a and 22.a).

121 Egyptians] Pronounced as four syllables.

122 observations] customs, observances (*OED* 1); pronounced as five syllables.

123 *Gehons*... waves] Gihon is one of the four rivers of Eden (Genesis 2: 13), here the Nile; this phrase is used by Spenser in *The Faerie Queene* (I.vii.43), Book I of which Marlowe probably read in manuscript (see *Two*, 4.3.119–24n).

125 God of Armes] Mars (the lover of Venus).

127 peremptory] Both incontrovertible and precluding all doubt or hesitation, *OED* 1.b and 3 (first cited use 1589); accented on the first and third syllables.

132 banefull] pernicious, injurious (*OED* 2, citing this example).

133 Thessalian drugs] Ellis-Fermor cites *The Golden Ass*, Lucan's *Pharsalia* (Book VI), Horace (*Odes*, I.xxvii.21) and Ovid (*Metamorphoses*, VII. 264 ff., and *Amores*, i.e. *All Ovids Elegies*, I.8.5 and III.6.27) on Thessaly as a land of witchcraft. 'Thessalian', *OED*, first cited use, 1590.

Mithradate] An antidote against poisons (*OED* 1.a), which Marlowe apparently understands as itself a poison. (The composition was named after Mithridates VI, king of Pontus, said to have rendered himself proof against poison by the constant use of poisons and antidotes: Marlowe perhaps supposed the poisons were themselves the antidotes, taken on a quasi-homoeopathic principle.)

135–90 Ah... nobility] The only occasion in either play when Tamburlaine is on stage alone.

137 passion] suffering, affliction (*OED sb.* 3).

139 discheweld] i.e. dishevelled.

140 *Flora*] Roman goddess of flowers and of spring.

142 resolved pearle] i.e. tears; on 'resolved' see 1.2.101n.

144 Beauty... Muses] Marlowe's invention; the mother of the Muses in classical mythology is Mnemosyne (Memory).

144–53 Beauty... life] Emendations have been suggested: 'Make in' for 'Making' (Bullen); 'These' for 'There' (Francis Cunningham). It seems better to suppose that the element of rhapsodic aspiration in Tamburlaine's tribute is conveyed by syntactic irregularity. Tamburlaine imagines Zenocrate's eyes as, by their sorrow, instructing the fundamental sources of human knowledge, and, by their brightness, giving light to the most profound darkness of the night sky; and even as perhaps able to divert him from his accustomed practice of showing no mercy to enemies who resist.

145 comments] furnishes with comments (*OED v.* 2, first cited use
1599, though *OED* notes that an example of the sense 'to devise, invent'
from 1554 may also assume this sense).

147 *Ebena*] An invented personification of Night, probably from Latin
'hebenus', ebony (and so black, though classical Latin has no adjectival
derivation from the noun). The rhythm of the line is defective. Ellis-
Fermor suggests that Marlowe may have written 'Ebenina'. Bullen
emends the line 'that when', and Brooke reports from Jakob Schipper's
rare *De versu Marlovii* the suggestion 'which when that'. Craik (this edn.)
suggests 'Thine eies'.

151 christal] clear and transparent like crystal (*OED* B 2.a).

154 consumes] Both engrosses the full attention of, and uses up (the
vital energy of) (*OED v.*[1] 1.e and 3).

158 conceit of foile] thought of defeat; cf. 1.2.64*n.* and 3.3.213*n.*

160 What... then] What, then, do my sufferings (provoked by Zenocrate's sorrow) suggest is the extraordinary power inherent in Beauty?

165 Quintessence] The 'fifth essence' of ancient and medieval philosophy, supposed to be the substance of which the heavenly bodies were
composed, and actually latent in all things (*OED sb.* 1).

still] extract by distillation (*OED v.*[2] 4).

168 wit] understanding, intellect (*OED sb.* 2.a).

169 period] end to be attained, goal (*OED sb.* 9, first cited use); J. S.
Cunningham notes the relevance of sense 10, a sentence consisting of
several clauses grammatically connected and rhetorically structured
(such as ll. 161–73).

173 vertue] power (*OED sb.* II. in various senses, esp. 9.d).

digest] reduce to a systematic (here, comprehensible) form (*OED v.* 2),
hence, express. H. J. Oliver suggests the word here may carry the
metaphorical implication he sees in the use of 'digestion' in the manuscript fragment of *The Massacre at Paris*, which he refers to the alchemical sense, 'preparing a substance by the action of gentle heat, concoction'
(*OED* 5.a) (*The Massacre at Paris*, London, 1968, 166). *OED*, however,
understands this as the first figurative use of the current modern sense
(1.d).

177 thoughts... faint] That is, thoughts about beauty, and, as a result,
about mercy (as at ll. 152–3).

178–90 Save... nobility] The most difficult passage of the play, almost
certainly textually corrupt, at least in ll. 184–7 (see Apparatus). Ellis-
Fermor (followed by Jump) supposes that an elided thought must be
understood: 'Excepting only that in a just reverence for beauty... [lies

one of the main sources of valour]' (Jump). Ellis-Fermor also conjectures that 'that in' should be transposed, giving the sense 'No effeminate thought ... except in the just applause of that beauty with whose instinct ...'. But the syntax, though complex, is complete without supposed elision or emendation (except of punctuation) if ll. 180–3 are understood as parenthetic: the framing syntax is 'in Beauties just applause ... I ... shall give the world to note'. Though Tamburlaine is struggling with an intuition which is unwelcome (because it suggests a potential for weakness), his drift is comprehensible: it is proper to be sensitive to beauty because it inspires soldierly aspirations; he is able both to respond to beauty (conceive) and do what even the greatest gods have at times failed to do—control that response (subdue).

178 applause] assent to a thing as worthy of praise (*OED sb.* 2.b).

179 instinct] Accented on the second syllable.

180 rapt] prompting (*OED sb.* 1).

184 stoopt the topmost] Deighton's combination of two separate emendations (see Apparatus) is defended by G. I. Duthie on the basis of probable scribal and compositorial errors: omission of a single letter (stopt/stoopt); misreading of manuscript *o* as *e* (topmost/tepmest) made sensible by transposition (tepmest/tempest). For the sense Duthie compares 1.2.199, a comparison which lends some support to the emendation 'maske' (l. 187). *English Studies 1948*, 101–26 (111). J. S. Cunningham retains the readings of *O1*, referring to 3.3.123: cf. J. Y. Liu, *N&Q* 195 (1950), 137–8.

186 lowly] *O1*'s 'lovely' is defensible, and is retained by many editors; but in the context of almost certain surrounding corruption Collier's conjecture is persuasive, particularly if one accepts the emendation 'stoopt', the sense of which it reinforces, so emphasizing the contrast between the gods and their mortal lovers.

shepheards flames] Referring to the description of the cottagers' fire in Golding's translation of Ovid's narrative of Baucis and Philemon, J. S. Cunningham takes these flames as literal; but they are primarily metaphoric—the flames of love experienced by gods whose passion caused them to disguise themselves as shepherds (as in the story of Jove's love for Mnemosyne, alluded to at 1.2.199).

187 maske] This emendation of *O1*'s 'martch' supposes a problematic misreading, but no sense of 'martch' seems appropriate to the context; elsewhere Marlowe uses 'maske' in the generalized sense of 'go' (see 4.4.17*n.*), though here some sense of disguise (see previous note) is also appropriate (*OED*, mask, *v.*[4] 5, to hide one's real form under an outward show).

188 give...to note] cause to believe (*OED*, give, *v.* 29.c, citing this example).

for...byrth] despite my lowly birth.

189 That] Ellis-Fermor finds the grammatical function of this word ambiguous: it 'may be a conjunction...or...a demonstrative adjective referring "virtue" back to "beauty" of l. 119, or to the power of conceiving and subduing it of l. 120'. Michael J. B. Allen likewise argues that 'That Vertue' refers back to 'beauty', and that beauty must be understood here in a Neoplatonic context: *RORD* 23 (1980), 21–31. The second of Ellis-Fermor's supposed possibilities is not consistent with the overall sense: Tamburlaine cannot both praise beauty as 'the sum of glorie' and exalt his own ability to subdue his sense of it. Ellis-Fermor's third proposed sense would be too difficult for an audience to make out when the immediate syntax can be construed so much more simply. The word is a conjunction.

Vertue] manly excellence, courage (*OED sb.* 7); but with some colouring of *virtù*, the fully developed powers of the human intellect and will. As Marlowe would probably be aware, *virtù* is a key but shifting term in the vocabulary of Machiavelli. It has often been studied as such, for example by Russell Price, *European Studies Review*, 3 (1973), 315–45, who shows that its sense includes (besides moral virtue) determination, courage, or ability in political and military affairs, and more generalized senses of power or talent (in relation to Marlowe and sixteenth-/seventeenth-century English usage, see esp. 335–7). Cf. 4.4.137 and *n*. On the relation of Machiavelli to the play as a whole, see Irving Ribner, *Comparative Literature*, 6 (1954), 348–56.

sum] ultimate goal, highest attainable point (*OED sb.*[1] 13.a).

189–90 Vertue...nobility] A transformation of the proverbial 'Virtue is the true nobility', Tilley, V85.

193 I] Ay.

201 no...us] i.e. no alternative but that we should be defeated. The phrase is proverbial: Tilley, W148 ('There is no way but one'); way, *OED*, *sb.*[1] 14.j, citing this example. Tamburlaine's reply implies the opposite sense, 'no alternative but that we should be victorious'.

211 from] away from (*OED* 5.b).

218 Furies] Cf. 2.7.53*n*.

Cocitus] A river of Hades (which Marlowe converts into a lake).

220 banefull] life-destroying (*OED* 1, first cited use 1593).

226 proper roomes] 'in their own particular places "where they belong"' (Jump); cf. 4.4.31*n*.

232 influence] Cf. 1.1.15*n*.

234 Cymerian *Stix*] Styx, a river of Hades; on 'Cymerian' cf. 3.2.77*n*.

236 aie] always (*OED adv.* 1.a), with understood ellipsis of a verb implying 'live on' after 'shall we' (l. 235). The construction is strained, and Dyce's emendation, 'stay', has been adopted by many editors. Craik (this edn.) points out that Robinson's conjecture, 'live', gains support from the probable misreading of 'aire' as 'lure' at 3.3.158.

237 bowels] Pronounced as two syllables.

retorqued] turned backwards (*OED*, citing this example only).

238 extasies] the state of being 'beside oneself', in a frenzy of passion (*OED sb.* 1).

239–40 *Mahomet* . . . Fortune] i.e. to whom we might pray.

241 infamous] deserving utter reprobation (*OED* 2.b, citing this example); accented on the second syllable.

slaveries] subjection like that of a slave (*OED sb.* 3.c, first cited use).

244 *Erebus*] Cf. 4.1.45*n*.

246 Ferriman] Charon, who ferried the souls of the dead across the rivers of the Underworld.

247 *Elisian*] Elysium, the abode of the blessed after death in classical mythology; the adjective as substantive (*OED* B, citing only this example and l. 465). For the unusual mid-speech rhyme cf. ll. 43–4.

249–50 build . . . aire] 'subsist on insubstantial hopes' (Pendry–Maxwell); cf. *OED*, castle, *sb.* 11.

251 oppression] Pronounced as four syllables.

254 obscure] dismal (*OED a.* 1.a).

256 noisome] both noxious and offensive (*OED* 1 and 3).

parbreak] vomit (*OED sb.*, first cited use). The word is notably used in Book I of *The Faerie Queene* (i.20), on Marlowe's probable reading of which in manuscript see *Two*, 4.3.119–24*n*.

Stygian Snakes] On Styx see l. 234*n*. As Ellis-Fermor notes, Ovid refers to the vomiting snakes in the hair of the Fury, Tisiphone (*Metamorphoses*, IV. 490). J. S. Cunningham compares Horace's reference to the snakes and bloody slaver of the guardian of Hades, the dog Cerberus (*Odes*, III.xi.17–20).

257 standing] stagnant, stale (*OED ppl.a.* 7.a, citing this example).

258 griefs] sufferings (*OED sb.* 1).

259 Engines . . . sight] i.e. eyes; *OED*'s first cited use of the figurative sense, 'instrument, organ', is 1590 (*sb.* 10.b).

264 Emperesse] Cf. 1.2.187*n*.

267 roomes] situations (*OED sb.*[1] 12.a).

abjection] humiliation, degradation (*OED* 2); pronounced as four syllables.

268 Smear'd] The line lacks a syllable; Marlowe may have written 'Smeared'.

269 Villanesse] (female) servant; see *OED*, villein, 1.b. *OED* records only one example of this female form, from 1611 (Cotgrave, 'a woman of servile condition'); it wrongly cites the present example as the earliest recorded use of 'villainess' in the sense 'a female villain'.

272 resolve] Cf. 1.1.118*n*.

ceasles] *OED*, first cited use.

273–4 Sharp . . . breake] 'Hunger cuts off at their source the thoughts of pity that Bajazeth would otherwise express to comfort Zabina' (Bevington–Rasmussen).

277 date] duration of life (*OED sb.*[2] 4).

278 sequel] remaining period (*OED sb.* 6.b, citing this example).

281 staid] stopped; cf. l. 88*n*.

282 expreslesse] inexpressible (*OED*, first cited use).

band] cursed (*OED ppl.a.* a).

inflictions] afflictions, punishments (*OED* b., first cited use); pronounced as four syllables.

286 banefull] destructive of well-being (*OED* 2); cf. ll. 132*n*. and 220*n*.

289 ministers] instruments (*OED sb.* 2.b).

decay] death (*OED sb.* 1.b).

294 rusty coach] The coach/chariot of Night can be found in many classical writers, including Virgil (*Aeneid*, V. 721). Its rust may have been suggested by *The Faerie Queene*, in which Night's 'yron charet' has 'coleblacke steedes . . . / That on their rustie bits did champ' (I.v.20), or (Woolf) by the ambiguity of the L. adj. *ferrugineus*, rust-coloured, dusky, used, for example, by Virgil of Charon's boat (*Aeneid*, VI. 303). In *Hero and Leander* 'ougly night' has a 'loathsome carriage' (ll.816–18).

295 Engyrt] encircled (*OED* 1, earliest cited use in *Edward II*, 18.46).

300 my . . . ayre] J. C. Maxwell (in J. S. Cunningham) suggests a source for this idea in Lucretius (*De rerum natura*, III. 455).

pin'd] exhausted by suffering (*OED ppl.a.*).

resolv'd] Cf. 1.1.118*n*.

301 excruciat] Cf. 1.1.113*n*.

310–19 Give . . . come] Some of this speech is confused or transformed reminiscence of actions presented in the play: 'give me the sworde' (cf. 4.4.42–3); 'I, even I' (cf. 3.3.166 ff.); 'Streamers, white' (cf. 4.1.49–63, etc.); 'Fling the meat' (cf. 4.4.43). Zabina may also refer to incidents of a kind readily surmisable by the audience, though not actually presented ('Let the souldiers be buried'). While 'Give him his liquor?' may be a reminiscence of 4.2.87–8, Perondinus records that Zabina was forced to serve drinks to the Scythian chieftains (Thomas–Tydeman, 109; and cf. Zenocrate's threat at 3.3.185). It makes better sense to think of Zabina not as refusing to serve her husband but as preferring death to serving her captors. 'My' (l. 314) should perhaps be understood as used vocatively (*OED* 2.a), 'child' in the general sense 'infant' (*OED sb.* 2.a), and 'go to' as an imperative expressing remonstrance (*OED v.* 93.b): Zabina guiltily juxtaposes the memory of an infant whose attentions she rejected with the memory of a child who suffered in the war against Tamburlaine. Not everything in the speech can be precisely placed or understood: it is a mixture of psychologically comprehensible material bursting out under pressure and the profoundly deranged.

312 wildefire] a composition of highly inflammable substances, readily ignited and difficult to extinguish, used in warfare (*OED* 3).

315 Streamers] Cf. 4.2.120*n*.

322 Thy] i.e. the blood of thy.

323 strowed] Pronounced as one syllable (strow'd).

327 God . . . armes] Mars.

331 fell] fierce (*OED a.* 1).

stout] A number of meanings are relevant: fierce, menacing, brave, hardy (*OED a.* 2.a and b, 3.a and b).

Tartarian] pertaining to Tartary (*OED B. adj.* a.).

333 chardg'd] levelled, placed ready for action (*OED v.* 21.a).

334 checke] strike (*OED v.*[1] 2.a).

338 Whose] Parallel to 'Whose' in l. 326.

345 motion] power of movement (*OED sb.* 2.c; first cited use 1603).

348–72 Earth . . . *Zenocrate*] Zenocrate here speaks the first of the choric laments with which Marlowe marks the other most significant deaths of the play: cf. *Two*, 2.4.15–37, 5.3.15–16/40–41, and 5.3.146–61.

348 Earth . . . entralles] Aristotle describes waterspouts as created by earthquakes and subterranean winds (*Meteorologica*, II.368a.26–32). Ellis-Fermor supposes that 'entralles' is here trisyllabic, and *OED* gives

'interails' as a possible (rare) spelling of the period. But Marlowe treats
the word as trisyllabic nowhere else: the line may simply be irregular.

353 Empery] the status and dignity of an emperor (*OED sb. 1*).

355, 358, 363, 369 Emperesse] Cf. 1.2.187*n*.

359 in conduct] under the guidance (*OED*, conduct, *sb.*[1] 1).

happy] Cf. 1.2.257*n*.

365–6 contempt . . . fortune] i.e. his refusal to make any accommoda-
tion with the expected turning of Fortune's wheel (by showing compassion for those fallen from power, prompted by the expectation that he
may come to partake of their condition).

366 respect] (contempt of) consideration (*OED sb.* 13.a).

367 ruthlesly] *OED*, first cited use.

369 In] As in.

373 resolv'd] convinced (*OED ppl.a.* 2).

374–5 fortune . . . more] Cf. 1.2.174–7.

375 stay] arrest the progress of, bring to a halt (*OED v.*[1] 20.a).

380 affecter] lover (*OED* 1, citing this example).

381 *Turnus . . . Eneas*] Rivals for the love of Lavinia (see l. 393) in
Virgil's *Aeneid*, Book VII of which is concerned with the war between
them. Though Lavinia had been previously betrothed to Turnus, she
eventually marries Aeneas. Cf. ll. 393–5.

384 presents] Cf. 1.1.117*n*.

386 fatall] destined, fated (*OED* 1).

388 rackt] torn apart (*OED v.*[3] 2.b).

391 use] have carried into effect (*OED v.* 6.a).

392 infamous] Cf. l. 241*n*.

393–5 the Gods . . . love] Cf. l. 380*n*.; fatally, cf. l. 385*n*.

394 Prevented] deprived (*OED v.* 6, citing this example).

396 Issue] termination (*OED sb.* 2.b).

398 their] i.e. of the gods (l. 393).

resistlesse] irresistible (*OED* 1, first cited use).

399 With vertue of] in consequence of (*OED*, virtue, 8.d, citing this
example only).

400 to] 'in accordance with' (Jump).

403SD *sound to*] Cf. 2.4.42SD*n*.

405 infamous] Cf. l. 241*n*.

souldiers] Cf. 2.2.63*n*.

415 Whose... griefs] 'whose apparent good fortune has never quieted her sorrow' (Bevington–Rasmussen).

416 conceit] Cf. 1.2.64*n*.

425 discourse] conversation (*OED sb.* 3; *OED*'s first cited example, of 1559, is, as here, of the now archaic combination with 'make').

425–6 sweet accidents... merits] 'unexpectedly good things that have happened to you, deserving as you are' (Bevington–Rasmussen).

426 worthles] unworthy of you (*OED* 3, first cited use 1592).

427 privy to] in the secret regarding (*OED a.* 4).

434 happy] Cf. 1.2.257*n*.

440 *Euphrates*] Accented on the first syllable.

443 of] with (*OED* 61).

446 gat] got.

449 dominions] Pronounced as four syllables (similarly at l. 509).

450 confirm'd] strengthened, firmly established (*OED ppl.a.*, first cited use 1594).

451 God... war] Cf. l. 327*n*.

roume] office, authority (*OED sb.*¹ 12.b).

455 fatall sisters] Cf. 1.2.174*n*.

460–1 swelling... showers] Kocher (237) quotes William Fulke, *A Most Pleasant Prospect into the Garden of Naturall Contemplation, to behold the naturall causes of all kinde of Meteors* (London, 1602; 1st edn., 1563): '[T]he Sunne... from places where blood hath beene spilt, draweth up great quantity of blood, and so it rayneth blood'.

461 resolv'd] Cf. 1.1.118*n*.

462 meteor] Cf. 1.1.11*n*.

464–6 *Styx... Charons... Elisian*] Cf. notes to ll. 234, 246, 247 above.

473 dispatcht] put an end to (*OED v.* 4.c, first cited use).

475 of... to] able to (*OED sb.*¹ 17.d).

479 manage] Cf. 2.7.16*n*.

482 Of force] of necessity (*OED sb.*¹ 19.a).

484 beseemes] befits (*OED* 2).

state] Cf. 1.1.99*n*.

487 for] as regards (*OED* 26.a).

inchastity] unchastity (*OED*, first cited use); cf. 1.1.40n.

488 record] call to witness (*OED v.*¹ 10.b, only cited example); accented on the first syllable.

489 further] more distant (*OED a.* 3).

494 adjoining] uniting (*OED*, adjoin, 1).

495, 508 *Persea*] Cf. 1.1.162n.

497 protestations] Pronounced as five syllables.

498 for . . . love] for your love of her.

501 forget . . . self] A set phrase, Dent, FF9, in the sense 'lose remembrance of my station' (here, my obligations).

505 worke us] bring about for us (*OED*, work, *v.* 10).

511–2 *Juno . . . Jove*] Cf. 2.3.21n. and 2.6.3–6n. Juno's reaction to Jove's victory seems to be Marlowe's invention.

513 shadowing] representing, imaging (*OED*, shadow, *v.* 7.a).

515 *Latonas* daughter] Diana (Greek Artemis), Roman goddess of the hunt, and so usually represented as armed with a bow and arrows.

518 *Asia*] Cf. 1.1.95n.

519 *Barbary . . . Inde*] i.e. from the western to the eastern extremities of Tamburlaine's empire. On Barbary cf. 3.1.1n. Bowers' emendation (see Apparatus) is supported both by the metre and by the fact that Marlowe nowhere else uses the form 'Indie'. Cf. 1.1.120 and *note*.

524 purchac'd] acquired, obtained (*OED v.* 4.a).

525 scarlet roabes] The apposition to armour implies a transition from military to civil authority; cf. l. 112n. It may also suggest the opposition war/peace. J. S. Cunningham cites 'The Plot of the Play, Called *Englands Joy*' (1602), in which 'Warre with a Scarlet Roabe of peace upon his Armour' appears in an emblematic pageant around Elizabeth I: W. W. Greg, *Dramatic Documents from the Elizabethan Playhouses* (Oxford, 1931), item VIII.

526 places of estate] chairs of state (*OED*, estate, *sb.* 4.c, citing this example).

529 *Alcides* poste] the doorpost of the temple of Hercules.

533 Emperesse] Cf. 1.2.187n.

535 our [celebrated] rites] See Apparatus; celebrated, performed with customary rites (*OED ppl.a.* 1, only cited example). The ungainly repetition 'solemne . . . solemnize' perhaps suggests more corruption than Dyce's simple emendation takes account of. Marlowe may have originally ended without a couplet, implicitly contrasting exequy with celebra-

tion: 'after all these solemne Exequies, / We wil our rites of mariage celebrate'. Or he may have ended with an alexandrine: 'We wil our celebrated mariage solemnize' ('celebrated' bearing its usual later sense of 'famed, renowned').

535SD *Finis...partis*] The end of the fifth and last Act of this first part.

PART 2

Dramatis Personae

CALYPHAS and AMYRAS] Both names are adapted from titles used in Islamic countries (modern calif, of which a sixteenth-century form was calipha; modern emir, of which early spellings included amir.) Though *OED* records no use of emir in English before the early seventeenth century, the word actually occurs in Nicolay's *Navigations* (1585, cf. *One*, 1.2.88n.), 'Emir, which may be interpreted, kinesman of the Prophet' (i.e. Mohammed) (iii. ch. 20). Seaton[2] (388) assumes Marlowe found both titles in Lonicerus, *Chronicorum Turcicorum* (1578). The one use of Amyras's name in the text (4.1.88) suggests that Marlowe thought of it as accented on the second syllable.

CELEBINUS] The name of one of the two sons of Bayazid in Perondinus (Thomas–Tydeman, 108); one of several sons of Bajazeth in Foxe, who gives 'Calepinus' as an alternative form of the name (Thomas–Tydeman, 137).

ORCANES ... Natolia] In Whetstone 'Orcan' is the name of one of the two sons of Callapine (Thomas–Tydeman, 92); the name is given in the form 'Orcannes' by Thomas Newton (see Introduction: Sources, pp. xxiii–xxiv). In the maps of Ortelius Natolia is the whole promontory of Asia Minor, covering little less than the area of modern Turkey. (Cf. 1.1.55–6.)

SORIA] Syria. This replaces the form 'Siria' used throughout Part 1. Cf. 1.1.47n.

AMASIA] In the maps of Ortelius a province in northern Asia Minor.

GAZELLUS ... Byron] In the maps of Ortelius Biron is just north of 'Bagdet' (Bagdad), which Ortelius identifies as 'olim (formerly) Babylonia' (cf. 4.3.6).

SIGISMUND] The name of an historical king of Hungary contemporary with Tamburlaine (reigned 1387–1437), who in Whetstone fights against Callapine (Thomas–Tydeman, 92). The events in which he is involved in the play are based on the life of a later king, Vladislaus III, and the battle of Varna (1444), at which he was killed (Thomas–Tydeman, 144–50). Roy W. Battenhouse argues that the connection between

Sigismund and Vladislaus was probably suggested to Marlowe by Foxe's *Acts and Monuments*: *ELR*, 3 (1973), 30–43. On Marlowe's possible reading of Foxe cf. *One*, 3.3.44*n*.

Buda] In Hungary; one of two cities amalgamated into the modern Budapest. The city is shown in Ortelius' map of Europe on the west bank of the Danube (opposite Pest on the east bank).

CALLAPINE] In Whetstone a son of Bajazeth who fights successfully against the sons of Tamburlaine (Thomas–Tydeman, 92).

ALMEDA] Accented on the first syllable (see 1.2.1).

BALSERA] The common Elizabethan form of Al Basrah (in Iraq), but Seaton[1] (24) plausibly suggests (on the basis of the geography implied by 3.3.1–4) that Marlowe may have misread Ortelius's 'Passera' (written with its first 's' long), on the northern (Natolian) frontier of Syria.

PERDICAS] In Whetstone (Bk. I, ch. 3, a book which contains Tamburlaine material) Perdicas is one of the successors of Alexander the Great.

Pioners] Cf. *One*, 3.1.58*n*.

Concubines] In reference to polygamous peoples, as Muslims: a 'secondary wife' whose position is recognized by law, but is inferior to that of a wife (*OED sb.* 1). While Mohammedan polygamy would confront an Elizabethan audience with a pattern of marriage unfamiliar and evidently non-Christian, given the presentation of Orcanes as sincerely religious it would be inconsistent to present the Turkish concubines as camp followers, 'harlots' in the usual Elizabethan sense (see 4.3.81–2*n*.).

David Bevington shows how, by having some actors take two or three roles, the speaking parts could be performed by thirteen men and four boys—or (as in Part 1) by eleven men and four boys if the roles of Amyras and Celebinus were played by boys (*From 'Mankind' to Marlowe*, 206–7).

Title

impassionate] impassioned (*OED a.*[1], earliest cited use).

Prologue

1–3 *The generall ... part*] On the relation of Part 1 to Part 2 see Introduction, xlii.

5 *Fates*] Cf. 1.2.174*n*.

throwes] For the singular noun and plural verb construction cf. *One*, 1.1.117*n*.

1.1

Location: on the banks of the river Danube. The league (l. 7) is a variable measure of distance, often understood as approximately five kilometres, in which case Natolia's army is near the border of modern Hungary.

OSD2 *traine*] retinue (*OED sb.*¹ 9.a).

drums] drummers (*OED sb.*¹ 3.a).

OSD3 *trumpets*] trumpeters (*OED sb.* 4.a).

1 Egregious] distinguished, renowned (*OED a.* 2.a, citing this example).

2 Plac'd] appointed to your offices (*OED v.* 2.a).

issue] offspring (*OED sb.* 6.a).

8 compleat] Cf. *One*, 1.2.42n. and *One*, 3.3.107n.

11 parle] Pronounced as two syllables (also at ll. 50 and 117); spelt 'parlee' at *One*, 1.2.137.

16 *Tamburlaine*] Ellis-Fermor points out that, in accordance with the modelling of the role of Sigismund on that of the historical Vladislaus III (see Dramatis Personae, notes), Tamburlaine's role here is somewhat modelled on that of the early-fifteenth-century Albanian ruler against the Ottomans, Scanderbeg (George Castriotis) (see Thomas–Tydeman, 144 ff.).

Asia] Cf. *One*, 1.1.95n.

17 *Guyrons* head] Guiron (which Marlowe apparently thought of as a river) is in Ortelius a town near the upper Euphrates, north-east of Aleppo (modern Halab, in Syria). Tamburlaine cannot have yet reached Guiron: in 1.3. he is still in north-eastern Egypt. Gazellus gives a more accurate view of Tamburlaine's progress at ll. 47–8.

18 fire] Pronounced as two syllables.

22 Sclavonians] An accepted spelling of 'Slavonians' (l.58), people of Slavic origin (*OED* 2). (Ortelius spells the name of the region 'Sclavonia'.)

Almans] Germans (*OED* 2).

Rutters] cavalry soldiers, especially German ones (*OED* 1).

Muffes] A depreciative term for Germans or Swiss (*OED sb.*¹ , earliest cited use).

23 Holbard] Cf. *One*, 4.1.25n.

24 hazard] endanger (*OED v.* 3, first cited use 1596).

that] that which.

25 Paralell] line of latitude (*OED sb.* 2.a).

26 *Gruntland*] In Ortelius, Groenlandt—Greenland; with 'oe' anglicized to 'u', and an added central 't'.

compast with] surrounded by (*OED v.*[1] 8.a).

27–8 Inhabited... Gyants] On the belief that the northern regions were inhabited by giants Jump cites R. I. Page, 'Lapland Sorcerers', *Saga-Book*, XVI (1963–4), 215–32, who offers illustrations from Saxo Grammaticus and later sources. Cf. *Doctor Faustus* [A text], 1.126, 'Lapland Gyants'.

28 hugie] Cf. *One*, 3.3.94*n*.

Polypheme] Polyphemus, the Cyclops, a one-eyed, man-eating giant (blinded by Odysseus, *Odyssey*, IX).

29 cut] cross (*OED v.* 16, earliest cited use 1634).

Artick line] *OED*, line, *sb.*[2], a circle of the terrestrial (or celestial) sphere, i.e. the Arctic circle.

32 champion] Cf. *One*, 2.2.40*n*.

mead] meadow (*OED*, mead[2], a).

33–8 *Danubius*... Sea] Marlowe envisages the Danube running into the Black Sea in two currents: one flowing east across the Black Sea to Trebizond (Trabzon, in northern Turkey); the other flowing south to the Bosporus, and so through the Dardanelles, and so into the Aegean Sea, at the eastern end of the Mediterranean (Seaton[1], 32–3).

37 Terrene main] Cf. *One*, 3.1.10*n*.

38 be... Sea] i.e. will be so renamed.

40 fleeting] floating, carried by the current (*OED*, fleet, *v.*[1] 2, latest cited use).

41 Argoses] merchant ships of the largest size and burden (*OED* a).

42 *Europe*... bull] The continent of Europe is imagined as Europa, daughter of Agenor, from whom it takes its name. To abduct Europa Zeus took the form of a bull and mingled with her father's herd. When Europa mounted him Zeus slipped into the sea and swam to Crete. Ovid tells the story in *Metamorphoses*, II. 836 ff.

43 Trapt] adorned (*OED ppl.a.*[2]).

44 weed] garment (*OED sb.*[2] 2).

45 Prorex] Cf. *One*, 1.1.89*n*.

47 *Cairon*] Cairo, capital of Egypt. As Seaton[1] (21) points out, Cairo is here named for the first time in either play, and it implies some revision of their geography. In Part 1 Egypt is thought of as centred on Memphis

and as including at least parts of Syria, which in Part 2 is a separate kingdom. Cf. *One*, 4.1.1*n*. and *Two*, 1.3.205*n*.

55 Empery] Cf. *One*, 1.1.126*n*.

59 Feare] inspire with fear, frighten (*OED v.* 1); i.e. it is Tamburlaine, not Sigismund and his allies, of whom Orcanes is afraid.

61 Albanees] Albanians (people from a district south-west of the Caspian Sea).

62 Cicilians] Perhaps Sicilians, but *OED* offers no example of this spelling; more probably, therefore, as suggested by Brooke, 'Cilicians', inhabitants of a district of Asia Minor (to which Marlowe refers in *All Ovids Elegies*, II.16.39).

63 Sorians] Syrians (cf. Dramatis Personae, note on Soria).

64 Illirians] In Ortelius 'Illyricum' lies east of the Adriatic (in the modern Balkan area).

Bythinians] Cf. *One*, 3.3.2*n*.

65 forcelesse] devoid of force, weak.

68 Plage] Cf. *One*, 4.4.131*n*.

69 *Lantchidol*] Ortelius's name for the Indian Ocean. Seaton[1] (31) points to the importance of the punctuation: ll.68–71 lead to l.72; ll.73–5 lead to l.76—though in fact correction, not, as Seaton supposes, retention of *O1*'s punctuation at ll. 72 and 75 is required (see Accidental emendations).

71 never . . . discovered] Cf. 5.3.155*n*.

73 midst . . . Tropick] i.e. the Canaries, just south of which the meridian intersects the tropic of Cancer.

74 *Amazonia*] Ortelius's *Amazonum Regio* is in southern Africa, just west of Mozambique (cf. 1.3.192).

75 *Archipellago*] i.e. the islands of the Aegean, above north Africa.

77SD *Enter*] *O1* begins a new scene at this point, but since the stage is not cleared and the action is continuous there is in effect no break of scene. Cf. *One*, 5.1.63SD*n*. and *Two*, 1.3.111SD*n*. and 127SD*n*.

drums and trumpets] Cf. OSD2*n*.

81 usde] did customarily (*OED*, use, *v.* 20.a).

88 Continent] land, earth (*OED sb.* 3.b, earliest cited use).

90 Quiver] *One*, 3.1.49 (see note there) shows a similar shift from singular noun to plural form of the verb; though since there 'all flesh', though grammatically singular, has an implied plural content

(all humankind), Oxberry and others may be right to emend here ('Quivers').

Axeltree of heaven] Cf. *One*, 4.2.50*n*.

92 fethered steele] i.e. steel-tipped arrows.

93 blink-ei'd] 'i.e., unable, in their fear, to look steadily upon the missiles' (Jump) (*OED* cites this example under blink, *a.*, habitually blinking).

94 County-Pallatine] County is an obsolete form of the title count, but the rank was higher than the English title conveys. Under the German Emperors the Count Palatine of the Rhine was one of the seven original electors of the Empire.

95 *Boheme*] Bohemia; accented on the first syllable.

Austrich] Austrian (not in *OED*).

100 princely Foule] The eagle. Pendry–Maxwell suggest the spread-eagle, as emblem of the Holy Roman Empire.

100–1 in . . . *Jove*] Heninger (85) cites Pliny on the supposition that the eagle was thought to be invulnerable to lightning (and so was the armour-bearer of Jupiter).

109 *Badgeths*] Bagdad's.

119 your General] i.e. Orcanes.

122 prest] prepared, ready for action (*OED a.* 1.a).

123 stand . . . tearmes] 'does not insist on unreasonable conditions' (Bevington–Rasmussen).

128 manage armes] Cf. *One*, 2.7.16*n*.

133–6 By him . . . inviolable] Marlowe follows Bonfinius on the treaty between the Ottoman ruler Amurath II and Vladislaus III (see Dramatis Personae, Sigismund, note), the breaking of which led to the battle of Varna (Thomas–Tydeman, 144–5).

135 protest] assert in formal and solemn terms (*OED v.* 1.a).

138 Alcaron] Cf. *One*, 3.3.76*n*.

147 confines] Cf. *One*, 1.1.39*n*.

151 Nations] Pronounced as three syllables.

155 Lanceres] (cavalry) soldiers armed with lances (*OED*, lancer², 1, earliest cited use); probably accented on the second syllable ('lanciers' was a possible spelling).

161 chiefe] the finest part (*OED a.* 5); the main part, the bulk, also seems a likely sense (7.b, first cited use 1833).

163 stay] Cf. *One*, 3.2.99*n*.

1.2

3 Western world] The Turkish empire (seen from an Asian perspective).

4 here] i.e. in Egypt.

12 moove] urge (*OED v.* 12.a).

17 further] in addition (*OED adv.* 3).

20 *Darotes* streames] The Nile. Ortelius places 'Derote' on the Nile delta, just north of Cairo. Darote is pronounced as three syllables.

25 Terrene sea] Cf. 3.1.10*n*.

33 straights] i.e. the Straits of Gibraltar.

34 Armados] large war vessels, either singly or in fleets (*OED* 3).

35 Fraughted] loaded (*OED v.* 1.a).

38 *Pigmalions* . . . gyrle] Pygmalion fell in love with a beautiful statue of a girl which he made. Venus brought the statue to life. Ovid tells the story in *Metamorphoses*, X. 243 ff.

39 *Io* metamorphosed] Io was loved by Jupiter, who transformed her to a heifer to shield her from the anger of Juno. Even in her new form she was of unusual beauty. The story is again from Ovid, *Metamorphoses*, I. 588 ff.

44 cloath of Arras] rich tapestry fabric, in which figures and scenes are woven in colours (*OED* 1).

46 Bassoes] Cf. *One*, Dramatis Personae, note.

47 Barbarian Steeds] horses from Barbary; cf. *One*, 3.1.1*n*. and *One*, 3.3.16*n*.

48 goest] walkest (*OED v.* 1.a), with following ellipsis of 'thou shalt have'.

49 Enchac'd] Cf. *One*, 1.2.96*n*.

50 faire . . . world] i.e. the light of the moon and stars.

51 *Phœbus*] the sun (here described as setting).

56 need we not] 'shall we not inevitably' (Ellis-Fermor).

60 close] concealed (*OED a.* 4.a).

62 bee . . . word] Proverbial, Dent W773.1.

66 mate] equal in eminence of dignity (*OED sb.*² 2).

69 style] title (*OED sb.* 18.a).

71 haughty] courageous (*OED* 2).

75 lingring] i.e. our lingering.

let] Cf. *One*, 4.4.57*n*.

77 straight] immediately, without delay (*OED* C. *adv.* 2.a).

1.3

OSD2 *drummes and trumpets*] Cf. 1.1.OSD2*n*.

2 illuminate] give light to (*OED v.* 1.a).

5 *Larissa*] In the maps of Ortelius a town on the coast of north-eastern Egypt (modern Al 'Arish). Having marched from Cairo via Alexandria (1.1.47–8), Tamburlaine has now turned east towards the Turkish empire, centred on Natolia.

6 parts] are divided (*OED v.* 1.a).

10 scathe] hurt, harm (*OED sb.* 2.a).

12 both the poles] each of the two points in the celestial sphere about which as fixed points the stars appear to revolve, being the points at which the earth's axis produced meets the celestial sphere (*OED sb.*[2] 1).

19 subdewed] Pronounced as two syllables (subdew'd).

21 amorous] inclined to love (*OED* 1), and so implying gentleness, and thence effeminacy.

22 as] as befits (Bevington–Rasmussen).

23–4 Water ... wit] In ancient and medieval physiology each of the four elements (water, air, earth, fire) was held to correspond to one of four supposed bodily fluids (respectively phlegm, blood, black bile, and choler) by the relative proportions of which a person's physical and mental character was determined. Any imbalance was regarded as unhealthy. The particular mixture of predominant water (phlegm, cold and moist) and air (blood, hot and moist) suggests a character that is mild and affectionate, lacking the determination and courage that would be supplied by earth (bile) and fire (choler). See Hoeniger, 102–9. Levinus Lemnius (trans. Thomas Newton, *The Touchstone of Complexions*, 1576) characterizes 'persons phlegmaticke' (cold and moist) as 'sleepie, lazye, slouthful, drowsie, heavie, lumpish, and nothinge quicke at their busynesse'; and 'persons meere [totally] Sanguine' (hot and moist) as 'for the most part starke fooles', though he allows that they are also 'gentle and quiet of nature ... not fumishe [hot-tempered], testy or soone angred' (fols. 111[v], 96 and 114[v]–115).

23 simbolisde] mixed, combined (*OED v.*[1] 1.c, earliest cited use).

25 white ... Downe] Conventional standards of comparison: Dent M931, D576.1.

27 blacke . . . steel] Likewise conventional: Tilley J49, Dent I89.11.

28 Bewraies] reveals (*OED v.* 4).

29 quaver] tremble (*OED v.* 1.a, citing this example).

36 list] wish, choose (*OED v.*¹ 2.b).

37 lovely] beautiful, handsome (*OED a.* 3.a, citing this example).

39 Trotting the ring] 'riding inside a ring designed for the *manège* or training of horses' (Bevington–Rasmussen). *OED*'s first cited use is 1602 (ring, *sb.*¹ 15.b).

tilting] thrusting at (using a weapon) (*OED v.*¹ 5.c).

40 tainted] touched, struck (esp. in tilting) (*OED v.*¹ 5.a, last cited use).

41 curvet] execute a leap in which the forelegs are raised together and equally advanced, and the hindlegs raised with a spring before the forelegs touch the ground (*OED sb.* and *v.*, first cited use of the verb 1592).

42 As] that.

44 proofe] of tried strength, hence (of armour) impervious, impenetrable (*OED a.* 1.a, earliest cited use 1592).

Curtle-axe] Cf. *One*, 1.2.42n.

46 harmelesse] free from harm, unhurt (*OED a.* 1).

51 compleat] perfect (*OED a.* 4), accented on the first syllable.

vertue] Cf. *One*, 4.4.137n.

54 if I live] A set phrase; Dent L375–6.1.

74 *Persea*] Cf. *One*, 1.1.162n.

76 Which] who.

wroth] wrathful, incensed (*OED a.* 1.a).

79 superficies] surface (*OED* 2 provides the nearest parallels); pronounced as five syllables (as at 3.4.48). Ellis-Fermor notes that Marlowe found the word in Paul Ive's *Practise of Fortification*, a pamphlet closely followed as a source in 3.2.62–82 (see note there, and Thomas–Tydeman, 154, where they suggest the sense 'surface-area'; Ive uses the word repeatedly). Bowers (1. 224) defends as possible *O1*'s 'superfluities', arguing that it is from the same root (L. *fluere*) as the rare 'superfluitance', that which floats on the surface. J. S. Cunningham points out, however, that *OED*'s first recorded instance of this is 1646.

86 Dismaies] Cf. *One*, 1.1.117n.

proove] Cf. *One*, 3.2.90n.

96 lovely] Cf. l.37n. (*OED* also cites this example).

99 Deputie] viceroy (*OED sb.* 2.a).

101 Pericranion] skull, cranium (*OED* 2, first cited use).

103 channell] According to *OED*, the neck or throat (*sb.*[1] 10, citing this example as the word's latest use). Craik (this edn.) suggests that Marlowe intended something solid able to arrest the passage of a sword: cf. *OED*, cannel-bone / channel-bone, neck-bone, or collar-bone.

107 *Larissa*] Cf. l. 5*n*.

110 it] presumably Natolia, the conquest of which Orcanes and his allies regard as Tamburlaine's current aim (cf. 1.1.49), a supposition which Theridamas here confirms (l. 121).

parcel] part (*OED sb.* 1.a).

Empery] Cf. *One*, 1.1.126*n*.

111SD *Enter*] *O1* begins a new scene at this point, but cf. 1.1.77SD*n*.

Drums and Trumpets] Cf. 1.1.0SD2*n*.

116 at...feet] in homage, as an expression of subjection (*OED*, foot, *sb.* 30.a).

SD *He*...TAMBURLAINE] This and the following related stage directions (ll. 127, 129, 137, 138 and 150) are based on Bevington–Rasmussen (see Apparatus), except that Bevington–Rasmussen understand the conventionally figurative 'at thy...feet' literally, and so involve Tamburlaine in some unlikely stooping.

122 Briggandines] Cf. *One*, 3.3.248*n*.

123 Meet] suitable, fit (*OED a.* 3.a).

127SD2 *Enter*] *O1* begins a new scene at this point, but cf. 1.1.77SD*n*.

130 my...*Fesse*] i.e. Techelles.

132 expert souldiers] Cf. *One*, 2.5.25*n*. and *One*, 2.2.63*n*.

133 *Azamor*] In the maps of Ortelius in Morocco, on the Atlantic coast just south of the Straits of Gibraltar.

134, 149 unpeopled] emptied of people (*OED v.* 1.a); cf. *One*, 3.3.34*n*.

143 infernall *Jove*] Pluto, ruler of the Underworld.

146 Furies...flags] Cf. *One*, 2.7.53*n*. Citing sources in Cicero and Ovid (e.g. *Metamorphoses*, VI. 430), Ellis-Fermor notes that the Furies are frequently represented in classical literature carrying firebrands (as at *One*, 5.1.218–19, and in *Lucans First Booke*, ll. 570–72).

148 *Tesella*] In Ortelius a town in north Africa just south of Oran (in modern Algeria).

Biledull] In Ortelius 'Biledulgerid' is a district of north Africa south of the coastal region 'Barbaria' (on which see *One*, 3.1.1*n*). Marlowe possibly shortened the name for metrical reasons (cf. l. 198*n*.), though (as often in Ortelius) the name is printed in two layers ('Biledul / gerid'), so the shortening may simply be Marlowe's error.

158 Campe] Cf. *One*, 2.5.26*n*.

160 *Boreas*] Cf. *One*, 1.2.206*n*.

rents] rends, tears (*OED v.*^{2} 1.a).

163–4 stones . . . men] When Zeus sent a flood to destroy men for their degeneracy, he spared Deucalion and his wife Pyrrha for their piety. After the flood, acting on the advice of Themis, they recreated the human race by throwing stones over their shoulders from which men and women sprang up. The story is told in Ovid, *Metamorphoses*, I. 274 ff.

165 lavish] extravagant outpouring. ('To make lavish' is a set phrase: *OED* cites a similar usage in *Massacre*, 24.102.)

166 winged Messenger] Mercury.

169 *Thetis*] A sea goddess.

170 *Boetes*] Cf. *One*, 1.1.207*n*.

174 *Barbary*] Cf. *One*, 3.1.1*n*.

176 laine in leagre] encamped to engage in a siege (*OED*, leaguer, *sb.*^{1} 1.b, first cited use; and see lay, *v.*^{1} 19).

178 *Guallatia*] In Ortelius 'Gualata' is a region (and a town) in the western Sahara (in modern Mauritania). Marlowe's version of the name should be pronounced as four syllables.

180 kept] had charge or control of (*OED v.* 16.a).

Gibralter] Accented on the first and last syllables; cf. *One*, 3.3.256*n*.

181 *Canarea*] The Canary Isles, off the coast of north-west Africa, near southern Morocco.

182 they] i.e. our soldiers.

183 alarms] calls to arms (*OED sb.* 4.a).

186–205 I have march'd . . . *Damasco*] In terms of the contemporary map Techelles describes a march from Egypt to eastern Angola, south along the coastal province ('Zanzibar' extends beyond the Cape of Good Hope), north across the River Congo to Niger, turning finally east into Chad, and thence to Damascus.

187 *Machda*] In Ortelius 'Machada', a town on a tributary of the Nile near the equator, given by Ortelius as the seat of Prester John (see

following note), to whose kingdom in north-east Africa Ortelius gives a whole separate map (1584 edn., f. 99). In terms of contemporary geography the town would be in southern Sudan.

188 *John* the great] Prester (or Presbyter) John, an alleged Christian priest or king, originally connected with the Orient, but from the fifteenth century supposed to reign in Ethiopia.

189 triple Myter] Implicitly comparing the priest-king Prester John with the Pope, whose diadem (often called the triple tiara) is encircled with three crowns.

191 *Cazates*] In Ortelius a town in *Amazonum regio* (in central southern Africa; see 1.1.74*n*.) on the shores of a large unnamed lake (not identifiable in terms of modern geography).

194–5 *Zansibar . . . Affrike*] In Ortelius Zanzibar is a province along the coast of southern Africa extending (in terms of modern geography) from southern Angola, through Namibia and South Africa, and round into Mozambique. (Ortelius correctly shows the island of Zanzibar off the east coast of central Africa.)

196 Ethiopian sea] In Ortelius the *Oceanus Æthiopicus*, the ocean between 'Zanzibar' (see preceding note) and South America (the modern South Atlantic).

197 neither . . . land] Perhaps based on the description in Ortelius of both north and south 'Zanzibar' as 'Deserta'.

198 *Manico*] In Orteilus 'Manicongo' is the name of a region (and a town) on the coast of west Africa, ten degrees south of the equator. The name was presumably shortened for metrical reasons (cf. l. 148*n*.).

200 *Byather*] Ortelius gives the name of this province as 'Biafar' (in modern terms, part of Cameroon).

201 *Cubar*] In Ortelius 'Guber' (the name of a district, a town, and a lake), part of an area described as '*Nigritarum Regio*'.

202 *Nubia*] Between the Nile and 'Borno lacus' (see following note), in modern terms part of Sudan.

203 *Borno*] In the modern Plain of Bornu, south of Lake Chad, which is possibly Tamburlaine's '*Borno* Lake' (5.3.137).

205 *Damasco*] As in Part 1, Marlowe apparently still thinks of Damascus as in Egypt (see l. 186). Cf. *One*, 4.1.1*n*. and *Two*, 1.1.47*n*. As Seaton[1] (30) points out, Damascus (the biblical form) is usual throughout Part 1, Damasco (the usual form in Ortelius) throughout Part 2, except at 3.2.125, where '*Damascus*' is a genitive form (i.e. '*Damasco*'s').

where ... before] i.e. where I encamped before starting this campaign (see *OED*, stay, *v.*[1] 8.a).

207 confines] Cf. *One*, 1.1.39n.

208 And ... *Europe*] The line lacks a syllable. Francis Cunningham emends 'And thence I made'; Elze conjectures 'Europa' a form for 'Europe' which Marlowe uses in *All Ovids Elegies* (I.10.2), but with the stress (as usual for the word) on the second syllable, not (as required here) on the first. Craik (this edn.) suggests the exceptional form, 'Europë'.

209 *Tyros*] The southern boundary of the province which Ortelius calls 'Podolia' (see l. 210n.), the modern River Dnestr, which flows into the Black Sea north of the Danube.

210 *Stoka*] In Ortelius 'Stoko', a town on the River Tyros (Dnestr).

Padalia] In Ortelius 'Podolia', a province to the north west of the Black Sea (in modern terms, part of the Ukraine).

Codemia] In Ortelius a town to the north-east of Stoko.

211 *Oblia*] In Ortelius 'Olbia', a town directly east of Codemia.

212 *Nigra Silva*] The 'Black Forest', in Ortelius extending north and east from 'Olbia', north of the Black Sea. Its dancing devils are not derived from Ortelius, though Seaton[1] (29) quotes the later map-maker Mercator to suggest that this colourful detail was a matter of popular superstition, not Marlowe's invention.

215 *Mare magiore*] The 'Great Sea', i.e. the Black Sea.

216 period] stop, end (to part of a course) (*OED sb.* 5.c, first cited use).

217 *Natolia*] i.e. Orcanes.

219 pensions] payments, wages (*OED sb.* 3.a).

cates] Cf. *One*, 4.4.115n.

221 *Lachrima Christi*] 'Christ's tears', a strong and sweet red wine of southern Italy (*OED*, first cited use 1611).

223 I] Ay.

him] i.e. Orcanes (cf. ll. 99–105, 161).

224 orient] lustrous, as coming anciently from the East (*OED a.* 2.a).

2.1

1 *Buda*] See Dramatis Personae, notes.

2 motion] emotion, desire (*OED sb.* 9.a).

3 valures] *OED*, valour, 1.c (a common form, 1580–1610).

5 bloods] lives (*OED sb.* 4.a).

7 *Zula*] In the maps of Ortelius Zula is north of the Danube, the principal city of 'Rascia' (a province east of Hungary).

8 *Verna*] In the maps of Ortelius 'Varna' is a city in Bulgaria, on the west coast of the Black Sea, south of the mouth of the Danube. Marlowe refers to it as though it were a province or country.

9 *Rome*] Probably Constantinople. The name was applied to Constantinople as the capital of the eastern Roman Empire, and the centre of eastern Christendom (Rome itself being the centre of the western Church). It is so used by Richard Knolles in his version of Bonfinius in *The General History of the Turks* (1603), which Marlowe may have read in manuscript: Hugh G. Dick, *Studies in Philology*, 46 (1949), 154–66. Seaton[1] (30) suggests that Marlowe may have been prompted by the wide break in Ortelius's map of Europe of the word Roma/nia, and the placing of the first element of the word just north of Constantinople.

10 Camp] Cf. *One*, 2.5.26*n*.

11 resteth] remains.

14 for . . . repaire] Because Tamburlaine is making his way there (i.e. to the places listed in ll. 19–20). (*OED*, repair, *sb.*[1] 4.a).

16–21 *Natolia . . . Jerusalem*] The army of Orcanes has travelled directly east through modern Turkey and then south into Arabia (see following notes) towards Tamburlaine on the north-east coast of Egypt.

16 *Natolia . . .* dismist] Orcanes has sent (the army has been redeployed from eastern Europe into Turkey); *OED*, dismiss, *v.* 1, send away in various directions.

18 *Cutheia . . . Orminius*] As Seaton[2] shows (389–90), Marlowe took the forms of these names from Lonicerus, not from Ortelius (who calls the town Chiutaie and the mountain Horminius). Cutheia, capital of Natolia, is modern Kütahya in western Turkey. Orminius is shown by Ortelius only on the map of Greece in his Parergon, where it is situated in Bythinia. In modern terms it corresponds to part of the Kuzey Anadolu Daglari range of mountains in northeastern Turkey.

19 *Belgasar*] In the maps of Ortelius 'Beglasar' is the next large town to the east of Cutheia in western Turkey.

20 *Acantha . . . Caesaria*] In the maps of Ortelius 'Acanta' is east and south of Beglasar; Antioch is on the north-western coast of Syria; and Caesaria is south of Antioch, on the coast of Judaea, north of Larissa (see 1.3.5*n*.).

30 record] witness (*OED sb*. 3.a).

31 should] would (Abbott, 322).

32 profession] acceptance of and conformity to the faith and principles of Christianity (*OED* 5.a); cf. l. 36; pronounced as four syllables.

33–6 No . . . injoine] Tilley illustrates different shades of proverbial wisdom on this issue: F33, 'No faith with heretics'; O7, 'An unlawful oath is better broken than kept'. The underlying argument could take sincerely religious forms; see e.g. Bishop Hugh Latimer, Second Sermon preached before Edward VI: 'All promises are not to be kept, specially if they be against the word of God' (ed. G. E. Corrie, Parker Society, 1844), 116. Nevertheless, any use of the argument for political advantage was likely to appear manipulative. The other notable example in Marlowe is the Machiavellian application of the idea by Barabas (*Jew*, 2.3.310–13). In Shakespeare the arguments of Cardinal Pandolf urging that Catholic Spain renege on its alliance with Protestant England (*King John*, 3.1.179–223) indicate a Protestant sense that the line of thought was a peculiarly Catholic justification of treachery. On this view the argument originated in Catholic attempts to justify the execution of the Czech Wycliffite reformer John Huss who, despite guarantees for his safe-conduct given by the Emperor Sigismund, was arrested at the Council of Constance and burned at the stake in 1415. This is discussed by Roy W. Battenhouse (*ELR* 3 (1973); cf. Dramatis Personae, Sigismund, note), as part of his argument that Marlowe drew on Foxe in relating Sigismund and Vladislaus III. As Battenhouse had earlier noted (*Marlowe's 'Tamburlaine'*, 66), Raleigh considers the issue (*The History of the World*, 1614, II.vi.8), basing his remarks on Joshua's keeping of his oath sworn to the deceitful Gibeonites (Joshua 9). Raleigh's discussion is especially pertinent because the second of his two modern examples of oath-breaking punished with disaster is that of Vladislaus III at Varna. Raleigh's moral conclusion is emphatic:

[T]o the end that the faithlesse subtiltie of man should borrow nothing in the future from his [Joshua's] example, who knowing well, that the promises he made in the name of God, were made to the living God, and not to the dying Man, he held them firme, and inviolable, notwithstanding that they, to whom he had sworne it, were worshippers of the Devil . . . I am not ignorant of their poore evasions, which play with the severity of Gods commandments in this kinde: But this indeed is the best answer. That he breaks no faith, that hath none to breake. For whosoever hath faith and the feare of God, dares not doe it.

For Marlowe's probable direct source in Bonfinius (cf. l. 9*n*.) see Thomas–Tydeman, 145–7. See also Kocher, 123, and Bawcutt, *Jew*, 122 (citing Catholic and Protestant discussions during the 1580s).

33 No whit] not in the least (*OED*, whit, *sb*.¹ 2.b).

35 accomplishments] fulfilments (here, of oaths) (*OED* 1).

37 plight] pledge (*OED v.*[1] 3).

38 pollycy] prudent course of action (*OED sb.*[1] 4.a). (Bevington–Rasmussen paraphrase l. 38 'is, according to the dictates of prudent statecraft, not'.)

39 assurance] guarantee (*OED* 1.a).

45 their religion] *O1*'s 'and' (see apparatus) is hypermetrical; 'religion' is pronounced as four syllables.

47 consumate] complete, perfect (*OED a.* 2.a). *OED* does not record *O1*'s 'consinuate'; and, like Oxberry's emendation 'continuate' (lasting), the word does not fit the metre. J. S. Cunningham compares the use of the verb in *Massacre*, 1.19–20, 'consumate / The rest, with hearing of a holy Masse'.

49 superstition] Pronounced as five syllables.

50 dispensive] subject to dispensation (*OED* 2, citing only this example).

53 blasphemous] impiously irreverent (*OED* 1, citing this example); accented on the second syllable.

Paganism,] J. S. Cunningham retains *O1*'s punctuation (see Accidental Emendations), so making ll. 51–3 a syntactically complete question. But, since it is then difficult to construe the syntax of ll. 54–9, it is better to take ll. 51–9 as a single unit within which ll. 51–3 are a conditional clause (Ando, 481).

54 *Saule*] Commanded by God to kill all the Amalekites, their flocks and herds, Saul spared their king, Agag, and some of the animals. As a result he lost the kingship of Israel (1 Samuel 15).

Balaam] Balaam was summoned by Balak, King of Moab, to curse the Israelites, but, in obedience to God's command, Balaam instead blessed them (Numbers 22–4). (The example does not illustrate Fredericke's argument as he implies.)

62 expedition] Cf. *One*, 3.3.20n.

2.2

2 *Orminius* mount] Cf. 2.1.18n.

4 Expect] wait for (*OED v.* 2.a).

6 *Larissa*] Cf. 1.3.5n.

7 tooles] weapons of war (*OED sb.* 1.b).

10 erst] formerly, hitherto (*OED* 5.a).

11 bid...armes] offer him battle (*OED*, arm, *sb.*² 6, citing this example).

15 as...haile] A standard comparison (Tilley H11).

17 partiall] biased (*OED* 1).

21 admitted] granted (*OED v.* 2.a).

23 unacquainted] unusual, unexampled (*OED ppl.a.* 2.a).

24 Arme, arme] The line is metrically defective without the extra syllable supplied by Craik's conjecture (see Apparatus).

25, 29, 36, 62 Christians] Pronounced as three syllables.

27 determines] resolves definitely (*OED* 18.a, citing this example).

29–33 Traitors...*Mahomet*] Ellis-Fermor points out that these lines follow closely the speech of Amurath II at the battle of Varna as given by Bonfinius (see Dramatis Personae, Sigismund, note; and Thomas–Tydeman, 149).

35 cares] Cf. *One*, 1.1.117*n*.

37 fleshly] *OED* cites this example under sense 7.b, 'tender, soft' (as opposed to 'stony'); but sense 3, 'unredeemed, unregenerate', better suits the context.

38 figure] image, likeness (*OED sb.* 9.a). Kocher (101) points out the underlying reference to Genesis 1: 26.

40 But...Christ] Kocher (101) compares Titus 1:16.

42 power...arme] Kocher (101) compares Exodus 7: 5; Cornelius (173) compares Jeremiah 27: 5. Closer than either is Deuteronomy, throughout which the power of the Lord's stretched out arm is a recurring motif (see e.g. 4: 34).

43 jealous] careful in guarding (*OED a.* 3). Kocher (101) compares Exodus 20: 5; Cornelius (173) compares Ezekiel 39: 25. Though the word does recall these and other biblical uses, its sense in such contexts is different (see *OED a.* 4.c).

47 vaile of *Cynthia*] Cf. 1.2.50*n*, and *One*, 4.2.35*n*. Pendry–Maxwell suggest that the moonlit sky is seen here as a barrier to mortal perception of the divine, though in fact Orcanes seems to have in mind the more unusual idea of a barrier to divine perception of the human ('Open... That he that sits on high...May...Behold...').

48 imperiall heaven] Cf. *One*, 2.7.15*n*.

49–51 he...Continent] As Kocher (97–100) demonstrates, these lines are in accordance with Elizabethan Anglican orthodoxy. Among his many biblical and theological citations, particularly close are Jeremiah 23: 24, 'Do not I fill heaven and earth? saith the Lord', and Augustine,

'Deus...solus incircumscriptus', quoted, as Kocher notes, in John Proctor, *The Fall of the late Arrian* (1549), which contains the list of reasons for doubting the divinity of Christ (with refutations) found amongst Marlowe's papers in Kyd's possession. On l. 50 Cornelius (173) cites Psalm 121: 4, 'He that keepeth Israel shall neither slumber nor sleep'.

50 circumscriptible] subject to limits of space.

51 Continent] containing agent or space (*OED sb.* I).

62 trustlesse] treacherous, untrustworthy (*OED* 1).

2.3

1 Discomfited] routed, completely overthrown (*OED v.* 1).

8 to...die] I put an end to any further possibility of sinning.

9 Conceive] beget, institute: see *OED* 1.c (unique cited use 1642), 13 (a legal use, in this case therefore metaphoric).

10 bathing] *OED* cites this example (5.b), noting that 'to bathe in blood' is a stock expression used figuratively to indicate a great amount of blood shed.

18 scaldes] is injured (by hot liquid) (*OED v.* 1.c, earliest cited use).

Tartarian] pertaining to Tartarus, infernal (*OED*, Tartarean, *a.*[1], first cited use 1623); cf. *One*, 1.1.71*n*.

19 banefull] poisonous (cf. *One*, 5.1.220*n*.).

20 *Zoacum*] As Seaton[2] showed (385–7), this is a form, derived from Lonicerus, of the word 'ezecum', the tree of Hell on which the damned feed. It is described in the Koran, 37.60–64. Lines 18–23 are closely based on this description as it appears in Lonicerus (see Thomas–Tydeman, 151–2).

21 ingraft] 'firmly rooted' (Jump) (*OED* cites this example under engraff, 1, referring it to non-metaphoric uses of engraft, 1.a).

22 *Flora*] Cf. *One*, 5.1.140*n*.

24–6 The Dyvils...end] Ellis-Fermor notes the combination of Christian and classical elements; for *Orcus* cf. *One*, 3.1.65*n*.

24 quencelesse] Cf. *One*, 2.6.33*n*.

27 foile] disgrace (*OED sb.*[2] 2.b); or defeat (cf. *One*, 3.3.213*n*).

29 his] Christ's.

30 *Cynthia*] Cf. *One*, 4.2.35*n*.

31 fortune of the wars] '*fortuna de la guerra*' seems to have been a proverbial phrase: *LLL*, 5.2.526; Jonson, *The Case is Altered*, 1.4.17.

32 proov'd ... myracle] 'offered as a demonstration of miraculous agency' (J. S. Cunningham); cf. *OED*, prove, *v*. 5.

36 miscreant] Cf. *One*, 3.3.236*n*.

38 wil] decree, give order (*OED v*.¹ 3.a).

watch ... ward] continuous guard (a set phrase, perhaps understood to mean operating both by night and day: *OED*, watch, *sb*. 7.a).

trunke] dead body (*OED sb*. 3).

40 give ... charge] take order for it immediately (*OED*, charge, *sb*. 13.b); straight, cf. *One*, 2.2.18*n*.

43 Our Army] i.e. the greater part of his army, sent to assist his allies against Tamburlaine; cf. 2.1.16–21.

brothers] *O1*'s 'brother' (retained by Bowers, J. S. Cunningham, and others) might possibly be an archaic plural, but *OED* records no use later than *c*.1400 (A. *a*).

44 *Amasia*] In the maps of Ortelius, a district of northern Natolia.

47 angry] grievous (*OED a*. 1).

2.4

0SD1 *Arras*] Cf. 1.2.44*n*., here used for the curtain enclosing the discovery space or (depending on the structure of the theatre) a removable booth placed on the stage. The main speakers (Zenocrate excepted) step forward on to the stage for the duration of the scene, and return to the discovery space (or booth) at its close (cf. l. 142SD).

0SD3 *tempering*] blending together the ingredients of (*OED v*. 3).

2–4 The ... beames] i.e. Zenocrate's eyes were the source of the sun's light; cf. *One*, 5.1.147–50.

4 enflamde] kindled (*OED* 1.a).

9 bowers] i.e. the place where the eyes are set.

10 tempered] refreshed, disposed favourably (*OED v*. 5, 6).

12 no ... Mate] no counterpart (*OED sb*.² 3.c). 'Second' is, strictly, supererogatory (there is no accepted 'first' counterpart): Tamburlaine's argument is that heaven has been provoked by Zenocrate's beauty rivalling the sun's.

14 dasled] overpowered, confounded (*OED v*. 4).

17, 21, 25, 29, 33 entertaine] receive (*OED v*. 12).

18 *Apollo*] The sun.

Cynthia] Cf. *One*, 4.2.35*n*.

ceaslesse lamps] The planets and stars.

22 christall springs] Referring to the heavenly river of life in Revelation 22: 1, where it sparkles like crystal (Kocher, 94). Ellis-Fermor sees also references to Psalm 46: 4 ('the rivers' which 'shall make glad the city of God') and to Aganippe, the fountain at the foot of Mount Helicon sacred to the Muses.

illuminates] Cf. 1.3.2*n*.

23 Refined] given clearer sight (*OED v.* 3.a).

24 tried] purified (*OED ppl.a.* 1).

runs] Cf. *One*, 1.1.117*n*.

26–7 The . . . kings] Cornelius (176) notes the reference to Isaiah 6: 2–3.

30 currious] skilfully, beautifully wrought (*OED* 7.a).

35 imperiall heaven] Cf. *One*, 2.7.15*n*.

40 And if] provided that (*OED*, and, *conj*. C. 1.b).

fit] mortal crisis, bodily state betokening death (*OED sb.*[1] 2.b).

43 That] Who (Abbott, 260).

fraile . . . flesh] Tilley F363, 'Flesh is frail'.

45 dated] having a fixed term (cf. *One*, 2.6.37*n*.).

46 Wanes] Cf. *One*, 1.1.117*n*. Though the antecedent here is, strictly, 'Emperesses', the form of the verb may be influenced by the intervening singular 'flesh'.

necessary] inevitable (*OED a.* 5.a).

50 Gives . . . stars] Cf. ll. 2–4.

Phœbus] Cf. *One*, 1.2.40*n*.

fixed stars] The sphere of the fixed stars was the eighth sphere of the pre-Copernican universe, below the outermost, the *primum mobile*, and the crystalline heaven, and above the sphere of Saturn (the farthest planet then known). S. K. Heninger reproduces sixteenth-century illustrations of the spheres in *The Cosmological Glass: Renaissance Diagrams of the Universe* (San Marino, Calif., 1977): see esp. 38. The fixed stars were 'fixed' not in the sense of being stationary but in that they appeared to maintain the same positions relative to one another.

51 Whose] Parallel to 'whose' in l. 49 (i.e. referring to 'life', not 'stars').

52–4 As . . . traine] These lines describe the conditions for a lunar eclipse (which can only take place at night, so the sun is necessarily absent). During an eclipse of the moon the sun and moon are diametrically opposite each other on different sides of the earth: the moon no longer reflects the sun's light because it is in the shadow cast by the earth. Marlowe's Serpent is the northern constellation *Draco*, the Dragon (see *OED*, dragon¹, 8.a and b). The Dragon's head is the ascending node of the moon's orbit with the ecliptic, the Dragon's tail the corresponding descending node. Kocher (228) gives a closely similar account of lunar eclipses from John Blagrave, *The Mathematical Jewel* (London, 1584). See also E. H. Neville, *TLS*, 12.7.1947, 351.

54 traine] tail (*OED sb.*¹ 5.c).

56 author] cause (*OED sb.* 1.c) (*Q*'s emendation).

58 fiery Element] Marlowe directly translates the medieval Latin (*elementum ignis*) for the sphere above 'the triple region of the aire' (see *One*, 4.2.30n.) and below the rotating spheres of the heavens. *OED*, element, *sb.* 10.b: one of the celestial spheres of ancient astronomy; and cf. *One*, 2.7.15n. Heninger (40) reproduces a sixteenth-century diagram.

59 make... kingdome] i.e. make a kingdom for you.

61 suspect... mine] 'imagine your death to follow as a consequence of mine' (Bevington–Rasmussen).

64–5 breast... rest] An unusual mid-speech couplet.

68 my... life] i.e. the life of immortality.

73–6 nobilitie... excellency] A double couplet, marking a formal close to Zenocrate's solemn farewell.

74 my... memorie] my last thoughts before death.

77SD *They... musicke*] i.e. a company of musicians (*OED sb.* 5). The musicians enter at this point, and should begin to play while Tamburlaine speaks (the stage direction at l. 95 meaning 'the music still sounding'). No undue pause is then required before Tamburlaine discovers Zenocrate's death at l. 96.

81 those Spheares] i.e. Zenocrate's eyes (cf. *One*, 1.2.176n.).

83 supplied with] occupied by (as a substitute) (*OED v.*¹ 9).

87 *Hellen*] Cf. *One*, 1.1.66n.

88 *Tenedos*] An island in the north-eastern Aegean off the coast of Troy, assembly point of the Greek fleet during the Trojan war.

90 Her] i.e. Zenocrate's.

93 *Lesbia... Corinna*] Women addressed and celebrated in the love poetry of Catullus and Ovid.

94 argument] theme, subject (*OED sb.* 6).

99 fatall Sisters] Cf. *One*, 1.2.174n.

100 triple mote] The three rivers of the Underworld (named at
3.2.13), perhaps, as Ellis-Fermor suggests, suggested by the Virgilian
Underworld's triple wall (*Aeneid*, VI. 549).

103 Cavalieros] In fortifications, constructions raised higher than, and
so commanding a view of, those around them (*OED*, cavalier, *sb*. 4, citing
this example).

114 rusty] having fallen out of use (*OED a.*¹ 6), and therefore needing
to be forced open.

114–15 *Janus*... war] Janus, the Roman god of beginnings, had a
covered passage (commonly referred to as a temple) dedicated to him
close by the forum in Rome. It was left open in times of war to indicate
that the god had gone to assist the Roman armies. The twin gates, and
their use in a formal declaration of war, are described by Virgil (*Aeneid*,
VII. 607–15). Marlowe refers to them, closed, to symbolize peace, in
Lucans First Booke (ll. 61–2).

117 *Tamburlain*... great] The first time Tamburlaine himself uses the
title phrase. The only other occasion is equally solemn (3.2.92).

129 her... thou] The shift of pronouns indicates that Tamburlaine
turns from thoughts of Zenocrate's soul to addressing her corpse.

130 Cassia] A fragrant shrub with both biblical and classical associa-
tions (*OED*, cassia¹, 3, first cited use 1594, though it would be known to
Marlowe from Coverdale's translation of Psalm 45 in the Elizabethan
Prayer Book).

Amber Greece] A usual sixteenth-century spelling of ambergris, a
wax-like substance, tropical in origin, used in perfumery.

131 lapt... lead] *OED* glosses as 'placed in a leaden coffin' (lap, *v.*²
3.a); but 5.3.226 ('Pierce through the coffin and the sheet of gold')
suggests rather 'wrapped in a sheet of lead' (and placed in a coffin).

133 *Mausolus*] King of Caria, who reigned 377–53 BC. His widow built
for him a huge memorial tomb (the Mausoleum) which was one of the
seven Wonders of the ancient world.

135 severall] different (*OED a.* 2.a).

137–8 This... Love] Marlowe may have had in mind various preced-
ents for Tamburlaine's rite of mourning. Plutarch (*The Lives of the Noble
Grecians and Romanes*, trans. Sir Thomas North, 1579) reports that
Alexander signified his sorrow for the death of Hephæstion by acts of
destruction and genocide. Richard II, as Holinshed records, destroyed the
House of Shene when his queen, Anne of Bohemia, died there in 1394.

140 statua] The word may mean either statue or (more loosely) an
image or effigy (*OED sb.* 1.a and b). *OED* accepts the emendation of

statue to statua in Shakespeare (*2HVI*, *RIII* and *Julius Caesar*) where a trisyllable is required, on the grounds that there is no evidence of the trisyllabic pronounciation statuë.

141 campe] Cf. *One*, 2.5.26*n*.

142SD *The . . . drawen*] Cf. OSD 1*n*.

3.1

OSD 4 *other*] others (*OED sb*. 4.a), i.e. the kings of Trebizond and Soria.

1 *Calepinus . . . Cybelius*] Seaton² (388–9) suggests that Marlowe derived these forms of Callapine's name (or title) from Lonicerus. He might also have found the form 'Cyriscelebes' in Thomas Newton (see Introduction: Sources, pp. xxiii–xxiv).

4 *Amasia*] Cf. 2.3.44*n*.

5 *Thracia*] The ancient name (given in Ortelius) of the district west of the Bosporus, modern north-western Turkey.

Carmonia] In the maps of Ortelius 'Carmania' is a province of south-eastern Natolia.

8 kings, *Natolia*] *O1*'s 'of' (see Apparatus) is hypermetrical and, since there is only one King of Natolia, gives a false meaning.

14 dismembred] divided up (*OED ppl.a.* 1.b).

16 *Persea*] Cf. *One*, 1.1.162*n*.

17 Do . . . supremacie] acknowledge and honour us (i.e. me) as overlord (as Bajazeth was forced to acknowledge Tamburlaine); as J. S. Cunningham notes, the usage is not recorded in *OED*.

19–20 As . . . infamies] 'That men would unanimously efface our noble names from the record of vile infamies' (Jump), where Bajazeth's illusage had caused them to be placed.

26 grievous] full of grief (*OED* 6, citing this example).

28–30 Fortune . . . inconstancie] Cf. Tilley F605, 'Fortune is constant only in inconstancy'. As J. S. Cunningham notes, the thought can be traced at least to Ovid, *Tristia*, 5.8.15–18, 'Fortuna volubilis . . . tantum constans in levitate sua est' ('Changeable fortune . . . is steadfast only in her own fickleness').

31 pitch] altitude, elevation (*OED sb.²* 18.c).

32 strong] performed with a powerful fighting force (*OED a.* 7.c).

fortunate] favoured by Fortune (*OED a.* 1).

35 happy] Cf. *One*, 1.2.257*n*.

36 surchardg'd] overwhelmed (*OED v.* 4.b, citing this example).

37 it] i.e. pity.

42 them] themselves.

43 drinke...river] 'To drink the ocean dry' was proverbial (Tilley O9); cf. *One*, 2.3.15–16n. and *Jew*, 5.5.120.

Euphrates] Cf. *One*, 5.1.440n. (similarly at l. 53).

46 *Scalonias*] As Seaton[1] (30) makes clear, 'Scalona' in the maps of Ortelius, better known to the Elizabethans under its biblical name, Ashkelon (modern Ashqelon in Israel), is a town south-west of Jerusalem, on the coast.

51 *Chio...Amasia*] In the maps of Ortelius 'Chia' is a town in central northern Natolia, on the shores of the Black Sea. Famastro is a town immediately east of Chia. On Amasia, cf. 2.3.44n.

52 *Mare-major*] The 'Great Sea', i.e. the Black Sea; cf. 1.2.215n.

53 *Riso, Sancina*] In the maps of Ortelius Riso is a town on the eastern shores of the Black Sea. 'Santina' is a town immediately north of Riso.

59 *Aleppo, Soldino*] In the maps of Ortelius Aleppo is a town in northern Syria (modern Halab). Soldino is a town on the Syrian coast, west of Aleppo.

64 battaile] army, body of troops in battle array (*OED sb.* 8.a).

pitcht] set in order for fighting (*OED v.*[1] 11.a).

65 use] custom (*OED sb.* 7.a).

65–6 beare...Moone] Kocher (242) cites Paulus Jovius, *A Short Treatise upon the Turkes Chronicles* (London, 1546) to show that this form of battle array ('bent after the fashion of the newe moone') was particularly associated with Bajazeth.

69 for] as for.

73 Gentleman] A man ranked by birth immediately below the nobility (*OED* 1.a).

74 That's...king] There's no importance attached to being of gentle birth as far as becoming a king is concerned (see *OED*, matter, *sb.*[1] 18.a). Marlowe adapts the proverbial 'A gentleman may make a king [and a clerk (i.e. cleric) may prove a pope]' (Dent G65).

3.2

1 this...towne] i.e. Larissa.

2 highest...aire] Cf. *One*, 4.2.30n.

3 exhalations] a body of vapour, usually enkindled (*OED* 3); pronounced as five syllables. Heninger (92) offers illustrations of various forms of fiery exhalations from *The Kalender of Sheepeherds* (1560).

4 meteors] Cf. *One*, 1.1.11*n*.

6 Over . . . Zenith] directly above me (*OED*, zenith, 1). Pendry–Maxwell suggest for 'zenith' a sense not recorded by *OED*, 'point of dominant (astrological) influence'.

12 Island] Marlowe apparently conceives of Hades as an island surrounded by a 'triple moat' of three rivers (cf. 2.4.100 and note).

maske] Cf. *One*, 4.4.17*n*.

15 Piller plac'd] With ellipsis of 'shall be'.

19 streamer] Cf. *One*, 4.2.120*n*.

20 Wrought] embroidered (*OED* 3.b).

23 table] tablet (*OED sb.* 2.a).

24 perfections] Pronounced as four syllables.

26 admyr'd] Cf. *One*, 1.2.204*n*.

29–32 cause . . . Hemi-spheare] 'Cause the stars of the southern latitudes (the loveliness of which cannot be seen by any but those who have crossed the equator) to make a pilgrimage to our northern latitudes'.

29 arke] the part of a circle a heavenly body appears to pass through above or below the horizon (*OED sb.* 2, citing this example).

31 Centers latitude] i.e the equator (see *OED*, centre, *sb.* 2.a; latitude, 4.a).

34 Thou] Addressing the portrait of Zenocrate.

36–39 At . . . will] 'At every town . . . I besiege, and when I encounter an army . . . your portrait shall be set on my . . . tent, the sight of which will . . .'. Dyce breaks the syntax at the end of l. 37, and emends 'Whose' to 'Those'; but the punctuation of *O1* suggests no need for emendation.

39 influence] Cf. *One*, 1.1.15*n*.

campe] Cf. *One*, 2.5.26*n*.

40 *Bellona*] Roman goddess of war.

41 sulphur . . . fire] Ellis-Fermor notes that this may be the so-called Greek fire, a combustible composition used for setting fire to an enemy's fortifications, etc. (*OED*, fire, *sb.* 8.b; cf. 'wildfire', *One*, 5.1.312*n*.); or that Marlowe may intend an early form of hand-grenade such as that described in Paul Ive, *The Practise of Fortification* (London, 1589), from which Marlowe took much of the detail about military practices in this scene (see notes on ll. 62 ff).

47 sea . . . teares] 'A sea (or ocean) of tears' was a set phrase (Dent T82.1).

62–82 Then . . . breach] Marlowe took much of the technical vocabulary of this speech, and much of its detail concerning contemporary military practices, from Paul Ive, *The Practise of Fortification* (London, 1589) (see detailed notes following, and Thomas–Tydeman, 153–6), a source which was first noticed by F.-C. Danchin, *Revue Germanique*, 8 (1912), 23–33. Ellis-Fermor (8–10) argues that Marlowe probably saw Ive's work in manuscript, perhaps through their mutual connection with the Walsingham family. Difficulties of interpretation suggest that Marlowe may sometimes have followed Ive's words without wholly envisaging their meanings.

62 fortifie] surround with defences (*OED v.* 8, citing this example).

63 champion] Cf. *One*, 2.2.40n.

64 which] Perhaps elliptical—'for which other kind of ground' (referring back loosely to l. 63); or Craik conjectures (this edn.) that a line may be missing between ll. 63 and 64 (but, if this is the case, Marlowe is not following Ive so closely that what it might have been can be conjectured).

quinque-angle] five-angled, *OED* first cited use (though Marlowe took the word from Ive).

64–7 For which . . . desperate] i.e. for a fort which has to be built on uneven (not 'champion') terrain the shape of an irregular pentagon is appropriate, because the obtuse-angled corners (which are easier to defend) can be situated on those parts of the ground which are strategically favourable to attackers, while the acute-angled corners (more difficult to defend) can be situated on parts of the ground difficult to assault (Ive, Bb2; Kocher, 254).

66 Whereas] where (*OED* 1).

68 Counterscarps] outer walls of the ditch which support the covered way (*OED* 1).

69 Narrow . . . steepe] It is the covered way that should be narrow, the sides of the ditch which should be steep.

70 Bulwarks] substantial defensive works of earth or other material (*OED sb.* 1.a), often a station for heavy artillery (Kocher, 250).

rampiers] ramparts (*OED*, rampire, *sb.* 1.a), usually surmounted by a parapet on which musketeers could stand, shielded by the wall (l. 77).

71 Cavalieros] Cf. 2.4.103n.

counterforts] buttresses to support a wall (*OED* 1.a, first cited use, though Marlowe took the word directly from Ive).

73–4 It . . . ditch] Ellis-Fermor notes that Marlowe follows Ive peculiarly closely in these lines: 'It must also have countermines, privie ditches, secret issuings out to defende the ditch' (Ive, Aa3^v; Thomas–Tydeman, 154). A privy (secret) ditch ran along the centre of a main ditch as an extra obstacle to infantry and to mines (Kocher, 252).

73 countermines] subterranean excavations made by the defenders of a fortress to intercept mines dug by the besiegers (*OED sb.* 1.a).

74 issuings] outlets (*OED vbl. sb.* 2, citing this example), permitting defenders to enter the ditch to drive out besiegers who might effect an entry (Kocher, 252).

75 Argins] embankments in front of a fort (*OED*, only citations from Ive and Marlowe), designed to cover defending infantry (Kocher, 252), or hinder the approach of attackers (Ive, Thomas–Tydeman, 154).

covered] concealed, secret (*OED ppl.a.* 2)—concealed by the argin (Ive, Dd4).

77 Parapets] protections against shot raised on the top of ramparts (*OED* 1).

Muscatters] *OED*, musketeer, first cited use.

78 Casemates] a vaulted chamber built in the thickness of the ramparts, with embrasures for the defence of the place (*OED* 1.a, which also cites Ive's definition of this word of variable signification: 'any ... edifice in the ditch that may be made to defend the ditch by' [Ive, Dd3^v]).

79 flanke] any part of a work so disposed as to defend another by flanking fire, especially the part of a bastion reaching from the curtain (see following note) to the face and defending the opposite face (*OED sb.*^{1} 7, first cited use).

80 curtaines] the plain walls of a fortified place, those parts of the walls that connect bulwarks (*OED sb.*^{1} 4.a).

81 Dismount] throw down from their supports (*OED v.* 6).

adverse part] opposite side, enemy.

82 Murther] slaughter, massacre (*OED v.* 1.d); E. A. J. Honigmann (in J. S. Cunningham) suggests a play on murderer, a small cannon (*OED* 2).

84 demonstration] Pronounced as five syllables.

85–90 make ... place] Two separate lessons are envisaged: how to build a dam; how to build a fortress at sea.

85 mount] rise (*OED v.* 1.e, earliest cited use 1594).

86 That] So that.

88 make] i.e. how to make.

91 souldiers] Cf. *One*, 2.2.63*n*.

96 Curtle-axe] Cf. *One*, 1.2.42*n*.

99 A . . . horse] Kocher (246–7) argues that 'mingled with' should here be understood as 'closely flanked by'—a defensive circular formation of pikemen which would be tactically orthodox. Proposed emendations suppose a high degree of compositorial misreading ('pikes and horse mangled with shot', *conj.* Mitford; 'pikes of mingled foot and horse', Francis Cunningham).

shot] soldiers armed with muskets or other firearms (*OED sb.*¹ 21.a).

101 sunny motes] particles of dust seen floating in sunbeams (*OED*, mote, *sb.*¹ 1.a), a standard comparison (Dent M1192).

104 overthwart] across (*OED prep.* 1).

107–8 Filling . . . blood] Cf. 'Good wine makes good blood', Tilley W461—a supposition of Elizabethan popular medicine echoed in Spenser (*The Faerie Queene*, V.vii.10), Shakespeare (*Much Ado*, 1.1.233–4), and Jonson (*Volpone*, 5.1.16).

107 aiery] like air in its lightness and buoyancy (*OED* 6, first cited use 1598). Pendry–Maxwell conjecture 'effervescent' (a sense not supported by *OED*), and note that 'air is the equivalent of the "humour" blood, both being hot and moist'.

108 concocted] digested (*OED v.* 4).

114 lance] cut, slit (*OED v.* 6.a, citing *One*, 1.2.146, spelling as here).

114–15 all . . . deepe] The punctuation of *O1* (see Apparatus) assumes that Marlowe here uses 'teach' absolutely, without an additional indirect object, which he otherwise does only once, in translating Ovid (*All Ovids Elegies*, 1.14.30, where the word is used in a rhyming position). It seems probable, therefore, that the *O1* compositor, perhaps misled by a stage direction centred and given a line to itself, created the un-Marlovian syntax which has been generally accepted.

120 Enchac'd] Cf. *One*, 1.2.96n.

124 the . . . Potentate] i.e. Bajazeth; cf. *One*, 1.2.16 (where Africa is apparently used to denote the Turkish empire) and note, and *One*, 3.1.23.

135 bravely] fearlessly (*OED adv.* 1).

149 Coward . . . runaway] i.e. Callapine. *O1*'s punctuation (see accidental emendations) suggests that 'coward' and 'faint-heart' be taken as nouns. Both are also adjectival forms, and it is as an adjective that *OED* cites this use of faint-heart (first cited example).

151 at . . . bay] at bay. All of *OED*'s sixteenth-century examples (*sb.*⁴ 3) retain, as here, some form of the article.

156 puissance] Pronounced as three syllables.

3.3

OSD 1 *traine*] Cf. 1.1.0SD 2*n*.

2 *pioners*] Cf. *One*, 3.1.58*n*. (similarly at l. 20).

3 *Balsera*] Cf. Dramatis Personae, notes.

hold] stronghold (cf. ll. 16 and 24).

6 Minions . . . Sakars] Various kinds of small artillery (the distinctions between which were not fixed).

trench] defensive ditch around the outer walls, the earth from which is thrown up as a parapet (*OED sb.* 3.a); for the tactics involved cf. ll. 25–6.

11 summon] give notice of (*OED v.* 6).

parle] Cf. 1.1.11*n*.

Drum] Cf. 1.1.0SD 2*n*.

13 friendes] Bowers (I. 225) tentatively defends *O1*'s 'friend' as a collective singular, but his example, *Julius Caesar*, 5.3.18 (*OED* B) is not a proper parallel (the use is adjectival, not, as here, substantival); and, as Bowers admits, the plurals in ll. 19 and 35 support emendation.

14SD 1 *battell*] Cf. 3.1.63*n*.

SD 2 *above*] i.e. in the gallery above the stage; cf. 5.1.0SD, '*upon the walles*'.

23 Argins . . . waies] Cf. 3.2.75*n*.

24 bulwarks] Cf. 3.2.70*n*.

25 ordinance] artillery (*OED* 2.a).

26 his] its.

ruine] fall (*OED sb.* 1.a), i.e. the fall of the breached fortification walls.

38 mounts] defensive earthworks (*OED sb.*[1] 2.a).

intrench] fortify with trenches (*OED* 1.b, citing this example); similarly at l. 42.

39 Cut . . . can] The present emendation (see Apparatus) assumes elision of the second syllable of 'water'; for 'that' with ellipsis of the following relative see *OED dem. pron.* 7.

44 it] i.e. the cast-up earth.

low] in a low position (*OED adv.* 1.a).

50 Jacobs staffe] a surveying instrument used for measuring distances and heights (in military contexts, in relation to gun ranges) (*OED* 2.b).

53 full] directly, straight (*OED adv.* C 3.a).

point blancke] in a horizontal line (*OED adv.* C 1, first cited use 1594).

54 see] see to.

55 battery] the fortified work within which the artillery is mounted (*OED* 5.a, first cited example).

56 Gabions] wicker baskets filled with earth (for use as shields) (*OED* 1).

60 cracke] a sudden loud noise (commonly applied to the roar of a cannon) (*OED sb.* 1.a).

60–61 crie . . . Sky] An emphatic end-of-speech couplet.

62 Trumpets . . . drums] Cf. 1.1.0SD2*n*.

alarum] sound a call to arms (*OED v.* 1.a, first cited use).

presently] Cf. *One*, 2.5.94*n*.

63 play . . . men] conduct yourselves heroically (*OED*, play, *v.* 34, to behave like).

3.4

2 cave] underground passage (Jump).

9 straineth] trickles (*OED v.*¹ 15.a, first cited use).

orifex] obs. erron. form of 'orifice' (*OED*'s first cited use, but not unique).

13 daies . . . sepulcher] Though 'sepulchre' could be stressed on the second syllable in the sixteenth century, elsewhere in the play Marlowe stresses it on the first (e.g. 3.5.19); 'and' (here omitted: see Apparatus) is therefore hypermetrical (probably an error, by eye-skip from the preceding line).

15 this] i.e. the dagger she draws.

16–17 Now . . . remaines] For the sources of Olympia's killing of her son and herself in Belleforest (*Cosmographie Universelle*, vol. ii, cols. 749–50), first identified by Seaton² (395–6), see Thomas–Tydeman, 157–8.

21 wheele] an instrument of torture (*OED sb.* 2.a).

24 lance] Cf. 3.2.114*n*.

29 tyrannise] exercise power cruelly (*OED* 3.a).

33SD *She . . . bodies*] Bowers' stage direction (see Apparatus) is endorsed by ll. 71–2. That Henslowe's company had some means of bringing fire on to the stage, or at least representing it satisfactorily, is clear from 5.1.178–86.

46 And . . . greater] Brooke's conjecture (see Apparatus), which attempts to address the line's faulty metre, requires that '*Mahomet*' be stressed on the second syllable, whereas it is stressed throughout the play

on the first (see *One*, 3.1.54*n*.). 'Thou shalt' may have been introduced by eye-skip from l. 39.

48–50 from . . . sits] i.e. through the full extent of the heavens, from the outermost to the innermost sphere.

48 superficies] the boundary that separates one part of space from another (*OED* 1); pronounced as five syllables.

49 imperiall Orbe] Cf. *One*, 2.7.15*n*.

50 bower . . . sits] i.e. the moon (cf. *One*, 4.2.35*n*.).

51 *Thetis*] Cf. 1.3.169*n*.

52 That] Who (i.e. Tamburlaine); cf. 2.4.43*n*.

53 God . . . armes] Cf. *One*, 5.1.327*n*.

54 fatall sisters] Cf. *One*, 1.2.174*n*.

57 *Rhamnusia*] Cf. *One*, 2.3.38*n*.

59 ugly] having an appearance which causes dread or horror (*OED a*. 1).

furies] Cf. *One*, 2.7.53*n*.

61 Over . . . Zenith] i.e. directly above whom (cf. 3.2.6*n*.).

62–3 Eagles . . . Trumpe] Wings and a trumpet are standard symbolic attributes of Fame in Renaissance emblem books, as, for example, in Cesare Ripa's *Iconologia* (1593).

64 adverse] opposite in position (*OED a*. 3, first cited use 1623).

that . . . line] the pole which was thought to form the axis on which the celestial spheres revolved (cf. *One*, 4.2.50*n*.).

75 frame] the action of framing, fashioning (*OED sb*. 2.a).

81 fatall] Cf. *One*, 5.1.386*n*.

86 *Natolia*] Here and in the following scene Marlowe transforms what is elsewhere in the play (and in the maps of Ortelius) a province into a town.

91 our] Theridamas (King of Argier) perhaps intends to emphasize his dignity by a royal plural (*OED* 1.c).

3.5

3 Here] i.e. nearby, to the south. Callapine and his army are not (as the line might imply) in Syria, but in eastern Natolia (cf. ll. 11–12 and note).

Alepo] Cf. 3.1.58*n*.

4 *Persea*] Cf. *One*, 1.1.162*n*.

5 the . . . leaves] Cf. *One*, 4.1.30–2.

6 *Idas*] Presumably the classical Mount Ida in Asia Minor (Natolia), from which the gods in Homer watch the Trojan War. (There is also a Mount Ida on Crete.)

11 *Phrigia*] A classical name for part of Asia Minor (not shown as such on the maps of Ortelius); in terms of the geography of *Tamburlaine* apparently a district of western Natolia.

14 play...men] Cf. 3.3.63n.

18 The...fought] The site of this unhistorical battle (about which Marlowe is perhaps intentionally imprecise) is later called '*Asphaltis*' (4.3.5), and '*Asphaltis* plaines' (4.3.68), and is connected with '*Limnasphaltis*', the lake near Babylon (5.1.17). 'Asphaltites Lacus' is one name for the Mare Mortuum or Dead Sea, but no use of such a name with reference to Marlowe's location is to be found in Ortelius or classical geography. Marlowe apparently intends the Euphrates basin, the bituminous nature of the waters of which he may have known from Plutarch's Life of Alexander (see 2.4.137–8n.), from Herodotus' description of Babylon (*Historia*, 1. 179), or from contemporary testimonies such as those known to Hakluyt (Seaton,[1] 25–6): see, for example, the voyage of Ralph Fitch:

By the river Euphrates two dayes journey from Babylon at a place called Ait, in a fielde neere unto it, it is a strange thing to see: a mouth that doth continually throwe foorth against the ayre boyling pitch with a filthy smoke: which pitch doth runne abroad into a great fielde which is always full thereof. The Moores say that it is the mouth of hell.

Hakluyt, *The Principal Navigations...of the English Nation*, ed. Edmund Goldsmid (Edinburgh, 16 vols. 1884–90), x. 23.

24 lake] underground dungeon, prison (*OED sb.*[4] 3.b).

28 pawes] Francis Cunningham emended to 'jaws', but 'paw' was used, not only for the feet of animals, but also for the claws of birds of prey (*OED sb.*[1] 1.b), and is used by Marlowe in a context similar to the present one (not of devils but of the Furies) in *Massacre*, 22.10.

29 entertaine] Cf. 2.4.17n.

34 shewed] perhaps mustered before (cf. *OED v.* 4.c, first cited use 1655; and *sb.*[1] 1.c from 1548); 'displayed to, as in a military march of inspection before a commander or sovereign' (Bevington–Rasmussen); pronounced as one syllable.

35 *Arabia* desart] A direct translation of Ortelius's 'Arabia Deserta', modern northern Saudi Arabia.

36–7 whose...*Semyramis*] The legendary queen Semiramis rebuilt Babylon and its hanging gardens.

36 Metropolis] capital (*OED* 2, first cited use).

39, 45 numbred] reckoned up our numbers (*OED v.* 2.a, citing this example).

40 *Asia* the lesse] A direct translation of Asia Minor; Asia pronounced as three syllables.

41 stout] Cf. *One*, 3.3.93*n.*

Bythinians] Cf. *One*, 3.3.2*n.*

43 knowes] Cf. *One*, 1.1.117*n.*

46 *Halla*] In Ortelius' map of the world (though it is not shown on his more detailed maps) Halla is a substantial city due east of Aleppo.

57SD2 *other*] Possibly a plural form: cf. 3.1.0SD4*n.*

62 he] Their death, i.e. Tamburlaine himself.

65–8 As . . . *Achilles*] Ellis-Fermor points out that this episode is not from the *Iliad*, but is treated in various narratives of the Trojan War, such as Lydgate's *Troy Book* (3. 3755 ff.).

66 overdare] daunt, overcome by daring, or surpass in daring (*OED v.* 2, first cited use).

74 fly] flee (*OED v.*[1] 11.a).

glove] Thrown down as a challenge to combat.

75 fearfull of] anxious about (*OED* 3.c, citing this example).

76 Thou . . . fight] You wish, relying on your individual superiority, to engage in single combat. Overmatch, a contest in which one side is more than a match for the other (*OED* 1, last cited use).

78 lance] Cf. 3.2.114*n.*

80 gratious aspect] favourable conjunction of the planets (cf. *One*, 1.1.13–14*n.*, and *One*, 1.2.92); gratious, pronounced as three syllables; aspect, accented on the second syllable.

81–2 join'd . . . world] i.e. never again will any birth be blessed by this particularly favourable astrological conjunction.

87 villaine] i.e. Almeda.

88 false] prove false to (*OED v.* 4).

91 abuses] injuries, wrongs (*OED sb.* 5, first cited use 1593).

93 Brigandine] Cf. *One*, 3.3.248*n.*

94 spoile] pillage, plunder (*OED v.*[1] 5).

96 lusty] vigorous (*OED* 5.a).

100 clogge] a block of wood attached to the leg or neck to prevent escape (*OED sb.* 2.a).

101 for] as a precaution against, to prevent you from (*OED* 23.d).

103 Viceroys] Many editors retain *O1*'s singular (see Apparatus), which Bevington–Rasmussen take as scornfully referring to Almeda. But Tamburlaine has in mind the kings with whom he is in dialogue (ll. 103–15), and on whom this cruelty is eventually visited. He does not turn his attention to Almeda after ll. 87–8 until drawn to notice him again by Celebinus at l. 116.

103–7 bits... planks] Allan Gilbert, *Rivista di Letterature Moderne*, 4 (1954), 208–10, shows that this is based ultimately on the account in Diodorus Siculus of the similar behaviour of the semi-legendary Egyptian ruler Sesostris:

whenever he intended to visit a temple or city he would remove the horses from his four-horse chariot and in their place yoke the kings and other potentates, taking them four at a time, in this way showing to all men, as he thought, that, having conquered the mightiest of other kings and those most renowned for their excellence, he now had no one who could compete with him for the prize of excellence. (*Bibliotheca historia*, trans. Oldfather, I. 58. 2)

Marlowe may have known this either directly, or through a reference in Lucan (*Pharsalia*, X. 277–8), or through the conjunction of a similar account of Sesostris with Tamburlaine's treatment of Bajazeth in Loys LeRoy's *De la Vicissitude ou variété des choses en l'univers* (1575): see Hallett Smith, '*Tamburlaine* and the Renaissance', *Elizabethan Studies and Other Essays in Honour of George F. Reynolds* (Boulder, 1945), 126–31 (129). Marlowe may also have known the *Jocasta* (1566) of George Gascoigne and Francis Kinwelmershe, in the dumbshow preceding the first act of which Sesostris appears driving a chariot drawn by four captive kings as an emblem of Ambition (Thomas–Tydeman, 165). The play was reprinted in *The pleasauntest workes of George Gascoigne Esquyre* (1587). As Hallett Smith points out, Nashe, in *Strange Newes* (1592), speaks of 'Tamberlaine drawne in a chariot by foure Kings' (*Works*, ed. McKerrow, i. 293).

113 Or... wrath] J. S. Cunningham finds this syntactically awkward if read as an alternative torment to that of the previous line, and reports the suggestion of E. A. J. Honigmann that 'thee' be emended to 'them'. But the syntax is clear if one supposes a not unusual ellipsis of 'to (bind)': see Abbott, 349.

115 journey] ride, drive (*OED v.* 3, first cited use).

127 livest] Pronounced as one syllable (liv'st).

not... Element] Not earth, air, fire, or water, i.e. nothing whatever. Cf. *One*, 1.2.236n.

131 *Ariadan*] Ortelius's map of Arabia shows this small town just as Callapine specifies, due south of Mecca in the region of modern Al Lith in Saudi Arabia.

132 *Mare Roso*] The 'Red Sea'.

136 Go too] An imperative expressing remonstrance (*OED v.* 93.b); cf. *One*, 5.1.310–19*n*.

138 give armes] exhibit armorial bearings (*OED sb.*[2] 15, citing this example): possibly, as several editors suppose, with a play on 'give alms' (*OED* 1.a), practise the charitable giving which, though enjoined on all, is particularly incumbent on those of your new rank. The following exchange takes up only the primary meaning, suggesting variously mocking heraldic devices for Almeda's coat of arms.

139 Scutchion] escutcheon, shield with armorial bearings (*OED sb.*[1] 1).

149 Camp] Cf. *One*, 2.5.26*n*.

150 Bugges] bugbears, bogeys (*OED sb.*[1] 1.a).

155 I] Ay.

165 aspect] Cf. *One*, 1.2.170*n*.

173SD *severally*] in (two) separate groups (see *OED* 1).

4.1

0SD1 *Alarme*] Cf. 1.3.183 (similarly at 51SD and 73SD).

issues] Cf. *One*, 1.1.117*n*.

the tent] Ernest L. Rhodes, in *Henslowe's Rose: the Stage & Staging* (Lexington, Kentucky U. P., 1976), 134–5, takes this tent to be represented by an opening in the wall of the stage, but some movable structure must have been arranged over a stage door to represent the tent, within which Calyphas (who never consents to issue from it, l. 31, until brought out by Tamburlaine, l. 91) is visible from the opening of the scene. The *O1* stage direction '*He* [Tamburlaine] *goes in*' (l. 90) could, taken by itself, mean either that Tamburlaine has something to enter or that he goes off stage; but it seems likely that J. S. Cunningham's added direction at l. 66 indicates Marlowe's intention: the tent is an on-stage structure.

5 swifter...thoughts] Based on the proverbial 'as swift as thought' (Tilley T240).

6 his] its (*OED poss. pron.* 3.c), i.e. the sword's.

conquering wings] Cf. *One*, 2.3.51, 57. Brereton (see Apparatus, followed in Kirschbaum's edition) proposes retaining the text of *O1*, simply modernizing the punctuation; but the construction is, as J. S. Cunningham remarks, un-Marlovian, and *O2*'s simple emendation seems preferable.

14 proper] Cf. *One*, 4.4.31*n*.

soile] disgrace (see *OED*, soil, *v.*[1] 3.a). The text here has been universally read as 'foile', but *O1*'s long *s* is clear. At *One*, 3.3.213 'soile' is emended to 'foile' (defeat), but, though that sense is possible here (and the foul-case error of long *s* for *f* easily made), the text as it stands also makes sense, and the reading of *O1* is, therefore, retained.

18 campe] Cf. *One*, 2.5.26*n*.

19 scar] Cf. *One*, 2.3.64*n*.

24 stil] Cf. *One*, 4.4.85*n*.

26 flesh ... swords] initiate us in fighting our first battle (*OED*, flesh, *v.* 3.a, first cited use); also *OED*'s first cited use of taintless—unstained, innocent.

28 conscience] Pronounced as three syllables.

32 house] family, lineage (*OED sb.*[1] 6).

33 tall] strong in combat, brave (*OED* 3); here perhaps specifically (following l. 27), 'brave enough to kill someone'; cf. *OED* citation of 1577; *Jew*, 3.2.7 (used of Mathias and Lodowick after they have killed each other); *Massacre*, 19.13 (said of the soldier who shoots the Guise); and Bevington and Rasmussen (eds.), *Doctor Faustus* (Manchester, 1993), A-text, I.iv.50*n*. (135).

34 toward] promising, forward (*OED a.* 3); accented on the first syllable.

35 For] as regards (*OED* 26.a, citing this example).

like] likely (*OED* A. *adj.* 9.a).

42–3 lofty ... *Tartary*] In Ortelius's map of Europe the Zona Mundi range of mountains appears in eastern Tartary (in northern Asia)—in modern terms, the northern range of the Ural Mountains, in north-eastern Russia.

45 bide] face, encounter (*OED v.* 7).

46 hautie] involving exalted courage (*OED* 2).

51SD *in*] i.e. offstage.

52 list] like, choose (*OED v.*[1] 1.b).

57 good] wealth (*OED* C. *sb.* 7.c)

66 Agreed] Cf. *One*, 3.2.113*n*.

68 *tara, tantaras*] imitating (and hence denoting) the sound of a trumpet or bugle (*OED* 1).

69 net] piece of fine mesh-work used as part of a dress, or a veil (*OED sb.*^{1} 3.a); 'suggesting also the snare in which Mars and Venus were caught by Vulcan as they made love; *Odyssey*, VIII. 300 ff ' (Bevington–Rasmussen).

and] and who.

76 coyle ... keepe] noisy disturbance they make (*OED*, coil, *sb.*^{2} 4.a); cf. 'to keep a foul coil', Tilley C505.

78 stoops] subdue (*OED v.*^{1} 7.a); for this and 'leads' (l. 77) cf. *One*, 1.1.117*n*.

79 sheep-like] submissively, pusillanimously (*OED*, citing this example).

sword] slaughter (*OED sb.* 3, citing this example).

81 illustrate] shed lustre, confer distinction upon (*OED v.* 4); accented on the second syllable.

82 tickle ... Spirits] are your spirits not eager (*OED*, tickle, *v.* 2).

87 magnanimity] Cf. *One*, 4.4.135*n*.

91 coward, villaine] Misled by emendations by Oxberry and Robinson elsewhere in the text (see Bowers, I. 225), Broughton argued for removing the comma here and understanding 'coward' as an adjective (cf. 3.2.149*n*.); but *O1*'s punctuation makes good sense and is consistent with Marlowe's usage elsewhere.

93–113 Image ... againe] Paul Kocher, *SP* 39 (1942), 207–25 (223–4) suggests that Marlowe here draws on an incident in Livy (VIII. vii) in which a father, Manlius Torquatus, orders the execution of his son Titus for an infringement of military discipline. Though this infringement is one of fighting when the son is forbidden to do so, and the father does not himself carry out the execution, there is a underlying similarity: in both cases the father feels his own military character impugned by his son's breach of military discipline. Livy concludes, 'The "orders of Manlius" ... became a type of severity with succeeding ages'. Kocher shows that the incident was often cited by Renaissance writers on military affairs as an exemplum.

94 obloquie] disgrace, cause of reproach (*OED* 2, first cited use 1589).

95 fired ... eies] i.e. set on fire with rage by what I see.

97 Shrowd] shelter, entertain (*OED v.*^{1} 2.a).

may] which may.

101 souldiers] Cf. *One*, 2.2.63*n*.

102 argument... Armes] i.e. implications for conduct and discipline of military life: an unusual usage, based metaphorically on argument, summary of the subject-matter of a book (*OED sb.* 7); arms, the practice of the military profession (*OED sb.*² 7), as at l. 103.

106 jealousie... warres] zeal for fighting as a profession or art (*OED*, jealousy, 2, last cited use 1565; war, *sb.*¹ 5.a).

108 joy'd... flesh] 'delighted in being born into this human flesh, ardent with vitality and aspiring to military deeds' (Bevington–Rasmussen).

109 foile] Cf. *One*, 3.3.213*n*.

110 Jaertis streame] In Ortelius' map of the Persian Empire the Jaxartes, called 'Chesel fl. olim (formerly) Iaxartes', runs north of Samarkand, west from Tartary into the Caspian Sea. In this map Samarkand is labelled 'magni Tamberlanis regia'. Perondinus places the city on the river, the modern Syr Darya (Thomas–Tydeman, 120).

112 distained] dishonoured (*OED v.* 2, citing this example).

113SD *stabs* CALYPHAS] This direction has been variously placed (see Apparatus). The argument for placing it at this point (as do Bevington–Rasmussen) is that l. 113 is the line which expresses the intention to stab. The argument for placing it at l. 122 (as does Dyce) is that this is the end of the syntactic unit with which that expression of intention begins; but immediately after l. 113 Tamburlaine turns from thoughts of his son's inadequacies to his own rivalry with Jove. The argument for placing it at the end of Tamburlaine's speech (as does Oxberry) is that the stage audience can then react immediately to what he has done; but after l.133 Tamburlaine's thoughts turn yet further from Calyphas to Orcanes and his allies.

114–17 A Forme... consists] i.e. the (cowardly) determining principle of Calyphas's soul makes it one not appropriate to give being to the god-like substance, his flesh, derived from his father Tamburlaine.

114 Forme] the essential determinant principle of a thing, its creative quality (*OED sb.* 4.a, noting its origin in Aristotle and use in Scholastic philosophy).

subject] the substance from which a thing is made (*OED sb.* 5, noting its origin in Aristotle, and citing the similar usage at 5.3.165).

essence] being, existence (*OED sb.* 1.a).

115 matter] that component of the essence of a being which has bare existence, but which requires the addition of a particular form (see l. 114*n*.) to constitue the being as determinately existent

(*OED sb.*[1] 6.a, noting its origin in Aristotle and use in Scholastic philosophy).

117 mould] distinctive nature; esp. of persons, native constitution, or character (*OED sb.*[2] 9). *OED* associates *sb.*[2] 9 with the form under which it cites this example: mould, *sb.*[1] 4.a, earth regarded as the material of the human body; but, while Tamburlaine may claim to be of the same character as Jove, he cannot mean, especially in the context of his repudiation of Calyphas (l. 125), that both their beings are made of earth. All the senses of 'mould', *sb.*[1] firmly retain a non-metaphorical sense of 'earth', which does not permit the otherwise plausible extension '(aetherial) substance'.

118 ambitious] Pronounced as four syllables.

120 turning...heaven] Cf. *One*, 2.7.25*n*.

121–2 earth...*Tamburlaine*] Kocher (85) notes the blasphemous echo of 1 Kings 8: 27.

121 region] Pronounced as three syllables.

122 state] Cf. *One*, 1.2.29.

123 thy] i.e. Jove's (from l. 113).

124 issue] Cf. 1.1.2*n*.

126 tartar] bitartrate of potash, deposited in the process of fermentation and adhering to the sides of wine-casks in the form of a hard crust (*OED sb.*[1] 1.d, first cited use in a figurative sense).

127 wit] Cf. *One*, 2.2.58*n*.

130 he...head] Cf. *One*, 2.3.21*n*. and 2.6.3–6*n*.; 'he that' suggests that Marlowe had in mind some single leading figure among the Titans such as Typhoeus.

131 *Atlas*] Cf. *One*, 2.1.11*n*.

133 for] Cf. 3.5.101*n*.

134 cankred] malignant, ill-natured (*OED ppl.a.* 6).

Asia] Cf. *One*, 1.1.95*n*.

139 Approove] find out by experience (*OED v.*[1] 9).

143–5 heaven...head] For the meteorology, cf. *One*, 5.1.460–1*n*.; and on these signs of the apocalypse, cf. *One*, 4.2.53*n*.

143 meteors] Cf. *One*, 1.1.11*n*. (and similarly at l. 203).

146 seething] pervaded by intense ceaseless inner agitation (*OED ppl. a.*, first cited use of this figurative sense).

147 bloods] deaths (*OED sb.* 3.a).

149 repute] regard as (*OED v.* 2.).

155 exercise] possess (and discharge the functions of) (*OED v.* 5.e, first cited use).

156 Scourge... God] Cf. *One*, 3.3.44*n*.

159 Pesants] rascals (*OED sb.* 1.c).

162 pavilions] Pronounced as four syllables (similarly at l. 208).

166 faint] spiritless, cowardly (*OED a.* 3).

168 dispose] dispose of, deal with (*OED v.* 1.c, only cited example).

likes] is pleasing to (*OED v.*[1] 1.c, citing this example).

173 *Radamanth... Eacus*] Rhadamanthus and Aeacus were sons of Zeus who, on account of their just lives on earth, became judges in the Underworld after their deaths.

175 Excell] *O1*'s 'Expell' (retained by many editors) can be given a plausible meaning: Tamburlaine's sufferings will relieve Orcanes and his associates of the impotent desire for revenge with which they are afflicted as a result of his cruelties (*OED*, expel, 1.a, drive out). But 'Excell' gives a simpler and more probable sense.

176 vertue] power (*OED* 9.d).

178 affections] feelings (*OED sb.* 2.a).

179 Artier] Cf. *One*, 2.7.10*n*.

181–2 moisture... Drie] For this association of bodily moisture with pity and dryness with rage cf. (the contrary) 1.3.23–4*n*.

181 remorsefull] compassionate (*OED* 2, first cited use 1591).

185 channels] Cf. 1.3.103*n*.

189–92 Cymbrian... bellowing] These lines, which draw on *The Faerie Queene* (I.viii.11), are further evidence that Marlowe read Book I of Spenser's poem in manuscript (cf. *One*, 5.1.256*n*. and *Two*, 4.3.119–24*n*.).

189 Cymbrian] The Cimbri ('furious *Cymbrians*' of Marlowe's *Lucans First Booke*, I. 257) were a Celtic people who invaded the Roman empire with some success in the late second century BC.

190 Run... about] i.e. run around complaining about.

Femals misse] loss of or being separated from their mates (*OED*, miss, *sb.*[1] 1.a, citing this example).

191 their following] following them.

191–92 following... bellowing] An unusual mid-speech couplet.

192 troublous] sorrowful (*OED* 3.b, citing this example).

193 Engines] Cf. *One*, 4.1.28*n*.

197 Incense] kindle, consume with fire (*OED v.*² 1.a).

199 For ... pride] Shed on account of the destruction by fire of his country's 'cities' and 'golden pallaces' (l. 195).

203–6 Making ... aire] Cf. 3.2.3*n*. Heninger's illustrations of fiery exhalations cited there actually include a burning lance.

205 tilting] Cf. 1.3.39*n*.

4.2

OSD *Enter*] Oxberry has Olympia '*discovered*', implying that (like 2.4) the scene begins with a curtain being drawn to reveal Olympia on the inner stage. Her situation, however, as one just escaped from confinement, is better expressed by Dyce's '*Enter*'.

4 Hath] Cf. *One*, 1.1.117*n*.

7 drift] purpose, intention (*OED sb.* 4.a).

12 close] concealed, secluded (*OED a.* 4.a).

cave] i.e. place of confinement (Theridamas's tent).

13 this invention] i.e. a flask or jar containing the ointment described at ll. 59 ff.

23 affections] Cf. 4.1.178*n*.; here pronounced as four syllables.

29 operation] influence, capacity to produce a given effect (*OED* 3.a).

30 Than ... wildernes] Than the moon has power to control the tides; the image is continued in the following lines ('at the full ... eb'). For *Cynthia* cf. *One*, 4.2.35*n*.

31 thy view] the sight of you.

41 turrets] i.e. raised platforms (Bevington–Rasmussen); *OED* offers no precise parallel, but see *sb.*¹ 3.

42 *Venus*] The Roman goddess of beauty and love.

47 period] sentence (*OED sb.* 10.a).

49 love ... be] Oxberry's emendation of *O1*'s punctuation gives, in place of a weak circumlocution, the sense 'fall in love in order to become'.

53 I ... wil] A set phrase, D1330.1.

55–82 Stay ... *Olympia*] For the principal source of this episode in Ariosto's story of Isabella and Rodomonte (*Orlando Furioso*, Cantos 38 and 39) see Thomas–Tydeman, 159–64. A. B. Taylor, *N&Q*, n.s., 34 (1987), 191–2, cites verbal echoes which suggest Marlowe also had in mind Golding's translation of Ovid's tale of Caenis/Caeneus, whose flesh was made invulnerable by Neptune (*Metamorphoses*, XII. 168 ff. and 459 ff.; Golding's translation, XII. 506–49).

55 honor] chastity (*OED sb.* 3.a).

60 Balsamum] aromatic resinous vegetable juice (*OED* 1, citing this example).

61 simplest] purest (*OED a.* 13).

extracts] *OED sb.*[1] 2.a, first cited use. Ellis–Fermor plausibly refers the phrase 'simplest extracts' to an alchemical context (cf. *OED*, simple, *a.* 13).

62 which the] With ellipsis of 'is' understood.

fourme] Cf. 4.1.112*n*.

63 Tempered] brought to a proper consistency (*OED v.* 10).

science metaphisicall] supernatural knowledge (*OED*, metaphysical, 3.b, first cited use).

68 noint] Aphetic form of 'anoint' (similarly at l. 79SD).

71 rebated] blunted (*OED v.*[1] 4.a).

73 precious] Pronounced as three syllables.

85 Rabies] Rabbis, learned authorities (*OED sb.*[1] 2.b).

87 Theoria] ? contemplation, survey (*OED* 1, citing only this instance). Under theory[1] 2 *OED* also cites Florio (1598, 1611), '*Theoria*, contemplation, speculation, deepe study, insight or beholding'.

88 *Elisian*] Cf. *One*, 5.1.247*n*.

89 eie . . . heaven] i.e. the sun.

90 From . . . light] That the stars received their light from the sun was an accepted view of the period. Kocher (224) cites, amongst others, Robert Recorde, *The Castle of Knowledge* (1556), 148. Greg notes that periods for the revolutions of the planets given in *Faustus* (A-text, II.iii.53–5) are closely similar to Recorde's (*Castle*, 272–9): W. W. Greg, *Marlowe's 'Doctor Faustus', 1604–1616* (Oxford, 1950), 337.

93 Fury] Cf. *One*, 2.7.53*n*.

94 *Dis*] Pluto, ruler of the Underworld.

95 maskes] lavish courtly entertainments combining music, dancing, drama, and spectacular elements (*OED* 2).

97 entertaine] Cf. 2.4.17*n*.

4.3

0SD1 *drawen . . . chariot*] Cf. 3.3.103–7*n*. Robert Cockcroft argues that emblematic significations based on Alciati's *Emblemata* and a variety of classical sources suggest ironies in the brutally heroic image of the chariot: *Renaissance and Modern Studies*, 12 (1968), 33–55. The known contemporary responses do not support this view: see Richard Levin in *Medieval & Renaissance Drama in England*, ed. J. Leeds Barroll III (New York, 1984), 51–70, (esp. 57–61). 'Tamberlyne brydell' is among the items inventoried in Henslowe's diary (320; see *One*, 4.2.0SD2–3n.).

1 pampered...*Asia*] Mary Matheson Wills (see *One*, 2.4.4–5n.) shows that Marlowe could have found the 'pampered Jades of Trace' (cf. l. 12) in Golding's translation of Ovid (IX. 238). It seems probable that Marlowe had this part of Golding's translation in mind, since Hercules is here referring to the horses of Diomedes, king of the Bistones (in Thrace), whose horses had 'Maungers full of flesh of men on which they fed a pace' (IX. 239; cf. ll. 12–13n.). The phrase 'pampered Jades' also occurs in George Gascoigne's verse satire, *The Steele Glas* (1576), as first noted by Emil Koeppel, *Englische Studien*, 1892 (see Introduction, Sources, *n.* 2); cf. Leonard Nathanson, *N&Q*, n.s., 5 (1958), 53–4.

Asia] Cf. *One*, 1.1.95n.

5 *Asphaltis*] Cf. 3.5.18n.

6 *Byron*] Cf. Dramatis Personae, Gazellus, note.

7 horse] A usual plural form in the sixteenth century (*OED sb.* 1.b).

eie...heaven] Cf. 4.2.89n.

8 blow...nosterils] Based on Virgil, *Aeneid*, XII. 115: 'Solis equi lucem...elatis naribus efflant' (the horses of the Sun—i.e. which draw the chariot of Apollo—breathe light from lifted nostrils'); 'nosterils' (as the spelling indicates) is trisyllabic.

9 gate] journey, course (*OED sb.*^{2} 6.a).

10 Governour] controller, i.e., here, driver of the chariot they draw (*OED* 2.a).

12–13 Jades...flesh] Referring to the eighth labour of Hercules (Alcides), the capture and taming of the horses of King Diomedes of Thrace, which had been fed on human flesh. Marlowe's 'Egeus' probably stems from a confusion with Hercules' fifth labour, the cleansing of the stables of Augeias, King of Elis.

14 wanton] Cf. *One*, 4.1.23n.

17 fit] suit (*OED v.*^{1} 4).

appetite] disposition (*OED sb.* 1).

19 Muscadell] a strong sweet wine (*OED* 1, citing this example).

21 racking] driving before the wind (*OED ppl. a.*^{1} 1, first cited use). The secondary sense suggested by Robert Cockcroft (see 0SD1n., 37),

'galloping at full stretch', misunderstands the form of equine movement involved (see *OED*, racking, *ppl. a.*[3] 1, and rack, *sb.*[6]).

23 fatall] ominous, foreboding (*OED* 4.c, first cited use).

24 right] altogether, to the full (*OED adv.* 5).

25 figure] Cf. 2.2.38*n*. (here Tamburlaine's whip).

28 two . . . kings] i.e. Orcanes and Jerusalem.

32 thou] Dis; cf. 4.2.94*n*.

34–8 Come . . . Queene] An allusion to the story of the seizure by Pluto/Dis of Proserpina, the daughter of the goddess of the earth and its fertility, Ceres, as she gathered flowers in a garden near Enna in Sicily. Proserpina thus became Queen of the Underworld. The story is told in Ovid, *Metamorphoses*, V. 385 ff.

37 Joying] enjoying (*OED*, joy, *v.* 4.a).

40 contemner] despiser, scorner (*OED* 1).

41 once] once for all (*OED* 3).

46 hedges] Any line of objects forming a barrier (*OED sb.* 3), here used for the teeth (with a play on the sense 'row of bushes surrounding a field', in l. 48).

49 their . . . pastures] 'their frisky tongues out of their mouths' (Bevington–Rasmussen). *OED* cites this use of 'colt' as its only figurative example of the sense 'young horse'; in this punning context 'colt's tooth' (milk-tooth, used figuratively to describe some unexpected or disruptive vigour: *OED* 8.b) is also relevant.

52 coach-horse] i.e. coach-horses' (possessive plural: cf. l. 7*n*.), *OED*, first figurative use; though, since the tongues being restrained are of those drawing Tamburlaine's chariot, the context suggests a play on the literal sense.

53SD *To* TREBIZON] J. S. Cunningham has Celebinus bridle Orcanes and address this remark to him. Bevington–Rasmussen follow this direction, though doubtfully, pointing out that Jerusalem too is threatened with bridling (though in terms that suggest no equipment for it is available, ll. 43–9), and that if Orcanes is bridled he must be released to speak at l. 77. It seems better to suppose that, following Usumcasane's redirection of attention to the kings already bridled (ll. 50–2), Celebinus here addresses one of them.

57 I] Ay.

59 unsackt] not plundered (*OED*, first cited use).

61 Raise . . . *Aldeboran*] Aldebaran (Alpha Tauri) is a particularly bright star among the seven Hyades, a group in the head of Taurus.

Tamburlaine looks to be stellified after his death in the manner of certain heroic figures of classical mythology.

62 Astracisme] constellation (*OED*, first cited use). Various explanations have been posited of how this 'astracisme' might be threefold. Kocher (227) suggests either the constellations south of, within, and north of the zodiac, or the levels of the cosmos—the elements, the planets and fixed stars, the empyrean. Woolf (265), following the reference to Taurus's 'eye' (Aldebaran), suggests three other prominent stars in the Hyades cluster (those which form Taurus's 'nose'). Pendry—Maxwell suggest the division of the cosmos into earth, planets, and stars. Another possiblity is the division of the zodiac into four trigons—groups of three stars (corresponding to the elements). If *OED* is right about the meaning of the rare 'astracisme', Kocher's first explanation seems the most plausible. But the precise nature of heavenly triplicity is less important than its correspondence with a tripartite earth in the following line.

63 triple world] i.e. Europe, Asia, and Africa—the world as known to Tamburlaine and his contemporaries.

65 prefer] advance, promote (*OED* 1.a).

66 abortive] coming to nothing, useless (*OED a.* 2, first cited use 1593).

70 tal] Cf. 4.1.33*n*.

Queens] With a play on 'quean', harlot, strumpet (*OED* 1).

73 serve . . . turnes] satisfy the sexual requirements of all of you (*OED*, turn, *sb.* 30.b).

75 Brawle] In the usual modern sense. Bevington–Rasmussen gloss 'brag loudly', citing *OED v.*[1] 2; but *OED*'s examples suggest that this sense may have fallen out of use by the late sixteenth century, and in any case Tamburlaine's threat of death is more realistic if understood as about fighting rather than boasting.

81–2 Live . . . heeles] 'Tamburlaine mocks Orcanes and the other defeated "slaves" by suggesting that if they really wished to spare their "guiltless dames" they should have lived continently and not marched to meet Tamburlaine in battle with "troops of harlots" at their heels' (Bevington–Rasmussen). However, Craik (this edn.) argues that the speech (following ll. 75–6) is still addressed to Tamburlaine's soldiers: he tells them to be 'continent' (i.e. moderate, satisfied with one concubine each) and that they must not aspire to have 'troops of harlots'; 'ye slaves' is jocular (cf. 'ye villaines', l. 83); 'sloothful' implies the unsoldierlike self-indulgence of such behaviour.

81 continent] i.e. sexually. Oxberry's emendation (see Apparatus), which gives a more precisely appropriate sense, is supported by the

requirements of the metre. (A word the first syllable of which can be stressed is required.)

83 honours] chastities (*OED sb.* 3.a); similarly at ll. 86, 87.

86 twere ... indeed] 'it is about time. (Said sardonically; Tamburlaine is scornfully amused at the notion of concubines' honour [chastity].)' (Bevington–Rasmussen).

89 Pageants] spectacles, as part of a public triumph (*OED sb.* 3); pronounced as three syllables (Dobson, 276: 'pagiaunt' was a possible sixteenth-century spelling).

Trulles] concubines (*OED* 1).

94 expedition] haste (*OED* 5, citing this example); pronounced as five syllables.

96 presently] Cf. *One*, 2.5.94*n*.

prest] ready (*OED a.* 1).

98 ye ... *Asia*] i.e. those as yet unconquered; *Asia* pronounced as three syllables.

100 controwleth] holds sway over (*OED v.* 4.a).

crownes] monarchs (*OED sb.* 4).

102 Euxine sea] Cf. *One*, 1.1.167*n*.

103 Terrene] Cf. *One*, 3.1.10*n*.

104 *Senus Arabicus*] The Red Sea, in Ortelius called 'Mar Rosso (cf. 3.5.132*n*.) olim (formerly) Sinus Arabicus'.

106 *Persea*] Cf. *One*, 1.1.162*n*.

108 *Jaertis* streame] Cf. 4.1.108*n*.

112 Turrets ... heavens] Susan Richards, *MLQ* 26 (1965), 375–87 (383) points to the parallel with the Tower of Babel (Genesis 11: 1–9). The line may also draw on Spenser's description of the Palace of Pride (*The Faerie Queene*, I.iv.4: 'That purest skye with brightnesse ... dismaid').

113 *Ilions*] Troy's.

114 Thorow] through.

118 three ... world] Cf. l. 63*n*.

119–24 Like ... blowen] These lines, based on *The Faerie Queene* I.vii.32, are the clearest indication in the play that Marlowe had read Book I of Spenser's poem in manuscript. T. W. Baldwin argues that Spenser borrowed from Marlowe (*ELH* 9 (1942), 157–87), but the contrary argument of W. B. C. Watkins (*ELH* 11 (1944), 249–65) has been generally accepted.

119 ymounted] Cited by *OED* as 'pseudo-arch. pa. pple.'; though Marlowe also uses 'ysprong' (*One*, 3.3.109), the form is distinctively Spenserian.

120–1 celestiall...*Selinus*] A town in Sicily (Selinunte, on the south-western coast), referred to in *Aeneid*, III. 705 as 'palmosa' (abounding in palm trees), and the site of a temple of Jupiter.

122 *Hericinas*] i.e. Venus's. Venus was referred to as 'Erycina' (as, for example, in Ovid, *Metamorphoses*, V. 363) after Mount Eryx, a mountain sacred to her in Sicily.

125 *Saturnes*...son] Jupiter (Jove, Zeus).

126 Mounted] mounted in; Abbott, 198.

127–8 path...starres] i.e. the Milky Way (as at l. 132). The idea that the Milky Way is the highway to the palace of Jupiter can be traced to Ovid, *Metamorphoses*, I. 168–76.

128 enchac'd] Cf. *One*, 1.2.96*n*.

5.1

osd 1 *upon the walles*] i.e. in the gallery; cf. 3.3.14sd.

9 submission] Pronounced as four syllables (similarly at l. 94; but as three syllables at l. 26).

14 of...conceit] that you consider valuable (*OED*, price, *sb.* 8.a; and cf. *One*, 1.2.64*n*.).

15 for all] in spite of (*OED* 23.a).

17 *Limnasphaltis*] Cf. 3.5.18*n*.

18–20 Makes...hel] i.e the bituminous waters of the lake surrounding the city make anything that falls into it an impregnably strong defence.

21 faintnesse] timorousness (*OED* 2).

24 ruth] pity (*OED sb.*[1] 1.a).

31 Christians] Pronounced as three syllables.

Georgia] In the maps of Ortelius Georgia is a province to the west of the Black Sea.

32 Whose...reliev'd] Cf. *One*, 3.3.46–58*n*.

33 Wil] Who will; Abbott, 244.

34 How...with cares] Marlowe nowhere else used 'environ' absolutely, with no indirect object, and it also seems unlikely that he would have written the pointlessly metrically incomplete line given in *O1*; but his usage elsewhere gives no ground for choosing between the proposed emendations of the end of the line (see Apparatus). (Marlowe's use of

'environ' elsewhere make less probable Wagner's conjectural emendation, 'Alas (*or* Ay me) how'.)

35 eternisde] Cf. *One*, 1.2.72*n*.

53 exquisite] intensely painful (*OED* 3.b); accented on the first syllable.

54 in . . . throat] i.e. repudiating it as false (*OED*, throat, *sb*. 3.c); 'in thy throat' was a set phrase (Dent T268.11).

60 prest] Cf. 1.1.122*n*.

61 that . . . parlie] that assault will endure no further consideration of parley (*OED*, bide, *v*. 9; regard, *sb*. 6.a)—i.e. once we begin a final assault there will be no further question of discussing terms of surrender.

65 woont . . . deepe] Bevington–Rasmussen remark the hyperbole: in the maps of Ortelius Babylon is over a hundred miles upstream from the coast.

69 *Belus*] The legendary founder of Babylon.

Ninus] The legendary founder of Nineveh, associated with Babylon as the husband of Semiramis (cf. 3.5.36–7*n*.).

Alexander] Alexander the Great took Babylon following his defeat of the Persian ruler Darius III at the battle of Arbela in 331 BC.

71 burst] broken, shattered suddenly (*OED v.* 7.a, citing this example).

72 with] by (*OED* 37.b).

73 *Semiramis*] Cf. l. 69*n*.

74 *Asia*] Cf. *One*, 1.1.95*n*.

75 trode . . . Meisures] danced in a stately manner (*OED*, measure, *sb*. 20.a, citing this example).

76 brave] Cf. *One*, 1.2.127*n*.

77 *Saturnia*] Juno (daughter of Saturn), a surname of Juno used by Ovid (*Metamorphoses*, III. 271 and elsewhere) and Virgil (*Aeneid*, I. 23, XII. 156).

83 usde . . . reckning] held in such low esteem (*OED*, reckoning, *vbl. sb*. 7.b).

86 vermillion tents] i.e. yesterday. Cf. *One*, 4.1.49–63*n*., and ll. 29–30 and l. 62SD2 of this scene.

87–90 threatened . . . earth] On such astrological phenomena regarded as prognosticative of disasters cf. 3.2.4–5, *Lucans First Booke*, ll. 524–30, and *Dido*, 4.4.117–19.

87 region] Cf. 4.1.119*n*.

88 Element . . . fire] Cf. 2.4.58n.

90 traines] tails (of comets), luminous trails (of other heavenly bodies) (*OED sb.*¹ 5.c).

93 quail'd] caused to quail (*OED v.*¹ 5).

95 ports] gates (*OED sb.*² 1.a).

97 *Cerberus*] The triple-headed dog, guardian of the entrance to the Underworld.

98 blacke *Jove*] i.e. Dis (cf. 4.2.94n.).

103 bloody tents] Cf. l. 86n.

104 anger . . . highest] embodiment of God's anger; cf. *One*, 3.3.44n.

113 dreadlesse] fearless (*OED* A.*a*. a).

114 scard] A play on the senses 'scarred' and 'scared' (the latter Tamburlaine's sardonic comment, drawing on the usual mind/body antithesis, on the governor's claim to have a fearless mind. Bullen, uniquely, modernized it as 'scared').

115–17 in . . . hid] Ellis-Fermor notes a parallel in Johannes Schiltberger's account of the sack of Babylon, *Bondage and Travels . . . in Europe, Asia, and Africa, 1396–1427* (published, in German, c.1475; trans. J. B. Telfer, London, Hakluyt Society, 1879); but it is unlikely that this could have been known to Marlowe.

124 execution] Pronounced as five syllables.

128 *Persea*] Cf. *One*, 1.1.162n. (similarly at l. 212).

132 presently] Cf. *One*, 2.5.94n.

133 Vild] vile.

140 abject] abase (*OED v.* 2); accented on the second syllable.

148 Bridle them] Craik (this edn.) suggests 'Bridle them then', which follows well from ll. 146–7 (and omission might easily have been caused by the similarity of 'them' and 'then'). But there is no certain need for emendation because the text as it stands makes sense, and Tamburlaine is elsewhere given prose, or a line that is metrically irregular, at moments of particular brutality (cf. *One*, 4.2.82 and *One*, 5.1.192–4, 213).

148SD2–3 *Souldiers . . . walles*] It may be (as Dyce's stage direction implies) that the governor was hung up in sight of the audience; or it may be that he was secured on the wall of the inner stage and 'discovered' at this point by the drawing of its curtain (cf. 2.4.0SD1n.).

149–50 brave] A sardonic play on the senses 'courageously' (*OED a.* 1.a, recalling ll. 112–19), and 'excellently' (*a.* 3, first cited use 1600), both with quasi-*adv.* function (*a.* sense 5, first cited use 1596).

152 have... withall] Here goes with a shot at him for a start (*OED*, have, 20; withall, *adv.* 2, citing this example; and see with, *prep.* 37.e).

158 like... Governour] i.e. in that, like the walls of the city, he is shot full of holes. On Marlowe's equation of Bagdad with Babylon cf. Dramatis Personae, Gazellus, note.

161 Burghers] citizens (*OED sb.* 1.a, first cited use; also used at 1.1.93).

165 *Assiria*] Cf. *One*, 1.1.89n. (The emendation is endorsed by Tamburlaine's references to Babylon as an Assyrian city in ll. 71 and 76.)

173 *Alcaron*] Cf. *One*, 3.3.76n.

176 Whom... God] In Marlowe's sources Tamburlaine is frequently presented as a pious Muslim (see, for example, Perondinus, ch. 23; Thomas–Tydeman, 119). Tamburlaine's apparent recantation here, however, seems inconsistent not so much with the sources as with his presentation earlier in the play as an anti-Islamic defender of Christians (cf. *One*, 3.3.46–58n. and ll. 31–3 of the present scene).

178 Wel said] Well done.

178SD *fire*] Cf. 3.4.33n.

187–8 Now... myracle] Battenhouse (173–4) sees here a reference to the mocking of Christ on the Cross (Matt. 27: 40; Mark 15: 30–32; Luke 23: 35–7). Kocher (88) argues against this reading, and quotes Paolo Giovio, *A Short Treatise upon the Turkes Chronicles* (trans. Peter Ashton, 1546)—one of Marlowe's possible sources for the play—who writes approvingly of the Tamburlainesque activities of the Sophy of Persia: he 'called Mahomet in despite, a bondeman, and a vyle bowghte drudge. The bookes of his lawe whersoever he founde theym, as false heresies & divilysh doctrine he brent them. Besyde thys he commaunded Mahomets temples to be throwen downe, and of them made stables and dogge kenels'.

195 Or vengeance] i.e. or why do you not send vengeance (from l. 191).

197 Abstracts... lawes] i.e. the Koran.

198 *Mahomet*... hell] The standard pre-Enlightenment Christian view, as in Dante (*Inferno*, XXVIII).

200 adore] worship (*OED* 1).

201 if... God] Elliptical: not, as Kocher understands it (89), 'if any God exists', but (following l. 200) 'if you wish to worship a God'. Lines 200–2 enjoin forsaking the false god of Mohammedanism and turning to the worship of the true God (who 'sits in heaven' and 'is God alone').

202 he . . . he] Kocher (87) cites parallels in Deuteronomy, 4: 35 and 32: 39.

206 fishes] Ellis-Fermor comments, 'Marlowe's imagination misled him slightly when he introduced fishes into the bituminous lake of Babylon'.

208 *Assafitida*] a resinous gum used in medicine and cookery.

209 fleet] float (cf. 1.1.40*n*.).

214 I] Ay.

215 remoov'd] removed from; Abbott, 198.

216 about] Oxberry's 'above' is plausible, particularly in view of the possibility of eye-skip from the following line. But, as Bowers comments (i. 225), the case is insufficiently certain to justify emendation.

218 distempered] sick, ailing (*OED ppl. a.*[1] 3.a); pronounced as three syllables (distemper'd).

221 ye vassals] i.e. Orcanes and Jerusalem, now drawing Tamburlaine's chariot (l. 148).

5.2

0SD2 *drums and trumpets*] Cf. 1.1.0SD2*n*.

3 *Euphrates*] Cf. *One*, 5.1.440*n*.

9 full . . . *Babylon*] i.e. fully recovered from the siege of Babylon (cf. ll. 7 and 58).

19 record] call to mind (*OED v.*[1] 4).

33 Chaplet] garland, coronal (*OED* 1.a).

45 drifts] purposes (*OED sb.* 4.a).

46 *Cynthia*] Cf. *One*, 4.2.35*n*.

48 selected] specially picked out (*OED ppl. a.*, first cited use).

49 severall] separate (*OED a.* 1.a).

52 sunder . . . armes] disperse our collected forces (cf.1.3.158*n*.); camps, cf. *One*, 2.5.26*n*. (similarly at l. 57).

54 eternize] Cf. 5.1.35.

58 Or that] before (*OED*, or, C. *conj.* 1.a).

rejoin'd] reunited again (*OED v.*[2] 1).

at full] completely (*OED*, full, B. *sb.* 1.a).

5.3

1 vanish] disappear (by ceasing to exist) (*OED v.* 2.c, first cited use with 'into').

4 bootlesse] unavailing, useless (*OED a.*[1] 3).

5 influence] Cf. *One*, 1.1.15*n*.

8 Cymerian] Cf. *One*, 3.2.77*n*. and *One*, 5.1.234.

19 desert... holinesse] that which deserves worship (*OED*, desert, *sb.*[1] 1.b, citing this example).

20 estates] positions, authorities (*OED sb.* 3.a).

22 Beare... burthen] do not join in the chorus (Bevington–Rasmussen) (*OED*, bear, *v.*[1] 20; burden, *sb.* 10). But Techelles may also be taken to mean 'do not tolerate the oppression caused you by your rejoicing enemies' (*OED*, bear, *v.*[1] 15.c; burden, *sb.* I).

29 see... head] Ellis-Fermor suggests a reference to Psalm 110: 1.

31 Sustaine... inexcellence] 'put up with so vile a shame' (Jump); inexcellence, *OED*, unique cited example.

34 they] i.e. the devils.

date is out] time is up (a set phrase: Dent D42.1), i.e. that their suffering in hell has come to an end.

35 puissant] powerful; pronounced as three syllables (cf. 3.2.156*n*.).

36 manage arms] Cf. *One*, 2.7.16*n*.

thy] i.e. heaven's.

37 feele] feel that; Abbott, 244.

38 note] sign, token by which something may be inferred (*OED sb.*[2] 7.a).

44 man] i.e. a mere mortal.

49 streamers] Cf. *One*, 4.2.120*n*.

53 invie] show malevolent feelings towards (*OED v.*[1] 1.a); accented on the second syllable.

56 Why] Interjection for emphasis (indicating that what follows is a rhetorical question already presupposing the kind of answer given in the following line) (*OED* 7.b).

58 chardge] Cf. *One*, 5.1.333*n*.

58–9 his... world] Cf. *One*, 2.1.11*n*.

62 *Apollo*] As the god who affords help and wards off evil Apollo also became god of medicine.

64 griefe] pain (*OED sb.* 6).

65 cannot... violent] 'Nothing violent can be permanent', Tilley N321. Marlowe refers to the proverb again in *Jew*, 1.1.129–30.

67–71 See... on] Among three portents of Tamburlaine's death in André Thevet's *Cosmographie Universelle* (1575), Seaton[2] (398–9) suggests a parallel to these lines in the first, which involves a man carrying a spear. Death's dart, however, is a conventional image (*OED*, dart, *sb.* 1.b), and in the context Death's appearance is not treated as a portent but as a figurative expression of Tamburlaine's state of mind.

73 barke] Death is identified with Charon, the ferryman who transports the shades of the dead across the rivers of the Underworld (cf. *One*, 5.1.246*n.* and *One*, 5.1.465).

76 stay] delay (*OED v.*^{1} 7.a).

80 governe] to govern; Abbott, 349.

82 Hipostasis] sediment (*OED* 1.a, citing this example). Robinson's emendation (see Apparatus) has commanded general assent.

83 obscure] dark in colour (*OED a.* 3).

84 accidentall] non-essential (*OED a.* 4), i.e. what should be subsidiary is predominant.

86 *Humidum . . . Calor*] moisture and heat.

87 parcell] part (*OED sb.* 1.a).

89 cleane] wholly (*OED adv.* 5.a).

91 Criticall] of decisive importance in relation to the issue (*OED* 5.a, first cited use 1649).

92 Chrisis] The point in the progress of a disease when an important development or change takes place which is decisive for recovery or death (*OED* 1): Hoeniger (184–5) assumes this sense only. However, Johnstone Parr, who gives a detailed and elaborately referenced account of the terms of Marlowe's imagined diagnosis, argues that the sense 'the conjunction of planets determining the issue of a disease' (*OED* 2, first cited use 1603) is also present: *PMLA* 59 (1944), 696–714. J. C. Maxwell, *TLS*, 4.1.1947, 9, pointing out that earlier in the same speech there is an agreed corruption of a Greek medical term (l. 82*n.*), suggests that 'Chrisis' might be a compositor's misreading of 'crasis', constitution, temperament (*OED* 1.a, first cited use 1616—but Marlowe would know the Greek root, and *OED* records the use of a secondary sense in 1602 [1.b]). The appropriateness of the sense to the context, and the likelihood of compositorial misreading of so unfamiliar a term, make this a plausible suggestion. (It does not, however, appear in the Pendry–Maxwell edition.)

93–7 Your . . . indure] i.e. 'the vital spirit . . . is unable to perform properly as the soul's . . . instrument because it has become too meager' (Hoeniger, 94).

93 Artier] Cf. *One*, 2.7.10*n.*

alongst] close by, parallel to (*OED prep.* 2).

94 lively] vital, necessary to life (*OED a.* 2).

spirits] subtle, high-refined substances supposed to permeate the blood (*OED sb.* 16.a).

96 Organnons] bodily organs (as instruments of the soul) (*OED* 1, first cited use).

97 by . . . art] according to the logic of medical science (cf. 4.1.100*n.*).

99 all] completely (*OED* C. *adv.* 2).

100 comfort] strengthen, invigorate (*OED v.* 4).

101SD 1 *Alarme*] Cf. 1.3.183*n.* (similarly at l. 115SD).

104 offers] dares, presumes (*OED v.* 5.b).

107 recur] cure me from (*OED*, recure, *v.* 1.a).

110 give offer] *OED* cites this example under offer, *sb.* 1, proposal; but Tamburlaine takes up the word from l. 104 and intends the more vigorous sense implied there (see note).

111 joy] rejoice that (*OED v.* 2.b, citing this example); Abbott, 244.

112 endure] strengthen (*OED* 1).

your . . . presence] yourself (following from 'endure'); your appearance in person (leading into l. 113) (*OED*, presence, 4.a, 1.a).

113 onely] of itself alone (*OED* A. *adv.* 2).

116 villaines, cowards] Robinson and other early editors emend 'villain cowards', so making the first word an adjective (mod. villainous); but *O1* makes good sense as it stands. Cf. 4.1.89 and *note*.

117 vanisht] caused to disappear (*OED v.* 4, citing this example).

123 disdainfull] Cf. *One*, 4.2.13*n.*

127 *Persea*] Cf. *One*, 1.1.162*n.*

128 *Armenia*] Cf. *One*, 1.1.162–5*n.*

129 *Bythinia*] Cf. *One*, 3.3.2*n.*

132–5 here . . . both] The construction of a canal from the Nile to the Red Sea was attributed to the semi-legendary Egyptian ruler Sesostris and to Pharaoh Ptolemy Philadelphus II (third century BC). Herodotus mentions such a canal constructed by Darius III (*Historia*, IV. 39). Marlowe may also have known of the attempts to construct a similar waterway by the Venetian republic in the early sixteenth century, which were revived by the Ottoman government of Egypt in 1586: Frederic C. Lane, *Venice: A Maritime Republic* (Baltimore, 1973), 293. Cf. *One*, 3.3.256 (and note), where Tamburlaine implies that he will build the Panama Canal.

133 Whereas] Cf. 3.2.66n.

Terren] Cf. *One*, 3.1.10n.

137–40 From . . . *Zansibar*] Tamburlaine here speaks as though he had in person carried out the conquests actually accomplished by Techelles (1.3.186–205).

137 *Nubia . . . Borno* Lake] Cf. 1.3. 202 and 203n.

139 Cutting] Cf. 1.1.29n.

147 westward . . . line] i.e. to the west of where the meridian cuts across the Tropic of Cancer—in the maps of Ortelius, off the west coast of Africa just west of the Canary Islands: Tamburlaine indicates the Americas.

150 Antypodes] those who dwell directly opposite to us on the globe (*OED* 1). As Ellis-Fermor points out, from Tamburlaine's geographical perspective this means South America, 'the source of Spanish gold and the riches of the fabulous El Dorado'. Marlowe ignores the fact that from Tamburlaine's temporal perspective the continent has not yet been discovered—and that in Part 1 Tamburlaine had proposed to discover it (cf. *One* 4.4.82n.).

151 And . . . unconquered] J. S. Cunningham proposes that 'unconquered' be pronounced as trisyllabic ('unconquer'd'), so making an abrupt tetrameter. But there are very few cases in *O1* where *ed* is given for *'d*: there can be little doubt that Marlowe intended the rhetorically more grand, full pentameter.

156 which . . . descried] In Ortelius's map of the world the whole Antarctic area (including vast outcrops of land to both east and west) is described as 'Terra Australis nondum cognita' (not yet known). In other maps 'terrae incognitae' appear in what is the modern South Pacific.

163 griefe] Cf. l. 64n.

165–6 Your . . . flesh] i.e your soul gives being to our bodies, the purely material substance of which is also derived from you. For essence, subjects, matter, cf. 4.1.112 and 113 notes; incorporate, combined in one substance (*OED ppl.a.* 1.a).

168 entertaine] maintain in existence (*OED v.* 4).

169–72 this . . . breasts] i.e. this body, no longer strong enough to contain its spirit, must disintegrate, sharing out that spirit equally between both of you.

171 imparting] giving a share of to each of a number of persons (*OED v.* 3).

his] its (cf. 4.1.6n.), i.e. the spirit's.

impressions] change produced in a passive subject by the operation of an external cause (*OED sb.* 4); pronounced as four syllables.

177, 183 proper] Cf. *One*, 4.4.31*n*.

178 Scourge] i.e. his whip.

179 estate] Cf. *One*, 5.1.526*n*.

184 and] Oxberry's minor emendation (see Apparatus) restores the metre, which is otherwise pointlessly irregular.

186–91 With... dignity] i.e. how hardhearted I should be if I were able to enjoy life physically or emotionally, if, instead of dissolving into extreme pain, my heart should be prompted to any joy at the thought of earthly dignity; resolv'd, cf. *One*, 1.1.118*n*.; motions, 2.1.2*n*.

188 resolved] melted (*OED ppl.a.* 5); the reduplication is unusual, but not out of keeping with the highly convoluted syntax of the speech (and cf. ll. 209–10 and note).

194 influence] Cf. *One*, 1.1.15*n*.

196–9 How... soverainty] i.e. how shall I, contrary to what I feel, continue to go on living when I wish only to die, and uselessly offer as my motivation for so doing the kingship which is in fact unwelcome to me.

200 thyne honor] 'your devotion to honour' (Bevington–Rasmussen).

201 magnanimitie] Cf. *One*, 4.4.135*n*.

204 steeled] inflexible, insensible to impression (*OED ppl. a.* 5).

stomackes] malice, spite (*OED sb.* 8.c).

208 damned spirit] i.e. spirit suffering pains like those of the damned (*OED*, damned, *ppl.a.* 2.a, used in an extended figurative sense).

209–10 send... agony] i.e. may heaven afflict me with my father's pains. It is not clear whether this is so that Amyras can suffer in total sympathetic identification with his father; or so that he can die before his father and will not therefore have to see him die; or so that he can suffer as a surrogate victim, and thereby reprieve his father.

211 hearse] coffin (similarly at l. 224SD).

212 fatall] in which I am fated to die (*OED* 5, with some colouring of 6).

213 parcell] Cf. l. 87*n*.

216 Joy] rejoice in (cf. 110*n*.).

223 his] i.e. Death's.

unquenched] unquenchable. Glossed by *OED* 1.b as 'unsuppressed' (first cited use in relation to feelings), but on the -*ed* suffix as equivalent to -*able*, see G. V. Smithers, *Shakespeare Survey*, 23 (1970), 27–37.

224 be... reverberate] recoil upon himself (*OED*, reverberate, *v.* 5.b, first cited use in this sense 1713; *ppl.a.* 1.a, citing this example).

226 when... sight] i.e. after death, when the faculties of the soul have become more acute, being no longer clogged by the relative grossness of the body.

232 that... guide] Cf. *One*, 4.2.49*n.*

233 *Phœbes*] Cf. *One*, 3.2.19*n.*

235 him] i.e. Phaeton.

awfull] awe-inspiring (*OED* I).

238 *Phyteus*] Apollo's, the sun's. B. P. Fisher, *N&Q*, n.s., 22 (1975), 247–8, notes that φύτιος ('generative') is given as an appellation of Helios (Apollo) or Zeus in the *Lexicon* of Hesychius of Alexandria (a work available to Marlowe, though not standard). But the appellation is so rare that this is more probably a distortion of Pythius, a common epithet for Apollo: C. Brennan, *Beiblatt zur Anglia*, 16 (1905), 207–9. Thomas Cooper (cf. *One*, 1.1.50*n.*) gives the spelling 'Phyton' as an alternative for Python, the fabulous serpent killed by Apollo, from which the epithet Pythius is derived. Dyce notes the same spelling in Lydgate's *Warres of Troy*—a work which may have been one of Marlowe's sources for *Dido*.

239 these... Jades] i.e. Orcanes and Jerusalem.

240 take... haire] 'Take Time (occasion) by the forelock, for she is bald behind', Tilley T311. Occasion is represented in this way in Elizabethan emblem books as, for example, in Whitney's *A Choice of Emblems* (1586), and similarly (drawing on emblematic conventions) in *The Faerie Queene* (II.iv.4), to signify that she can only be grasped by those who seize their opportunity before she has passed by.

241 *Hyppolitus*] Hippolytus fell from his chariot with his hands entangled in the reins and was dragged to death by his horses. The story is told in Ovid, *Metamorphoses*, XV. 497 ff.

244 temper] mental constitution (*OED sb.* 9, first cited use 1595).

245 *Phaeton*] Cf. l. 232*n.*

252 his] its (cf. 4.1.6*n.*).

253 timelesse] untimely (*OED* 1.a, citing this example).

THE MASSACRE AT PARIS

*For Norma Jean Esche
and Phyllis Glenice Marsh*

CONTENTS

The Massacre at Paris

ACKNOWLEDGEMENTS

My thanks go to the following for their help. Roma Gill initially offered the project and supplied a xerox copy of the Bodleian Malone octavo. Anglia Polytechnic University generously gave me a sabbatical semester in early 1997 to complete the work. Two libraries made available the two extremely rare 1818 editions of *The Massacre at Paris*: the Alderman Library of the University of Virginia kindly provided a microfilm of Broughton and the Foley Library of Gonzaga University in Spokane, Washington kindly supplied a xerox copy of Oxberry. But my greatest professional thanks must go to Tom Craik, whose generosity of time, spirit, and suggestion went far beyond the standard general editor's role and improved the edition immeasurably. The imperfections that remain are entirely my own. Nigel Wheale lent aid and support, as is his wont. Finally, I must thank my glorious family, Rosalind, Ben, and Nick, whose time was sometimes massacred by this project, but whose insistent distractions held us all together.

E JE

SELECT BIBLIOGRAPHY TO
THE MASSACRE AT PARIS

Bakeless, John Ronald. 'The Martyrdom of Ramus in Marlowe's *The Massacre at Paris*', *PLL* 9 (1973), 363–79.

Bono, Paola. '*The Massacre at Paris* (1592): Contributi del gruppo di ricerca sulla communicazione teatrale in Inghilterra', in *Le forme del teatro*, ed. Giorgio Melchiori (Rome, 1979–81), 11–52.

Briggs, Julia. 'Marlowe's *Massacre at Paris*: A Reconsideration', *RES* 34 (1983), 257–78.

Dickens, A. G. 'The Elizabethans and St. Bartholomew', in *The Massacre of St. Bartholomew*, ed. Alfred Soman (The Hague, 1974), 52–70.

Erikson, Roy. 'Construction in Marlowe's *The Massacre at Paris*', in *Papers from the First Nordic Conference for English Studies*, ed. S. Johansson and B. Tysdahl (Oslo, 1981), 41–54.

Kirk, Andrew M. 'Marlowe and the Disordered Face of French History', *SEL* 35 (1995), 193–213.

Kocher, Paul H. 'Contemporary Pamphlet Backgrounds for Marlowe's *The Massacre at Paris*', *MLQ* 8 (1947), 157–73, 309–18.

—— 'François Hotman and Marlowe's *The Massacre at Paris*', *PMLA* 56 (1941), 349–68.

Lanbin, Georges. 'Marlowe et la France', *EA* 19 (1966), 55–9.

Potter, David. 'Marlowe's *Massacre at Paris* and the Reputation of Henri III of France', in *Christopher Marlowe and English Renaissance Culture*, eds. Darryll Grantley and Peter Roberts (Aldershot, 1996), 70–95.

Smith, Robert A. H. 'Four Notes on *The Massacre at Paris*', *N & Q* 237 (1992), 308–9.

Stroup, Thomas B. 'Ritual in Marlowe's Plays', *CompD* 7 (1973), 198–221.

REFERENCES AND ABBREVIATIONS

Texts and Editions (of Marlowe and Others)

Bennett	*'The Jew of Malta' and 'The Massacre at Paris'*, ed. H. S. Bennett (London, 1931).
Bowers	*The Complete Works of Christopher Marlowe*, ed. Fredson Bowers, (Cambridge, 1973; 2nd ed., 1981).
Broughton & Oxberry	*The Massacre at Paris*, ed. James Broughton (London, 1818) and *The Massacre at Paris*, ed. W. Oxberry (London, 1818).
Bullen	*The Works of Christopher Marlowe*, ed. A. H. Bullen (London, 1885).
Contention	Shakespeare, *The First part of the Contention betwixt the two famous Houses of Yorke and Lancaster...* (London, 1594), ed. William Montgomery, MSR (Oxford, 1985).
Craik	T. W. Craik; suggestion to editor.
Cunningham	*The Works of Christopher Marlowe*, ed. Francis Cunningham (London, 1870).
Dyce[1]	*The Works of Christopher Marlowe*, ed. Alexander Dyce (London, 1850).
Dyce[2]	*The Works of Christopher Marlowe, a New Edition, Revised and Corrected*, ed. Alexander Dyce (London, 1858).
Folger MS	Manuscript leaf of *The Massacre at Paris* in the Folger Library, MS. J. b. 8
Forker	Marlowe, *Edward II*, ed. Charles R. Forker (Manchester, 1994).
Gill	*The Plays of Christopher Marlowe*, ed. Roma Gill (Oxford, 1971).
Golding	Arthur Golding, trans., *Ovid's Metamorphoses* (London, 1567), ed. John Frederick Nims (New York, 1965).
Greg	*The Massacre at Paris*, ed. W. W. Greg, MSR (Oxford, 1929 for 1928).
Kyd	*The Works of Thomas Kyd*, ed. Frederick S. Boas (Oxford, 1901).
Malone MS	hand-written notes by Edmund Malone in the Bodleian copy of O.

O	*The Massacre at Paris* (London, no date).
Oliver	*'Dido Queen of Carthage' and 'The Massacre at Paris'*, ed. H. J. Oliver (London, 1968).
Pendry-Maxwell	Christopher Marlowe, *Complete Plays and Poems*, ed. E. D. Pendry and J. C. Maxwell (London, 1976).
Robinson	*The Works of Christopher Marlowe*, ed. G. Robinson (London, 1826).
Shakespeare	*William Shakespeare. The Complete Works: Original Spelling Edition*, ed. Stanley Wells and Gary Taylor (Oxford, 1986).
Spenser, *Faerie Queene*	Edmund Spenser, *The Faerie Queene*, 2 vols., ed. J. C. Smith (Oxford, 1909).
1 Troublesome Reign	*The Troublesome Reign of King John*, Part 1, ed. Geoffrey Bullough, *Narrative and Dramatic Sources of Shakespeare*, iv (London, 1962).
True Tragedy	Shakespeare, *The true Tragedie of Richard Duke of Yorke* ... (London, 1595), ed. W. W. Greg, Shakespeare Quarto Facsimiles, (Oxford, 1958).

Other References

Abbott	E. A. Abbott, *A Shakespearian Grammar* (Macmillan, London, 1869; 2nd edn., 1870).
Dent	R. W. Dent, *Proverbial Language in English Drama Exclusive of Shakespeare, 1495–1616. An Index* (University of California Press, Los Angeles, 1984).
MED	*Middle English Dictionary*, ed. Kurath, Kuhn, Reidy, Lewis (University of Michigan Press, Ann Arbor, 1956–present).
MSR	The Malone Society Reprints.
OED	*The Oxford English Dictionary*, 2nd edn., prepared by J. A. Simpson and E. S. C. Weiner (Clarendon Press, Oxford, 1989).
Partridge	Eric Partridge, *Shakespeare's Bawdy: A Literary and Psychological Essay and a Comprehensive Guide* (Routledge & Kegan Paul, London, 1947; 3rd edn., 1968).

Rubinstein   Frankie Rubinstein, *A Dictionary of Shakespeare's Sexual Puns and their Significance* (Macmillan, London, 1984; 2nd ed., 1989).

Sugden   Edward H. Sugden, *A Topographical Dictionary to the Works of Shakespeare and his Fellow Dramatists* (Manchester University Press, Manchester, 1925).

Tilley   M. P. Tilley, *A Dictionary of the Proverbs in England in the Sixteenth and Seventeenth Centuries* (University of Michigan Press, Ann Arbor, 1950).

Welsh   Robert Ford Welsh, 'The Printing of the Early Editions of Christopher Marlowe's Plays', unpublished thesis, University Microfilms, Ann Arbor, 1964.

Periodicals

CompD   *Comparative Drama*
EA   *Etudes Anglaises*
EHR   *English Historical Review*
ELH   *ELH: A Journal of English Literary History*
JQ   *Journalism Quarterly*
MLQ   *Modern Language Quarterly*
N&Q   *Notes and Queries*
PLL   *Papers on Language and Literature*
PMLA   *Publications of the Modern Language Association*
RES   *Review of English Studies*
SEL   *Studies in English Literature*
SQ   *Shakespeare Quarterly*

Biblical quotations are from the 1560 Geneva Bible. References to Marlowe are to *The Complete Works of Christopher Marlowe* (Clarendon Press: i. *Translations*, ed. Roma Gill, 1987; ii. *Doctor Faustus*, ed. Gill, 1990; iii. *Edward II*, ed. Richard Rowland, 1994; iv. *The Jew of Malta*, ed. Gill, 1995; v. *1 Tamburlaine* and *2 Tamburlaine*, ed. David Fuller, 1998). Quotations from Shakespeare are from *William Shakespeare. The Complete Works; Original Spelling Edition*, ed. Stanley Wells and Gary Taylor (Clarendon Press, Oxford, 1986). In this edition plays are numbered throughout by lines, without act and scene division. References are therefore as in *William Shakespeare. The Complete Works: Compact Edition*, ed. Stanley Wells and Gary Taylor (Clarendon Press, Oxford, 1988) unless otherwise specified.

subst.   substantially

TEXTUAL INTRODUCTION

I. The Octavo and Date

The Massacre at Paris was not entered in the Stationers' Register; it survives in an undated octavo printed by Edward Allde for Edward White. The title-page is THE / MASSACRE / AT PARIS: / With the Death of the Duke / of Guise. / As it was plaide by the right honourable the / Lord high *Admirall* his Seruants. / Written by *Christopher Marlow*. / [Device, McKerrow 290] / AT LONDON / Printed by *E. A.* for *Edward White*, dwelling neere / the little North doore of S.Paules / Church, at the signe of / the Gun. Ten copies of the octavo survive, in: the British Museum; the Bodleian Library; the Pepys Library, Magdalene College, Cambridge; the Dyce Collection in the Victoria and Albert Museum; the Library of Congress; the Folger Library; the Huntington Library; the Newberry Library (the C.W. Clark copy); the Chapin Library, Williamstown, Massachusetts; and the private collection of Mr. Robert A. Taylor of Princeton, New Jersey (the White–Rosenbach copy).

The octavo collates A – D$_8$, with the text beginning on A3r and ending on D3v. A1 is blank except for the signature 'A' on the recto. A2r is the title-page and not signed; A2v is blank, as are D$_7$–D$_8$. The text is clean in that there are few typographical errors, but it is often heavily inked, sometimes making legibility difficult, particularly of punctuation. Composition and printing of sheets A–D were by formes from cast-off copy, the outer forme first. There is some evidence, based on type piece distribution, of 'a delay in the composition of D outer, and an ensuing delay in the presswork' (Welsh, 58). Oliver's collation of all extant copies of the octavo confirmed Greg's discovery (and Welsh's analysis) of variants in the running title. Oliver also produces evidence of further press-corrections on three pages: D1 uncorrected 'diceast', corrected to 'deceast'; D2v 'dy the King' to 'by the King'; and D4v 'the President . . . send' to 'the President . . . sends'. Welsh notes, 'In the octavo the [double-"s"] ligature is used for all instances of double-"s" followed by "e", "a", "u", and "w"; however, in all instances in which the double-"s" is followed by "i", two separate letters are used for double-"s": before "i", the first "s" is the long "s" and the second is always the short "s" ' (37–8). He found exactly the same practice with regard to the use of the double-'s' ligature in the undated octavo of *The Spanish Tragedy*. He notes a similar, but not exactly the same, pattern for two other plays printed by Allde, *The Battle of Alcazar* (1594) and *The Wars of Cyrus* (1594). The use of the double-'s' ligature in *The Massacre at Paris* and *The Spanish Tragedy* coupled with identical spellings consistently used for several frequently occurring words — 'doe', 'goe', 'then' (for 'than'), 'heer(e)', 'freend', 'Ile', 'bloud', and '-es' as opposed to '-esse' word endings — convincingly argues for the same compositor setting both plays near the same time (39–42). The contention that the same compositor set *The Battle of Alcazar* and *The Wars of Cyrus* is less persuasive because the identical spellings of the test words are not as consistently used.[1] This method of typesetting by outer then inner formes, the fairly even distribution of certain spelling peculiarities, and the unusual treatment of the double-'s' ligatures throughout the text indicate that one compositor set the whole of the octavo.[2]

The precise date of the octavo is difficult to establish. Since time has not allowed fresh investigation of all the octavos, Welsh remains the best discussion of the problem.[3] There are four pieces of hard evidence. First, Henry III of France died on 2 August (old style 23 July) 1589, and since his death is dramatized, the play could not have been written (or printed) before this date. Second, the first written reference to *The Massacre at Paris* is a note in Henslowe's *Diary* for 30 January 1593, 'Rd at the tragedey of the gvyse 30 iij li xiiij s', and marked 'ne'.[4] The 'ne' is sometimes used by Henslowe to indicate the first production of a new play, and the takings, the highest sum recorded since 3 March 1591 at 'harey the vj' (another play marked 'ne'), may support such a meaning in this case. These first two pieces of evidence obviously supply the range

---

[1] Bowers, pp. 356–7.

[2] Oliver asserts that two compositors set the text, but offers no proof (p. lx).

[3] Neither Greg (pp. v–ix) nor Oliver (pp. xlix–l) supplies convincing evidence for his conclusion, and Bowers (pp. 355–7) is essentially a summary of Welsh (pp. 33–49).

[4] Greg (p. vi) says 'according to Henslowe on the 30th, but this is clearly an error for the 26th', and he may be correct, but since he offers no justification for his assertion, and since R. A. Foakes and R. T. Rickert, eds., *Henslowe's Diary*, Cambridge, 1961, p. 20 do not comment on the date, nor mention it in their Introduction (pp. xxvi–xxvii), Henslowe's date is used throughout this Introduction.

for the date of composition, between August of 1589 and late 1592. Third, Welsh discovered that 'the head-piece which appears on A$_3$ of the octavo was badly damaged on its lower right side in 1602 or 1603' (34), and it is not damaged in *The Massacre at Paris* octavo. Fourth, Welsh advanced an extremely persuasive argument that the compositor of *The Massacre at Paris* set *The Spanish Tragedy*, also printed by Allde for White and also undated, but confidently thought to be 1592.[5]

We thus have a *terminus post quem* of 1589 based on internal historical evidence, and a *terminus ante quem* of 1602–3 based on bibliographical evidence of the damaged head-piece. The two other dates, 1592, coinciding with the undated octavo of *The Spanish Tragedy*, and 30 January 1593, the date of the entry in Henslowe's *Diary*, are incompatible. So, either we have a date for *The Massacre at Paris* octavo of 1592 and Henslowe's 'ne' does not mean a first performance, or we have a date of printing in late 1593 or 1594, the necessary time required for the play to be performed and printed as the octavo, a text usually identified as one of a group thought to be highly corrupted through memorial reconstruction.

That it is a 'bad' text is beyond question. Early editors often cavalierly emended or 'improved' the text without authority, a practice that has continued to some extent down to at least one edition currently in print; but, in the absence of persuasive argument or evidence, emendation must be kept to the minimum in exactly the same way as if one were editing a 'good' text. We do, however, possess one portion of 'good' text for *Massacre*, a manuscript leaf preserved in the Folger Library, Folger MS. J. b. 8.

II. The *Massacre* Leaf

The manuscript leaf of *The Massacre at Paris*, or Folger MS. J. b. 8, as it is now known, was first mentioned by John Payne Collier in 1825: 'A curious MS. fragment of one quarto leaf of this tragedy [*Massacre*] came into the hands of Mr. Rodd of Newport-street not long since, which, as it very materially differs from the printed

---

[5] See W. W. Greg and Nichol Smith, eds., *The Spanish Tragedy* by Thomas Kyd , MSR, Oxford, 1949 for 1948, p. ix, and Philip Edwards, ed., *The Spanish Tragedy* by Thomas Kyd, Revels, London, 1959, pp. xxvii–xxix.

edition, is here inserted *literatim*'.[6] Collier then prints an inaccurate transcript of the leaf. He printed another transcript, less inaccurate, after having acquired the document, in his own *History of English Dramatic Poetry to the Time of Shakespeare* in 1831 (III, pp. 134–5). The document subsequently passed through the hands of J. O. Halliwell-Phillips, Marsden J. Perry, and finally Henry Clay Folger to the Folger Library, where it now remains.

The *Massacre* leaf has received considerable critical attention,[7] not least because it is a unique example of a single scene of a Renaissance play in MS. It has sometimes been thought to be a forgery, mainly because Collier discovered it. That Collier was a notorious forger of early documents is not open to doubt, but to suppose that everything he touched was forged is, in itself, weak thought; in this case, he made an honest and lasting discovery for Marlowe studies. Although Collier never claimed that the leaf was in Marlowe's hand, others have, and this claim has tended to cloud judgement and to confuse argument concerning authenticity. The following discussion argues that the leaf is a genuine playhouse document, but not, as has been so often asserted (most recently in Bowers), Marlowe's autograph. Readers may wish to refer to a new transcript of the leaf prepared for this edition and printed in the Appendix.[8]

The manuscript is written on two sides of a paper fragment, measuring $7\frac{1}{8}$ inches high and $7\frac{7}{8}$ inches wide, of a folio leaf of foolscap. The watermark, a well-known pitcher device, appears

[6] Isaac Reed, Octavius Gilchrist, and the editor [J. Payne Collier], eds., *A Select Collection of Old Plays. In Twelve Volumes. A New Edition: With Additional Notes and Corrections*, VIII, London, 1825, p. 244.

[7] Greg, pp. xi–xvi; S. A. Tannenbaum, *Shakesperian Scraps*, New York, 1933, pp. 177–86; Joseph Q. Adams, 'The "Massacre at Paris" Leaf', *The Library*, Fourth Series, XIV, 1934, 447–69; J. M. Nosworthy, 'The Marlowe Manuscript', *The Library*, Fourth Series, XXVI, 1945, 158–71; A. D. Wraight and Virginia F. Stern, *In Search of Christopher Marlowe: A Pictorial Biography*, London, 1965, pp. 224–32; Oliver, p. lviii; P. J. Croft, *Autograph Poetry in the English Language: Facsimiles of Original Manuscripts from the Fourteenth to the Twentieth Century*, i, London, 1973, p. xiv; R. E. Alton, 'Marlowe Authenticated', *TLS*, 26 April 1974, 446–7; Antony G. Petti, *English Literary Hands from Chaucer to Dryden*, London, 1977, pp. 84–5; P. J. Croft, 'Autograph Copies', *TLS*, 24 February 1978, 241; Peter Beal, compiler, *Index of English Literary Manuscripts*, 1/2, London, 1980, p. 325; Bowers, p. 358.

[8] As so often in matters textual, I am heavily indebted to W. W. Greg, who offers the finest unedited transcript of the entire leaf to date at the end of the Adams article cited above; Petti prints an excellent transcript of the recto. The entire leaf is photographically reproduced in Adams and Bowers; the recto only in Oliver and Petti.

near the top, so what remains is the lower half of a folio leaf. The writing is regular throughout and evenly inked, except, of course, when slight corrections are made or when the quill either starts to run out of ink or begins anew after dipping.[9]

R. E. Alton's detailed comparison of the leaf with the Marlowe signature, discovered in 1939, strongly suggests that the hand is not autograph. His work deserves extended quotation, as he takes issue with Wraight and Stern's contention that the differences between leaf and signature are merely simplifications of letter forms.

There are between the signature and the leaf many striking variations of detail which are not susceptible to such an explanation: that the ascending loop of *h* should have acquired an angle, or that in all positions, including the final, the descender of *y* should have been all but doubled in length, can hardly be called simplifications, nor can the *Massacre* scribe's remorseless separation of letters be excused as 'a necessity for a man who has much writing to do'.

Alton goes on to mention three more points:

first, while it is true that a shorter stroke joins *st* ligature in the leaf, the real difference is that *st* in the signature has a bold clockwise curve absent from the leaf; secondly, while the saucer shaped *r* of the leaf is superficially 'simpler' than the two-stemmed *r* of the signature, the clockwise movements of the latter are reversed in the leaf; and thirdly, whereas the signature has a wholly angular *a*, the leaf has a rounded variety made of a loop and a curve which are both counter-clockwise. These are details which illustrate one general tendency and it is on general appearance rather than detail that a judgment finally depends.

He concludes that:

The signature is full of character, with firm alternations of pressure and pronounced horizontals: the hand of the leaf is flat, lacking in currency and grace. It would be hard to conceive of two hands which belonged to the same type (the Secretary script) and yet were more distant in general appearance and in detail; the dissimilarities go far beyond the discrepancies to be expected between a man's signature and his normal hand. (pp. 446-7)

The writing itself contains several errors and corrections which are noted in the apparatus in the Appendix: they include, for instance, the *A* in line 1 originally written as the *s* of the following

---

[9] See Adams and Petti (who says that the hand of the leaf is 'uneven in inking') for a much more detailed description than is possible here.

word, *souldier*, and then altered to its present form; *key* in line 2 originally written as *Cey*, then corrected; the *h* of *exhalatione* in line 22 written over an *a*. These are the kind of errors normally found in the work of a partially attentive copyist, not a forger;[10] in other words, what we have is a scribal copy of an unknown original, an authentic document; but why the copy was made remains unexplained. Also unexplained remains the question of why anyone would forge this bit of *Massacre*.[11] Collier could not have done it; he 'was simply not capable of this standard of palaeographical forgery in the 1820s and 1830s (when he announced the discovery of the leaf)', and his later forgeries 'are characterised by jerky and angular letters in contrast to the competent, if disjunct, letter formation in the leaf'.[12] In the final analysis, I suppose that only scientific examination of ink and paper will prove the authenticity of the leaf, but until then, there is no reason to doubt.

III. Memorial Reconstruction

The octavo of *The Massacre at Paris* is one of several texts from the period known as 'bad quartos', a vague and misleading term meaning that the play as we have it is in a corrupt form. The level of corruption of such texts varies widely from the severe to the less severe. Although we do not have a complete 'good' text with which to compare *Massacre*, we can safely say that the octavo text is severely corrupted; it seems for the most part to have come to us through the filter of one or more memories of the actors who took part in a performance.[13] Indeed, in the most recent study of all of the suspected bad texts of the period, *Massacre* resides in an élite group of only four plays for which a strong case can be made for memorial reconstruction.[14] Thus the standard characteristics of such a text are here in abundance. They include excessive overall shortness of the text and shortness of speeches within it. *Massacre* is about 1,250 lines long, or about half the length of an average play of

[10] Alton, p. 446.

[11] R. E. Alton, private correspondence.

[12] Laurie E. Maguire, *Shakespearean Suspect Texts: The 'Bad' Quartos and their Contexts*, Cambridge, 1996, p. 377.

[13] Some sections of the text, most notably Scene 2, may derive from sources other than memorial reconstruction, perhaps even manuscript. Attempts to identify the parts played by actors who reconstructed the text have been less than persuasive, but see Tannenbaum.

[14] Maguire, p. 324, and see pp. 279–81 for a full description of *Massacre*.

the period, such as Marlowe's *Edward II*. There are only 3 speeches of over 25 lines or more and only another 12 of 12 or more lines; the majority are of one or two lines. A comparison with the only fragment of 'good' text that we have of *Massacre*, the beginning of Scene 19, demonstrates the memorial compression: in this edition, 36 lines shrink to 16; several lines disappear from the speaking parts of the Soldier and Guise, and the one line that Mugeroun had in the original evaporates completely.

Another major characteristic of a bad text memorially reconstructed is repetition, both from itself and from other works; *Massacre* contains a high proportion of repeated catchphrases such as 'my Lord', 'my good Lord', 'your majesty', and 'I will'; it also contains, as we shall see, a significant number of borrowings from other plays of the period. Finally, such texts often contain a high proportion of metrical irregularities (one can often hear verse 'behind' what is clearly prose in *Massacre*) and confusions of meaning which might be put down to lapses of memory, but this is much more difficult to assess with any degree of assurance.[15]

Repetition within the text and from other plays of the period as an indicator of memorial reconstruction is one of degree: in isolation each repetition may not indicate corruption and can perhaps be justified on its own merits, but when taken together they may indicate memories at work other than that of the author, although even here one needs to exercise caution. What follows is a selective list of the repetitions, beginning with the internal ones. Speech prefixes in square brackets indicate the speaker only and not a speech prefix on the same line.

[CHARLES] Prince *Condy*, and my good Lord Admirall (1.2)

NAVARRE. Prince *Condy* and my good Lord Admiral (1.27)

[GUISE] Cheefe standard bearer to the Lutheranes (6.12)

[GUISE] Cheef standard bearer to the Lutheranes (6.40)

GUISE. *Tue, tue, tue,*
Let none escape . . . (7.1–2)

[GUISE] *Tue, tue, tue,* let none escape (12.7)

GUISE. Come dragge him away and throw him in a ditch. (7.10)

[GUISE] Sirs, take him away and throw him in some ditch. (11.18)

---

[15] Maguire uses the term 'weakened verse', p. 196.

[QUEENE MOTHER] As I doe live, so surely shall he dye (11.40)

[KING] But as I live, so sure the *Guise* shall dye (19.95)

[NAVARRE] And *Guise* for *Spaine* hath now incenst the King
(16.14)

[NAVARRE] This is the *Guise* that hath incenst the King (16.32)

[CARDINALL] My brother *Guise* hath gathered a power of men
(14.55)

KING. My Lord of *Guise*, we understand
    That you have gathered a power of men (19.18–19)

[EPERNOUNE] That the *Guise* durst stand in armes against the
    King   (19.74)

[NAVARRE] That the *Guise* hath taken armes against the King
(20.2)

CAPTAINE. Come on sirs, what, are you resolutely bent,
    Hating the life and honour of the *Guise*?   (21.1–2)

KING. But are they resolute and armde to kill,
    Hating the life and honour of the *Guise*? (21.19–20)

QUEENE MOTHER. I, but my Lord, let me alone for that,
    For *Katherine* must have her will in *France*:
    As I doe live, so surely shall he dye.
    And *Henry* then shall weare the diadem.
    And if he grudge or crosse his Mothers will,
    Ile disinherite him and all the rest:
    For Ile rule *France*, but they shall weare the crowne:
    And if they storme, I then may pull them downe.
    Come my Lord let us goe.   *Exeunt.* (11.38–46)

QUEENE MOTHER. Tush man, let me alone with him,
    To work the way to bring this thing to passe:
    And if he doe deny what I doe say,
    Ile dispatch him with his brother presently.
    And then shall *Mounser* weare the diadem:
    Tush, all shall dye unles I have my will.
    For while she lives *Katherine* will be Queene.
    Come my Lord, let us goe seek the *Guise*,
    And then determine of this enterprise.   *Exeunt.* (14.61–9)

We are, perhaps, closer to noting corruptions when we consider some of the repetitions in *Massacre* from other plays of the period. It is usually thought that these echoes would have found their way into *Massacre* through actors remembering bits from other plays in which they would have recently performed. The following is, again, a selective list of such echoes, beginning with Marlowe's own work.

QUEENE MOTHER. My Lord Cardinall of *Loraine*, tell me,
How likes your grace my sonnes pleasantnes?
His minde you see runnes on his minions   (14.44–6)

QUEEN. Look *Lancaster* how passionate he is,
And still his minde runs on his minion. (*Edward II*, 6.3–4)

[DUMAINE] Come let us away and leavy men,
Tis warre that must asswage this tyrantes pride. (23.21–2)

[EDWARD] Come *Edmund* lets away, and levie men,
Tis warre that must abate these Barons pride. (*Edward II*, 6.98–9)

[KING] These bloudy hands shall teare his triple Crowne,
And fire accursed *Rome* about his eares.
Ile fire his crased buildings and incense
The papall towers to kisse the holy earth.   (24.61–4)

[EDWARD] Proud *Rome*, that hatchest such imperiall groomes,
For these thy superstitious taperlights,
Wherewith thy antichristian churches blaze,
Ile fire thy crased buildings, and enforce
The papall towers, to kisse the lowlie ground
                                    (*Edward II*, 4.97–101)

There are also echoes from Shakespeare's work.

[ADMIRALL] Oh fatall was this mariage to us all. (3.37)

[HUMPHREY] Ah Lords, fatall is this marriage canselling our states (*Contention*, sig. A3)

[GUISE] And he shall follow my proud Chariots wheeles (21.54)

[GLOSTER] That erst did follow thy prowd Chariot-Wheeles
                                    (*2 Henry VI*, 2.4.14)

[HUMPHREY] That erst did follow thy proud Chariot wheeles
                                    (*Contention*, sig. D2)

FRIER. O my Lord, I have beene a great sinner in my dayes, and the deed is meritorious. (23.28–9)

[SUFFOLKE] But that my heart accordeth with my tongue,
Seeing the deed is meritorious (*2 Henry VI*, 3.1.269–70)

ADMIRALL. O let me pray before I dye. (6.28)

SEROUNE. O let me pray before I take my death. (8.7)

SEROUNE. O let me pray unto my God. (8.14)

RUTLAND. Oh let me pray, before I take my death
(*3 Henry VI*, 1.3.36)

RUT[LAND]. Oh let me praie, before *I* take my death.
(*True Tragedy*, sig. A8)

QUEENE MOTHER. What art thou dead, sweet sonne speak to thy
Mother.   (13.16)

QUEENE MARGARET. Oh, *Ned*, sweet *Ned*, speake to thy Mother
Boy   (*3 Henry VI*, 5.5.50)

QUEEN. Ah, *Ned*, speake to thy mother boy? (*True Tragedy*, sig.
E5)

[QUEENE MOTHER] And he nor heares, nor sees us what we doe
(13.18)

[WARWICKE] And he nor sees, nor heares vs, what we say
(*3 Henry VI*, 2.6.63)

[WARWICKE] And he nor sees nor heares vs what we saie
(*True Tragedy*, sig. C4v)

[NAVARRE] And makes his footstoole on securitie (16.41)

[KING EDWARD] And made our Footstoole of Security
(*3 Henry VI*, 5.7.14)

[EDWARD] And made our footstoole of securitie
(*True Tragedy*, sig. E7v)

[NAVARRE] And we are grac'd with wreathes of victory (18.2)

[KING EDWARD] And we are grac'd with wreaths of Victorie
(*3 Henry VI*, 5.3.2)

EDW[ARD]. Thus farre our fortunes keepes an vpward
Course, and we are grast with wreathes of victorie.
(*True Tragedy*, sig. C4)

[DUMAINE] Sweet Duke of *Guise* our prop to leane upon,
　　Now thou art dead, heere is no stay for us　　(23.4–5)

EDWARD　Sweet Duke of Yorke, our Prop to leane vpon,
　　Now thou art gone, wee haue no Staffe, no Stay.
　　　　　　　　　　　　　　　　(*3 Henry VI*, 2.1.68–9)

EDW[ARD].　Sweet Duke of *Yorke* our prop to leane vpon,
　　Now thou art gone there is no hope for vs (*True Tragedy*, sig. B4)

GUISE.　Yet *Cæsar* shall goe forth. (21.66)

[CÆSAR]　Yet *Cæsar* shall go forth (*Julius Caesar*, 2.2.28)

This last exact parallel has led to a great deal of speculation as to
the relationship between *Massacre* and *Julius Caesar*, but no con-
clusive proof can be drawn from the meagre phrase.

There is finally, one more parallel that deserves citation.

[DUCHESSE].　Sweet *Mugeroune*, tis he that hath my heart,
　　And *Guise* usurpes it, cause I am his wife　　(15.4–5)

[ALICE]　Sweet Mosbie is the man that hath my hart:
　　And he vsurpes it, hauing nought but this,
　　That I am tyed to him by marriage.
　　　　　　　　　　　(*Arden of Faversham*, sig. A3)

These parallels taken in their entirety certainly indicate a tendency
to memorial corruption on the part of the reporter or reporters of
Massacre. Who they were remains a mystery. Oliver's hypothesis
is that they were three actors who played the roles of Guise,
Anjoy–Henry III, and one doubling 'some of the minor roles
such as the Cardinal and the Soldier' (Oliver, lix). He bases his
hypothesis on speech lengths and certain spelling habits, for the
latter of which he presents no evidence. My work on the text does
not lead me to any conclusions on the problem. The actor who
played Guise, if he was a reporter, certainly got quite a bit of
Scene 2 down well, but how then can we account for the absence
of so many lines from Scene 19, which we know were lost because
of the Folger leaf? For what it is worth, I suspect that there were
at least two kinds of copy text behind the octavo: one, the memorially reconstructed sections of the text; and two, at least some
printed or written copy, most clearly in evidence in the longer
scenes of the play, including Scenes 2, 21, and 24. But, like so
much else with *Massacre*, this too is mere speculation.

IV. Broughton and Oxberry

The two earliest modern editions of *The Massacre at Paris* were both published in 1818: one bears the editor's name, W. Oxberry, on the title-page; the other does not name the editor, but has been referred to as 'Chappell' by Bowers. The actual editor was identified in 1971 by N. W. Bawcutt as James Broughton.[16] Bawcutt was working on his Revels edition of *The Jew of Malta* when he made the discovery, and he was able to prove, from entries in *Blackwood's Edinburgh Magazine*, that Broughton's *The Jew of Malta* preceded Oxberry's into print by about one month. His collation of the two editions demonstrated their independence: 'There was, indeed, no connection at all between his [Broughton's] work and Oxberry's's' (450). The same cannot be said of the two *Massacre* editions; a collation of them has demonstrated that they are virtually the same text. There are variants between them, most notably in stage directions, and Broughton is divided into acts and scenes with locations indicated, but both share a very large number of substantive variants from the original octavo. For example, both print the following variants in the first eighteen lines of Scene 17: 4 goe] go'st; 5 suffer] suffer't; 8 to] *omitted*; 10 So] How; 10 of] *omitted*; 11 SD] *placed after l. 14*; 16 thus] *placed after* be; and 18 Kings] Kings beside. As one can see even from such a small sampling, it is statistically impossible for each editor to have come to so many of the same variants independently. The question now is which text came first.

The 'Prolegomena' to Broughton ends with this assertion: 'The present is the only reprint that has appeared'. It would be extremely helpful to have more evidence to corroborate the assertion, such as independent entries in *Blackwood's Edinburgh Magazine* for each publication, as Bawcutt had for the two early editions of *The Jew of Malta*. There is an entry for June 1818 (345) announcing the publication of volumes II and III, *Edward II* and *Doctor Faustus* respectively, in which Broughton identifies himself as the editor of the Marlowe edition. He completed his collection with volumes IV and V, *Lust's Dominion* and *The Massacre at Paris* respectively; but there are no subsequent announcements in *Blackwood's Edinburgh Magazine* marking the publication of either

---

[16] N. W. Bawcutt, 'James Broughton's Edition of Marlowe's Plays', *N & Q* 216 (1971), 449–452.

volume.[17] I have also been unable to locate any information as to the precise month of publication for the Oxberry *Massacre*. Since the question of which edition came first is still open, I have adopted the strategy of citing both editors in alphabetic order when noting a substantive variant in the two editions.

V. Editorial Procedures

Written editorial procedures for *The Complete Works of Christopher Marlowe* do not exist; however, this edition conforms as closely as possible to practice that Roma Gill used in volumes I, II, and IV, and to David Fuller's practice in this volume.

The copy-text for this edition of *The Massacre at Paris* is the first Octavo held in the Bodleian Library, containing Edmond Malone's textual annotations. Transcriptions of letters of the text follow the practice of the complete Marlowe edition: letters are transcribed in the original form, whether italic or Roman, upper or lower case; the long s is printed as a lower-case s; and where the early modern printer used u and v and i and j interchangeably, the letter in current common usage is printed. All exceptions to these procedures are noted in the accidental emendations. Words run together are printed as such when usage conforms to acceptable early modern practice (e.g., 'wilbe', 'shalbe', etc.), but are silently separated when seemingly inconsistent with early modern usage (e.g., 'hebeen', 'onethat', 'thisis', etc.). All changes of punctuation within the spoken text and stage directions are noted in the accidentals.

Abbreviations, such as ampersands and contractions of titles and names, are expanded and noted in the accidentals.

The punctuation in speech prefixes has been silently normalized to a full stop, and the spelling of names in speech prefixes has been silently standardized throughout to the most often used full form in the text. The only exception to this rule concerns the 'QUEENE MOTHER' prefix, which is sometimes in the original '*Old Qu.*' or a variant thereof, or simply '*Queene*' or a variant thereof. In each case the change is recorded. In two cases (Scenes 1 and 14), both concerning two different kings of France, Christian-name speech

---

[17] The final two volumes were reviewed, along with the previous three, by J. T. M. in *The European Magazine, and London Review* 79 (1821), 309–15, 413–18.

prefixes are not altered to the usual type-name because the copy-text versions make perfect sense. The typographical form of speech prefixes follows the practice of the entire edition: all names are printed in Roman capitals. Names in stage directions are also printed to conform to the rest of the edition: all proper names follow copy-text spelling and are printed in Roman capitals, and generic names are printed in Roman capitals only when they are speaking parts (e.g., '*the* KING' or 'CUTPURSE', but 'Attendant' or 'Soldier').

All changes of typography in the spoken text and stage directions are noted in the accidental collation. Scene divisions and lineation are mainly those of Roma Gill's earlier Oxford World's Classics edition of the play. All substantive variants from the copy-text are noted; each is followed by the earliest editor to make the emendation. There is no historical collation of substantive variants; and all additions to the copy-text except expansions of abbreviations in speech prefixes are placed within square brackets.

GENERAL INTRODUCTION

I. Sources

We now have an excellent collection and discussion of Marlowe's sources in Thomas and Tydeman's recent publication, to which the following brief summary is indebted.[1]

Marlowe relied heavily upon an account of the massacre written by the Huguenot lawyer, François Hotman, who used the pseudonym Ernestus Varamundus. This account first appeared in Latin in 1573 and was translated into English in the same year as *A true and plaine report of the Furious outrages of Fraunce, & the horrible and shameful slaughter of Chastillion the Admirall, and diuers other Noble and excellent men, and of the wicked and straunge murder of godlie persons, committed in many Cities of Fraunce, without any respect of sorte, kinde, age, or degree. By Ernest Varamvnd of Freseland.* It was reprinted in 1574 as Book X of a more extensive history by Jean de Serres, entitled *The Three Partes of Commentaries, Containing the whole and perfect discourse of the Ciuill warres of Fraunce, vnder the raignes of Henry the second, Frances the second, and of Charles the ninth.* Marlowe clearly knew the work in one of its forms and used it as the major, but not unique, source for material in Scenes 1 to 9 and Scene 11.[2] In addition, he probably used a number of pro-Protestant pamphlets and a Latin work of Jean de Serres which was translated into English by Arthur Golding, *The lyfe of the most godly, valeant and noble capteine and mainterner of the trew Christian Religion in Fraunce, Iasper Colignie Shatilion, sometyme greate Admirall of Fraunce* (1576). Marlowe may also have used Simon Goulart's *Mémoires de l'Etat de France sous Charles Neuvième* (1576) for incidents not found in Hotman, including, among other things, the mention of the gallows at Montfaucon, Guise stamping on the dead Admiral, and the death of Ramus.[3]

[1] Vivien Thomas and William Tydeman, eds., *Christopher Marlowe: The Plays and their Sources*, London and New York, 1994.

[2] See Paul H. Kocher, 'François Hotman and Marlowe's *The Massacre at Paris*', *PMLA* 56 (1941), 349–68; 'Contemporary Pamphlet Backgrounds for Marlowe's *The Massacre at Paris*', *MLQ* 8 (1947), 151–73, 309–18.

[3] Jacques Ramel, '*Le Massacre de Paris* de Christopher Marlowe et *Les Mémoires de l'État de France sous Charles Neuvième*', *Confluents* 5 (1979), 5–18.

For roughly the second half of the play, that is, for the events covering the period from the end of the massacre of 1572 to the death of Henry III in 1589, sources 'must remain far more conjectural and certainly have no equivalent for Hotman on the Massacre'.[4] Because we are in the realm of conjecture the Commentary does not quote from these sources. This is a confused and confusing period of French history, and there remain extant a number of pamphlets from the period. Marlowe appears to have drawn on material sympathetic to both sides for many of the events of the play and, in particular, for his ambiguous presentation of Henry III.[5] He would also have drawn on hearsay and on his own experiences; 'his personal contacts were wide enough for him to have absorbed information and ideas from diplomats like Walsingham, Stafford and Cobham, soldiers and courtiers like Raleigh as well as merchants who knew France', and he worked abroad as a government agent.[6] His own knowledge also possibly informed his presentation of Ramus' death; he was studying at Cambridge when the Ramist controversy was at its height.[7]

In a very important study of Marlowe's sources, Julia Briggs identifies a substantial amount of the material in the second half of the play as coming from pro-Catholic pamphlets, including Henry's dismissal of his counsellors in Scene 20, Guise's courage at his assassination, Henry's summons of Guise's son to view his dead father, and the mocking of the Cardinal of Lorraine at his death.[8]

There is nothing in Marlowe's sources for the relationship between the Guise and Catherine de Medici, although her outburst in Scene 22 after Guise's death is in the League pamphlet, Le martyre des deux frères; but, as Thomas–Tydeman point out (254), she is more concerned there for the consequences to Henry

[4] David Potter, 'Marlowe's *Massacre at Paris* and the Reputation of Henri III of France', in Darryll Grantley and Peter Roberts, eds., *Christopher Marlowe and English Renaissance Culture*, Aldershot, 1996, p. 73.

[5] Potter, pp. 70–95.

[6] Potter, p. 75, and see R. B. Wernham, 'Christopher Marlowe at Flushing in 1592', *EHR* 91 (1976), 344–5, and Constance Brown Kuriyama, 'Marlowe's Nemesis: The Identity of Richard Baines', in Kenneth Friedenreich, Roma Gill, and Constance B. Kuriyama, eds., *'A Poet and a filthy Play-maker': New Essays on Christopher Marlowe*, New York, 1988, pp. 343–60.

[7] But see Kocher, *PMLA* 56, 361, and John Bakeless, 'Christopher Marlowe and the Newsbooks', *JQ* 14 (1937), 18–22, who both think that the incident may come from *Le Tocsin contre les Massacreurs* (1579).

[8] Julia Briggs, 'Marlowe's *Massacre at Paris*: A Reconsideration', *RES* 34 (1983), 257–78.

than for Guise. Similarly, Ramus' friend Talaeus is not in the source materials; he had in fact been dead for 10 years before Ramus' murder.[9] Likewise, no contemporary source has been found for the Mugeroun cuckolding episode, although Thomas–Tydeman print a later account of it by Jacques-Auguste de Thou first published in 1609 (282–3). Finally, Henry's assassination scene does not depend on any one source, though a number of the details can be found in Antony Colynet, *The True History of the Civil Wars of France* . . . (1591).

II. The Play

The major difficulty with a critical response to *Massacre* is the corrupt state of the text, and one must preface any discussion with the proviso that, by any standard, the play as we have it is a very inferior piece of art because of excessive corruption caused by memorial reconstruction. Most critical response has failed to get beyond this fairly basic point, and the play is either condemned outright or partially redeemed by isolating Guise as a Marlovian hero characteristically overreaching himself, or as a pure Machiavellian villain;[10] thus both the earliest critics and many modern commentators see *Massacre* as crude and simplistic. But very recent criticism, reacting to the long tradition of negative response outlined below, offers much more sophisticated and interesting responses to what remains of it.

Although Edward Phillips first mentions *Massacre* in a curiously non-judgemental way, simply grouping it with *Edward II* as one of Marlowe's tragedies not to be forgotten,[11] the opinions of the earliest editors are much more characteristic of the low opinion in which it was held:

It has in fact no particular excellence of any kind sufficient to render the oblivion in which it has so long reposed a matter either of surprise or regret . . . . Marlowe evidently hurried through his task with all possible

[9] See John Ronald Glenn, 'The Martyrdom of Ramus in Marlowe's *The Massacre at Paris*', *PLL* 9 (1973), 365–79.

[10] See e.g. Harry Levin, *A Study of Christopher Marlowe: The Overreacher*, London, 1954, pp. 104–8; Douglas Cole, *Suffering and Evil in the Plays of Christopher Marlowe*, Princeton, 1962, pp. 144–58.

[11] Edward Phillips, *Theatrum Poetarum Anglicanorum* . . . (London, 1675), as quoted in Millar MacLure, ed., *Marlowe: The Critical Heritage 1588–1896*, London, Boston, and Henley, 1979, p. 51.

dispatch; the events of years are crowded into the compass of as many pages; and in the composition of the dialogue, brevity alone seems to have been studied. He has not, however, forgotten to interlard it with invectives against Popery, compliments to Queen Elizabeth, and other clap-traps, which were, doubtless, mightily relished and applauded by our ancestors of the sixteenth century.[12]

There is little, if any thing in this tragedy deserving praise; the language seldom rises above mediocrity, the characters are drawn with the indistinct faintness of shadows, and the plot is contemptible: events in themselves full of horror and such as should strike the soul with awe, become ludicrous in the extreme by injudicious management. The whole is in fact not so much a tragedy, as a burlesque upon tragedy; even the asperity of criticism is blunted by such gross absurdities, and loses its keenness in the overwhelming sensation of disgust. Had our task been that of selection, we should have omitted this monstrous farce altogether.[13]

The early editors attribute far more fault to Marlowe than he deserves, mainly because they did not know that the text was a memorial reconstruction; thus the point about hurried composition and some faults of the language are no longer seen as the playwright's responsibility, but several of the points made remain standard negative criticisms of the play to the present day, most notably the anti-Catholicism, the thinly drawn characterization, and its odd generic classification. And the absolute condemnation of the work as a play is also reflected in modern criticism by Wilbur Sanders: 'If space were to be allotted to a play only in proportion to its dramatic merit, I should not be writing this chapter on *Massacre*.'[14]

One more damaging criticism, that Marlowe slavishly followed his anti-Catholic sources, and thus produced little more than pro-Protestant propaganda, was added to the critical history in three articles by Kocher on the sources of *Massacre*. These articles are masterly works of source study, but the critical conclusions that Kocher draws have been challenged and overturned in the best piece written on *Massacre* to date, another article on Marlowe's sources by Julia Briggs.[15]

---

[12] Broughton, 'Prolegomena'.
[13] Oxberry, 'Remarks'.
[14] Wilbur Sanders, *The Dramatist and the Received Idea: Studies in the Plays of Marlowe & Shakespeare*, Cambridge, 1968, p. 20.
[15] Briggs, 257–78.

Briggs takes issue with Wilbur Sanders, who, following Kocher, condemns *Massacre* as a play of purely pro-Protestant propaganda; she demonstrates that Marlowe did not follow his Protestant sources in a slavish manner, but instead presented the events of a whole section of the play, those dealing with the murder of the Guise and his brother, 'not from the Huguenot viewpoint at all, but from the League viewpoint' (263). Briggs lists four places in the play where Marlowe follows League sources in support of her argument. First, Marlowe condenses the time between Henry's personal reassurance of his support to Guise (21.39–46) and Guise's assassination, thus emphasizing Henry's hypocrisy; second, Guise shows personal courage in the face of death (21.59–85); third, Guise's son is introduced to view his father's dead body (21.116–123); and fourth, the Cardinal of Loreine is mocked before his death (22.1–11) (265–7). The result of all of these pro-Catholic emphases, as Briggs tells us, is not to justify the League point of view, but to remind us of events we have already witnessed. Henry's hypocritical reassurance parallels Charles's to the Admiral (5.1–20); Guise's dying bravely parallels the Admiral at his death (6.25–30); the mockery of the Cardinal before his death recalls the earlier mockeries of the Admiral, Seroune, and others before their deaths (6.28–9, 7.8–9, 8.7–15, 9.54–56). In this reading of *Massacre*, 'The play's structure thus turns on the ironic relation between the massacre of the Huguenots and the murder of the Guise brothers' (268). Once we have an ironic perspective on the events of the play [16] critical response to *Massacre* becomes much more intriguing; in particular pro-Protestant events, such as Henry's change of sides from being a Huguenot killer in the massacre (scenes 6, 7, and 9) to a League hater (24.56–70, 90–106), seem part of a pattern of mutual duplicity. And Navarre, too, might also fit the pattern as he moves from being a fairly ineffectual figure in the early parts of the play to emerge as a force of enormous power, after rebelling against a rightful king.

Far from being a 'problem' of characterization (Oliver, p. lxiv), Navarre changes from a figure firmly dependent upon a providential history early in *Massacre* (see, for instance, 1.55–7, 3.24–5, and 13.6–7) into one who becomes a type of Machiavellian leader,

---

[16] See Judith Weil, *Christopher Marlowe: Merlin's Prophet*, Cambridge, 1977, pp. 82–104, on whose argument Briggs builds.

seizing opportunity as he rebels against a legitimate monarch (13.30–40). In this view Navarre's early reliance upon Providence parallels Charles's reliance upon his mother and Henry's upon his minions, but Navarre's later emergence as a figure of power and action parallels Guise, the play's main figure of Machiavellian dynamism. This is 'a transformation that inscribes a rift in his identity, and one that casts doubt on his role as either passive Christian or as dynamic leader, indicating instability in the self underlying both roles'.[17]

Briggs notes a final irony: that, historically, the dying Henry urged Navarre to convert to Catholicism, and that 'Henry IV's first public commitment was not to the Huguenots—it was an undertaking to defend the French Catholic Church' (271). This last fact takes us into an interesting speculation about how an audience of the time actually 'heard' Massacre. Was it a play that served as a warning against religious extremes, presenting repeated atrocity as a sickening and disgusting spectacle to be avoided? Or was it one which presented recent history as foreign absurdity, something to be witnessed and entertained by, but certainly nothing to do with 'us'? As Briggs puts it, 'The scenes of the massacre may be viewed either as a subtle, perhaps even a humane, analysis of contemporary crowd violence and religious hatred, or as a black comedy that paradoxically invites its audience to laugh at helpless Protestant victims. Either way, it must be conceded that the Massacre is something more than a tract on their behalf' (278). And, either way, the renewed language of rabid anti-Catholicism with which the play ends may be a signal of renewed intolerance which will lead directly back to the patterns of repetitive violence already witnessed earlier in the drama.

III. Staging

Most of the staging in Massacre is relatively straightforward, easily played on a stage with a couple of doors for entrances and exits; but Scenes 6, 9, and 21 are much more complex, demanding multiple areas for the action. The following offers one or two suggestions for realizing several of these moments of the play, which may be confusing when read, but which almost always

[17] Andrew M. Kirk, 'Marlowe and the Disordered Face of French History', SEL 35 (1995), 194–213.

become less confusing if one remembers that continuity and location on the Elizabethan stage could be very fluid indeed.

Scene 6 opens with the Guise and his henchmen entering the
main stage '*to the massacre*' and discussing how they intend to
make the Admiral their first victim. Gonzago exits with '*others*'
(19SD), and they all re-enter five lines later '*into the* ADMIRALS
house, and he in his bed' (24SD). Guise, Anjoy, and the rest have
remained behind on the main stage. Gonzago then kills the
Admiral, and Guise orders him to throw the body 'down' (33).
The question here is what part of the stage could represent the
Admiral's house, the area into which Gonzago and the '*others*'
enter at 6.24. The Guise's order to throw the body down would
seem to indicate an upper acting area, and this would certainly
make sense. But the beginning of Scene 5 opens with the stage
direction '*Enter the* ADMIRALL *in his bed*', and then presents 21
lines of dialogue between the Admiral and the King. It may well
be, as Oliver suggests (108–9), that the Admiral does not need to
be in the same place '*in his bed*'; he could be discovered or thrust
out onto the main stage at the beginning of Scene 5 and above in
Scene 6; but, even allowing for Elizabethan fluidity of action, the
appearance of Admiral and bed in two different locations seems
inconsistent in such a short space of time (45 lines, to be exact). It
is more likely that, whatever option is chosen, the Admiral and his
bed are in the same space twice, and the upper acting area makes
the stage business of throwing the body down slightly more
credible than throwing it from one area of the main stage to
another, or from the discovered inner acting space onto the main
stage.

Scene 9 also requires at least two clearly separate acting spaces.
It begins with Ramus entering '*in his studie*', a stage direction that
recalls the opening of *Doctor Faustus* ('*Enter* FAUSTUS *in his
studie*'), and which probably indicates some sort of inner acting
space. Taleus enters the study to warn Ramus that the Guisians
are 'hard at thy doore', and then exits from the study through a
window, 'Ile leap out at the window' (9). As he attempts to escape,
perhaps crossing the main stage from the inner acting area, he
meets Gonzago and Retes, who spare him because he is a Catholic
(15). Then Ramus enters, again exiting from the study onto the
main stage, where, after Guise, Anjoy, and others enter, he is
eventually killed. An alternative staging might utilize an upper

acting area as the location of Ramus' study, which might make
more sense of Taleus' exit line about leaping 'out at the window'.
It might also point a nice staging parallel between this action and
that implied in Scene 8, where, after Mountsorrell knocks at a
door, Seroune comes 'down' to speak with him and is murdered:
Guise and his accomplices inhabit the middle or main region of
the stage, which becomes a killing area, and some of the 'innocent'
characters like the Admiral, Ramus, and Seroune often occupy the
'higher' regions, but are dragged down to be killed.

Further on in Scene 9 there is another 'door' scene: Anjoy
knocks to gain access to Navarre, Condy, and their two schoolmasters, but after he knocks, the latter group enters (9.69SD):
literal action would demand the opposite, that is, Anjoy entering
to the group, but this is probably an example of the fluidity of
location. It could be staged as Anjoy going to a door, or to a
curtained-off inner acting area, while the others remain at a distance (front stage and to one side) till they 'enter' by joining Anjoy
and the other four. After they 'enter', the area in which they all
now stand has become the opposite side of the door or curtained-
off inner acting area.

The Guise's final interview with King Henry in Scene 21 again
requires two separate acting areas, but they seem to blend
together, becoming first one location and then another. We seem
to be on the main stage at the beginning of the scene when the
Captain of the Guard and the Murderers enter. But then the
Murderers exit and, after the King and Epernoune enter, we
seem to be in a private apartment of some sort, an area clearly
separated from the main stage, because as Guise enters he has to
knock to gain access to it (25SD). In another 'door' scene, Guise is
surprised to meet someone of rank, such as Epernoune, answering
his knock. Perhaps after the Murderers exit the King and Epernoune enter on one side of the stage, or even in an inner acting
area where the Captain joins them. At any rate, their space has
now become a 'private' area. When Guise asks the whereabouts of
the King, Epernoune tells him that he has 'Mounted his royall
Cabonet' (27). The word 'Mounted' is probably not a literal
indication of an upper acting area; however, the metaphorical
sense of 'above' is clearly suggested, although only for the King.
As Guise enters to join the King, Henry speaks two lines which
function almost as an aside, but which indicate just how fluid the

location is: 'Come Guise and see thy traiterous guile outreacht, /
And perish in the pit thou mad'st for me' (32–3). The area now is
about to become a metaphorical 'pit', the lowest level of the acting
space, but a pit only for Guise. It soon becomes literally a pit after
the King, Epernoune, and the Captain exit and the Murderers
enter. The point might be nicely underscored in staging terms if
the private apartment was an inner acting area and Guise was
trapped within it by his assassins; but the irony could also be that
he is now trapped on the main stage that he commanded as a
killing area in the earlier scenes of the play.

IV. Stage History

As noted above, the likely first performance of *The Massacre at
Paris* was 30 January 1592/3 by the Lord Strange's Men at the
Rose theatre. Henslowe subsequently notes performances by the
Admiral's Men of 'the Gwies' or 'the masacar' (variously spelled)
on the following dates in 1594, with generally diminishing returns:
19 June (54*s*.), 25 June (36*s*.), 3 July (31*s*.), 8 July (27*s*.), 16 July
(31*s*.), 27 July (22*s*.), 8 August (23*s*. 6*d*.), 17 August (20*s*.), 7
September (17*s*. 6*d*.), 25 September (14*s*.). *Massacre* then seems
to have left the stage until a probable revival late in 1598. It is then
mentioned by Henslowe on 19 November 1598 when he lent 'w^m
B*o*rne' 12*s*., 'wch he sayd yt was to Imbrader his hatte for th*e*
gwisse'. On 27 November 1598 Henslowe lent 'w^m birde ales
[alias] borne', 20*s*. 'to bye a payer of sylke stokens to play*e* the
gwiss*e* in'. The next mention, probably relating to another revival,
is for 3 November 1601, when Henslowe lent 'w^m Jube' £3 'to bye
stamell cllath for A clocke [cloak] for th*e* gwisse', and the Admiral's Men Company 30*s*. 'to lend the littell tayller to bye fuschen
[fustian] and lynynge for th*e* clockes for the masaker of france'.
There are later entries on 8, 13, and 26 November 1601 for
payments to the tailor, Radford, the first for 20*s*. for 'mackeynge
of sewtes' for 'th*e* gwess*e*', and the latter two for 20*s*. and 24*s*. 6*d*.
for settling his bill for work related to 'the gwisse'. The final entry
relating to *Massacre* in Henslowe is for the purchase of 3 'bookes'
from Alleyn in January 1601/2, one of which was 'the massaker of
france' and may not be related to a performance.[18]

---

[18] Foakes and Rickert, eds., *Henslowe's Diary*, pp. 20, 22–4, 76, 82, 183–5, 187.

The next record of a *Massacre* production is 21, 22, and 23 October 1940 by the Yale Dramatic Association, an amateur group, directed by Burton G. Shevelove.[19] The Marlowe Society (of London) revived the play at the Chanticleer Theatre in London on 30 January 1963 to mark the 370th anniversary of its first performance at the Rose on 30 January 1593; the performance 'proved an unexpected, resounding success'.[20] The next performance appears to be in 1981 by the Glasgow Citizens' Theatre (reviewed by Robert Cushman in *The Observer*, 8 February 1981). The Royal Shakespeare Company then produced the play at The Other Place on 15 and 16 October 1985 in Stratford-upon-Avon; Paul Marcus directed.[21] There was also a radio version on BBC Radio 3, directed by Alan Drury and Michael Earley, in 1993. It may just be coincidence, but it is curious that *Massacre*, as 'bad' a text as it is, has received renewed attention in Britain during the eighties and early nineties: perhaps the portrayal of the naked ambition of the Guise, in particular, struck a chord in a country where personal ambition and acquisition appeared to be institutionalized in its political structures.

[19] John Bakeless, *The Tragical History of Christopher Marlowe*, ii, Cambridge, Mass., 1942, p. 91.

[20] A. D. Wraight, *Christopher Marlowe and Edward Alleyn*, Chichester, 1993, p. 382.

[21] This production appears not to have been reviewed, but it is briefly discussed in Maguire, 1996, pp. 204–5.

THE
MASSACRE
AT PARIS:

With the Death of the
Duke of Guise

[Dramatis Personae

CHARLES IX, King of France
Duke of ANJOY, brother of Charles, later King Henry III
King of NAVARRE, later King Henry IV
Prince of CONDY, his brother
Lord High ADMIRALL
Duke of GUISE
Duke DUMAINE, brother of Guise
CARDINALL of Lorraine, brother of Guise
YONG GUISE, Guise's son
EPERNOUNE
PLESHE
MUGEROUN, King Henry III's minion
Duke of JOYEUX, King Henry III's minion
COSIN, Captain of the King's Guard
GONZAGO
RETES
MOUNTSORRELL
BARTUS
LOREINE, a Protestant preacher
SEROUNE
RAMUS
TALEUS
Two LORDS of Poland

A Jacobin FRIER
POTHECARIE
SOULDIER
Admiral's MAN
CUTPURSE
MESSENGER
Three MURTHERERS
SURGEON
SOULDIERS
English Agent
Two Scholmaisters
PROTESTANTS
Attendants

QUEENE MOTHER of France, Catherine de' Medici, mother of
    Charles IX, Duke of Anjoy, and Queen Margret of Navarre

OLD QUEENE of Navarre, mother of the King of Navarre
Queen MARGRET of Navarre, wife of the King of Navarre and daughter
  of Catherine de' Medici
DUCHESSE of Guise, wife of Guise
SEROUNE's wife
MAID to Duchess of Guise]

Dramatis Personae] *Broughton and Oxberry subst.*

THE
MASSACRE
AT PARIS

With the Death of the Duke of Guise.

[Scene 1]

Enter CHARLES *the French King, the* QUEENE MOTHER, *the King of* NAVARRE, *the Prince of* CONDYE, *the Lord high* ADMIRALL, *and* [MARGRET] *the Queene of* NAVARRE, *with others.*

CHARLES. Prince of *Navarre* my honourable brother,
Prince *Condy*, and my good Lord Admirall,
I wishe this union and religious league,
Knit in these hands, thus joyn'd in nuptiall rites,
May not desolve, till death desolve our lives,   5
And that the native sparkes of princely love,
That kindled first this motion in our hearts,
May still be feweld in our progenye.
NAVARRE. The many favours which your grace hath showne,
From time to time, but specially in this,   10
Shall binde me ever to your highnes will,
In what Queen Mother or your grace commands.
QUEENE MOTHER. Thanks sonne *Navarre*, you see we
    love you well,
That linke you in mariage with our daughter heer:
And as you know, our difference in Religion   15
Might be a meanes to crosse you in your love.
CHARLES. Well Madam, let that rest:
And now my Lords the mariage rites perfourm'd,
We think it good to goe and consumate
The rest, with hearing of a holy Masse: 20

Scene 1] *Bullen, as all following scene divisions*   0SD3 MARGRET] *Broughton and Oxberry*

Sister, I think your selfe will beare us company.

QUEENE MARGRET. I will my good Lord.

CHARLES. The rest that will not goe (my Lords) may stay:
Come Mother
Let us goe to honor this solemnitie.   25

QUEENE MOTHER. Which Ile desolve with bloud and
crueltie.   [*Aside*.]

Exit [CHARLES] *the* KING, QUEENE MOTHER,
and [MARGRET] *the Queene of* NAVAR, [*with others*,] *and*
manet NAVAR, *the Prince of* CONDY, *and the Lord high*
ADMIRALL.

NAVARRE. Prince *Condy* and my good Lord Admiral,
Now *Guise* may storme but doe us little hurt:
Having the King, Queene Mother on our sides,
To stop the mallice of his envious heart,   30
That seekes to murder all the Protestants:
Have you not heard of late how he decreed,
If that the King had given consent thereto,
That all the protestants that are in *Paris*,
Should have been murdered the other night?   35

ADMIRALL. My Lord I mervaile that th'aspiring *Guise*,
Dares once adventure without the Kings consent,
To meddle or attempt such dangerous things.

CONDY. My Lord you need not mervaile at the *Guise*,
For what he doth the Pope will ratifie: 40
In murder, mischeefe, or in tiranny.

NAVARRE. But he that sits and rules above the clowdes,
Doth heare and see the praiers of the just:
And will revenge the bloud of innocents,
That *Guise* hath slaine by treason of his heart,   45
And brought by murder to their timeles ends.

ADMIRALL. My Lord, but did you mark the Cardinall,
The *Guises* brother, and the Duke *Dumain*:
How they did storme at these your nuptiall rites,
Because the house of *Burbon* now comes in,   50

26SD 1] *Broughton and Oxberry*   26SD2 CHARLES] *Broughton and Oxberry*
subst.   26SD3 MARGRET] *Broughton and Oxberry subst.*   *with others*] *Broughton and*
Oxberry subst.

And joynes your linnage to the crowne of *France*?
NAVARRE. And thats the cause that *Guise* so frowns at us,
   And beates his braines to catch us in his trap:
   Which he hath pitcht within his deadly toyle.
   Come my Lords lets go to the Church and pray,   55
   That God may still defend the right of *France*:
   And make his Gospel flourish in this land.   *Exeunt.*

[Scene 2]

Enter the Duke of GUISE.

GUISE. If ever *Hymen* lowr'd at marriage rites,
   And had his alters deckt with duskie lightes:
   If ever sunne stainde heaven with bloudy clowdes,
   And made it look with terrour on the worlde:
   If ever day were turnde to ugly night,   5
   And night made semblance of the hue of hell,
   This day, this houre, this fatall night,
   Shall fully shew the fury of them all.
   Apothecarie.

Enter the POTHECARIE.

POTHECARIE. My Lord.   10
GUISE. Now shall I prove and guerdon to the ful,
   The love thou bear'st unto the house of *Guise*:
   Where are those perfumed gloves which I sent
   To be poysoned, hast thou done them? speake,
   Will every savour breed a pangue of death?   15
POTHECARIE. See where they be my good Lord,
   And he that smelles but to them, dyes.
GUISE. Then thou remainest resolute.
POTHECARIE. I am my Lord, in what your grace commaundes
   Till death.   20
GUISE. Thankes my good freend, I wil requite thy love.
   Goe then, present them to the Queene *Navarre*:
   For she is that huge blemish in our eye,
   That makes these upstart heresies in *Fraunce*:

Be gone my freend, present them to her straite.   25
                                        Exit POTHECARIE.
Souldyer.

                    Enter a SOULDIER.

SOULDIER. My Lord.
GUISE. Now come thou forth and play thy tragick part,
    Stand in some window opening neere the street,
    And when thou seest the Admirall ride by,   30
    Discharge thy musket and perfourme his death:
    And then Ile guerdon thee with store of crownes.
SOULDIER. I will my Lord.   *Exit* SOULDIER.
GUISE. Now *Guise*, begins those deepe ingendred thoughts
    To burst abroad those never dying flames,   35
    Which cannot be extinguisht but by bloud.
    Oft have I leveld, and at last have learnd,
    That perill is the cheefest way to happines,
    And resolution honors fairest aime.
    What glory is there in a common good,   40
    That hanges for every peasant to atchive?
    That like I best that flyes beyond my reach:
    Set me to scale the high Peramides,
    And thereon set the Diadem of *Fraunce*,
    Ile either rend it with my nayles to naught,   45
    Or mount the top with my aspiring winges,
    Although my downfall be the deepest hell.
    For this, I wake, when others think I sleepe,
    For this, I waite, that scornes attendance else:
    For this, my quenchles thirst whereon I builde,   50
    Hath often pleaded kindred to the King.
    For this, this head, this heart, this hand and sworde,
    Contrives, imagines and fully executes,
    Matters of importe, aimde at by many,
    Yet understoode by none.   55
    For this, hath heaven engendred me of earth,
    For this, this earth sustaines my bodies waight,
    And with this wait Ile counterpoise a Crowne,

25SD] *Dyce*[2]; *placed at end of line 26 in O, presumably because of the lack of space at the end of line 25*

Or with seditions weary all the worlde:
For this, from *Spaine* the stately Catholickes   60
Sends Indian golde to coyne me French ecues:
For this have I a largesse from the Pope,
A pension and a dispensation too:
And by that priviledge to worke upon,
My policye hath framde religion.   65
Religion: *O Diabole.*
Fye, I am ashamde, how ever that I seeme,
To think a word of such a simple sound,
Of so great matter should be made the ground.
The gentle King whose pleasure uncontrolde,   70
Weakneth his body, and will waste his Realme,
If I repaire not what he ruinates:
Him as a childe I dayly winne with words,
So that for proofe, he barely beares the name:
I execute, and he sustaines the blame.   75
The Mother Queene workes wonders for my sake,
And in my love entombes the hope of *Fraunce*:
Rifling the bowels of her treasurie,
To supply my wants and necessitie.
Paris hath full five hundred Colledges,   80
As Monestaries, Priories, Abbyes and halles,
Wherein are thirtie thousand able men,
Besides a thousand sturdy student Catholicks,
And more: of my knowledge in one cloyster keeps,
Five hundred fatte Franciscan Fryers and priestes.   85
All this and more, if more may be comprisde,
To bring the will of our desires to end.
Then *Guise*
Since thou hast all the Cardes within thy hands
To shuffle or cut, take this as surest thing: 90
That right or wrong, thou deale thy selfe a King.
I, but *Navarre*: *Navarre*, tis but a nook of *France*,
Sufficient yet for such a pettie King:
That with a rablement of his hereticks,
Blindes *Europs* eyes and troubleth our estate: 95
Him will we——   *Pointing to his Sworde.*

92 I, but *Navarre*:] *Craik (this edn.)*; I but, *Navarre, O*

But first lets follow those in *France*,
That hinder our possession to the crowne:
As *Cæsar* to his souldiers, so say I:
Those that hate me, will I learn to loath.   100
Give me a look, that when I bend the browes,
Pale death may walke in furrowes of my face:
A hand, that with a graspe may gripe the world,
An eare, to heare what my detractors say,
A royall seate, a scepter and a crowne: 105
That those which doe beholde, they may become
As men that stand and gase against the Sunne.
The plot is laide, and things shall come to passe:
Where resolution strives for victory.   *Exit.*

[Scene 3]

Enter the King of NAVAR *and Queen* [MARGRET], *and his*
MOTHER QUEEN, *the Prince of* CONDY, *the* ADMIRALL,
and the POTHECARY *with the gloves, and gives them to the*
olde Queene.

POTHECARIE. Maddame,
   I beseech your grace to accept this simple gift.
OLD QUEENE. Thanks my good freend, holde, take thou this
   reward.
POTHECARIE. I humbly thank your Majestie.
                                          Exit POTHECARIE.
OLD QUEENE. Me thinkes the gloves have a very strong
   perfume,   5
   The sent whereof doth make my head to ake.
NAVARRE. Doth not your grace know the man that gave them you?
OLD QUEENE. Not wel, but do remember such a man.
ADMIRALL. Your grace was ill advisde to take them then,
   Considering of these dangerous times.   10
OLD QUEENE. Help sonne *Navarre* I am poysoned.
QUEENE MARGRET. The heavens forbid your highnes
   such mishap.
NAVARRE. The late suspition of the Duke of *Guise*,

Might well have moved your highnes to beware
How you did meddle with such dangerous giftes.   15
QUEENE MARGRET. Too late it is my Lord if that be true
To blame her highnes, but I hope it be
Only some naturall passion makes her sicke.
OLD QUEENE. O no, sweet *Margret*, the fatall poyson
Workes within my head, my brain pan breakes,   20
My heart doth faint, I dye.   *She dyes.*
NAVARRE. My Mother poysoned heere before my face:
O gracious God, what times are these?
O graunt sweet God my daies may end with hers,
That I with her may dye and live againe.   25
QUEENE MARGRET. Let not this heavy chaunce my dearest
    Lord,
(For whose effects my soule is massacred)
Infect thy gracious brest with fresh supply,
To agravate our sodaine miserie.
ADMIRALL. Come my Lords let us beare her body hence,   30
And see it honoured with just solemnitie.
              As they are going, the SOULDIER *dischargeth*
                        his Musket at the Lord ADMIRALL.
CONDY. What are you hurt my Lord high Admiral?
ADMIRALL. I my good Lord, shot through the arme.
NAVARRE. We are betraide, come my Lords, and let us
goe tell the King of this.   35
ADMIRALL. These are the cursed Guisians that doe seeke
    our death.
Oh fatall was this mariage to us all.

    They beare away the [OLD] QUEENE *and goe out.*

[Scene 4]

Enter [CHARLES] *the* KING, QUEENE MOTHER, *Duke of*
GUISE, *Duke* ANJOY, *Duke* DEMAYNE [*and* COSIN].

QUEENE MOTHER. My noble sonne, and princely Duke of
    Guise,

37SD OLD] *Dyce*[1]   OSD1 CHARLES] *Broughton and Oxberry*   OSD2 *and*
COSIN] *Oliver subst.*

Now have we got the fatall stragling deere
Within the compasse of a deadly toyle,
And as we late decreed we may perfourme.

KING. Madam, it wilbe noted through the world,   5
An action bloudy and tirannicall:
Cheefely since under safetie of our word,
They justly challenge their protection:
Besides my heart relentes that noble men,
Onely corrupted in religion,   10
Ladies of honor, Knightes and Gentlemen,
Should for their conscience taste such rutheles ends.

ANJOY. Though gentle mindes should pittie others paines,
Yet will the wisest note their proper greefes:
And rather seeke to scourge their enemies,   15
Then be themselves base subjects to the whip.

GUISE. Me thinkes my Lord, *Anjoy* hath well advisde
Your highnes to consider of the thing,
And rather chuse to seek your countries good,
Then pittie or releeve these upstart hereticks.   20

QUEENE MOTHER. I hope these reasons may serve my princely
    Sonne,
To have some care for feare of enemies.

KING. Well Madam, I referre it to your Majestie,
And to my Nephew heere the Duke of *Guise*:
What you determine, I will ratifie.   25

QUEENE MOTHER. Thankes to my princely sonne, then tell me
    Guise,
What order wil you set downe for the Massacre?

GUISE. Thus Madame.
They that shalbe actors in this Massacre,
Shall weare white crosses on their Burgonets,   30
And tye white linnen scarfes about their armes.
He that wantes these, and is suspected of heresie,
Shall dye, be he King or Emperour. Then Ile have
A peale of ordinance shot from the tower, at which
They all shall issue out and set the streetes.   35
And then the watchword being given, a bell shall ring,
Which when they heare, they shall begin to kill:
And never cease untill that bell shall cease,
Then breath a while.

Enter the Admirals MAN.

KING. How now fellow, what newes? 40
MAN. And it please your grace the Lord high Admirall,
  Riding the streetes was traiterously shot,
  And most humbly intreates your Majestie
  To visite him sick in his bed.
KING. Messenger, tell him I will see him straite. 45
                              Exit MESSENGER.
What shall we doe now with the Admirall?
QUEENE MOTHER. Your Majesty were best goe visite him,
  And make a shew as if all were well.
KING. Content, I will goe visite the Admirall.
GUISE. And I will goe take order for his death.   *Exit* GUISE.

[Scene 5]

Enter the ADMIRALL *in his bed.*

KING. How fares it with my Lord high Admiral,
  Hath he been hurt with villaines in the street?
  I vow and sweare as I am King of *France*,
  To finde and to repay the man with death:
  With death delay'd and torments never usde, 5
  That durst presume for hope of any gaine,
  To hurt the noble man their soveraign loves.
ADMIRALL. Ah my good Lord, these are the Guisians,
  That seeke to massacre our guiltles lives.
KING. Assure your selfe my good Lord Admirall, 10
  I deeply sorrow for your trecherous wrong:
  And that I am not more secure my selfe,
  Then I am carefull you should be preserved.
  Cosin, take twenty of our strongest guarde,
  And under your direction see they keep 15
  All trecherous violence from our noble freend,
  Repaying all attempts with present death,
  Upon the cursed breakers of our peace.

43 humbly] *Broughton and Oxberry*; humble *O*

And so be pacient good Lord Admirall,
And every hower I will visite you. 20
ADMIRALL. I humbly thank your royall Majestie.

Exeunt omnes.

[Scene 6]

Enter GUISE, ANJOY, DUMAINE, GONZAGO, RETES,
MONTSORRELL, *and Souldiers to the massacre.*

GUISE. *Anjoy, Dumaine, Gonzago, Retes,* sweare
By the argent crosses in your burgonets,
To kill all that you suspect of heresie.
DUMAINE. I sweare by this to be unmercifull.
ANJOY. I am disguisde and none knows who I am, 5
And therfore meane to murder all I meet.
GONZAGO. And so will I.
RETES. And I.
GUISE. Away then, break into the Admirals house.
RETES. I, let the Admirall be first dispatcht. 10
GUISE. The Admirall
Cheefe standard bearer to the Lutheranes,
Shall in the entrance of this Massacre,
Be murdered in his bed.
Gonzago conduct them thither, and then 15
Beset his house that not a man may live.
ANJOY. That charge is mine: Swizers keepe you the streetes,
And at ech corner shall the Kings garde stand.
GONZAGO. Come sirs follow me.

Exit GONZAGO *and others with him.*

ANJOY. *Cosin*, the Captaine of the Admirals guarde,
Plac'd by my brother, will betray his Lord: 20
Now *Guise* shall catholiques flourish once againe,
The head being of, the members cannot stand.
RETES. But look my Lord, ther's some in the Admirals house.

Enter [GONZAGO *and others*] *into the* ADMIRALS *house, and
he in his bed.*

24SDI GONZAGO *and others*] *Robinson subst.* ('*They enter into the house of the Admiral, who
is in bed.*')

ANJOY. In lucky time, come let us keep this lane,   25
  And slay his servants that shall issue out.
GONZAGO. Where is the Admirall?
ADMIRALL. O let me pray before I dye.
GONZAGO. Then pray unto our Ladye, kisse this crosse.

                                              Stab him.

ADMIRALL. O God forgive my sins.   *[Dyes.]*
GUISE. *Gonzago*, what, is he dead?   31
GONZAGO. I my Lord.
GUISE. Then throw him down.

             [The body of the ADMIRALL *is thrown down.]*

ANJOY. Now cosin view him well,
  It may be it is some other, and he escapte.   35
GUISE. Cosin tis he, I know him by his look.
  See where my Souldier shot him through the arm.
  He mist him neer, but we have strook him now.
  Ah base *Shatillian* and degenerate,
  Cheef standard bearer to the Lutheranes,   40
  Thus in despite of thy Religion,
  The Duke of *Guise* stampes on thy liveles bulke.
ANJOY. Away with him, cut of his head and handes.
  And send them for a present to the Pope:
  And when this just revenge is finished,   45
  Unto mount *Faucon* will we dragge his coarse:
  And he that living hated so the crosse,
  Shall being dead, be hangd thereon in chaines.
GUISE. *Anjoy, Gonzago, Retes*, if that you three,
  Will be as resolute as I and *Dumaine*:   50
  There shall not a Hugonet breath in *France*.
ANJOY. I sweare by this crosse, wee'l not be partiall,
  But slay as many as we can come neer.
GUISE. *Mountsorrell*, goe shoote the ordinance of,
  That they which have already set the street   55
  May know their watchword, then tole the bell,
  And so lets forward to the Massacre.
MOUNTSORRELL. I will my Lord.   *Exit* MOUNTSORRELL.
GUISE. And now my Lords let us closely to our busines.
ANJOY. *Anjoy* will follow thee.   60

              30SD] *Dyce*[1]   33SD] *Dyce*[1]

DUMAINE. And so will *Dumaine.*

> *The ordinance being shot of, the bell tolles.*

GUISE. Come then, lets away.   *Exeunt.*

[Scene 7]

The GUISE *enters againe, with all the rest, with their Swords drawne, chasing the Protestants.*

GUISE. *Tue, tue, tue,*
    Let none escape, murder the Hugonets.
ANJOY. Kill them, kill them.   *Exeunt.*

Enter LOREINE *running, the* GUISE *and the rest pursuing him.*

GUISE. *Loreine, Loreine,* follow *Loreine.* Sirra,
    Are you a preacher of these heresies?   5
LOREINE. I am a preacher of the word of God,
    And thou a traitor to thy soule and him.
GUISE. 'Dearely beloved brother', thus tis written.   *he stabs him.*
ANJOY. Stay my Lord, let me begin the psalme.
GUISE. Come dragge him away and throw him in a ditch.   10
       Exeunt.

[Scene 8]

Enter MOUNTSORRELL *and knocks at* SEROUNS *doore.*

SEROUNS WIFE. Who is that which knocks there?   [*Within.*]
MOUNTSORRELL. *Mountsorrell* from the Duke of *Guise.*
SEROUNS WIFE. Husband come down, heer's one would speak
    with you from the Duke of *Guise.*   [*Within.*]

Enter SEROUNE.

SEROUNE. To speek with me from such a man as he?   5

Sc.8   1SD] *Broughton and Oxberry*   4SD] *Dyce*[1]

MOUNTSORRELL. I, I, for this *Seroune*, and thou shalt ha't.

            shewing his dagger.

SEROUNE. O let me pray before I take my death.

MOUNTSORRELL. Despatch then quickly.

SEROUNE. O Christ my Saviour.

MOUNTSORRELL. Christ, villaine,   10

 Why darst thou presume to call on Christ,

 Without the intercession of some Saint?

 Sanctus Jacobus hee was my Saint, pray to him.

SEROUNE. O let me pray unto my God.

MOUNTSORRELL. Then take this with you. *Stab him. Exit*. 15

[Scene 9]

Enter RAMUS *in his studie*.

RAMUS. What fearfull cries comes from the river *Sene*,

 That frightes poore *Ramus* sitting at his book?

 I feare the Guisians have past the bridge,

 And meane once more to menace me.

Enter TALEUS.

TALEUS. Flye *Ramus* flye, if thou wilt save thy life.   5

RAMUS. Tell me *Taleus*, wherfore should I flye?

TALEUS. The Guisians are

 Hard at thy doore, and meane to murder us:

 Harke, harke they come, Ile leap out at the window.

          [*Exit from studie*.]

RAMUS. Sweet *Taleus* stay.   10

Enter GONZAGO *and* RETES.

GONZAGO. Who goes there?

RETES. Tis *Taleus*, *Ramus* bedfellow.

GONZAGO. What art thou?

TALEUS. I am as *Ramus* is, a Christian.

RETES. O let him goe, he is a catholick.   *Exit* TALEUS. 15

---

 6 ha't] *Malone MS*; hate *O* 13 *Sanctus*] *Broughton and Oxberry*; *Sancta O* 1
Sene] *Malone MS*; *Rene O* 9SD] *This edn.* 15SD 1] *placed below l. 15 and to the
right of following* SD *at margin in O, presumably because of the lack of space at end of line 15*

Enter RAMUS [*from his studie*].

GONZAGO. Come *Ramus*, more golde, or thou shalt have the stabbe.

RAMUS. Alas I am a scholler, how should I have golde?
All that I have is but my stipend from the King,
Which is no sooner receiv'd but it is spent.

Enter the GUISE *and* ANJOY[, DUMAINE, MOUNTSORRELL *and Soldiers*].

ANJOY. Who have you there?   20

RETES. Tis *Ramus*, the Kings professor of Logick.

GUISE. Stab him.

RAMUS. O good my Lord,
Wherein hath *Ramus* been so offencious?

GUISE. Marry sir, in having a smack in all,   25
And yet didst never sound anything to the depth.
Was it not thou that scoftes the *Organon*,
And said it was a heape of vanities?
He that will be a flat decotamest,
And seen in nothing but Epetomies,   30
Is in your judgment thought a learned man.
And he forsooth must goe and preach in *Germany*:
Excepting against Doctors actions,
And *ipse dixi* with this quidditie,
Argumentum testimonii est inartificiale.   35
To contradict which, I say *Ramus* shall dye:
How answere you that? your *nego argumentum*
Cannot serve, sirra, kill him.

RAMUS. O good my Lord, let me but speak a word.

ANJOY. Well, say on.   40

RAMUS. Not for my life doe I desire this pause,
But in my latter houre to purge my selfe,
In that I know the things that I have wrote,
Which as I heare one *Shekius* takes it ill,
Because my places being but three, contains all his: 45

15SD2 *from his studie*] *This edn.*
and Oxberry subst. ('and the rest'). 19SD, DUMAINE . . . *Souldiers*] *Dyce;*[1] *Broughton*
34 *ipse*] *Malone MS; ipsi* O   35 *testimonii est*
inartificiale] *Dyce*[1] (*who credits the Rev. J. Mitford*); *testimonis est in arte fetialis* O   44
Shekius] *Dyce*[1]; *Shekins (possibly turned 'u')* O

I knew the *Organon* to be confusde,
And I reduc'd it into better forme.
And this for *Aristotle* will I say,
That he that despiseth him, can nere
Be good in Logick or Philosophie.   50
And thats because the blockish Sorbonests,
Attribute as much unto their workes,
As to the service of the eternall God.

GUISE. Why suffer you that peasant to declaime?
Stab him I say and send him to his freends in hell.   55
ANJOY. Nere was there Colliars sonne so full of pride. *kill him.*
GUISE. My Lord of *Anjoy*, there are a hundred Protestants,
Which we have chaste into the river *Sene*,
That swim about and so preserve their lives:
How may we doe? I feare me they will live.   60
DUMAINE. Goe place some men upon the bridge,
With bowes and dartes to shoot at them they see,
And sinke them in the river as they swim.
GUISE. Tis well advisde *Dumain*, goe see it strait be done.

                              [*Exit* DUMAINE.]
And in the mean time my Lord, could we devise,   65
To get those pedantes from the King *Navarre*,
That are tutors to him and the prince of *Condy* ——
ANJOY. For that let me alone, Cousin stay you heer,
And when you see me in, then follow hard.

He knocketh, and enter the King of NAVARRE *and Prince of*
CONDY, *with their scholmaisters.*

How now my Lords, how fare you?   70
NAVARRE. My Lord, they say
That all the protestants are massacred.
ANJOY. I, so they are, but yet what remedy:
I have done what I could to stay this broile.
NAVARRE. But yet my Lord the report doth run,   75
That you were one that made this Massacre.
ANJOY. Who I? you are deceived, I rose but now.

---

51 Sorbonests] *Broughton and Oxberry*; thorbonest *O*   58 *Sene*] *Malone MS*;
Rene *O*   64SD] *Dyce*[1]

Enter [to them] GUISE [*with* GONZAGO, RETES,
MOUNTSORRELL, *and Souldiers*].

GUISE. Murder the Hugonets, take those pedantes hence.
NAVARRE. Thou traitor *Guise*, lay of thy bloudy hands.
CONDY. Come let us goe tell the King.   80
                    Exeunt [CONDY *and* NAVARRE].
GUISE. Come sirs,
  Ile whip you to death with my punniards point.   *he kils them.*
ANJOY. Away with them both.
            Exit ANJOY [*with Souldiers carrying the bodies*].
GUISE. And now sirs for this night let our fury stay.
  Yet will we not that the Massacre shall end: 85
  Gonzago poste you to *Orleance*,
  Retes to *Deep*, *Mountsorrell* unto *Roan*,
  And spare not one that you suspect of heresy.
  And now stay that bel that to the devils mattins rings.
  Now every man put of his burgonet,   90
  And so convey him closely to his bed.   *Exeunt.*

[Scene 10]

Enter ANJOY, *with two* LORDS *of Poland.*

ANJOY. My Lords of *Poland* I must needs confesse,
  The offer of your Prince Electors, farre
  Beyond the reach of my desertes:
  For *Poland* is as I have been enformde,
  A martiall people, worthy such a King,   5
  As hath sufficient counsaile in himselfe,
  To lighten doubts and frustrate subtile foes.
  And such a King whom practise long hath taught,
  To please himselfe with mannage of the warres,
  The greatest warres within our Christian bounds,   10
  I meane our warres against the Muscovites:
  And on the other side against the Turke,
  Rich Princes both, and mighty Emperours:

77SD *to them, with...Souldiers*] *Dyce*[1] *subst.*   80SD CONDY *and* NAVARRE]
Broughton and Oxberry   83SD *with...bodies*] *Dyce*[1] *subst.*

Yet by my brother *Charles* our King of *France*,
And by his graces councell it is thought,   15
That if I undertake to weare the crowne
Of *Poland*, it may prejudice their hope
Of my inheritance to the crowne of *France*:
For if th'almighty take my brother hence,
By due discent the Regall seat is mine.   20
With *Poland* therfore must I covenant thus,
That if by death of *Charles*, the diadem
Of *France* be cast on me, then with your leaves
I may retire me to my native home.
If your commission serve to warrant this,   25
I thankfully shall undertake the charge
Of you and yours, and carefully maintaine
The wealth and safety of your kingdomes right.
LORD. All this and more your highnes shall commaund,
   For *Polands* crowne and kingly diadem.   30
ANJOY. Then come my Lords, lets goe.   *Exeunt*.

[Scene 11]

Enter two [SOULDIERS] *with the* ADMIRALS *body*.

1. Now sirra, what shall we doe with the Admirall?
2. Why let us burne him for an heretick.
1. O no, his bodye will infect the fire, and the fire the aire,
   and so we shall be poysoned with him.
2. What shall we doe then?   5
1. Lets throw him into the river.
2. Oh twill corrupt the water, and the water the fish, and
   by the fish our selves when we eate them.
1. Then throw him into the ditch.
2. No, no, to decide all doubts, be rulde by me, lets hang   10
   him heere upon this tree.
1. Agreede.   *They hang him*.

OSD SOULDIERS] *Craik* (*this edn.*)

Enter the Duke of GUISE, *and* QUEENE MOTHER, *and the*
CARDINALL.

GUISE. Now Madame, how like you our lusty Admirall?

QUEENE MOTHER. Beleeve me *Guise* he becomes the place so
    well,

    As I could long ere this have wisht him there.   15

    But come lets walke aside, th'air's not very sweet.

GUISE. No by my faith Madam.

    Sirs, take him away and throw him in some ditch.

                    [SOULDIERS] *carry away the dead body*.

    And now Madam as I understand,

    There are a hundred Hugonets and more,   20

    Which in the woods doe holde their synagogue:

    And dayly meet about this time of day,

    And thither will I to put them to the sword.

QUEENE MOTHER. Do so sweet *Guise*, let us delay no time,

    For if these straglers gather head againe,   25

    And disperse themselves throughout the Realme of *France*,

    It will be hard for us to worke their deaths.

    Be gone, delay no time sweet *Guise*.

GUISE. Madam   29

    I goe as whirl-windes rage before a storme.   *Exit* GUISE.

QUEENE MOTHER. My Lord of *Loraine* have you markt of late,

    How *Charles* our sonne begins for to lament

    For the late nights worke which my Lord of *Guise*

    Did make in *Paris* amongst the Hugonites?

CARDINALL. Madam, I have heard him solemnly vow,   35

    With the rebellious King of *Navarre*,

    For to revenge their deaths upon us all.

QUEENE MOTHER. I, but my Lord, let me alone for that,

    For *Katherine* must have her will in *France*:

    As I doe live, so surely shall he dye.   40

    And *Henry* then shall weare the diadem.

    And if he grudge or crosse his Mothers will,

    Ile disinherite him and all the rest:

    For Ile rule *France*, but they shall weare the crowne:

    And if they storme, I then may pull them downe.   45

    Come my Lord let us goe.   *Exeunt*.

    18SD SOULDIERS] *Craik (this edn.)*   46] let *Dyce*[1]; lets *O*

[Scene 12]

Enter five or sixe PROTESTANTS *with bookes, and kneele*
together. Enter also the GUISE *[and others].*

GUISE. Downe with the Hugonites, murder them.
PROTESTANT. O *Mounser de Guise*, heare me but speake.
GUISE. No villain, that toung of thine,
  That hath blasphemde the holy Church of *Rome*,
  Shall drive no plaintes into the *Guises* eares,   5
  To make the justice of my heart relent:
  Tue, tue, tue, let none escape: *kill them.*
  So, dragge them away.   *Exeunt.*

[Scene 13]

Enter the King of FRANCE, NAVAR *and* EPERNOUNE *staying*
him: enter QUEENE MOTHER, *and the* CARDINALL *[with*
PLESHE *and Attendants].*

KING. O let me stay and rest me heer a while,
  A griping paine hath ceasde upon my heart:
  A sodaine pang, the messenger of death.
QUEENE MOTHER. O say not so, thou kill'st thy mothers heart.
KING. I must say so, paine forceth me complaine.   5
NAVARRE. Comfort your selfe my Lord and have no doubt,
  But God will sure restore you to your health.
KING. O no, my loving brother of *Navarre*.
  I have deserv'd a scourge I must confesse,
  Yet is there pacience of another sort,   10
  Then to misdoe the welfare of their King:
  God graunt my neerest freends may prove no worse.
  O holde me up, my sight begins to faile,
  My sinnewes shrinke, my braines turne upside downe,   14
  My heart doth break, I faint and dye.   *He dies.*
QUEENE MOTHER. What art thou dead, sweet sonne speak to thy
  Mother.

Sc. 12 OSD2 *and others]* Broughton *and* Oxberry   Sc. 13 OSD2–3 *with* PLESHE]
Broughton *and* Oxberry *subst.*   OSD3 *and Attendants]* Dyce¹

O no, his soule is fled from out his breast,
And he nor heares, nor sees us what we doe:
My Lords, what resteth there now for to be done,
But that we presently despatch Embassadours   20
To *Poland*, to call *Henry* back againe,
To weare his brothers crowne and dignity?
Epernoune, goe see it presently be done,
And bid him come without delay to us.

EPERNOUNE. Madam, I will.   *Exit* EPERNOUNE.

QUEENE MOTHER. And now my Lords after these funerals be
    done,   26
We will with all the speed we can, provide
For *Henries* coronation from *Polonie*:
Come let us take his body hence.

                    All goe out, but NAVARRE *and* PLESHE.

NAVARRE. And now *Navarre* whilste that these broiles
    doe last,   30
My opportunity may serve me fit,
To steale from *France*, and hye me to my home.
For heers no saftie in the Realme for me,
And now that *Henry* is cal'd from *Polland*,
It is my due by just succession: 35
And therefore as speedily as I can perfourme,
Ile muster up an army secretly,
For feare that *Guise* joyn'd with the King of *Spaine*,
Might seeme to crosse me in mine enterprise.
But God that alwaies doth defend the right,   40
Will shew his mercy and preserve us still.

PLESHE. The vertues of our true Religion,
Cannot but march with many graces more:
Whose army shall discomfort all your foes,
And at the length in *Pampelonia* crowne,   45
In spite of *Spaine* and all the popish power,
That holdes it from your highnesse wrongfully,
Your Majestie her rightfull Lord and Soveraigne.

NAVARRE. Truth *Pleshe*, and God so prosper me in all,
As I entend to labour for the truth,   50
And true profession of his holy word:
Come *Pleshe*, lets away whilste time doth serve.   *Exeunt.*

[Scene 14]

Sound Trumpets within, and then all crye vive le Roy *two or three times.*

Enter HENRY *crownd*: QUEENE [MOTHER], CARDINALL, *Duke of* GUISE, EPERNOONE, *the kings Minions* [JOYEUX *and* MUGEROUN], *with others, and the* CUTPURSE.

ALL. Vive le Roy, vive le Roy.   *Sound Trumpets.*

QUEENE MOTHER. Welcome from *Poland Henry* once agayne,
Welcome to *France* thy fathers royall seate,
Heere hast thou a country voide of feares,
A warlike people to maintaine thy right,   5
A watchfull Senate for ordaining lawes,
A loving mother to preserve thy state,
And all things that a King may wish besides:
All this and more hath *Henry* with his crowne.

CARDINALL. And long may *Henry* enjoy all this and more.   10

ALL. Vive le Roy, vive le Roy.   *Sound trumpets.*

HENRY. Thanks to you al. The guider of all crownes,
Graunt that our deeds may wel deserve your loves:
And so they shall, if fortune speed my will,
And yeeld your thoughts to height of my desertes.   15
What saies our Minions, think they *Henries* heart
Will not both harbour love and Majestie?
Put of that feare, they are already joynde,
No person, place, or time, or circumstance,
Shall slacke my loves affection from his bent: 20
As now you are, so shall you still persist,
Remooveles from the favours of your King.

MUGEROUN. We know that noble mindes change not their
    thoughts
For wearing of a crowne: in that your grace,
Hath worne the *Poland* diadem, before   25
You were invested in the crowne of *France*.

HENRY. I tell thee *Mugeroun* we will be freends,

OSD1 le] *Broughton and Oxberry*; la O (*also at lines* 1 *and* 11)   OSD3 MOTHER]
Robinson   OSD4–5 JOYEUX *and*] *Oliver*   OSD5 MUGEROUN] *Broughton and*
Oxberry   1 le...le] *Broughton and Oxberry*; la...la O (*also at line* 11)

And fellowes to, what ever stormes arise.

MUGEROUN. Then may it please your Majestie to give me leave,
To punish those that doe prophane this holy feast.   30

> *He cuts of the* CUTPURSE *eare, for cutting of the*
> *golde buttons off his cloake.*

HENRY. How meanst thou that?

CUTPURSE. O Lord, mine eare.

MUGEROUN. Come sir, give me my buttons and heers your eare.

GUISE. Sirra, take him away.

HENRY. Hands of good fellow, I will be his baile   35
For this offence: goe sirra, worke no more,
Till this our Coronation day be past:
And now
Our solemne rites of Coronation done,
What now remaines, but for a while to feast,   40
And spend some daies in barriers, tourny, tylte,
And like disportes, such as doe fit the Court?
Lets goe my Lords, our dinner staies for us.

> *Goe out all, but the* QUEENE [MOTHER] *and the* CARDINALL.

QUEENE MOTHER. My Lord Cardinall of *Loraine*, tell me,
How likes your grace my sonnes pleasantnes?   45
His minde you see runnes on his minions,
And all his heaven is to delight himselfe:
And whilste he sleepes securely thus in ease,
Thy brother *Guise* and we may now provide,
To plant our selves with such authoritie,   50
As not a man may live without our leaves.
Then shall the Catholick faith of *Rome*,
Flourish in *France*, and none deny the same.

CARDINALL. Madam, as in secrecy I was tolde,
My brother *Guise* hath gathered a power of men,   55
Which as he saith, to kill the Puritans,
But tis the house of *Burbon* that he meanes.
Now Madam must you insinuate with the King,
And tell him that tis for his Countries good,
And common profit of Religion.   60

QUEENE MOTHER. Tush man, let me alone with him,
To work the way to bring this thing to passe:

And if he doe deny what I doe say,
Ile dispatch him with his brother presently.
And then shall *Mounser* weare the diadem: 65
Tush, all shall dye unles I have my will.
For while she lives *Katherine* will be Queene.
Come my Lord, let us goe seek the *Guise*,
And then determine of this enterprise.   *Exeunt.*

[Scene 15]

Enter the Duchesse of GUISE, *and her* MAIDE.

DUCHESSE. Goe fetch me pen and inke.
MAID. I will Madam.   *Exit* MAID.
DUCHESSE. That I may write unto my dearest Lord.
  Sweet *Mugeroune*, tis he that hath my heart,
  And *Guise* usurpes it, cause I am his wife: 5
  Faine would I finde some means to speak with him
  But cannot, and therfore am enforst to write,
  That he may come and meet me in some place,
  Where we may one injoy the others sight.

Enter the MAID *with* [Pen,] *Inke and Paper.*

So, set it down and leave me to my selfe.   [*Exit* MAID.]
She writes. O would to God this quill that heere doth write,
Had late been pluckt from out faire *Cupids* wing: 12
That it might print these lines within his heart.

Enter the GUISE.

GUISE. What, all alone my love, and writing too:
  I prethee say to whome thou writes?   15
DUCHESSE. To such a one my Lord, as when she reads my lines,
  Will laugh I feare me at their good aray.
GUISE. I pray thee let me see.
DUCHESSE. O no my Lord, a woman only must
  Partake the secrets of my heart.   20

68 Lord] *Broughton and Oxberry*; Lords *O*   9SD *Pen,] Dyce*[1]   10SD] *Broughton*
and Oxberry

GUISE. But Madam I must see.   *he takes it.*
Are these your secrets that no man must know?
DUCHESSE. O pardon me my Lord.
GUISE. Thou trothles and unjust, what lines are these?
     Am I growne olde, or is thy lust growne yong,   25
     Or hath my love been so obscurde in thee,
     That others needs to comment on my text?
     Is all my love forgot which helde thee deare?
     I, dearer then the apple of mine eye?
     Is *Guises* glory but a clowdy mist,   30
     In sight and judgement of thy lustfull eye?
     Mor du, wert not the fruit within thy wombe,
     Of whose encrease I set some longing hope:
     This wrathfull hand should strike thee to the hart.
     Hence strumpet, hide thy head for shame,   35
     And fly my presence if thou looke to live.   *Exit* [DUCHESSE].
     O wicked sexe, perjured and unjust,
     Now doe I see that from the very first,
     Her eyes and lookes sow'd seeds of perjury,
     But villaine he to whom these lines should goe,   40
     Shall buy her love even with his dearest bloud.   *Exit.*

[Scene 16]

Enter the King of NAVARRE, PLESHE *and* BARTUS, *and their train, with drums and trumpets.*

NAVARRE. My Lords, sith in a quarrell just and right,
     We undertake to mannage these our warres
     Against the proud disturbers of the faith,
     I meane the *Guise*, the Pope, and King of *Spaine*,
     Who set themselves to tread us under foot,   5
     And rent our true religion from this land:
     But for you know our quarrell is no more,
     But to defend their strange inventions,
     Which they will put us to with sword and fire:
     We must with resolute mindes resolve to fight,   10

36SD DUCHESSE] *Broughton and Oxberry*

In honor of our God and countries good.
Spaine is the counsell chamber of the pope,
Spaine is the place where he makes peace and warre,
And *Guise* for *Spaine* hath now incenst the King,
To send his power to meet us in the field.   15
BARTUS. Then in this bloudy brunt they may beholde,
The sole endevour of your princely care,
To plant the true succession of the faith,
In spite of *Spaine* and all his heresies.
NAVARRE. The power of vengeance now incampes it selfe,   20
Upon the hauty mountains of my brest:
Plaies with her goary coulours of revenge,
Whom I respect as leaves of boasting greene,
That change their coulour when the winter comes,
When I shall vaunt as victor in revenge.   25

Enter a MESSENGER.

How now sirra, what newes?
MESSENGER. My Lord, as by our scoutes we understande,
A mighty army comes from *France* with speed:
Which are already mustered in the land,
And meanes to meet your highnes in the field.   30
NAVARRE. In Gods name, let them come.
This is the *Guise* that hath incenst the King,
To leavy armes and make these civill broyles:
But canst thou tell who is their generall?
MESSENGER. Not yet my Lord, for thereon doe they stay: 35
But as report doth goe, the Duke of *Joyeux*
Hath made great sute unto the King therfore.
NAVARRE. It will not countervaile his paines I hope.
I would the *Guise* in his steed might have come,
But he doth lurke within his drousie couch,   40
And makes his footstoole on securitie:
So he be safe he cares not what becomes
Of King or Country, no not for them both.
But come my Lords, let us away with speed,
And place our selves in order for the fight.   *Exeunt.* 45

[Scene 17]

Enter the King of FRANCE, *Duke of* GUISE, EPERNOUNE,
and Duke JOYEUX.

KING. My sweet *Joyeux*, I make thee Generall,
　　Of all my army now in readines,
　　To march against the rebellious King *Navarre*:
　　At thy request I am content thou goe,
　　Although my love to thee can hardly suffer,　　　　5
　　Regarding still the danger of thy life.
JOYEUX. Thanks to your Majestie, and so I take my leave.
　　Farwell to my Lord of *Guise* and *Epernoune*.
GUISE. Health and harty farwell to my Lord *Joyeux*.

Exit JOYEUX.

KING. So kindely Cosin of *Guise* you and your wife　　10
　　Doe both salute our lovely Minions.

he makes hornes at the GUISE.

　　Remember you the letter gentle sir,
　　Which your wife writ
　　To my deare Minion, and her chosen freend?
GUISE. How now my Lord, faith this is more then need,　15
　　Am I thus to be jested at and scornde?
　　Tis more then kingly or Emperious.
　　And sure if all the proudest Kings
　　In Christendome, should beare me such derision,
　　They should know how I scornde them and their mockes.　20
　　I love your Minions? dote on them your selfe,
　　I know none els but holdes them in disgrace:
　　And heer by all the Saints in heaven I sweare,
　　That villain for whom I beare this deep disgrace,
　　Even for your words that have incenst me so,　　　25
　　Shall buy that strumpets favour with his blood,
　　Whether he have dishonoured me or no.
　　Par la mor du, Il mora.　　　　　　　　　*Exit.*
KING. Beleeve me this jest bites sore.
EPERNOUNE. My Lord, twere good to make them frends　30
　　For his othes are seldome spent in vaine.

Enter MUGEROUN.

KING. How now *Mugeroun*, metst thou not the *Guise* at the
　　doore?

MUGEROUN. Not I my Lord, what if I had?
KING. Marry if thou hadst, thou mightst have had the stab,
    For he hath solemnely sworne thy death.   35
MUGEROUN. I may be stabd, and live till he be dead,
    But wherfore beares he me such deadly hate?
KING. Because his wife beares thee such kindely love.
MUGEROUN. If that be all, the next time that I meet her,
    Ile make her shake off love with her heeles.   40
    But which way is he gone? Ile goe make a walk
    On purpose from the Court to meet with him.   *Exit.*
KING. I like not this, come *Epernoune*
    Lets goe seek the Duke and make them freends.   *Exeunt.*

[Scene 18]

Alarums within. The Duke JOYEUX *slaine.*

Enter the King of NAVARRE[, *with* BARTUS,] *and his traine.*

NAVARRE. The Duke is slaine and all his power dispearst,
    And we are grac'd with wreathes of victory:
    Thus God we see doth ever guide the right,
    To make his glory great upon the earth.
BARTUS. The terrour of this happy victory,   5
    I hope will make the King surcease his hate:
    And either never mannage army more,
    Or else employ them in some better cause.
NAVARRE. How many noble men have lost their lives,
    In prosecution of these cruell armes,   10
    Is ruth and almost death to call to minde:
    But God we know will alwaies put them downe,
    That lift themselves against the perfect truth,
    Which Ile maintaine so long as life doth last,
    And with the Queene of *England* joyne my force,   15
    To beat the papall Monarck from our lands,
    And keep those relicks from our countries coastes.
    Come my Lords now that this storme is overpast,
    Let us away with triumph to our tents.   *Exeunt.*

OSD2 , *with* BARTUS,] *Dyce*[1] *subst.*

[Scene 19]

Enter a SOULDIER *[with a muskett].*

SOULDIER. Sir, to you sir, that dares make the Duke a
cuckolde, and use a counterfeite key to his privie Chamber doore: And although you take out nothing but your
owne, yet you put in that which displeaseth him, and so
forestall his market, and set up your standing where you   5
should not: and whereas hee is your Landlord, you will
take upon you to be his, and tyll the ground that he
himself should occupy, which is his own free land. If it
be not too free there's the question: and though I come
not to take possession (as I would I might) yet I meane to   10
keepe you out, which I will if this geare holde: what are
ye come so soone? have at ye sir.

Enter MUGEROUN.

He shootes at him and killes him.

Enter the GUISE *[attended].*

GUISE. Holde thee tall Souldier, take thee this and flye.

Exit SOULDIER.

Lye there the Kings delight, and *Guises* scorne.
Revenge it *Henry* as thou list or dare,   15
I did it only in despite of thee.   *[Attendants] Take him away.*

Enter the KING *and* EPERNOUNE.

KING. My Lord of *Guise*, we understand
That you have gathered a power of men:
What your intent is yet we cannot learn,
But we presume it is not for our good.   20
GUISE. Why I am no traitor to the crowne of *France*.
What I have done tis for the Gospell sake.
EPERNOUNE. Nay for the Popes sake, and thine owne benefite.
What Peere in *France* but thou (aspiring *Guise*)
Durst be in armes without the Kings consent?   25

OSD *with a muskett*] Folger MS   12SD3 *attended*] Broughton and Oxberry
subst.   16SD1 *Attendants*] Broughton and Oxberry subst.

I challenge thee for treason in the cause.

GUISE. Ah base *Epernoune*, were not his highnes heere,
Thou shouldst perceive the Duke of *Guise* is mov'd.

KING. Be patient *Guise* and threat not *Epernoune*,
Least thou perceive the King of *France* be mov'd.   30

GUISE. Why I am a Prince of the *Valoyses* line,
Therfore an enemy to the *Burbonites*.
I am a juror in the holy league,
And therfore hated of the Protestants.
What should I doe but stand upon my guarde?   35
And being able, Ile keep an hoast in pay.

EPERNOUNE. Thou able to maintaine an hoast in pay,
That livest by forraine exhibition?
The Pope and King of *Spaine* are thy good frends,
Else all *France* knowes how poor a Duke thou art.   40

KING. I, those are they that feed him with their golde,
To countermaund our will and check our freends.

GUISE. My Lord, to speak more plainely, thus it is:
Being animated by Religious zeale,
I meane to muster all the power I can,   45
To overthrow those sexious Puritans:
And know my Lord, the Pope will sell his triple crowne,
I, and the catholick *Philip* King of *Spaine*,
Ere I shall want, will cause his Indians,
To rip the golden bowels of *America*.   50
Navarre that cloakes them underneath his wings,
Shall feele the house of *Lorayne* is his foe:
Your highnes needs not feare mine armies force,
Tis for your safetie and your enemies wrack.

KING. *Guise*, weare our crowne, and be thou King of *France*,   55
And as Dictator make or warre or peace,
Whilste I cry *placet* like a Senator.
I cannot brook thy hauty insolence,
Dismisse thy campe or else by our Edict,
Be thou proclaimde a traitor throughout *France*.   60

GUISE. The choyse is hard, I must dissemble.   [*Aside.*]
My Lord, in token of my true humilitie,

31 Why] Dyce¹ *subst.* (Why,); Why ? *O*   61SD] *Broughton and Oxberry*

And simple meaning to your Majestie,
I kisse your graces hand, and take my leave,
Intending to dislodge my campe with speed.   65
KING. Then farwell *Guise*, the King and thou are freends.

Exit GUISE.

EPERNOUNE. But trust him not my Lord, for had your
    highnesse
Seene with what a pompe he entred *Paris*,
And how the Citizens with gifts and shewes
Did entertaine him,   70
And promised to be at his commaund:
Nay, they fear'd not to speak in the streetes,
That the *Guise* durst stand in armes against the King,
For not effecting of his holines will.
KING. Did they of *Paris* entertaine him so?   75
Then meanes he present treason to our state.
Well, let me alone, whose within there?

Enter one with a pen and inke.

Make a discharge of all my counsell straite,
And Ile subscribe my name and seale it straight.
My head shall be my counsell, they are false: 80
And *Epernoune* I will be rulde by thee.
EPERNOUNE. My Lord,
I think for safety of your royall person,
It would be good the *Guise* were made away,
And so to quite your grace of all suspect.
KING. First let us set our hand and seale to this,   85
And then Ile tell thee what I meane to doe.   *he writes.*
So, convey this to the counsell presently.   *Exit one.*
And *Epernoune* though I seeme milde and calme,
Thinke not but I am tragicall within:
Ile secretly convay me unto *Bloyse*,   90
For now that *Paris* takes the *Guises* parte,
Heere is no staying for the King of *France*,
Unles he meane to be betraide and dye:
But as I live, so sure the *Guise* shall dye.   *Exeunt.*

[Scene 20]

Enter the King of NAVARRE *reading of a letter, and* BARTUS.

NAVARRE. My Lord, I am advertised from *France*,
That the *Guise* hath taken armes against the King,
And that *Paris* is revolted from his grace.
BARTUS. Then hath your grace fit oportunitie,
To shew your love unto the King of *France*:   5
Offering him aide against his enemies,
Which cannot but be thankfully receiv'd.
NAVARRE. *Bartus*, it shall be so, poast then to *Fraunce*,
And there salute his highnesse in our name,
Assure him all the aide we can provide,   10
Against the Guisians and their complices.
Bartus be gone, commend me to his grace,
And tell him ere it be long, Ile visite him.
BARTUS. I will my Lord.   *Exit.*

Enter PLESHE.

NAVARRE. *Pleshe.*   15
PLESHE. My Lord.
NAVARRE. *Pleshe*, goe muster up our men with speed,
And let them march away to *France* amaine:
For we must aide the King against the *Guise*.
Be gone I say, tis time that we were there.   20
PLESHE. I goe my Lord.   [*Exit.*]
NAVARRE. That wicked *Guise* I feare me much will be
The ruine of that famous Realme of *France*:
For his aspiring thoughts aime at the crowne,
And takes his vantage on Religion,   25
To plant the Pope and popelings in the Realme,
And binde it wholy to the Sea of *Rome*:
But if that God doe prosper mine attempts,
And send us safely to arrive in *France*,
Wee'l beat him back, and drive him to his death,   30
That basely seekes the ruine of his Realme.   *Exit.*

21SD] *Broughton and Oxberry*   31SD] *Broughton and Oxberry; Exeunt O*

[Scene 21]

Enter the CAPTAINE *of the guarde, and three* MURTHERERS.

CAPTAINE. Come on sirs, what, are you resolutely bent,
  Hating the life and honour of the *Guise*?
  What, will you not feare when you see him come?
1. Feare him said you? tush, were he heere, we would kill
  him presently.   5
2. O that his heart were leaping in my hand.
3. But when will he come that we may murther him?
CAPTAINE. Well, then I see you are resolute.
1. Let us alone, I warrant you.
CAPTAINE. Then sirs take your standings within this
    Chamber,   10
  For anon the *Guise* will come.
ALL. You will give us our money?
CAPTAINE. I, I, feare not: stand close, so, be resolute:
                                        [*Exeunt* MURTHERERS.]
  Now fals the star whose influence governes *France*,
  Whose light was deadly to the Protestants: 15
  Now must he fall and perish in his height.

Enter the KING *and* EPERNOUNE.

KING. Now Captain of my guarde, are these murtherers ready?
CAPTAINE. They be my good Lord.
KING. But are they resolute and armde to kill,
  Hating the life and honour of the *Guise*?   20
CAPTAINE. I warrant ye my Lord.
KING. Then come proud *Guise* and heere disgordge thy brest,
  Surchargde with surfet of ambitious thoughts:
  Breath out that life wherein my death was hid,
  And end thy endles treasons with thy death.   25

Enter the GUISE *and knocketh.*

GUISE. *Halla verlete hey*: *Epernoune*, where is the King?
EPERNOUNE. Mounted his royall Cabonet.
GUISE. I prethee tell him that the *Guise* is heere.

13SD] *Broughton and Oxberry*

EPERNOUNE. And please your grace the Duke of *Guise*, doth
    crave
    Accesse unto your highnes.   30
KING. Let him come in.
    Come *Guise* and see thy traiterous guile outreacht,
    And perish in the pit thou mad'st for me.

                  The GUISE *comes to the* KING.

GUISE. Good morrow to your Majestie.
KING. Good morrow to my loving Cousin of *Guise*.   35
    How fares it this morning with your excellence?
GUISE. I heard your Majestie was scarsely pleasde,
    That in the Court I bare so great a traine.
KING. They were to blame that said I was displeasde,
    And you good Cosin to imagine it.   40
    Twere hard with me if I should doubt my kinne,
    Or be suspicious of my deerest freends:
    Cousin, assure you I am resolute,
    Whatsoever any whisper in mine eares,
    Not to suspect disloyaltye in thee,   45
    And so sweet Cuz farwell.

           Exit KING [*with* EPERNOUNE *and* CAPTAINE].

GUISE. So,
    Now sues the King for favour to the *Guise*,
    And all his Minions stoup when I commaund:
    Why this tis to have an army in the fielde.   50
    Now by the holy sacrament I sweare,
    As ancient Romanes over their Captive Lords,
    So will I triumph over this wanton King,
    And he shall follow my proud Chariots wheeles.
    Now doe I but begin to look about,   55
    And all my former time was spent in vaine:
    Holde Sworde,
    For in thee is the Duke of *Guises* hope.

           Enter one of the MURTHERERS.

    Villaine, why dost thou look so gastly? speake.
3. O pardon me my Lord of *Guise*.   60
GUISE. Pardon thee, why what hast thou done?

    46SD *with* EPERNOUNE] *Broughton and Oxberry subst.*   *and* CAPTAINE] *Oliver subst.*

3. O my Lord, I am one of them that is set to murder you.

GUISE. To murder me villaine?

3. I my Lord, the rest have taine their standings in the next
    roome, therefore good my Lord goe not foorth.   65

GUISE. Yet *Cæsar* shall goe forth.
    Let mean consaits, and baser men feare death:
    Tut they are pesants, I am Duke of *Guise*:
    And princes with their lookes ingender feare.

[*Enter two* MURTHERERS.]

1. Stand close, he is comming, I know him by his voice.   70

GUISE. As pale as ashes, nay then tis time to look about.

ALL. Downe with him, downe with him.   *They stabbe him.*

GUISE. Oh I have my deaths wound, give me leave to speak.

2. Then pray to God, and aske forgivenes of the King.

GUISE. Trouble me not, I neare offended him,   75
    Nor will I aske forgivenes of the King.
    Oh that I have not power to stay my life,
    Nor immortalitie to be reveng'd:
    To dye by Pesantes, what a greefe is this?
    Ah *Sextus*, be reveng'd upon the King,   80
    Philip and *Parma*, I am slaine for you:
    Pope excommunicate, *Philip* depose,
    The wicked branch of curst *Valois* his line.
    Vive la messe, perish Hugonets,
    Thus *Cæsar* did goe foorth, and thus he dyed.   *He dyes.*

Enter CAPTAINE *of the Guarde.*

CAPTAINE. What, have you done?   86
    Then stay a while and Ile goe call the King,
    But see where he comes.

[*Enter the* KING, EPERNOUNE *and Attendants.*]

My Lord, see where the *Guise* is slaine.

KING. Ah this sweet sight is phisick to my soule,   90
    Goe fetch his sonne for to beholde his death: [*Exit Attendant.*]
    Surchargde with guilt of thousand massacres,

69SD] *Oxberry subst., but placed after line* 71; *placed after line* 72 *by Oliver*   88SD
Enter... EPERNOUNE] *Broughton and Oxberry subst.*   *and Attendants*] *Dyce*[1]
91SD] *Dyce*[1]

Mounser of *Loraine* sinke away to hell,
And in remembrance of those bloudy broyles,
To which thou didst alure me being alive: 95
And heere in presence of you all I sweare,
I nere was King of *France* untill this houre:
This is the traitor that hath spent my golde,
In making forraine warres and civile broiles.
Did he not draw a sorte of English priestes,   100
From *Doway* to the Seminary at *Remes*,
To hatch forth treason gainst their naturall Queene?
Did he not cause the King of *Spaines* huge fleete,
To threaten *England* and to menace me?
Did he not injure *Mounser* thats deceast?   105
Hath he not made me in the Popes defence,
To spend the treasure that should strength my land,
In civill broiles between *Navarre* and me?
Tush, to be short, he meant to make me Munke,
Or else to murder me, and so be King.   110
Let Christian princes that shall heare of this,
(As all the world shall know our *Guise* is dead)
Rest satisfied with this that heer I sweare,
Nere was there King of *France* so yoakt as I.
EPERNOUNE. My Lord heer is his sonne.   115

                   Enter the GUISES *sonne.*

KING. Boy, look where your father lyes.
YONG GUISE. My father slaine, who hath done this deed?
KING. Sirra twas I that slew him, and will slay
     Thee too, and thou prove such a traitor.
YONG GUISE. Art thou King, and hast done this bloudy
       deed?   120
Ile be revengde.   *He offereth to throwe his dagger.*
KING. Away to prison with him, Ile clippe his winges
     Or ere he passe my handes, away with him.

                              Exit BOY [*guarded*].

But what availeth that this traitors dead,
When Duke *Dumaine* his brother is alive,   125
And that young Cardinall that is growne so proud?

123SD *guarded*] *Broughton and Oxberry subst.* ('*The attendants bear off the boy.*')

Goe to the Governour of *Orleance*,
And will him in my name to kill the Duke.
                    [*Exit* CAPTAINE *of the Guarde*.]
Get you away and strangle the Cardinall,
                        [*Exeunt* MURTHERERS.]
These two will make one entire Duke of *Guise*,   130
Especially with our olde mothers helpe.
EPERNOUNE. My Lord, see where she comes, as if she droupt
    To heare these newes.

               Enter QUEENE MOTHER.

KING. And let her droup, my heart is light enough.
    Mother, how like you this device of mine?   135
    I slew the *Guise*, because I would be King.
QUEENE MOTHER. King, why so thou wert before.
    Pray God thou be a King now this is done.
KING. Nay he was King and countermanded me,
    But now I will be King and rule my selfe,   140
    And make the Guisians stoup that are alive.
QUEENE MOTHER. I cannot speak for greefe: when thou wast
        borne,
    I would that I had murdered thee my sonne.
    My sonne: thou art a changeling, not my sonne.
    I curse thee and exclaime thee miscreant,   145
    Traitor to God, and to the realme of *France*.
KING. Cry out, exclaime, houle till thy throat be hoarce,
    The *Guise* is slaine, and I rejoyce therefore:
    And now will I to armes, come *Epernoune*:
    And let her greeve her heart out if she will.   150
                    Exit the KING *and* EPERNOUNE.
QUEENE MOTHER. Away, leave me alone to meditate.
            [*Exeunt Attendants bearing away* GUISE.]
    Sweet *Guise*, would he had died so thou wert heere:
    To whom shall I bewray my secrets now,
    Or who will helpe to builde Religion?
    The Protestants will glory and insulte,   155
    Wicked *Navarre* will get the crowne of *France*,

The Popedome cannot stand, all goes to wrack,
And all for thee my *Guise*, what may I doe?
But sorrow seaze upon my toyling soule,
For since the *Guise* is dead, I will not live.   *Exit.*   160

[Scene 22]

Enter two [MURTHERERS] *dragging in the* CARDENALL.

CARDINALL. Murder me not, I am a Cardenall.
1. Wert thou the Pope thou mightst not scape from us.
CARDINALL. What, will you fyle your handes with Churchmens
     bloud?
2. Shed your bloud? O Lord no: for we entend to strangle you.
CARDINALL. Then there is no remedye but I must dye?   5
1. No remedye, therefore prepare your selfe.
CARDINALL. Yet lives my brother Duke *Dumaine*, and many
     moe:
     To revenge our deaths upon that cursed King,
     Upon whose heart may all the furies gripe,
     And with their pawes drench his black soule in hell.   10
1. Yours my Lord Cardinall, you should have saide.
                              Now they strangle him.
     So, pluck amaine,
     He is hard hearted, therfore pull with violence.
     Come take him away.   *Exeunt.*

[Scene 23]

Enter Duke DUMAYN *reading of a letter, with others.*

DUMAINE. My noble brother murthered by the King,
     Oh what may I doe, for to revenge thy death?
     The Kings alone, it cannot satisfie.
     Sweet Duke of *Guise* our prop to leane upon,
     Now thou art dead, heere is no stay for us: 5
     I am thy brother, and ile revenge thy death,
     And roote *Valoys* his line from forth of *France*,

Sc. 22 OSD MURTHERERS] *Broughton and Oxberry*

And beate proud *Burbon* to his native home,
That basely seekes to joyne with such a King,
Whose murderous thoughts will be his overthrow.   10
Hee wild the Governour of *Orleance* in his name,
That I with speed should have beene put to death.
But thats prevented, for to end his life,
And all those traitors to the Church of *Rome*,
That durst attempt to murder noble *Guise*.   15

Enter the FRIER.

FRIER. My Lord, I come to bring you newes, that your
brother the Cardinall of *Loraine* by the Kings consent is
lately strangled unto death.
DUMAINE. My brother Cardenall slaine and I alive?
O wordes of power to kill a thousand men.   20
Come let us away and leavy men,
Tis warre that must asswage this tyrantes pride.
FRIER. My Lord, heare me but speak:
I am a Frier of the order of the Jacobyns,
That for my conscience sake will kill the King.   25
DUMAINE. But what doth move thee above the rest to doe
the deed?
FRIER. O my Lord, I have beene a great sinner in my
dayes, and the deed is meritorious.
DUMAINE. But how wilt thou get opportunitye?   30
FRIER. Tush my Lord, let me alone for that.
DUMAINE. Frier come with me,
We will goe talke more of this within.   *Exeunt.*

[Scene 24]

Sound Drumme and Trumpets, and enter the King of FRANCE,
and NAVARRE, EPERNOUNE, BARTUS, PLESHE *and*
Souldiers.

KING. Brother of *Navarre*, I sorrow much,
That ever I was prov'd your enemy,

14 And] *Malone MS*; His life, and O

And that the sweet and princely minde you beare,
Was ever troubled with injurious warres:
I vow as I am lawfull King of *France*,   5
To recompence your reconciled love,
With all the honors and affections,
That ever I vouchsafte my dearest freends.
NAVARRE. It is enough if that *Navarre* may be
    Esteemed faithfull to the King of *France*:   10
    Whose service he may still commaund till death.
KING. Thankes to my Kingly Brother of *Navarre*.
    Then heere wee'l lye before *Lutetia* walles,
    Girting this strumpet Cittie with our siege,
    Till surfeiting with our afflicting armes,   15
    She cast her hatefull stomack to the earth.

Enter a MESSENGER.

MESSENGER. And it please your Majestie heere is a Frier
    of the order of the Jacobins, sent from the President of
    Paris, that craves accesse unto your grace.
KING. Let him come in.   [*Exit* MESSENGER.]

Enter FRIER *with a Letter.*

EPERNOUNE. I like not this Friers look.   21
    Twere not amisse my Lord, if he were searcht.
KING. Sweete *Epernoune*, our Friers are holy men,
    And will not offer violence to their King,
    For all the wealth and treasure of the world.   25
    Frier, thou dost acknowledge me thy King?
FRIER. I my good Lord, and will dye therein.
KING. Then come thou neer, and tell what newes thou bringst.
FRIER. My Lord,
    The President of *Paris* greetes your grace,   30
    And sends his dutie by these speedye lines,
    Humblye craving your gracious reply.
KING. Ile read them Frier, and then Ile answere thee.
FRIER. *Sancte Jacobe*, now have mercye upon me.

13 *Lutetia*] Broughton and Oxberry *subst.* (Lutetia's); Lucrecia *O*   20SD1] *Dyce*[1]
34 *Jacobe*] *Dyce*[1]; *Jacobus O*

He stabs the King with a knife as he readeth the letter, and then
the King getteth the knife and killes him.

EPERNOUNE. O my Lord, let him live a while.   35
KING. No, let the villaine dye, and feele in hell,
  Just torments for his trechery.
NAVARRE. What, is your highnes hurt?
KING. Yes *Navarre*, but not to death I hope.
NAVARRE. God shield your grace from such a sodaine death: 40
  Goe call a surgeon hether strait.   [*Exit Souldier.*]
KING. What irreligeous Pagans partes be these,
  Of such as holde them of the holy church?
  Take hence that damned villaine from my sight.
            [*Souldiers carry out the* FRIER'S *body.*]
EPERNOUNE. Ah, had your highnes let him live,   45
  We might have punisht him to his deserts.
KING. Sweet *Epernoune* all Rebels under heaven,
  Shall take example by his punishment,
  How they beare armes against their soveraigne.
  Goe call the English Agent hether strait, [*Exit Souldier.*] 50
  Ile send my sister *England* newes of this,
  And give her warning of her trecherous foes.

          [*Enter a* SURGEON.]

NAVARRE. Pleaseth your grace to let the Surgeon search your
      wound?
KING. The wound I warrant ye is deepe my Lord,
  Search Surgeon and resolve me what thou seest.   55
                        The SURGEON *searcheth.*

          Enter the English Agent.

  Agent for *England*, send thy mistres word,
  What this detested Jacobin hath done.
  Tell her for all this that I hope to live,
  Which if I doe, the Papall Monarck goes
  To wrack, and antechristian kingdome falles.   60
  These bloudy hands shall teare his triple Crowne,

41SD, 44SD, 50SD] *Dyce*¹ *subst., but Craik (this edn.) suggests 'Souldier' or 'Souldiers', as*
appropriate, for Dyce's 'Attendant' or 'Attendants'   48 his] *Broughton and Oxberry; their*
O   52SD] *Broughton and Oxberry*

And fire accursed *Rome* about his eares.
Ile fire his crased buildings and incense
The papall towers to kisse the holy earth.
Navarre, give me thy hand, I heere do sweare,   65
To ruinate that wicked Church of *Rome*,
That hatcheth up such bloudy practises.
And heere protest eternall love to thee,
And to the Queene of *England* specially,
Whom God hath blest for hating Papestry.   70

NAVARRE. These words revive my thoughts and comforts me,
To see your highnes in this vertuous minde.

KING. Tell me Surgeon, shall I live?

SURGEON. Alas my Lord, the wound is dangerous,
For you are stricken with a poysoned knife.   75

KING. A poysoned knife? what, shall the French king dye,
Wounded and poysoned, both at once?

EPERNOUNE. O that that damned villaine were alive againe,
That we might torture him with some new found death.

BARTUS. He died a death too good,   80
The devill of hell torture his wicked soule.

KING. Ah curse him not sith he is dead,
O the fatall poyson workes within my brest,
Tell me Surgeon and flatter not, may I live?

SURGEON. Alas my Lord, your highnes cannot live.   85

NAVARRE. Surgeon, why saist thou so? the King may live.

KING. Oh no *Navarre*, thou must be King of *France*.

NAVARRE. Long may you live, and still be King of *France*.

EPERNOUNE. Or else dye *Epernoune*.

KING. Sweet *Epernoune* thy King must dye.   90
My Lords fight in the quarrell of this valiant Prince,
For he is your lawfull King and my next heire:
Valoyses lyne ends in my tragedie.
Now let the house of *Bourbon* weare the crowne,
And may it never end in bloud as mine hath done.   95
Weep not sweet *Navarre*, but revenge my death.
Ah *Epernoune*, is this thy love to me?
Henry thy King wipes of these childish teares,
And bids thee whet thy sword on *Sextus* bones,
That it may keenly slice the Catholicks.   100
He loves me not that sheds most teares,

But he that makes most lavish of his bloud.
Fire *Paris* where these trecherous rebels lurke.
I dye *Navarre*, come beare me to my Sepulchre.
Salute the Queene of *England* in my name,   105
And tell her *Henry* dyes her faithfull freend.   *He dyes.*
NAVARRE. Come Lords, take up the body of the King,
That we may see it honourably interde:
And then I vow for to revenge his death,
As *Rome* and all those popish Prelates there,   110
Shall curse the time that ere *Navarre* was King,
And rulde in *France* by *Henries* fatall death.

They march out with the body of the King, lying on foure mens
shoulders with a dead march, drawing weapons on the ground.

FINIS.

ACCIDENTAL EMENDATIONS

Scene 1

0SD1 QUEENE MOTHER] *Queene Mother*   0SD3 ADMIRALL] *Admirall*
7 hearts,] ~:   10 this,] ~:   13 QUEENE MOTHER] *Old Qu* (*also at line* 26 (*Old Q*))
15 know,...Religion] ~ₐ...~,   19–21 We...consumate / The rest, with...Masse: /
Sister...company] We...consumate the rest, / With...Masse: Sister...company
22 Lord.] ~,   24–5 Come Mother / Let...solemnitie] Come Mother let...
solemnitie   26SD2 QUEENE] Q   26SD3 *Queene*] Q.   27 *Condy*] Condy
Lord] L.   29 Queene] Qu.   34 *Paris*] Paris   39 Lord] L.   48 brother,] ~ₐ   51 *France*] France (*also at line* 56)   52 the] yᵉ

Scene 2

8 all.] ~,   19–20 I...commaundes / Till death] I...commaundes till
death   21 love.] ~,   24 *Fraunce*] Fraunce (*also at lines* 44 *and* 77) 25 *Exit*
POTHECARIE] Exit *Pothe*   26SD *Enter a* SOULDIER] Enter a Souldier
27 Lord.] ~,   33SD *Exit* SOULDIER] Exit *Souldi*   34 *Guise,...* thoughts]
~ₐ...~,   42 reach:] ~,   58 wait] wiat   60 *Spaine*] Spaine   Catholickes]
~,   65 religion.] ~,   67 ashamde,] ~ₐ   80 *Paris*] Paris   84 more:]
~ₐ   88–90 Then *Guise* / Since...Cardes within...hands / To...thing] Then *Guise*
since...Cardes, / Within...hands to...thing   92 *France*] France (*also at line*
97)   95 *Europs*] Europs   96 we——] weₐ

Scene 3

0SD2 MOTHER QUEEN] *Mother Queen*   1–2 Maddame, / I...gift] Maddam,
I...gift   3 holde,] ~ₐ   4SD POTHECARIE] Po   9 them] thē
14 beware] ~:   27 (For] *text*; For (*catchword*)   31SD1 SOULDIER] *Souldier*
ADMIRALL] *Admirall*   32 Lord] L.   33 Lord,] ~ₐ   36 Guisians] *Guisians*

Scene 4

2 deere] ~:   10–12 Onely...religion, / Ladies...honor, Knightes...Gentlemen,
/ Should...ends] Onely...religion, Ladies...honor, / Knightes...Gentlemen,
should...ends   17 advisde] ~,   22 enemies.] ~:   30 Burgonets,] ~:
33–5 Shall...Emperour. Then...have / A...tower, at which / They...streetes]
Shall...Emperour. / Then...have a...tower, / At which they...streetes
39SD *Admirals* MAN] Admirals *man*   45SD MESSENGER] *Messenger*

Scene 5

3 *France*] France   9 Guisians] *Guisians*   14 *Cosin*] Cosin   15 keep] ~,

Scene 6

1–2 *Anjoy...Retes,* sweare / By...burgonets] *Anjoy...Retes,* /
Sweare by...
burgonets   5 am,] ~ .   9 house.] ~,   10 I,] Iₐ   11–12 The Admirall
/ Cheefe...Lutheranes] The...Admirall cheefe...Lutheranes   14–16 Be...bed. /
Gonzago... thither, and then / Beset...live] Be...bed. *Gonzago...* thither, / And then
beset...live   17 mine:] ~,   20 *Cosin*] Cosin   34–5 Now...well, /
It...escapte] Now...well, it...escapte   39 *Shatillian*] Shatillian   39–40
Ah...degenerate, / Cheef...Lutheranes] Ah...degenerate, cheef...Lutheranes

46 *Faucon*] Faucon   51 *France*] France   58 Lord.] ~, *Exit* MOUNT-
SORRELL] ~ . Mount

Scene 7

1–2 *Tue...tue,* / Let...Hugonets] *Tue...tue,* let...Hugonets   4 *Loreine.*] ~,
8 'Dearely...brother'] ͵~...~͵

Scene 8

9 SEROUNE] *Seronne* (*text*); *Seroun* (*catchword*)   10–13 Christ, villaine, /
Why...Christ, / Without...Saint? / *Sanctus*...him] Christ, villaine, why...Christ,
without...Saint? *Sancta*...him

Scene 9

3 Guisians] *Guisians* (*also at line* 7)   5 life.] ~,   7–9 The...are / Hard...us:
/ Harke...window] The...are hard...us: harke...window   23–4 O...Lord, /
Wherein...offencious?] O...Lord, wherein...offencious.   27 *Organon*] Organon
(*also at line* 46)   30 Epetomies,] ~:   32 *Germany*] Germany   37–8
How...*argumentum*/Cannot...him] How...*argumentum* cannot...him   44 ill,] ~:
57 Protestants,] ~.   64 GUISE.] *Guise.* (*text*); *Guise* (*catchword*)   67 That] that
Condy——] ~.   71–2 My...say / That...massacred] My...say that...
massacred   77 I?] ~,   81–2 Come sirs, / Ile...point] Come sirs, Ile...
point   85 end:] ~,   86 *Orleance*] Orleance   87 *Deep*] Deep   *Roan*]
Roan   89 And] and   the] yᵉ   90 Now] *text*; Now. (*catchword*)

Scene 10

0SD LORDS] *Lords*   1 *Poland*] Poland (*also at lines* 4, 17 *and* 21)   9 warres,] ~.
14 *France*] France (*also at lines* 18 *and* 23)   16 That] that   28 The]
the   30 *Polands*] Polands

Scene 11

14 QUEENE MOTHER] *Queene* (*also* (*Qu*) *at lines* 24, 31 *and* 38)   16 th'air's]
thair's   26 *France*] France (*also at lines* 39 *and* 44)   29–30 Madam / I...storme]
Madam I...storme   31 *Loraine*] Loraine   32 lament] ~:   34 *Paris*]
Paris   38 Lord,] ~ ͵

Scene 12

0SD1 PROTESTANTS] *Protestants*   4 *Rome*] Rome

Scene 13

0SD1 FRANCE] *France*   0SD2 QUEENE] Qu.   4 QUEENE MOTHER] *Qu* (*also*
(*Queene*) *at lines* 16 *and* 26)   16 Mother.] ~,   19–22 done,...dignity?] ~ ?...~.
21 *Poland*] Poland   25 EPERNOUNE] Eper   27 can, provide] ~͵ ~,
28 *Polonie*] Polonie   29SD PLESHE] *P*leshe   32 *France*] France   34 *Polland*] Polland   38 King] K.   *Spaine*] Spaine (*also at line* 46)   45 *Pampelonia*]
Pampelonia   47 wrongfully,] ~:   52 serve.] ~,   52 *Exeunt*] Ezeunt

Scene 14

0SD3 *crownd*] crownd   0SD5 CUTPURSE] *Cutpurse*   1 Roy.] ~,   2 QUEENE
MOTHER] *Qu* (*also at lines* 44 (*Queene*) *and* 61)   *Poland*] Pola nd (*also at line* 25
(Poland))   3 *France*] France (*also at line* 53)   10 and] &   20 bent:] ~,
21 persist,] ~.   26 You] you   *France.*] France: 38–9 And now / Our...

done] And now our . . . done   42 And] and   44 *Loraine*] Loraine   51 As]
as   52 *Rome*] Rome

Scene 15

OSD MAIDE.] *Maide,*   7 But] but   16–17 To . . . lines, / Will . . . aray]
To . . . lines, will . . . aray   19–20 O . . . must / Partake . . . heart] O . . . must
partake . . . heart

Scene 16

2 warres] ~:   4 *Spaine*] Spaine (*also at lines* 12, 13, 14 *and* 19)   6 land:] ~.
22 Plaies] plaies   25 SD MESSENGER] *Messenger*   28 *France*] France
38 hope.] ~,   42 becomes] ~,

Scene 17

OSD I FRANCE] *France*   2–3 readines, . . . *Navarre*:] ~: . . . ~,   8 *Epernoune.*] ~,
10–14 So . . . wife / Doe . . . Minions. / Remember . . . sir, / Which . . . writ / To . . . freend]
So . . . wife doe . . . Minions. / Remember . . . sir, which . . . writ to . . . freend   18–19
And . . . Kings / In Christendome . . . derision,] And . . . Kings in / Christendome . . .
derision: 21 Minions?] ~,   24 disgrace,] ~:   26 blood,] ~.
41–4 But . . . walk / On . . . him. / I . . . *Epernoune* / Lets . . . freends] But . . . walk
on . . . him. / I . . . *Epernoune* lets . . . freends   41 gone?] ~,

Scene 18

15 Queene] Q.   *England*] England   force,] ~:

Scene 19

OSD SOULDIER] *Souldier*   1–2 Sir . . . cuckolde, and] Sir . . . cuckolde, /
And   13SD SOULDIER] Soul   17–20 My . . . understand / That . . . men: /
What . . . learn, / But . . . good] My . . . understand that . . . men, what . . . learn, but . . .
good   21 *France*] France (*also at lines* 24, 30, 40, 55, 60 *and* 92)   28 Duke]
D.   30 King] Kiug   38 exhibition?] ~.   39 *Spaine*] Spaine (*also at line*
48)   47 crowne,] ~.   50 *America*] America   57 Senator.] ~,   58 I] *I*
(*also at lines* 61 *and* 64)   63 Majestie,] ~:   67 highnesse] ~,   68 *Paris*]
Paris (*also at lines* 75 *and* 91)   70–1 Did . . . him, / And . . . commaund] Did . . . him,
and . . . commaund   82–3 My Lord, / I . . . person] My Lord, I . . . person   90
Bloyse] Bloyse

Scene 20

1 *France*] France (*also at lines* 5, 18, *and* 23)   3 *Paris*] Paris   8 *Fraunce*]
Fraunce   11 Guisians] *Guisians*   15 *Pleshe.*] Pleshe,   22 NAVARRE]
Nauar (*text*); *Nauarre* (*catchword*)   be] ~,   27 *Rome*] Rome   29 *France*,]
France: 31 *Exit*] Exeunt

Scene 21

OSD CAPTAINE] *Captaine* MURTHERERS] *murtherers*   10 Chamber,] ~.
12 money?] ~.   13 I, I] *I, I*   not:] ~,   so,] ~∧   14 *France*] France (*also at
lines* 97, 114, 146 *and* 156)   29–30 And . . . crave / Accesse . . . highnes] And . . . crave
accesse . . . highnes   47–8 So, / Now . . . *Guise*] So, now . . . *Guise*   49 I] *I* (*also at
lines* 51, 53, 55, 62, 64, 68, 70, 73, 96 *and* 97)   50 fielde.] ~,   57–8 Holde
Sworde, / For . . . hope] Holde Sworde, for . . . hope   58SD MURTHERERS]
Murtherers   60 3.] *Mur.* (*also at lines* 62 *and* 64)   63 villaine?] ~.   66–69
Yet . . . forth. / Let . . . death: / Tut . . . pesants, I . . . *Guise*: / And . . . feare] Yet . . . forth,

let...death: tut...pesants, / I...*Guise*: and...feare   69 lookes] ~,   72SD
him] him   75 him,] ~.   81 *Philip*] Philip (*also at line* 82)   *Parma*]
Parma   84 *messe*] messa   85SD2 CAPTAINE] *Captaine*   86–8 What,...
done? / Then...King, / But...comes] What...done? then...King, but...
comes   92 massacres,] ~:   94 broyles,] ~:   99 In] *In*   101 *Doway*]
Doway   *Remes*] Remes   103 *Spaines*] Spaines   104 *England*] England
107 land,] ~:   116 lyes.] ~,   118–19 Sirra...slay / Thee...traitor] Sirra...slay
thee...traitor   122–3 Away...winges / Or...him] Away...winges or... him
127 *Orleance*] Orleance   132–3 My...droupt / To...newes] My... droupt to...
newes   133SD QUEENE] *Queene*   137 QUEENE MOTHER] *Queene* (*also at lines*
142 *and* 151)   141 Guisians] *Guisians*   142 greefe:] ~,   151 meditate.]
~,

Scene 22

        0SD CARDENALL] *Cardenall*   3 What,] ~∧   4 bloud?] ~,   5 dye?] ~ .
8 King,] ~.   12–13 So...amaine, / He...violence] So...amaine, he...violence

Scene 23

        7 *France*] France   8 home,] ~.   9 King,] ~.   11 *Orleance*]
Orleance   13 life,] ~.   14 And] and   *Rome*] Rome   17 *Loraine*]
Loraine   23 speak:] ~,

Scene 24

        0SD1 FRANCE] *France*   5 *France*] France (*also at lines* 10, 87, 88 *and* 112)
9 be] ~.   16SD MESSENGER] *Messenger*   19 *Paris*] Paris (*also at lines* 30 *and*
103)   20SD2 FRIER] *Frier*   26 King?] ~:   29–32 My Lord, / The...
grace, / And...lines, / Humblye...reply] My Lord the...grace, and...lines,
humblye...reply   36–7 No...hell, / Just...trechery] No...hell, just...trechery
39 *Navarre*] Navarre (*also at lines* 87, 96 *and* 104)   47–9 Sweet...heaven,
/ Shall...punishment, / How...soveraigne] Sweet...heaven, shall... punishment,
how...soveraigne   51 *England*] England (*also at lines* 56, 69 *and* 105)
53 wound?] ~.   55SD1 SURGEON] *Surgeon*   SD2 *English Agent*] English
Agent   59–60] Which...goes / To wrack, and...falles] Which...goes to wrack,
/ And...falles   62 *Rome*] Rome (*also at lines* 66 *and* 110)   63 incense] ~,
74–5 Alas...dangerous, / For...knife] Alas...dangerous, for...knife   76 knife?
what,] ~, ~∧   80–1 He...good, / The...soule] He...good, the...soule
82 KING.] *King*. (*text*); *King*, (*catchword*)   82–4 Ah...dead, / O...brest, / Tell...live]
Ah...dead, O...brest, tell...live   103 lurke.] ~.   107 King,] ~.

COMMENTARY

This commentary follows the same principles as that for *Tamburlaine* above.

[Dramatis Personae]

CHARLES] Charles IX (1550–74), called (until 1560) duke of Orleans, king of France from 1560. He remained under his mother's domination, incapable of choosing and following a policy of his own; his health was poor and he was mentally unstable. The massacre apparently haunted Charles until his death.

ANJOY] Henry, duke of Anjou (1551–89), later Henry III (1574), elected to the throne of Poland in May 1573, married Louise de Vaudémont on 15 February 1575, laid siege to Paris with Navarre in 1589. He was assassinated on 1 August 1589 by Jacques Clément, but, before dying, acknowledged Henry of Navarre as his heir.

NAVARRE] Henri de Bourbon, king of Navarre (1553–1610), later Henry IV, first Bourbon King of France (1589), married Margaret on 18 August 1572 before the main portal of Notre Dame. He was ordered by Charles IX to abjure his Protestant faith after the massacre, and he did; the conversion was obviously of dubious sincerity. He was held for 3½ years at the courts of Charles IX and Henry III, then escaped (1576) with the consent of Catherine de' Medici. After the death of Francis, Henry III's brother, in 1584, he became heir presumptive to the French throne, from where he lent grudging support to Elizabeth until his serious conversion to Catholicism in 1593.

CONDY] Henry I de Bourbon, second prince of Bourbon (1552–88). His father's death (13 March 1569) left him and his cousin, Henry of Navarre, as titular leaders of the Huguenots. He was caught in Paris during the massacre, where he had been forced to profess Catholicism.

ADMIRALL] Gaspard de Coligny, seigneur de Châtillon (1519–72), admiral of France (1552) and leader of the Huguenots during the early years of the Wars of Religion (1562–98). He became sole leader upon the death of the first prince de Condé at the battle of Jarnac in 1569, and was assassinated on 24 August 1572.

GUISE] Henri I de Lorraine, third duke of Guise (1550–88). He was 13 years old at the time of his father's death, for incitement of which Coligny was formally accused by the duchess of Guise (Guise's mother) and her brothers-in-law. After an attempt on the Admiral's life failed,

Guise attended a secret meeting (23 August 1572) that planned the massacre of St Bartholomew's Day. On 24 August he personally supervised Coligny's murder, thereby avenging his father's death, but otherwise took no part in the massacre and even sheltered about a hundred Huguenots in his house. He was chief of the Catholic party and the Holy League during the Wars of Religion; murdered 23 December 1588.

DUMAINE] Charles de Lorraine, duke of Mayenne (1554–1611), succeeded as head of the Holy League after his brother Guise's death in 1588, remained leader until 1595. He was absent from France at the time of the massacre.

CARDINALL] Louis II de Lorraine, second cardinal of Guise, archbishop of Reims (1555–88). Marlowe either confuses or conflates him with Guise's uncle, Charles (d. 1574) who was Cardinal of Lorraine and also a fellow conspirator with the Queen Mother, Catherine de' Medici. Oliver suggests the possibility that 'Marlowe read carelessly in Varamund, who calls the Cardinal of Lorraine "brother to the Duke of Guise, which (as is aboue sayde) was slayne in the first warre"—i.e., brother to Francis, Duke of Guise, not to Henry'.

YONG GUISE] Charles de Lorraine, fourth duke of Guise (1571–1640). On the day of his father's assassination he was arrested and transferred to the Château of Tours in which he was imprisoned for 3 years, escaping in 1591.

EPERNOUNE] Jean-Louis de Nogaret de La Valete, duke d'Épernon (1554–1642), favourite friend and counsellor of Henry III.

PLESHE] Philippe Duplessis-Mornay (1549–1623), friend and close associate of Henry of Navarre. He was a political philosopher, theologian, and Huguenot leader whose written work advocated the right of rebellion against monarchy.

GONZAGO] Louis de Gonzague, duke of Nevers and Rethel (1539–95), a military officer.

RETES] Count of Retz, a marshal, an Italian nobleman close to the Queen Mother who had been a leader in the French privy council for some time.

MOUNTSORRELL] 'Called by Varamund "Monsorel" and may be identified with the historical Montsoreau' (Oliver).

BARTUS] Guillaume de Salluste du Bartas (1544–90), a Gascon gentleman who, in 1566, after a studious youth, took up arms in the service of Navarre; he was a Protestant writer and poet.

SEROUNE] Called by Varamund Masson de Rivers, but not further identified.

RAMUS] Petrus Ramus = Pierre de la Ramée (1515–72) French philosopher, logician, and rhetorician; converted to Protestantism in 1561 and murdered two days after the outbreak of the massacre.

TALEUS] Audomarus Talæus = Omer Talon, reformed Ciceronian rhetoric upon the principles applied by Ramus to the rearrangement of Aristotle's *Organon*.

QUEENE MOTHER] Catherine de' Medici (1519–89), a shrewd and accomplished political figure, who became the focus of rabid negative propaganda; in fact, she neither dominated Henry III nor sought to rule in his place, but actually allowed her own exploitation and supplied his deficiencies.

OLD QUEENE] Jeanne d'Albert, married Antoine duke of Vendôme (1518–62), refused suit of Francis of Lorraine, second duke of Guise (1519–63), and remained one of the most dangerous and persistent enemies of the Guises. She announced her Calvinism at Christmas 1560 and died in Paris on 9 June 1572 of a respiratory illness.

MARGRET] Margaret of Valois (1553–1615), daughter of Catherine de' Medici. She had an early liaison with Henry, duke of Guise, but married Henry de Bourbon, king of Navarre, on 18 August 1571, five days before the outbreak of the massacre.

DUCHESSE] Catherine of Cleves, daughter of Francis of Cleves, duke of Nevers, and Margaret of Bourbon.

Scene 1

1 brother] Commonly used for 'brother-in-law', which is Navarre's new relationship to Charles through marriage.

3 union . . . league] sacred alliance, i.e. between the houses of Valois and Navarre and their adherents.

4 these hands] i.e. of Henry and Margaret.

6 native] natural (*OED a.* 1.a).

7 motion] desire (*OED sb.* 9.a).

8 still] in future (*OED adv.* 4.c).

feweld] fed with fuel (*OED*, fuel, *v.* 1, first cited use).

12] 'Catherine, who—contrary to earlier French practice—had been virtually Regent of France during her son's minority, retained much of the real power after her legal authority ended' (Oliver).

18–23] From Varamund: 'When the day came, the mariage was with royall pompe solemnized before the great Churche of *Paris*, and a certaine forme of wordes so framed, as disagreed with the Religion of neither side, was by the Kings commaundement pronounced by the

Cardinall of *Burbon* the King of *Nauars* vncle: and so the matrimonie celebrate with great ioye of the King and all good men, the bryde was with great traine and pompe led into the Church to heare Masse, and in the meane time the brydgrome who mislyked these ceremonies, togither with *Henrie* Prince of *Conde*, sonne of *Lewes*, and the Admirall, and other noble men of the same Religion, walked without the Church dore, wayting for the Brides returne.' (Oliver, 167–8).

19 consumate] complete (*OED v.* 1).

25 this solemnitie] the marriage.

26SD4 *manet*] remains [on stage] (Latin).

30 envious] full of ill-will (*OED* 2).

46 timeles] untimely, premature (*OED* 1).

48 brother] See *Dramatis Personae*, CARDINALL*n*.

50–1] Navarre's father, Antoine de Bourbon, married Jeanne d'Albret, heiress of Navarre (the 'Old Queene' of Scene 3) in 1548 and became king of Navarre in 1554. The present marriage to the French king's sister gives Navarre an indirect claim to the French throne.

53 beates his braines] eagerly schemes. *OED*, beat, *v.*¹ 29, 'to think persistently and laboriously', citing this example; proverbial (Tilley, B602).

54 toyle] 'a net or nets set so as to enclose a space into which the quarry is driven, or within which the game is known to be' (*OED sb.*² 1); 'probably the trap and the toil are the same thing' (Bennett).

Scene 2

1–2] Bennett compares Ovid, *Metamorphoses*, X. 1–7: at the marriage of Orpheus and Eurydice, Hymen's 'torch with drizling smoke / Was dim' (Golding).

2 duskie] dim, obscure (*OED* 2).

11 prove] test (*OED v.* B.1).

guerdon] reward.

13 perfumed gloves] Varamund (Oliver, 167) relates that the poisoned gloves were 'dressed by one *Renat* the Kings Apothicarie, an Italian'. That Guise was responsible appears to be Marlowe's invention, as is the time of the Queen-Mother's death (actually two months before the marriage of Scene 1). The charge of poisoning appears to be unfounded, and her death due to pleurisy.

15 savour] smell, perfume, aroma (*OED sb.* 2); but l. 15 suggests that the sense here may be 'act of smelling' (not in *OED*).

23 blemish . . . eye] Oliver suggests an allusion to Matt. 7: 3, 'And why seest thou the mote that is in thy brothers eye, and perceivest not the beame that is in thine owne eye?', but more probably 'in our eye' means 'always before us, in our sight' (Bennett; *OED*, eye, *sb.*¹ 4.c), and 'blemish' is a moral defect (*OED sb.* 3 *fig.*). For Guise's use of 'our', cf. ll. 87, 95, and 98.

24 makes] brings about (*OED v.*¹ 9), i.e. foments.

31 perfourme] bring about (*OED v.* 4).

32 store] abundance (*OED sb.* 4.a).

34 begins] begin. Abbott (333) notes the frequency of third person plural in -s and (335) of inflection in -s preceding a plural subject, as here.

35 burst abroad] cause to burst or issue forth widely (*OED*, burst, *v.* 14, citing this example).

35–6 flames . . . bloud] Proverbial: Dent B465.1, 'Only BLOOD can quench the fire'.

37 leveld] guessed (*OED*, level *v.*¹ 8.b).

38–9 That . . . aime] Oliver compares 'Danger and delight grow both upon one stalk' (Tilley, D28) and 'The more Danger the more honor' (Tilley, D35).

40 common] ordinary.

41 hanges] i.e. like fruit on a tree, within reach. The idea in ll. 41–2 may have been suggested by the torments of Tantalus: 'But both the fruit from hand, and floud from mouth / Did flie abacke, and made him vainely swinke' (Spenser, *Faerie Queene*, II.vii.58).

peasant] low fellow, rascal (*OED* 1.c).

42 That . . . reach] Cf. Tilley, M282, 'A Man must not roam above his reach', and *Doctor Faustus*, Prologue, 21, 'His waxen wings did mount above his reach.'

43 Peramides] pyramids (here, cf. l. 45, used as a singular noun, as in *Doctor Faustus*, 7.42); four syllables, as always in Marlowe. 'Any structure of pyramidal form, as a spire, pinnacle, obelisk, etc.' (*OED*, pyramid, 3).

45 it] i.e. the 'Peramides' of line 43.

46 aspiring winges] Cf. *1 Tamburlaine*, 2.7.20 ('aspyring minds') and 1.2.237 ('aspire celestiall thrones').

49 attendance] 'the action or condition of an inferior in waiting the leisure, convenience, or decision of a superior' (*OED* 4). Word-play, as 'wait' and 'attend' are synonymous in sixteenth-century usage.

52–3 this head . . . executes] 'The head contrives, the heart imagines, and the hand and the sword execute' (Bennett). All three verbs are used transitively with 'Matters', l. 54. Cf. Kyd, *Cornelia*, 4.1.176–7, 'As if he wanted hands, sence, sight, or hart, / He doth, deuiseth, sees, nor dareth ought.'

imagines] conceives as a thing to be performed (*OED* 3).

54 importe] importance; stressed on the second syllable.

aimde] guessed (*OED*, aim, *v.* 3).

60 stately] haughty, domineering (*OED* 2.a).

61 Sends] Cf. l. 34*n.*

to coyne me] with which I may coin myself. To do so was a criminal offence, even though Guise uses gold and not baser metal. Marlowe himself was charged with counterfeiting, a capital offence, but the charges were dropped (see Charles Nicholl, *The Reckoning: The Murder of Christopher Marlowe*, London, 1992, pp. 235 ff).

ecues] crowns (French *écu*). An 'ecu' was actually a French silver coin: *OED*'s first cited use is 1704.

62 largesse] free gift of money (*OED* 2.b).

63 pension] regular payment (to a person of rank, *OED* sb. 3.c).

dispensation] licence to do what ecclesiastical law forbids (*OED* 8).

65 policye] political cunning (*OED sb.*[1] 3), with Machiavellian associations.

framde] shaped, fashioned (*OED*, frame, *v.* 5), as a building material.

66 *Diabole*] An oath: 'the devil!' Cf. Lancaster's oath '*Diablo*', *Edward II*, 4.319.

67 how ever] i.e. however unashamed.

69 so great matter] i.e. Guise's ambitious scheme.

ground] basis, foundation (*OED sb.* 5.a).

74] 'So that the result (*OED*, proof, *sb.* 7) is that he is king merely in name.'

75] Oliver compares Lorenzo's Machiavellian boast: Kyd, *The Spanish Tragedy*, 3.4.40, 'I lay the plot: he prosecutes the point.'

77] 'And wholly commits (*OED*, entomb, 2) the welfare of France to my (presumed) love.'

84 more] furthermore (*OED a.* C.6).

keeps] dwell (*OED v.* 37, and cf. l. 34*n.*).

86 comprisde] included (*OED* 6).

88–91] Cf. *The Tragical Reign of Selimus* (anonymous, 1594), ll.1539–44: 'Will fortune fauour me yet once againe? / And will she thrust the cards into my hands? / Well if I chance but once to get the decke, / To deale about and shufle as I would: / Let *Selim* neuer see the day-light spring, / Vnlesse I shuffle out my selfe a king.' (ed. W. Bang, 1909 for 1908, MSR; rpt. Oxford, 1964). To have all the cards in one's hands is proverbial for being in control (Dent, C78.11, citing l. 89).

92 *Navarre: Navarre*] The repetition may indicate that Guise first names Navarre as an impediment and then considers his kingdom (Craik).

95 our estate] i.e. the realm of France.

97 follow] pursue (*OED* 5).

98 possession to] Perhaps elliptical for 'progress to the possession of'.

99 As...souldiers] Caesar's remark does not appear to have been identified.

101–2] Cf. *1 Tamburlaine*, 2.1.21 and *2 Tamburlaine*, 1.3.77–8.

103 gripe] lay hold of, seize (*OED*, *v.*¹ 2), perhaps, as elsewhere in Marlowe, as an animal seizes its prey: cf. 22.9 below; *Edward II*, 19.7–9; and *1 Tamburlaine*, 2.7.48–9.

107 As...Sunne] i.e. blinded. Cf. Dent, S971.1, 'He that gazes upon the SUN shall at last be blind (fig.)', only cited example.

against] into.

Scene 3

2 accept] O's 'except' is probably an auditory error. *OED* (except, *v.* 6. 'To receive, accept. *Obs.* [A frequent sense of L. *excipere*; but in some at least of the examples the word is a mistake for ACCEPT.]') gives no good warrant for it in this context. Cf. *Arden of Faversham* (ed. M. L. Wine, Revels, London, 1973), 7.31, 'So you will except [*Q1–2*; accept *Q3*] of my company'.

3 holde] An imperative usage, meaning 'Here! take it!', i.e., the 'reward' (*OED v.* 15.b).

5 gloves...perfume] Bennett notes that gloves were often highly perfumed and cites Shakespeare, *Much Ado*, 3.4.57–8, 'These gloues the Counte sent me, they are an excellent perfume.'

10 Considering of] Abbott (178) notes the old usage of 'of' following a verbal noun.

11 poysoned] Not historically true (see 2.13*n.*); from Varamund: 'Not long before this, *Ioane* Queene of *Nauarre* aboue mentioned, died in the

Court at *Paris*, of a sodaine sicknesse, beeing about the age of fortie and three yeres, where as the suspition was great that she dyed of poyson, and hir body being for that cause opened by the Phisitions, there were no tokens of poyson espied. But shortely after, by the detection of one *A. P.* it hath ben founde that she was poysoned with a venomed smell of a payre of perfumed gloues' (Oliver, 167).

13 late suspition] 'recent suspecting' or 'recent grounds for suspecting' (*OED*, suspicion, 1.a and c) (Oliver).

15 meddle] deal or concern (yourself) (*OED* 8), not necessarily, as now, expressive of disapprobation.

18 naturall] as opposed to unnatural poisoning.

passion] a painful affection or disorder of the body or of some part of it (*OED sb*. 4.a).

20 brain pan] that which contains the brain, the skull (*OED*)—used figuratively here to suggest extreme pain.

25 dye . . . againe] Navarre alludes to the central Christian doctrine of everlasting life in eternity after death.

26 heavy] A word with multiple meanings in this context: of great import, serious (*OED a.*[1] 12); hard to bear, grievous (*OED a.*[1] 23); distressing, sorrowful (*OED a.*[1] 25.a).

chaunce] 'the falling out or happening of events' (*OED sb*. 1).

27 effects] accomplishment, fulfilment (*OED sb*. 7.a).

31SD *As* . . . ADMIRALL] From Varamund: 'About noone, when he was in returning home from the Counsell, with a greate companie of noblemen and Gentlemen, beholde, a Harquebuzier out of a window of a house neere adioyning, shot yᵉ Admiral with two bullets of leade through both the armes.' (Oliver, 168).

Scene 4

1–4] From Varamund: 'After noone the Queene mother led out the King, the Duke of *Aniow*, *Gonzague*, *Tauaignes*, the Counte *de Rhetz* called *Gondin*, into hir gardens called *Tegliers*. This place bicause it was somewhat farre from resort, she thought most fit for this their laste consultation. There she shewed them, howe those whome they hadde long bene in waite for, were nowe sure in hold, & the Admirall lay in his bed maymed of both his armes and could not stir, the King of *Nauar* and Prince of *Conde* were fast lodged in the Castle, the gates were kept shut all nyghte, and watches placed, so as they were so snared that they coulde no way escape, and the captaines thus taken, it was not to be feared that any of the Religion woulde from thenceforth stir any more. Now was a notable opportunitie (saide she) offred to dispatch the matter.' (Oliver, 171–2).

2 fatall] condemned by fate; doomed (*OED* 2, citing this as example).

stragling] straying apart from companions or the main body (*OED ppl. a.*) and thus exposed to attack. Cf. *1 Tamburlaine*, 2.4.16: 'fearful coward, stragling from the camp'.

deere] i.e. the Protestants; cf. 'They', l. 8.

3 compasse] enclosing limit of a space (*OED sb.*¹ 7.a).

toyle] See 1.54*n*.

5–12] Charles's statement of honourable behaviour here, followed soon after by his capitulation using specious logic, recalls Sigismond's behaviour in *2 Tamburlaine*, 2.1.42–8 and 60–3; both men also see their deaths as being deserved (13.9 below and *2 Tamburlaine* 2.3.1–9).

5–6] 'Madam, what we are about to do will be perceived (*OED*, note, *v.*² 1.b) or adversely recorded (*v.*² 4) as a bloody and tyrannical action throughout the world'.

8 challenge] claim (*OED v.* 5).

9 relentes] melts (*OED v.*¹ 1.*fig.*).

11 Ladies] The only indication in the text that women are to be included in the massacre. Perhaps suggested by Varamund: 'but be it that the Admirall and a fewe other of his confederates and followers had conspired, why yet proceeded the outragious crueltie vpon the reste that were innocent, why vpon ancient matrones, why vpon noble Ladies & yong Gentlewomen and virgins that came thither for the honor of the wedding? why were so manye women greate with childe, against the lawes of all nations and of nature, before their deliuery thrown into the Ryuer?' (Oliver, 178).

13 gentle] noble, courteous (*OED a.* and *sb.* A. 3.a).

14 proper] own.

16 Then] Than.

24 Nephew] Kinsman (*MED*, neveu, 1.f; not in *OED*).

25 determine] decide (*OED* 5).

ratifie] to confirm by giving formal sanction (*OED* 1).

29–39] From Varamund: 'and the token to set vpon them, should be giuen, not with a trumpet, but with tocksein or ringing of the great bel of the Palace, which they knewe to be accustomed onely in great cases: and the marke for them to be knowne from other, should be a white linnen cloth hanged about their lefte arme, and a white crosse pinned vppon their cappes.' (Oliver, 173).

30 Burgonets] A burgonet is either a very light casque, or steel cap, for the use of the infantry, especially pikemen, or a helmet with a visor, so fitted to the gorget or neck-piece that the head could be turned without exposing the neck (*OED*).

35 set] to beset (a place) for the purpose of intercepting or capturing a person (*OED v*¹. 118.b, latest cited use; cf. 6.16 and 6.55).

40–9] Cf. Varamund: 'While these things were doing, and the Admirals wounde in dressing, *Theligny* went by his commaundement to the king, and moste humbly besought him in the name of his father in lawe, that his Maiestie would voutsafe to come vnto him, for that his life seemed to be in perill, and that he hadde certaine things to say, greatly importing to the Kings safetie, which he well knewe that none in his Realme durst declare to his maiestie. The King courteously answered that he would willingly go to him, and within a little while after he sette forwarde. The Queene mother went with him, and the Duke of *Aniow*, the Duke of *Monpensier*, a most affectionate subiect to the church of *Rome*, the Count *de Rhetz*, the Queene mothers great familiar, *Chauigny* and *Entragny*, whiche afterwarde were chiefe ringleaders in the butcherie of *Paris*.' (Oliver, 169).

41 And] If (Abbott 101).

50] Editors are divided on whether or not to end a scene here: Gill and Pendry–Maxwell do; Greg, Bennett, Bowers, and Oliver do not. Both lines 49 and 50 sound like exit cues, but the octavo notes only one exit, that of Guise; the Queen Mother also has no exit, nor does she speak in the presence of the Admiral. Perhaps new action, and thus a new scene, begins above after at least the king enters the Admiral's living quarters; his entourage might be with him, or might wait.

Scene 5

osd *in his bed*] The bed would most likely have been thrust onto the stage with the Admiral in it: cf. Middleton, *A Chaste Maid in Cheapside* (ed. R. B. Parker, Revels, London, 1969), 3.2.0SDI, '*A bed thrust out upon the stage*, ALLWIT′S *Wife in it*', and *Othello*, First Folio, 5.2.0SD, '*Enter Othello, and Desdemona in her bed*'. Alternatively, the stage business might have taken place on an upper acting area: the Guise orders his followers to throw 'down' the Admiral's body at 6.33 below. See Richard Hosley, 'The Staging of Desdemona's Bed', *SQ* 14 (1963), 57–65 on the staging of bed scenes, and Introduction, p. 313.

1–7] Cf. Varamund: 'When the King had louingly saluted the Admirall as he was wont to do, and had gently asked him some questions concerning his hurt and the state of his health, and the Admirall had answered with such a milde and quiet countenaunce, that all they that were present wondered at his temperance and patience, the King being much moued (as it seemed) sayd, The hurt my Admirall is done to thee, but the dishonour to me: but by the death of God (saith he) I swear I wil so seuerely reuenge bothe the hurte and the dishonor, that it shall neuer be forgotten.' (Oliver, 169).

2 with] by (Abbott 193).

8–18] In Varamund, the Admiral's friends ask the King for a guard. He readily agrees, saying 'that he was fully determined to prouide aswell for the Admirals safetie as for his owne'. 'Therewith the Duke of *Aniow* the Kings brother commanded *Cossin* Captaine of the Kings guarde, to place a certaine band of souldiers to warde the Admiralles gate.' (Oliver, 171).

9 massacre] kill indiscrimately (*OED v.* 1, citing this example).

12 And ... selfe] 'And that I am no more concerned about my own safety or security' (Oliver).

13 Then] Than.

14 *Cosin*] Bennett first identified the word as a proper name here. Cf. also 6.20.

17 present] immediate.

20 hower] hour (pronounced as two syllables).

Scene 6

2 argent] of, or resembling, silver; silvery white (*OED* B. cites this as earliest example of adjectival use).

2 burgonets] See 4.30*n*.

6 all] i.e. all Protestants, not every person.

11–12] See *Dramatis Personae*, ADMIRALL *n*. Line 12 is duplicated verbatim at l. 40; see Introduction, p. 299.

13 entrance] beginning or commencement (*OED sb.* 4.a).

17 charge] responsibility (*OED sb.* 12). There may be an irony here because the word also means 'the duty or responsibility of taking care *of* (a person or thing)' (*OED sb.* 13.a).

Swizers] Swiss guards (*OED*, Switzer, 2), well-known mercenaries, and particularly as bodyguards for royalty; cf. Shakespeare, *Hamlet*, 4.5.95.

keepe] guard, defend, protect (*OED v.* 14.b).

19SD *others*] i.e. some soldiers.

20–1] Cf. Varamund: 'There coulde hardly a man be founde more hatefull against the Admiralles part, nor more affected to the *Guisians*, than this *Cossin*, whiche the successe playnly proued, as hereafter shall appeare.' (Oliver, 171).

23 The...stand] Proverbial, 'If the HEAD is off, no beast can live' (Dent, H257.1).

24SD] Probably an entry to an acting space above: see l. 33, 5.0SD*n*. and Introduction, p. 313.

28–9] The Admiral, being Protestant, would pray directly to God, but Gonzago, being Catholic, insists on an intermediary, the Virgin Mother, and puns on his weapon as a 'crosse', that is, the figure made by the cross-piece dividing the blade of a sword or dagger from the hilt, and serving as a guard to the hand (*OED sb*. 14.b).

33–48] Much of the action derives from Varamund: 'When they were broken into the Admiralles chamber, *Benuese* came to him, and bending his drawne sworde vpon him, said, Art not thou the Admirall? he with a quiet and constant countenance, (as we haue since vnderstode by themselues) answered, I am so called. And then seeing the sworde drawne vpon him, he sayde, yong man, consider my age and the weake case that I am now in. But the fellowe after blaspheming God, fyrste thrust his sworde into the Admiralles breste, and then also stroke him vpon the head, and *Attin* shot him through ye brest with a pistol. When the Admiral was with this wound not yet throughly deade, *Benuese* gaue him the thirde wounde vpon the thygh, and so he fell down for deade. When the duke of *Guise*, which stayed in the courte with the other noblemen, heard this, he cried out alowde, hast thou done *Benuese*? he answered, I haue done. Then said the Duke of *Guise*, our *Cheuelier* (meaning King *Henries* bastard abouesaide) vnlesse he see it with his eyes will not beleeue it: throw him down at the window. Then *Benuese* with the helpe of his fellowes toke vp the Admirals body and threwe it downe through the windowe. When by reason of the wound in his head, and his face couered with bloud they could not well discerne him, the Duke of *Guise* kneeled down on the ground and wiped him with a napkin and sayde, now I know him, it is he. And therewithal going out at the gate with the rest of the Lordes, he cryed out to the multitude in armour, saying: my companions we haue had a good lucky beginning: now let vs go forward to the rest, for it is the Kings commaundement: which words he did ofte repeat aloud, saying: Thus the King commaundeth: This is the Kings wil, this is his pleasure. And then he commaunded ye token to be giuen by ringing tocksein with ye great bel of the palace, & alarme to be raysed, and he caused it to be published, that the conspiratours were in armour and about to kill the King. Then a certaine Italian of *Gonzagues* band, cut off the Admirals head, & sent it preserued with spices to *Rome* to the Pope and the Cardinall of *Loreine*. Other cut off his hands, and other his secrete partes. Then the common laborers and rascalles three days togither dragged the deade bodie thus mangled and berayed with bloude and filth, through the streates, and afterward drewe it out of the towne to the common gallowes, and hanged it vp with a rope by the feete.' (Oliver, 174–5).

33SD] The desecration of the body, both here, at l. 42, and in Scene 11, recalls other atrocities in Marlowe: cf. the treatment of Sigismond's corpse in *2 Tamburlaine*, 2.3.14–17, 38–9, and, particularly, the Governor of Babylon's execution while hanging in chains (*2 Tamburlaine*, 5.1.147 SD2 ff.), which is similar to the Guise's order for the Admiral's body to be hung in chains (l. 48). See also *Edward II*, 2.29–30: 'Weele hale him from the bosome of the king, / And at the court gate hang the pessant up'. A contemporary audience might have recalled the heads displayed on London Bridge, which was part of the punishment for treason.

38 neer] narrowly, only by a little (*OED adv.*² 9 cites this as an example and notes the meaning as *Obs. rare*). *OED* also quotes Greene, *Orlando Furioso*, 443–4, (ed. W. W. Greg, MSR, Oxford, 1907), 'The Foxe is scapde, but here's his case: / I mist him nere, twas time for him to trudge'.

39 *Shatillian*] English spelling of 'Châtillon', pronounced as three syllables here. Bennett notes that Golding's title-page of *The lyfe of... Iasper Colignie Shatilion* (1576) uses a similar spelling and that 'Châtillon' is the family name of Coligny.

41 in despite of] in contempt or scorn of; in contemptuous defiance of (*OED, despite, sb.* 5.a cites this as an example).

42 bulke] 'the trunk, the body generally' (*OED sb.*¹ 2).

46 mount *Faucon*] Montfaucon. Oliver notes that bodies were normally allowed to decay on the gibbets there; he also points out that Marlowe is using other authorities (e.g. Golding, cited in Bennett's 5.33n.) or possibly his own knowledge, because Varamund does not mention Montfaucon, only 'the common gallowes'.

48 thereon] The antecedent is probably 'the crosse' of l. 47, but may be 'mount *Faucon*' of l. 46. (For the association of cross = tree = gallows see 11.11 and *n.*).

51 breath] breathe (variant spelling).

52 partiall] Punning upon the meanings 'unduly favouring one side', the opposite of 'impartial' (*OED* 1.a) and 'dealing with only a part', 'sparing' (*OED* 2.d).

55 set] See 4.35 and *n.*

57 lets forward] let's go forward (with ellipsis of 'go': *OED*, forward, B. *adv.* 4.b).

59 closely] attentively (*OED* 6). Oliver glosses 'secretly', but there is nothing secret about the massacre from now on (Craik).

Scene 7

1 *Tue*] French for 'kill' (tuer); *OED* defines as '*Obs.* [? a. F. *tue* kill.] A hunting cry' and illustrates with a single quotation from 1602 Carew, *Cornwall*, I. 22, 'The Captaine hunters, discouering his sallies by their Espyals doe lay their souldier-like Hounds, his borne enemies, in ambush betweene him [the Fox] and home, and so with *Har* and *Tue* pursue him to the death'. Bennett notes that the same cry with the same spelling occurs in *A Larum for London* (1602) (ed. W. W. Greg, MSR, Oxford, 1913), l. 1128. The dramatic situation is also exactly the same, that is, killers pursuing their human prey.

3SD2 LOREINE] Oliver suggests that this is the Leranne whom Varamund (quoted by Oliver, 176) described as being wounded but escaping during the general massacre of Navarre's and Condy's companions in the Louvre (see 9.65–83*n*.). He follows Ethel Seaton's suggestion that because 'Follow Loreine' was the war-cry of the Guise (Lorraine) faction (review of Bennett in *RES* 9, 1933, 330), there may be a pun on the victim's name 'in line with the other jesting associated with each of the murders'. But there is no connection between this incident and that of 9.65–83; the victim is 'a preacher of the word of God' and is undoubtedly killed (ll. 8SD and 10); it may be that LOREINE here and in the speech prefix l. 6 is guesswork by the compiler of the Octavo, based entirely on Guise's exclamation at l. 4 (Craik).

8 'Dearely . . . brother'] A sardonic application of 'Dearly beloved brethren', the opening phrase of the priest's exhortation to the congregation at morning and evening prayer to join him in the general confession (Craik); cf. *Doctor Faustus*, 2.26–7, where Wagner quotes the unctuous speech forms of the religious Puritans: 'I will set my countnance like a precisian, and begin to speake thus: truly my deare brethren'.

9] The joke is, presumably, that Anjoy wishes to emulate Guise's 'praying'.

Scene 8

1–15] Varamund describes the murder of Masson de Rivers at Angiers, on which this incident is based. 'This man was a pastor of the church, and esteemed a singular man both in vertuousnesse of life, and in excellence of wit and learning, and was the first that had layd the foundacion of the Churche at Paris. As sone as the slaughter was begon at *Paris*, *Monsorel* a most cruell enimie of the Religion, was sente to *Angiers* in post to preuente al other that might carie tidings of the murdering. As sone as he came into ye towne, he caused himself to be brought to *Massons* house. There he met *Massons* wife in the entrie, and gently saluted hir, and after the maner of Fraunce, specially of the Court, he kissed hir, and asked hir where hir husband was, she answered, that he was walking in the garden, and by and by she brought *Monsorell* to hir husbande, who gently embraced *Masson* and sayde vnto him: Canst thou tell why I am come hither? it is to kyll thee by the Kings commaundement at this very instant time, for so hath the King commaunded, as thou mayste perceiue by these letters, and therewith he shewed him his dagge ready charged. *Masson* answered that he was not guiltie of any crime, howbeit this one thing only he besought him, to giue him space to call to the mercie of God, and to commende his spirit into Gods hande. Which prayer as soone as he had ended in fewe wordes, he meekely receiued the death offered by the other, and was shot through with a pellet, and dyed.' (Oliver, 178–9).

6 ha't] have it: emendation is necessary to clarify meaning.

7–15] See 6.28–9 and *n*.

7] The line is identical with *3 Henry VI*, 1.3.36 and *True Tragedy*, sig. A8; see Introduction, p. 302.

11 Why] Not a question but an indignant interjection (*OED* 7) (Craik).

13 *Sanctus Jacobus*] Saint James (Latin).

was] Curiously, Mountsorrell speaks of his faith in the past even as he insists on the (catholic) imperative of seeking a saint's intercession.

Scene 9

0SD] The direction may indicate the use of an inner acting area (cf. *Doctor Faustus*, 1.0SD: '*Enter* FAUSTUS *in his Study*' and *The Jew of Malta*, 1.0SD: '*Enter* BARABAS *in his Counting-house, with heapes of gold before him*') or, possibly, an upper acting area as in Scene 6 (see 6.24SD*n*., 6.33, and Introduction, pp. 314–14).

1 comes] See 2.34*n*.

4 once more] From l. 16 it seems that the 'Guisians' have previously extorted money from Ramus; perhaps this is an indication of lost action or dialogue which would have made the meaning clear.

9 Harke, harke] Often an indication of off-stage noise, probably knocking; cf. Middleton, *The Witch* (ed. Edward J. Esche, Garland, New York, 1992), 4.3.29 and 31; see also his Introduction, p. 61.

9SD] The stage business which follows at ll. 11–15 and Ramus' second entry at l. 15 seems to indicate that Gonzago and Retes enter (l. 10) onto a stage area which is not representative of the 'studie'; thus, if Taleus is to meet them, he must leave the 'studie' at some point. See Introduction, pp. 313–14 for possibilities of staging this scene.

12 bedfellow] One who shares a bed with another, but not in a sexual sense here.

16 more golde] See l. 4n.

24 offencious] offensive, transgressive (*OED* cites this as unique example).

25 smack in] slight or superficial knowledge of (*OED*, smack, *sb.*¹ 3.b).

all] everything, but possibly, more specifically, the 'Whole system of things, the Universe' (*OED* B.3; first cited use is 1598).

27 *Organon*] 'The title of Aristotle's logical treatises; = "instrument" of all reasoning' (*OED*). 'In the sixteenth century the university curriculum was based on the study of Aristotle, although his supremacy was disputed in Cambridge (while Marlowe was a student there) by the intellectual reformer Petrus Ramus' (*Doctor Faustus*, 1.5*n.*).

28 heape of vanities] Bennett notes that 'Ramus in the thesis for his degree (1536) had ventured to uphold the view that "Everything that Aristotle taught is false". Then in 1543 he published a criticism of the old logic entitled *Aristotelicae Animadversiones*.'

29 flat] absolute, unqualified (*OED a.* 6.a), but perhaps also 'prosaic, dull' (*OED a.* 7).

decotamest] 'One who dichotomizes, or classifies by dichotomy' (*OED* 1, first cited use), which in logic is the division of a whole into parts, specifically, the 'Division of a class or genus into two lower mutually exclusive classes or genera; binary classification' (*OED* 1.a). 'Marlowe is being academic: Aristotle had rejected dichotomy as a scientific method of classification and had maintained that it assumed knowledge it aimed at giving' (Oliver).

30 seen] versed, expert (*OED ppl. a.*, 2, which quotes Shakespeare, *Shrew*, 1.2.131–2, 'a schoole-master / Well seene in Musicke').

Epetomies] brief statements of main points in a work, abridgements (*OED* 1).

32 preach in *Germany*] 'Ramus lectured for a time at the University of Heidelberg' (Bennett). 'Preach' may also have Protestant overtones because the Reformation began in Germany.

33 Excepting against] Objecting or taking exception to (*OED*, except, *v.* 2).

actions] deeds. But in the present scholastic context Dyce²'s emendation 'axioms' (*OED* 2, '*Logic*. A proposition (whether true or false).') is attractive (Craik).

34 *ipse dixi*] 'I have spoken'; the argument that a statement is true because the speaker has made it (Oliver).

quidditie] 'A subtlety or captious nicety in argument; a quirk, quibble. (Alluding to scholastic arguments on the "quiddity" of things.)' (*OED* 2); cf. *Doctor Faustus*, 1.164.

35] i.e. 'an assertion based on the authority of the person making it is in itself insufficient proof or incapable of proof. This is a fair summary of Ramus' position—but Guise grimly proceeds to make such an assertion (that Ramus shall die) and says *this* assertion *is* capable of proof—and "proves" it by killing him' (Oliver).

37 *nego argumentum*] Literally 'I deny (the validity of) your argument', but, as Bennett points out, 'A term commonly used in disputation in the schools of the Universities of the Middle Ages'.

42 latter] last.

purge my selfe] clear myself of a charge or suspicion of guilt (*OED* purge *v.*¹ 5.a), and Oliver adds, 'not necessarily by recantation'.

43 know] understand or comprehend with clearness and feeling of certainty (*OED v.* 10.a).

44 *Shekius*] 'Ramus' opponent in a famous published philosophical dispute, culminating in the 1571 *Rami Defensio pro Aristotele adversus Jacobum Shecium*' (Oliver).

takes it] The quasi-redundant use of 'it' with verb (Abbott 226, and see *OED*, take, *v.* 42).

45 places] subjects or topics = Latin *loci* in formal logic or rhetoric.

contains] cf. 2.34*n*.

47 reduc'd] To 'reduce' something is to bring it into a 'certain form or character' (*OED,* reduce, *v.* 15.a, first cited use), thus making an 'epitome' (see l. 30*n*.2).

51 And thats because] There seems to be a disconnection of sense here, possibly because some of the speech is lost.

blockish] stupid, obtuse.

Sorbonests] doctors and students at the Sorbonne, 'a theological college at Paris founded by Robert de Sorbon early in the 13th century' and specifically 'the faculty of theology in the old University of Paris, of great importance down to the 17th century' (*OED,* Sorbonne, 1).

54 declaime] The Guise is again being sardonic, as the full *OED*, 1 definition makes clear: 'to make a speech on a set subject or theme as an exercise in public oratory or disputation'.

56 Colliars sonne] A typical Marlovian class insult: cf. *2 Tamburlaine*, 3.5.77, 'Shepheards issue, base borne *Tamburlaine*', and *Edward II*, 2.30, where Gaveston is referred to as a 'pessant'. Ramus' father was a charcoal burner.

56SD] The form and context of this stage direction, the imperative marking the murder of an individual, probably indicates that Anjoy alone kills Ramus (cf. '*Stab him*', 6.29 and 8.15).

62 dartes] arrows (*OED* 1).

63 sinke] i.e. cause them to sink (*OED v.* 16) by killing them.

65–83] Cf. Varamund: 'While these things were thus a doing in the towne, the King of *Nauarre* and the Prince of *Conde*, whome the King had lodged in his owne Castle of the *Louure*, were by the Kings commaundement sent for and conueyed vnto him. But their company, their seruitours of their Chambers, their friendes retaining to them, their scholemasters, and those that had the bringing vp of them, crying out aloude to the Kings fidelitie for succour, were thrust out of the Chambers, and by the Kyngs guarde of Switzers hewed in pieces and slaughtered in the Kings owne sight.' (Oliver, 175).

66 pedantes] schoolmasters, teachers (but often without implication of contempt) (*OED* 1).

69 hard] closely (behind).

69SD] The logic of Anjoy knocking and the others entering may seem strained, but Anjoy's going 'in' (l. 69) probably marks a new acting area of the stage into which Guise and his followers enter later (l. 77); see Introduction, p. 314.

74 stay] to appease, allay (strife, tumult); to reduce to order, bring under control (rebellious elements) (*OED v*¹. 28, citing this as example).

broile] confused disturbance, tumult or turmoil (*OED sb.*¹ 1).

76 made] brought about (*OED*, make, *v.*¹ 9.a).

80SD] Oliver suggests a possible lacuna in the text here which would have explained why Navarre and Condy are spared, but this is guess-work. We simply are not told why Guise does not kill them, but clearly he was not planning to (see ll. 65–7); Navarre's next amicable appearance with Charles (Scene 13) is not surprising because we are clearly prepared for it (see 11.35–7). Varamund does, however, offer explanations: 'The Queenes opinion [i.e. that the Admiral, Navarre and Condy, being all in vulnerable situations, could all be destroyed, and Protestantism in France with them] was allowed. Howbeit it was thought best, partly for his age, and partly for the affinities sake, that the King of *Nauars* life should be saued. As for the Prince of *Conde*, it was doubted whether it were best to spare him for his age, or to put him to death for hatred of his fathers name. But herein the opinion of *Gonzague* toke place, that he should with feare of death and torment, be drawne from the Religion. So that counsell brake vp, with appoyntment that the matter should be put in execution the nexte night earely afore day, and that the ordering and doing of all shoulde be committed to the Duke of *Guise*.' (Oliver, 172).

82 whip you] The Guise matches his black humour to the professions of his victims, the schoolmasters: as they whip schoolboys, so the Guise whips them.

84–8] Cf. Varamund: 'This butcherly slaughter of *Paris* thus performed, and foure hundred houses (as is abouesayde) sacked, immediatly messengers were sent in post into all the partes of the Realme, with oft shifting their horsses for hast, to commaunde all other Cities in the Kings name to followe the example of *Paris*, and to cause to be killed as many as they had among them of the reformed Religion.' (Oliver, 176).

84 stay] cease (*OED v.*^{1} 3).

85 will we not] we do not wish.

89 stay] 'To cause (a bell) to cease ringing' (*OED v.*^{1} 23.d, first cited use).

mattins] One of the canonical hours of the breviary; properly, as here, a midnight office (*OED* 1.a).

90 burgonet] See 4.30*n*.

91 convey him] steal away (*OED*, convey, *v.* 7).

closely] secretly, covertly (*OED* 3).

Scene 10

2 Prince Electors] 'Princes entitled to elect the King or Emperor' (Oliver).

9 mannage] the direction or control (*OED sb.* 5). Marlowe often uses the related verb in reference to military activities (cf. 16.2, 18.7 and *1 Tamburlaine*, 3.1.34 and *2 Tamburlaine*, 5.3.36).

21 covenant] make it a condition of an agreement (*OED v.* 3, citing this as example). No source has yet been found for this agreement.

Scene 11

OSD] Is the body headless and handless as suggested by 6.43?

1–12] This action does not necessarily contradict Guise's order at 6.46–8; the setting may be the 'mount *Faucon*' of 6.46, and the 'tree' of l. 11 a gallows (*OED sb*. B.4.b and 6.48*n*.).

13 lusty] Guise is using the word in a context that gives a multiplicity of ironic meanings, including, at least, 'healthy, strong' (*OED* 5.a), and 'arrogant, self-confident' (*OED* 6).

21 synagogue] assembly (*OED* 4, citing this as example).

24, 28 sweet *Guise*] No source has yet been found for the Queen-Mother's attraction to Guise; Marlowe may, of course, simply be inventing for the dramatic effect of blackening her character.

25 straglers] See 4.2*n*.2.

gather head] increase in strength (*OED*, head, *sb.*^{1}, 31).

32 for to] to (Abbott 152; cf. l. 37, 13.19, 21.91, 23.13, and 24.109).

38 let . . . that] leave that to me (14.61 and 19.77 contain a similar phrase).

Scene 12

OSD] This is a dramatization of the 'synagogue' to which Guise referred earlier (see 11.21 and *n*.)

5 plaintes] lamentations (*OED sb*. 1), i.e. appeals for pity.

7] The verbatim repetition from 7.1–2 may be faulty reporting (Oliver and Introduction, p. 299), but may just as likely be a deliberate repetition marking Guise's fanatical violence.

Scene 13

OSD1 *staying*] supporting (*OED* stay *v.*^{2} 1).

1 stay] stop (*OED v.*^{1} 1.b).

2 griping paine] 'There was a rumour that Charles, like the Queen-Mother in Scene iii, had been poisoned' (Gill), but there is no historical evidence; the literary symptoms of the two deaths, however, are very close: cf. ll. 13–15 and 3.19–21. See 2.103*n*. for 'griping'.

9–12] These are among the most confusing lines in the play. Oliver paraphrases thus: 'although I have deserved a scourge, there are two kinds of response to evil; one is patient suffering, the other the undoing of the King; I pray that my nearest friends are of the better kind—and have not been responsible for my death!' This interpretation is weakened by its substitution of '*the* King' for '*their* King' (Craik). Cunningham emended 'there', l. 10, to 'their', and many editors follow him: he paraphrased ll. 10–12 as 'There are persons (you yourself, and my Protestant subjects, for instance) from whom I have deserved a scourge, but *their* feelings would never lead them to poison their king; God grant that my dearest relations may prove to have been no worse than those who ought to be my enemies.' Bowers, following Cunningham, paraphrases, 'I must confess that my unjust actions (to the Protestants) have made me deserve their retaliation as scourges for my sins. However, I credit them with patient submission to these wrongs, as God requires, and do not believe that they have murdered me in revenge. May God grant that my nearest friends are no more culpable in my death than these innocent Protestants.' (p. 406). Bullen notes, ' "Scourge" must surely be the scourge of God. Navarre had said, "God will surely restore you", to which the king answers, "I have deserved a scourge" from God. Before l. 10 a line or more referring to the massacre of the Protestants must have dropped out.'

11 misdoe] harm or injure (*OED* 3).

15SD] Charles's death occurred on 30 May 1574.

16] Perhaps an echo of Shakespeare, *3 Henry VI*, 5.5.50, and *True Tragedy*, sig. E5; see Introduction, p. 302.

17 his . . . breast] Thought to happen literally at the point of death: see, for instance, Donne, 'A Valediction: Forbidding Mourning', first stanza.

18] Perhaps an echo of Shakespeare, *3 Henry VI*, 2.6.63 and *True Tragedy*, sig. C4v; see Introduction, p. 302.

20, 23 presently] immediately.

28 *Polonie*] Poland (*OED* A. 1, first and only cited use is 1634).

30 broiles] See 9.74*n*.2.

31 serve me fit] conveniently afford me an occasion (*OED*, serve, $v.^1$ 25, citing *3 Henry VI*, 4.8.77; 'fit' not in *OED* as adverb, but see *a*. 7).

32] Navarre did not leave Paris until 1576, two years after Charles died. Compressing time and action like this is standard dramatic licence in history plays of the period.

steale] withdraw secretly or surreptitiously (*OED* $v.^1$ 9.a).

hye me] hasten, hurry (*OED* $v.^1$ 3).

35 It] i.e. the throne of France. If Navarre ignores the legitimate claim of Alençon, Henry III's brother (who did not die till 1584), then this might be an early indication of his self-serving political acumen. On the other hand, Alençon has not yet been mentioned in the play, though he will be later (see 14.65 and 21.105).

37] A destabilizing action and one for which Guise is attacked later (see 19.17 ff.); Guise is raising an army in France, Navarre in Navarre (ll. 32, 37).

39 seeme] think fit (*OED v.*² 9.b, an archaic usage when Marlowe wrote).

43 march] used figuratively (*OED v.*2 1.c, first cited use is 1684), i.e. an army of virtues is on Navarre's side.

44 Whose] The antecedent is 'vertues' of l. 42.

45 *Pampelonia*] Pamplona, the capital of Navarre, held by Spain at this time, as ll. 46–7 indicate, but Navarre's reasoning is confusing. He was talking of his claim to France at ll. 34–5, but he now seems to be talking of his claim to the Navarrese capital, and this, in turn, seems to retro-act on ll. 36–9, since the King of Spain is involved. Perhaps 'all the popish power' (l. 46) is at least partly localized in '*Guise*' (l. 38) (Craik).

Scene 14

OSD 1 vive le Roy] (long) live the King.

OSD 4 *Minions*] favourites 'of a sovereign, prince, or other great person; *esp*. opprobriously, one who owes everything to his patron's favour, and is ready to purchase its continuance by base compliances', creatures (*OED sb.*¹, 1.c), but, more specifically, 'homosexual lovers' (see ll.16–22, 17.21–2, and 19.14). The latter sense is not in *OED* although 1.c. illustrates meaning with quotation from *Edward II*, 4.87; 1.a gives sexual connotations, but only in relation to women. 'Minion' is a derivative of the French *mignon* = darling boy, and often in Marlowe's work carries meaning of homoerotic desire (cf. *Edward II*, 4.30 where Edward uses the word non-pejoratively, as Henry does here, to describe his favourite, Gaveston), but the term also carries contemptuous meaning, as in *Edward II*, 1.133 and, possibly, at l. 46 below.

3 fathers] i.e. Henry II's (1519–1559), duke of Orleans to 1547, king of France 1547–59.

12 guider . . . crownes] i.e. God.

14 speed] carries out (*OED v.* 8.a).

15 And . . . desertes] The sense is obscure. In ll. 14–15 Henry seems to be promising that, if Fortune carries out his wishes, his deeds will requite (*OED*, yield, *v.* B.1) their good opinions of him (*OED*, thought, 4.g) to the height of his *desires* (for which Octavo's 'desertes' may be an error induced by 'deserve', l. 13) (Craik).

15 to height] omission of definite article (Abbott 89).

16–17 What... Majestie] Henry's rhetorical question ironically alludes to a proverbial idea (Tilley, L495, 'Love and lordship like no fellowship') derived, as Bennett notes, from Ovid, *Metamorphoses*, ii.1057–8: 'Betweene the state of Majestie and love is set such oddes, / As that they can not dwell in one.' Cf. *Edward II*, 4.13 and *n.*

20 slacke] reduce the force or strength of.

affection] sexual desire, often related to sodomy: see Rubinstein and cf. *Edward II*, 4.151.

his] its (Abbott 228).

bent] purpose, intention (*OED*, *sb.*², 7).

21 still persist] constantly remain or always continue to be (*OED*, persist, *v.* 2).

22 Removeles] Incapable of being removed (*OED*, cited as unique example).

26 invested in] installed (with the customary rites and ceremonies) (*OED*, invest, *v.* 4).

crowne] sovereignty (of which a crown is a symbol) (*OED sb.* 3).

28 fellowes] 'equals', a completely inappropriate relationship, as an example from *OED*, fellow, *sb.* 5.a illustrates: Tasso, *Godfrey of Bulloigne*, trans. Edward Fairfax, 1.12, 'His fellowes late, shall be his subjects now' (eds. Kathleer M. Lea and T.M. Gang, Oxford, 1981).

30SD] Editors note the absence of a direct source, but the severed ear may recall the apostle Peter's behaviour in the Garden of Gethsemane when he cut off Malchus' ear: Matt. 26: 51; Mark 14: 47; Luke 22: 50; John 18: 10 (only John names Peter as the disciple who commits the offence). The stage action here recalls Gaveston's physical abuse of the Bishop of Coventry in *Edward II*, 1.186SD. Mugeroun's attack is presumably synchronous with Henry's question, which relates to Mugeroun's words and not to his actions. The stage direction might also indicate a previous event now lost: the Cutpurse might have cut off Mugeroun's gold buttons earlier in the scene.

34–5] Guise and Henry address an attendant officer.

41 barriers] a martial exercise or exhibition in the fifteenth and sixteenth centuries. The nature of the exercise varies; it sometimes appears to be jousting, sometimes men fighting together with short-swords in a confined space (see *OED sb.* 2.a,b and quotations).

tourny] 'Originally, A martial sport or exercise of the middle ages, in which a number of combatants, mounted and in armour, and divided into two parties, fought with blunted weapons and under certain restrictions, for the prize of valour; later, A meeting at an appointed time and place for knightly sports and exercises' (*OED*, tournament, 1.a).

tylte] 'A combat or encounter (for exercise or sport) between two armed men on horseback, with lances or similar weapons, the aim of each being to throw his opponent from the saddle; = JOUST *sb.* 1; also, the exercise of riding with a lance, or the like, at a mark, as the quintain' (*OED sb.*² 1.a).

42 disportes] pastimes, games (*OED sb.* 2).

doe fit] are suitable for or become (*OED*, fit, *v.*¹ 3).

45 pleasantnes] cheerfulness, good humour (*OED*, pleasant, *a.* (*adv.*) 2).

46] The line closely recalls *Edward II*, 6.4, 'And still his minde runs on his minion'.

48 securely] in (culpable) self-assurance.

49 provide] see to it or take care (*OED v.* 2.a).

50 plant] establish or set up (*OED v.* 5.c); cf. 16.18 and 20.26.

55 power] fighting force, army (*OED sb.*¹ 9).

63–4] Cf. ll.39–40; both threats are unsubstantiated by history.

65 *Mounser*] Alençon: see 13.35*n*.

Scene 15

4–5] Bennett notes the similarity to *Arden of Faversham*, sig. A3; see Introduction, p. 303.

4 *Mugeroune*] Not, historically, the Duchess's real lover, who was Saint-Mégrin.

11–12 quill . . . wing] A commonplace.

15 writes] second person singular, 's' or 'es' after 't' (Abbott 340).

17 aray] attire, dress (*OED sb.* 11.b); ironical.

24 trothles] disloyal, untrustworthy (*OED* 1, 2, citing this as example).

unjust] faithless, dishonest (*OED* 2).

26–7] Bennett notes 'a metaphor from the scholiasts. The gloss or comment on the obscure text of a classical or sacred author was one of the greatest occupations of the medieval scholar.' The 'text' here is the Duchess, not Guise (Oliver) upon which 'others', such as Mugeroun, 'comment' because Guise's 'love' has been 'obscurde' by the Duchess's faithlessness.

29 dearer . . . eye] Proverbial (Tilley, A290).

32 *Mor du*] 'death of God', an oath: see 17.28 and *n*.

wert not] were it not for (Oliver).

fruit . . . wombe] The Duchess is pregnant.

33 Of] On.

37 perjured] pronounced as three syllables with stress on second.

40 villaine he] that villain.

Scene 16

1 sith] since.

2 mannage] See 10.9n.

3 proud . . . faith] A common description for repellent political opponents, which, as Forker (2.5.9n.) notes, has several parallels: *Edward II*, 9.9, 'Thou proud disturber of thy countries peace'; *1 Troublesome Reign*, 7.1059, 'Proud, and disturber of thy Countreyes peace'; Peele, *Edward I*, 5.831, 'the proude disturber of our state', *The Dramatic Works of George Peele*, ii (ed. Frank S. Hook, New Haven and London, 1961).

6 rent] rend.

7 But for] But because, but since (*OED*, but, 29.b, citing this as example).

8 But] Than.

defend] ward off, repel (*OED v.* 1).

strange] extreme (*OED a.* 9).

inventions] methods, instruments, i.e. of oppression or torture (*OED* 9); pronounced as four syllables.

9 put us to] subject us to (*OED v.*[1] 26.a).

14 for] in support of (*OED* 7.a, Abbott 150).

incenst] incited (*OED*, incense, *v.*[2] 4).

King] i.e. King Henry of France.

16 brunt] assault, violent attack (*OED sb.*[1] 2); cf. *Doctor Faustus*, 1.95, 'stranger engines for the brunt of warre'.

19 *Spaine*] i.e. the King of Spain, Philip.

20–5] This passage has, simultaneously, an undoubtedly Marlovian sound and an equally undoubtedly un-Marlovian syntax. Many editors note substantial difficulty here. It is probable that a line has been omitted before l. 22 (providing a feminine subject, perhaps 'Ate', for the verb 'Plaies'), and that another, referring to Navarre's vainglorious enemies, has been omitted before l. 23 (Craik). Robert A. H. Smith suggests transposing lines 21 and 22 for better sense: *N & Q* 237 (1992), 309.

23 respect] consider, look upon (*OED v.* 2.c, first cited use).

28–31] Although the verbs change number twice in ll. 28–30, the army is probably understood as plural.

32] A close repetition of l. 14; for 'incenst' see l. 14*n*. and cf. *Edward II*, 1.184, 'As then I did incense the parlement'.

33 broyles] See 9.74*n*.2.

35 thereon . . . stay] 'it is for this they wait' (Bennett).

38 It] i.e. the post of general. Navarre sardonically implies that Joyeux will get himself killed for his trouble—as proves to be the case (Craik).

countervaile] make an equal return for, reciprocate (*OED v.* 2.b).

39 steed] place (*OED*, stead, *sb.* 12.d).

40 lurke] hide (himself) (*OED* 1.a), idle (1.b).

drousie] indicating sleepiness, soporific (*OED* 3 quotes Spenser, *Faerie Queene*, II.iii.1, '[He] Vprose from drowsie couch').

41 on] of.

securitie] a feeling of safety or freedom from danger (*OED* 3). The line is very similar to *3 Henry VI*, 5.7.14 and *True Tragedy*, sig. E7v; see Introduction, p. 302.

Scene 17

5 suffer] allow (Joyeux's going) to take place (*OED* 18.a).

6 Regarding still] Always taking into account (*OED*, regard, *v.* 3.b).

11SD *makes hornes*] holds the fist with two fingers extended like a pair of horns, as an insulting gesture, thus indicating cuckoldry (*OED*, horn, *sb.* 7.b).

14 freend] a lover or paramour (*OED sb.* 4).

15 faith] an interjection meaning 'in truth', 'really' (*OED sb.* 12.b).

17 Emperious] befitting an emperor or supreme ruler (*OED*, imperious, 1, citing this example).

20 mockes] derisive or contemptuous actions or speeches (*OED sb.*¹ 1).

21 dote] to be infatuatedly fond of (*OED v.*¹ 3).

22 disgrace] dishonour, shame (*OED sb.* 3), but possibly an error for 'despite' ('dispite', variant sixteenth-century spelling), anticipating 'disgrace' in l. 24; 'to hold or have in despite', i.e. to have or show contempt or scorn for (*OED*, despite, *sb.* 1.b; latest example is 1526) (Craik).

25 incenst] angered.

28 *Par . . . mora*] 'par la mort dieu, il mourra', an oath, 'By the death [of] God, he shall die'.

36] 'I may die by being stabbed, but after Guise dies (so he will not kill me)' or 'He may stab me, but I will kill him'. There may be a bawdy, probably homosexual, quibble here with 'stab'd': cf. *Edward II*, 5.43.

38 beares] double entendre, i.e. to bear during intercourse (Partridge, bear).

40] i.e. Mugeroun will seduce her. Oliver compares 'the series of improper jests' in *Much Ado*, 3.4.36–46. Cf. also Beaumont, *The Knight of the Burning Pestle* (ed. Sheldon P. Zitner, Revels, Manchester, 1984), 5.5.201–2, 'When the young man's——, [*sic*: Zitner suggests 'hand's a friskin'; Craik thinks 'prick's in' is more probable] / Up goes the maiden's heels'.

41 make] Editors from Broughton and Oxberry often emend to the colloquial 'take', and there is the argument of an eye slip from the previous line, but 'make' is perfectly intelligible and, as Oliver notes, 'suggests the deliberateness of the decision'; Mugeroun is, after all, seeking out Guise 'On purpose' (l. 42).

Scene 18

OSD1 *The . . . slaine*] All editors emend by placing this stage direction within quotation marks and adding '*A cry*' before it, but it is difficult to believe that a battle scene and killing of a main character would be 'off stage' in this play. Although Bennett suggests a dumb-show representation of the Duke's death, it is more likely to have been fully played on stage.

OSD2 *traine*] followers (*OED sb*.1 9.a), frequent in Marlowe; cf. for instance, *2 Tamburlaine*, where it is used nine times (e.g. 1.1.OSD2, 2.1.OSD2, 3.4.33SD2).

2] This line appears verbatim in *3 Henry VI*, 5.3.2 and *True Tragedy*, sig. C4; see Introduction, p. 302.

6 surcease] abandon (*OED v. arch.* 3).

7 mannage] See 10.9*n*.

10 prosecution . . . armes] the continuation of this savage war (*OED*, prosecution, 1 and *OED*, arm, *sb*.2.6).

11 ruth] matter or occasion of sorrow or regret (*OED*, ruth[1], 4.a).

17 relicks] specific Roman Catholic artefacts, 'such as a part of the body or clothing, an article of personal use, or the like, which remains as a memorial of a departed saint, martyr, or other holy person, and as such is carefully preserved and held in esteem or veneration' (*OED* 1.a). The idea is of an aggressive Catholicism coercing Navarre's subjects, as in Scene 16, with the relics as objects of compulsory worship.

coastes] borders (*OED sb.* 5); but for an English audience the word would also suggest the sea-coasts and the recent defeat of the Spanish Armada (Craik).

Scene 19

1–16] Another version of this section of the scene exists in MS form: see Appendix and Introduction, pp. 295–8.

1–12] These lines contain numerous *double entendres* and sexual innuendoes; only the less obvious are glossed.

5 forestall . . . standing] 'The metaphor is from the stealing of another's market or trade by setting up a stall in an unauthorized place' (Oliver); standing = erection (Partridge, stand). Forestalling the market is normally the buying up of goods beforehand in order to raise their price (*OED v.* 2.b).

8 occupy] 1. possess, 2. have intercourse with; cf. Shakespeare, *Romeo and Juliet*, 2.3.92 and *2 Henry IV*, 2.4.115 (ed. Giorgio Melchiori, New Cambridge, 1989, following 1600 quarto).

11 geare] equipment (i.e. the musket) (*OED sb.* 2); matter (i.e. plan of assassination) (11).

holde] remains unbroken (*OED v.* 16); continues (23.a).

13 Holde thee] Here! Take it! (*OED v.* 15.b).

tall] brave, valiant (*OED* 3).

. this] Probably a purse of money.

18 have . . . men] Repetition of a phrase from 14.55; see *n.* for 'power'.

25 in armes] in active readiness to fight (*OED,* arm, *sb.*² 4.b), i.e. with an army raised.

26 cause] matter in dispute (*OED sb.* 8.c); cf. *2 Henry VI*, 3.1.289, 'What counsaile giue you in this weightie cause?'

28, 30 mov'd] angered (*OED,* move, *v.* 9.b).

31 Prince . . . line] There is some confusion here. Guise was not, strictly speaking, a member of the royal family of Valois (which he curses at 21.83); he was a member of the Lorraine family (which he states at l. 52). Paul H. Kocher ('Contemporary Pamphlet Backgrounds for Marlowe's *The Massacre at Paris*', *MLQ* 8 (1947), 311) suggests that Guise may be claiming kinship through the marriage of his cousin, Mary Queen of Scots, to the King's eldest brother, Francis II.

32 *Burbonites*] Navarre's family (see 1.50–1 and *n.*).

33 juror] one who swears allegiance to some body or cause (*OED* 4, first cited use).

the holy league] La Sainte Ligue, organized in 1576 under the leadership of Guise, to oppose concessions granted to the Protestants (Huguenots) by King Henry III. Henry III ordered its dissolution in September of 1577, but it revived in importance in 1584, when the Protestant leader, Henry of Navarre, became heir to the crown. It in fact forced Henry III to proscribe the Protestant religion in July 1585. Henry III had Guise assassinated in December of 1588 to put a decisive end to the League's popular support, which was in control of most of France and continued to challenge his authority. Henry III failed to destroy the League, which, after his assassination in 1589, waned in power only after Henry IV's conversion to Catholicism.

35 stand . . . guarde] be vigilant or cautious (*OED*, guard, *sb*. 5.a).

36, 37 hoast] an army.

38 exhibition] support, maintenance (*OED* 1). Philip II of Spain paid Guise a pension from 1578 to his death.

40 Else] Otherwise (*OED* 4.a). Oliver notes that Marlowe could have obtained the information about the alleged source of Guise's finances from various pamphlets.

42 countermaund] oppose (*OED v.* 5).

check] repress (*OED v.*¹ 13); perhaps 'taunt' (*OED v.*¹ 10).

44 animated] inspired (*OED* 3).

46 sexious] i.e. sectious, meaning, perhaps, 'sectarian' (*OED*, only cited use). Many editors follow Oxberry's and Broughton's emendation 'factious'.

47 triple crowne] the papal tiara (*OED*, triple, *a*. 5), 'the three crowns of which symbolised perhaps the Church militant, suffering, and triumphant' (eds. David Bevington and Eric Rasmussen, *Doctor Faustus*, B-text, 3.1.83*n*., Revels, Manchester, 1993).

48–50 cause . . . *America*] The Guise is alluding to wealth derived from the American tribute to Spain: cf. 'Indian golde', 2.61 and *Doctor Faustus*, 1.131–2.

51 them] i.e. the sexious Puritans.

54 wrack] ruin (*OED sb.*1 3.b).

55–7 *Guise* . . . Senator] Henry's sarcasm towards his powerful political opponent recalls Edward's to his nobles in *Edward II*, 4.36–7: 'Here *Mortimer*, sit thou in *Edwards* throne, / *Warwicke* and *Lancaster*, weare you my crowne'. The political allusion ('Dictator . . . Senator') is to Roman government.

57 *placet*] Latin for 'it pleases me'. 'The word is part of the form used in the old Universities when a question is put to the vote: "Placetne vobis, domini doctores? placetne vobis, magistri?" (Does it please you, Doctors? does it please you, Masters?); the answer being "Placet", or "Non placet". ' (*OED* 1, first cited use).

58 hauty] arrogant.

63 meaning] intention (*OED vbl. sb.*[1] 1).

65 dislodge] shift the position of (*OED* 1.b).

68 pompe] Probably a combination of meanings: splendour (*OED* 1); triumphal procession (2); ostentatious display (3).

74 effecting] accomplishing (*OED*, effect, *v.* 1).

his holines] i.e. the Pope's.

76 present] immediate (*OED a.* 9.a.).

77 let me alone] leave it to me (i.e. to take action).

78 discharge] a document for conveying dismissal from service (*OED sb.* 4.c).

84] i.e. 'and in such a way to clear you from all suspicion' (Oliver). Quite = quit = acquit (*OED*, quit, *v.* 2.b).

89 tragicall] excited with tragic feeling (*OED* 2.b, first cited use). There may be other meanings. Bennett suggests 'perhaps used here in opposition to *mild and calm*, to refer to Henry's plans against the Guise, which he is determined shall be fatal to that prince' (see l. 94); 'tragicall' may also mean the opposite of 'milde and calme' (l. 88) in another way: thus 'within', the King has that which is appropriate to tragedy, that is, the 'serious and stately' or the 'grave' and 'formidable' (*OED* 2), perhaps even the 'heroic'.

90 convay] See 9.91*n*.1.

Bloyse] Bloise, containing the famous château of the family of Orleans, where Guise was assassinated.

Scene 20

1 advertised] (four syllables, with stress on the second) informed, notified (*OED* 1).

4 fit] appropriate (*OED a.* 1.a).

11 complices] accomplices, specifically, an associate in crime, a confederate with the principal offender (*OED* 2 quotes *Contention*, sig. H2, 'To quell these Traitors and their compleases').

18 amaine] in full force (*OED adv.* 1); at full speed (2); without delay (2.b).

25 vantage] *OED sb.* 5.b cites this as an example of the phrase 'to take...vantage (of)', and refers to 'advantage' *sb.* 5.b: 'To use any favourable condition which it [here, religion] yields; to avail oneself of. Often in a bad sense: To seize an accidental or unintended opportunity of profiting'.

26 popelings] Either adherents, followers, or ministers of the pope; papists; in sixteenth c. mostly, popish ecclesiastics (*OED*, popeling, 1) or little or petty popes; those who act as popes on a small scale (*contemptuous*) (2).

28 mine] interchangeable with 'my' (Abbott 237).

Scene 21

1 bent] determined (*OED ppl. a.* 3).

5 presently] immediately.

6 heart...hand] Proverbial (Dent, H331.2).

9 I...you] A common phrase indicating assurance of a fact (*OED*, warrant, *a.* 5), here, that the murderers are determined to kill Guise.

10, 64 standings] stations (*OED vbl. sb.* 4, citing *1 Tamburlaine*, 1.2.150), but also punning on a stand from which to shoot game (*OED vbl. sb.* 4.c).

13 I] i.e. 'Aye' = 'Yes'.

close] concealed (*OED a.* A.4); cf. l. 70.

14 the star] i.e. Guise.

16 in] at (Abbott 163).

22 disgordge] discharge or empty (*OED* 2, first cited use, and also quotes Shakespeare, *2 Henry IV*, 1.3.97–8, 'So, so, (thou common Dogge) did'st thou disgorge / Thy glutton-bosome of the Royal *Richard*').

23 Surchargde] Overburdened, overloaded (*OED*, surcharge, *v.* 3.b).

surfet] surfeit = excessive amount.

25SD] For staging options, see Introduction, pp. 314–15.

26 *Halla verlete hey*] 'Holà, varlet, hé' = 'Hullo there, page!' 'Guise expects a page or attendant to come to the door, and the actor should seem startled when no less a person than Epernoun appears.' (Oliver).

27 Mounted] Ascended (into) (*OED*, mount, *v.* 8.a).

Cabonet] private apartment (*OED*, cabinet, 3).

33 pit] pitfall, trap (metaphorical) (*OED sb.*¹ 1.g).

38 bare] bore.

traine] See 18.0SD2*n*.

41 Twere . . . me] It would be to my serious disadvantage (*OED*, hard, *adv.* 2.c).

kinne] See 19.31*n*.

51–4] Recalls the fantasy of Gaveston in *Edward II*, 1.172–4 and the achievement of Tamburlaine in *1 Tamburlaine*, 4.2. Both Guise and Gaveston seem to ignore the irony of Caesar's ultimate demise.

53 wanton] lascivious (*OED* lists no examples of homosexual use, as here; cf. also *Edward II*, 4.198–9 and 402).

54] The line is similar to *2 Henry VI*, 2.4.14 and *Contention*, sig. D2; see Introduction, p. 301.

55 look about] be on the watch, i.e. for my profit (*OED*, look, *v.* 25).

56] i.e. because now I can achieve infinitely greater things.

57 Holde] Keep whole, unbroken (*OED v.* 16).

59 gastly] full of fear, inspired by fear (*OED a.* 3). Oliver points out that Shakespeare uses the word in the same sense in *Julius Caesar*, 1.3.23–4, 'a hundred gastly Women, / Transformed with their feare'.

66] The line occurs verbatim in Shakespeare, *Julius Caesar*, 2.2.28; either it is proverbial or the reporter has introduced it (see Oliver, p. lvii).

67 consaits] conceits, imaginations, intellects (an extension of *OED* 2, particularly 2.b) (Oliver).

69 ingender] produce (*OED*, engender, 5.b).

71 As . . . ashes] There are several options here. Dyce[1] takes these words to refer to Guise and conjectures that he must have seen himself in a mirror. Bennett thinks that 'Guise evidently refers to the ghastly look of the murderer', who enters at l.58SD, and notes l. 59. A third possibility is that Guise is referring to the looks of the two murderers' who just entered at l. 69SD.

look about] be on the look-out (*OED*, look, *v.* 25), i.e. for danger.

74 Then . . . God] i.e. make your peace with Heaven. It is not necessary to suppose that the intercession of saints is being pointedly rejected: Guise does not take it in that sense (Craik).

75 him] ambiguous: either the King or God may be meant.

77 stay] i.e. save (*OED v.*[1] 20, to hinder from going away).

80 *Sextus*] Pope Sixtus V, Felice Peretti (1520–1590). He was Guise's ally, strongly supporting the Holy League and the Armada. He also excommunicated Navarre in 1585.

81 *Philip*] Philip II, King of Spain, who 'was also a strong supporter of the Duke of Guise, to whom he gave a pension of 600,000 golden crowns' (Bennett).

Parma] 'Alexander Farnese (1545–1592), Duke of Parma, was the great leader of the Spanish forces who subjected the Netherlands, and one of the most doughty soldiers against whom Henry IV was destined to fight' (Bennett). Gill comments, 'From 1579 to 1592 the Prince of Parma was Spanish governor-general of the United Provinces of the Netherlands', and suggests that Marlowe's interest derives from his time there (*Doctor Faustus*, 1.93n.): see R. B. Wernham, 'Christopher Marlowe in Flushing in 1592', *EHR* 91 (1976), 344–5.

83 *Valois* his] Valois', an early form of the possessive (Abbott 217).

84 *Vive la messe*] Long live the mass.

85 Thus . . . died] A direct answer to l. 66, and a final underscoring of hubristic irony.

90 phisick] moral or spiritual remedy (*OED sb*. 5.b).

92 Surchargde] Overburdened (cf. l. 23).

93 Mounser of *Loraine*] Guise is never so called elsewhere, and as the title Monsieur was given to the princely members of a royal house (cf. 14.65 and 21.105) it is inappropriate unless the King is using it with irony. The context of strong invective raises the possibility that the word should be 'Monster' (of which Mounster was a sixteenth-c. spelling); cf. Shakespeare, *Tempest*, 3.2.18, 'Weel not run Monsieur Monster' (Craik).

94 broyles] See 9.74n.2.

97] Oliver notes that this comment was recorded by many historians and became famous.

100 sorte] group (*OED sb*.^{2} 17.a), or, alternatively, 'multitude' (*OED sb*.^{2} 19); examples cited from the latter indicate that, when used without a qualifying adjective, as here, the sense could be derogatory.

101 *Doway . . . Remes*] 'Douai, in Belgium, was a famous theological college established in 1568, under William Parsons. It was under the patronage of the King of Spain, and in 1578 the insurgents against Spain, urged on by Queen Elizabeth's emissaries, expelled the students from Douai, as being partisans of the enemy. Allen, the principal, moved his students to Rheims under the protection of Guise, and it was here that the Douai version of the Scriptures was begun' (Bennett).

102] Bennett offers the suggestion that the line might refer to the Babington plot of 1586, but the reference is a general one and there were so many plots and rumours of plots in the period that it is difficult to be certain.

103 huge fleete] i.e. the Armada of Spain, defeated in 1588.

105 *Mounser*] Alençon, who died in 1584 leaving Navarre heir to the throne. The unspecified injury does not seem to imply that Guise caused Alençon's death.

108 strength] strengthen, fortify (*OED v.* 1).

109 make me Munke] cause me to behave like a monk (i.e. in abjuring a secular life, as, for example, Shakespeare's Henry VI) or, as Oliver suggests, 'make me a virtual prisoner in a monastery'.

114 yoakt] subjugated, oppressed (*OED*, yoke, *v.* 6).

122 clippe . . . winges] Proverbial (Tilley, W498).

123 Or . . . handes] before he passes out of my hands.

127 *Orleance*] A mistake for 'Lyons' repeated at 23.11.

128 will] order (*OED v.*¹ B.3).

130] 'These two, joined together, will make an opposition as forceful and as dangerous as one whole Duke of Guise.'

133 newes] tidings (*OED sb.* (*pl.*) 2.a), regularly regarded as a plural noun, hence modified by 'these'.

135 device] 'an ingenious or clever expedient; often one of an underhand or evil character' (*OED* 6).

139 countermanded me] opposed my commands (*OED*, countermand, *v.* 5 cites *Edward II*, 11.187–8, 'proud rebels that are up in armes, / And do confront and countermaund their king'); cf. 19.42.

141 stoup] yield obedience (*OED v.*¹ 2.a).

144 changeling] 'A child secretly substituted for another in infancy; *esp.* a child (usually stupid or ugly) supposed to have been left by fairies in exchange for one stolen' (*OED* 3).

145 exclaime] proclaim loudly (*OED v.* 3, earliest cited use).

miscreant] heretic, unbeliever (*OED* B.1); villain (B.2).

151SD] The added stage direction makes the following a reflective soliloquy, but if O is correct, then it is just possible that the Queen Mother is addressing the corpse.

152 he] i.e. the King.

so] provided that, so long as (*OED* 26.a).

153 bewray] divulge, reveal (*OED* 4), confide.

155 insulte] exult contemptuously (*OED v.* 1).

157 stand] last (*OED v.* B.41).

wrack] destruction (*OED sb.*¹ 2); cf. 19.55.

158 for] because of, on account of (*OED* 21.a, Abbott 150), i.e. (in exchange) for.

159 toyling] struggling, labouring (*OED ppl. a.*, second cited example).

Scene 22

2 scape] escape.

3 fyle] defile, pollute (*OED v.*² 1).

7 moe] more (*OED a.* (*sb.*) and *adv.* B.4.e.).

8 our deaths] i.e. his and Guise's.

9 gripe] See 2.103*n*.

10 pawes] claws (*OED sb.*¹ 1.b).

drench] immerse, plunge, overwhelm (*OED v.* 6). Bennett compares Orcanes imagining Tamburlaine's fall 'to the lake of hell: / Where legions of devils . . . Stretching their monstrous pawes, grin with their teeth, / And guard the gates to entertaine his soule' (*2 Tamburlaine*, 3.5.24–9).

12 pluck amaine] pull with full force (*OED*, pluck, *v.* 4.a; see 20.18*n*.).

13 hard hearted] unmerciful, incapable of being moved to pity or tenderness (*OED*); here with the suggestion 'tough-hearted', i.e. difficult to kill (Craik).

Scene 23

3] Henry III's death by itself cannot compensate or atone for (my brother's death) (see *OED*, satisfy, 2).

4–5] Cf. *3 Henry VI*, 2.1.68–9, and *True Tragedy*, sig. B4; see Introduction, p. 303 and Oliver, pp. lv–lvi.

5 stay] support (*OED sb.*² 1.b).

7 *Valoys* his] See 21.83*n*.

10 his] i.e. Navarre's.

11 Hee] i.e. Henry III.

13 prevented] baffled by precautionary measures (*OED*, prevent, 5).

for to] to; see 11.32*n*. The implied sense is 'leaving me free to'.

13–14 his life, / And] O's repetition of 'His life' at the beginning of l. 14 is a compositor's eye slip; the repetition also destroys the metre, which is fairly regular through Dumaine's speech.

15SD FRIER] He was, in fact, a Dominican named Jacques Clément.

21–2] Cf. *Edward II*, 6.98–9, 'Come *Edmund* lets away, and levie men, / Tis warre that must abate these Barons pride'.

24 Jacobyns] i.e. Dominicans, members of the order of St Dominic. 'Originally applied to the French members of the order, from the church of *Saint Jacques* (S. Jacobus) which was given to them, and near which they built their first convent' (*OED, Jacobin, sb.*[1] and *a.*).

29 the . . . meritorious] Cf. *2 Henry VI*, 3.1.270; see Introduction, pp. 302.

31] Cf. 11.38 for similarly worded line.

Scene 24

8 vouchsafte] bestowed (upon).

11 Whose] i.e. Navarre's.

he] i.e. the King of France.

13 lye] encamp, take up a position (*OED* v.[1] B.5.b).

Lutetia] The Roman name (i.e. *Lutetia Parisiorum*) for what afterwards became Paris (Sugden, p. 323).

14 Girting] Encircling (*OED*, gird, v.[1] 5.b, often said of a siege).

strumpet Cittie] 'so called because it had proved faithless to the King, by espousing the cause of Guise' (Oliver), but for an English audience the phrase might also suggest the 'Strumpet of Rome' or the 'Babylonian strumpet'.

15–16] The city will be given so much warfare that the excess will cause it to vomit up its stomach, that is, its pride onto the earth. Oliver notes that 'hatefull' may, mean both 'hated' and 'full of hate'.

18 Jacobins] See 23.24*n*.

President] 'The appointed governor or lieutenant of a province, or division of a country, a dependency, colony, city, etc.' (*OED sb.* 1.a); cf. *Edward II*, 4.68.

27 therein] in that affair or matter (*OED* 2). The Friar speaks equivocally.

31 speedye] prompt (*OED* 3.a) or hasty, quick-written (Bennett, following, presumably, *OED* 5.a).

34 *Sancte Jacobe*] See 8.13*n*.

34SD] The notion that a king often killed his attackers became cliché: cf. the king's death in Shakespeare's *Richard II* 5.5.105–7, for instance.

41 strait] immediately (*OED*, straight, *a.*, *sb.* and *adv.* C.2.a).

42 partes] acts (*OED sb.* 11).

43 such . . . them] those who consider or regard themselves as (*OED*, hold, *v.* B.12.d).

46 to] to the full extent (of) (*OED prep.*, *conj.*, *adv.* A.14).

50 English Agent] At this time Sir Edward Stafford was the English ambassador to France, but, as Bennett notes, he was actually called home in March and did not return till September; thus he was not available when Henry III was assassinated on 2 August 1589. No audience would notice the historical mistake. Roma Gill suggests (privately) that Marlowe is in fact bringing his patron, Sir Thomas Walsingham (1568–1630), onto the stage, but the 'Agent' is more likely to be Sir Francis Walsingham (1530?–90), who was not actually in France at this historical moment, but had been there from December 1570 to April 1573 as the English ambassador. He was in Paris during the massacre, where he sheltered many English Protestant visitors who took refuge under his roof and eventually escaped unharmed.

51 sister *England*] i.e. Elizabeth I.

53 search] probe (*OED v.* 8) as a means of diagnosing the severity of the injury.

55 resolve] inform, tell (*OED v.* 17.a).

59–67] Part of the Protestant anti-Catholic propaganda; cf. *Edward II*, 4.96–103 for a similar, but anachronistic, sentiment. Although ll. 63–4 are very close to *Edward II*, 4.100–1 ('Ile fire thy crased buildings, and enforce / The papall towers, to kisse the lowlie ground'), there is no justifiable reason to emend 'incense' to 'enforce' (Dyce[1]) or 'holy' to 'lowlie' (Dyce[2]). I am not as certain as Oliver that the two lines are 'apparently a poor recollection of the two from *Edward II*' and that we 'can almost see the reporter's memory running on to the wrong set of rails' (p. lvii).

61 triple Crowne] Cf. 19.47 and see *n.*

63 crased] 'The usual sense is cracked or rotten (*OED* 1)' (Rowland, *Edward II*, 4.100*n.*), but here the context may admit the figurative meaning 'diseased' (*OED* 4) or 'unsound' (*OED* 3).

66 ruinate] overthrow (*OED v.* 5.a).

67 practises] conspiracies, plots, intrigues (*OED*, practice, 6.c).

79 new found death] newly discovered method of execution.

93] Henry III was the last of the Valois family to rule France; they had done so for 261 years.

94 house of *Bourbon*] To which Navarre belonged; see 1.50–1*n*.

99 *Sextus* bones] Pope Sixtus V died 27 August 1590; he was, therefore, alive as the King now speaks, but 'remembered' as dead when the play was probably written or reported.

100 slice] Bennett notes that Marlowe regularly uses 'slice' in the sense of 'cut, as with a sword' in *1 Tamburlaine*; cf. 4.2.3 and 4.4.47.

102 makes most lavish] makes the most extravagant outpouring or expenditure (*OED* lavish, *sb.*, cites this example).

109 I . . . death] Navarre actually did no such thing; he accepted the Roman Catholic faith in 1593. For 'for to' see 11.32*n*.

110 As] So that (*OED* B.21.a).

112 fatall] Probably all of the following from *OED*: destined, fated (1); ominous (4.c, citing *2 Tamburlaine*, 4.3.23 as first example in 1590); fraught with destiny, fateful (5); ruinous (6). Cf. *Doctor Faustus*, 10.31.

112SD2 *dead march*] 'A piece of solemn music played at the funeral procession' (*OED*, dead, *a.* (*sb.*[1], *adv.*) D.2); Brockbank notes in his edition of Shakespeare, *Coriolanus* (Arden, London, 1975), 5.6.154SD*n.*, that 'Funeral music was rarely heard on the Elizabethan stage', and compares *2 Tamburlaine*, 3.2.0SD.

drawing weapons] pulling after them, thus dragging (*OED*, draw, B.2.a); perhaps removing swords from sheaths and pointing downward (*OED*, draw, B.33.a); perhaps 'trailing pikes', as was the usual practice at funerals; cf. the end of Shakespeare, *Coriolanus*.

APPENDIX
Folger MS. J. b. 8

[recto]

Enter A ſouldier wᵗ *a Mu*ſkett

     Now ſer to you yᵗ dares make advke a Cuckolde

     and vſe a Counterfeyt key to his privye Chamber

ſouldier thoughe you take out none but yoʳ owne treaſure

     yett you putt in yᵗ diſpleaſes him/ And fill vp his rome yᵗ   5

     he ſhold occupie. Herein ſer you foreſtalle the markett

     and ſett vpe yoʳ ſtandinge where you ſhold not: But you will

     ſaye you leave him rome enoughe beſides: thats no anſwere

     hes to have the Choyce of his owne freeland/ Yf it be

     not to free theres the queſtione/ Now ſer where he is   10

     your landlorde. you take vpon you to be his/ and will needs

     enter by defaulte/ whatt thoughe you were once in poſſeſſion

     yett Comminge vpon you once vnawares he frayde you

     out againe. therefore your entrye is mere Intrvſione

     this is againſte the lawe ſer: And thoughe I Come not   15

     to keep poſſeſſione as I wold I mighte. yet I Come to

     keepe you out ſer. yow are wellcome ſer have at you

Enter minion   *He* Kills him

minion Trayterouſe guiſe ah thow haſt mvrthered me

                              Enter guiſe   20

     Hold thee tale ſoldier take the this and flye   *Exit.*

---

1 *A*] left leg formed out of ſ probably as soon as written   2 Cuckolde] C
superscribed on what appears to be the beginning of k as soon as written   3
key] first written as Cey, then k superscribed on C   4 ſouldier] r blotted, or
possibly altered from *t*. The marginal speech-prefixes here and at ll. 21–2, 30–1,
fall mid-speech (the repeated one at 30–1 acting as a reminder following the page-
turn).   15 ſer] first written as ſeo, then r written over o

Guiſe

 thus fall Imperfett exhalatione

 wch our great ſonn of fraunce Cold not effecte

 a fyery Meteor in the fermament

 lye there the Kinges delyght and guiſes ſcorne   25

 revenge it henry if thow liſte or darſt

 I did it onely in deſpight of thee

 [verso]

 fondlie haſt thow in Cenſte the guiſes ſowle

 y^t of it ſelf was hote enoughe to worke

 thy Iuſt degeſtione wt extreameſt ſhame   30

Guiſe the armye I have gathered now ſhall ayme

 more at thie end then exterpatione

 and when thow thinkſt I have forgotten this

 and y^t thow moſt repoſeſt one my faythe

 then will I wake thee from thie foliſhe dreame   35

 and lett thee ſee thie ſelf my pryſoner *Exe*unt

---

22 exhalatione] h superscribed on a as soon as written   24 Meteor] second e superscribed on o as soon as written   31 armye] r superscribed on, possibly a   32
exterpatione] superscribed on t as soon as written   36 *Exe*unt] un lacks a minim

13 frayde] frightened, afraid (*OED v.*¹ 1); cf. *1 Tamburlaine*, 5.1.64.

30 degeſtione] *OED*, digestion, 1.d, the figurative sense of the physiological
process (first cited use); alternatively 'dissolution by heat' (*OED*, digest, *v.* 10).

32 exterpatione] rooting out, extermination (*OED* 3), i.e. of the king's sup-
porters or, possibly, of the Huguenots (Oliver).